INTRODUCTION TO LAW

Feminist Legal Theory, 7

The Law and Economics School of Jurisprudential Thought, *8*

Regulations and Order of Administrative Agencies, *12*

Specialized Courts Hear Commercial Disputes, *30*

The Process of Choosing a Supreme Court Justice, *34*

I'll Take You to the U.S. Supreme Court!—Not!, *35*

Ford Explorer SUV Rollover Lawsuit Settled for $22 Million, *54*

Money Laundering, 77

Corporate Criminal Liability, *81*

Miranda, *86*

Federal Antiterrorism Act of 2001, *87*

The Constitution of the United States of America, *101*

Constitutional Violations, *104*

Wal-Mart Shopper Wins, *127*

Liability for Frivolous Lawsuits, *129*

Ouch! The Coffee's Too Hot!, *133*

Evolution of the Modern Law of Contracts, *155*

A Contract Is a Contract Is a Contract, *157*

"Heads I Win, Tails You Lose," *164*

Fraud, *167*

Article 2 (Sales) of the Uniform Commercial Code, *175*

Article 2A (Leases) of the Uniform Commercial Code, *176*

Estray Statutes, *189*

Recording Statutes, *197*

Government Regulation Versus Compensable "Taking" of Real Property, *204*

Same-Sex Marriages, *217*

Common Law Marriage, *219*

Child Abuse, *220*

Surrogacy, *221*

Family Support Act, *229*

Palimony, *231*

The Right to Die and Living Wills, *250*

Liability of General Partners, *268*

Limited Partner Liable on Personal Guarantee, *271*

Accounting Firms Operating as LLPs, *273*

DreamWorks SKG, LLC, *276*

S Corporations, *281*

The Sarbanes-Oxley Act of 2002, *286*

Employment-At-Will, *304*

Minimum Wage and Overtime Pay, *312*

Principal Liable for Repo Man's Tort, *314*

Family and Medical Leave Act, *323*

Klondike Bar's Unsecured Claim Melts, *336*

Material Person's Liens, *339*

Super-Priority Liens, *343*

Kmart Emerges from Bankruptcy, *353*

Federal Patent Statute, *363*

American Inventors Protection Act, *364*

Federal Copyright Revision Act, *366*

Federal Lanham Trademark Act, *371*

Administrative Procedure Act, *388*

Do-Not-Call Registry, *389*

A Hidden Source of Protein in Peanut Butter, *391*

Clean Air Act, *399*

Indoor Air Pollution: A Frontier for Environmental Litigation, *400*

Superfund, *401*

Environmental Protection, *402*

INTRODUCTION TO LAW
ITS DYNAMIC NATURE

Henry R. Cheeseman

CLINICAL PROFESSOR OF BUSINESS LAW
DIRECTOR OF THE LEGAL STUDIES PROGRAM
MARSHALL SCHOOL OF BUSINESS
UNIVERSITY OF SOUTHERN CALIFORNIA

Upper Saddle River, New Jersey

Library of Congress Cataloging-in-Publication Data

Cheeseman, Henry R.
Introduction to law : Its dynamic nature / Henry R. Cheeseman.— 1st ed.
p. cm.
ISBN 0-13-112373-4
1. Law—United States. 2. Law and ethics. I. Title.

KF385.C44 2005
349.73—dc22

2004012050

Director of Production and Manufacturing: Bruce Johnson
Executive Editor: Elizabeth Sugg
Managing Editor-Editorial: Judy Casillo
Editorial Assistant: Cyrenne Bolt de Freitas
Marketing Manager: Leigh Ann Sims
Managing Editor-Production: Mary Carnis
Manufacturing Buyer: Ilene Sanford
Production Liaison: Denise Brown
Production Editor: Gay Pauley/Holcomb Hathaway
Composition: Carlisle Communications, Ltd.
Interior Design: Aerocrafter Charter Art Service
Director, Image Resource Center: Melinda Reo
Manager, Rights and Permissions: Zina Arabia
Interior Image Specialist: Beth Brenzel
Cover Image Specialist: Karen Sanatar
Image Permission Coordinator: Robert Farrell
Design Director: Cheryl Asherman
Senior Design Coordinator: Christopher Weigand
Cover Image: Omni Communications, Inc./Frank Siteman
Cover Design: Kevin Kall
Cover Printer: Phoenix Color
Printer/Binder: Courier Westford

Photo Credits, by page number: **3,** John Neubauer/PhotoEdit; **27,** David R. Frazier/David R. Frazier Photolibrary, Inc.; **34,** U.S. Department of Agriculture; **36,** Jeff Greenberg/PhotoEdit; **47,** John Neubauer/PhotoEdit; **69,** John Neubauer/PhotoEdit; **83,** Jeff Greenberg/PhotoEdit; **99,** PhotoEdit; **100,** Library of Congress; **125,** Billy E. Barnes/ PhotoEdit; **128,** Tony Freeman/PhotoEdit; **136,** Robert W. Ginn/PhotoEdit; **153,** Billy E. Barnes/PhotoEdit; **162,** Michael Newman/ PhotoEdit; **172,** Cathy Melloan/PhotoEdit; **187,** Bob Rowan; Progressive Image/Corbis/Bettmann; **196,** Ron Chapple/Getty Images, Inc.–Taxi; **215,** Paul Conklin/ PhotoEdit; **217,** Betts Anderson Loman/ PhotoEdit; **239,** Keith Brofsky/Getty Images, Inc.–Photodisc; **242,** Jeff Greenberg/PhotoEdit; **263,** Bruce Ayers/Getty Images Inc.–Stone Allstock; **270,** Joseph Nettis/Stock Boston; **301,** Michael Newman/PhotoEdit; **335,** Mikael Karlsson/ Arresting Images; **361,** Jose L. Pelaez/Corbis/Stock Market; **366,** Clever Bryant/PhotoEdit; **367,** John Elk III/Stock Boston; **385,** Owen Franken/Stock Boston.

Pearson Education Ltd.
Pearson Education Australia Pty. Limited
Pearson Education Singapore Pte. Ltd.
Pearson Education North Asia Ltd.
Pearson Education Canada, Ltd.
Pearson Educación de Mexico, S.A. de C.V.
Pearson Education—Japan
Pearson Education Malaysia Pte. Ltd.

10 9 8 7 6 5 4 3 2
ISBN 0-13-112373-4

Contents

Preface xii

PART I THE LEGAL ENVIRONMENT 1

1

THE NATURE OF LAW AND CRITICAL LEGAL THINKING 3

Introduction 3
What Is Law? 4
Definition of Law 4
Functions of the Law 4
INFORMATION TECHNOLOGY: Students Plug Into the Internet and the Law 5
Flexibility of the Law 5
ETHICAL PERSPECTIVE: Fairness of the Law 6
Schools of Jurisprudential Thought 6
History of American Law 8
INTERNATIONAL PERSPECTIVE: Adoption of English Common Law in America 9
Law Courts 9
Chancery (Equity) Courts 9
INTERNATIONAL PERSPECTIVE: The Civic Law System 10
Merchant Courts 10
Sources of Law in the United States 10
Constitutions 10
Treaties 11
Codified Law 11
Executive Orders 11
Judicial Decisions 12
Doctrine of Stare Decisis 12
Priority of Law in the United States 12
Critical Legal Thinking 13
Key Terms 13
CASE FOR DISCUSSION: *Gratz v. Bollinger and the Regents of the University of Michigan* 14
CASE FOR DISCUSSION: *Grutter v. Bollinger and the University of Michigan Law School* 15
ETHICAL PERSPECTIVE: Nike Cleans Up Its Act in Vietnam 16
Briefing a Case 16
Briefing the Case—Example 18
Brief of the Case: PGA Tour Inc. v. Martin 22
LEGAL TERMINOLOGY 23
CHAPTER SUMMARY 23
INTERNET EXERCISES AND CASES 25
Working the Web 25
Critical Legal Thinking Questions 25
Case for Briefing 25
Cases for Discussion 26

2

THE AMERICAN COURT SYSTEM 27

Introduction 27
State Court System 27
Limited-Jurisdiction Trial Court 28
General-Jurisdiction Trial Court 28
Intermediate Appellate Court 28
Highest State Court 28
Federal Court System 29
Special Federal Courts 30
U.S. District Courts 30
U.S. Courts of Appeals 30
U.S. Supreme Court 31
CASE FOR DISCUSSION: *Pizza Hut, Inc. v. Papa John's International, Inc.* 32
Decisions by the U.S. Supreme Court 33
Jurisdiction of Federal and State Courts 35
Authority of Courts 36
CASE FOR DISCUSSION: *Carnival Cruise Lines, Inc. v. Shute* 38
INFORMATION TECHNOLOGY: Obtaining Personal Jurisdiction in Cyberspace 39
INTERNATIONAL PERSPECTIVE: Comparison of Japanese and American Legal Systems 39
LEGAL TERMINOLOGY 40
CHAPTER SUMMARY 41
INTERNET EXERCISES AND CASES 44
Working the Web 44
Critical Legal Thinking Questions 44
Case for Briefing 44
Cases for Discussion 45

3

Civil Litigation and Alternative Dispute Resolution 47

Introduction 47
The Pleadings 48
Complaint and Summons 48
Answer 49
Cross-Complaint and Reply 49
Intervention and Consolidation 49
Statute of Limitations 49
CASE FOR DISCUSSION: ***Swierkiewicz v. Sorema N.A.*** 50
INFORMATION TECHNOLOGY: E-Filings in Court 51
Discovery 51
Depositions 51
CASE FOR DISCUSSION: ***Norgart v. The Upjohn Company*** 52
Interrogatories 53
Production of Documents 53
Physical and Mental Examinations 53
Pretrial Motions 53
Motion for Judgment on the Pleadings 53
Motion for Summary Judgment 53
Settlement Conference 54
The Trial 54
Jury Selection 55
Opening Statements 55
The Plaintiff's Case 55
The Defendant's Case 56
Rebuttal and Rejoinder 56
Closing Arguments 56
Jury Instructions 56
Jury Deliberation 56
Entry of Judgment 56
CASE FOR DISCUSSION: ***Ferlito v. Johnson & Johnson Products, Inc.*** 57
The Appeal 58
Alternative Dispute Resolution 58
Arbitration 58
ETHICAL PERSPECTIVE: Firestone Tires Shred 59
Mediation and Conciliation 59
Minitrial 60
Fact-Finding 60
Judicial Referee 60
LEGAL TERMINOLOGY 60
CHAPTER SUMMARY 61
INTERNET EXERCISES AND CASES 64
Working the Web 64
Critical Legal Thinking Questions 64
Case for Briefing 65
Cases for Discussion 66

4

Criminal Law and Ethics 69

Introduction 69
Definition of a Crime 70
Penal Codes and Regulatory Statutes 70
Parties to a Criminal Action 70
Classification of Crimes 70
Felonies 70
Misdemeanors 71
Violations 71
Essential Elements of a Crime 71
Criminal Act 71
Criminal Intent 71
INFORMATION TECHNOLOGY: Federal Law Helps Victims of Identity Fraud 72
Criminal Acts as Basis for Tort Actions 72
Criminal Procedure 72
Arrest 73
Indictment or Information 73
Arraignment 73
CASE FOR DISCUSSION: ***Atwater v. City of Lago Vista, Texas*** 74
Plea Bargaining 75
Crimes Affecting Business 75
Robbery 75
Burglary 75
Larceny 75
Theft 76
Receiving Stolen Property 76
Arson 76
Forgery 76
Extortion 76
Credit-Card Crimes 76
Bad Check Legislation 77
White-Collar Crimes 77
Embezzlement 77
Criminal Fraud 78
Mail and Wire Fraud 78
Bribery 78
ETHICAL PERSPECTIVE: Hughes Aircraft Downed as a Criminal Conspirator 79
Racketeer Influenced and Corrupt Organizations Act (RICO) 79

INTERNATIONAL PERSPECTIVE: The Foreign Corrupt Practices Act 80
Inchoate Crimes 80
Criminal Conspiracy 81
Attempt to Commit a Crime 81
Aiding and Abetting the Commission of a Crime 81
INFORMATION TECHNOLOGY: Information Infrastructure Protection (IIP) Act 82
Constitutional Safeguards 82
Fourth Amendment Protection Against Unreasonable Searches and Seizures 82
Fifth Amendment Privilege Against Self-Incrimination 83
CASE FOR DISCUSSION: ***Kyllo v. United States*** 84
Fifth Amendment Protection Against Double Jeopardy 85
Sixth Amendment Right to a Public Jury Trial 85
Eighth Amendment Protection Against Cruel and Unusual Punishment 85
INTERNATIONAL PERSPECTIVE: Hiding Money in Offshore Banks 86
Law and Ethics 87
CASE FOR DISCUSSION: ***Wal-Mart Stores, Inc. v. Samara Brothers, Inc.*** 88
ETHICAL PERSPECTIVE: Enron Corporation Plunges Into Bankruptcy 89
ETHICAL PERSPECTIVE: Sarbanes-Oxley Act Prompts Public Companies to Adopt Code of Ethics 91
LEGAL TERMINOLOGY 91
CHAPTER SUMMARY 92
INTERNET EXERCISES AND CASES 96
Working the Web 96
Critical Legal Thinking Questions 96
Case for Briefing 96
Cases for Discussion 97

5

CONSTITUTIONAL LAW AND FREEDOMS 99

Introduction 99
Basic Constitutional Concepts 100
Federalism and Delegated Powers 100
The Doctrine of Separation of Powers 100
Checks and Balances 101
The Supremacy Clause 101
CASE FOR DISCUSSION: ***Geier v. American Honda Motor Co., Inc.*** 102
ETHICAL PERSPECTIVE: Cigarette Companies Assert Supremacy Clause 103
The Commerce Clause 104
CASE FOR DISCUSSION: ***Reno, Attorney General of the United States v. Condon, Attorney General of South Carolina*** 105
State Police Power 106
The Bill of Rights 106
Freedom of Speech 106
INTERNATIONAL PERSPECTIVE: Foreign Commerce Clause 107
Freedom of Religion 108
CASE FOR DISCUSSION: ***Fax.com, Inc. v. United States*** 109
CASE FOR DISCUSSION: ***United States v. Playboy Entertainment Group, Inc.*** 110
INFORMATION TECHNOLOGY: Broad Free Speech Rights Granted in Cyberspace 111
Other Constitutional Clauses 111
The Equal Protection Clause 111
The Due Process Clause 112
The Privileges and Immunities Clause 113
Administrative Agencies 113
Federal Administrative Agencies 113
INTERNATIONAL PERSPECTIVE: Constitution of the People's Republic of China 114
State Administrative Agencies 114
Administrative Law 114
Legislative Powers of Administrative Agencies 115
Executive Powers of Administrative Agencies 115
Judicial Powers of Administrative Agencies 115
LEGAL TERMINOLOGY 115
CHAPTER SUMMARY 117
INTERNET EXERCISES AND CASES 120
Working the Web 120
Critical Legal Thinking Questions 120
Case for Briefing 120
Cases for Discussion 121

PART II BASIC LAW 123

6

TORTS AND PRODUCT LIABILITY 125

Introduction 125
Intentional Torts Against Persons 126
Assault 126
Battery 126
False Imprisonment 126
Defamation of Character 127

Misappropriation of the Right to Publicity 128
Invasion of the Right to Privacy 128
Intentional Infliction of Emotional Distress 129
CASE FOR DISCUSSION: *Roach v. Stern* 130
Intentional Torts Against Property 131
Trespass to Land 131
Trespass to and Conversion of Personal Property 131
Unintentional Torts (Negligence) 131
Elements of Negligence 131
Special Negligence Doctrines 134
Negligent Infliction of Emotional Distress 134
Negligence Per Se 134
Res Ipsa Loquitur 134
CASE FOR DISCUSSION: *James v. Meow Media, Inc.* 135
Good Samaritan Laws 136
Dram Shop Acts 136
Guest Statutes 137
Fireman's Rule 137
"Danger Invites Rescue" Doctrine 137
Social Host Liability 137
Liability of Landowners 137
Liability of Common Carriers and Innkeepers 138
Defenses Against Negligence 138
Superseding or Intervening Event 138
Assumption of the Risk 138
CASE FOR DISCUSSION: *Cheong v. Antablin* 139
Contributory Negligence 140
Comparative Negligence 140
Product Liability 140
Restatement of Torts 140
Liability Without Fault 141
All in the Chain of Distribution Are Liable 141
Parties Who Can Recover for Strict Liability 141
Damages Recoverable for Strict Liability 142
CASE FOR DISCUSSION: *Shoshone Coca-Cola Bottling Co. v. Dolinski* 143
ETHICAL PERSPECTIVE: General Motors Hit with Billion-Dollar Judgment 144
LEGAL TERMINOLOGY 144
CHAPTER SUMMARY 145
INTERNET EXERCISES AND CASES 149
Working the Web 149
Critical Legal Thinking Questions 149
Case for Briefing 149
Cases for Discussion 150

7

CONTRACTS AND E-COMMERCE 153

Introduction 153
Definition of and Parties to a Contract 154
Parties to a Contract 154
Requirements of a Contract 154
Agreement 155
Requirements of the Offer 155
Termination of the Offer 156
Acceptance 156
Express and Implied Contracts 156
Consideration 157
CASE FOR DISCUSSION: *Wrench LLC v. Taco Bell Corporation* 158
Gift Promises 159
Capacity to Contract 159
Minors 159
CASE FOR DISCUSSION: *Alden v. Presley* 160
INFORMATION TECHNOLOGY: Nondisclosure Agreements 161
Mentally Incompetent Persons 161
Intoxicated Persons 161
Lawful Object 161
Illegality—Contracts Contrary to Public Policy 162
Statute of Frauds—Writing Requirement 162
Contracts Involving Interests in Land 162
CASE FOR DISCUSSION: *Flood v. Fidelity & Guaranty Life Insurance Co.* 163
One-Year Rule 164
Contracts for the Sale of Goods 164
Formality of the Writing 164
ETHICAL PERSPECTIVE: Unconscionable Contract 165
Required Signature 165
INFORMATION TECHNOLOGY: The Federal Electronic Signature Act 166
Assignment of Rights 166
Third-Party Beneficiaries 168
Performance 169
Covenants 169
Conditions Precedent 169
Complete Performance 169
Substantial Performance Minor Breach 169
Inferior Performance Material Breach 170
Remedies 170
Monetary Damages 170
CASE FOR DISCUSSION: *Lim v. The .TV Corporation International* 171
Mitigation of Damages 172

ETHICAL PERSPECTIVE: State Farm: Not Such a Good Neighbor 173
Equitable Remedies 173
The Uniform Commercial Code (UCC) 174
INFORMATION TECHNOLOGY: Uniform Computer Information Transactions Act (UCITA) 176
INTERNATIONAL PERSPECTIVE: U.N. Convention on Contracts for the International Sale of Goods (CISG) 177
LEGAL TERMINOLOGY 177
CASE FOR DISCUSSION: *Brumfield v. Death Row Records, Inc.* 178
CHAPTER SUMMARY 179
INTERNET EXERCISES AND CASES 183
Working the Web 183
Critical Legal Thinking Questions 183
Case for Briefing 183
Cases for Discussion 184

8

REAL AND PERSONAL PROPERTY 187

Introduction 187
Personal Property 187
Gifts of Personal Property 188
Mislaid, Lost, and Abandoned Property 188
ETHICAL PERSPECTIVE: Honest Citizen 190
Bailments 190
CASE FOR DISCUSSION: *Sisters of Charity of the Incarnate Word v. Meaux* 191
Mutual-Benefit Bailments 192
Innkeepers 192
Real Property 192
Freehold Estates 193
Estates in Fee 193
Life Estate 193
Future Interests 194
Reversion 194
Remainder 194
Concurrent Ownership 194
Joint Tenancy 194
Tenancy in Common 195
Tenancy by the Entirety 196
Community Property 196
Condominiums 196
Cooperative 197
Transfer of Ownership of Real Property 197
CASE FOR DISCUSSION: *Cunningham v. Hastings* 198
Sale of Real Estate 199
Marketable Title 199
Adverse Possession 199
ETHICAL PERSPECTIVE: Modern-Day Squatters 200
Easements 200
CASE FOR DISCUSSION: *Walker v. Ayres* 201
Landlord–Tenant Relationship 202
Types of Tenancy 202
The Lease 203
Implied Warranty of Habitability 203
Land-Use Control 204
CASE FOR DISCUSSION: *Guinnane v. San Francisco City Planning Commission* 205
LEGAL TERMINOLOGY 206
CHAPTER SUMMARY 207
INTERNET EXERCISES AND CASES 210
Working the Web 210
Critical Legal Thinking Questions 210
Case for Briefing 211
Cases for Discussion 212

9

FAMILY LAW 215

Introduction 215
Premarriage Issues 215
Engagement 216
Promise to Marry 216
Marriage 216
Marriage Requirements 216
Financial Support 217
CASE FOR DISCUSSION: *Baker v. State of Vermont* 218
Spousal Abuse 219
Parents and Children 219
Parents' Rights and Duties 219
Paternity Actions 220
Adoption 221
Agency Adoption 221
Independent Adoption 222
Court Approval of Adoptions 222
Marriage Termination 222
Annulment 223
Divorce 223
Child Custody 224
CASE FOR DISCUSSION: *Giha v. Giha* 225
Factors for Determining Child Custody 226
Visitation Rights 226

Joint Custody 226
Guardian Ad Litem 227
Financial Considerations Associated with the Termination of a Marriage 227
Division of Assets 227
Separate Property 227
Marital Property 227
Division of Debts 228
Child Support 228
Spousal Support 229
Prenuptial Agreements 230
LEGAL TERMINOLOGY 231
CHAPTER SUMMARY 232
INTERNET EXERCISES AND CASES 236
Working the Web 236
Critical Legal Thinking Questions 236
Case for Briefing 236
Cases for Discussion 237

10

WILLS, TRUSTS, AND ESTATES 239

Introduction 239
Wills 239
Requirements for Making a Will 240
Attestation by Witnesses 240
Changing a Will 240
Revoking a Will 242
Special Types of Wills 242
Holographic Wills 242
Noncupative Wills 242
Types of Testamentary Gifts 242
CASE FOR DISCUSSION: *In the Matter of the Estate of Reed* 243
Ademption 244
Abatement 244
Per-Stirpes *and* Per-Capita *Distribution* 244
CASE FOR DISCUSSION: *Opperman v. Anderson* 245
INFORMATION TECHNOLOGY: Videotaped and Electronic Wills 247
Special Issues Concerning Wills 247
Simultaneous Deaths 247
Joint and Mutual Wills 247
Undue Influence 248
Intestate Succession 248
Probate 248
CASE FOR DISCUSSION: *Robison v. Graham* 249
Trusts 250
Express Trusts 252
Implied Trusts 253
Special Types of Trusts 253
Termination of a Trust 253
Living Trusts 253
LEGAL TERMINOLOGY 255
CHAPTER SUMMARY 256
INTERNET EXERCISES AND CASES 259
Working the Web 259
Critical Legal Thinking Questions 259
Case for Briefing 259
Cases for Discussion 260

PART III ADVANCED LAW 261

11

BUSINESS ORGANIZATIONS 263

Introduction 263
Sole Proprietorship 264
Creation of a Sole Proprietorship 264
Personal Liability of Sole Proprietors 264
General Partnership 264
Formation of a Partnership 265
The Partnership Agreement 266
Contract Liability 267
Tort Liability 267
Dissolution of Partnerships 267
Limited Partnership 268
General and Limited Partners 268
Formation of Limited Partnerships 269
Limited Partnership Agreement 270
Liability of General and Limited Partners 270
Limited Liability Partnership (LLP) 270
Articles of Partnership 271
Limited Liability Company (LLC) 271
Formation of an LLC 272
Members' Limited Liability 273
Corporations 273
Classifications of Corporations 277
Incorporation Procedure 277
Shareholders 281
Disregard of the Corporate Entity 282
Board of Directors 282
CASE FOR DISCUSSION: *Kinney Shoe Corp. v. Polan* 283
INFORMATION TECHNOLOGY: Delaware Amends Corporation Code to Recognize Electronic Communications 284

Corporate Officers 284
ETHICAL PERSPECTIVE: Directors' and Officers' Duty of Loyalty 285
Duty of Care 285
INTERNATIONAL PERSPECTIVE: The Multinational Corporation 287
Franchise 288
CASE FOR DISCUSSION: *Martin v. McDonald's Corporation* 289
Licensing 290
LEGAL TERMINOLOGY 290
CHAPTER SUMMARY 291
INTERNET EXERCISES AND CASES 297
Working the Web 297
Critical Legal Thinking Questions 298
Case for Briefing 298
Cases for Discussion 299

12

AGENCY, EMPLOYMENT, AND EQUAL OPPORTUNITY LAW 301

Introduction 301
Agency 302
Persons Who Can Initiate an Agency Relationship 302
Kinds of Employment Relationships 303
Employer–Employee Relationship 303
Principal–Agent Relationship 303
Principal–Independent Contractor Relationship 303
Formation of the Agency Relationship 304
Contract Liability to Third Parties 307
CASE FOR DISCUSSION: *Holiday Inns, Inc. v. Shelburne* 308
Tort Liability to Third Parties 309
Termination of an Agency and Employment Contract 312
Independent Contractor 313
Liability of Independent Contractor and Principal 314
ETHICAL PERSPECTIVE: Microsoft Violates Employment Law 315
Workers' Compensation 315
Employment-Related Injury 316
Exclusive Remedy 316
Occupational Safety and Health Act 316
Specific and General Duty Standards 316
CASE FOR DISCUSSION: *Smith v. Workers' Compensation Appeals Board* 317
Title VII of the Civil Rights Act of 1964 318
Scope of Coverage of Title VII 318
Race, Color, and National Origin Discrimination 318
CASE FOR DISCUSSION: *National Association for the Advancement of Colored People, Newark Branch v. Town of Harrison, New Jersey* 319
Sex Discrimination 320
Sexual Harassment 320
Religious Discrimination 320
Bona Fide Occupational Qualification (BFOQ) 320
Age Discrimination in Employment Act (ADEA) 321
CASE FOR DISCUSSION: *Harris v. Forklift Systems, Inc.* 322
Americans With Disabilities Act (ADA) 323
Labor Union Law 324
Collective Bargaining 324
Strikes and Picketing 324
LEGAL TERMINOLOGY 325
CHAPTER SUMMARY 326
INTERNET EXERCISES AND CASES 331
Working the Web 331
Critical Legal Thinking Questions 331
Case for Briefing 331
Cases for Discussion 332

13

CREDIT, SURETYSHIP, AND BANKRUPTCY 335

Introduction 335
Unsecured and Secured Credit 336
Unsecured Credit 336
Secured Credit 337
Security Interests in Real Property 337
Mortgages 337
Notes and Deeds of Trust 337
Recording Statutes 338
Foreclosure 339
Deficiency Judgments 339
Security Interests in Personal Property 340
Written Security Agreement 341
Perfection by Filing a Financing Statement 341
Perfection by Possession of Collateral 341
CASE FOR DISCUSSION: *In Re Greenbelt Cooperative Inc.* 342
Surety and Guaranty Arrangements 343
Surety Arrangement 343
Guaranty Arrangement 343
Federal Bankruptcy Law 343
CASE FOR DISCUSSION: *General Motors Acceptance Corporation v. Daniels* 344

"Fresh Start" *345*
Types of Bankruptcy *345*
Chapter 7 Liquidation Bankruptcy 345
Filing a Petition *345*
Automatic Stay *346*
Property of the Bankruptcy Estate *346*
Exempt Property *346*
State Law Exemptions *346*
Voidable Transfers *346*
Priority of Distribution *347*
CASE FOR DISCUSSION: ***In Re Witwer*** 348
Discharge *349*
CASE FOR DISCUSSION: ***Kawaauhau v. Geiger*** 350
Chapter 13 Consumer Debt Adjustment 351
Filing the Petition *351*
Plan of Payment *351*
Discharge *351*
Chapter 11 Reorganization Bankruptcy 351
Reorganization Proceeding *352*
Plan of Reorganization *352*
Executory Contracts *352*
LEGAL TERMINOLOGY 352
CHAPTER SUMMARY 354
INTERNET EXERCISES AND CASES 358
Working the Web 358
Critical Legal Thinking Questions 358
Case for Briefing 358
Cases for Discussion 359

14

INTELLECTUAL PROPERTY AND INTERNET LAW 361

Introduction 361
INFORMATION TECHNOLOGY: Economic Espionage Act 362
Trade Secrets 362
Patents 363
INFORMATION TECHNOLOGY: Amazon.com Loses Its One-Click Patent 364
ETHICAL PERSPECTIVE: Inventor Wipes Ford's and Chrysler's Windshields Clean 365
Patent Infringement *365*
Public-Use Doctrine *365*
Copyrights 366
Registration of Copyrights *366*
Copyright Infringment *367*
Fair-Use Doctrine *367*
INFORMATION TECHNOLOGY: Copyrighting Software 367
CASE FOR DISCUSSION: ***Newton v. Beastie Boys*** 368
INFORMATION TECHNOLOGY: Digital Millennium Copyright Act 369
INFORMATION TECHNOLOGY: NET Act: Criminal Copyright Infringement 369
Trademarks 370
Distinctiveness of a Mark *370*
Marks That Can Be Trademarked *370*
Trademark Infringement *371*
Generic Names *371*
The Internet 373
World Wide Web *373*
Electronic Mail *373*
Domain Names *374*
CASE FOR DISCUSSION: ***E. & J. Gallo Winery v. Spider Webs Ltd.*** 375
INFORMATION TECHNOLOGY: Anticybersquatting Act Passed by Congress 376
LEGAL TERMINOLOGY 376
INFORMATION TECHNOLOGY: Armani Outmaneuvered for Domain Name 376
CHAPTER SUMMARY 376
INTERNET EXERCISES AND CASES 381
Working the Web 381
Critical Legal Thinking Questions 381
Case for Briefing 382
Cases for Discussion 383

15

ADMINISTRATIVE LAW, CONSUMER, INVESTOR, AND ENVIRONMENTAL PROTECTION 385

Introduction 385
Administrative Law 385
General Government Regulation *386*
Specific Government Regulation *386*
Delegation of Powers *386*
Administrative Agencies *387*
Licensing Powers of Administrative Agencies *387*
Consumer Protection 388
Federal Food, Drug, and Cosmetic Act *388*
Regulation of Food *388*
Regulation of Drugs *390*
Regulation of Cosmetics *390*
Food Labeling *390*
Product Safety *391*

INTERNATIONAL PERSPECTIVE: United Nations Biosafety Protocol for Genetically Altered Foods 392
Safety Labeling 392
Unfair and Deceptive Practices 392
INFORMATION TECHNOLOGY: Anti-Spam Statute 393
CASE FOR DISCUSSION: *Federal Trade Commission v. Colgate-Palmolive Co.* 394
Investor Protection 395
The Securities and Exchange Commission (SEC) 395
Issuance of Securities 395
Registration Statement 395
Prospectus 396
Insider Trading 396
CASE FOR DISCUSSION: *Securities and Exchange Commission v. Edwards* 397
Environmental Protection 398
Environmental Impact Statement 398
Air Pollution 399
Toxic Air Pollutants 399
Water Pollution 399
Thermal Pollution 400
Wetlands 401
Hazardous Waste 401
Endangered Species and Wildlife Protection 402
CASE FOR DISCUSSION: *Tennessee Valley Authority v. Hill, Secretary of the Interior* 403
LEGAL TERMINOLOGY 404
CHAPTER SUMMARY 405
INTERNET EXERCISES AND CASES 409
Working the Web 409
Critical Legal Thinking Questions 409
Case for Briefing 410
Cases for Discussion 411

APPENDIX A
CASES FOR BRIEFING 413

APPENDIX B
THE CONSTITUTION OF THE UNITED STATES 431

APPENDIX C
ANALYSIS USING THE CODE OF ETHICS FOR THE NATIONAL ASSOCIATION OF LEGAL ASSISTANTS, INC. 439

APPENDIX D
BASIC CITATION REFERENCE GUIDE 451

APPENDIX E
GLOSSARY OF LATIN TERMS AND PHRASES 455

GLOSSARY 459

CASE INDEX 485

SUBJECT INDEX 487

Dedication

Life

the taste of water
the scent of jasmine
the feel of silk
the quiet of Zen
the thunder of death

Henry Cheeseman

Every effort has been made to provide accurate and current Internet information in this book. However, the Internet and information posted on it are constantly changing, so it is inevitable that some of the Internet addresses listed in this textbook will change.

Preface

To the Instructors

The editors would like to point out that Henry Cheeseman's award-winning teaching style and extensive knowledge of every aspect of the law comes shining through every page in this book. ***Introduction to Law***, along with all of Henry Cheeseman's publications, is recognized as a complete teaching package. All course materials for teaching with Professor Cheeseman's books are prepared with you in mind.

Features of the Book

Students learn how to engage in ethical, analytical reasoning with every topic from legal fundamentals to areas of substantive law. The features of the book encourage students to apply critical thinking, organizational and summation skills, and legal research tools to solve specific legal problems. These features include:

- Chapter Outline, Objectives, Terminology, and Summary in every chapter
- Special boxed examples, graphics, photos, and diagrams illustrating essential points
- In each chapter, one or more Cases for Discussion, with questions, as well as the chapter-end feature Cases for Discussion, which includes additional cases and one ethics case
- Guidelines for briefing a case and one Case for Briefing activity in each chapter
- Sidebars highlighting information about text topics and the legal profession
- Ethical Perspective, Information Technology, and International Perspective feature boxes
- Working the Web research exercises and Critical Legal Thinking Questions

Course Support

Introduction to Law can be taught in the classroom or in a distance-learning environment with the tools listed below. Visit **www.prenhall.com/legal_studies** for online access to these materials or information about more materials available from Pearson Prentice Hall.

- **Instructor's Manual** with Test Item File and PowerPoint slides—Classroom support free to instructors with lecture notes and PowerPoint files for overheads and handouts.
- **Pearson TestGen**—Free, computerized test generating program helps you create quizzes, tests, and examinations quickly and easily with automated answer keys. Questions can be selected at random or individually and are also available as Word files in the downloadable version of the Instructor's Manual.
- **Free Companion Website**—This site is available for use as a classroom study enhancement tool. Students use it as an online study guide and review with immediate feedback and hints.
- **BlackBoard course**—Fully classroom-tested online course available for distance learning students. It is a complete package with student study review, reference links, sample documents, and handouts as well as course management features available through professor-only access.

- **VersusLaw® online legal research access**—One-semester subscription access code cards (0-13-118514-4) are free packaged with any Pearson Legal Series title. Student access allows them to work from anywhere there is an Internet connection.
- **LexiBrief™ and The Lexiverse Dictionary**—Both on one CD-ROM (0-13-112310-6) that can be packaged for free with any Pearson Legal Series textbook, these tools help students develop skills for a successful career in any legal industry.
- **Paralegal Videos**—Select at least one free video for your classroom from the range of videos offered through the Kapio'lani Community College program and Pearson Prentice Hall. Contact your Pearson Prentice Hall representative or visit **www.prenhall.com/legal_studies** for details.

To the Students

Each semester, as I stand up in front of a new group of students in my law class, I am struck by the thought that, cases and statutes aside, I know two very important things that they have yet to learn. The first is that I draw as much from them as they do from me. Their youth, enthusiasm, questions, and even the doubts a few of them hold about the relevance of law to their futures, fuel my teaching. They don't know that every time they open their minds to look at a point from a new perspective or critically question something they have taken for granted, I get a wonderful reward for the word that I do.

The other thing I know is that both teaching and learning the legal and ethical environment are all about stories. The stories I tell provide the framework on which students will hang everything they learn about the law in my class. It is my hope that long after the facts about the specific language of the statutes and legal principles have faded, they will retain that framework. Several years from now, "unintentional torts" may draw only a glimmer of recognition with students who learn about them in my class this year. However, they will likely recall the story of the woman who sued McDonalds for serving her coffee that was too hot and caused her injuries. The story sticks and give students the hook on which to hang the concepts.

I reminded myself of these two facts when I sat down to write *Introduction to Law.* My goal is to present law and ethics in a way that will spur students to ask questions, to go beyond rote memorization. Law is an evolving outgrowth of its environment, and that environment keeps changing. In addition to the social, ethical, and international contexts I have incorporated in *Introduction to Law,* this book also emphasizes coverage of e-commerce and the Internet as two vital catalysts to the law and a key part of its environment.

It is my wish that my commitment to these goals shines through in this labor of love, and I hope you have as much pleasure in using it as I have had in creating it for you.

A Helping Hand

The editors at Pearson Prentice Hall want you to know that other materials are available to help you in your studies. Visit **www.prenhall.com/legal_studies** to find Resources to help you with your course work. The **Companion Website** can help you study and review the information in this book, and practice test taking. You may share the results of your self-test with your professor or keep them to yourself. Use the feedback from the Companion Website as a guide for further study and practice. In addition, numerous Web links are available for reference and further investigation.

Your professor can order this book shrink-wrapped with free time-limited access to **VersusLaw®**, an online legal research service. The access code for VersusLaw® allows you to research at your leisure for one semester.

The book can also be packaged with **LexBrief™** software designed to help you develop the analytical, organizational, and summation skills needed to have a successful career in the industry. On the same CD-ROM you will have a copy of **The Lexiverse Dictionary**, a customized, stand-alone dictionary for legal students.

ACKNOWLEDGMENTS

When I first began writing this book, I was a solitary figure researching cases and statutes in the law library and online, and writing the text at my desk. As rime passed, others entered upon the scene—editors, reviewers, production personnel—and touched the project and made it better. Although my name appears on the cover of this book, it is no longer mine alone. I humbly thank the following persons for their contributions to this project.

Contributors

I would like to personally thank the following reviewers, who spent considerable time and effort reviewing the manuscripts for *Introduction to Law*, and whose comments, suggestions, and criticisms are seen in the final product: Laura Barnard, Lakeland Community College; Adam Epstein, Central Michigan University; Kent Kauffman, Ivy Tech State College; Taylor Morton, Golden West University, and Stephen Pan, Las Vegas College.

For this first edition of *Introduction to Law* a special group of people from Pearson Prentice Hall have come together along with Enika Schulze, Consulting Editor, who is in charge of producing the extensive supplements that support *Introduction to Law*. The supplements have been produced by a remarkable team of authors: Craig Simonsen and Kent Kaufmann.

Personal Acknowledgments

My family: My wife Shou-Yi Kang; my parents, Henry B. and Florence, deceased; my twin brother Gregory and his wife Lana; my sister Marcia; my nephew Gregory and niece Nikki, and the two new additions to the family, Lauren and Addison.

The students at the Marshall School of Business at the University of Southern California. Their spirit, energy, and joy are contagious, and I love teaching them (and as important, their teaching me).

While writing this Preface and Acknowledgment, I have thought about the thousands of hours I have spent researching, writing, and preparing this manuscript. I loved every minute, and the knowledge gained has been sufficient reward for the endeavor.

I hope this book and its supplementary materials will serve you as well as they have served me.

Personal Note

With joy and sadness, emptiness and fullness, honor and humility,
I surrender the fruits of this labor.

Henry R. Cheeseman

PART I

The Legal Environment

- Chapter 1 The Nature of Law and Critical Legal Thinking
- Chapter 2 The American Court System
- Chapter 3 Civil Litigation and Alternative Dispute Resolution
- Chapter 4 Criminal Law and Ethics
- Chapter 5 Constitutional Law and Freedoms

Part I introduces the reader to the legal environment. Chapter 1 provides an overview of the nature of the law and introduces the reader to the process of critical legal thinking. Chapter 2 covers the American legal system, including a description of the federal court system and a typical state court system. Chapter 3 addresses in depth the civil litigation process for beginning and maintaining a lawsuit. The chapter also includes alternative dispute resolution such as arbitration. The topics of Chapter 4 are criminal law and criminal procedure, as well as ethical concepts. Chapter 5 discusses major constitutional clauses and the freedoms they endow.

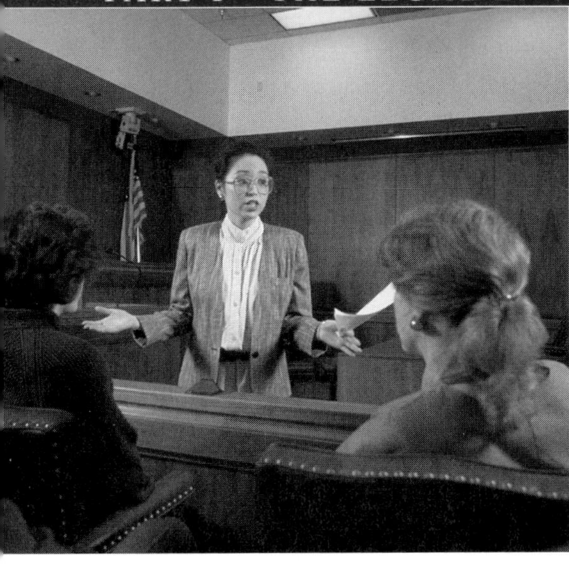

1 The Nature of Law and Critical Legal Thinking

Where there is no law, there is no freedom.

—JOHN LOCKE, *SECOND TREATISE OF GOVERNMENT*, SEC. 57

CHAPTER OBJECTIVES

After studying this chapter, you should be able to

1. Define *law* and describe the functions of law.
2. Trace the development of the U.S. legal system.
3. List and describe the sources of law in the United States.
4. Explain the international civil law legal system used in some other countries.
5. Apply critical legal thinking in analyzing judicial decisions.

CHAPTER OUTLINE

- Introduction
- What Is Law?
- Schools of Jurisprudential Thought
- History of American Law
- Sources of Law in the United States
- Critical Legal Thinking
- Case for Discussion: *Gratz v. Bollinger and the Regents of the University of Michigan*
- Case for Discussion: *Grutter v. Bollinger and the University of Michigan Law School*
- Legal Terminology
- Chapter Summary
- Internet Exercises and Cases

INTRODUCTION

Every society makes and enforces laws that govern the conduct of the individuals, businesses, and other organizations that function within it. In the words of Judge Learned Hand, "Without law we cannot live; only with it can we insure the future which by right is ours. The best of men's hopes are enmeshed in its success."[1]

Although U.S. law is based primarily on English common law, other legal systems, such as Spanish and French civil law, also influenced it. The sources of law in this country are the U.S. Constitution, state constitutions, federal and state statutes, ordinances, administrative agency rules and regulations, executive orders, and judicial decisions by federal and state courts.

Businesses that are organized in the United States are subject to its laws. They are also subject to the laws of other countries in which they operate. Businesses organized in other countries must obey the laws of the United States when doing business here. In addition, businesspeople owe a duty to act ethically in the conduct of their affairs, and businesses owe a responsibility not to harm society.

---

[1] *The Spirit of Liberty*, 3d ed (New York: Alfred A. Knopf, 1960).

SIDEBAR

The Meaning of Law
"Let every American, every lover of liberty, every well-wisher to his posterity, swear by the blood of the Revolution never to violate in the least particular the laws of the country, and never to tolerate their violation by others."

Abraham Lincoln, Speech, 1837

This chapter delves into the nature and definition of law, its philosophy or jurisprudence, and the history and sources of law. The chapter also presents two cases for discussion and a writing assignment in which you will apply critical thinking to a U.S. Supreme Court case.

What Is Law?

The law consists of rules that regulate the conduct of individuals, businesses, and other organizations within society. It is intended to protect persons and their property from unwanted interference from others. In other words, the law forbids persons from engaging in certain undesirable activities.

Consider the following passage:

> Hardly anyone living in a civilized society has not at some time been told to do something or to refrain from doing something, because there is a law requiring it, or because it is against the law. What do we mean when we say such things? Most generally, how are we to understand statements of the form "x is law"? This is an ancient question. In his *Memorabilia* (I, ii), Xenophon reports a statement of the young Alcibiades, companion of Socrates, who in conversation with the great Pericles remarked that "no one can really deserve praise unless he knows what a law is."
>
> At the end of the 18th century, Immanuel Kant wrote of the question "What is law?" that it "may be said to be about as embarrassing to the jurist as the well-known question 'What is truth?' is to the logician."[2]

SIDEBAR

Definition of the Law
That which must be obeyed and followed by citizens subject to sanctions or legal consequences; a body of rules of action or conduct prescribed by controlling authority, and having binding legal force.

Definition of Law

The concept of **law** is broad. Although it is difficult to state a precise definition, *Black's Law Dictionary* gives one that is sufficient for this text:

> Law, in its generic sense, is a body of rules of action or conduct prescribed by controlling authority, and having binding legal force. That which must be obeyed and followed by citizens subject to sanctions or legal consequences is a law.[3]

Functions of the Law

The law is often described by the function it serves within a society. The primary *functions* served by the law in this country are:

1. Keeping the peace, which includes making crimes out of certain activities.
2. Shaping moral standards (e.g., laws that discourage drug and alcohol abuse).
3. Promoting social justice (e.g., statutes that prohibit discrimination in employment).
4. Maintaining the status quo (e.g., laws preventing the forceful overthrow of the government).
5. Facilitating orderly change (e.g., laws requiring study, debate, and public input before votes on new statutes).
6. Facilitating planning (e.g., well-designed commercial laws that allow businesses to plan their activities, allocate their productive resources, and assess the risks they take).

---

[2]Introduction, *The Nature of Law: Readings in Legal Philosophy*, ed. M.P. Golding (New York: Random House, 1966).
[3]*Black's Law Dictionary*, 5th ed (St. Paul, MN: West, 1979).

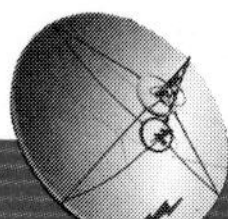

INFORMATION TECHNOLOGY

STUDENTS PLUG INTO THE INTERNET AND THE LAW

Every year millions of students arrive on college campuses and unpack an array of items—clothes, books, furniture, decorations, and their computers. College students used to be judged by the size of their stereo speakers; today it is their computer and their Internet savvy. Ninety percent of college students now own personal computers.

The Internet has revolutionized campus life. Computer kiosks abound around college campuses, occupying more space in libraries, dorm rooms, and hallways of athletic departments. Traditional libraries have become obsolete for many students as they conduct almost all of their research online. More than 80 percent of college students check out the Web daily, while others communicate through email, pick up course assignments, download course notes, and socialize online. Current university and college students use modern technology and are leading their parents, employers, and sometimes even their professors into the new world of high technology. Today's college students are the leaders of the e-generation.

Universities and colleges are now rated not only on how well they are connected with alumni but also on how well they are connected to computer technology. Some universities have installed software that allows their students to sit anywhere on campus with their laptops and "plug" into the school's network. The computer is no longer just a study tool; it has become totally integrated into the lives of college students. Students of the new generation study online, shop online, and even date online.

7. Providing a basis for compromise (approximately 90 percent of all lawsuits are settled prior to trial).
8. Maximizing individual freedom (e.g., the rights of freedom of speech, religion, and association granted by the First Amendment to the U.S. Constitution).

Flexibility of the Law

U.S. law evolves and changes along with the norms of society, technology, and the growth and expansion of commerce in the United States and the world. The following quote by Judge Jerome Frank discusses the value of the adaptability of law.

> Law must be stable and yet it cannot stand still.
>
> —Roscoe Pound

> The law always has been, is now, and will ever continue to be, largely vague and variable. And how could this be otherwise? The law deals with human relations in their most complicated aspects. The whole confused, shifting helter-skelter of life parades before it—more confused than ever, in our kaleidoscopic age.
>
> Men have never been able to construct a comprehensive, eternalized set of rules anticipating all possible legal disputes and formulating in advance the rules which would apply to them. Situations are bound to occur which were never contemplated when the original rules were made. How much less is such a frozen legal system possible in modern times?
>
> The constant development of unprecedented problems requires a legal system capable of fluidity and pliancy. Our society would be straightjacketed were not the courts, with the able assistance of the lawyers, constantly overhauling the law and adapting it to the realities of ever-changing social, industrial, and political conditions; although changes cannot be made lightly, yet rules of law must be more or less impermanent, experimental and therefore not nicely calculable.

ETHICAL PERSPECTIVE

FAIRNESS OF THE LAW

On the whole, the American legal system is one of the most comprehensive, fair, and democratic systems of law ever developed and enforced. Nevertheless, some misuses and oversights of our legal system—including abuses of discretion and mistakes by judges and juries, unequal applications of the law, and procedural mishaps—allow some guilty parties to go unpunished.

In *Standefer v. United States* [447 U.S. 10, 100 S. Ct. 1999, 1980 U.S. Lexis 127 (1980)] the Supreme Court *affirmed* (let stand) the criminal conviction of a Gulf Oil Corporation executive for aiding and abetting the bribery of an Internal Revenue Service agent. The agent had been acquitted in a separate trial. In writing the opinion of the Court, Chief Justice Warren Burger stated, "This case does no more than manifest the simple, if discomforting, reality that different juries may reach different results under any criminal statute. That is one of the consequences we accept under our jury system."

1. Do you think the law is fair? Or as fair as it can be?
2. Can you cite an instance in which you believe the law was not applied fairly?

SIDEBAR

Brown v. Board of Education

One of the main attributes of American law is its *flexibility.* It is generally responsive to cultural, technological, economic, and social changes. For example, laws that are no longer viable—such as those that restricted the property rights of women—are often repealed.

Sometimes it takes years before the law reflects the norms of society. Other times, society is led by the law. An example of the law leading the people is the Supreme Court's landmark decision in *Brown v. Board of Education* [347 U.S. 483, 74 S. Ct. 686, 1954 U.S. Lexis 2094 (1954)]. The Court's decision overturned the old "separate but equal" doctrine that condoned separate schools for black children and white children.

> Much of the uncertainty of law is not an unfortunate accident; it is of immense social value.[4]

Schools of Jurisprudential Thought

The philosophy or science of the law is referred to as **jurisprudence**. There are several different philosophies about how the law developed, ranging from the classical natural theory to modern theories of law and economics and critical legal studies. Legal philosophies can generally be grouped into the major categories discussed in the paragraphs that follow.

- The **Natural Law School** of jurisprudence postulates that the law is based on what is "correct." Natural law philosophers emphasize a **moral theory of law**—that is, law should be based on morality and ethics. Natural law is "discovered" by man through the use of reason and choosing between good and evil. Documents such as the U.S. Constitution, the Magna Carta, and the United Nations Charter reflect this theory.
- The **Historical School** of jurisprudence believes that the law is an aggregate of social traditions or customs that have developed over the centuries. It believes that changes in the norms of society will gradually be reflected in the law. To these legal philosophers, the law is an evolutionary process. Thus, historical legal scholars look to past legal decisions (precedent) to solve contemporary problems.
- The **Analytical School** of jurisprudence maintains that the law is shaped by logic. Analytical philosophers believe that results are reached by applying principles of logic to the specific facts of the case. The emphasis is on the logic of the result rather than on how the result is reached.

[4]*Law and the Modern Mind* (New York: Brentano's, 1930).

Feminist Legal Theory

In the past, the law treated men and women unequally. For example, women were denied the right to vote, could not own property if they were married, were unable to have legal abortions, and could not hold the same jobs as men. The enactment of statutes and the interpretation of constitutional provisions by the courts have changed all of these things. The Nineteenth Amendment to the U.S. Constitution gave women the right to vote. States have repealed constraints on the ability of women to own property. The famous U.S. Supreme Court decision in *Roe v. Wade* [410 U.S. 959 (1973)] gave women the constitutional right to have an abortion.

Title VII of the Civil Rights Act of 1964 prohibits employment discrimination based on sex. In addition, the equal protection clause of the U.S. and state constitutions provides that women cannot be treated differently than men (and vice versa) by the government unless some imperative reason warrants different treatment.

But is it enough for women to be treated like men? Should the female perspective be taken into account when legislators and judges develop, interpret, and apply the law? A body of scholarship known as feminist legal theory or feminist jurisprudence has been created around just such a theory.

The "battered woman's syndrome" illustrates how this type of theory works. It has been introduced into evidence to prove self-defense in homicide cases where a woman is accused of killing her husband or another male. This defense asserts that sustained domestic violence against a woman may justify such a murder. Although many courts have rejected this defense, some courts have recognized battered woman's syndrome as a justifiable defense.

Some other areas of the law where a woman's perspective might differ from a man's include male-only combat rules in the military, rights to privacy, family law, child custody, surrogate motherhood, job security for pregnant women, rape, sexual assault, abortion, and sexual harassment. Even the traditional "reasonable man standard," so prevalent in American law, is attacked as being gender-biased.

- The **Sociological School** of jurisprudence asserts that the law is a means of achieving and advancing certain sociological goals. The followers of this philosophy, known as *realists*, believe that the purpose of law is to shape social behavior. Sociological philosophers are unlikely to adhere to past law as precedent.
- The philosophers of the **Command School** of jurisprudence believe that the law is a set of rules developed, communicated, and enforced by the ruling party rather than a reflection of the society's morality, history, logic, or sociology. This school maintains that the law changes when the ruling class changes.

"Before we begin today, may I say that both my client and I were astonished that Your Honor was not nominated for the Supreme Court?"

The Law and Economics School of Jurisprudential Thought

Should free market principles, like the supply-and-demand and cost-benefit theories, determine the outcome of lawsuits and legislation? A growing number of judges and legal theorists think so. These people are members of the **Law and Economics School** (or the "Chicago School") of jurisprudence, which had its roots at the University of Chicago. According to the Law and Economics School, the central goal of legal decision making should be to promote market efficiency.

For example, proponents of law and economics theory suggest that the practice of appointing counsel, free of charge, to prisoners who bring civil rights cases should be abolished. If a prisoner cannot find a lawyer who will take the case on a contingency-fee basis, it probably means that the case is not worth bringing. Naysayers warn that certain rights and liberties must be safeguarded even if to do so is unpopular or costly from an economic point of view.

TABLE 1.1 *Comparison of schools of jurisprudential thought.*

School	Philosophy
Natural Law	Postulates that law is based on what is "correct." It emphasizes a moral theory of law—that is, law should be based on morality and ethics.
Historical	Believes that law is an aggregate of social traditions and customs.
Analytical	Maintains that law is shaped by logic.
Sociological	Asserts that the law is a means of achieving and advancing certain sociological goals.
Command	Believes that the law is a set of rules developed, communicated, and enforced by the ruling party.
Critical Legal Studies	Maintains that legal rules are unnecessary and that legal disputes should be solved by applying arbitrary rules based on fairness.
Law and Economics	Believes that promoting market efficiency should be the central concern of legal decision-making.

- The **Critical Legal Studies School** proposes that legal rules are unnecessary and are used as an obstacle by the powerful to maintain the status quo. Critical legal theorists (the "*Crits*") argue that legal disputes should be solved by applying arbitrary rules that are based on broad notions of what is "fair" in each circumstance. Under this theory, subjective decision-making by judges would be permitted.

History of American Law

When the American colonies were first settled, the English system of law was generally adopted as the system of jurisprudence. This was the foundation from which American judges developed a common law in America.

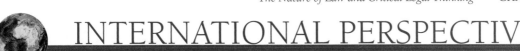

INTERNATIONAL PERSPECTIVE

ADOPTION OF ENGLISH COMMON LAW IN AMERICA

All the states of the United States of America except Louisiana base their legal systems primarily on English common law. Because of its French heritage, Louisiana bases its law on the *civil law* (see discussion of international legal systems later in this chapter). Elements of California and Texas law, as well as that of other southwestern states, are rooted in civil law.

In the United States, the law, equity, and merchant courts have been merged. Thus, most U.S. courts permit the aggrieved party to seek both law and equitable orders and remedies.

The importance of common law to the American legal system is described in the following excerpt from Justice Douglas's opinion in the 1841 case of *Penny v. Little* [4 Ill. 301, 1841 Ill. Lexis 98 (IL 1841)]:

The common law is a beautiful system, containing the wisdom and experiences of ages. Like the people it ruled and protected, it was simple and crude in its infancy and became enlarged, improved, and polished as the nation advanced in civilization, virtue, and intelligence. Adapting itself to the conditions and circumstances of the people and relying upon them for its administration, it necessarily improved as the condition of the people was elevated. The inhabitants of this country always claimed the common law as their birthright, and at an early period established it as the basis of their jurisprudence.

English common law was law developed by judges who issued their opinions when deciding a case. The principles announced in these cases became *precedent* for later judges deciding similar cases. The English common law can be divided into cases decided by the law courts, equity courts, and merchant courts.

Law Courts

Prior to the Norman Conquest of England in 1066, each locality in England was subject to local laws as established by the lord or chieftain in control of the local area. There was no countrywide system of law. After 1066, William the Conqueror and his successors to the throne of England began to replace the various local laws with one uniform system of law. To accomplish this, the king or queen appointed loyal followers as judges in all local areas. These judges were charged with administering the law in a uniform manner in courts that were called **law courts.** Law at this time tended to emphasize form (legal procedure) over the substance (merit) of the case. The only relief available at law courts was a monetary award for damages.

Chancery (Equity) Courts

Because of the unfair results and the limited remedy available in the law courts, a second set of courts—the **Court of Chancery** (or **equity court**)—was established. These courts were under the authority of the Lord Chancellor. Persons who believed that the decision of the law court was unfair or that the law court could not grant an appropriate remedy could seek relief in the Court of Chancery. Rather than emphasizing legal procedure, the Chancery Court inquired into the merits of

INTERNATIONAL PERSPECTIVE

THE CIVIL LAW SYSTEM

One of the major legal systems that has developed in the world in addition to the Anglo-American common law system is the **Romano-Germanic civil law system.** This legal system, commonly called the **civil law**, dates to 450 B.C., when Rome adopted the Twelve Tables, a code of laws applicable to the Romans. A compilation of Roman law, called the *Corpus Juris Civilis* (the Body of Civil Law), was completed in A.D. 534. Later, two national codes—the French Civil Code of 1804 (the Napoleonic Code) and the German Civil Code of 1896—became models for countries that adopted civil codes.

In contrast to the Anglo-American common law, where laws are created by the judicial system as well as by congressional legislation, the Civil Code and parliamentary statutes that expand and interpret it are the sole sources of the law in most civil law countries. Thus, the adjudication of a case is simply the application of the code or the statutes to a particular set of facts. In some civil law countries, court decisions do not have the force of law.

Today, followers of civil law include Austria, Belgium, Greece, Indochina, Indonesia, Japan, Latin America, the Netherlands, Poland, Portugal, South Korea, Spain, Sub-Saharan Africa, Switzerland, and Turkey.

the case. The Chancellor's remedies were called *equitable remedies* because they were shaped to fit each situation. Equitable order and remedies of the Court of Chancery took precedence over the legal decisions and remedies of the law courts.

Merchant Courts

As trade developed in the Middle Ages, the merchants who traveled about England and Europe developed certain rules to solve their commercial disputes. These rules, known as the "law of merchants" or the Law Merchant, were based upon common trade practices and usage. Eventually, a separate set of courts was established to administer these rules. This court was called the **Merchant Court**. In the early 1900s, the Merchant Court was absorbed into the regular law court system of England.

SOURCES OF LAW IN THE UNITED STATES

In more than 200 years since the founding of the United States and adoption of the English common law, the lawmakers of this country have developed a substantial body of law. The *sources of modern law* in the United States are constitutions, treaties, codified law, executive orders, and judicial decisions, including the doctrine of *stare decisis.*

Constitutions

The **Constitution of the United States of America** is the *supreme law of the land.* This means that any law—whether federal, state, or local—that conflicts with the U.S. Constitution is unconstitutional and, therefore, unenforceable.

TABLE 1.2 *Summary of sources of law in the United States.*

Source of Law	**Description**
Constitutions	The U.S. Constitution establishes the federal government and enumerates its powers. Powers not given to the federal government are reserved to the states. State constitutions establish state governments and enumerate their powers.
Treaties	The President, with the advice and consent of the Senate, may enter into treaties with foreign countries.
Codified Law: Statutes and Ordinances	Statutes are enacted by Congress and state legislatures. Ordinances are enacted by municipalities and local government agencies. They establish courses of conduct that covered parties must follow.
Administrative Agency Rules and Regulations	Administrative agencies are created by the legislative and executive branches of government. They may adopt rules and regulations that regulate the conduct of covered parties.
Executive Orders	Issued by the President and governors of states, executive orders regulate the conduct of covered parties.
Judicial Decisions	Courts decide controversies. In doing so, a court issues decisions that state the holding of the case and the rationale the court used in reaching that decision.

Critical Legal Thinking

Judges apply *legal reasoning* in reaching a decision in a case. That is, the judge must specify the issue presented by the case, identify the key facts in the case and the applicable law, and then apply the law to the facts to come to a conclusion that answers the issue presented. This process is called critical legal thinking. Skills of analysis and interpretation are important in deciding legal cases.

Key Terms

Before you embark upon the study of law, you should know the following key legal terms.

- **Plaintiff:** The party who originally brought the lawsuit.
- **Defendant:** The party against whom the lawsuit has been brought.
- **Petitioner or appellant:** The party who has appealed the decision of the trial court or lower court. The petitioner may be either the plaintiff or the defendant, depending on who lost the case at the trial court or lower court level.
- **Respondent or appellee:** The party who must answer the petitioner's appeal. The respondent may be either the plaintiff or the defendant, depending upon which party is the petitioner. In some cases, both the plaintiff *and* the defendant may disagree with the trial court's or lower court's decision, and both parties may appeal the decision.

CASE FOR DISCUSSION

Gratz v. Bollinger and the Regents of the University of Michigan

539 U.S. 244, 123 S.Ct. 2411, 2003 U.S. Lexis 4801 (2003) — Supreme Court of the United States

FACTS

Jennifer Gratz, a Caucasian resident of the state of Michigan, applied for admission to the College of Literature, Science, and the Arts at the University of Michigan, a state government–supported university. In its review of applicants, the University of Michigan considered high school grade point average; standardized test scores (i.e., SAT, ACT); high school quality, curriculum strength, geography, and alumni relationships; and leadership. Each item was assigned a certain number of points for each applicant. If an applicant received 100 points, he or she would be guaranteed admission to the university. Minority applicants, defined as Blacks, Hispanics, and Native Americans, were automatically given 20 points, or one-fifth of the points needed to guarantee admission. Gratz was originally placed in a postponed decision category, but was ultimately rejected for admission. A minority applicant with Gratz's score, with the extra 20 points, would have been admitted.

Gratz brought a class action lawsuit against the University of Michigan, alleging that the University violated the Equal Protection Clause of the Fourteenth Amendment to the U.S. Constitution. Plaintiff Gratz sought damages for past violations and an injunction prohibiting the university from continuing to discriminate on the basis of race in violation of the Fourteenth Amendment. The district court granted the university's motion for summary judgment and upheld the university's policy of adding 20 points to minority applicants' applications for admission. The U.S. Supreme Court granted certiorari to hear the appeal of this issue.

ISSUE

Does the University of Michigan's automatic award of 20 points to minority applicants for admission to the university's undergraduate College of Literature, Sciences, and the Arts violate the Equal Protection Clause of the Fourteenth Amendment to the U.S. Constitution?

COURT'S REASONING

The Equal Protection Clause of the Fourteenth Amendment states that "no State shall . . . deny to any person within its jurisdiction the equal protection of the laws." The U.S. Supreme Court has held that the government can treat persons differently if there is a compelling state interest for doing so and the law is narrowly tailored to accomplish the state's interest. The Supreme Court held that all racial qualifications reviewable under the Equal Protection Clause must be analyzed using the strict scrutiny test.

The Supreme Court has held that having diversity in a university student body is a compelling state interest. The Court held, however, that the University of Michigan's admissions program that automatically added 20 points to a minority applicant's score was not narrowly tailored to accomplish this compelling interest.

The Supreme Court found that the University of Michigan's policy had the effect of making the fact of race decisive for virtually every minimally qualified minority applicant. The Supreme Court held that the University's policy did not pass the strict scrutiny test. The Court noted that the University should consider each applicant on an individual basis, and that an applicant's race should be just one factor of many factors used in deciding whether to admit an applicant. The Supreme Court rejected the University's contention that it was not possible to examine individually each of the thousands of applications it received each year.

DECISION AND REMEDY

The U.S. Supreme Court held that the University of Michigan's undergraduate admission policy that automatically assigned 20 points, or one-fifth of the points needed to guarantee admission, to minority applicants did not pass the strict scrutiny test and was not narrowly tailored to accomplish the compelling state interest of obtaining a diverse student population. The Supreme Court held that the University of Michigan had violated the Equal Protection Clause of the Fourteenth Amendment. The Supreme Court reversed the decision of the district court and remanded the case for further proceedings.

QUESTIONS

1. What is the difference between the Supreme Court's decision in this case and its decision in the *Grutter v. Bollinger* case (see p. 15)? Explain.
2. Did the University of Michigan act socially responsible by using the plus 20-point program for minority applicants?
3. After this decision, can race still be used in university admissions decisions? Explain.

CASE FOR DISCUSSION

Grutter v. Bollinger and the University of Michigan Law School

539 U.S. 306, 123 S.Ct. 2325, 2003 U.S. Lexis 4800 (2003) Supreme Court of the United States

FACTS

Barbara Grutter, a Caucasian resident of the state of Michigan, applied to the Law School of the University of Michigan, a state government–supported institution, in 1996 with a 3.8 undergraduate grade point average and a 161 LSAT score. The Law School received 3,500 applications for a class of 350 students. The Law School used race as one of the factors in considering applicants for admission. The race of minority applicants, defined as Blacks, Hispanics, and Native Americans, was considered as a "plus factor" in considering their applications to law school. Caucasians and Asians were not given such a plus factor. Evidence showed that the Law School accepted approximately 35 percent of minority applicants, but that if race was not considered in admissions only 10 percent of these applicants would have been admitted.

When the Law School rejected Grutter's application, she brought a class action lawsuit against the Law School of the University of Michigan, alleging that its use of a minority's race as a plus factor in admissions violated the Equal Protection Clause of the Fourteenth Amendment to the U.S. Constitution. The district court held in favor of plaintiff Grutter, finding that the Law School's use of race as a factor in admissions violated the Equal Protection Clause. The court of appeals reversed. The U.S. Supreme Court granted certiorari to hear the appeal.

ISSUE

Does the University of Michigan Law School's use of race as a plus factor in accepting minority applicants for admission to the Law School violate the Equal Protection Clause of the Fourteenth Amendment?

COURT'S REASONING

The Equal Protection Clause of the Fourteenth Amendment states "no State shall . . . deny to any person within its jurisdiction the equal protection of the laws." The Supreme Court applies a strict scrutiny test whenever the government treats a person differently because of his or her race. To withstand such scrutiny, the government must prove a compelling state interest for such different treatment of persons based on race. The Supreme Court held that having a diverse student body at an educational institution was a compelling state interest sufficient to justify using a minority applicant's race as a plus factor in selecting a student body.

The Supreme Court held that once a state has demonstrated a compelling state interest for treating persons differently because of their race, the state's action must be narrowly tailored to accomplish this state interest. The Supreme Court stated, "A university may consider race or ethnicity only as a 'plus' in a particular student's file. Here, the Law School engages in a highly individualized, holistic review of each applicant's file, giving serious consideration to all ways an applicant might contribute to a diverse educational environment. The Law School affords this individualized consideration to applicants of all races. The Law School's race-conscious admissions policy does not unduly harm nonminority applicants. We expect that 25 years from now, the use of racial preferences will no longer be necessary to further the interest approved today."

DECISION AND REMEDY

The U.S. Supreme Court held that the University of Michigan Law School's policy of using race as a plus factor in admitting minority applicants furthers a compelling state interest and is narrowly tailored to accomplish that interest. The Supreme Court affirmed the decision of the court of appeals that held that the Law School's race-conscious admissions policy does not violate the Equal Protection Clause of the Fourteenth Amendment to the U.S. Constitution.

QUESTIONS

1. What does the Equal Protection Clause provide? Should the government ever be allowed to treat persons differently because of their race? Explain.
2. Is it socially responsible for the University of Michigan Law School to consider a minority applicant's race as a plus factor in its admissions decisions?
3. Is anyone hurt by the University of Michigan Law School's race-conscious admissions policy? Explain.

ETHICAL PERSPECTIVE

NIKE CLEANS UP ITS ACT IN VIETNAM

Nike produces basketball, running, and other athletic shoes that it sells in the United States and worldwide. Nike has more than 40 percent of the athletic shoe market. The majority of Nike's shoes are produced by subcontractors located in some of the poorest countries of the world. In 1997, Nike faced a public relations and ethical nightmare: It was being charged with selling shoes made by slave and child laborers who worked in horrid conditions.

In Vietnam, where Nike has 12 percent of its shoes manufactured, subcontractors worked employees 8 hours per day, 6 days per week, and paid them as little as $40 per month in wages. These workers, who were mostly women in their 20s, worked under terrible conditions. They were subject to hot and noisy working environments, exposed to toxic chemicals and fumes, and mistreated by the managers.

These conditions were brought to light not by Nike but by humanitarian organizations. After first vehemently denying the allegations, Nike backed down and agreed to improve the working conditions at its subcontractors in Vietnam.

Nike took the following steps:

- Required many managers at the subcontractors to be fired for their abusive conduct.
- Reduced toxic petroleum-based compounds used in making Nike shoes.
- Banned its subcontractors from paying below Vietnam's minimum wage of $45 per month.
- Installed Nike managers in the subcontractors' plants to monitor working conditions.
- Opened the manufacturing plants to outside inspectors.

Nike stated that it has taken the necessary steps to prohibit and prevent abuses by its subcontractors in Vietnam and that its decision to have its shoes made in Vietnam is an economic one. Critics contend that Nike is outsourcing the production of its shoes to workers in poor countries that do not have the same worker protections as provided in the United States.

Briefing a Case

It is often helpful for a student to "brief" a case to clarify the legal issues involved and to gain a better understanding of the case.

The procedure for a student briefing a case is as follows. The student must summarize, or brief, the court's decision in no more than 400 words (some professors may shorten or lengthen this limit). The assignment's format is highly structured, consisting of five parts, each of which is numbered and labeled:

Part	Maximum Words
1. *Case name, citation,* and *court*	25
2. Summary of the *key facts* in the case	125
3. The *issue* presented by the case, stated as a one-sentence question answerable only by *yes* or *no*	25
4. The court's resolution of the issue (the *holding*)	25
5. A summary of the *court's reasoning* justifying the holding	200
Total words	400

Briefing a case consists of making a summary of each of the following items of the case.

1. **Case name, citation, and court:** The name of the case should be placed at the beginning of each briefed case. The case name usually contains the names of the parties to the lawsuit. For example, *PGA TOUR, Inc. v. Martin.* Where there are multiple plaintiffs or defendants, however, some of the names of the parties may be omitted from the case name. Abbreviations are often used in case names as well.

   The case citation, which consists of a number plus the year in which the case was decided, such as "532 U.S. 661, 121 S.Ct. 1879, 2001 U. S. Lexis 4115 (2001)," is set forth below the case name. The case citation identifies the book in the law library or the Internet site where the case may be found. For example, the case in the above citation may be found in volume 532 of the *United States Reports* at page 661, in volume 121 of the *Supreme Court Reporter*, page 1879, and on the Lexis Web site at 2001 U.S. Lexis 4115. The name of the court that decided the case should be set forth below the case name.
2. **Summary of the key facts in the case:** The important facts of a case should be stated briefly. Extraneous facts and facts of minor importance should be omitted from the brief. The facts of the case can usually be found at the beginning of the case, but not necessarily. Important facts may be found throughout the case.
3. **Issue presented by the case:** In the briefing of a case, it is crucial to identify the issue presented to the court to decide. The issue on appeal is most often a legal question, although questions of fact are sometimes the subject of an appeal. The issue presented in each case is usually quite specific and should be asked in a one-sentence question that is answerable only by a *yes* or *no*. For example, the issue statement, "Is Mary liable?" is too broad. A more proper statement of the issue would be, "Is Mary liable to Joe for breach of the contract made between them based on her refusal to make the payment due on September 30?"
4. **Holding:** The "holding" is the decision reached by the present court. It should be *yes* or *no*. The holding should also state which party won.
5. **Summary of the court's reasoning:** When an appellate court or a supreme court issues a decision, which is often called an *opinion*, the court will normally state the reasoning it used in reaching its decision. The rationale for the decision may be based on the specific facts of the case, public policy, prior law, or other matters. In stating the reasoning of the court, the student should reword the court's language into the student's own language. This summary of the court's reasoning should pick out the meat of the opinion and weed out the nonessentials.

Briefing the Case—Example

The following is an excerpted decision by the Supreme Court of the United States. The case is presented in the language of the Supreme Court. Following the case is a brief of the case using the previous model.

Case Name, Citation, and Court

PGA TOUR, Inc. v. Martin, 532 U.S. 661, 121 S.Ct. 1879, 2001 U.S. LEXIS 4115 (2001), Supreme Court of the United States

Opinion of the Court

Issue

OPINION, STEVEN, JUSTICE This case raises two questions concerning the application of the Americans with Disabilites Act of 1990 [42 U.S.C. § 12101 et seq.] to a gifted athlete: first, whether the Act protects access to professional golf tournaments by a qualified entrant with a disability; and second, whether a disabled contestant may be denied the use of a golf cart because it would "fundamentally alter the nature" of the tournaments to allow him to ride when all other contestants must walk.

Facts

Petitioner: PGA TOUR, Inc.

Petitioner PGA TOUR, Inc., a nonprofit entity formed in 1968, sponsors and cosponsors professional golf tournaments conducted on three annual tours. About 200 golfers participate in the PGA TOUR; about 170 in the NIKE TOUR; and about 100 in the SENIOR PGA TOUR. PGA TOUR and NIKE TOUR tournaments typically are four-day events, played on courses leased and operated by petitioner. The revenues generated by television, admissions, concessions, and contributions from cosponsors amount to about $300 million a year, much of which is distributed in prize money. The "Conditions of Competition and Local Rules," often described as the "hard card," apply specifically to petitioner's professional tours. The hard cards for the PGA TOUR and NIKE TOUR required players to walk the golf course during tournaments, but not during open qualifying rounds. On the SENIOR PGA TOUR, which is limited to golfers age 50 and older, the contestants may use golf carts. Most seniors, however, prefer to walk.

Respondent: Casey Martin

Casey Martin is a talented golfer. As an amateur, he won 17 Oregon Golf Association junior events before he was 15, and won the state championship as a high school senior. He played on the Stanford University golf team that won the 1994 National Collegiate Athletic Association (NCAA) championship. As a professional, Martin qualified for the NIKE TOUR in 1998 and 1999, and based on his 1999 performance, qualified for the PGA TOUR in 2000. In the 1999 season, he entered 24 events, made the cut 13 times, and had six top-10 finishes, coming in second twice and third once.

Martin is also an individual with a disability as defined in the Americans with Disabilities Act of 1990 (ADA or Act). Since birth he has been afflicted with Klippel-Trenaunay-Weber Syndrome, a degenerative circulatory disorder that obstructs the flow of blood from his right leg back to his heart. The disease is progressive; it causes severe pain and has atrophied his right leg. During the latter part of his college career, because of the progress of the disease, Martin could no longer walk an 18-hole golf course. Walking not only caused him pain, fatigue, and anxiety, but also created a significant risk of hemorrhaging, developing blood clots, and fracturing his tibia so badly that an amputation might be required.

When Martin turned pro and entered petitioner's Qualifying-School, the hard card permitted him to use a cart during his successful progress through the first two stages. He made a request, supported by detailed medical records, for permission to use a golf cart during the third stage. Petitioner refused to review those records or to waive its walking rule for the third stage. Martin therefore filed this action.

District Court's Decision 994 F.Supp. 1242, 1998 U.S. Dist. Lexis 1980 [District: Oregon (1998)]

At trial, petitioner PGA TOUR did not contest the conclusion that Martin has a disability covered by the ADA, or the fact that his disability prevents him from walking the course during a round of golf. Rather, petitioner asserted that the condition of walking is a substantive rule of competition, and that waiving it as to any individual for any reason would fundamentally alter the nature of the competition. Petitioner's evidence included the testimony of a number of experts, among them some of the greatest golfers in history. Arnold Palmer, Jack Nicklaus, and Ken Venturi explained that fatigue can be a critical factor in a tournament, particularly on the last day when psychological pressure is at a maximum. Their testimony makes it clear that, in their view, permission to use a cart might well give some players a competitive advantage over other players who must walk.

The judge found that the purpose of the rule was to inject fatigue into the skill of shot-making, but that the fatigue injected "by walking the course cannot be deemed significant under normal circumstances." Furthermore, Martin presented evidence, and the judge found, that even with the use of a cart, Martin must walk over a mile during an 18-hole round, and that the fatigue he suffers from coping with his disability is "undeniably greater" than the fatigue his able-bodied competitors endure from walking the course. As a result, the judge concluded that it would "not fundamentally alter the nature of the PGA TOUR's game to accommodate him with a cart." The judge accordingly entered a permanent injunction requiring petitioner to permit Martin to use a cart in tour and qualifying events.

Court of Appeals Decision 204 F.3d 994, 2000 U.S. App. Lexis 3376 [9th Circuit (2000)]

The Court of Appeals concluded that golf courses remain places of public accommodation during PGA tournaments. On the merits, because there was no serious dispute about the fact that permitting Martin to use a golf cart was both a reasonable and a necessary solution to the problem of providing him access to the tournaments, the Court of Appeals regarded the central dispute as whether such permission would "fundamentally alter" the nature of the PGA TOUR or NIKE TOUR. Like the District Court, the Court of Appeals viewed the issue not as "whether use of carts generally would fundamentally alter the competition, but whether the use of a cart by Martin would do so." That issue turned on "an intensively fact-based inquiry," and, the court concluded, had been correctly resolved by the trial judge. In its words, "all that the cart does is permit Martin access to a type of competition in which he otherwise could not engage because of his disability."

Federal Statute Being Interpreted

Congress enacted the ADA in 1990 to remedy widespread discrimination against disabled individuals. To effectuate its sweeping purpose, the ADA forbids discrimination against disabled individuals in major areas of public life, among them employment (Title I of the Act), public services (Title II), and public accommodations (Title III). At issue now is the applicability of Title III to petitioner's golf tours and qualifying rounds, in particular to petitioner's treatment of a qualified disabled golfer wishing to compete in those events.

U.S. Supreme Court's Reasoning

It seems apparent, from both the general rule and the comprehensive definition of "public accommodation," that petitioner's golf tours and their qualifying rounds fit comfortably within the coverage of Title III, and Martin within its protection. The events occur on "golf courses," a type of place specifically identified by the Act as a public accommodation. Section 12181(7)(L). In this case, the narrow dispute is whether allowing Martin to use a golf cart, despite the walking requirement that applies to the PGA TOUR, the NIKE TOUR, and the third stage of the Qualifying-School, is a modification that would "fundamentally alter the nature" of those events.

As an initial matter, we observe that the use of carts is not itself inconsistent with the fundamental character of the game of golf. From early on, the essence of the game has been shot-making—using clubs to cause a ball to progress from the teeing ground to a hole some distance away with as few strokes as possible. Golf carts started appearing with increasing regularity on American golf courses in the 1950s. Today they are everywhere. And they are encouraged. For one thing, they often speed up play, and for another, they are great revenue producers. There is nothing in the rules of golf that either forbids the use of carts or penalizes a player for using a cart.

Petitioner, however, distinguishes the game of golf as it is generally played from the game that it sponsors in the PGA TOUR, NIKE TOUR, and the last stage of the Qualifying-School—golf at the "highest level." According to petitioner, "the goal of the highest-level competitive athletics is to assess and compare the performance of different competitors, a task that is meaningful only if the competitors are subject to identical substantive rules." The waiver of any possibly "outcome-affecting" rule for a contestant would violate this principle and therefore, in petitioner's view, fundamentally alter the nature of the highest level athletic event. The walking rule is one such rule, petitioner submits, because its purpose is "to inject the element of fatigue into the skill of shot-making," and thus its effect may be the critical loss of a stroke. As a consequence, the reasonable modification Martin seeks would fundamentally alter the nature of petitioner's highest level tournaments.

The force of petitioner's argument is, first of all, mitigated by the fact that golf is a game in which it is impossible to guarantee that all competitors will play under exactly the same conditions or that an individual's ability will be the sole determinant of the outcome. For example, changes in the weather may produce harder greens and more head winds for the tournament leader than for his closest pursuers. A lucky bounce may save a shot or two. Whether such happenstance events are more or less probable than the likelihood that a golfer afflicted with Klippel-Trenaunay-Weber Syndrome would one day qualify for the NIKE TOUR and PGA TOUR, they at least demonstrate that pure chance may have a greater impact on the outcome of elite golf tournaments than the fatigue resulting from the enforcement of the walking rule.

Further, the factual basis of petitioner's argument is undermined by the District Court's finding that the fatigue from walking during one of petitioner's 4-day tournaments cannot be deemed significant. The District Court credited the testimony of a professor in physiology and expert on fatigue, who calculated the calories expended in walking a golf course (about five miles) to be approximately 500 calories—"nutritionally less than a Big Mac." What is more, that energy is expended over a 5-hour period, during which golfers have numerous intervals for rest and refreshment. In fact, the expert concluded, because golf is a low intensity activity, fatigue from the game is primarily a psychological phenomenon in which stress and motivation are the key ingredients. And even under conditions of severe heat and humidity, the critical factor in fatigue is fluid loss rather than exercise from walking. Moreover, when given the option of using a cart, the majority of golfers in petitioner's tournaments have chosen to walk, often to relieve stress or for other strategic reasons. As NIKE TOUR member Eric Johnson testified, walking allows him to keep in rhythm, stay warmer when it is chilly, and develop a better sense of the elements and the course than riding a cart. As we have demonstrated, the walking rule is at best peripheral to the nature of petitioner's athletic events, and thus it might be waived in individual cases without working a fundamental alteration.

Holding and Remedy

Under the ADA's basic requirement that the need of a disabled person be evaluated on an individual basis, we have no doubt that allowing Martin to use a golf cart would not fundamentally alter the nature of petitioner's tournaments. As we have discussed, the purpose of the walking rule is to subject players to fatigue, which in turn may influence the outcome of tournaments. Even if the rule does serve that purpose, it is an uncontested finding of the District Court that Martin "easily endures greater fatigue even with a cart than his able-bodied competitors do by walking." The purpose of the walking rule is therefore not compromised in the slightest by allowing Martin to use a cart. A modification that provides an exception to a peripheral tournament rule without impairing its purpose cannot be said to "fundamentally alter" the tournament. What it can be said to do, on the other hand, is to allow Martin the chance to qualify for and compete in the athletic events petitioner offers to those members of the public who have the skill and desire to enter. That is exactly what the ADA requires. As a result, Martin's request for a waiver of the walking rule should have been granted.

The judgment of the Court of Appeals is affirmed. It is so ordered.

Dissenting Opinion

DISSENTING OPINION, SCALIA, JUSTICE In my view today's opinion exercises a benevolent compassion that the law does not place it within our power to impose. The judgment distorts the text of Title III, the structure of the ADA, and common sense. I respectfully dissent.

The Court, for its part, assumes that conclusion for the sake of argument, but pronounces respondent to be a "customer" of the PGA TOUR or of the golf courses on which it is played. That seems to me quite incredible. The PGA TOUR is a professional sporting event, staged for the entertainment of a live and TV audience. The professional golfers on the tour are no more "enjoying" (the statutory term) the entertainment that the tour provides, or the facilities of the golf courses on which it is held, than professional baseball players "enjoy" the baseball games in which they play or the facilities of Yankee Stadium. To be sure, professional ballplayers *participate* in the games, and *use* the ball fields, but no one in his right mind would think that they are *customers* of the American League or of Yankee Stadium. They are themselves the entertainment that the customers pay to watch. And professional golfers are no different. A professional golfer's practicing his profession is not comparable to John Q. Public's frequenting "a 232-acre amusement area with swimming, boating, sunbathing, picnicking, miniature golf, dancing facilities, and a snack bar."

Having erroneously held that Title III applies to the "customers" of professional golf who consist of its practitioners, the Court then erroneously answers—or to be accurate simply ignores—a second question. The ADA requires covered businesses to make such reasonable modifications of "policies, practices, or procedures" as are necessary to "afford" goods, services, and privileges to individuals with disabilities; but it explicitly does not require "modifications that would fundamentally alter the nature" of the goods, services, and privileges. Section 12182(b)(2)(A)(ii). In other words, disabled individuals must be given access to the same goods, services, and privileges that others enjoy.

A camera store may not refuse to sell cameras to a disabled person, but it is not required to stock cameras specially designed for such persons. It is hardly a feasible judicial function to decide whether shoe stores should sell single shoes to one-legged persons and if so at what price, or how many braille books the Borders or Barnes and Noble bookstore chains should stock in each of their stores. Eighteen-hole golf courses, 10-foot-high basketball hoops, 90-foot baselines, 100-yard football fields—all are arbitrary and none is essential. The only support for any of them is tradition and (in more modern times) insistence by what has come to be regarded as the ruling body of the sport—both of which factors support the PGA TOUR's position in the present case. One can envision the parents of a Little League player with attention deficit disorder trying to convince a judge that their son's disability makes it at least 25 percent more difficult to hit a pitched ball. (If they are successful, the only thing that could prevent a court order giving the kid four strikes would be a judicial determination that, in baseball, three strikes are metaphysically necessary, which is quite absurd.)

Agility, strength, speed, balance, quickness of mind, steadiness of nerves, intensity of concentration—these talents are not evenly distributed. No wild-eyed dreamer has ever suggested that the managing bodies of the competitive sports that test precisely these qualities should try to take account of the uneven distribution of God-given gifts when writing and enforcing the rules of competition. And I have no doubt Congress did not authorize misty-eyed judicial supervision of such a revolution. The year was 2001, and "everybody was finally equal" (K. Vonnegut, in *Animal Farm and Related Readings*, 1997, p. 129).

Brief of the Case: *PGA Tour, Inc. v. Martin*

1. **Case name, citation, and court:**
   PGA TOUR, Inc. v. Martin
   532 U.S. 661, 121 S.Ct. 1879, 2001 U. S. LEXIS 4115 (2001)
   Supreme Court of the United States
2. **Key facts:**
   a. PGA TOUR, Inc. is a nonprofit organization that sponsors professional golf tournaments.
   b. The PGA establishes rules for its golf tournaments. A PGA rule requires golfers to walk the golf course and not use golf carts.
   c. Casey Martin is a professional golfer who suffers from Klippel-Trenaunay-Weber Syndrome, a degenerative circulatory disorder that atrophied Martin's right leg and causes him pain, fatigue, and anxiety when walking.
   d. When Martin petitioned the PGA to use a golf cart during golf tournaments, the PGA refused.
   e. Martin sued the PGA, alleging discrimination against a disabled individual in violation of the Americans with Disabilities Act of 1990, a federal statute.
3. **Issue:** Does the Americans with Disabilities Act require the PGA to accommodate Martin by permitting him to use a golf cart while playing in PGA tournaments?
4. **Holding:** Yes. The Supreme Court held that the PGA must allow Martin to use a golf cart when competing in PGA golf tournaments. Affirmed.
5. **Court's reasoning:** The Supreme Court held that:
   a. Martin was disabled and covered by the act.
   b. Golf courses are "public accommodations" covered by the act.
   c. The use of golf carts is not a fundamental characteristic of the game of golf.
   d. Other than the PGA rule, there is no rule of golf that forbids the use of golf carts.
   e. It is impossible to guarantee that all players in golf will play under the exact same conditions, so allowing Martin to use a golf cart gives him no advantage over other golfers.
   f. Martin, because of his disease, will probably suffer more fatigue playing golf using a golf cart than other golfers will suffer without using a cart.

g. The PGA's "walking rule" is only peripheral to the game of golf and not a fundamental part of golf.
h. Allowing Martin to use a golf cart will not fundamentally alter the PGA's highest-level professional golf tournaments.

LEGAL TERMINOLOGY

Administrative agencies
Analytical School
Civil law
Codified law
Command School
Constitution of the United States of America
Court of Chancery (Equity)
Critical Legal Studies School
English common law
Executive branch
Executive order
Historical School
Judicial branch
Judicial decision
Jurisprudence
Law
Law and Economics School
Law court
Legislative branch
Merchant court
Moral theory of law
Natural Law School
Ordinances
Precedent
Romano-Germanic civil law system
Sociological School
Stare decisis
Statute
Treaty

chapter summary

THE NATURE OF LAW AND CRITICAL LEGAL THINKING	
What Is Law?	
Definition	A body of rules of action or conduct prescribed by controlling authority and having binding legal force.
Functions	1. Keep the peace 2. Shape moral standards 3. Promote social justice 4. Maintain the status quo 5. Facilitate orderly change 6. Facilitate planning 7. Provide a basis for compromise 8. Maximize individual freedom
Fairness	Although the American legal system is one of the fairest and most democratic systems of law, abuses and mistakes in the application of the law still occur.
Flexibility	The law must be flexible to meet social, technological, and economic changes. *(continued)*

Schools of Jurisprudential Thought	
Natural Law	Postulates that law is based on what is "correct"; it emphasizes a moral theory of law—that is, law should be based on morality and ethics.
Historical	Believes that law is an aggregate of social traditions and customs.
Analytical	Maintains that law is shaped by logic.
Sociological	Asserts that the law is a means of achieving and advancing certain sociological goals.
Command	Believes that the law is a set of rules developed, communicated, and enforced by the ruling party.
Critical Legal Studies	Maintains that legal rules are unnecessary and that legal disputes should be solved by applying arbitrary rules based on fairness.
Law and Economics	Believes that promoting market efficiency should be the central concern of legal decision-making.

History of American Law	
Foundation of American Law	English common law (judge-made law) forms the basis of the legal systems of most states in this country. Louisiana bases its law on the French civil code.

Sources of Law in the United States	
Constitutions	The U.S. Constitution establishes the federal government and enumerates its powers. Powers not given to the federal government are reserved to the states. State constitutions establish state governments and enumerate their powers.
Treaties	The President, with the advice and consent of the Senate, may enter into treaties with foreign countries.
Codified Law	1. *Statutes* are enacted by the U.S. Congress and state legislatures. 2. *Ordinances* and statutes are passed by municipalities and local government bodies to establish courses of conduct that covered parties must follow.
Administrative Agency Rules and Regulations	Administrative agencies are created by the legislative and executive branches of government; they may adopt rules and regulations that govern the conduct of covered parties.
Executive Orders	Issued by the President and governors of states, executive orders regulate the conduct of covered parties.
Judicial Decisions	Courts decide controversies by issuing decisions that state the holding of each case and the rationale the court used to reach that decision.
Doctrine of *Stare Decisis*	Means "to stand by the decision"; provides for adherence to precedent.

WORKING THE WEB

Visit the Web sites listed below for more information about the topics covered in this chapter.

1. For a broad overview of legal history, visit **jurist.law.pitt.edu/sg_hist.htm.**
2. To better understand the conceptual differences between law versus equity, see **www.law.cornell.edu/topics/equity.html.**
3. For a working definition of basic legal categories, visit "common law," *The Columbia Encyclopedia*, Sixth Edition, 2001, at **www.bartleby.com/65/co/commonla.html.**

CRITICAL LEGAL THINKING QUESTIONS

1. Define *law*. What are the intended purposes of law?
2. List and describe the functions of the law.
3. Is the law always fair? Explain.
4. Is the law flexible? Does flexibility or lack of it add strength to the law? Explain.
5. Describe feminist legal theory. Give an example of the application of feminist legal theory.
6. Describe the Sociological School of jurisprudence. Contrast it to the Analytical and Natural Law Schools of jurisprudence.
7. Describe the *common law*. How does this differ from *civil law?* Explain.
8. List and describe the major sources of law in the United States.
9. Define *stare decisis*. Does it add stability to the law? Explain.
10. Describe the procedure for briefing a case.

CASE FOR BRIEFING

Read Case 1 in Appendix A *(Harris v. Forklift Systems, Inc.)*. Review and brief the case using the *Critical Legal Thinking* "Briefing the Case" example described in this chapter.

1.1 *W. C. Ritchie & Co. v. Wayman*

91 N.E. 695, 1910 Ill. Lexis 1958 (1910)
Supreme Court of Illinois

FACTS In 1909, the state legislature of Illinois enacted a statute called the "Woman's 10-Hour Law." The law prohibited women who were employed in factories and other manufacturing facilities from working more than 10 hours per day. The law did not apply to men. W. C. Ritchie & Co., an employer, brought a lawsuit that challenged the statute as being unconstitutional in violation of the Equal Protection Clause of the Illinois constitution. In upholding the statute, the Illinois Supreme Court stated,

> *It is known to all men (and what we know as men we cannot profess to be ignorant of as judges) that woman's physical structure and the performance of maternal functions place her at a great disadvantage in the battle of life; that while a man can work for more than 10 hours a day without injury to himself, a woman, especially when the burdens of motherhood are upon her, cannot; that while a man can work standing upon his feet for more than 10 hours a day, day after day, without injury to himself, a woman cannot; and that to require a woman to stand upon her feet for more than 10 hours in any one day and perform severe manual labor while thus standing, day after day, has the effect to impair her health, and that as weakly and sickly women cannot be mothers of vigorous children.*
>
> *We think the general consensus of opinion, not only in this country but in the civilized countries of Europe, is, that a working day of not more than 10 hours for women is justified for the following reasons: (1) the physical organization of women, (2) her maternal function, (3) the rearing and education of children, (4) the maintenance of the home; and these conditions are, so far, matters of general knowledge that the courts will take judicial cognizance of their existence.*
>
> *Surrounded as women are by changing conditions of society, and the evolution of employment which environs them, we agree fully with what is said by the Supreme Court of Washington in the* Buchanan *case; "Law is, or ought to be, a progressive science."*

ISSUE Is the statute fair? Would the statute be lawful today? Should the law be a "progressive science"?

ETHICS CASE

1.2 *Rostker, Director of the Selective Service v. Goldberg*

453 U.S. 57, 101 S.Ct. 2646, 1981 U.S. Lexis 126 (1981)
Supreme Court of the United States

FACTS In 1975, after the war in Vietnam, the U.S. government discontinued draft registration for men in this country. In 1980, after the Soviet Union invaded Afghanistan, President Jimmy Carter asked Congress for funds to reactivate draft registration. President Carter suggested that both males and females be required to register. Congress allocated funds only for the registration of males. Several men who were subject to draft registration brought a lawsuit that challenged the law as being unconstitutional in violation of the Equal Protection Clause of the U.S. Constitution. The U.S. Supreme Court upheld the constitutionality of the draft registration law, reasoning as follows:

> *The question of registering women for the draft not only received considerable national attention and was the subject of wide-ranging public debate, but also was extensively considered by Congress in hearings, floor debate, and in committee. The foregoing clearly establishes that the decision to exempt women from registration was not the "accidental by-product of a traditional way of thinking about women."*
>
> *This is not a case of Congress arbitrarily choosing to burden one of two similarly situated groups, such as would be the case with an all-black or all-white, or an all-Catholic or all-Lutheran, or an all-Republican or all-Democratic registration. Men and women are simply not similarly situated for purposes of a draft or registration for a draft.*

Justice Thurgood Marshall dissented, stating that "The Court today places its imprimatur on one of the most potent remaining public expressions of 'ancient canards about the proper role of women.' It upholds a statute that requires males but not females to register for the draft, and which thereby categorically excludes women from a fundamental civic obligation. I dissent."

ISSUE Was the decision fair? Has the law been a "progressive science" in this case? Is it ethical for males, but not females, to have to register for the draft?

2 The American Court System

The law wherein, as in a magic mirror, we see reflected, not only our own lives, but the lives of all men that have been! When I think of this majestic theme, my eyes dazzle.

—OLIVER WENDELL HOLMES, *THE LAW*, SPEECHES 17 (1913)

CHAPTER OBJECTIVES

After studying this chapter, you should be able to

1. Describe state court systems.
2. Describe the federal court system.
3. Explain how a justice is chosen for the U.S. Supreme Court.
4. Define *jurisdiction* and compare federal and state court jurisdiction.
5. Explain how jurisdiction is obtained in cyberspace.

CHAPTER OUTLINE

- Introduction
- State Court System
- Federal Court System
- Case for Discussion: *Pizza Hut, Inc. v. Papa John's International, Inc.*
- Jurisdiction of Federal and State Courts
- Case for Discussion: *Carnival Cruise Lines, Inc. v. Shute*
- Legal Terminology
- Chapter Summary
- Internet Exercises and Cases

U.S. Courts:

www.uscourts.gov

INTRODUCTION

The two major court systems in the United States are: (1) the federal court system, and (2) the court systems of the 50 states and the District of Columbia. Each of these systems has jurisdiction to hear different types of lawsuits. The process of bringing, maintaining, and defending a lawsuit is called **litigation**. Litigation is a difficult, time-consuming, and costly process that must comply with complex procedural rules. Although it is not required, most parties employ a lawyer to represent them when they are involved in a lawsuit.

This chapter covers the various court systems, the jurisdiction of courts to hear and decide cases, and the litigation process.

STATE COURT SYSTEM

Each state and the District of Columbia have separate court systems. Most **state court systems** include the following:

- Limited-jurisdiction trial courts
- General-jurisdiction trial courts

- Intermediate appellate courts
- A supreme court (or highest state court)

Limited-Jurisdiction Trial Court

State **limited-jurisdiction trial courts**, which sometimes are referred to as inferior trial courts, hear matters of a specialized or limited nature. Examples of those courts, in many states, are traffic courts, juvenile courts, justice-of-the-peace courts, probate courts, family law courts, and courts that hear misdemeanor criminal law cases and civil cases involving lawsuits less than a certain dollar amount. Because these courts are trial courts, evidence can be introduced and testimony given. Most limited-jurisdiction courts keep a record of their proceedings. Their decisions usually can be appealed to a general-jurisdiction court or an appellate court.

Many states also have created **small-claims courts** to hear civil cases involving small dollar amounts (e.g., $5,000 or less). Generally, the parties must appear individually and cannot have a lawyer represent them. The decisions of small claims courts are often appealable to general-jurisdiction trial courts or appellate courts.

General-Jurisdiction Trial Court

Every state has a **general-jurisdiction trial court**. These courts often are called **courts of record** because the testimony and evidence at trial are recorded and stored for future reference. These courts hear cases that are not within the jurisdiction of limited-jurisdiction trial courts, such as felonies, civil cases above a certain dollar amount, and so on. Some states divide their general-jurisdiction courts into two divisions, one for criminal cases and another for civil cases. General-jurisdiction trial courts hear evidence and testimony. The decisions handed down by these courts are appealable to an intermediate appellate court or to the state supreme court, depending on the circumstances.

Intermediate Appellate Court

In many states, **intermediate appellate courts** (also called appellate courts or courts of appeal) hear appeals from trial courts. These courts review the trial court record to determine any errors at trial that would require reversal or modification of the trial court's decision. Thus, the appellate court reviews either pertinent parts or the whole trial court record from the lower court. No new evidence or testimony is permitted. The parties usually file legal **briefs** with the appellate court, stating the law and facts that support their positions. Appellate courts usually grant a short oral hearing to the parties. Appellate court decisions are appealable to the state's highest court. In less populated states that do not have an intermediate appellate court, trial court decisions can be appealed directly to the state's highest court.

Highest State Court

Each state has a highest court in its court system. In most states this is called the **state supreme court**. The function of a state supreme court is to hear appeals

EXHIBIT 2.1 *Typical state court system.*

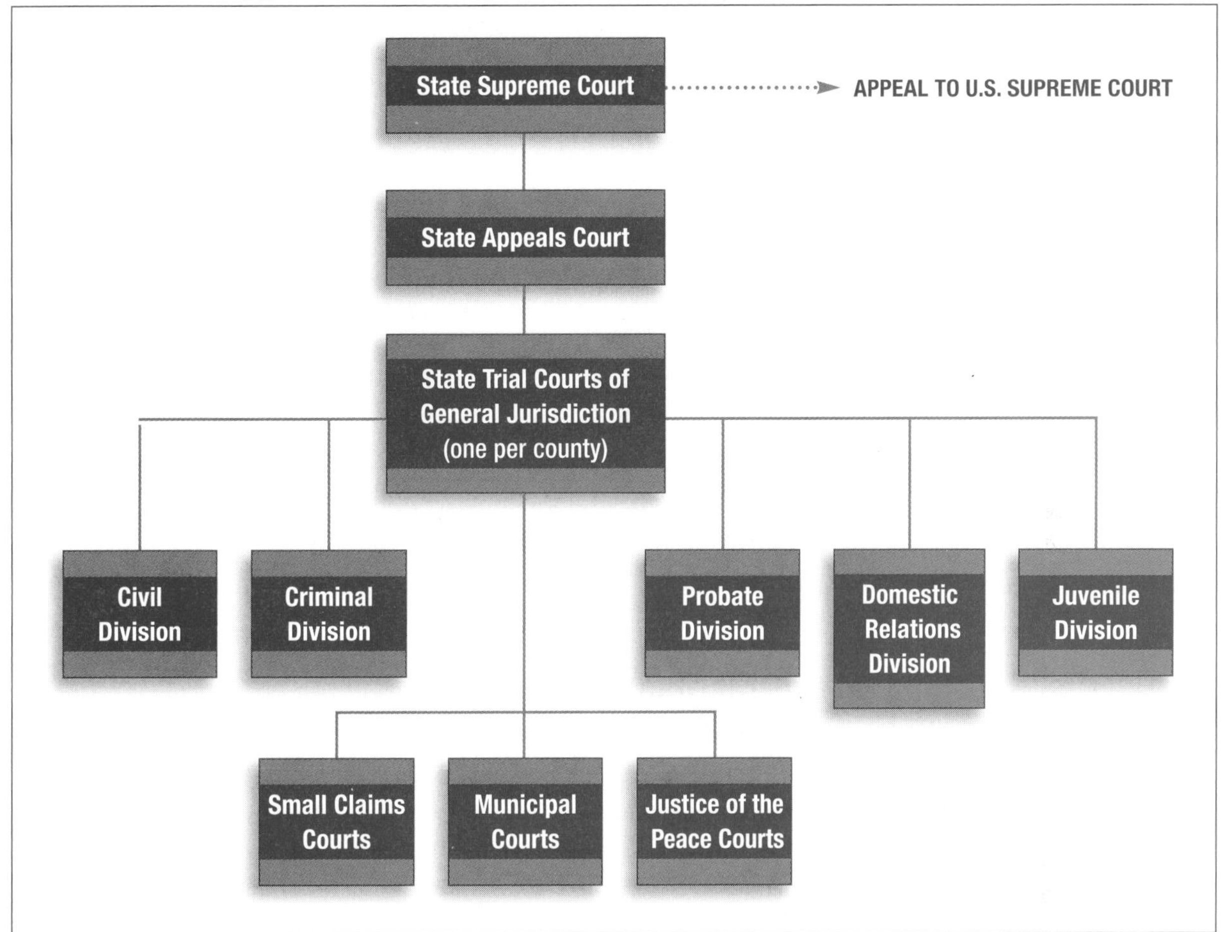

from intermediate state courts and certain trial courts. The **highest state court** hears no new evidence or testimony. The parties usually submit pertinent parts of or the entire lower court record for review. The parties also submit legal briefs to the court and usually are granted a brief oral hearing. Decisions of state supreme courts are final, unless a question of law is involved that is appealable to the U.S. Supreme Court. Exhibit 2.1 depicts a typical state court system.

Federal Court System

Article III of the U.S. Constitution provides that the federal government's judicial power is vested in one "supreme court." This court is the **U.S. Supreme Court.** The Constitution also authorizes Congress to establish "inferior" federal courts. Pursuant to this power, Congress has established special federal courts, U.S. district courts, and U.S. courts of appeal. Federal judges are appointed for life by the President with the advice and consent of the Senate (except bankruptcy court judges, who are appointed for 14-year terms, and U.S. Magistrate Judges, who are appointed for an 8-year term).

Specialized Courts Hear Commercial Disputes

In most states, the same judges who hear and decide criminal, landlord–tenant, matrimonial, medical malpractice, and other nonbusiness-related cases also hear most business and commercial disputes. The one major exception to this standard has been the state of Delaware, where a special Chancery Court hears and decides business litigation. This special court, which deals mainly with cases involving corporate government disputes, has earned a reputation for its expertise in handling and deciding corporate matters. Perhaps the existence of this special court and a corporation code that tends to favor corporate management are the primary reasons that more than 60 percent of the corporations listed on the New York Stock Exchange are incorporated in Delaware.

New York is one state that is following Delaware's lead in this area. New York has designated courts within its general court system to hear commercial disputes. These courts, which began operating in 1993, hear contract, sales, shareholder, business-related, and other commercial cases.

Businesses tend to favor special commercial courts because the judges presiding over them are expected to have the expertise to handle complex commercial lawsuits. Also, the courts are expected to be more efficient in deciding business-related cases, thereby saving time and money for the parties.

U.S. Tax Court:
www.ustaxcourt.gov/

U.S. Court of Federal Claims:
www.uscfc.uscourts.gov/

U.S. Court of International Trade:
www.cit.uscourts.gov/

Special Federal Courts

The **special federal courts** established by Congress have limited jurisdiction. They include:

- **U.S. tax court:** Hears cases involving federal tax laws
- **U.S. claims court:** Hears cases brought against the United States
- **U.S. Court of International Trade:** Hears cases involving tariffs and international commercial disputes
- **U.S. bankruptcy court:** Hears cases involving federal bankruptcy laws

U.S. District Courts

The **U.S. district courts** are the federal court system's trial courts of general jurisdiction. The District of Columbia and each state have at least one federal district court; the more populated states have more than one. The geographical area that each court serves is referred to as a *district.* There presently are 96 federal district courts. The federal district courts are empowered to impanel juries, receive evidence, hear testimony, and decide cases. Most federal cases originate in federal district courts.

U.S. Courts of Appeals

The **U.S. courts of appeals** are the federal court system's intermediate appellate courts. The federal court system has 13 circuits. **Circuit** refers to the geographical area served by the court. Eleven are designated by a number, such as the First Circuit, Second Circuit, and so on. The Twelfth Circuit court is located in Washington, DC, and is called the District of Columbia Circuit.

As appellate courts, these circuit courts hear appeals from the district courts located in their circuit, as well as from certain special courts and federal administrative agencies. The courts review the record of the lower court or administrative agency proceedings to determine if any error would warrant reversal or modification of the lower court decision. Circuit courts do not hear new evidence or testimony. The parties file legal briefs with the court and are given a short oral hearing. Appeals usually are heard by a three-judge panel. After the panel tenders a decision, a petitioner can request a review *en banc* by the full court.

The Thirteenth Circuit court of appeals was created by Congress in 1982. Called the **Court of Appeals for the Federal Circuit** and located in Washington, DC, this court has special appellate jurisdiction to review the decisions of the claims court, the Patent and Trademark Office, and the Court of International Trade. This court of appeals was created to provide uniformity in the application of federal law in certain areas, particularly patent law.

U.S. Court for the Federal Circuit:
www.fedcir.gov/

The map in Exhibit 2.2 shows the 13 federal circuit courts of appeals.

U.S. Supreme Court

The highest court in the land, the U.S. Supreme Court, is located in Washington, DC. This court is composed of nine justices who are nominated by the President and confirmed by the Senate. The President appoints one justice as **Chief Justice**, who is responsible for administration of the Supreme Court. The other eight justices are **associate justices**.

The Supreme Court, which is an appellate court, hears appeals from federal circuit courts of appeals and, under certain circumstances, from federal district courts, special federal courts, and the highest state courts. The Supreme Court

EXHIBIT 2.2 *Federal circuit courts of appeals.*

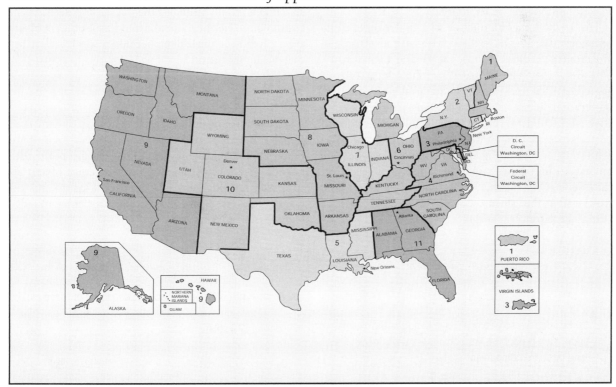

CASE FOR DISCUSSION

Pizza Hut, Inc. v. Papa John's International, Inc.

227 F.3d 489, 2000 U.S.App. Lexis 23444 (2000) — United States Court of Appeals, Fifth Circuit

FACTS

Pizza Hut, Inc., the largest pizza chain in the United States, operates over 7000 restaurants. Papa John's International, Inc. is the third largest pizza chain in the United States with over 2050 locations. In May 1995, Papa John's adopted a new slogan, "Better Ingredients. Better Pizza" and applied for and received a federal trademark for this slogan. Papa John's spent over $300 million building customer recognition and goodwill for this slogan. The slogan has appeared on millions of signs, shirts, menus, pizza boxes, napkins, and other items, and has regularly appeared as the "tag line" at the end of Papa John's radio and television advertisements.

On May 1, 1997, Pizza Hut launched a new advertising campaign in which it declared "war" on poor quality pizza. The advertisements touted the "better taste" of Pizza Hut's pizza and "dared" anyone to find a better pizza. A few weeks later Papa John's launched a comparative advertising campaign that touted the superiority of Papa John's pizza over Pizza Hut's pizza. Papa John's claimed it had superior sauce and dough to Pizza Hut. Many of these advertisements were accompanied by Papa John's slogan "Better Ingredients. Better Pizza."

In 1998, Pizza Hut filed a civil action in federal district court charging Papa John's with false advertising in violation of Section 43(a) of the federal Lanham Act. The district court found that Papa John's slogan "Better Ingredients. Better Pizza," standing alone, was mere puffery and did not constitute false advertising. The district court found, however, that Papa John's claims of superior sauce and dough were misleading and that Papa John's slogan "Better Ingredients. Better Pizza" became tainted because it was associated with these misleading statements. The district court enjoined Papa John's from using the slogan "Better Ingredients. Better Pizza." Papa John's appealed.

ISSUE

Is Papa John's slogan, "Better Ingredients. Better Pizza," false advertising in violation of Section 43(a) of the Lanham Act?

COURT'S REASONING

The court of appeals noted that statements of general opinion—referred to as "puffery"—are not actionable under Section 43(a) of the Lanham Act. The court stated that "puffery" is defined as "an exaggerated, blustering, and boasting statement which no reasonable buyer would be justified in relying on" or "a general claim of superiority over comparative products that is so vague that it can be understood as nothing more than a mere expression of opinion." The court of appeals found that Papa John's slogan "Better Ingredients. Better Pizza" is a statement of opinion and is not a statement of fact upon which consumers would be justified in relying. The court also held that Papa John's claims of superior sauce and dough over that of Pizza Hut's was not material because Pizza Hut had failed to show that these statements would influence the purchasing decisions of consumers. The court did not find Papa John's comparative advertising misleading because it was based on actual consumer tests.

DECISION AND REMEDY

The court of appeals held that Papa John's trademarked slogan "Better Ingredients. Better Pizza" was mere puffery and a statement of opinion that did not violate Section 43(a) of the Lanham Act. The court of appeals reversed the judgment of the district court and remanded the case to the district court for entry of judgment for Papa John's.

QUESTIONS

1. What is the role of an appellate court? Explain.
2. Do businesses sometimes make exaggerated claims about their products? Are consumers smart enough to "see through" companies' "puffery"?
3. If the court of appeals had found in favor of Pizza Hut, what would have been the effect on advertising in this country? Explain.

EXHIBIT 2.3 *Federal court system.*

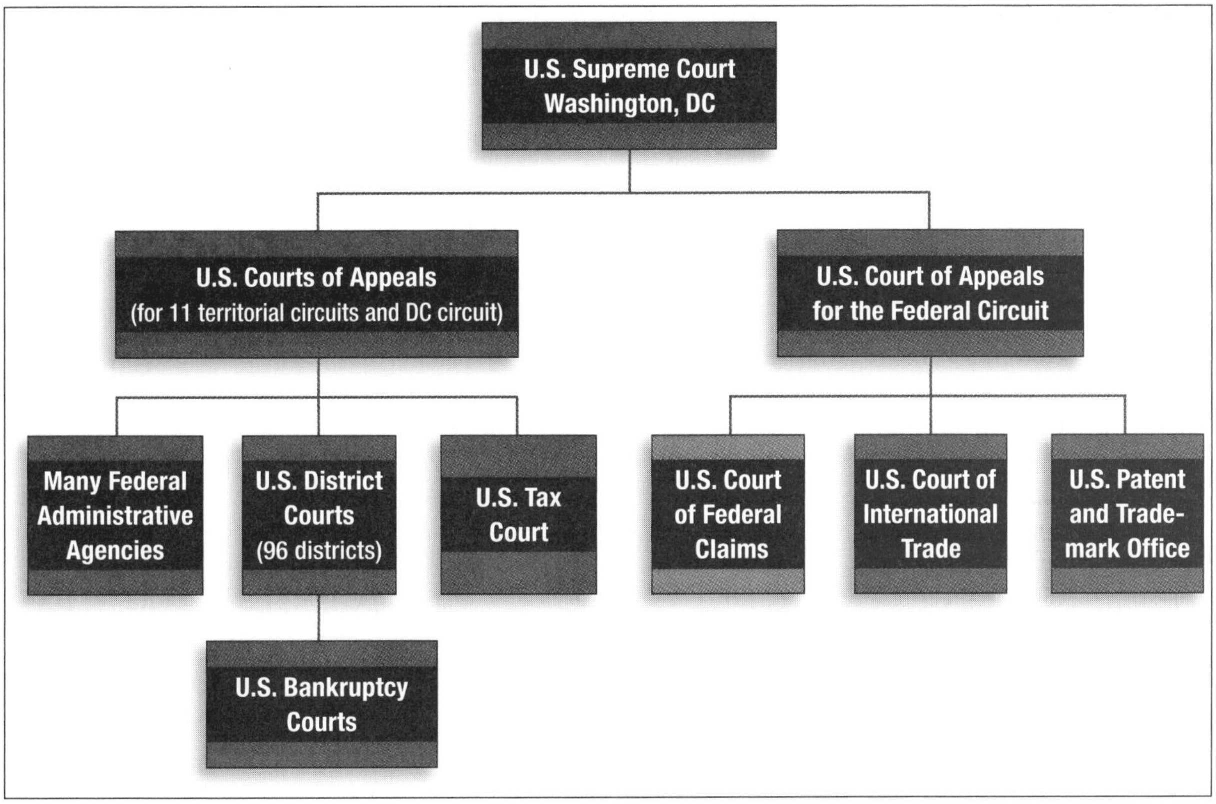

U.S. Supreme Court
Washington, DC

U.S. Courts of Appeals
(for 11 territorial circuits and DC circuit)

U.S. Court of Appeals
for the Federal Circuit

Many Federal Administrative Agencies

U.S. District Courts (96 districts)

U.S. Tax Court

U.S. Court of Federal Claims

U.S. Court of International Trade

U.S. Patent and Trademark Office

U.S. Bankruptcy Courts

hears no evidence or testimony. As with other appellate courts, the lower court record is reviewed to determine whether an error has been committed that warrants a reversal or modification of the decision. Legal briefs are filed, and the parties are granted a brief oral hearing. The Supreme Court's decision is final.

Exhibit 2.3 illustrates the federal court system.

SIDEBAR

U.S. Supreme Court
The Supreme Court was created by Article III of the U.S. Constitution. The Supreme Court is the highest court in the land. It is located in Washington, DC.

Decisions by the U.S. Supreme Court

The U.S. Constitution gives Congress the authority to establish rules for the appellate review of cases by the U.S. Supreme Court, except in the rare case where mandatory review is required. Congress has given the Supreme Court discretion to decide what cases it will hear.

A petitioner must file a **petition for certiorari** asking the Supreme Court to hear the case. If the Court decides to review a case, it will issue a **writ of certiorari**. Because the Court issues only about 100 to 150 opinions each year, writs usually are granted only in cases involving constitutional and other important issues.

Each justice of the Supreme Court, including the Chief Justice, has an equal vote. The Supreme Court can issue the following types of decisions:

- **Unanimous decision:** If all of the justices voting agree as to the outcome and reasoning used to decide the case, it is a unanimous opinion. Unanimous decisions are precedent for later cases.

Supreme Court of the United States:
www.supremecourtus.gov

The Process of Choosing a Supreme Court Justice

In an effort to strike a balance of power between the executive and legislative branches of government, Article II, Section 2, of the U.S. Constitution gives the President the power to appoint Supreme Court justices "with the advice and consent of the Senate." In recent years, however, many conservative and liberal critics have charged that this process has become nothing more than a political tennis match in which the hapless nominee is the ball.

President George H. Bush was given the chance to cast a conservative shadow over the Court's decisions when Justice Thurgood Marshall retired in 1991. Marshall, who served 24 years, was one of the most liberal members of the Court. Also, he had been the only black person to serve on the Supreme Court. In 1991, Bush nominated Clarence Thomas, a black conservative serving as a judge of the U.S. court of appeals in the District of Columbia, to replace Marshall. Thomas grew up in rural Georgia and graduated from Yale Law School. After a heated political debate, Thomas was confirmed by the U.S. Senate with a 52–48 vote in October 1991.

The election of Bill Clinton as President swung the pendulum back to the Democrats. President Clinton got an early opportunity to nominate a candidate when Justice Byron R. White, a Democrat-appointed member of the Court, retired.

President Clinton nominated Judge Ruth Bader Ginsburg to serve on the Supreme Court. Justice Ginsburg was considered a moderate liberal. Ginsburg was approved by a bipartisan vote of the Senate and took office for the Supreme Court's 1993–1994 term. She is the second woman to serve on the Court, joining Sandra Day O'Connor, who was nominated by President Ronald Reagan. Ginsburg is also the first Jewish person to serve on the Court since Justice Abe Fortas resigned in 1969.

U.S. Supreme Court building, Washington DC.

- **Majority decision:** If a majority of the justices agree to the outcome and reasoning used to decide the case, it is a majority opinion. Majority decisions are precedent for later cases.
- **Plurality decision:** If a majority of the justices agree to the outcome of the case, but not to the reasoning for reaching the outcome, it is a plurality opinion. A plurality decision settles the case but is not precedent for later cases.
- **Tie decision:** Sometimes the Supreme Court sits without all nine justices being present, because of illness or conflict of interest, or because a justice has not been confirmed to fill a vacant seat on the court. In the case of a tie vote, the lower court's decision is affirmed. These votes are not precedent for later cases.

A justice who agrees with the outcome of a case but not the reason proffered by other justices can issue a **concurring opinion** setting forth his or her reasons for deciding the case. A justice who does not agree with a decision can file a **dissenting opinion** that sets forth the reasons for his or her dissent.

I'll Take You to the U.S. Supreme Court!—Not!

As textbooks say, in the United States you can appeal your legal case all the way to the U.S. Supreme Court. In reality, however, the chance of ever having your case heard by the highest court is slim to none. Each year, more than 7,000 petitioners pay the $300 filing fee to ask the Supreme Court to hear their case. In addition, these petitioners usually pay big law firms from $30,000 to $100,000 or more to write the appeal petition. In recent years, the Supreme Court has accepted fewer than 100 of these cases for full review each term.

Each of the nine Supreme Court justices has three law clerks—recent law school graduates usually chosen from the elite law schools across the country—who assist them. The justices rarely read the appellate petitions but, instead, delegate this task to their law clerks. The clerks then write a short memorandum discussing the key issues raised by the appeal and recommend to the justices whether they should grant or deny a review. The justices meet once a week to discuss which cases merit a review. The votes of four justices are necessary to grant an appeal and schedule an oral argument before the Court ("rule of four"). Written opinions by the justices are usually issued many months later.

So what does it take to win a review by the Supreme Court? The U.S. Supreme Court usually decides to hear cases involving major constitutional questions such as freedom of speech, freedom of religion, equal protection, and due process. The Court, therefore, rarely decides such day-to-day legal issues as breach of contract, tort liability, or corporations law unless they involve more important constitutional or federal law questions. So the next time you hear someone say, "I'll take you to the U.S. Supreme Court!" just say, "Not!"

JURISDICTION OF FEDERAL AND STATE COURTS

Article III, Section 2, of the U.S. Constitution sets forth the **jurisdiction** of federal courts. Federal courts have *limited jurisdiction* to hear cases involving:

- **Federal questions:** cases arising under the U.S. Constitution, treaties, and federal statutes and regulations. There is no dollar-amount limit on federal question cases that can be brought in federal court.
- **Diversity of citizenship:** cases between (a) citizens of different states, (b) a citizen of a state and a citizen or subject of a foreign country, and (c) a citizen of a state and a foreign country where the foreign country is the plaintiff. A corporation is considered to be a citizen of the state in which it is incorporated and in which it has its principal place of business. The reason for providing diversity of citizenship jurisdiction was to prevent state court bias against nonresidents. The federal court must apply the appropriate state's law in deciding the case. The dollar amount of the controversy must exceed $75,000. If this requirement is not met, the action must be brought in the appropriate state court.

Federal courts have **exclusive jurisdiction** to hear cases involving federal crimes, antitrust, bankruptcy, patent and copyright cases, suits against the United States, and most admiralty cases. State courts cannot hear these cases.

State and federal courts have **concurrent jurisdiction** to hear cases involving diversity of citizenship and federal questions over which federal courts do not have

SIDEBAR

Supreme Court Decision

The U.S. Supreme Court's decisions are precedent for all the other courts in the country. In *Bush v. Gore* [531 U.S. 98, 121 S.Ct. 525, 2000 U.S. Lexis 8430 (2000)] the Supreme Court decided that George W. Bush had been elected President of the United States.

EXHIBIT 2.4 *Jurisdiction of federal and state courts.*

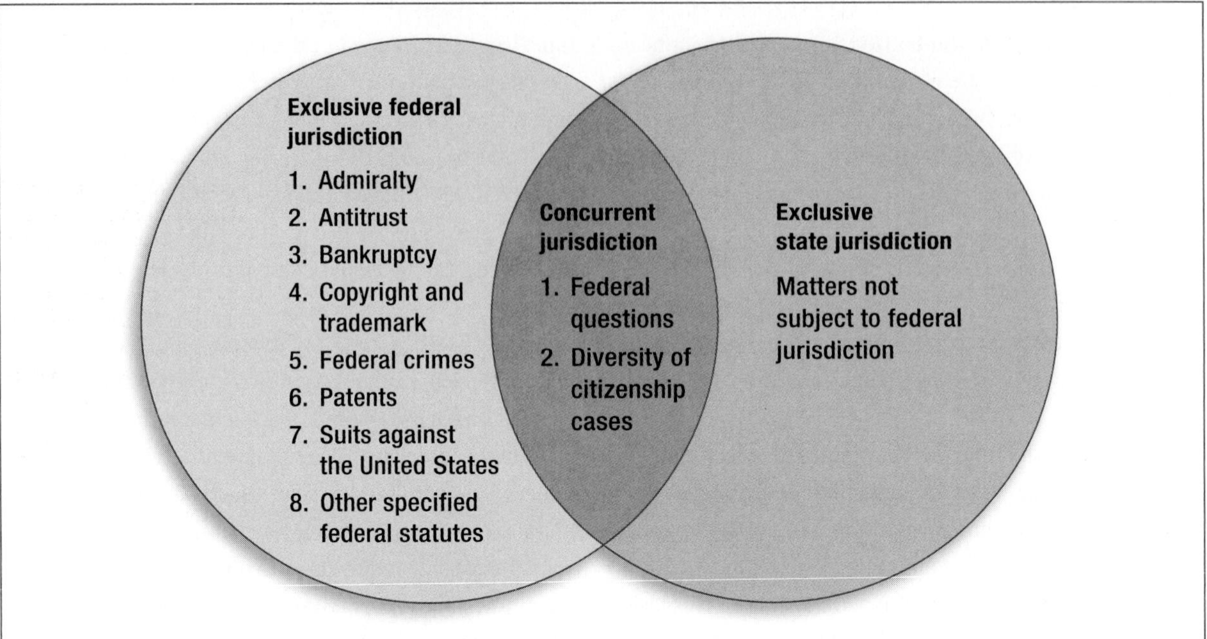

exclusive jurisdiction (e.g., cases involving federal securities laws). If a plaintiff brings a case involving concurrent jurisdiction in state court, the defendant can remove the case to federal court. If a case does not qualify to be brought in federal court, it must be brought in the appropriate state court. Exhibit 2.4 illustrates the overlapping jurisdiction.

Exterior of brick Franklin County Courthouse with manicured lawn, Framington, Maine.

Authority of Courts

Not every court has the authority to hear all types of cases. First, to bring a lawsuit in a court, the plaintiff must have *standing to sue.* In addition, the court must have *jurisdiction* to hear the case, and the case must be brought in the proper *venue.*

Standing to sue. To bring a lawsuit, a plaintiff must have **standing to sue**. The plaintiff must have some stake in the outcome of the lawsuit.

Consider this example: Linda's friend Jon is injured in an accident caused by Emily. Jon refuses to sue. Linda cannot sue Emily on Jon's behalf because she does not have an interest in the result of the case.

Courts hear and decide actual disputes involving specific controversies. Hypothetical questions will not be heard and trivial lawsuits will be dismissed.

Types of jurisdiction. A court must have **jurisdiction** to hear and decide a case. There are two types of jurisdiction: (1) subject-matter jurisdiction and (2) in personam, in rem, or quasi in rem jurisdiction.

1. **Subject-matter jurisdiction.** Some courts have only limited jurisdiction to hear and decide a case. A court must have subject-matter jurisdiction over the type of case. For example, federal courts have jurisdiction to hear only certain types of cases (discussed later in this chapter) and certain state courts, such as probate courts and small-claims courts, can hear only designated types of cases. If a court does not have subject-matter jurisdiction, it cannot hear the case.
2. **In personam, in rem,** and **quasi in rem jurisdictions.** Jurisdiction over the person is called in personam jurisdiction, or *personal jurisdiction.* By filing a lawsuit with a court, a **plaintiff** gives the court in personam jurisdiction over himself or herself. The court must also have in personam jurisdiction over the **defendant**, which usually is obtained by having that person served a summons within the territorial boundaries of the state (i.e., **service of process**).

   Service of process usually is accomplished by personally serving the summons and complaint on the defendant. If this is not possible, alternative forms of notice, such as mailing the summons or publishing a notice in a newspaper, may be permitted. A corporation is subject to personal jurisdiction in the state in which it is incorporated, has its principal office, or is doing business. A party who disputes the jurisdiction of a court can make a **special appearance** in that court to argue against the imposition of jurisdiction. Service of process is not permitted during such an appearance.

> Let every American, ever lover of liberty, every well-wisher to his posterity, swear by the blood of the Revolution never to violate in the least particular the laws of the country, and never to tolerate their violation by others.
>
> —Abraham Lincoln

A court may have jurisdiction to hear and decide a case because it has jurisdiction over the property of the lawsuit. This is called **in rem jurisdiction** ("jurisdiction over the thing"). For example, a state court would have jurisdiction to hear a dispute over the ownership of a piece of real estate located within the state. This is so even if one or more of the disputing parties lives in another state or states.

Sometimes a plaintiff who obtains a judgment against a defendant in one state will try to collect the judgment by attaching property of the defendant that is located in another state. This is permitted under **quasi in rem jurisdiction** or **attachment jurisdiction**.

Long-arm statutes. In most states, a state court can obtain jurisdiction over persons and businesses located in another state or country through the state's **long-arm statute**. These statutes extend a state's jurisdiction to nonresidents who were not served a summons within the state. The nonresident must have had some **minimum contact** with the state [*International Shoe Co. v. Washington*, 326 U.S. 310, 66 S.Ct. 154, 1945 U.S. Lexis 1447 (1945)]. In addition, maintenance of the suit must uphold the traditional notions of fair play and substantial justice.

The exercise of long-arm jurisdiction is generally permitted over nonresidents who have (1) committed torts within the state (e.g., caused an automobile accident in the state), (2) entered into a contract either in the state or that affects the state (and allegedly breached the contract), or (3) transacted other business in the state that allegedly caused injury to another person.

Parties to a contract may include a **forum-selection clause** designating a certain court to hear any dispute concerning nonperformance of the contract. In the

CASE FOR DISCUSSION

Carnival Cruise Lines, Inc. v. Shute

499 U.S. 585, 111 S.Ct. 1522. 1991 U.S. Lexis 2221 (1991) Supreme Court of the United States

FACTS

Mr. and Mrs. Shute, residents of the state of Washington, purchased passage for a 7-day cruise on the *Tropicale*, a cruise ship operated by Carnival Cruise Lines, Inc. (Carnival). They paid the fare to the travel agent, who forwarded the payment to Carnival's headquarters in Miami, Florida. Carnival prepared the tickets and sent them to the Shutes. Each ticket consisted of five pages, including contract terms. The ticket contained a forum-selection clause that designated the state of Florida as the forum for any lawsuits arising under or in connection with the ticket and cruise.

The Shutes boarded the *Tropicale* in Los Angeles and set sail for Puerto Vallarta, Mexico. While the ship was on its return voyage and in international waters off the Mexican coast, Mrs. Shute was injured when she slipped on a deck mat during a guided tour of the ship's galley. Upon return to Washington, she filed a negligence lawsuit against Carnival in U.S. district court in Washington, seeking damages.

Carnival filed a motion for summary judgment contending that the suit could be brought only in a court located in the state of Florida. The district court granted Carnival's motion. The court of appeals reversed, holding that Mrs. Shute could sue Carnival in Washington. Carnival appealed to the U.S. Supreme Court.

ISSUE

Is the forum-selection clause in Carnival Cruise Lines' ticket enforceable?

COURT'S REASONING

The Supreme Court stated that as an initial matter it did not adopt the court of appeals' determination that a nonnegotiated forum-selection clause in a form ticket contract is never enforceable simply because it is not the subject of bargaining. The Supreme Court held that including a reasonable forum clause in form contract of this kind is permissible for several reasons: (1) A cruise line has a special interest in limiting the fora in which it potentially could be subject to suit. Because a cruise ship typically carries passengers from many locales, it is not unlikely that a mishap on a cruise could subject the cruise line to litigation in several different fora. (2) A clause establishing the forum for dispute resolution has the salutary effect of dispelling any confusion where suits arising from the contract must be brought and defended, sparing litigants the time and expense of pretrial motions to determine the correct forum, and conserving judicial resources that otherwise would be devoted to deciding those motions. (3) Passengers who purchase tickets containing a forum clause like that at issue in this case benefit in the form of reduced fares reflecting the savings that the cruise line enjoys by limiting the fora in which it may be sued.

DECISION AND REMEDY

The forum-selection clause in Carnival's ticket is fair and reasonable and therefore enforceable against Mrs. Shute. If she wishes to sue Carnival, she must do so in a court in the state of Florida, not in a court in the state of Washington. The U.S. Supreme Court reversed the decision of the court of appeals.

QUESTIONS

1. Should forum-selection clauses be enforced? Why or why not?
2. Did Carnival Cruise Lines act ethically by placing the forum-selection clause in its tickets?
3. Do forum-selection clauses serve any legitimate business purpose? Explain.

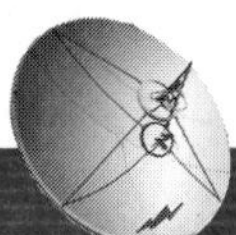

INFORMATION TECHNOLOGY

OBTAINING PERSONAL JURISDICTION IN CYBERSPACE

Obtaining personal jurisdiction over a defendant located in another state has always been a difficult issue for the courts. States have enacted long-arm statutes that permit the courts located in one state to reach out and make people in another state come to court and defend themselves. To make sure this is not overly burdensome, the U.S. Supreme Court has held that out-of-state defendants must have had certain "minimum contacts" with the state before they are made to answer to a lawsuit there [*International Shoe Co. v. Washington,* 326 U.S. 310, 66 S.Ct. 154, 1945 U.S. Lexis 1447 (1945)].

Today, with the advent of the Internet and the ability of persons and businesses to reach millions of people in other states electronically, application of the *International Shoe* minimum-contacts standard is even more difficult.

Several courts have decided cases involving the reach of a state's long-arm statute to obtain jurisdiction over someone in another state because of his or her Internet activities. In one case, Zippo Manufacturing Company (Zippo) sued Zippo Dot Com, Inc. (Dot Com) in federal district court in Pennsylvania. Zippo manufactures its well-known line of Zippo tobacco lighters in Bradford, Pennsylvania, and sells them worldwide. Dot Com, a California corporation with its principal place of business and its servers located in Sunnyvale, California, operates an Internet Web site that transmits information and sexually explicit material to its subscribers. Of Dot Com's 140,000 paying subscribers worldwide, 3,000 are located in Pennsylvania.

Zippo sued Dot Com in federal district court in Pennsylvania for trademark infringement. Dot Com alleged that it was not subject to personal jurisdiction in Pennsylvania. The district court applied the *International Shoe* minimum-contact standard and held that Dot Com was subject to personal jurisdiction under the Pennsylvania long-arm statute and ordered Dot Com to defend itself there. [*Zippo Manufacturing Company v. Zippo Dot Com, Inc.,* 952 F.Supp. 1119, 1997 U.S. Dist. Lexis 1701 (W.D.Pa. 1997)]

INTERNATIONAL PERSPECTIVE

COMPARISON OF JAPANESE AND AMERICAN LEGAL SYSTEMS

Businesses often complain that there are too many lawyers and too much litigation in the United States. Currently there are more than 800,000 lawyers and more than 20 million lawsuits per year in this country. In contrast, Japan, a country with about half the population of the United States, has only 15,000 lawyers and little litigation. Why the difference?

Much of the difference is cultural: Japan nurtures the attitude of avoiding confrontation. Litigious persons in Japan are looked down upon. Thus, companies rarely do battle in court. Instead, they opt for private arbitration of most of their disputes. Other differences are built into the legal system itself. For example, there is only one place to study to become a *bengoshi,* or lawyer, in Japan—the government-operated National Institute for Legal Training. Only 2 percent of 35,000 applicants are accepted annually, and only 400 new *bengoshi* are admitted to Japan's exclusive legal club per year.

There are other obstacles, too. For example, no class actions or contingency-fee arrangements are allowed. Plaintiffs must pay their lawyers a front fee of up to 8 percent of the damages sought, plus a nonrefundable filing fee to the court of one-half of 1 percent of the damages. To make matters even more difficult, no discovery is permitted and plaintiffs are denied access to an opponent's potential evidence before trial. And even if the plaintiff wins the lawsuit, damage awards are low.

The Japanese bias against courtroom solutions remains strong. The current system is designed to save time and money and to preserve long-term relationships. The belief that disputes can be solved amicably without litigation is a concept that U.S. businesses are starting to embrace.

second case discussed in this chapter, the U.S. Supreme Court upheld a forum-selection clause in a contract.

Venue. **Venue** requires lawsuits to be heard by the court with jurisdiction nearest the location in which the incident occurred or where the parties reside. For example, Harry, a Georgia resident, commits a felony crime in Los Angeles County, California. The California Superior Court—located in Los Angeles—is the proper venue because the crime was committed there, the witnesses are probably from the area, and so on.

Occasionally, pretrial publicity may prejudice jurors located in the proper venue. In these cases, a *change of venue* may be requested so that a more impartial jury can be found. The courts generally frown upon *forum shopping* (looking for a favorable court without a valid reason).

LEGAL TERMINOLOGY

Associate justice
Brief
Chief Justice
Circuit
Concurrent jurisdiction
Concurring opinion
Court of Appeals for the Federal Circuit
Court of record
Defendant
Dissenting opinion
Diversity of citizenship
Exclusive jurisdiction
Federal question
Forum-selection clause
General-jurisdiction trial court
Highest state court
In personam jurisdiction
In rem jurisdiction
Intermediate appellate court (court of appeals)
Jurisdiction
Limited-jurisdiction trial court
Litigation
Long-arm statute
Majority decision
Minimum contact
Petition for certiorari
Plaintiff
Plurality decision
Quasi in rem jurisdiction (attachment jurisdiction)
Service of process
Small-claims court
Special appearance
Special federal court
Standing to sue
State court system
State supreme court
Subject-matter jurisdiction
Tie decision
Unanimous decision
U.S. bankruptcy court
U.S. claims court
U.S. court of appeals
U.S. Court of International Trade
U.S. district courts
U.S. Supreme Court
U.S. tax court
Venue
Writ of certiorari

chapter summary

THE AMERICAN COURT SYSTEM

State Court Systems	
Limited-Jurisdiction Trial Court	State courts that hear matters of a specialized or limited nature (e.g., misdemeanor criminal matters, traffic tickets, civil matters under a certain dollar amount). Many states have created small claims courts that hear small-dollar-amount civil cases (e.g., under $5,000) where the parties cannot be represented by lawyers.
General-Jurisdiction Trial Court	State courts that hear cases of a general nature that are not within the jurisdiction of limited-jurisdiction trial courts.
Intermediate Appellate Court	State courts that hear appeals from state trial courts. The appellate court reviews the trial court record in making its decision; no new evidence is introduced at this level.
Highest State Court	Each state has a highest court in its court system. This court hears appeals from appellate courts, and where appropriate, trial courts. This court reviews the record in making its decision; no new evidence is introduced at this level. Most states call this court the supreme court.
Federal Court System	
Special Federal Courts	Federal courts that have specialized or limited jurisdiction. They include: 1. *U.S. tax court:* Hears cases involving federal tax laws. 2. *U.S. claims court:* Hears cases brought against the United States. 3. *U.S. Court of International Trade:* Hears cases involving tariffs and international commercial disputes. 4. *U.S. bankruptcy court:* Hears cases involving federal bankruptcy law.
U.S. District Courts	Federal trial courts of general jurisdiction that hear cases not within the jurisdiction of specialized courts. Each state has at least one U.S. district court; more populated states have several district courts. The area served by each of these courts is called a *district.*
U.S. Courts of Appeals	Intermediate federal appellate courts that hear appeals from district courts located in their circuit, and in certain instances from special federal courts and federal administrative agencies. There are 12 geographical circuits in this country; 11 serve areas encompassing several states, and another is located in Washington, DC. The 13th circuit court—the Court of Appeals for the Federal Circuit, is located in Washington, DC, and reviews patent, trademark, and international trade cases.
U.S. Supreme Court	Highest court of the federal court system. It hears appeals from the circuit courts and, in some instances, from special courts and U.S. district courts. The Court, located in Washington, DC, is composed of nine justices, one of whom is named Chief Justice. *(continued)*

Decisions by U.S. Supreme Court	1. *Petition of certiorari and writ of certiorari:* To have a case heard by the U.S. Supreme Court, a petitioner must file a *petition for certiorari* with the Court. If the Court decides to hear the case, it will issue a *writ of certiorari.*
Voting by the U.S. Supreme Court	1. *Unanimous decision:* All of the justices agree as to the outcome and reasoning used to decide the case; the decision becomes precedent. 2. *Majority decision:* A majority of the justices agrees as to the outcome and reasoning used to decide the case; the decision becomes precedent. 3. *Plurality decision:* A majority of the justices agrees to the outcome but not to the reasoning; the decision is not precedent. 4. *Tie decision:* If there is a tie vote, the lower court's decision stands; the decision is not precedent. 5. *Concurring opinion:* A justice who agrees as to the outcome of the case but not the reasoning used by other justices may write a concurring opinion setting forth his or her reasoning. 6. *Dissenting opinion:* A justice who disagrees with the outcome of a case may write a dissenting opinion setting forth his or her reasoning for dissenting.
Jurisdiction of Federal and State Courts	
Jurisdiction of Federal Courts	Federal courts may hear the following cases: 1. *Federal question:* Cases arising under the U.S. Constitution, treaties, and federal statutes and regulations; there is no dollar-amount limit. 2. *Diversity of citizenship:* Cases between (a) citizens of different states and (b) citizens of a state and citizen or subject of a foreign country; federal courts must apply the appropriate state law in such cases. The controversy must exceed $75,000 for the federal court to hear the case.
Jurisdiction of State Courts	State courts hear some cases that may be heard by federal courts. 1. *Exclusive jurisdiction:* Federal courts have exclusive jurisdiction to hear cases involving federal crimes, antitrust, and bankruptcy, patent and copyright cases, suits against the United States, and most admiralty cases. State courts may not hear these matters. 2. *Concurrent jurisdiction:* State courts have concurrent jurisdiction to hear cases involving diversity of citizenship cases and federal question cases over which the federal courts do not have exclusive jurisdiction. The defendant may have the case removed to federal court.
Standing to Sue	To bring a lawsuit, the plaintiff must have some stake in the outcome of the lawsuit.
Subject-Matter Jurisdiction	The court must have jurisdiction over the subject matter of the lawsuit; each court has limited jurisdiction to hear only certain types of cases.
In Personam Jurisdiction (or Personal Jurisdiction)	The court must have jurisdiction over the parties to a lawsuit. The plaintiff submits to the jurisdiction of the court by filing the lawsuit there. Personal jurisdiction is obtained over the defendant through *service of process.*

In Rem Jurisdiction	A court may have jurisdiction to hear and decide a case because it has jurisdiction over the property at issue in the lawsuit (e.g., real property located in the state).
Quasi In Rem Jurisdiction (or Attachment Jurisdiction)	A plaintiff who obtains a judgment against a defendant in one state may utilize the court system of another state to attach property of the defendant located in the second state.
Long-Arm Statutes	These statutes permit a state to obtain personal jurisdiction over an out-of-state defendant as long as the defendant had the requisite minimum contact with the state. The out-of-state defendant may be served process outside the state in which the lawsuit has been brought.
Forum-Selection Clause	This clause in a contract designates the court that will hear any dispute arising out of the contract.
Venue	A case must be heard by the court that has jurisdiction nearest to where the incident at issue occurred or where the parties reside. A *change of venue* will be granted if prejudice would occur because of pretrial publicity or another reason.

WORKING THE WEB

Visit the Web sites listed below for more information about the topics covered in this chapter.

1. The Law, Commerce & Technology Center, University of Washington Law, provides online information about Internet issues, biotechnology, electronic commerce, and technology news in the Northwest. Visit **www.law.washington.edu/lct/.**
2. Check out the latest developments at the Business Law—Committee on Cyberspace Law Home Page, **www.abanet.org/buslaw/cyber/home.html.**
3. An ongoing series of publications and seminars can be found at the Online Education—Berkman Center for Internet and Society, **cyber.harvard.edu/online/.**

CRITICAL LEGAL THINKING QUESTIONS

1. Delineate the courts of a typical state court system. What courts make up your state's court system?
2. Describe the following special federal courts: (1) U.S. tax court, (2) U.S. claims court, (3) U.S. Court of International Trade, and (4) U.S. bankruptcy court.
3. Describe U.S. district courts. What types of cases do they hear?
4. Describe U.S. courts of appeals. How many are there? Explain the function of the Court of Appeals for the Federal Circuit.
5. Describe the U.S. Supreme Court. What are the functions of the Chief Justice? What are the functions of the associate justices?
6. Explain the process of choosing a Supreme Court justice. Do you you think this process is political or not? Explain.
7. Define the following types of decisions of the U.S. Supreme Court: (1) unanimous decision, (2) majority decision, (3) plurality decision, and (4) tie decision.
8. Federal courts have limited jurisdiction to hear cases. Describe the following types of jurisdiction: (1) federal question jurisdiction and (2) diversity of citizenship jurisdiction.
9. Describe the difference between subject-matter jurisdiction and in personam jurisdiction. What is the purpose of a long-arm statute?
10. Define *venue.* Give an example of when a change of venue would be granted.

CASE FOR BRIEFING

Read Case 2 in Appendix A *(Anheuser-Busch, Inc. v. Schmoke).* Review and brief the case using the *Critical Legal Thinking* "Briefing the Case" example described in Chapter 1.

2.1 *Nutrilab, Inc. v. Schweiker*

713 F.2d 335, 1983 U.S. App. Lexis 25121 (1983)
United States Court of Appeals, Seventh Circuit

FACTS Nutrilab, Inc. manufactures and markets a product known as "Starch Blockers." The purpose of the product is to block the human body's digestion of starch as an aid in controlling weight. On July 1, 1982, the U.S. Food and Drug Administration classified Starch Blockers as a drug and requested that the product be removed from the market until the FDA approved of its use. The FDA claimed that it had the right to classify new products as drugs and prevent their distribution until their safety is determined. Nutrilab disputes the FDA's decision and wants to bring suit to halt the FDA's actions.

ISSUE Do the federal courts have jurisdiction to hear this case?

2.2 *Allison v. ITE Imperial Corporation*

729 F. Supp. 45, 1990 U.S. Dist. Lexis 607 (1990)
U.S. District Court, Southern District of Mississippi

FACTS James Clayton Allison, a resident of the state of Mississippi, was employed by the Tru-Amp Corporation as a circuit-breaker tester. As part of his employment, Allison was sent to inspect, clean, and test a switch gear located at the South Central Bell Telephone Facility in Brentwood, Tennessee. On August 26, 1988, he attempted to remove a circuit breaker manufactured by ITE Corporation (ITE) from a bank of breakers, when a portion of the breaker fell off. The broken piece fell behind a switching bank and, according to Allison, caused an electrical fire and explosion. Allison was severely burned in the accident. Allison brought suit against ITE in a Mississippi state court, claiming more than $50,000 in damages.

ISSUE Can this suit be removed to federal court?

2.3 *Brooks v. Magnaverde Corporation*

619 P.2d 1271, 1980 Okla. Civ. App. Lexis 118 (1980)
Court of Appeals of Oklahoma

FACTS Sean O'Grady, a professional boxer, was managed by his father, Pat. Sean was a contender for the world featherweight title. On January 30, 1978, Pat entered into a contract with Magnaverde Corporation, a Los Angeles–based business, to co-promote a fight between Sean and the current featherweight champion. The fight was scheduled to take place on February 5, 1978, in Oklahoma City, Oklahoma.

To promote the fight, Pat O'Grady scheduled a press conference for January 30, 1978. At the conference, Pat was involved in a confrontation with a sportswriter named Brooks. He allegedly struck Brooks in the face. Brooks brought suit against Pat O'Grady and Magna Verde Corporation in an Oklahoma state court. Court records showed that the only contact Magnaverde had had with Oklahoma was that a few of its employees had taken several trips to Oklahoma in January 1978 to plan the title fight. The fight was never held.

Oklahoma has a long-arm statute. Magnaverde was served by mail and made a special appearance in Oklahoma state court to argue that Oklahoma does not have jurisdiction over it.

ISSUE Does Oklahoma have jurisdiction over Magnaverde Corporation?

ETHICS CASE

2.4 *Harris v. Time, Inc.*

191 Cal.App. 3d 449, 237 Cal.Rptr. 584, 1987 Cal. App. Lexis 1619 (1987)
Court of Appeal of California

FACTS One day Joshua Gnaizda, a 3-year-old, received what he (or his mother) thought was a tantalizing offer in the mail from Time, Inc. The front of the envelope contained a see-through window that revealed the following statement: "Joshua Gnaizda, I'll give you this versatile new calculator watch free just for opening the envelope before Feb. 15, 1985." Beneath the offer was a picture of the calculator watch itself. When Joshua's mother opened the envelope, she realized that the see-through window had not revealed the full text of Time's offer. Not viewable through the see-through window were the following words: "And mailing this Certificate today." The certificate required Joshua to purchase a subscription to *Fortune* magazine in order to receive the free calculator watch.

Joshua (through his father, a lawyer) sued *Time* in a class action, seeking compensatory damages in an amount equal to the value of the calculator watch and $15 million in punitive damages. The trial court dismissed the lawsuit as being too trivial for the court to hear. Joshua appealed.

ISSUE Should Joshua be permitted to maintain his lawsuit against Time, Inc.? Did Time act ethically? Should Joshua's father have sued for $15 million?

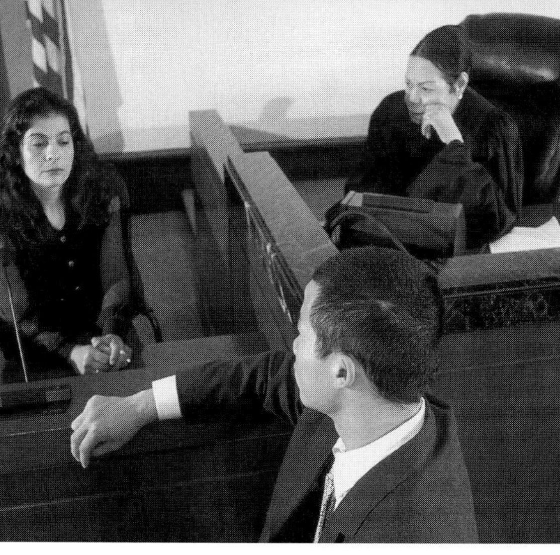

3 Civil Litigation and Alternative Dispute Resolution

I was never ruined but twice; once when I lost a lawsuit, and once when I won one. —VOLTAIRE

CHAPTER OBJECTIVES

After studying this chapter, you should be able to

1. Apply a cost-benefit analysis for bringing and defending a lawsuit.
2. Describe the pretrial litigation process.
3. Describe how a case proceeds through trial and the phases of a trial.
4. Describe how a trial court decision is appealed.
5. Explain the use of arbitration and other nonjudicial methods of alternative dispute resolution.

CHAPTER OUTLINE

- Introduction
- The Pleadings
- Case for Discussion: *Swierkiewicz v. Sorema N.A.*
- Discovery
- Case for Discussion: *Norgart v. The Upjohn Company*
- Pretrial Motions
- Settlement Conference
- The Trial
- Case for Discussion: *Ferlito v. Johnson & Johnson Products, Inc.*
- The Appeal
- Alternative Dispute Resolution
- Legal Terminology
- Chapter Summary
- Internet Exercises and Cases

INTRODUCTION

The process of bringing, maintaining, and defending a lawsuit is called **litigation.** Litigation is a difficult, time-consuming, and costly process that must comply with complex procedural rules. Although it is not required, most parties employ a lawyer to represent them when they are involved in a lawsuit.

Several forms of *nonjudicial* dispute resolution have developed in response to the expense and difficulty of bringing a lawsuit. These methods, collectively called **alternative dispute resolution,** are being used more and more often to resolve commercial disputes.

Students should have a good foundation in the procedures of the litigation process and methods of alternative dispute resolution. These facets of litigation are explained in this chapter.

THE PLEADINGS

The paperwork that is filed with the court to initiate and respond to a lawsuit is referred to as the **pleadings.** The major pleadings are the **complaint,** the **answer,** the **cross-complaint,** and the **reply.**

Complaint and Summons

The law, in its majestic equality, forbids the rich as well as the poor to sleep under bridges.
—Anatole France

To initiate a lawsuit, the party who is suing, the **plaintiff,** must file a complaint with the proper court. The complaint must name the parties to the lawsuit, allege the ultimate facts and law violated, and contain a "prayer for relief" for a remedy to be awarded by the court. The complaint can be as long as necessary, depending on the complexity of the case. A sample complaint appears in Exhibit 3.1.

Once a complaint has been filed with the court, the court issues a **summons,** a court order directing the defendant to appear in court and answer the complaint.

EXHIBIT 3.1 *Sample complaint.*

In the United States District Court for the District of Idaho

John Doe
Plaintiff

Civil No. 2-1005

v.

COMPLAINT

Jane Roe
Defendant

The plaintiff, by and through his attorney, alleges:

1. The plaintiff is a resident of the State of Idaho, the defendant is a resident of the State of Washington, and there is diversity of citizenship between the parties.
2. The amount in controversy exceeds the sum of $75,000, exclusive of interest and costs.
3. On January 10, 2005, plaintiff was exercising reasonable care while walking across the intersection of Sun Valley Road and Main Street, Ketchum, Idaho, when defendant negligently drove her car through a red light at the intersection and struck plaintiff.
4. As a result of the defendant's negligence, plaintiff has incurred medical expenses of $104,000 and suffered severe physical injury and mental distress.

WHEREFORE, plaintiff claims judgment in the amount of $1,000,000, interest at the maximum legal rate, and costs of this action.

By ______________________________
Edward Lawson
Attorney for Plaintiff
100 Main Street
Ketchum, Idaho

The complaint and summons are served on the defendant by a sheriff, another government official, or a private process server.

Answer

The defendant must file an answer to the plaintiff's complaint. The defendant's answer is filed with the court and served on the plaintiff. In the answer, the defendant admits or denies the allegations contained in the plaintiff's complaint. A judgment will be entered against a defendant who admits all of the allegations in the complaint. The case will proceed if the defendant denies all or some of the allegations. If the defendant does not answer the complaint, a **default judgment** is entered against him or her. A default judgment establishes the defendant's liability. The plaintiff then has only to prove damages.

In addition to answering the complaint, a defendant's answer can assert **affirmative defenses.** For example, if a complaint alleges that the plaintiff was personally injured by the defendant, the defendant's answer could state that he or she acted in self-defense. Another affirmative defense would be an assertion that the plaintiff's lawsuit is barred because the **statute of limitations** (time within which to bring the lawsuit) has expired.

Cross-Complaint and Reply

A defendant who believes that he or she has been injured by the plaintiff can file a cross-complaint against the plaintiff in addition to an answer. In the cross-complaint, the defendant, now the **cross-complainant,** sues the plaintiff, now the **cross-defendant,** for damages or some other remedy. The original plaintiff must file a reply (answer) to the cross-complaint. The reply, which can include affirmative defenses, must be filed with the court and served on the original defendant.

Intervention and Consolidation

If other persons have an interest in a lawsuit, they may intervene and become parties to the lawsuit. As an example of an **intervention,** a bank that has made a secured loan on a piece of real estate can intervene in a lawsuit between parties who are litigating ownership of the property.

If several plaintiffs have filed separate lawsuits stemming from the same factual situation against the same defendant, the court can consolidate the cases into one case if it would not cause undue prejudice to the parties. As an example of **consolidation,** suppose a commercial airplane crashes, killing and injuring many people. The court could consolidate all of the lawsuits against the defendant airline company.

Statute of Limitations

A statute of limitations establishes the time period during which a plaintiff must bring a lawsuit against a defendant. If a lawsuit is not filed within this period, the plaintiff loses his or her right to sue. A statute of limitations begins to "run" at the time the plaintiff first has the right to sue the defendant (e.g., when the accident happens, or when the breach of contract occurs).

Federal and state governments have established statutes of limitations for each type of lawsuit. Most are from one to four years, depending on the type of lawsuit. For example, a one-year statute of limitations is common for ordinary negligence

SIDEBAR

Cost–Benefit of a Lawsuit

The choice of whether to bring or defend a lawsuit should be analyzed like any other business decision. This includes performing a **cost–benefit analysis** of the lawsuit. For the plaintiff, it may be wise not to sue. For the defendant, it may be wise to settle. The following factors should be considered in deciding whether to bring or settle a lawsuit:

- The probability of winning or losing.
- The amount of money to be won or lost.
- Lawyers' fees and other costs of litigation.
- Loss of time by managers and other personnel.
- The long-term effects on the relationship and reputations of the parties.
- The amount of prejudgment interest provided by law.
- The aggravation and psychological costs associated with a lawsuit.
- The unpredictability of the legal system and the possibility of error.
- Other factors peculiar to the parties and lawsuit.

CASE FOR DISCUSSION

Swierkiewicz v. Sorema N.A.

534 U.S. 506, 122 S.Ct. 992, 2002 U.S. Lexis 1374 (2002) — Supreme Court of the United States

FACTS

In April 1989, Akos Swierkiewicz, a native of Hungary, began working for Sorema N.A., a reinsurance company headquartered in New York. Swierkiewicz was initially employed as senior vice president and chief underwriting officer. Nearly six years later the chief executive officer of the company demoted Swierkiewicz to a marketing position, and he was removed of his underwriting responsibilities. Swierkiewicz's underwriting responsibilities were transferred to a 32-year-old employee with less than one year of underwriting experience. Swierkiewicz, who was 53 years old at the time and had 26 years of experience in the insurance industry, was then dismissed by Sorema. Swierkiewicz sued Sorema to recover monetary damages for alleged age and national origin discrimination in violation of federal antidiscrimination laws. Sorema moved to have Swierkiewicz's complaint dismissed. The district court dismissed Swierkiewicz's complaint for not being specific enough, and the court of appeals affirmed. Swierkiewicz appealed to the U.S. Supreme Court.

ISSUE

Under the notice pleading system, was plaintiff Swierkiewicz's complaint sufficiently stated to permit the case to go to trial?

COURT'S REASONING

The Supreme Court noted that Federal Rule of Civil Procedure 8(a)(2) provides that a complaint must include only "a short and plain statement of the claim showing that the pleader is entitled to relief." Under a notice pleading system, such a statement must simply give the defendant fair notice of what the plaintiff's claim is and the grounds upon which it rests. The Supreme Court stated, "The Federal Rules reject the approach that pleading is a game of skill in which one misstep by counsel may be decisive to the outcome."

Applying the relevant standard, the Supreme Court held that petitioner Swierkiewicz's complaint easily satisfied the requirements of Rule 8(a) because it gave respondent Sorema N.A. fair notice of the basis for petitioner's claims. Petitioner alleged that he had been terminated on account of his national origin in violation of Title VII and on account of his age in violation of the Age Discrimination in Employment Act.

DECISION AND REMEDY

The U.S. Supreme Court held that plaintiff Swierkiewicz's complaint met the requirements of notice pleading and was sufficient to withstand Sorema's motion to dismiss. The Supreme Court reversed the judgment of the court of appeals and remanded the case for further proceedings.

QUESTIONS

1. Describe "notice pleading." What is the public policy supporting notice pleading?
2. Did Sorema act ethically in trying to dismiss plaintiff Swierkiewicz's complaint? Explain.
3. Does notice pleading cause any problems for either of the parties to a lawsuit? Is the defendant put on sufficient notice of the charges against it by notice pleading?

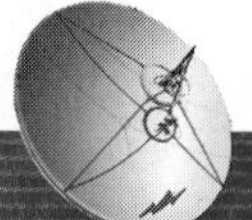

INFORMATION TECHNOLOGY

E-FILINGS IN COURT

When litigation ensues, the clients, lawyers, and judges involved in the case usually are buried in paper—pleadings, interrogatories, documents, motions to the court, briefs, and memorandums; the list goes on and on. By the time a case is over, reams of paper are stored in dozens, if not hundreds, of boxes. Further, court appearances, no matter how small the matter, must be made in person. For example, lawyers often wait hours for a 10-minute scheduling or other conference with the judge. Additional time is required to drive to and from court, which in an urban area could amount to hours.

Some forward-thinking judges and lawyers envision a day when the paperwork and hassle are reduced or eliminated in a "virtual courthouse." Technology supports the electronic filing—**e-filing**—of pleadings, briefs, and other documents related to a lawsuit. E-filing includes using CD-ROMs for briefs, scanning evidence and documents into a computer for storage and retrieval, and e-mailing correspondence and documents to the court and the opposing counsel. Scheduling and other conferences with the judge or opposing counsel would be held via telephone conferences and e-mail.

Many courts have instituted e-filing. In some courts e-filing is now mandatory. Companies such as Microsoft and Lexis-Nexis have developed systems to manage e-filings of court documents.

actions. Thus, if on July 1, 2004, Otis negligently causes an automobile accident in which Cha-Yen is injured, Cha-Yen has until July 1, 2005, to bring a negligence lawsuit against Otis. If she waits longer than that, she loses her right to sue him.

A lawyer without history of literature is a mechanic, a mere working mason: if he possesses some knowledge of these, he may venture to call himself an architect.
—Sir Walter Scott

DISCOVERY

The legal process provides for a detailed pretrial procedure called **discovery.** During discovery, both parties engage in various activities to discover facts of the case from the other party and witnesses prior to trial. Discovery serves several functions, including preventing surprise, allowing parties to prepare thoroughly for trial, preserving evidence, saving court time, and promoting the settlement of cases. The major forms of discovery are as follows:

Depositions

A **deposition** is the oral testimony given by a party or witness prior to trial. The person giving the deposition is called the **deponent.** The **parties** to the lawsuit must give their depositions, if called upon by the other party to do so. The deposition of a **witness** can be given voluntarily or pursuant to a **subpoena** (court order). The deponent can be required to bring documents to the deposition. Most depositions are taken at the office of one of the attorneys.

The deponent is placed under oath and then asked oral questions by one or both of the attorneys. The questions and answers are recorded in written form by a court reporter. Depositions can also be videotaped. The deponent is given an

CASE FOR DISCUSSION

Norgart v. The Upjohn Company

21 Cal.4th 383, 87 Cal.Rptr.2nd 453, 1999 Cal. Lexis 5308 (1999) Supreme Court of California

FACTS

Kristi Norgart McBride lived with her husband in Santa Rosa, California. Kristi suffered from manic-depressive mental illness (now called bipolar disorder). In this disease, the person cycles between manic (ultrahappy, expansive, extrovert) episodes to depressive episodes. The disease is often treated with prescription drugs.

In April 1984, Kristi attempted suicide. A psychiatrist prescribed an antianxiety drug. In May 1985, Kristi attempted suicide again by overdosing on drugs. The doctor prescribed Halcion, a hypnotic drug, and added Darvocet-N, a mild narcotic analgesic. On October 16, 1985, after descending into a severe depression, Kristi committed suicide by overdosing on Halcion and Darvocet-N.

On October 16, 1991, exactly six years after Kristi's death, Leo and Phyllis Norgart, Kristi's parents, filed a lawsuit against the Upjohn Company, the maker of Halcion, for wrongful death based on Upjohn's alleged failure to warn of the unreasonable dangers of taking Halcion. The trial court granted Upjohn's motion for summary judgment based on the fact that the one-year statute of limitations for wrongful death actions had run out. The court of appeals reversed, and Upjohn appealed to the supreme court of California.

ISSUE

Is the plaintiff's action for wrongful death barred by the one-year statute of limitations?

COURT'S REASONING

The court noted that the statute of limitations has a purpose to protect defendants from the stale claims of dilatory plaintiffs. It has as a related purpose to stimulate plaintiffs to assert fresh claims against defendants in a diligent fashion. The court stated that under the statute of limitations, a plaintiff must bring a cause of action from wrongful death within one year of accrual—that means that the date of accrual of a cause of action for wrongful death is the date of death. The Norgarts had to bring the cause of action for wrongful death within one year of accrual. The court stated, "They did not do so. Pursuant to this rule, the Norgarts were too late, exactly five years too late."

DECISION AND REMEDY

The supreme court of California held that the defendant, the Upjohn Company, was entitled to judgment as a matter of law based on the fact that the one-year statute of limitations for wrongful death actions had run, thus barring the plaintiff's lawsuit. The supreme court reversed the decisions of the court of appeals.

QUESTIONS

1. What is the public policy behind having statutes of limitations? What is the public policy against having such statutes? Which policy should dominate and why?
2. Was it ethical for the Upjohn Company to avoid facing the merits of the lawsuit by asserting the one-year statute of limitations?
3. What are the business implications for having statutes of limitations?

opportunity to correct his or her answers prior to signing the deposition. Depositions are used to preserve evidence (e.g., if the deponent is deceased, ill, or not otherwise available at trial) and impeach testimony given by witnesses at trial.

Interrogatories

Interrogatories are written questions submitted by one party to a lawsuit to another party. The questions can be very detailed. In addition, it might be necessary to attach certain documents to the answers. A party is required to answer the interrogatories in writing within a specified time period (e.g., 60 to 90 days). An attorney usually helps with preparation of the answers. The answers are signed under oath.

Production of Documents

Often, particularly in complex business cases, a substantial portion of the lawsuit may be based on information contained in documents (e.g., memoranda, correspondence, company records, and such). One party to a lawsuit may request that the other party produce all documents that are relevant to the case prior to trial. This is called **production of documents.** If the documents sought are too voluminous to be moved or are in permanent storage, or if production of the documents would disrupt the ongoing business of the party who is to produce them, the requesting party may be required to examine the documents at the other party's premises.

Physical and Mental Examinations

In cases that concern the physical or mental condition of a party, a court can order the party to submit to certain **physical or mental examinations** to determine the extent of the alleged injuries. This would occur, for example, where the plaintiff has been injured in an accident and is seeking damages for physical injury and mental distress.

Pretrial Motions

Parties to a lawsuit can make several **pretrial motions** to try to dispose of all or part of a lawsuit prior to trial. The two major pretrial motions are the motion for judgment on the pleading and the motion for summary judgment.

Motion for Judgment on the Pleadings

Either party can make a **motion for judgment on the pleadings** once the pleadings are complete. This motion alleges that if all of the facts presented in the pleadings are true, the party making the motion would win the lawsuit when the proper law is applied to these facts. In deciding this motion, the judge cannot consider any facts outside the pleadings.

Motion for Summary Judgment

The trier of the fact (i.e., the jury, or, if no jury, the judge) determines factual issues. A **motion for summary judgment** asserts that there are no factual disputes to be decided by the jury and that the judge should apply the relevant law to the undisputed facts to decide the case. Motions for summary judgment, which can be made by either party, are supported by evidence outside the pleadings. Affidavits

SIDEBAR

Payment of Attorney's Fees

In most civil lawsuits each party is responsible for paying its own attorney's fees, whether the party wins or loses. This is called the "American rule." The court can award attorney's fees to the winning party if a statute so provides, the parties have so agreed (e.g., in a contract), or the losing party has acted maliciously or pursued a frivolous case.

An attorney in a civil lawsuit can represent the plaintiff on an hourly, project, or contingency fee basis. Hourly fees usually range from $75 to $500 per hour, depending on the type of case, the expertise of the lawyer, and the locality of the lawsuit. Under a **contingency fee arrangement,** the lawyer receives a percentage of the amount recovered for the plaintiff upon winning or settling the case. Contingency fees normally range from 20 to 50 percent of the award or settlement, with the average being about 35 percent. Lawyers for defendants in lawsuits are normally paid on an hourly basis.

from the parties and witnesses, documents (e.g., a written contract between the parties), depositions, and such are common forms of evidence.

If, after examining the evidence, the court finds no factual dispute, it can decide the issue or issues raised in the summary judgment motion. This may dispense with the entire case or with part of the case. If the judge finds that a factual dispute exists, the motion will be denied and the case will go to trial.

Settlement Conference

Federal court rules and most state court rules permit the court to direct the attorneys or parties to appear before the court for a **pretrial hearing,** or **settlement conference.** One of the major purposes of such hearings is to facilitate settlement of the case. Pretrial conferences are often held informally in the judge's chambers. If no settlement is reached, the pretrial hearing is used to identify the major trial issues and other relevant factors. More than 90 percent of all cases are settled before they go to trial.

The Trial

Pursuant to the Seventh Amendment to the U.S. Constitution, a party to an action at law is guaranteed the right to a **jury trial** in cases in federal court. Most state constitutions contain a similar guarantee for state court actions. If either party requests a jury, the trial will be by jury. If both parties waive their right to a jury, the

Ford Explorer SUV Rollover Lawsuit Settled for $22 Million

On June 23, 1992, Nabil Boury was driving a 1992 Ford Explorer SUV on the Eisenhower Expressway in Chicago with five passengers in the vehicle. When another car clipped the Explorer on the driver's-side rear wheel well, the Explorer immediately rolled over. By the time it came to rest, the Explorer had rolled over three times, ejecting several of the passengers. Boury's sister and another teenager were killed, Boury's cousin lost vision in one eye, and another passenger was rendered a quadriplegic; Boury and his mother suffered minor injuries.

After the accident, the injured persons and the estates of the two deceased teenagers sued Ford Motor Company in a product liability lawsuit, alleging that there was a defect in the design of the Explorer SUV that caused it to roll over. The plaintiffs sued Michelin Tire Corporation, alleging that the Michelin tires on the SUV were inappropriate for the vehicle and that Michelin had not warned of this fact. The plaintiffs sued Packey Webb Ford, the car dealer that sold the Explorer, for putting Michelin tires on the SUV in a size and type specifically contrary to the warnings in the Ford owner's manual. The plaintiffs also sued Cassidy Tire Company, the distributor of the Michelin tires.

Several months before the case was to proceed to trial in the fall of 2001, the parties reached settlement. Ford agreed to pay $8 million, Packey Webb $10.5 million, Cassidy Tire $3 million, and Michelin Tire $500,000. The plaintiffs reached a separate agreement as to how to divide the settlement proceeds. This is just one example of the hundreds of thousands of civil lawsuits that are settled every year.

Boury v. Ford Motor Company, Cook County Circuit Court, Illinois (2001).

trial will be without a jury. In non-jury trials, the judge sits as the **trier of fact.** These trials also are called **waiver of trial** or **bench trial.** At the time of trial, the parties usually submit **trial briefs** to the judge, which contain legal support for their side of the case.

Trials are usually divided into the following phases:

- **Jury selection**
- Opening statements
- Plaintiff's case
- Defendant's case
- Rebuttal and rejoinder
- Closing arguments
- Jury instructions
- Jury deliberation
- **Entry of judgment**

Sancho: But if this is hell, why do we see no lawyers?

Clarindo: They won't receive them, lest they bring lawsuits here.

Sancho: If there are no lawsuits here, hell's not so bad.

—Lope de Vega,
The Star of Seville, Act 3, Scene 2

Jury Selection

The pool of potential jurors is usually selected from voter or automobile registration lists. Individuals are selected to hear specific cases through the process called ***voir dire*** ("to speak the truth"). Lawyers for each party and the judge can ask prospective jurors questions to determine if they would be biased in their decision. Biased jurors can be prevented from sitting on a particular case.

Once the appropriate number of jurors is selected (usually 6 to 12 jurors), they are **impaneled** to hear the case and are sworn in. The trial is ready to begin. A jury can be **sequestered** (separated from family, etc.) when warranted. Jurors are paid minimum fees for the service.

Opening Statements

Each party's attorney is allowed to make an **opening statement** to the jury. In opening statements, attorneys usually summarize the main factual and legal issues of the case and describe why they believe their client's position is valid. The information given in this statement is not considered as evidence.

The Plaintiff's Case

Plaintiffs bear the **burden of proof** to persuade the trier of the fact of the merits of their case. This is called the **plaintiff's case.** The plaintiff's attorney will call witnesses to give testimony.

Pieces of evidence, each by itself insufficient, may together constitute a significant whole and justify by their combined effect a conclusion.

—Lord Wright,
Grant v. Australian Knitting Mills, Ltd. (1936)

After a witness has been sworn in, the plaintiff's attorney examines (questions) the witness. This is called **direct examination.** Documents and other evidence can be introduced through each witness.

After the plaintiff's attorney has completed his or her questions, the defendant's attorney can question the witness. This is called **cross-examination.** The defendant's attorney can ask questions only about the subjects that were brought up during the direct examination.

After the defendant's attorney completes his or her questions, the plaintiff's attorney can ask questions of the witness. This is called **redirect examination.** The defendant's attorney can then again ask questions of the witness. This is called **recross examination.**

The Defendant's Case

The **defendant's case** proceeds after the plaintiff has concluded his or her case. The defendant's case must (1) rebut the plaintiff's evidence, (2) prove any affirmative defenses asserted by the **defendant,** and (3) prove any allegations contained in the defendant's cross-complaint. The defendant's witnesses are examined in much the same way as the plaintiff's attorney cross-examines each witness. This is followed by redirect and recross examination.

Rebuttal and Rejoinder

Human beings do not ever make laws; it is the accidents and catastrophes of all kinds happening in every conceivable way that make law for us.
—Plato, *Laws IV.709*

After the defendant's attorney has completed calling witnesses, the plaintiff's attorney can call witnesses and put forth evidence to rebut the defendant's case. This is called a **rebuttal.** The defendant's attorney can call additional witnesses and introduce other evidence to counter the rebuttal. This is called the **rejoinder.**

Closing Arguments

At the conclusion of the evidence, each party's attorney is allowed to make a **closing argument** to the jury. Both attorneys try to convince the jury to render a verdict for their client by pointing out the strengths in the client's case and the weaknesses in the other side's case. Information given by the attorneys in their closing statements is not evidence.

Jury Instructions

Once the closing arguments are completed, the judge reads **jury instructions** (or **charges**) to the jury. These instructions inform the jury about what law to apply when they decide the case. For example, in a criminal trial the judge will read to the jury the statutory definition of the crime charged. In an accident case, the judge will read the jury the legal definition of **negligence.**

Jury Deliberation

The jury then retires to the jury room to deliberate its findings. **Jury deliberation** can take from a few minutes to many weeks. After deliberation, the jury assesses penalties in criminal cases.

Entry of Judgment

After the jury has returned its **verdict,** in most cases the judge will enter **judgment** to the successful party based on the verdict. This is the official decision of the court. The court may, however, overturn the verdict if it finds bias or jury misconduct. This is called a **judgment notwithstanding the verdict** or **judgment n.o.v.** or **j.n.o.v.**

In a civil case, the judge may reduce the amount of monetary damages awarded by the jury if he or she finds the jury to have been biased, emotional, or inflamed. This is called **remittitur.** The trial court usually issues a **written memorandum** setting forth the reasons for the judgment. This memorandum, together with the trial transcript and evidence introduced at trial, constitutes the permanent **record** of the trial court proceeding. In the following Case for Discussion, the court was asked to grant a judgment notwithstanding the verdict.

CASE FOR DISCUSSION

Ferlito v. Johnson & Johnson Products, Inc.

771 F.Supp. 196, 1991 U.S. Dist. Lexis 11747 (1991) United States District Court, Eastern District of Michigan

FACTS

Susan and Frank Ferlito were invited to a Halloween party. They decided to attend as Mary (Mrs. Ferlito) and her little lamb (Mr. Ferlito). Mrs. Ferlito constructed a lamb costume for her husband by gluing cotton batting manufactured by Johnson & Johnson Products, Inc. (JJP) to a suit of long underwear. She used the same cotton batting to fashion a headpiece, complete with ears. The costume covered Mr. Ferlito from his head to his ankles, except for his face and hands, which were blackened with paint.

At the party, Mr. Ferlito attempted to light a cigarette with a butane lighter. The flame passed close to his left arm, and the cotton batting ignited. He suffered burns over one-third of his body.

The Ferlitos sued JJP to recover damages, alleging that JJP failed to warn them of the ignitability of cotton batting. The jury returned a verdict for Mr. Ferlito in the amount of $555,000 and for Mrs. Ferlito in the amount of $70,000. JJP filed a motion for judgment notwithstanding the verdict (j.n.o.v.).

ISSUE

Should defendant JJP's motion for j.n.o.v. be granted?

COURT'S REASONING

The court noted that if, after reviewing the evidence, the court is of the opinion that reasonable minds could not come to the result reached by the jury, then the motion for j.n.o.v. should be granted. At trial, both plaintiffs testified that they knew that cotton batting burns when exposed to flame. The court stated, "Because both plaintiffs were already aware of the danger, a warning by Johnson & Johnson would have been superfluous." Mrs. Ferlito testified that the idea for the costume was hers alone. As described on the product's package, its intended uses are for cleansing, applying medications, and infant care. The court concluded that the plaintiffs failed to demonstrate the forseeability of an adult male encapsulating himself from head to toe in cotton batting and then lighting up a cigarette.

DECISION AND REMEDY

The trial court granted defendant Johnson & Johnson's motion for j.n.o.v. By doing so, the court vacated the verdict entered by the jury in favor of Mr. and Mrs. Ferlito. The court of appeals affirmed the grant of j.n.o.v.

QUESTIONS

1. Should trial courts have the authority to enter a j.n.o.v., or should jury verdicts always be allowed to stand? Explain your answer.
2. Did the Ferlitos act ethically in suing JJP in this case? Were they responsible for their own injuries?
3. What would have been the business implications had JJP been found liable?

SIDEBAR

Discourage Litigation

Discourage litigation. Persuade your neighbors to compromise whenever you can. Point out to them how the nominal winner is often a real loser—in fees, and expenses, and waste of time. As a peacemaker the lawyer has a superior opportunity of being a good man. There will still be business enough.

Abraham Lincoln,
Notes on the Practice of Law (1850)

THE APPEAL

In a civil case, either party can **appeal** the trial court's decision once a final judgment is entered. Only the defendant can appeal in a criminal case. The appeal is made to the appropriate appellate court. A **notice of appeal** must be filed within a prescribed time after judgment is entered (usually within 60 or 90 days). The appealing party is called the **appellant, or petitioner.** The responding party is called the **appellee,** or **respondent.** The appellant is often required to post a bond (e.g., one-and-one-half times the judgment) on appeal.

The parties may designate all or relevant portions of the trial record to be submitted to the appellate court for review. The appellant's attorney may file an **opening brief** with the court that sets forth legal research and other information to support his or her contentions on appeal. The appellee can file a **responding brief** answering the appellant's contentions. Appellate courts usually permit a brief oral argument at which each party's attorney is heard.

An appellate court will reverse a lower court decision if it finds an **error of law** in the record. An error of law occurs if the jury was improperly instructed by the trial court judge, prejudicial evidence was admitted at trial when it should have been excluded, prejudicial evidence was obtained through an unconstitutional search and seizure, and the like. An appellate court will not reverse a **finding of fact** unless such finding is unsupported by the evidence or is contradicted by the evidence.

ALTERNATIVE DISPUTE RESOLUTION

The use of the court system to resolve business and other disputes can take years and cost thousands, if not millions, of dollars in legal fees and expenses. In commercial litigation, the normal business operations of the parties are often disrupted. To avoid or lessen these problems, businesses are increasingly turning to methods of alternative dispute resolution (ADR) and other aids to resolving disputes. The most common form of ADR is **arbitration.** Other forms of ADR are **mediation, conciliation, minitrial, fact-finding,** and a **judicial referee.**

Arbitration

In arbitration, the parties choose an impartial third party to hear and decide the dispute. This neutral party is called the **arbitrator.** Arbitrators are usually selected from members of the American Arbitration Association (AAA) or another arbitration association. Labor union agreements, franchise agreements, leases, and other commercial contracts often contain **arbitration clauses** that require disputes arising out of the contract to be submitted to arbitration. If there is no arbitration clause, the parties can enter into a **submission agreement** whereby they agree to submit a dispute to arbitration after the dispute arises.

Evidence and testimony are presented to the arbitrator at a hearing held for this purpose. Less formal evidentiary rules are usually applied in arbitration hearings than at court. After the hearing, the arbitrator reaches a decision and enters an **award.** The parties often agree in advance to be bound by the arbitrator's decision and award. If the parties have not so agreed, the arbitrator's award can be appealed to court. The court gives great deference to the arbitrator's decision.

Congress enacted the **Federal Arbitration Act** to promote the arbitration of disputes. About half of the states have adopted the **Uniform Arbitration Act.** This

ETHICAL PERSPECTIVE

FIRESTONE TIRES SHRED

On October 16, 1998, 14-year-old Jessica LeAnn Taylor, a junior high school cheerleader, was a passenger in a Ford Explorer SUV being driven to a homecoming football game. She never made it to the game. On the way, the left-rear Firestone ATX tire shredded, causing the SUV to roll over, killing Jessica. Randy Roberts, a small-town lawyer from East Texas, was hired by Jessica's parents to take on corporate giants Firestone Tire Company, which made the tire, and Ford Motor Company, which manufactured the Explorer SUV.

When attorney Roberts sought to discover any consumer complaints or other lawsuits that had been brought against Firestone concerning shredding tires, Firestone refused to disclose any documents but told Roberts that it knew of only one other similar accident. Undeterred, Roberts brought the issue to court, and the judge ordered Firestone to hand over the documents. The information, which was released in February 2000, showed that 1,100 complaints had been reported to Firestone about its ATX and Wilderness tires shredding, and 57 lawsuits had been filed already.

Attorney Roberts notified the National Highway Traffic Safety Administration (NHTSA), the federal government administrative agency responsible for automobile safety, about the findings. The NHTSA instituted an investigation, which further found that more than 80 people had died and more than 250 people had been injured in accidents involving shredding Firestone ATX and Wilderness tires, the majority on Ford Explorer SUVs. The Firestone tires tended to shred under hot temperatures. Further investigation showed that there had been deaths and injuries in other countries, including Saudi Arabia, Venezuela, Colombia, Ecuador, and other countries.

With mounting pressure, in August 2000 Firestone recalled more than 6 million ATX and Wilderness tires, the largest tire recall in U.S. history. Consumers all over America flocked to have their Firestone ATX and Wilderness tires replaced.

Hundreds of civil lawsuits now have been filed against Firestone and Ford, alleging design defect, defect in manufacturing, and failure to warn. The lawsuits seek not only compensatory damages for the loss of loved ones and to pay for injuries, but also seek large punitive damage awards to punish Firestone and Ford for acting recklessly. It will take years for all the trials and appeals to be sorted out to determine who is financially culpable. In the meantime, substantial ethical issues have been raised questioning the conduct of Firestone and Ford.

1. Do you think Firestone acted quickly enough in instituting the recall of its ATX and Wilderness tires?
2. Did Ford act ethically in this case? Should it have done anything earlier? Explain.
3. If you were a juror in Jessica's parents' lawsuit against Firestone and Ford, would you award punitive damages? Why or why not?

act promotes the arbitration of disputes at the state level. Many federal and state courts have instituted programs to refer legal disputes to arbitration or another form of alternative dispute resolution.

Mediation and Conciliation

In mediation, the parties choose a neutral third party to act as the **mediator** of the dispute. Unlike an arbitrator, a mediator does not make a decision or award. Instead, the mediator acts as a conveyor of information between the parties and assists them in trying to reach a settlement of the dispute. A mediator often meets separately with each of the parties. A settlement agreement is reached if the mediator is successful. If not, the case proceeds to trial. In a conciliation, the parties choose an interested third party, the **conciliator,** to act as the mediator.

Minitrial

A minitrial is a session, usually lasting a day or less, in which the lawyers for each side present their cases to representatives of each party who have authority to settle the dispute. In many cases, the parties hire a neutral person (e.g., a retired judge) to preside over the minitrial. Following the presentations, the parties meet to try to negotiate a settlement.

Fact-Finding

Fact-finding is a process whereby the parties hire a neutral person to investigate the dispute. The fact-finder reports his or her findings to the adversaries and may recommend a basis for settlement.

Judicial Referee

If the parties agree, the court may appoint a judicial referee to conduct a private trial and render a judgment. Referees, who are often retired judges, have most of the powers of a trial judge, and their decisions stand as a judgment of the court. The parties usually reserve their right to appeal.

LEGAL TERMINOLOGY

Affirmative defenses
Alternative dispute resolution (ADR)
Answer
Appeal
Appellant
Appellee
Arbitration
Arbitration clause
Arbitrator award
Bench trial
Burden of proof
Charges
Civil litigation
Closing argument
Complaint
Conciliation
Conciliator
Consolidation
Contempt of court
Contingency fee arrangement
Cost-benefit analysis
Cross-complainant
Cross-complaint
Cross-defendant
Cross-examination
Default judgment
Defendant
Defendant's case
Deponent
Deposition
Direct examination
Discovery
E-filing
Error of law
Fact-finding
Federal Arbitration Act
Finding of fact
Impaneling
Interrogatories
Intervention
Judgment
Judgment notwithstanding the verdict (j.n.o.v.)
Judicial referee

Jury deliberation
Jury instructions
Jury selection
Jury trial
Litigation
Mediation
Mediator
Minitrial
Motion for judgment on the pleadings
Motion for summary judgment
Negligence
Notice of appeal
Opening brief
Opening statement
Parties
Petitioner
Physical or mental examination
Plaintiff
Plaintiff's case
Pleadings
Pretrial hearing
Pretrial motions
Production of documents
Rebuttal
Record
Recross examination
Redirect examination
Rejoinder
Remittitur
Reply
Respondent
Responding brief
Sequester
Settlement conference
Statute of limitations
Submission agreement
Subpoena
Summons
Trial briefs
Trier of fact
Uniform Arbitration Act
Verdict
Voir dire
Waiver of trial
Witness
Written memorandum

chapter summary

CIVIL LITIGATION AND ALTERNATIVE DISPUTE RESOLUTION

The Pleadings

Pleadings	Pleadings consist of paperwork that initiates and responds to a lawsuit. Pleadings include: 1. *Complaint:* Filed by the plaintiff with the court and served with a *summons* on the defendant. It sets forth the basis of the lawsuit. 2. *Answer:* Filed by the defendant with the court and served on the plaintiff. It usually denies most allegations of the complaint. 3. *Cross-complaint:* Filed and served by the defendant if he or she counter-sues the plaintiff. The defendant is the *cross-complainant* and the plaintiff is the *cross-defendant.* The cross-defendant must file and serve a *reply* (answer). 4. *Intervention:* A person who has an interest in a lawsuit may intervene and become a party to the lawsuit. 5. *Consolidation:* Separate cases against the same defendant arising from the same incident may be consolidated by the court into one case if it would not cause prejudice to the parties. *(continued)*

Discovery	
Discovery	Discovery is the pretrial litigation process for discovering facts of the case from the other party and witnesses. Discovery consists of: 1. *Depositions:* Oral testimony given by a *deponent*, either a party or witness. Depositions are transcribed. 2. *Interrogatories:* Written questions submitted by one party to the other party. They must be answered within a specified period of time. 3. *Production of documents:* A party to a lawsuit may obtain copies of all relevant documents from the other party. 4. *Physical and mental examination:* These examinations of a party are permitted upon order of the court where injuries are alleged that could be verified or disputed by such examination.
Pretrial Motions	
Dismissals and Pretrial Judgments	1. *Motion for judgment on the pleadings:* Alleges that if all facts as pleaded are true, the moving party would win the lawsuit. No facts outside the pleadings may be considered. 2. *Motion for summary judgment:* Alleges that there are no factual disputes, so the judge may apply the law and decide the case without a jury. Evidence outside the pleadings may be considered (e.g., affidavits, documents, depositions).
Settlement Conference	
Settlement Conference	Conference prior to trial between the parties in front of the judge to facilitate the settlement of the case. Also called *pretrial hearing.* If a settlement is not reached, the case proceeds to trial.
The Trial	
Phases of a Trial	1. *Jury selection:* Done through a process called *voir dire.* Biased jurors are dismissed and replaced. 2. *Opening statements:* Made by the parties' lawyers. Are not evidence. 3. *The plaintiff's case:* The plaintiff bears the burden of proof. The plaintiff calls witnesses and introduces evidence to try to prove his or her case. 4. *The defendant's case:* The defendant calls witnesses and introduces evidence to rebut the plaintiff's case and to prove affirmative defenses and cross-complaints. 5. *Rebuttal and rejoinder:* The plaintiff and defendant may call additional witnesses and introduce additional evidence. 6. *Closing arguments:* Made by the parties' lawyers. Are not evidence. 7. *Jury instructions:* Judge reads instructions to the jury as to what law they are to apply to the case. 8. *Jury deliberation:* Jury retires to the jury room and deliberates until it reaches a *verdict.*

	9. *Entry of judgment:* The judge may: a. Enter the verdict reached by the jury as the court's *judgment.* b. Grant a motion for *judgment n.o.v.* if the judge finds the jury was biased. This means that the jury's verdict does not stand. c. Order *remittitur* (reduction) of any damages awarded if the judge finds the jury to have been biased or emotional.
The Appeal	
Appeal	Both parties in a civil suit and the defendant in a criminal trial may appeal the decision of the trial court. *Notice of appeal* must be filed within a specified period of time. The appeal must be made to the appropriate appellate court.
Alternative Dispute Resolution (ADR)	
Description of ADR	*Nonjudicial* means of solving legal disputes. ADR usually saves time and money of costly litigation.
Types of ADR	1. *Arbitration:* An impartial third party, called the arbitrator, hears and decides the dispute. The arbitrator makes an award. The award is appealable to a court if the parties have not given up this right. Arbitration is designated by the parties pursuant to: a. *Arbitration clause:* Agreement contained in a contract stipulating that any dispute arising out of the contract will be arbitrated. b. *Submission agreement:* Agreement made after the dispute arises to submit a dispute to arbitration. 2. *Mediation:* A neutral third party, called a *mediator,* assists the parties in trying to reach a settlement of their dispute. The mediator does not make an award. 3. *Conciliation:* An interested third party, called a *conciliator,* assists the parties in trying to reach a settlement of their dispute. The conciliator does not make an award. 4. *Minitrial:* A short session in which the lawyers for each side present their case to representatives of each party who have the authority to settle the dispute. 5. *Fact-finding:* The parties hire a neutral third person, called a *fact-finder,* to investigate the dispute and report his or her findings to the adversaries. 6. *Judicial referee:* With the consent of the parties, the court appoints a judicial referee (usually a retired judge or lawyer) to conduct a private trial and render a judgment. The judgment stands as the judgment of the court and may be appealed to the appropriate appellate court.

WORKING THE WEB

Visit the Web sites listed below for more information about the topics covered in this chapter.

1. Go to **www.adr.org/** and choose **Rules** and then **Ethics and Standards** from the sidebar menu. Study the rules of ethics for arbitrators. How do they compare with the rules of professional conduct for attorneys?
2. At the International Chamber of Commerce Web site **www.iccwbo.org/court/english/news_archives/2001/adr.asp,** you will find information about rules and procedures for settlement of international commercial disputes. Under what circumstances would you advise a client to elect ICC arbitration rules as compared with AAA rules?
3. Go to the U.S. Supreme Court site at **www.supremecourtus.gov.** Find a case from your state that recently has been appealed to the court. Outline the procedural steps involved in the process.
4. The site **guide.lp.findlaw.com/10fedgov/judicial/appeals_courts.html** contains links to each of the federal judicial circuits. Find your jurisdiction and review the cases available there. What is the oldest case you can find? The most recent? Compare your search results with the same two questions, looking at state court cases available in your state.

CRITICAL LEGAL THINKING QUESTIONS

1. Describe the following types of pleadings: (1) complaint, (2) answer, (3) cross-complaint, and (4) reply.
2. What is intervention? What is consolidation?
3. What is a statute of limitations? What is the public policy for having statutes of limitations?
4. Describe the following types of discovery: (1) deposition, (2) interrogatory, (3) production of documents, and (4) physical and mental examination.
5. Describe the following types of pretrial motions: (1) motion for judgment on the pleadings and (2) motion for summary judgment.
6. What is a settlement conference?
7. Describe the following phases of a trial: (1) jury selection, (2) opening statements, (3) plaintiff's case, (4) defendant's case, (5) rebuttal and rejoinder, (6) closing arguments, (7) jury instructions, (8) jury deliberation, (9) entry of judgment.
8. Describe the process of appeal. Who are the parties to an appeal?
9. What is alternative dispute resolution? What purposes are served by alternative dispute resolution?

10. Describe the following types of alternative dispute resolution: (1) arbitration, (2) mediation, (3) conciliation, (4) minitrial, (5) fact-finding, and (6) judicial referee.

CASE FOR BRIEFING

Read Case 3 in Appendix A *(Gnazzo v. G.D. Searle & Co.)*. Review and brief the case using the *Critical Legal Thinking* "Briefing the Case" example described in Chapter 1.

CASES FOR DISCUSSION

3.1 *Conrad v. Delta Airlines, Inc.*

494 F.2d 914 1974 U.S. App. Lexis 9186 (1974)
United States Court of Appeals, Seventh Circuit

FACTS Captain Conrad was a pilot for Delta Airlines. In 1970, Conrad was forced to resign by the airline. He sued, alleging that he was discharged because of his pro-union activities and not because of poor job performance, as claimed by Delta.

During discovery, a report written by a Delta flight operations manager was produced, which stated: "More than a few crew members claimed that Conrad professed to being a leftist-activist. His overactivity with the local pilots' union, coupled with inquiries regarding company files to our secretary, led to the conclusion that potential trouble will be avoided by acceptance of his resignation."

Conrad claims that the report is evidence of the anti-union motivation for his discharge. Delta made a summary judgment motion to the trial court.

ISSUE Should Delta's summary judgment motion be granted?

3.2 *Haviland & Co., Incorporated v. Montgomery Ward & Co.*

31 F.R.D. 578, 1962 U.S. Dist. Lexis 5964 (1962)
United States District Court, Southern District of New York

FACTS Haviland & Company filed suit against Montgomery Ward & Company in U.S. district court, claiming that Ward used the trademark "Haviland" on millions of dollars' worth of merchandise. As the owner of the mark, Haviland & Company sought compensation from Ward. Ward served notice to take the deposition of Haviland & Company's president, William D. Haviland. The attorneys for Haviland told the court that Haviland was 80 years old, lived in Limoges, France, and was too ill to travel to the United States for the deposition. Haviland's physician submitted an affidavit confirming these facts.

ISSUE Must Haviland give his deposition?

3.3 *Simblest v. Maynard*

427 F.2d 1, 1970 U.S. App. Lexis 9265 (1970)
United States Court of Appeals, Second Circuit

FACTS On November 9, 1965, Mr. Simblest was driving a car that collided with a fire engine at an intersection in Burlington, Vermont. The accident occurred on a night on which a power blackout left most of the state without lights. Mr. Simblest, who was injured in the accident, sued the driver of the fire truck for damages.

During the trial, Simblest testified that when he entered the intersection, the traffic light was green in his favor. All of the other witnesses testified that the traffic light had gone dark at least 10 minutes before the accident. Simblest testified that the accident was caused by the fire truck's failure to use any warning lights or sirens. Simblest's testimony was contradicted by four witnesses who testified that the fire truck had used both its lights and sirens. The jury found that the driver of the fire truck had been negligent and rendered a verdict for Simblest. The defense made a motion for judgment n.o.v.

ISSUE Who wins?

ETHICS CASE

3.4 *Burnham v. Superior Court of California*

495 U.S. 604, 110 S.Ct. 2105, 1990 U.S. Lexis 2700 (1990)
Supreme Court of the United States

FACTS Dennis and Francis Burnham were married in 1976 in West Virginia. In 1977, the couple moved to New Jersey, where their two children were born. In July 1987, the Burnhams decided to separate. Mrs. Burnham, who intended to move to California, was to have custody of the children. Mr. Burnham agreed to file for divorce on the grounds of "irreconcilable differences." In October 1987, Mr. Burnham threatened to file for divorce in New Jersey on the grounds of "desertion."

After unsuccessfully demanding that Mr. Burnham adhere to the prior agreement, Mrs. Burnham brought suit for divorce in California state court in early January 1988. In late January, Mr. Burnham visited California on a business trip. He then visited his children in the San Francisco Bay area, where his wife resided. He took the older child to San Francisco for the weekend. Upon returning the child to Mrs. Burnham's home, he was served with a court summons and a copy of Mrs. Burnham's divorce petition. He then returned to New Jersey. Mr. Burnham made a special appearance in the California court and moved to quash the service of process.

ISSUE Did Mr. Burnham act ethically in trying to quash the service of process? Did Mrs. Burnham act ethically in having Mr. Burnham served on his visit to California? Is the service of process good?

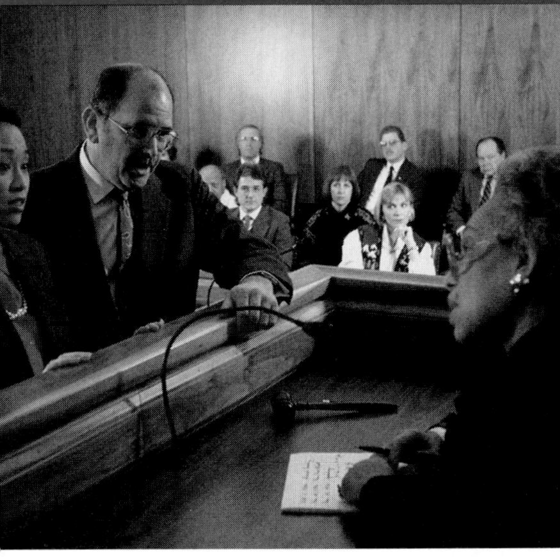

4 Criminal Law and Ethics

It is better that ten guilty persons escape, than that one innocent suffer.

—SIR WILLIAM BLACKSTONE, *COMMENTARIES ON THE LAWS OF ENGLAND* (1809)

CHAPTER OBJECTIVES

After studying this chapter, you should be able to

1. Define and list the essential elements of a crime.
2. Describe criminal procedure and the criminal trial.
3. Define major white-collar crimes.
4. Explain the constitutional safeguards provided to defendants in criminal cases.
5. Define and apply ethical principles to business.

CHAPTER OUTLINE

- Introduction
- Definition of a Crime
- Classification of Crimes
- Essential Elements of a Crime
- Criminal Acts as Basis for Tort Actions
- Criminal Procedure
- Case for Discussion: *Atwater v. City of Lago Vista, Texas*
- Crimes Affecting Business
- White-Collar Crimes
- Inchoate Crimes
- Constitutional Safeguards
- Case for Discussion: *Kyllo v. United States*
- Law and Ethics
- Case for Discussion: *Wal-Mart Stores, Inc. v. Samara Brothers, Inc.*
- Legal Terminology
- Chapter Summary
- Internet Exercises and Cases

INTRODUCTION

For members of society to coexist peacefully and for commerce to flourish, people and their property must be protected from injury by other members of society. Federal, state, and local governments' **criminal laws** are intended to accomplish this by providing an incentive for persons to act reasonably in society and imposing penalties on persons who violate them.

The United States has one of the most advanced and humane criminal law systems in the world. It differs from many other criminal law systems in several respects. First, a person charged with a crime in the United States is *presumed innocent until proven guilty*. The **burden of proof** is on the government to prove that the accused is guilty of the crime charged. Further, the accused must be found guilty "beyond a reasonable doubt." Conviction requires unanimous jury vote.

Under many other legal systems, a person accused of a crime is presumed guilty unless the person can prove that he or she is not. A person charged with a crime in the United States also is provided substantial constitutional safeguards during the criminal justice process—the protections against unreasonable search and seizure, against self-incrimination, against double jeopardy, and against cruel and unusual punishment, as well as the right to a public jury trial.

In addition to obeying criminal laws, business owners, managers, and members of boards of directors should abide by ethical principals when conducting business. This chapter discusses crimes, white-collar crimes, criminal procedure, constitutional protections, and business ethics.

Definition of a Crime

Law cannot persuade, where it cannot punish.

—Thomas Fuller

A **crime** is defined as any act done by an individual in violation of those duties that he or she owes to society and for the breach of which the law provides that the wrongdoer shall make amends to the public. Many activities have been considered crimes throughout the ages, whereas other crimes are of recent origin.

Penal Codes and Regulatory Statutes

Statutes, as described in Chapter 1, are the primary source of criminal law. Most states have adopted comprehensive **penal codes** that define in detail the activities considered to be crimes within their jurisdiction and the penalties that will be imposed for committing these crimes. A comprehensive federal criminal code defines federal crimes [Title 18 of the U.S. Code]. In addition, state and federal regulatory statutes often provide for criminal violations and penalties. The state and federal legislatures are continually adding to the list of crimes.

The penalty for committing a crime may be the imposition of a fine, imprisonment, both, or some other form of punishment (e.g., probation). Generally, imprisonment is imposed to

1. Incapacitate the criminal so he or she will not harm others in society.
2. Provide a means to rehabilitate the criminal.
3. Deter others from similar conduct.
4. Inhibit personal retribution by the victim.

Parties to a Criminal Action

In a criminal lawsuit, the government (not a private party) is the **plaintiff.** Representing the plaintiff is a lawyer, called the **prosecutor, district attorney,** or, in the federal system, United States Attorney. The accused is the **defendant.** The **defense attorney** represents the accused. If the accused cannot afford a defense lawyer, the government will provide one free of charge, called a **public defender.**

Classification of Crimes

All crimes can be classified into one of these categories: felonies, misdemeanors, or violations.

Felonies

The most serious kind of crime is called a **felony.** Felonies include crimes that are ***mala in se***—inherently evil. Most crimes against the person (murder, rape, and the like) and certain business-related crimes (such as embezzlement and bribery) are felonies in most jurisdictions. Felonies usually are punishable by imprisonment. In some jurisdictions, certain felonies (e.g., first-degree murder) are punishable by death. Federal law and some state laws require mandatory sentencing for specified crimes. Many statutes define different degrees of crimes (e.g., first-, second-, and third-degree murder), with each degree earning different penalties.

Misdemeanors

Misdemeanors are less serious than felonies. They are crimes ***mala prohibita***—not inherently evil but prohibited by society. This category includes many crimes against property, such as robbery, burglary, and violations of regulatory statutes. Misdemeanors carry lesser penalties than felonies. Misdemeanors usually are punishable by fine and/or imprisonment for one year or less.

Violations

Crimes such as traffic violations and jaywalking are neither felonies nor misdemeanors. Called **violations,** these crimes usually are punishable by a fine. Occasionally, a few days of imprisonment are imposed.

Essential Elements of a Crime

For a person to be found guilty of most crimes, a criminal act and criminal intent must be proven.

> The magnitude of a crime is proportionate to the magnitude of the injustice which prompts it. Hence, the smallest crimes may be actually the greatest.
>
> —Aristotle

Criminal Act

The defendant must have actually performed the prohibited act. Under the common law, actual performance of the criminal act is called the ***actus reus*** (guilty act). Under the Model Penal Code, the prohibited act may be analyzed in terms of conduct, circumstances, and results. Killing someone without legal justification is an example of *actus reus*. Sometimes the omission of an act constitutes the requisite *actus reus*. For example, a crime has been committed if a taxpayer who is under a legal duty to file a tax return fails to do so. Merely thinking about committing a crime is not a crime because no action has been taken.

Criminal Intent

To be found guilty of a crime, the accused must be found to have possessed the requisite subjective state of mind (i.e., specific or general intent) when the act was performed. This is called the ***mens rea*** (evil intent) under the traditional Common Law analysis and *culpable mental state* under the Model Penal Code. The Model Penal Code has four levels of culpable mental state:

1. Purposefully (or intentionally)
2. Knowingly
3. Recklessly
4. With criminal negligence

Specific intent is found where the accused purposefully, intentionally, or with knowledge commits a prohibited act. **General intent** is found where there is a showing of recklessness or a lesser degree of mental culpability. The individual criminal statutes state whether the crime requires a showing of specific or general

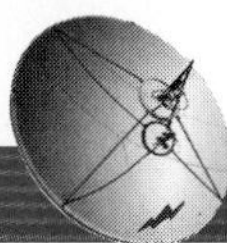

INFORMATION TECHNOLOGY

FEDERAL LAW HELPS VICTIMS OF IDENTITY FRAUD

For centuries, some people—for various purposes, mostly financial in nature—have attempted to take the identity of other persons. Today, taking on the identity of another can be extremely lucrative, earning the spoils of another's credit cards, bank accounts, Social Security benefits, and such. The use of new technology—computers and the Internet—has made such identity fraud even easier. But the victim of such fraud is left with funds stolen, a dismantled credit history, and thousands of dollars in costs in trying to straighten out the mess.

Identity fraud is the fastest growing financial fraud in the United States. Credit reporting firms say identity fraud cases have increased from 10,000 in 1990 to more than five million cases per year.

To combat such fraud, Congress passed the **Identity Theft and Assumption Deterrence Act** of 1998. This law criminalizes identity fraud, making it a federal felony punishable with prison sentences ranging from 3 to 25 years. The Act also appoints a federal administrative agency, the Federal Trade Commission (FTC), to help victims restore their credit and erase the impact of the imposter. Law-enforcement officials suggest that you:

1. Never put your Social Security number on any document unless it is legally required.
2. Obtain and review copies of your credit report at least twice each year.
3. Use passwords other than maiden names and birthdays on bank accounts and other accounts that require personal identification numbers (PINs).

intent. Juries may infer an accused's intent from the facts and circumstances of the case. There is generally no crime if the requisite *mens rea* cannot be proven. Thus, no crime is committed if one person accidentally injures another person.

Some statutes impose criminal liability based on **strict liability** or **absolute liability.** A finding of *mens rea* is not required. Criminal liability is imposed if the prohibited act is committed. Absolute liability is often imposed by regulatory statutes, such as environmental laws.

Criminal Acts as Basis for Tort Actions

An injured party may bring a **civil tort action** against a wrongdoer who has caused the party injury during the commission of a criminal act. Civil lawsuits are separate from the government's criminal action against the wrongdoer. In many cases, a person injured by a criminal act will not sue the criminal to recover civil damages. This is because the criminal is often **judgment-proof**—that is, the criminal does not have the money to pay a civil judgment. Table 4.1 compares civil and criminal law.

SIDEBAR

Criminal Procedure Federal rules of criminal procedure govern all criminal proceedings in the courts of the United States (federal courts). [FRCP Rule 1]

Criminal Procedure

The court procedure for initiating and maintaining a criminal action is quite detailed. It encompasses both pretrial procedures and the actual trial. Pretrial criminal procedure consists of several distinct stages: *arrest*, *indictment* or *information*, *arraignment*, and possible *plea bargaining*.

TABLE 4.1 *Civil and criminal law compared.*

Issue	Civil Law	Criminal Law
Party who brings the action	Plaintiff	Government
Trial by jury	Yes, except actions for equity	Yes
Burden of proof	Preponderance of evidence	Beyond a reasonable doubt
Jury vote	Judgment for plaintiff requires specific jury vote (e.g., 9 of 12 jurors)	Conviction requires unanimous jury vote
Sanctions and penalties	Monetary damages and equitable remedies (e.g., injunction, specific performance)	Imprisonment, capital punishment, fine, probation

Arrest

Before the police can arrest a person for committing a crime, they usually must obtain an **arrest warrant** based upon a showing of **probable cause**—the substantial likelihood that the person either committed or is about to commit a crime. If the police do not have time to obtain a warrant (e.g., if the police arrive during the commission of a crime, when a person is fleeing from the scene of the crime, or when it is likely that evidence will be destroyed), the police still may arrest the suspect. **Warrantless arrests,** too, are judged by the probable-cause standard. After a person is arrested, he or she is taken to the police station for **booking**—the administrative proceeding for recording the arrest, fingerprinting, and so on.

Indictment or Information

Accused persons must be formally charged with a crime before they can be brought to trial. This usually is done by the issuance of a *grand jury indictment* or a *magistrate's information statement.* Evidence of serious crimes, such as murder, is usually presented to a **grand jury.** Most grand juries consist of between 6 and 24 citizens who are charged with evaluating the evidence presented by the government. Grand jurors sit for a fixed time, such as one year. If the grand jury determines that there is sufficient evidence to hold the accused for trial, it issues an **indictment.** Note that the grand jury does not determine guilt. If an indictment is issued, the accused will be held for later trial.

The criminal is to go free because the constable has blundered.
—C.J. Cardozo, *People v. Defore* (1926)

For lesser crimes (burglary, shoplifting, and such), the accused will be brought before a **magistrate** (judge). A magistrate who finds that there is enough evidence to hold the accused for trial will issue **information.** The case against the accused is dismissed if neither an indictment nor information is issued.

Arraignment

If an indictment or information is issued, the accused is brought before a court for an **arraignment** proceeding during which the accused is (1) informed of the charges against him or her and (2) asked to enter a **plea.** The accused may plead *guilty, not guilty,* or *nolo contendere.* A plea of **nolo contendere** means that the

CASE FOR DISCUSSION

Atwater v. City of Lago Vista, Texas

532 U.S. 318, 121 S.Ct. 1536, 2001 U.S. Lexis 3366 (2001) Supreme Court of the United States

FACTS

Texas law requires that front-seat drivers and passengers must wear seat belts, and that a driver must secure any small child riding in front. In March 1997, Gail Atwater was driving her pickup truck in Lago Vista, Texas, with her three-year-old son and five-year-old daughter in the front seat. None of them was wearing a seat belt. Bart Turek, a Lago Vista police officer, observed the seat-belt violation and pulled Atwater over. A friend of Atwater's arrived at the scene and took charge of the children. Turek handcuffed Atwater, placed her in his squad car, and drove her to the police station. Atwater was booked, her "mug shot" was taken, and she was placed in a jail cell for about one hour until she was released on a $310 bond.

Atwater ultimately pleaded no contest to the misdemeanor seat-belt offenses and paid a $50 fine. Atwater sued the City of Lago Vista and the police officer for compensatory and punitive damages for allegedly violating her Fourth Amendment right to be free from unreasonable seizure. The district court ruled against Atwater and the court of appeals affirmed. The U.S. Supreme Court granted certiorari to hear the appeal.

ISSUE

Does the Fourth Amendment permit police to make a warrantless arrest pursuant to a minor criminal offense?

COURT'S REASONING

The U.S. Supreme Court stated there was no support for Atwater's position. The Court noted that both the legislative tradition of granting warrantless misdemeanor arrest authority and the judicial tradition of sustaining such statutes against constitutional attack for more than a century uniformly recognized the constitutionality of extending warrantless arrest power to misdemeanors without limitation to breaches of the peace. The Court held that if an officer has probable cause to believe that an individual has committed even a very minor criminal offense in his presence, he may, without violating the Fourth Amendment, arrest the offender.

DECISION AND REMEDY

The U.S. Supreme Court held that the Fourth Amendment permits police officers to make a warrantless arrest pursuant to a minor criminal offense. The Supreme Court affirmed the judgments of the district court and the court of appeals.

QUESTIONS

1. Do you agree with the U.S. Supreme Court's decision in this case? Why or why not?
2. Did the police officer act ethically in this case? Should he have used more discretion?
3. What would be the consequences if the Supreme Court had held in favor of Atwater?

accused agrees to the imposition of a penalty but does not admit guilt. A *nolo contendere* plea cannot be used as evidence of liability against the accused at a subsequent civil trial. Corporate defendants often enter this plea. The government has the option of accepting a *nolo contendere* plea or requiring the defendant to plead guilty or not guilty. Depending on the nature of the crime, the accused may be released upon posting bail.

Plea Bargaining

Sometimes the accused and the government enter into a **plea bargain** agreement. The government engages in plea bargaining to save costs, avoid the risks of a trial, and prevent further overcrowding of the prisons. This type of arrangement allows the accused to admit to a lesser crime than charged. In return, the government agrees to impose a lesser penalty or sentence than might have been obtained had the case gone to trial. In the federal system, more than 90 percent plead guilty rather than go to trial.

Crimes Affecting Business

Many crimes are committed against business property, often involving the theft, misappropriation, or fraudulent taking of property. The most important types of crimes against business property are discussed next.

There can be no equal justice where the kind of trial a man gets depends on the amount of money he has.
—J. Black, *Griffin v. Illinois* (1956)

Robbery

At common law, **robbery** is defined as the taking of personal property from another person by the use of fear or force. For example, if a robber threatens to physically harm a storekeeper unless the victim surrenders the contents of the cash register, this is robbery. If a criminal pickpockets somebody's wallet, it is not robbery because there has been no use of force or fear. Robbery with a deadly weapon is generally considered *aggravated robbery* (or armed robbery) and carries a harsher penalty.

Burglary

At common law, **burglary** was defined as "breaking and entering a dwelling at night" with the intent to commit a felony. Modern penal codes have broadened this definition to include daytime thefts and thefts from offices and commercial and other buildings. In addition, most modern definitions of burglary have abandoned the "breaking-in" element. Thus, unauthorized entering of a building through an unlocked door is sufficient. Aggravated burglary (or armed burglary) carries stiffer penalties.

Larceny

At common law, **larceny** is defined as the wrongful and fraudulent taking of another person's personal property. Most personal property—including tangible property, trade secrets, computer programs, and other business property—is subject to larceny. The stealing of automobiles and car stereos, pickpocketing, and such are larceny. Neither the use of force nor the entry of a building is required. Some states distinguish between *grand larceny* and *petit larceny*, depending on the value of the property taken.

SIDEBAR

Sentencing Guidelines
In order to make sentencing for the conviction of federal crimes more uniform, the United States Sentencing Commission adopted Sentencing Guidelines [U.S.C. § 3551 et seq.]. These guidelines establish minimum sentences, maximum sentences, and provide a range for sentences that may be imposed by a court upon persons and businesses convicted of federal crimes.

When a convicted criminal is sentenced, the court usually is bound by the sentencing guidelines. A court may depart from the sentencing guidelines based on evidence produced at trial and information provided by the prosecuting attorney, the defense attorney, and a pretrial services officer who reviews the case.

In sentencing, the court can impose time in prison, set fines to be paid to the government, and order monetary restitution to be paid to crime victims. A court can also impose probation on convicted defendants either as an original penalty or to be served upon release from jail.

Theft

Some states have dropped the distinction among the crimes of robbery, burglary, and larceny. Instead, these states group these crimes under the general crime of **theft.** Most of these states distinguish between *grand theft* and *petit theft*, depending upon the value of the property taken.

Receiving Stolen Property

It is a crime for a person to (1) knowingly receive stolen property, and (2) intend to deprive the rightful owner of that property. Knowledge and intent can be inferred from the circumstances. The stolen property can be any tangible property (e.g., personal property, money, negotiable instruments, stock certificates, and so on).

Arson

At common law, **arson** was defined as the malicious or willful burning of the dwelling of another person. Modern penal codes expanded this definition to include the burning of all types of private, commercial, and public buildings. Thus, in most states, an owner who burns his or her own building to collect insurance proceeds can be found liable for arson. If arson is found, the insurance company does not have to pay the proceeds of any insurance policy on the burned property.

Forgery

The crime of **forgery** occurs if a written document is fraudulently made or altered and that change affects the legal liability of another person. Examples of forgery are counterfeiting, falsifying public records, and the material altering of legal documents. One of the most common forms of forgery is the signing of another person's signature to a check or changing the amount of a check. Note that signing another person's signature without intent to defraud is not forgery. For instance, forgery has not been committed if one spouse signs the other spouse's payroll check for deposit in a joint checking or savings account at the bank.

Extortion

The crime of **extortion** means the obtaining of property from another, with his or her consent, induced by wrongful use of actual or threatened force, violence, or fear. For example, extortion occurs when a person threatens to expose something about another person unless that other person gives money or property. The truth or falsity of the information is immaterial. Extortion of private persons is commonly called *blackmail.* Extortion of public officials is called *extortion "under color of official right."*

Credit-Card Crimes

Substantial purchases in the United States are made with credit cards. This poses a problem if someone steals and uses another person's credit cards. Many states have enacted statutes that make the misappropriation and use of credit cards a separate crime. In other states, credit-card crimes are prosecuted under the forgery statute.

Money Laundering

When criminals make money from illegal activities, they are often faced with the problem of having large sums of money and no record of how this money was earned. This could easily tip the government off to their illegal activities. In order to "wash" the money and make it look like it was earned legitimately, many criminals purchase legitimate businesses and run the money through that business to clean it before the criminal receives the money. The legitimate business would have "cooked" books showing faked expenditures and receipts, in which the illegal money is buried. Restaurants, motels, and other cash businesses make excellent money laundries.

To address this problem the federal government enacted the **Money Laundering Control Act** [18 U.S.C. §1957]. This act makes it a crime to

- Knowingly engage in a *monetary transaction* through a financial institution involving property worth more than $10,000. For example, this would include making deposits, withdrawals, transactions between accounts, or obtaining monetary instruments such as cashiers' checks, money orders, and travelers' checks from a bank or other financial institution.
- Knowingly engage in a *financial transaction* involving the proceeds of an illegal activity. For example, this would include buying real estate, automobiles, personal property, intangible assets, or anything of value with money obtained from illegal activities.

Thus, money laundering itself is now a federal crime. The money that is washed could have been made from illegal gambling operations, drug dealing, fraud, and other crimes, including white-collar crimes. Persons convicted of money laundering can be fined up to $500,000 or twice the value of the property involved, whichever is greater, and sentenced to up to 20 years in federal prison. In addition, violation of the act subjects any property involved in or traceable to the offense to forfeiture to the government.

Bad Check Legislation

Many states have enacted *bad check legislation*, which makes it a crime for a person to make, draw, or deliver a check at a time when that person knows that funds in the account are insufficient to cover the amount of the check. Some states require proof that the accused intended to defraud the payee of the check.

In our complex society the accountant's certificate and the lawyer's opinion can be instruments for inflicting pecuniary loss more potent than the chisel or the crowbar.

—Justice Blackmun

White-Collar Crimes

Crimes that are prone to be committed by businesspersons are often referred to as **white-collar crimes.** These crimes usually involve cunning and deceit rather than physical force. Many of the white-collar crimes are discussed in the paragraphs that follow.

Embezzlement

Unknown at common law, the crime of **embezzlement** is now a statutory crime. Embezzlement is the fraudulent conversion of property by a person to whom that property was entrusted. Typically, embezzlement is committed by an employer's employees, agents, or representatives (e.g., accountants, lawyers, trust officers,

"Sweetie, show the Hazlitts the watercolors you made in jail."

treasurers). Embezzlers often try to cover their tracks by preparing false books, records, or entries.

The key element here is that the stolen property was *entrusted* to the embezzler. This differs from robbery, burglary, and larceny, in which property is taken by someone not entrusted with the property. For example, embezzlement has been committed if a bank teller absconds with money that was deposited by depositors; the employer (the bank) entrusted the teller to take deposits from its customers.

Criminal Fraud

Obtaining title to property through deception or trickery constitutes the crime of **criminal fraud,** also known as **false pretenses** or **deceit.** Consider this example: Robert Anderson, a stockbroker, promises Mary Greenberg, a prospective investor, that he will use any money she invests to purchase interests in oil wells. Based on this promise, Ms. Greenberg decides to make the investment. Mr. Anderson never intended to invest the money. Instead, he used the money for his personal needs. This is criminal fraud.

Mail and Wire Fraud

Federal law prohibits the use of mails or wires (e.g., telegraph or telephone) to defraud another person. These crimes are called **mail fraud** and **wire fraud,** respectively. The government often prosecutes a suspect under these statutes if there is insufficient evidence to prove the substantive crime that the criminal was attempting to commit or did commit. Wire-fraud statutes are sometimes used to prosecute Internet fraud.

Bribery

Bribery is one of the most prevalent forms of white-collar crime. A bribe can be in the form of money, property, favors, or anything else of value. The crime of commercial bribery prohibits the payment of bribes to private persons and businesses. This type of bribe is often called a *kickback* or a *payoff.* Intent is a necessary element of this crime. The offeror of a bribe commits the crime of bribery when the bribe is tendered. The offeree is guilty of the crime of bribery when he or she accepts the bribe. The offeror can be found liable for the crime of bribery even if the person to whom the bribe is offered rejects the bribe.

Consider this example: Harriet Landers is the purchasing agent for the ABCD Corporation and is in charge of purchasing equipment to be used by the corporation. Neal Brown, the sales representative of a company that makes equipment that can be used by the ABCD Corporation, offers to pay her a 10 percent kickback if she buys equipment from him. She accepts the bribe and orders the equipment. Both parties are guilty of bribery.

At common law, the crime of bribery was defined as the giving or receiving of anything of value in corrupt payment for an "official act" by a public official. Public

ETHICAL PERSPECTIVE

HUGHES AIRCRAFT DOWNED AS A CRIMINAL CONSPIRATOR

Hughes Aircraft Co., Inc. (Hughes), an aircraft manufacturer, contracted with the U.S. government to manufacture microelectronic circuits, known as "hybrids," which are used as components in weapons defense systems. The contract required Hughes to perform tests on each hybrid. A Hughes employee, Donald LaRue, was the supervisor responsible for ensuring the accuracy of the hybrid testing process. LaRue falsely reported that all tests had been performed and that each hybrid had passed the test. When LaRue's subordinates called his actions to the attention of LaRue's supervisors, the supervisors did nothing about it. Instead, they responded that LaRue's decisions were his own and were not to be questioned.

The United States sued Hughes and LaRue, charging criminal conspiracy to defraud the government. At trial, LaRue was acquitted, but Hughes was convicted of criminal conspiracy and fined $3.5 million. Hughes appealed its conviction, asserting that it should not be convicted of criminal conspiracy if its alleged co-conspirator, LaRue, was acquitted.

Should Hughes be acquitted as a matter of law because the same jury that convicted Hughes acquitted its alleged co-conspirator of the charge of criminal conspiracy? No. The court of appeals held that Hughes may be found guilty of criminal conspiracy even though its co-conspirator had been acquitted of the same crime.

The court of appeals, as a matter of law, held that the inconsistency of the jury verdicts of two defendants charged with criminal conspiracy does not mean that the convicted defendant should also be acquitted. The court noted that the jury may have been more lenient with defendant LaRue, an individual, than they were with Hughes, the corporate defendant. Moreover, the court stated that the jury could have found Hughes guilty of the required act of conspiracy based on evidence provided at trial by the other Hughes employees that were called as witnesses. [*United States v. Hughes Aircraft Company, Inc.*, 20 F.3d 974, 1994 U.S. App. Lexis 5603 (9th Cir. 1994)]

1. Did LaRue act ethically in this case? What do you think his motive was for justifying the tests? Explain.
2. Did LaRue's supervisors act ethically when they ignored subordinates' notices of LaRue's actions?
3. Was the conviction of Hughes Aircraft Co., Inc. warranted? Explain.

officials include legislators, judges, jurors, witnesses at trial, administrative agency personnel, and other government officials. Modern penal codes also make it a crime to bribe public officials. For example, a developer who is constructing an apartment building cannot pay the building inspector to overlook a building code violation.

Racketeer Influenced and Corrupt Organizations Act (RICO)

Organized crime has a pervasive influence on many parts of the U.S. economy. In 1980, Congress enacted the Organized Crime Control Act. **The Racketeer Influenced and Corrupt Organizations Act (RICO)** is part of this Act [18 U.S.C. §§ 1961–1968]. Originally, RICO was intended to apply only to organized crime, but the broad language of the RICO statute has been used against non–organized crime defendants as well. RICO, which provides for both criminal and civil penalties, is one of the most important laws affecting business today.

RICO makes it a federal crime to acquire or maintain an interest in, use income from, or conduct or participate in the affairs of an "enterprise" through a "pattern" of "racketeering activity." An "enterprise" is defined as a corporation, a

INTERNATIONAL PERSPECTIVE

THE FOREIGN CORRUPT PRACTICES ACT

It is well known that the payment of bribes is pervasive in conducting international business. To prevent American companies from engaging in this type of conduct, the U.S. Congress enacted the **Foreign Corrupt Practices Act of 1977 (FCPA)** [15 U.S.C. §78m]. The FCPA makes it illegal for American companies, or their officers, directors, agents, or employees, to bribe a foreign official, a foreign political party official, or a candidate for foreign political office. A bribe is illegal only where it is meant to influence the awarding of new business or the retention of a continuing business activity.

The FCPA imposes criminal liability where a person pays the illegal bribe himself or herself, or supplies a payment to a third party or an agent, knowing that it will be used as a bribe. A firm can be fined up to $2 million, and an individual can be fined up to $100,000 and imprisoned for up to five years for violations of the FCPA.

The 1988 amendments to the FCPA created two defenses. One excuses a firm or person charged with bribery under the FCPA if the firm or person can show that the payment was lawful under the written laws of that country. The other allows a defendant to show that a payment was a reasonable and bona fide expenditure related to the furtherance or execution of a contract. This latter exemption is difficult to interpret.

Some people argue that American companies are placed at a disadvantage in international markets where commercial bribery is commonplace and firms from other countries are not hindered by laws similar to the FCPA.

partnership, a sole proprietorship, another business or organization, or the government. *Racketeering activity* consists of a number of specifically enumerated federal and state crimes, including activities such as gambling, arson, robbery, counterfeiting, dealing in narcotics, and so on. Business-related crimes, such as bribery, embezzlement, mail fraud, wire fraud, and the like, also are considered racketeering.

To prove a *pattern of racketeering*, at least two predicate acts must be committed by the defendant within a 10-year period. For example, committing two different frauds would be considered a pattern. Individual defendants found criminally liable for RICO violations can be fined up to $25,000 per violation, imprisoned for up to 20 years, or both. In addition, RICO provides for the *forfeiture* of any property or business interests (even interests in a legitimate business) that were gained because of RICO violations. This provision allows the government to recover investments made with monies derived from racketeering activities. The government also may seek civil penalties for RICO violations. These include injunctions, orders of dissolution, reorganization of businesses, and divestiture of the defendant's interest in an enterprise.

INCHOATE CRIMES

In addition to the substantive crimes discussed, a person can be held criminally liable for committing an **inchoate crime,** which includes incomplete crimes and crimes committed by nonparticipants. The most important inchoate crimes are discussed below.

Criminal Conspiracy

When two or more persons enter into an *agreement* to commit a crime it is termed **criminal conspiracy.** To be liable for a criminal conspiracy, the conspirators must take an *overt act* to further the crime. The crime itself does not have to be committed, however.

Consider this example: Two securities brokers agreed over the telephone to commit a securities fraud. They also obtained a list of potential victims and prepared false financial statements necessary for the fraud. Because they entered into an agreement to commit a crime and took overt action, the brokers are guilty of the crime of criminal conspiracy even if they didn't carry out the securities fraud. The government usually brings criminal conspiracy charges if (1) the defendants have been thwarted in their efforts to commit the substantive crime, or (2) insufficient evidence is available to prove the substantive crime.

Attempt to Commit a Crime

The **attempt to commit a crime** is itself a crime. For example, suppose a person wants to kill his or her neighbor. He shoots at her but misses. The perpetrator is not liable for the crime of murder, but he is liable for the crime of attempted murder.

SIDEBAR

Computer Crime
The use of computers to commit business crimes is increasing. Businesses must implement safeguards to prevent computer crimes.

Aiding and Abetting the Commission of a Crime

Sometimes persons assist others in the commission of a crime. The act of **aiding and abetting** the commission of a crime is itself a crime. This concept, which is very broad, encompasses rendering support, assistance, or encouragement to the commission of a crime. Harboring a criminal after he or she has committed a crime is also considered aiding and abetting.

Corporate Criminal Liability

A corporation is a fictitious legal person that is granted legal existence by the state only after meeting certain requirements. A corporation cannot act on its own behalf. Instead, it must act through *agents* such as managers, representatives, and employees.

The question of whether a corporation can be held criminally liable has intrigued legal scholars for some time. Originally, under the common law, it was generally held that corporations lacked the criminal mind (*mens rea*) to be held criminally liable. Modern courts, however, are more pragmatic. These courts have held that corporations are criminally liable for the acts of their managers, agents, and employees. In any event, because corporations cannot be put in prison, they usually are sanctioned with fines, loss of a license or franchise, and the like.

Corporate directors, officers, and employees are individually liable for crimes they personally commit, whether for personal benefit or on behalf of the corporation. In addition, under certain circumstances a corporate manager can be held criminally liable for the criminal activities of his or her subordinates. To be held criminally liable, the manager must have failed to supervise the subordinate appropriately. This is an evolving area of the law.

INFORMATION TECHNOLOGY

INFORMATION INFRASTRUCTURE PROTECTION (IIP) ACT

The Internet and Information Age ushered in a whole new world for education, business, and consumer transactions. But with it followed a new rash of digital crimes. Prosecutors and courts wrestled over how to apply existing laws written in a nondigital age to new Internet-related abuses.

In 1996, Congress responded by enacting the **Information Infrastructure Protection Act (IIP Act)**. In this federal law, Congress addressed computer-related crimes as distinct offenses. The IIP Act provides protection for any computer connected to the Internet.

The IIP Act makes it a federal crime for anyone intentionally to access and obtain information from a protected computer without authorization. The IIP Act does not require that the defendant accessed a protected computer for commercial benefit. Thus, persons who transmit a computer virus over the Internet or hackers who trespass into Internet-connected computers may be criminally prosecuted under the IIP Act. Even merely observing data on a protected computer without authorization is sufficient to meet the requirement that the defendant has accessed a protected computer. Criminal penalties for violating the IIP Act include imprisonment for up to 10 years and fines.

The IIP Act gives the federal government a much-needed weapon for directly prosecuting cyber-crooks, hackers, and others who enter, steal, destroy, or look at others' computer data without authorization.

Constitutional Safeguards

> At the present time in this country there is more danger that criminals will escape justice than that they will be subjected to tyranny.
>
> —J. Holmes, *Kepner v. United States* (1904)

When our forefathers drafted the U.S. Constitution, they included provisions that protect persons from unreasonable government intrusion and provide safeguards for those accused of crimes. Although these safeguards originally applied only to federal cases, the Fourteenth Amendment's Due Process Clause made them applicable to state criminal law cases as well. The most important constitutional safeguards and privileges are discussed in the following paragraphs.

Fourth Amendment Protection Against Unreasonable Searches and Seizures

The *Fourth Amendment* to the U.S. Constitution protects persons and corporations from overzealous investigative activities by the government. It protects the rights of the people from **unreasonable search and seizure** by the government and permits people to be secure in their persons, houses, papers, and effects.

"Reasonable" search and seizure by the government is lawful. **Search warrants** based on probable cause are necessary in most cases. These warrants specifically state the place and scope of the authorized search. General searches beyond the specified area are forbidden. **Warrantless searches** generally are permitted only (1) incident to arrest, (2) where evidence is in "plain view," or (3) where evidence likely will be destroyed. Warrantless searches also are judged by the **probable-cause standard.**

Evidence obtained from an unreasonable search and seizure is considered tainted evidence ("fruit of a poisonous tree"). Under the **exclusionary rule,** such evidence can be prohibited from introduction at a trial or administrative proceeding against the person searched. This evidence, however, is freely admissible against other persons. The U.S. Supreme Court created a **good-faith exception** to the exclusionary rule. This exception allows evidence otherwise obtained illegally to be introduced as evidence against the accused if the police officers who conducted the unreasonable search reasonably believed they were acting pursuant to a lawful search warrant.

Generally, the government does not have the right to search business premises without a search warrant. But certain hazardous and regulated industries—such as sellers of firearms and liquor, coal mines, vehicle dismantling and automobile junkyards, and the like—are subject to warrantless searches if proper statutory procedures are met. A business also may give consent to search the premises, including employee desks and computers, because of the lack of privacy in those items.

Lighted Sevier County Courthouse, completed 1896, at dusk, Great Smoky Mountains, Sevierville, TN.

Fifth Amendment Privilege Against Self-Incrimination

The *Fifth Amendment* to the U.S. Constitution provides that no person "shall be compelled in any criminal case to be a witness against himself." Thus, a person cannot be compelled to give testimony against himself or herself, although nontestimonial evidence (fingerprints, body fluids, and the like) may be required. A person who asserts this right is described as having "taken the Fifth." This protection applies to federal cases and is extended to state and local criminal cases through the Due Process Clause of the Fourteenth Amendment.

The protection against **self-incrimination** applies only to natural persons who are accused of crimes. Therefore, artificial persons (such as corporations and partnerships) cannot raise this protection against incriminating testimony. Thus, business records of corporations and partnerships are not protected from disclosure, even if they incriminate individuals who work for the business. But certain "private papers" of businesspersons (such as personal diaries) are protected from disclosure.

Immunity from prosecution. On occasion, the government wants to obtain information from a suspect who has asserted his or her Fifth Amendment privilege against self-incrimination. The government can try to achieve this by offering the suspect **immunity from prosecution,** in which the government agrees not to use any evidence given by a person who has been granted immunity against that person. Once immunity is granted, the suspect loses the right to assert his or her Fifth Amendment privilege. Grants of immunity often are given when the government wants the suspect to give information that will lead to the prosecution of other, more important criminal suspects. Partial grants of immunity also are available. For example, a suspect may be granted immunity from prosecution for a serious crime but not a lesser crime, in exchange for information.

SIDEBAR

Fifth Amendment
It is improper for a jury to infer guilt from the defendant's exercise of his or her constitutional right to remain silent.

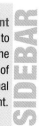

Kyllo v. United States

533 U.S. 27, 121 S.Ct. 2038, 2001 U.S. Lexis 4487 (2001) — Supreme Court of the United States

FACTS

In 1992, government agents suspected that marijuana was being grown in the home of Danny Kyllo, which was part of a triplex building in Florence, Oregon. Indoor marijuana growth typically requires high-intensity lamps. In order to determine whether an amount of heat was emanating from Kyllo's home consistent with the use of such lamps, federal agents used a thermal imager to scan the triplex. Thermal imagers detect infrared radiation and produce images of the radiation. The scan of Kyllo's home, which was performed from an automobile on the street, showed that the roof over the garage and a side wall of Kyllo's home were "hot." The agents used this scanning evidence to obtain a search warrant authorizing a search of Kyllo's home. During the search, the agents found an indoor growing operation involving more than 100 marijuana plants.

Kyllo was indicted for manufacturing marijuana, a violation of federal criminal law. Kyllo moved to suppress the imaging evidence and the evidence it led to, arguing that it was an unreasonable search that violated the Fourth Amendment to the U.S. Constitution. The trial court disagreed with Kyllo and let the evidence be introduced and considered at trial. Kyllo then entered a conditional guilty plea and appealed the trial court's failure to suppress the challenged evidence. The court of appeals affirmed the trial court's decision admitting the evidence. The U.S. Supreme Court granted certiorari to hear the appeal.

ISSUE

Is the use of a thermal-imaging device aimed at a private home from a public street to detect relative amounts of heat within the home a "search" within the meaning of the Fourth Amendment?

COURT'S REASONING

The U.S. Supreme Court stated, "At the very core of the Fourth Amendment stands the right of a man to retreat into his own home and there be free from unreasonable government intrusion." With few exceptions, a warrantless search of a home is unconstitutional. The Court noted, however, that the visual observation of a house is no "search" at all. The case involves officers on a public street engaged in more than naked-eye surveillance of a home. The Supreme Court held, "We think that obtaining by sense-enhancing technology any information regarding the interior of the home that could not otherwise have been obtained without physical intrusion into a constitutionally protected area constitutes a search." On the basis of this criterion, the information obtained by the thermal imager in this case was the product of a search.

DECISION AND REMEDY

The U.S. Supreme Court held that the use of a thermal-imaging device aimed at a private home from a public street to detect relative amounts of heat within the home is a "search" within the meaning of the Fourth Amendment. The Supreme Court reversed the decision of the court of appeals and remanded the case for further proceedings.

QUESTIONS

1. Is the Fourth Amendment's prohibition against unreasonable search and seizure an easy standard to apply? Explain.
2. Did the police act ethically in obtaining the evidence in this case? Did Kyllo act ethically in trying to suppress the evidence?
3. How can the government catch "entrepreneurs" such as Kyllo? Explain.

Attorney–client privilege and other privileges. To obtain a proper defense, the accused person must be able to tell his or her attorney facts about the case without fear that the attorney will be called as a witness against the accused. The **attorney–client privilege** is protected by the Fifth Amendment. Either the client or the attorney can raise this privilege. For the privilege to apply, the information must be told to the attorney in his or her capacity as an attorney, and not as a friend or neighbor or other such relationship.

The following privileges also have been recognized under the Fifth Amendment:

1. Psychiatrist/psychologist–patient privilege,
2. Priest/minister/rabbi–penitent privilege,
3. Spouse–spouse privilege, and
4. Parent–child privilege.

There are some exceptions. For example, a spouse or a child who is beaten by a spouse or a parent may testify against the accused.

SIDEBAR

Immunity
Some persons who are granted immunity are placed in witness protection programs. They are usually given a new identity, relocated, and found a job.

SIDEBAR

Accountant–Client Privilege?
Clients usually supply information and documents to their accountants. The U.S. Supreme Court has found that there is no accountant–client privilege under federal law [*Couch v. U.S.*, 409 U.S. 322, 93 S.Ct. 611, 1973 U.S. Lexis 23 (1973)]. Thus, an accountant can be called as a witness in a case against a client involving federal securities laws, federal mail or wire fraud, federal RICO, or other federal crimes. Approximately 20 states have enacted special statutes that create an accountant–client privilege at the state level. An accountant cannot be called as a witness against a client in a court action in a state court where these statutes are in effect.

Fifth Amendment Protection Against Double Jeopardy

The **double jeopardy** clause of the *Fifth Amendment* protects persons from being tried twice for the same crime. For example, if the state tries a suspect for the crime of murder and the suspect is found innocent, the state cannot bring another trial against the accused for the same crime. But if the same criminal act involves several different crimes, the accused may be tried for each of the crimes without violation of the double jeopardy clause. Suppose the accused kills two people during a robbery. The accused may be tried for two murders and the robbery.

If the same act violates the laws of two or more jurisdictions, each jurisdiction may try the accused. For instance, if an accused person kidnaps a person in one state and brings the victim across a state border into another state, the act violates the laws of two states and the federal government. Thus, three jurisdictions can prosecute the accused without violating the double jeopardy clause.

Sixth Amendment Right to a Public Jury Trial

The *Sixth Amendment* guarantees that criminal defendants have these rights:

1. The right to be tried by an impartial jury of the state or district in which the accused crime was committed.
2. The right to confront (cross-examine) the witnesses against the accused.
3. The right to have the assistance of a lawyer.
4. The right to have a speedy trial.

The *Speedy Trial Act* requires that a criminal defendant be brought to trial within 70 days after indictment [18 U.S.C. § 3161(c)(1)]. The court may grant continuances to serve the "ends of justice."

Eighth Amendment Protection Against Cruel and Unusual Punishment

The *Eighth Amendment* protects criminal defendants from **cruel and unusual punishment.** For example, it prohibits the torture of criminals. This clause, however, does not prohibit capital punishment.

Miranda

Most people have not read and memorized the provisions of the U.S. Constitution. The U.S. Supreme Court recognized this fact when it decided the landmark case *Miranda v. Arizona* in 1966 [384 U.S. 436, 86 S.Ct. 1603, 1996 U.S. Lexis 2817 (1966)]. In that case, the Supreme Court held that the Fifth Amendment privilege against self-incrimination is not useful unless a criminal suspect has knowledge of this right. Therefore, the Supreme Court required that the following warning—colloquially called the "*Miranda* rights"—be read to a criminal suspect before he or she is interrogated by the police or other government officials.

- You have the right to remain silent.
- Anything you say can and will be used against you.
- You have the right to consult a lawyer, and to have a lawyer present with you during interrogation.
- If you cannot afford a lawyer, a lawyer will be appointed free of charge to represent you.

Any statements or confessions obtained from a suspect prior to being read his *Miranda* rights can be excluded from evidence at trial. In 2000, the U.S. Supreme Court upheld *Miranda* in *Dickerson v. United States* [530 U.S. 428, 120 S.Ct. 2326, 2000 U.S. Lexis 4305 (2000)]. The Supreme Court stated, "We do not think there is justification for overruling *Miranda*. *Miranda* has become embedded in routine police practice to the point where the warnings have become part of our national culture."

INTERNATIONAL PERSPECTIVE

HIDING MONEY IN OFFSHORE BANKS

Little did Christopher Columbus know in 1503 when he sailed past the Cayman Islands in the Caribbean that these tiny islands would become a bastion of international finance in the late 20th and early 21st centuries. These tiny islands of 35,000 people host about 600 banks with more than $500 million in deposits. Why is so much money being hoarded there? The answer is: bank secrecy laws.

Every nation has banking laws, but all banking laws are not equal. What the Cayman Islands' banking law provides is confidentiality. In most instances, no party other than the depositor has the right to know the identity of the depositor, account number, or amount in the account. In fact, most accounts are held in the name of trusts instead of the depositor's actual name. This bank secrecy law has attracted many persons—in some instances, crooks who wish to park their illegally gotten gains. Often the bank is no more than a lawyer's office.

There are several other bank secrecy hideouts around the world, including the Bahamas in the Caribbean, the country of Liechtenstein in Europe, the Isle of Jersey off Great Britain, and the micro-island of Niue in the South Pacific. These tiny countries and islands follow the adage: "Write a good law and they will come."

Federal Antiterrorism Act of 2001

The devastating terrorist attacks on the World Trade Center in New York and the Pentagon in Washington, DC, on September 11, 2001, shocked the nation. The attacks were organized and orchestrated by terrorists who crossed nations' borders easily, secretly planned and prepared for the attacks undetected, and financed the attacks using money located in banks in the United States, Great Britain, and other countries. In response, Congress enacted a new federal Antiterrorism Act that assists the government in detecting, investigating, and prosecuting terrorists. The bill was signed into law on October 26, 2001. The act contains the following main features:

- **Special Intelligence Court.** The act authorizes a Special Intelligence Court to issue expanded wiretap orders and subpoenas to obtain evidence of suspected terrorism.
- **Nationwide search warrant.** The act creates a nationwide search warrant to obtain evidence of terrorist activities.
- **Roving wiretaps.** The act permits "roving wiretaps" on a person suspected of involvement in terrorism so that any telephone or electronic device used by the person may be monitored.
- **Sharing of information.** The act permits evidence obtained by government law enforcement and intelligence agencies to be shared among the agencies.
- **Detention of noncitizens.** The act gives the federal government authority to detain a nonresident in the United States for up to seven days without filing charges against that person. Nonresidents who are certified by a court as a threat to national security may be held for up to six months without a trial.
- **Bioterrorism provision.** The act makes it illegal for people or groups to possess substances that can be used as biological or chemical weapons for any purpose besides a "peaceful" one.
- **Anti-money laundering provisions.** The act requires U.S. banks to determine sources of large overseas private bank accounts and to disclose information about such accounts to U.S. investigators. The U.S. Treasury Department may cut off all dealings in the United States of foreign banking institutions located in nations with bank secrecy laws that refuse to disclose information about bank accounts to U.S. investigators.

Proponents argue that the federal Antiterrorism Act is needed to detect and prevent terrorist activities, and to investigate and prosecute terrorists. Critics of the act argue that constitutional freedoms are trampled on by the provisions of the act.

Law and Ethics

Sometimes the rule of law and the golden rule of **ethics** demand the same response by the person confronted with a problem. For example, federal and state laws make bribery unlawful. A person violates the law if he or she bribes a judge for a favorable decision in a case. Ethics would also prohibit this conduct.

The law may permit something that would be ethically wrong. Consider this example: Occupational safety laws set standards for emissions of dust from toxic chemicals in the workplace. Suppose a company can reduce the emissions below the legal standard by spending additional money. The only benefit from the expenditure would be better employee health. Ethics would require the extra expenditure; the law would not.

SIDEBAR

Ethics

Ethical considerations can no more be excluded from the administration of justice, which is the end and purpose of all civil laws, than one can exclude the vital air from his room and live.

—John F. Dillon
Laws and Jurisprudence of England and America
Lecture 1 (1894)

CASE FOR DISCUSSION

Wal-Mart Stores, Inc. v. Samara Brothers, Inc.

529 U.S. 205, 123 S.Ct. 1339, 2000 U.S. Lexis 2197 (2000) Supreme Court of the United States

FACTS

Samara Brothers, Inc. (Samara) is a designer and manufacturer of children's clothing. The core of Samara's business is its annual new line of spring and summer children's garments. Samara sold its clothing to retailers, who in turn sold the clothes to consumers. Wal-Mart Stores, Inc. (Wal-Mart) operates a large chain of budget warehouse stores that sell thousands of items at very low prices. In 1995, Wal-Mart contacted one of its suppliers, Judy-Philippine, Inc. (JPI), about the possibility of making a line of children's clothes just like Samara's successful line. Wal-Mart sent photographs of Samara's children's clothes to JPI (the name "Samara" was readily discernible on the labels of the garments) and directed JPI to produce children's clothes exactly like those in the photographs. JPI produced a line of children's clothes for Wal-Mart that copied the designs, colors, flower patterns, and so on of Samara's clothing. Wal-Mart then sold this line of children's clothing in its stores, making a gross profit of over $1.15 million on these clothes sales during the 1996 selling season.

Samara discovered that Wal-Mart was selling the knockoff clothes at a price that was lower than Samara's retailers were paying Samara for its clothes. After sending unsuccessful cease and desist letters to Wal-Mart, Samara sued Wal-Mart, alleging product trade dress infringement in violation of Section 43(a) of the Lanham Trademark Act. Although not finding that Samara's clothes had acquired a secondary meaning in the minds of the public, the district court held in favor of Samara and awarded damages. The court of appeals affirmed. Wal-Mart appealed to the U.S. Supreme Court.

ISSUE

Must a product's design have acquired a secondary meaning before it is protected as trade dress under Section 43(a) of the Lanham Trademark Act?

COURT'S REASONING

The Lanham Act, in Section 43(a), gives a designer and producer a cause of action for the use by any person of "any word, term, name, symbol, or device, or any combination thereof which is likely to cause confusion as to the origin, sponsorship, or approval of his or her goods." It is this provision that is at issue in this case. The U.S. Supreme Court held that "trade dress" of a design for apparel needs to have acquired a *secondary meaning* in the mind of the public before the design is protected under Section 43(a) of the Lanham Trademark Act. After the Supreme Court established this rule, it remanded the case for a factual determination as to whether Samsara's apparel designs had acquired a secondary meaning.

DECISION AND REMEDY

The U.S. Supreme Court held that a product's design has to have acquired a secondary meaning in the public's eye before it is protected as trade dress under Section 43(a) of the Lanham Trademark Act. The Supreme Court reversed the decision of the court of appeals and remanded the case for further proceedings.

QUESTIONS

1. What is trade dress? What is secondary meaning?
2. Was it ethical for Wal-Mart to copy Samara Brothers' design for children's clothing? What was Wal-Mart's motive?
3. What were the economic consequences of the U.S. Supreme Court's decision? Who are the winners? Who are the losers?

ETHICAL PERSPECTIVE

ENRON CORPORATION PLUNGES INTO BANKRUPTCY

By the year 2000, Enron Corporation, a Houston-based energy company, had become the sixth-largest corporation in America. Its rise to this status was meteoric and the company's stock was trading at over $90 per share. The company's main business was brokering energy between buyers and sellers. It also engaged in building huge energy projects worldwide, as well as speculating in oil and gas futures on the world's commodities markets.

But all was not well with the corporation. Enron had created hundreds of partnerships, many located in offshore tax havens. These partnerships were used to borrow money from banks and other creditors and to engage in speculative business dealings. Enron booked its investments and money from these partnerships as assets, but the debts of these partnerships and much of the self-dealing with and among these partnerships were not reported on Enron's consolidated financial statements. Enron executives purposefully created this maze of entities to perpetrate accounting fraud. Thus, Enron looked profitable when in fact it was not. Enron was able to run this charade for years before the bubble finally burst.

In 2002, reporters and securities analysts began investigating Enron's financial empire. As rumors of Enron's "creative accounting" reached the public, the price of Enron's stock began to fall. Many of Enron's top executives sold their Enron shares before the stock price plummeted. Other investors without inside information were not so lucky, and lost their investment as the price of Enron stock tumbled to less than 50 cents per share.

The Securities and Exchange Commission, a federal government agency, announced it was investigating the Enron affair. Officers and employees at Enron began to shred thousands of documents relevant to the investigation. Andersen LLP, one of the "Big Five" accounting firms in the United States, had been Enron's auditor for years. Andersen was making between $2 million and $4 million per month providing audit and other services to Enron. Andersen's malpractice or fraud contributed to Enron being able to conceal its fraud from the investing public. Several of Andersen's partners in the Houston office responsible for auditing Enron also shredded thousands of documents pertaining to the Enron audits. Once alerted, the court issued an injunction prohibiting the destruction of any more documents by Enron or Andersen.

In late 2002, Enron Corporation filed for Chapter 11 bankruptcy. By that time, billions of dollars of shareholder wealth had been wiped out. Enron's employees, who had their pension funds invested in Enron stock, saw their dreams of a comfortable retirement evaporate. And bondholders, banks, suppliers, and other creditors lost billions of dollars in unpaid debts. Enron became the largest company in America ever to file for bankruptcy. Some parts of its business were sold to other energy companies, but the majority of its businesses were worthless. Andersen LLP unraveled and eventually went out of business.

1. Did Enron executives act ethically when they sold their stock before the Enron collapse?
2. Did Enron executives and Andersen partners act ethically in shredding documents?

Another alternative occurs where the law demands certain conduct but a person's ethical standards are contrary. As an example: Federal law prohibits employers from hiring certain illegal alien workers. Suppose an employer advertises the availability of a job and receives no responses except from a person who cannot prove he or she is a citizen of the United States or does not possess a required visa. The worker and his or her family are destitute. Should the employer hire him or her? The law says no, but ethics says yes. (See Exhibit 4.1.)

> Ethics precede laws as man precedes society.
>
> —Jason Alexander

EXHIBIT 4.1 *Law and ethics.*

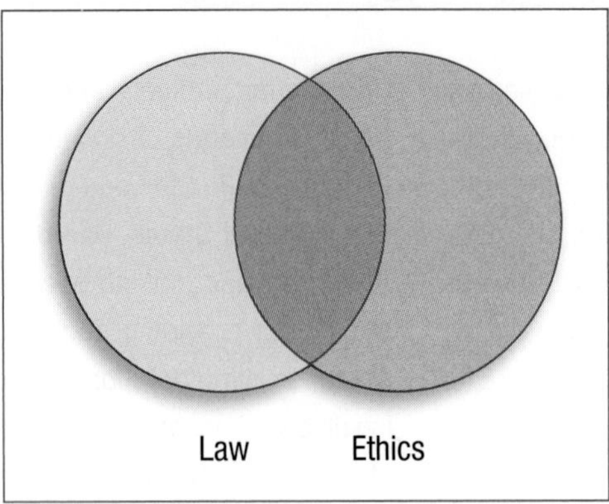

EXHIBIT 4.2 *Sample code of ethics.*

BIG CHEESE CORPORATION

Code of Ethics

Big Cheese Corporation's mission includes the promotion of professional conduct in the practice of general management and financial management worldwide. Big Cheese's Chief Executive Officer (CEO), Chief Financial Officer (CFO), corporate Controller, and other employees of the finance organization and other employees of the corporation hold an important and elevated role in the corporate governance of the corporation. They are empowered and uniquely capable to ensure that all constituents' interests are appropriately balanced, protected, and preserved.

This Code of Ethics embodies principles which we are expected to adhere to and advocate. The CEO, CFO, finance organization employees, and other employees of the corporation are expected to abide by this Code of Ethics and all business conduct standards of the corporation relating to areas covered by this Code of Ethics. Any violation of the Code of Ethics may result in disciplinary action, up to and including termination of employment. All employees will:

- Act with honesty and integrity, avoiding actual or apparent conflicts of interest in their personal and professional relations.
- Provide stakeholders with information that is accurate, fair, complete, timely, objective, relevant, and understandable, including in our filings with and other submissions to the U.S. Securities and Exchange Commission.
- Comply with rules and regulations of federal, state, provincial and local governments, and other appropriate private and public regulatory agencies.
- Act in good faith, responsibly, with due care, competence and diligence, without misrepresenting material facts or allowing one's independent judgment to be subordinated.
- Respect the confidentiality of information acquired in the course of one's work except when authorized or otherwise legally obligated to disclose. Confidential information acquired in the course of one's work will not be used for personal advantage.
- Share knowledge and maintain professional skills important and relevant to stakeholders' needs.
- Proactively promote and be an example of ethical behavior as a responsible partner among peers, in the work environment, and in the community.
- Achieve responsible use, control, and stewardship over all Big Cheese's assets and resources that are employed or entrusted to us.
- Not unduly or fraudulently influence, coerce, manipulate, or mislead any authorized audit or interfere with any auditor engaged in the performance of an internal or independent audit of Big Cheese's financial statements or accounting books and records.

ETHICAL PERSPECTIVE

SARBANES-OXLEY ACT PROMPTS PUBLIC COMPANIES TO ADOPT CODE OF ETHICS

In the late 1990s and early 2000s, many large corporations in the United States were found to have engaged in massive financial frauds. These frauds often were perpetrated by the Chief Executive Officer (CEO) and other senior officers of the companies. Financial officers, such as the Chief Financial Officer (CFO) and Controller, also were found to have been instrumental in creating these frauds. In response, Congress enacted the **Sarbanes-Oxley Act of 2002,** which made certain conduct illegal and established criminal penalties for violations.

In addition, Sarbanes-Oxley prompts companies to encourage senior officers of public companies to act ethically in their dealings with shareholders, employees, and other constituents. Section 406 of the Sarbanes-Oxley Act requires a public company to disclose whether it has adopted a code of ethics for senior financial officers, including its principal financial officer and principal accounting officer. In response, public companies have adopted codes of ethics for their senior financial officers. Many public companies have included all officers and employees in the coverage of their codes of ethics.

A typical code of ethics appears in Exhibit 4.2 on the preceding page.

LEGAL TERMINOLOGY

Absolute liability
Actus reus
Aiding and abetting
Arraignment
Arrest warrant
Arson
Attempt to commit a crime
Attorney–client privilege
Booking
Bribery
Burden of proof
Burglary
Civil tort action
Code of ethics
Crime
Criminal conspiracy
Criminal fraud
Criminal law
Cruel and unusual punishment
Deceit
Defendant
Defense attorney
District attorney as prosecutor
Double jeopardy
Embezzlement
Ethics
Exclusionary rule
Extortion
False pretenses
Felony
Foreign Corrupt Practices Act
Forgery
General intent
Good-faith exception
Grand jury
Hung jury
Identity Theft and Assumption Deterrence Act
Immunity from prosecution
Inchoate crime
Indictment
Information
Information Infrastructure Protection Act (IIP)
Judgment-proof
Larceny
Magistrate
Mail fraud

Mala in se
Mala prohibita
Mens rea
Misdemeanor
Money Laundering Control Act
Nolo contendere
Penal code
Plaintiff
Plea
Plea bargain
Probable cause
Probable-cause standard
Prosecutor
Public defender
Racketeer Influenced and Corrupt Organizations Act (RICO)
Robbery
Sarbanes-Oxley Act
Search warrant
Self-incrimination
Specific intent
Strict liability
Theft
Unreasonable search and seizure
Violation
Warrantless arrest
Warrantless search
White-collar crimes
Wire fraud

chapter summary

CRIMINAL LAW AND ETHICS

What Is a Crime?	
Specifics of a Criminal Trial	1. The accused is *presumed innocent until proven guilty.* 2. The plaintiff (the government) bears the *burden of proof.* 3. The government must prove *beyond a reasonable doubt* that the accused is guilty of the crime charged. 4. The accused does not have to testify against himself or herself.
Definition of Crime	A crime is any act done by a person in violation of those duties that he or she owes to society and for the breach of which the law provides a penalty.
Penal Codes	Penal codes are state and federal statutes that define many crimes. Criminal conduct is also defined in many *regulatory statutes.*
Parties to a Criminal Lawsuit	1. *Plaintiff:* The government, which is represented by the *prosecuting attorney* (or *prosecutor*). 2. *Defendant:* The person or business accused of the crime, who is represented by a *defense attorney.*
Classification of Crimes	1. *Felonies:* The most serious kinds of crimes. *Mala in se* (inherently evil). Usually punishable by imprisonment. 2. *Misdemeanors:* Less serious crimes. *Mala prohibita* (prohibited by society). Usually punishable by fine and/or imprisonment for less than one year. 3. *Violations:* Not a felony nor a misdemeanor. Generally punishable by a fine.
Elements of a Crime	1. *Actus reus:* Guilty act. 2. *Mens rea:* Evil intent.

Criminal Procedure and Process	
Pretrial Criminal Procedure	1. *Arrest:* Made pursuant to an *arrest warrant* based upon a showing of "probable cause," or, where permitted, by a *warrantless arrest.* 2. *Indictment or information:* Grand juries issue *indictments;* magistrates (judges) issue *information.* These formally charge the accused with specific crimes. 3. *Arraignment:* The accused is informed of the charges against him or her and enters a *plea* in court. The plea may be *not guilty, guilty,* or *nolo contendere.* 4. *Plea bargaining:* Government and the accused may negotiate a settlement agreement wherein the accused agrees to admit to a lesser crime than charged.
Crimes Affecting Business	
Robbery	The taking of personal property from another by fear or force.
Burglary	The unauthorized entering of a building to commit a felony.
Larceny	The wrongful taking of another's property other than from his person or building.
Theft	The wrongful taking of another's property, whether by robbery, burglary, or larceny.
Receiving Stolen Property	A person knowingly receiving stolen property with the intent to deprive the rightful owner of that property.
Arson	The malicious and willful burning of a building.
Forgery	Fraudulently making or altering a written document that affects the legal liability of another person.
Extortion	Threat to expose something about another person unless that person gives up money or property.
Credit-Card Crime	The misappropriation or use of another person's credit card.
Bad Check Legislation	Legislation making it a crime to make, draw, or deliver a check by a person when that person knows that there are insufficient funds in the account to cover the check.
White-Collar Crimes	
Definition	Crimes that are prone to be committed by businesspersons that involve cunning and trickery rather than physical force.
Embezzlement	The fraudulent conversion of property by a person to whom the property was entrusted.
Criminal Fraud	Obtaining title to another's property through deception or trickery. Also called *false pretenses* or *deceit.* *(continued)*

Mail Fraud	The use of mail to defraud another person.
Wire Fraud	The use of wire (telephone or telegraph) to defraud another person.
Bribery	The offer of payment of money or property or something else of value in return for an unwarranted favor. The payee of a bribe is also guilty of the crime of bribery. 1. *Commercial bribery* is the offer of a payment of a bribe to a private person or business. This is often referred to as a *kickback* or *payoff.* 2. Bribery of public officials for an "official act" is a crime.
Racketeer Influenced and Corrupt Organizations Act (RICO)	Makes it a federal crime to acquire or maintain an interest in, use income from, or conduct or participate in the affairs of an "enterprise" through a "pattern" of "racketeering activity." Criminal penalties include the *forfeiture* of any property or business interests gained by a RICO violation.
Inchoate Crimes	
Definition	Crimes that are incomplete or that are committed by nonparticipants.
Criminal Conspiracy	When two or more persons enter into an *agreement* to commit a crime and take some *overt act* to further the crime.
Attempt to Commit a Crime	The successful or unsuccessful attempt to commit a crime.
Aiding and Abetting the Commission of a Crime	Rendering support, assistance, or encouragement to the commission of a crime, or knowingly harboring a criminal after he or she has committed a crime.
Constitutional Safeguards	
Fourth Amendment Protection Against Unreasonable Searches and Seizures	Protects persons and corporations from *unreasonable searches and seizures.* 1. *Reasonable searches and seizures* based on *probable cause* are lawful: a. *Search warrant:* Stipulates the place and scope of the search. b. *Warrantless search:* Permitted only: i. Incident to an arrest. ii. Where evidence is in plain view. iii. Where it is likely that evidence will be destroyed. 2. *Exclusionary rule:* Evidence obtained from an unreasonable search and seizure is *tainted evidence* that may not be introduced at a government proceeding against the person searched. 3. *Business premises:* Protected by the Fourth Amendment, except that certain *regulated industries* may be subject to warrantless searches authorized by statute.
Fifth Amendment Privilege Against Self-Incrimination	Provides that no person "shall be compelled in any criminal case to be a witness against himself." A person asserting this privilege is said to have "taken the Fifth." 1. *Nontestimonial evidence:* Unprotected evidence (e.g., fingerprints, body fluids, etc.). 2. *Businesses:* Apply only to natural persons; businesses cannot assert the privilege.

	3. *Miranda rights:* Criminal suspects must be informed of their Fifth Amendment rights before they can be interrogated by the police or government officials. 4. *Immunity from prosecution:* Granted by the government to obtain otherwise privileged evidence. The government agrees not to use the evidence given against the person who gave it. 5. *Attorney–client privilege:* An accused's lawyer cannot be called as a witness against the accused. 6. *Other privileges:* The following privileges have been recognized, with some limitations: a. Psychiatrist/psychologist–patient b. Priest/minister/rabbi–penitent c. Spouse–spouse d. Parent–child 7. *Accountant–client privilege:* None recognized at the federal level. Some states recognize this privilege in state law actions.
Fifth Amendment Protection Against Double Jeopardy	Protects persons from being tried twice by the same jurisdiction for the same crime. If the act violates the laws of two or more jurisdictions, each jurisdiction may try the accused.
Sixth Amendment Right to a Public Jury Trial	Guarantees criminal defendants the following rights: 1. To be tried by an impartial jury 2. To confront the witness 3. To have the assistance of a lawyer 4. To have a speedy trial
Eighth Amendment Protection Against Cruel and Unusual Punishment	Protects criminal defendants from cruel and unusual punishment. Capital punishment is permitted.
Law and Ethics	
Comparison	The law sometimes reflects ethics. Often ethics is broader than the law.

WORKING THE WEB

Visit the Web sites listed below for more information about the topics covered in this chapter.

1. Check on the U.S. Department of Justice Web site for information about computer-related crimes: **www.usdoj.gov/criminal.**
2. See **www.hg.org/crime.html** for a comprehensive list of criminal law resources. Find the listing for your jurisdiction and research state laws relating to white-collar crime.
3. For international crime, see **www.usinfo.state.gov/usa/infousa/laws/majorlaw/ fcpa.htm** regarding the U.S. Foreign Corrupt Practices Act. Compare that legislation with the OECD approach at **www.law.vanderbilt.edu/journal/32-05/32-5-2.html.**

CRITICAL LEGAL THINKING QUESTIONS

1. Define *crime*. What are penal codes?
2. Define the following elements of a crime: *actus reus* and *mens rea*.
3. Describe the differences between a civil lawsuit and a criminal lawsuit. Are these differences warranted?
4. What is an indictment? What is an arraignment?
5. Define *extortion*. What are the elements of this crime? How is it different from *bribery*? What are the elements of bribery?
6. Define money laundering. Why did Congress make this a crime?
7. Describe the crime prohibited by the Foreign Corrupt Practices Act. What public policy underlies this act?
8. Describe the crime prohibited by the Information Infrastructure Protection Act. What is the purpose of this act?
9. Describe the protection afforded by the Fourth Amendment to the U.S. Constitution discussed in this chapter. Is the protection necessary?
10. Describe the protection afforded by the Fifth Amendment to the U.S. Constitution discussed in this chapter. Is the protection necessary?

CASE FOR BRIEFING

Read Case 4 in Appendix A *(Schalk v. Texas)*. Review and brief the case using the *Critical Legal Thinking* "Briefing the Case" example described in Chapter 1.

4.1 *People v. Paulson*

216 Cal.App.3d 1480, 265 Cal.Rptr. 579, 1990 Cal. App. Lexis 10 (1990)
Court of Appeal of California

FACTS Lee Stuart Paulson owns the liquor license for "My House," a bar in San Francisco. The California Department of Alcoholic Beverage Control is the administrative agency that regulates bars in that state. The California Business and Professions Code, which the department administers, prohibits "any kind of illegal activity on licensed premises." On February 11, 1988, an anonymous informer tipped the department that narcotic sales were occurring on the premises of "My House" and that the narcotics were kept in a safe behind the bar on the premises.

A special department investigator entered the bar during its hours of operation, identified himself, and informed Paulson that he was conducting an inspection. The investigator, who did not have a search warrant, opened the safe without seeking Paulson's consent. Twenty-two bundles of cocaine, totaling 5.5 grams, were found in the safe. Paulson was arrested. At his criminal trial, Paulson challenged the lawfulness of the search.

ISSUE Was the warrantless search of the safe a lawful search?

4.2 *Center Art Galleries–Hawaii, Inc. v. United States*

875 F.2d 747, 1989 U.S. App. Lexis 6983 (1989)
United States Court of Appeals, Ninth Circuit

FACTS The Center Art Galleries–Hawaii sells artwork. Approximately 20 percent of its business involves art by Salvador Dali. The federal government, which suspected the center of fraudulently selling forged Dali artwork, obtained identical search warrants for six locations controlled by the center. The warrants commanded the executing officer to seize items which were "evidence of violations of federal criminal law." The warrants did not describe the specific crimes suspected and did not stipulate that only items pertaining to the sale of Dali's work could be seized. There was no evidence of any criminal activity unrelated to that artist.

ISSUE Is the search warrant valid?

4.3 *United States v. John Doe*

465 U.S. 605, 104 S.Ct. 1237, 1984 U.S. Lexis 169 (1984)
Supreme Court of the United States

FACTS John Doe is the owner of several sole-proprietorship businesses. In 1980, during the course of an investigation of corruption in awarding county and municipal contracts, a federal grand jury served several subpoenas on John Doe demanding the production of certain business records. The subpoenas demanded the production of the following records: (1) general ledgers and journals, (2) invoices, (3) bank statements and canceled checks, (4) financial statements, (5) telephone-company records, (6) safe-deposit box records, and (7) copies of tax returns. John Doe filed a motion in federal court seeking to quash the subpoenas, alleging that producing these business records would violate his Fifth Amendment privilege of not testifying against himself.

ISSUE Do the records have to be disclosed?

ETHICS CASE

4.4 *People v. Shaw*

10 Cal.App.4th 969, 12 Cal.Rptr.2d 665, 1992 Cal. App. Lexis 1256 (1992)
Court of Appeal of California

FACTS In 1979, Leo Shaw, an attorney, entered into a partnership agreement with three other persons to build and operate an office building. From the outset, it was agreed that Shaw's role was to manage the operation of the building. Management of the property was Shaw's contribution to the partnership; the other three partners contributed the necessary capital.

In January 1989, the other partners discovered that the loan on the building was in default and that foreclosure proceedings were imminent. Upon investigation, they discovered that Shaw had taken approximately $80,000 from the partnership's checking account. After heated discussions, Shaw repaid $13,000. In May 1989, when no further payment was forthcoming, a partner filed a civil suit against Shaw and notified the police. The state filed a criminal complaint against Shaw on March 15, 1990.

On April 3, 1990, Shaw repaid the remaining funds as part of a civil settlement. At his criminal trial in November 1990, Shaw argued that repayment of the money was a defense to the crime of embezzlement.

ISSUE Did Shaw act ethically in this case? Would your answer be different if he had really only "borrowed" the money and had intended to return it?

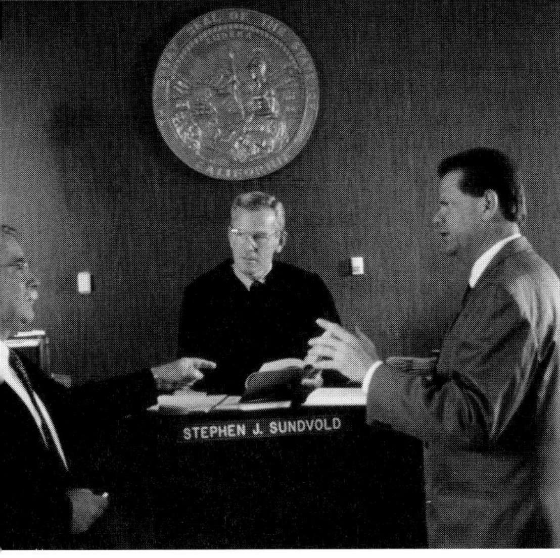

5 Constitutional Law and Freedoms

The nation's armor of defense against the passions of men is the Constitution. Take that away, and the nation goes down into the field of its conflicts like a warrior without armor.

—HENRY WARD BEECHER, *PROVERBS FROM PLYMOUTH PULPIT*, 1887

CHAPTER OBJECTIVES

After studying this chapter, you should be able to

1. Describe the concept of federalism and the doctrine of separation of powers.
2. Define and apply the Supremacy Clause of the U.S. Constitution.
3. Explain the federal government's authority to regulate foreign commerce and interstate commerce.
4. Explain how speech is protected by the First Amendment.
5. Explain the doctrines of equal protection and due process.

CHAPTER OUTLINE

- Introduction
- Basic Constitutional Concepts
- The Supremacy Clause
- Case for Discussion: *Geier v. American Honda Motor Co., Inc.*
- The Commerce Clause
- Case for Discussion: *Reno v. Condon*
- The Bill of Rights
- Case for Discussion: *Fax.com, Inc. v. United States*
- Case for Discussion: *United States v. Playboy Entertainment Group, Inc.*
- Other Constitutional Clauses
- Administrative Agencies
- Legal Terminology
- Chapter Summary
- Internet Exercises and Cases

INTRODUCTION

Prior to the American Revolution, each of the 13 original colonies operated as a separate sovereignty under the rule of England. In September 1774, representatives of the colonies met as a Continental Congress. In 1776, the colonies declared independence from England and the American Revolution ensued.

The chapter examines the major provisions of the U.S. Constitution and the amendments to the Constitution that have been adopted. Of particular importance, this chapter discusses how these provisions affect the operations of business in this country. The Constitution, with amendments, is set forth as Appendix B to this book.

Congress and the executive branch of government have created more than 100 federal **administrative agencies.** These agencies are intended to provide resources and expertise in dealing with complex commercial organizations and businesses. In addition, state governments have created many state administrative

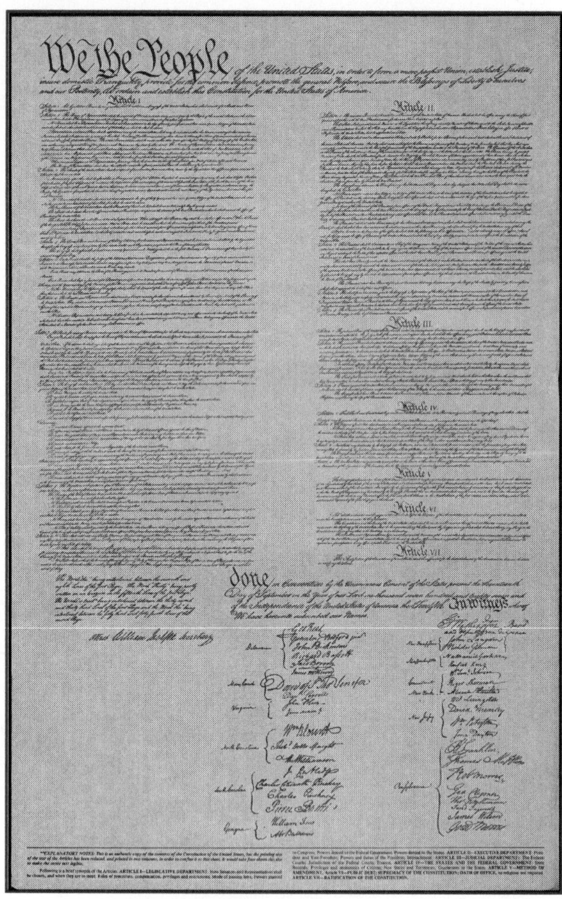

The Constitution of the United States.

agencies. Thousands of **rules and regulations** have been adopted and enforced by federal and state administrative agencies.

This chapter covers constitutional law and freedoms.

Basic Constitutional Concepts

The U.S. Constitution is a unique document that provides rights and protections to individuals and businesses. Some important constitutional concepts are discussed in the following paragraphs.

Federalism and Delegated Powers

Our country's form of government is referred to as **federalism.** That means that the federal government and the 50 state governments share powers.

When the states ratified the Constitution, they delegated certain powers to the federal government. These are called **enumerated powers.** The federal government is authorized to deal with national and international affairs. Any powers that are not specifically delegated to the federal government by the Constitution are reserved to the state governments. State governments are empowered to deal with local affairs.

SIDEBAR

The Constitution
The Constitution of the United States is not a mere lawyers' document: It is a vehicle of life, and its spirit is always the spirit of the age.

Woodrow Wilson
Constitutional Government in the United States
69 (1927)

The Doctrine of Separation of Powers

The three branches of federal government are as follows.

1. Article I of the Constitution established the **legislative branch** of government. This branch is bicameral; that is, it consists of the Senate and the House of Representatives. Collectively, they are referred to as *Congress.* Each state has two senators. The number of representatives to the House of Representatives is determined according to the population of each state. The current number of representatives is determined from the 2000 census.
2. Article II of the Constitution established the **executive branch** of government by providing for the election of the President and Vice President. The President is not elected by popular vote but instead is selected by the **electoral college,** whose representatives are appointed by state delegations.
3. Article III established the **judicial branch** of the government by instituting the Supreme Court and providing for the creation of other federal courts by Congress.

The Constitution of the United States of America

In 1778, the Continental Congress formed a *federal government* and adopted the **Articles of Confederation.** The Articles of Confederation created a federal Congress composed of representatives of the 13 new states. The Articles of Confederation was a particularly weak document that gave limited power to the newly created federal government. For example, it did not provide Congress with the power to levy and collect taxes, to regulate commerce with foreign countries, or to regulate interstate commerce among the states.

The **Constitutional Convention** was convened in Philadelphia in May 1787. The primary purpose of the Convention was to strengthen the federal government. After substantial debate, the delegates agreed to a new U.S. Constitution. The Constitution was reported to Congress in September 1787. State ratification of the Constitution was completed in 1788. Many amendments, including the **Bill of Rights**, have been added to the Constitution since that time.

The U.S. Constitution serves two major functions:

1. It creates the three branches of the federal government (i.e., the executive, legislative, and judicial branches) and allocates powers to these branches.
2. It protects individual rights by limiting the government's ability to restrict those rights.

The Constitution itself provides that it may be amended to address social and economic changes.

Checks and Balances

Certain **checks and balances** are built into the Constitution to ensure that no one branch of the federal government becomes too powerful. Some of the checks and balances in our system of government are the following.

1. The judicial branch has authority to examine the acts of the other two branches of government and determine whether these acts are constitutional.
2. The executive branch can enter into treaties with foreign governments only with the advice and consent of the Senate.
3. The legislative branch is authorized to create federal courts and determine their jurisdiction and to enact statutes that change judicially made law.

> The American Constitution is, so far as I can see, the most wonderful work ever struck off at a given time by the brain and purpose of man.
>
> —W.E. Glastone

The Supremacy Clause

The **Supremacy Clause** establishes that the federal Constitution, treaties, federal laws, and federal regulations are the supreme law of the land [Article VI, Section 2]. State and local laws that conflict with valid federal law are unconstitutional. The concept of federal law taking precedence over state or local law is commonly called the **preemption doctrine.**

Congress may expressly provide that a particular federal statute *exclusively* regulates a specific area or activity. No state or local law regulating the area or activity is valid if there is such a statute. More often, though, federal statutes do not expressly provide for exclusive jurisdiction. In these instances, state and local governments have *concurrent jurisdiction* to regulate the area or activity. However, any

CASE FOR DISCUSSION

Geier v. American Honda Motor Company, Inc.

529 U.S. 861, 120 S.Ct. 1913, 2000 U.S. Lexis 3425 (2000) Supreme Court of the United States

FACTS

In 1987, the United States Department of Transportation, a federal administrative agency, adopted a Federal Motor Vehicle Safety Standard that required automobile manufacturers to equip 10 percent of their 1987 vehicles with passive restraints, including automatic seat belts or air bags. In 1992, Alexis Geier, driving a 1987 Honda Accord automobile in the District of Columbia, collided with a tree and was seriously injured. The car was equipped with manual shoulder and lap belts that were buckled up at the time of the accident; the car was not equipped with air bags, however. Geier sued the car's manufacturer, the American Honda Motor Company, Inc. to recover damages under the District of Columbia's tort law, alleging that American Honda had negligently and defectively designed the car because it lacked a driver's side air bag. The trial court dismissed Geier's lawsuit, finding that the District of Columbia's tort law conflicted with the federal passive restraint safety standard and was therefore preempted under the Supremacy Clause of the U.S. Constitution. The court of appeals affirmed. Geier appealed to the U.S. Supreme Court.

ISSUE

Does the federal passive restraint safety standard preempt the District of Columbia's common law tort law?

COURT'S REASONING

Petitioner Geier's tort action depends upon her claim that the manufacturer had a duty to install an air bag when it manufactured her 1987 Honda Accord. The petitioner's position would have required all manufacturers to have installed air bags in the entire District of Columbia–related portion of their 1987 new car fleet. The federal safety standard at that time required only 10 percent of a manufacturer's nationwide fleet be equipped with any passive restraint device at all. The Supreme Court stated that the language of the federal passive restraint standard was clear enough: The federal standard sought a gradually developing mix of passive restraint devices for safety-related reasons. Thus, the rule of state tort law for which petitioner Geier argues would stand as an "obstacle" to the accomplishment of the federal objective. Hence the tort action is preempted.

DECISION AND REMEDY

The U.S. Supreme Court held that the federal passive restraint safety standard preempted the District of Columbia's tort law under which petitioner Geier sued. The U.S. Supreme Court affirmed the dismissal of Geier's lawsuit against American Honda.

QUESTIONS

1. What would be the consequences if there were no Supremacy Clause? Explain.
2. Do you think American Honda owed a duty to equip all of its 1987 vehicles with air bags even though federal law did not require this?
3. Do laws ever protect—rather than harm—businesses? Do you think defendant American Honda would say "There are too many laws" in this case?

ETHICAL PERSPECTIVE

CIGARETTE COMPANIES ASSERT SUPREMACY CLAUSE

Businesspersons often complain that there are too many laws. In some cases, however, business executives actually like a law because it works in their favor. Consider the following case. Rose Cipollone began smoking cigarettes in 1942, when she was 17 years old. She continued to smoke between one and two packs of cigarettes per day until the early 1980s. Cipollone first smoked Chesterfield cigarettes, manufactured by Liggett Group, Inc. She then switched to L&M filter cigarettes, also made by Liggett Group. Cipollone subsequently switched to Virginia Slims cigarettes, manufactured by Phillip Morris, Inc. Finally, she smoked Parliament cigarettes, also made by Phillip Morris.

In 1981, Cipollone was diagnosed with lung cancer. Even though her doctor advised her to quit smoking, she was unable to do so. Cipollone continued to smoke heavily until June 1982, when her lung was removed, but even after that she smoked in secret. She stopped smoking only in 1983, after she had become terminally ill with cancer. On August 1, 1983, she sued those cigarette manufacturers for personal injuries. Cipollone died on October 21, 1984, but her heir continued to prosecute the case.

In 1965, Congress enacted the Federal Cigarette Labeling and Advertising Act, which required cigarette manufacturers to place on cigarette packages a warning of the dangers of smoking. The act requires one of the following warning labels, which must be rotated every quarter, to be placed on each cigarette package after the words "SURGEON GENERAL'S WARNING":

1. Smoking Causes Lung Cancer, Heart Disease, Emphysema, and May Complicate Pregancy.
2. Cigarette Smoke Contains Carbon Monoxide.
3. Quitting Smoking Now Greatly Reduces Serious Risks to Your Health.
4. Smoking by Pregnant Women May Result in Fetal Injury, Premature Birth, and Low Birth Weight.

The cigarette company defendants argued that the warnings on cigarette packages—which are mandated by the Federal Cigarette Labeling and Advertising Act—preempted Cipollone's state tort action against them.

The U.S. Supreme Court held that the federal act preempted Cipollone's state law claims based on failure to warn of the dangers of smoking. The Court held that the Federal Cigarette Labeling and Advertising Act was a valid federal law that, under the Supremacy Clause of the U.S. Constitution, was precedent over conflicting state law failure-to-warn claims.

The Supreme Court did rule, however, that the act did not bar lawsuits against cigarette companies for claims based on fraudulent misrepresentation or conspiracy among cigarette companies to misrepresent or conceal material facts about the dangers of cigarette smoking. Therefore, if they can prove fraud—that is, intentional conduct whereby the cigarette companies knew of the dangers of cigarette smoking and either lied to the public or concealed this information—smokers can win against cigarette companies. The Supreme Court reversed the court of appeals and allowed Cipollone's heirs to proceed against the defendants on this issue. Worn down, Cipollone's heirs dropped the lawsuit after this U.S. Supreme Court ruling. [*Cipollone v. Liggett Group, Inc.,* 505 U.S. 504, 112 S.Ct. 2608, 1992 U.S. Lexis 4365 (1992)]

1. Do you think cigarette companies knew of the dangers of smoking during the period when Cipollone smoked? Did they conceal this information from her?
2. What would be the economic consequences if courts were to hold cigarette companies liable to injured smokers? Who would gain? Who would suffer?

Constitutional Violations

The United States is the world's leading democracy. The country, however, has had many blemishes on its citizens' constitutional rights. For example, slavery was not outlawed in the United States until the Thirteenth Amendment was added to the U.S. Constitution in 1865. Women did not receive the right to vote in federal elections until the Nineteenth Amendment was added to the U.S. Constitution in 1920. During World War II, Japanese Americans were involuntarily placed in camps. During the McCarthy hearings of the 1950s, citizens who were Communists or associated with Communists were blackballed from their occupations, most notably in the film industry. Not until the mid-1960s did equal opportunity laws outlaw discrimination in the workplace based on race and sex.

state or local law that "directly and substantially" conflicts with valid federal law is preempted under the Supremacy Clause.

THE COMMERCE CLAUSE

SIDEBAR

Commerce Regulation
The federal government may regulate:

1. *Interstate* commerce that crosses state borders.
2. *Intrastate* commerce that affects interstate commerce.

The **Commerce Clause** of the U.S. Constitution grants Congress the power "to regulate commerce with foreign nations, and among the several states, and with Indian tribes" [Article 1, Section 8, clause 3]. Because this clause authorizes the federal government to regulate commerce, it has a greater impact on business than any other provision in the Constitution. Among other things, this clause is intended to foster the development of a national market and free trade among the states.

The Commerce Clause also gives the federal government the authority to regulate **interstate commerce.** Originally, the courts interpreted this clause to mean that the federal government could regulate only commerce that moved *in* interstate commerce. The modern rule, however, allows the federal government to regulate activities that *affect* interstate commerce.

Under the **effects on interstate commerce test,** the regulated activity does not itself have to be in interstate commerce. Thus, any local activity, or **intrastate commerce,** that has an effect on interstate commerce is subject to federal regulation. Theoretically, this test subjects a substantial amount of business activity in the United States to federal regulation.

For example, in the famous case of *Wickard, Secretary of Agriculture v. Filburn,* [317 U.S. 111, 63 S.Ct. 82, 1942 U.S. Lexis 1046 (1942)], a federal statute limited the amount of wheat a farmer could plant and harvest for home consumption. Filburn, a farmer, violated the law. The U.S. Supreme Court upheld the statute on the grounds that it prevented nationwide surpluses and shortages of wheat. The Court reasoned that wheat grown for home consumption would affect the supply of wheat available in interstate commerce.

In several more recent cases, the U.S. Supreme Court held that the federal government had enacted statutes beyond its interstate commerce–clause powers. For example, in *United States v. Lopez,* the Supreme Court invalidated the Gun-Free School Zone Act, a federal statute that made it a crime knowingly to possess a firearm in a school zone [514 U.S. 549, 115 S.Ct. 1624, 1995 U.S. Lexis 3039 (1995)]. The Court found that no commercial activity was being regulated.

CASE FOR DISCUSSION

Reno, Attorney General of the United States v. Condon, Attorney General of South Carolina

528 U.S. 141, 120 S.Ct. 666, 2000 U.S. Lexis 503 (2000) — Supreme Court of the United States

FACTS

State departments of motor vehicles (DMVs) register automobiles and issue drivers' licenses. State DMVs require automobile owners and drivers to provide personal information, which includes a person's name, address, telephone number, vehicle description, Social Security number, medical information, and a photograph, as a condition for registering an automobile or obtaining a driver's license. Many states DMVs sold this personal information to individuals, advertisers, and businesses. These sales generated significant revenues for the states.

After receiving thousands of complaints from individuals whose personal information had been sold, the Congress of the United States enacted the Driver's Privacy Protection Act of 1994 (DPPA) [18 U.S.C. §§ 2721–2775]. This federal statute prohibits a state from selling the personal information of a person unless the state obtains that person's affirmative consent to do so. South Carolina sued the United States, alleging that the Commerce Clause was violated by the federal government by adopting the DPPA. The district court and the court of appeals held for South Carolina. The U.S. Supreme Court granted review.

ISSUE

Was the Driver's Privacy Protection Act properly enacted pursuant to the interstate commerce–clause power granted to the federal government by the U.S. Constitution?

COURT'S REASONING

The Supreme Court reasoned that the motor vehicle information that the states have historically sold is used by insurers, manufacturers, direct marketers, and others engaged in interstate commerce to contact drivers with customized solicitations. The information is also used in the stream of interstate commerce by various public and private entities for matters related to interstate motoring. The Supreme Court held that because drivers' information is an article of commerce, its sale or release into the interstate stream of business is sufficient to support congressional regulation, and therefore the Driver's Privacy Protection Act is a proper exercise of Congress's authority to regulate interstate commerce under the Commerce Clause.

DECISION AND REMEDY

The U.S. Supreme Court held that Congress had the authority under the Commerce Clause to enact the federal Driver's Privacy Protection Act. The Supreme Court reversed the decisions of the district court and court of appeals, which held in favor of South Carolina.

QUESTIONS

1. How often do you think one government (the federal government) saves people from the intrusiveness of another government (state or local government)?
2. Was it ethical for the states to sell the personal information of automobile owners and drivers?
3. Who were the winners from this decision? Who were the losers?

State Police Power

SIDEBAR

Police Power
States may enact laws that protect or promote the public health, safety, morals, and general welfare as long as the laws do not unduly burden interstate commerce.

The states did not delegate all power to regulate business to the federal government. They retained the power to regulate intrastate and much interstate business activity that occurs within their borders. This is commonly referred to as states' **police power.**

Police power permits states (and, by delegation, local governments) to enact laws to protect or promote the *public health, safety, morals, and general welfare.* This includes the authority to enact laws that regulate the conduct of business. Zoning ordinances, state environmental laws, corporation and partnership laws, and property laws are enacted under this power.

State and local laws cannot impose an **undue burden on interstate commerce.** If they do, they are unconstitutional because they violate the Commerce Clause. For example, if the federal government has chosen not to regulate an area that it has the power to regulate (*dormant Commerce Clause*), but the state does regulate it, the state law cannot unduly burden interstate commerce.

The Bill of Rights

SIDEBAR

The Bill of Rights
The first 10 amendments to the Constitution are called the Bill of Rights. They were added to the U.S. Constitution in 1791.

In 1791, the 10 amendments that are commonly referred to as the Bill of Rights were approved by the states and became part of the U.S. Constitution. The Bill of Rights guarantees certain fundamental rights to natural persons and protects these rights from intrusive government action. Most of these rights have also been found applicable to so-called artificial persons (i.e., corporations).

In addition to the Bill of Rights, 17 amendments have been incorporated into the Constitution. These amendments cover a variety of topics. For instance, they have abolished slavery, prohibited discrimination, authorized a federal income tax, given women the right to vote, and specifically recognized that persons 18 years of age and older have the right to vote.

Originally, the Bill of Rights limited intrusive action by the federal government only. Intrusive actions by state and local governments were not limited until the **Due Process Clause** of the Fourteenth Amendment was added to the Constitution in 1868. The Supreme Court has applied the **incorporation doctrine** and held that most of the fundamental guarantees contained in the Bill of Rights are applicable to state and local government action.

Some of the most important amendments are discussed next.

Freedom of Speech

One of the most honored freedoms guaranteed by the Bill of Rights is the **freedom of speech** of the First Amendment. Many other constitutional freedoms would be meaningless without it. The First Amendment's Freedom of Speech Clause protects speech only, not conduct. The U.S. Supreme Court places speech into three categories: (1) *fully protected,* (2) *limited protected,* and (3) *unprotected speech.*

I disapprove of what you say, but I will defend to the death your right to say it.

—Voltaire

1. **Fully protected speech:** Fully protected speech is speech that the government cannot prohibit or regulate. Political speech is an example of such speech. For example, the government could not enact a law that forbids citizens from criticizing the current administration. The First Amendment protects oral, written, and symbolic speech.

INTERNATIONAL PERSPECTIVE

FOREIGN COMMERCE CLAUSE

The Commerce Clause of the U.S. Constitution gives the federal government the exclusive power to regulate commerce with foreign nations. Direct and indirect regulation of foreign commerce by state or local governments that discriminates against foreign commerce violates the **Foreign Commerce Clause** and is therefore unconstitutional.

Consider the following examples: The state of Michigan is the home of General Motors Corporation and Ford Motor Company, the two largest automobile manufacturers in the United States. Suppose the Michigan state legislature enacts a law imposing a 100 percent tax on any automobile imported from a foreign country that is sold in Michigan but does not impose the same tax on domestic automobiles sold in Michigan. The Michigan tax violates the Foreign Commerce Clause and therefore is unconstitutional and void.

If, on the other hand, Michigan enacts a law that imposes a 100 percent tax on all automobiles sold in Michigan, domestic and foreign, the law does not discriminate against foreign commerce and therefore does not violate the Foreign Commerce Clause. But the federal government could enact a 100 percent tax on all foreign automobiles but not domestic automobiles sold in the United States, and that law would be valid.

2. **Limited protected speech:** The Supreme Court has held that certain types of speech are limited protected speech under the First Amendment. The government cannot forbid this type of speech, but it can subject this speech to time, place, and manner restrictions. The following types of speech are accorded limited protection:
   - **Offensive speech:** Offensive speech is speech that offends many members of society. (It is not the same as obscene speech, however.) The Supreme Court has held that offensive speech may be restricted by the government under time, place, and manner restrictions. For example, the Federal Communications Commission (FCC) can regulate the use of offensive language on television by limiting such language to time periods when children would be unlikely to be watching (e.g., late at night).
   - **Commercial speech:** Commercial speech, such as advertising, was once considered unprotected by the First Amendment. The Supreme Court's landmark decision in *Virginia State Board of Pharmacy v. Virginia Citizens Consumer Council, Inc.* [425 U.S. 748, 96 S.Ct. 1817, 1976 U.S. Lexis 55 (1976)] changed this rule. In that case, the Supreme Court held that a state statute prohibiting a pharmacist from advertising the price of prescription drugs was unconstitutional because it violated the Freedom of Speech Clause. But the Supreme Court held that commercial speech is subject to proper time, place, and manner restrictions. For example, a city could prohibit billboards along its highways for safety and aesthetic reasons as long as other forms of advertising (e.g., print media) were available.

3. **Unprotected speech:** The Supreme Court has held that the following types of speech are unprotected speech; they are not protected by the First Amendment and may be totally forbidden by the government:
   - Dangerous speech (including such things as yelling "fire" in a crowded theater when there is no fire).
   - Fighting words that are likely to provoke a hostile or violent response from an average person.
   - Speech that incites the violent or revolutionary overthrow of the government; the mere abstract teaching of the morality and consequences of such action is protected.
   - Defamatory language.
   - Child pornography.
   - Obscene speech.

   The definition of obscene speech is quite subjective. One Supreme Court justice stated, "I know it when I see it" [Justice Stewart in *Jacobellis v. Ohio.* 378 U.S. 184, 84 S.Ct. 1676, 1964 U.S. Lexis 822 (1963)]. In *Miller v. California* [413 U.S. 15, 93 S.Ct. 2607, 1973 U.S. Lexis 149 (1973)], the Supreme Court determined that speech is obscene when:
   - The average person, applying contemporary community standards, would find that the work, taken as a whole, appeals to the prurient interest.
   - The work depicts or describes, in a patently offensive way, sexual conduct specifically defined by the applicable state law.
   - The work, taken as a whole, lacks serious literary, artistic, political, or scientific value.

"No! No!" said the Queen. "Sentence first—verdict afterward."
—Lewis Carroll, *Alice in Wonderland*

Freedom of Religion

The U.S. Constitution requires federal, state, and local governments to be neutral toward religion. The First Amendment actually contains two separate religion clauses. They are:

1. **The Establishment Clause:** Prohibits the government from either establishing a state religion or promoting one religion over another. Thus, it guarantees that there will be no state-sponsored religion. The Supreme Court used this clause as its reason for ruling that an Alabama statute that authorized a one-minute period of silence in schools for "meditation or voluntary prayer" was invalid [*Wallace v. Jaffree*, 472 U.S. 38, 105 S.Ct. 2479, 1985 U.S. Lexis 91 (1985)]. The Court held that the statute endorsed religion.
2. **The Free Exercise Clause:** Prohibits the government from interfering with the free exercise of religion in the United States. Generally, this clause prevents the government from enacting laws that either prohibit or inhibit individuals from participating in or practicing their chosen religion. For example, in *Church of Lukumi Babalu Aye, Inc. v. City of Hialeah, Florida* [508 U.S. 520, 113 S.Ct. 2217, 1993 U.S. Lexis 4022 (1993)], the U.S. Supreme Court held that a city ordinance that prohibited ritual sacrifices of animals (chickens) during church services violated the Free Exercise Clause. Of course, this right to be free from government intervention in the practice of religion is not absolute. For example, human sacrifices are unlawful and are not protected by the First Amendment.

The ultimate justification of the law is to be found, and can only be found, in moral considerations.
—Lord MacMillan

CASE FOR DISCUSSION

Fax.com, Inc. v. United States

323 F.3d 649, 2003 U.S. App. Lexis 5469 (2003) **United States Court of Appeals, Eighth Circuit**

FACTS

The use of fax machines has made the conduct of business and individuals' transactions more efficient. However, faxes have also spurred a growth industry that sends unsolicited advertising "junk faxes" to fax machines all over the country. The recipients of these junk faxes complained to the government that these faxes tied up their fax machines and cost them money to receive and process. In order to regulate this practice, Congress enacted a provision in the Telephone Consumer Protection Act of 1991 (TCPA) that outlaws junk faxes. Fax.com, Inc., which provides promotional services to clients, continued to transmit unsolicited advertisements to fax machines of potential customers. In response to numerous consumer complaints, the United States government sued Fax.com for violating the TCPA. Fax.com argued in defense that the TCPA's regulation of unsolicited faxes violated its free speech rights under the First Amendment to the U.S. Constitution. The U.S. government argued that junk faxes were commercial speech that it could regulate in this manner. The U.S. district court held that the TCPA violated Fax.com's free speech rights and dismissed the government's lawsuit. The U.S. government appealed.

ISSUE

Is the federal government's prohibition against unsolicited commercial advertising faxes a constitutionally permitted regulation of commercial speech?

COURT'S REASONING

The court of appeals held that unsolicited advertising faxes—junk faxes—were commercial speech. The court cited legislative history of the passage of the TCPA as well as evidence from the district court that proved that unsolicited junk faxes caused recipients of these faxes substantial costs and time loss. The court of appeals held that the federal government's enactment of the TCPA that prohibits junk faxes was a constitutional "time, place, and manner" regulation of commercial speech and did not violate Fax.com's free speech rights. The court stated, "There is a substantial governmental interest in protecting the public from the cost shifting and interference caused by unwanted fax advertisements."

DECISION AND REMEDY

The court of appeals held that the TCPA's prohibition against unsolicited advertising faxes was a lawful constitutional regulation of commercial speech. The court of appeals reversed the district court's judgment dismissing the government's lawsuit and remanded the case for further proceedings.

QUESTIONS

1. What is "commercial speech"? How can commercial speech be regulated by the government? Explain.
2. Did Fax.com act ethically in sending unsolicited junk faxes to unsuspecting parties?
3. Was Fax.com making profits from its endeavors? Did it shift costs to the recipients of its junk faxes? What will be the effect of the court of appeals' ruling?

CASE FOR DISCUSSION

United States v. Playboy Entertainment Group, Inc.

529 U.S. 803, 120 S.Ct. 1878, 2000 U.S. Lexis 3427 (2000) Supreme Court of the United States

FACTS

Many entertainment companies, including Playboy Entertainment Group, Inc., produce and distribute sexually explicit adult entertainment features for transmission over cable television stations. These shows are usually offered on a pay-per-view subscription service. Cable operators provide viewers with a converter box that attaches to the television set and scrambles these sexually explicit materials so they can be viewed only by subscribers who pay the subscription fee. However, with today's analog television sets, there often occurs "signal bleed" of either a blurred visual image or muted audio transmission of these materials. Digital television eliminates the signal bleed problem, but it will be years before digital technology becomes prevalent.

To address the signal bleed problem, Congress enacted Section 505 of the Telecommunications Act of 1996, which requires cable operators not to transmit sexually explicit materials during the hours from 6:00 A.M. to 10:00 P.M. if the signal bleed problem can occur. Thus, in this instance cable operators could not make their sexually explicit adult entertainment available for 16 hours each day.

Playboy Entertainment Group, Inc., a cable operator of Playboy Television and Spice, two adult entertainment cable television networks, sued the federal government alleging that Section 505 violated its free speech rights guaranteed by the U.S. Constitution. The district court declared Section 505 unconstitutional. The court found it feasible to allow cable operators to block individual cable boxes in the home, so Section 505 therefore was an overly broad restriction on content-based speech. The U.S. Supreme Court agreed to hear the case on direct appeal.

ISSUE

Is Section 505 an overly broad restriction on content-based speech that violates the free speech rights of Playboy Entertainment Group, Inc.?

COURT'S REASONING

The U.S. Supreme Court noted that the programming in this case is not alleged to be obscene and that adults have a constitutional right to view it. The Supreme Court stated that the only reasonable way for a substantial number of cable operators to comply with the letter of Section 505 is to "time channel," which silences the protected speech for two-thirds of the day in every home in a cable service area, regardless of the presence or likely presence of children or of the wishes of the viewers. Thirty to 50 percent of all adult programming is viewed by households prior to 10 P.M., when the safe-harbor period begins. The Supreme Court stated, "To prohibit this much speech is a significant restriction of communication between speakers and willing adult listeners, communication which enjoys First Amendment protection." The Court cited the fact that cable systems have the capacity to block unwanted channels on a household-by-household basis.

DECISION AND REMEDY

The U.S. Supreme Court held that Section 505 was an overly broad restriction on legal content-based speech and was therefore an unconstitutional violation of free speech rights. The Supreme Court affirmed the judgment of the district court.

QUESTIONS

1. Do you think that Section 505 was an overly broad restriction on free speech rights? Why or why not?
2. Why do you think Congress enacted Section 505 rather than require each home to choose individually to block the challenged programming?
3. What economic consequences did the Supreme Court's ruling have for Playboy Entertainment and other adult entertainment cable companies?

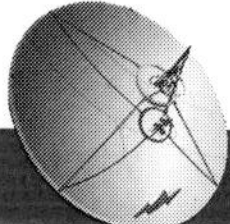

INFORMATION TECHNOLOGY

BROAD FREE SPEECH RIGHTS GRANTED IN CYBERSPACE

Once or twice a century a new medium comes along that presents new problems for applying freedom of speech rights. This time it is the Internet. In 1996 Congress enacted the **Computer Decency Act,** which made it a felony to knowingly make "indecent" or "patently offensive" materials available on computer systems, including the Internet, to persons under 18 years of age. Immediately, more than 50 cyberspace providers and users filed a lawsuit challenging the Act as a violation of their free-speech rights granted under the First Amendment to the Constitution. The U.S. district court agreed with the plaintiffs and declared the Act an unconstitutional violation of the Freedom of Speech Clause.

On appeal, the U.S. Supreme Court agreed and held that the Act was an unconstitutional violation of free speech rights. The Supreme Court concluded that the Internet allows an individual to reach an audience of millions at almost no cost, setting it apart from TV, radio, and print media, which are prohibitively expensive to use. The Court stated, "As the most participatory form of mass speech yet developed, the Internet deserves the highest protection from government intrusion." The Court declared emphatically that the Internet must be given the highest possible level of First Amendment free-speech protection.

Proponents of the Act argued that it was necessary to protect children from indecent materials. The Supreme Court reasoned that limiting the content on the Internet to what is suitable for a child resulted in unconstitutionally limiting adult speech. The Court noted that children are far less likely to trip over indecent material on the Internet than on TV or radio because the information must be actively sought out on the Internet. The Court noted that less obtrusive means for protecting children are available, such as requiring parents to regulate their children's access to materials on the Internet and placing filtering and blocking software on computers to control what their children see on the Internet [*Reno v. American Civil Liberties Union,* 521 U.S. 844, 117 S.Ct. 2329, 1997 U.S. Lexis 4037 (1997)]. [*Note:* It still remains a crime under existing laws to transmit *obscene* materials over the Internet.]

OTHER CONSTITUTIONAL CLAUSES

The Fourteenth Amendment was added to the U.S. Constitution in 1868. Its original purpose was to guarantee equal rights to all persons after the Civil War. The provisions of the Fourteenth Amendment prohibit discriminatory and unfair action by the government. Several of these provisions—namely the *Equal Protection Clause*, the *Due Process Clause*, and the *Privileges and Immunities Clause*—have important implications.

> The law is not a series of calculating machines where definitions and answers come tumbling out when the right levers are pushed.
>
> —William O. Douglas,
> *A Safeguard of Democracy* (1948)

The Equal Protection Clause

The **Equal Protection Clause** provides that a state cannot "deny to any person within its jurisdiction the equal protection of the laws." Although this clause expressly applies to state and local government action, the Supreme Court has held that it also applies to federal government action.

SIDEBAR

Equal Protection Clause
A clause that provides that a state cannot "deny to any person within its jurisdiction the equal protection of the laws."

This clause prohibits state, local, and federal governments from enacting laws that classify and treat "similarly situated" persons differently. Artificial persons, such as corporations, are also protected. Note that this clause is designed to prohibit invidious discrimination; it does not make the classification of individuals unlawful per se.

The Supreme Court has adopted three different standards for reviewing equal protection cases. They are:

1. **Strict scrutiny test:** Any government activity or regulation that classifies persons based on a *suspect class* (i.e., race) is reviewed for lawfulness using a strict scrutiny test. Under this standard, most government classifications of persons based on race are found to be unconstitutional. For example, a government rule permitting persons of one race, but not of another race, to receive government benefits would violate this test.
2. **Intermediate scrutiny test:** The lawfulness of government classifications based on *protected classes* other than race (such as sex or age) are examined using an intermediate scrutiny test. Under this standard, the courts determine whether the government classification is "reasonably related" to a legitimate government purpose. For example, a rule prohibiting persons over a certain age from serving in military combat would be lawful, but a rule prohibiting persons over a certain age from acting as government engineers would not be.
3. **Rational basis test:** The lawfulness of all government classifications that do not involve suspect or protected classes is examined using a rational basis test. Under this test, the courts will uphold government regulation as long as there is a justifiable reason for the law. This standard permits much of the government regulation of business. For example, providing government subsidies to farmers but not to other occupations is permissible.

The Due Process Clause

The Due Process Clause provides that no person shall be deprived of "life, liberty, or property" without due process of the law. It is contained in both the Fifth and Fourteenth Amendments. The Due Process Clause of the Fifth Amendment applies to federal government action; that of the Fourteenth Amendment applies to state and local government action. The government is not prohibited from taking a person's life, liberty, or property, but the government must follow due process to do so. There are two categories of due process: *substantive* and *procedural.*

Substantive due process. **Substantive due process** requires that government statutes, ordinances, regulations, or other laws be clear on their face and not overly broad in scope. The test of whether substantive due process is met is whether a "reasonable person" could understand the law to be able to comply with it. Laws that do not meet this test are declared *void for vagueness.*

Suppose, for example, that a city ordinance were to make it illegal for persons to wear "clothes of the opposite sex." Such an ordinance would be held unconstitutional as void for vagueness because a reasonable person could not clearly determine whether his or her conduct violates the law.

Procedural due process. **Procedural due process** requires that the government must give a person proper *notice* and *hearing* of the legal action before that person is deprived of his or her life, liberty, or property. The government action must be fair.

For example, if the government wants to take a person's home by eminent domain to build a highway, the government must (1) give the homeowner sufficient notice of its intention, and (2) provide a hearing. Under the **Just Compensation Clause** of the Fifth Amendment, the government must pay the owner just compensation for taking the property.

Public policy: That principle of the law which holds that no subject can lawfully do that which has a tendency to be injurious to the public or against the public good.

—Lord Truro,
Egerton v. Brownlow (1853)

The Privileges and Immunities Clause

The purpose of the U.S. Constitution is to promote nationalism. If the states were permitted to enact laws favoring their residents over out-of-state residents, the concept of nationalism would be defeated. Both Article IV of the Constitution and the Fourteenth Amendment contain a **Privileges and Immunities Clause** prohibiting states from enacting laws that unduly discriminate in favor of their residents.

For example, a state cannot enact a law that prevents residents of other states from owning property or businesses in that state. Only invidious discrimination is prohibited. Thus, state universities are permitted to charge out-of-state residents higher tuition than in-state residents. Note that this clause applies only to citizens; corporations are not protected.

Administrative Agencies

Administrative agencies are generally established with the goal of creating a body of professionals who are experts in a particular field. These experts have delegated authority to regulate an individual industry or a specific area of commerce.

Administrative agencies are created by federal, state, and local governments. They range from large, complex federal agencies, such as the Department of Health and Human Resources, to local zoning boards. Many administrative agencies are given the authority to adopt rules and regulations that enforce and interpret statutory law (the rule-making power of administrative agencies is discussed later in this chapter).

Federal Administrative Agencies

The most pervasive government regulations have developed from the statutes enforced by and the rules and regulations adopted by **federal administrative agencies.** The majority of federal administrative agencies—such as the Justice Department, the Department of Housing and Urban Development, the Labor Department, the Transportation Department, and the Commerce Department—are part of the executive branch of government.

Congress has established many federal administrative agencies. These agencies are independent of the executive branch and have broad regulatory powers over key areas of the national economy. Many of these independent agencies are discussed separately in this book.

INTERNATIONAL PERSPECTIVE

CONSTITUTION OF THE PEOPLE'S REPUBLIC OF CHINA

CHAPTER TWO
THE FUNDAMENTAL RIGHTS AND DUTIES OF CITIZENS
[SELECTED PROVISIONS]

Article 33
All citizens of the People's Republic of China are equal before the law.

Article 34
All citizens of the People's Republic of China who have reached the age of 18 have the right to vote and stand for election, regardless of ethnic status, race, sex, occupation, family background, religious belief, education, property status or length of residence, except persons deprived of political rights according to law.

Article 35
Citizens of the People's Republic of China enjoy freedom of speech, of the press, of assembly, of association, of procession and of demonstration.

Article 36
Citizens of the People's Republic of China enjoy freedom of religious belief. No state organ, public organization or individual may compel citizens to believe in, or not to believe in, any religion; nor may they discriminate against citizens who believe in, or do not believe in, any religion.

Article 41
Citizens of the People's Republic of China have the right to criticize and make suggestions regarding any state organ or functionary.

Article 48
Women in the People's Republic of China enjoy equal rights with men in all spheres of life, in political, economic, cultural, social and family life.

State Administrative Agencies

All states have created administrative agencies to enforce and interpret state law. For example, most states have a corporations department to enforce state corporations law, a banking department to regulate the operation of banks, fish and game departments, and workers' compensation boards. **State administrative agencies** also have a profound effect on business. In addition, local governments and municipalities create administrative agencies, such as zoning commissions, to administer local law.

Administrative Law

Administrative law is a combination of substantive and procedural law. Each federal administrative agency is empowered to administer a particular statute or statutes. For example, the Securities and Exchange Commission (SEC) is authorized to enforce the Securities Act of 1933, the Securities Exchange Act of 1934, and other federal statutes dealing with securities markets. These statutes are the *substantive law* that is enforced by the agency.

Because the U.S. Constitution does not stipulate that administrative agencies are a separate branch of the government, they must be created by the legislative or executive branch. When an administrative agency is created, it is delegated certain powers. The agency has only the legislative, judicial, and executive powers that are delegated to it. This is called the **delegation doctrine.**

Legislative Powers of Administrative Agencies

Administrative agencies usually are delegated certain *legislative powers*. Many federal statutes expressly authorize an administrative agency to issue **substantive rules.** A substantive regulation is much like a statute: It has the force of law and must be adhered to by covered persons and businesses. Violators may be held civilly or criminally liable, depending on the rule. All substantive rules are subject to judicial review.

Executive Powers of Administrative Agencies

Administrative agencies are usually granted **executive powers** such as the investigation and prosecution of possible violations of statutes, administrative rules, and administrative orders. To perform these functions successfully, the agency must often obtain information from the persons and businesses under investigation as well as from other sources.

Judicial Powers of Administrative Agencies

Many administrative agencies have the judicial authority to adjudicate cases through an administrative proceeding. Such a proceeding is initiated when an agency serves a complaint on a party the agency believes has violated a statute or administrative rule or order. The person on whom the complaint is served is called the **respondent.**

Administrative law judges (ALJs) preside over administrative proceedings. They decide questions of law and fact concerning the case. There is no jury. The ALJ is an employee of the administrative agency. The ALJ's decision is issued in the form of an **order.** The order must state the reasons for the ALJ's decision. The order becomes final if it is not appealed. An appeal consists of a review by the agency. The agency review can result in new findings of fact and law.

An administration agency rule, order, or decision may be appealed to the appropriate federal court (in federal agency actions) or state court (in state agency actions). (See Exhibit 5.1.)

SIDEBAR

Administrative Procedure Act
In 1946, Congress enacted the **Administrative Procedure Act (APA)** [5 U.S.C. §§ 551 et seq.]. This act establishes certain administrative procedures that federal administrative agencies must follow in conducting their affairs. For example, the APA establishes notice and hearing requirements, rules for conducting agency adjudicative actions, and procedures for rule-making. Most states have enacted administrative procedural acts that govern state administrative agencies.

LEGAL TERMINOLOGY

Administrative agency
Administrative law judge (ALJ)
Administrative Procedure Act (APA)
Articles of Confederation
Bill of Rights
Checks and balances
Commerce Clause
Commercial speech
Computer Decency Act
Constitutional Convention
Delegation doctrine
Due Process Clause
Effects on interstate commerce test
Electoral college
Enumerated powers
Equal Protection Clause
Establishment Clause
Executive branch
Executive powers
Federal administrative agency
Federalism
Foreign Commerce Clause
Free Exercise Clause
Freedom of speech
Fully protected speech
Incorporation doctrine
Intermediate scrutiny test
Interstate commerce

EXHIBIT 5.1 *Appeal of a federal administrative agency rule, order, or decision.*

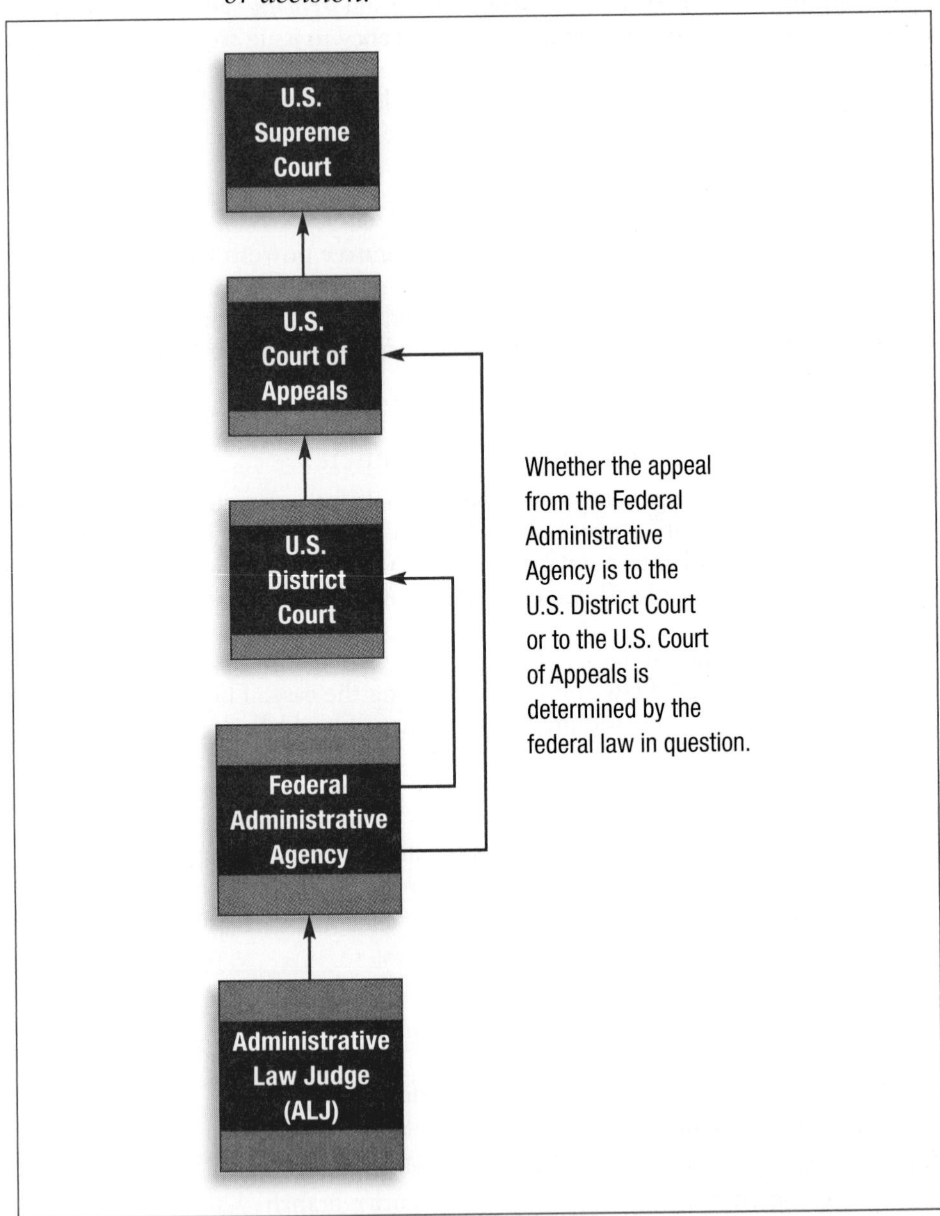

Intrastate commerce
Judicial branch
Just Compensation Clause
Legislative branch
Limited protected speech
Order
Offensive speech
Police power
Preemption doctrine
Privileges and Immunities Clause
Procedural due process
Rational basis test
Respondent
Rules and regulations

Strict scrutiny test
State administrative agency
Substantive due process
Substantive rules
Supremacy Clause
Undue burden on interstate commerce
Unprotected speech

chapter summary

CONSTITUTIONAL LAW AND FREEDOMS

Basic Constitutional Concepts

The U.S. Constitution	The Constitution consists of 7 articles and 26 amendments. It establishes the three branches of the federal government, enumerates their powers, and provides important guarantees of individual freedom. The Constitution was ratified by the states in 1788.
Basic Constitutional Concepts	1. *Federalism:* The Constitution created the federal government. The federal government and the 50 state governments share powers in this country. 2. *Delegated powers:* When the states ratified the Constitution, they delegated certain powers to the federal government. These are called *enumerated powers.* 3. *Reserved powers:* Those powers not granted to the federal government by the Constitution are reserved to the states. 4. *Separation of powers:* Each branch of the federal government has separate powers. These powers are: a. Legislative branch—power to make the law. b. Executive branch—power to enforce the law. c. Judicial branch—power to interpret the law. 5. *Checks and balances:* Certain checks and balances are built into the Constitution to ensure that no one branch of the federal government becomes too powerful.

The Supremacy Clause

The Supremacy Clause	Stipulates that the U.S. Constitution, treaties, and federal law (statutes and regulations) are the *supreme law of the land.* State or local laws that conflict with valid federal law are unconstitutional. This is called the *preemption doctrine.*

The Commerce Clause

The Commerce Clause	1. *Purpose:* Authorizes the federal government to regulate commerce with foreign nations, among the states, and with Indian tribes. 2. *Interstate commerce:* Under the broad *effects test,* the federal government may regulate any activity (even intrastate commerce) that *affects* interstate commerce. 3. *Undue burden on interstate commerce:* Any state or local law that causes an undue burden on interstate commerce is unconstitutional as a violation of the Commerce Clause.

(continued)

The Bill of Rights	
The Bill of Rights	Consists of the first 10 amendments to the Constitution, which establish basic individual rights. The Bill of Rights was ratified in 1791.
Freedom of Speech	1. *Freedom of Speech Clause:* Clause of the First Amendment that guarantees that the government shall not infringe on a person's right to speak. Protects oral, written, and symbolic speech. This right is not absolute—that is, some speech is not protected and other speech is granted only limited protection. 2. *Fully protected speech:* Speech that cannot be prohibited or regulated by the government. 3. *Limited protected speech:* The following types of speech are granted only limited protection under the Freedom of Speech Clause—that is, they are subject to governmental *time, place, and manner restrictions.* a. Offensive speech b. Commercial speech 4. *Unprotected speech:* The following speech is not protected by the Freedom of Speech Clause: a. Dangerous speech b. Fighting words c. Speech that advocates the violent overthrow of the government d. Defamatory language e. Child pornography f. Obscene speech
Freedom of Religion	The two religion clauses in the First Amendment are: 1. *Establishment Clause:* Prohibits the government from establishing a state religion or promoting religion. 2. *Free Exercise Clause:* Prohibits the government from interfering with the free exercise of religion. This right is not absolute: for example, human sacrifices are forbidden.
Other Constitutional Clauses	
Equal Protection Clause	Prohibits the government from enacting laws that classify and treat "similarly situated" persons differently. This standard is not absolute. The U.S. Supreme Court has applied the following tests to determine if the Equal Protection Clause has been violated: 1. *Strict scrutiny test:* Applies to *suspect classes* (e.g., race and national origin). 2. *Intermediate scrutiny test:* Applies to other *protected classes* (e.g., sex and age). 3. *Rational basis test:* Applies to government classifications that do not involve a suspect or protected class.
Due Process Clause	Provides that no person shall be deprived of "life, liberty, or property" without due process. The two categories of due process are: 1. *Substantive due process:* Requires that laws be clear on their face and not overly broad in scope. Laws that do not meet this test are *void for vagueness.*

	2. *Procedural due process:* Requires that the government give a person proper *notice* and *hearing* before that person is deprived of his or her life, liberty, or property. An owner must be paid *just compensation* if the government takes his or her property.
Privileges and Immunities Clause	Prohibits states from enacting laws that unduly discriminate in favor of their residents over residents of other states.
Administrative Agencies	
Administrative Agencies	1. *Administrative agencies:* Created by federal and state legislative and executive branches. Consist of professionals having an area of expertise in a certain area of commerce, who interpret and apply designated statutes. 2. *Administrative rules and regulations:* Administrative agencies are empowered to adopt rules and regulations that interpret and advance the laws they enforce. 3. *Administrative Procedure Act:* Act that establishes procedures (e.g., notice, hearing, and such) to be followed by federal agencies in conducting their affairs. States have enacted their own procedural acts to govern state agencies.

WORKING THE WEB

Visit **www.infoctr.edu/fwl,** the Web site for the Federal Law Locator. Try the following:

1. Check on the product safety record for selected products at the U.S. Consumer Product Safety Commission site. For example, "CPSC, Burger King Corporation Announce Voluntary Recall of Pokemon Ball."
2. Find and compare the U.S. Constitution to the Washington State Constitution, available at **www.access.wa.gov** How are they similar? How are they different?
3. Locate the municipal code for your city. Find the law on loitering in public places. Is it constitutional?
4. Find and review the USA Patriot Act of 2001. Is it constitutional?

CRITICAL LEGAL THINKING QUESTIONS

1. Describe each of the following constitutional concepts: (1) federalism, (2) enumerated powers, (3) doctrine of separation of powers, and (4) checks and balances.
2. What does the Supremacy Clause provide? What purpose does it serve?
3. What does the Commerce Clause provide? What purpose does it serve?
4. Explain the difference between *interstate* commerce and *intrastate* commerce. Describe the "effects" test for determining whether interstate commerce exists.
5. What does the Freedom of Speech Clause of the First Amendment provide? Define the following three types of speech: (1) fully protected speech, (2) limited protected speech, and (3) unprotected speech.
6. Describe the protections afforded by the following two freedom of religion clauses: (1) Establishment Clause and (2) Free Exercise Clause.
7. What does the Equal Protection Clause provide? Describe the differences among the following three tests: (1) strict scrutiny test, (2) intermediate scrutiny test, and (3) rational basis test.
8. Describe the protections afforded by (1) substantive due process and (2) procedural due process.
9. What does the Privileges and Immunities Clause provide?
10. What are administrative agencies? What powers do administrative agencies have?

CASE FOR BRIEFING

Read Case 5 in Appendix A *(Lee v. Weisman).* Review and brief the case using the *Critical Legal Thinking* "Briefing the Case" example described in Chapter 1.

5.1 *Heart of Atlanta Motel v. United States*

379 U.S. 241, 85 S.Ct. 348, 1964 U.S. Lexis 2187 (1964)
Supreme Court of the United States

FACTS The Heart of Atlanta Motel, located in the state of Georgia, has 216 rooms available to guests. The motel is readily accessible to interstate highways 75 and 85 and to state highways 23 and 41. The motel solicits patronage from outside the state of Georgia through various national advertising media, including magazines of national circulation, and it maintains more than 50 billboards and highway signs within the state. Approximately 75 percent of the motel's registered guests are from out of state.

Congress enacted the Civil Rights Act of 1964, which made it illegal for public accommodations to discriminate against guests based on their race. Prior to that, the Heart of Atlanta Motel had refused to rent rooms to blacks. After the act was passed, it alleged that it intended to continue not to rent rooms to blacks. The owner of the motel brought an action to have the Civil Rights Act of 1964 declared unconstitutional, alleging that Congress, in passing the act, had exceeded its powers to regulate commerce under the Commerce Clause of the U.S. Constitution.

ISSUE Who wins and why?

5.2 *Ray, Governor of Washington v. Atlantic Richfield Co.*

435 U.S. 151, 98 S.Ct. 988, 1978 U.S. Lexis 18 (1978)
Supreme Court of the United States

FACTS In 1972, Congress enacted a federal statute, called the Ports and Waterways Safety Act, that established uniform standards for the operation of boats on inland waterways in the United States. The act coordinated its provisions with those of foreign countries so that there was a uniform body of international rules applying to vessels that traveled between countries. Pursuant to the act, a federal rule was adopted that regulated the design, length, and size of oil tankers, some of which traveled the waters of the Puget Sound area in the State of Washington. Oil tankers from various places entered Puget Sound to bring crude oil to refineries located in Washington.

In 1975, the State of Washington enacted a statute that established different designs, smaller lengths, and smaller sizes for oil tankers serving Puget Sound than allowed by the federal law. Oil tankers used by the Atlantic Richfield Company (ARCO) to bring oil into Puget Sound met the federal standards but not the state standards. ARCO sued to have the state statute declared unconstitutional.

ISSUE Who wins and why?

5.3 *Federal Communications Commission v. Pacifica Foundation*

438 U.S. 726, 98 S.Ct. 3026, 1978 U.S. Lexis 135 (1978)
Supreme Court of the United States

FACTS Satiric humorist George Carlin recorded a 12-minute monologue entitled "Filthy Words" before a live audience in a California theater. He began referring to "the words you couldn't say on the public airwaves—the ones you definitely couldn't say, ever." He proceeded to list those words and repeat them again and again in a variety of colloquialisms.

At about 2:00 P.M. on October 30, 1973, a New York radio station owned by Pacifica Foundation broadcast the "Filthy Words" monologue. A man who heard the broadcast while driving with his young son complained to the FCC, the federal administrative agency in charge of granting radio licenses and regulating radio broadcasts. The FCC administers a statute that forbids the use of any offensive language on the radio. The FCC found that Carlin's monologue violated this law and censured the Pacifica Foundation for playing the monologue.

ISSUE Can the FCC prohibit Pacifica Foundation from playing the Carlin monologue on the radio? Explain your answer.

ETHICS CASE

5.4 *United States v. Eichman*

496 U.S. 310, 110 S.Ct. 2404, 1990 U.S. Lexis 3087 (1990)
Supreme Court of the United States

FACTS In 1989, Congress enacted the Flag Protection Act, which made it a crime to knowingly mutilate, deface, physically defile, burn, or trample the U.S. flag. The law provided for fines and up to one year in prison upon conviction [18 U.S.C. §700]. Certain individuals set fire to several U.S. flags on the steps of the U.S. Capitol in Washington, DC, to protest various aspects of the federal government's foreign and domestic policy. In a separate incident, other individuals set fire to a U.S. flag to protest the act's passage. All of these individuals were prosecuted for violating the act.

The district courts held the act unconstitutional in violation of the defendants' First Amendment free speech rights and dismissed the charges. The government appealed to the U.S. Supreme Court, which consolidated the two cases.

ISSUE Who wins and why? Does the flag burner exhibit any morals?

PART II

Basic Law

- Chapter 6 Torts and Product Liability
- Chapter 7 Contracts and E-Commerce
- Chapter 8 Real and Personal Property
- Chapter 9 Family Law
- Chapter 10 Wills, Trusts, and Estates

There are certain basic substantive areas of the law that students should know. Part II covers many of these areas. Chapter 6 focuses on the area of tort law, which includes intentional torts and negligence. This chapter also includes strict liability and product liability. Chapter 7 explores common law, e-commerce contracts, and commercial law derived from the Uniform Commercial Code (UCC). Chapter 8 provides a discussion of real property law, personal property law, and bailments. Chapter 9 is devoted to the many facets of family law, including marriage, dissolution of marriages, and rights of children. Chapter 10 covers the topics of wills, trusts, and estates. This part of the book provides readers with information about a great number of laws that they will encounter in their business and personal lives.

6 Torts and Product Liability

Negligence is not actionable unless it involves the invasion of a legally protected interest, the violation of a right. Proof of negligence in the air, so to speak, will not do. —C. J. CARDOZO, *PALSGRAF V. LONG ISLAND RAILROAD CO.*, 248 N.Y. 339, 162 N.E. 99, 1928 N.Y. LEXIS 1269 (1928)

CHAPTER OBJECTIVES

After studying this chapter, you should be able to

1. List and describe intentional torts against persons and against property.
2. List and explain the elements necessary to prove negligence.
3. Apply special negligence doctrines such as negligence per se, negligent infliction of emotional distress, and *res ipsa loquitur*.
4. Describe the different legal theories of product liability.
5. Describe and apply the doctrine of strict liability.

CHAPTER OUTLINE

- Introduction
- Intentional Torts Against Persons
- Case for Discussion: *Roach v. Stern*
- Intentional Torts Against Property
- Unintentional Torts (Negligence)
- Special Negligence Doctrines
- Case for Discussion: *James v. Meow Media, Inc.*
- Defenses Against Negligence
- Case for Discussion: *Cheong v. Antablin*
- Product Liability
- Case for Discussion: *Shoshone Coca-Cola Bottling Co. v. Dolinski*
- Legal Terminology
- Chapter Summary
- Internet Exercises and Cases

INTRODUCTION

Tort is the French word for a "wrong." Tort law protects a variety of injuries and provides remedies for them. Under tort law an injured party can bring a **civil lawsuit** to seek compensation for a wrong done to the party or to the party's property. Many torts originate in common law. The courts and legislatures have extended tort law to reflect changes in modern society.

Tort damages are monetary damages sought from the offending party, intended to compensate the injured party for the injury suffered. These may consist of past and future medical expenses, loss of wages, pain and suffering, mental distress, and other damages caused by the defendant's tortious conduct. If the victim of a tort dies, his or her beneficiaries can bring a **wrongful death action** to recover damages from the defendant. **Punitive damages,** which are awarded to punish the defendant, may be recovered in **intentional tort** and strict liability cases. Other remedies, such as **injunctions,** may be available, too.

Tort lawsuits make up a substantial portion of the civil lawsuits in this country. Therefore, a reader should have a knowledge of the major tort principles and the elements of each tort. This chapter covers various tort laws, including intentional torts, negligence, and strict liability.

Intentional Torts Against Persons

The law protects a person from unauthorized touching, restraint, or other contact. In addition, the law protects a person's reputation and privacy. Violations of these rights are actionable as torts. Intentional torts against the person are discussed in the paragraphs that follow.

Assault

Assault is (1) the threat of immediate harm or offensive contact, or (2) any action that arouses reasonable apprehension of imminent harm. Actual physical contact is unnecessary. Threats of future harm are not actionable. For example, suppose a 6-foot-5-inch, 250-pound male makes a fist and threatens to punch a 5-foot, 100-pound woman. If the woman is afraid that the man will physically harm her, she can sue him for assault. If she is a black-belt karate champion and laughs at the threat, there is no assault because the threat does not cause any apprehension.

Battery

Battery is unauthorized and harmful or offensive physical contact with another person. Basically, the interest protected here is each person's reasonable sense of dignity and safety. For example, intentionally hitting someone is considered battery because it is harmful. Note that there does not have to be direct physical contact between the victim and the perpetrator. If an injury results, throwing a rock, shooting an arrow or a bullet, knocking off a hat, pulling a chair out from under someone, and poisoning a drink are all instances of actionable battery. The victim need not be aware of the harmful or offensive contact (e.g., it may take place while the victim is asleep). Assault and battery often occur together, although they do not have to (e.g., the perpetrator hits the victim on the back of the head without any warning).

"I'm a lawyer, so I'll try the torte."

Sometimes a person acts with the intent to injure one person but actually injures another. The **doctrine of transferred intent** applies to these situations. Under this doctrine, the law transfers the perpetrator's intent from the target to the actual victim of the act. The victim then can sue the defendant.

False Imprisonment

The intentional confinement or restraint of another person without authority or justification

Wal-Mart Shopper Wins

On Christmas Eve 1995, LaShawna Goodman went to the local Wal-Mart store in Opelika, Alabama, to do some last-minute holiday shopping. She brought along her two young daughters and a telephone, which she had purchased earlier at Wal-Mart, to exchange. She presented the telephone and receipt to a Wal-Mart employee, who took the telephone. Unable to find another telephone she wanted, Goodman retrieved the previously purchased telephone from the employee, bought another item, and left.

Outside, Ms. Goodman was stopped by Wal-Mart security personnel and was accused of stealing the phone. Goodman offered to show the Wal-Mart employees the original receipt, but the Wal-Mart employees detained her and called the police. Ms. Goodman was handcuffed in front of her children. Wal-Mart filed criminal charges against Ms. Goodman.

At the criminal trial Ms. Goodman was acquitted of all charges. Now it was Ms. Goodman's turn: She filed a civil lawsuit against Wal-Mart Stores, Inc., to recover damages for falsely accusing her of stealing the telephone. She presented the evidence as outlined. Wal-Mart asserted the defense that it was in its rights to have detained Ms. Goodman as it did and to prosecute Ms. Goodman based on its investigation. Wal-Mart asserted that the merchant protection statute protected its actions in this case.

The jury did not accept Wal-Mart's plea that it had acted reasonably. The jury rejected Wal-Mart's defenses, including the shopkeeper's privilege and its allegations that it had not maliciously prosecuted her. The jury determined that Ms. Goodman should be awarded $200,000 in compensatory damages for her suffering. The jury then decided that Wal-Mart had acted so badly in this case that it tacked on punitive damages in its award to Ms. Goodman, just to teach Wal-Mart a lesson.

The Supreme Court of Alabama upheld liability, the award of $200,000 compensatory damages, and an award of $600,000 in punitive damages. [*Wal-Mart Stores, Inc. v. Goodman*, 789 So.2d 166, 2000 Ala. Lexis 548 (2000)]

and without that person's consent constitutes **false imprisonment.** The victim may be restrained or confined by physical force, barriers, threats of physical harm, or the perpetrator's false assertion of legal authority (i.e., false arrest). A threat of future harm or moral pressure is not considered false imprisonment. The false imprisonment must be complete. For example, merely locking one door to a building when other exits are not locked is not false imprisonment. A person is not obliged to risk danger or an affront to his or her dignity by attempting to escape.

Shoplifting causes substantial losses to merchants each year. Almost all states have enacted **merchant protection statutes,** also known as the **shopkeeper's privilege.** These statutes allow merchants to stop, detain, and investigate suspected shoplifters without being held liable for false imprisonment if

1. There are reasonable grounds for the suspicion,
2. Suspects are detained for only a reasonable time, and
3. Investigations are conducted in a reasonable manner.

Defamation of Character

A person's reputation is a valuable asset. Therefore, every person is protected during his or her lifetime from false statements by others. This protection ends upon a person's death. The tort of **defamation of character** requires a plaintiff to prove that (1) the defendant made an *untrue statement of fact* about the plaintiff, and (2) the statement was intentionally or accidentally *published* to a third party. In this context, "publication" simply means that a third person heard or saw the untrue statement. It does not just mean appearance in newspapers, magazines, or books.

The term for an oral defamatory statement is **slander.** A false statement that appears in a letter, newspaper, magazine, book, photograph, movie, video, and the like is called **libel.** Most courts hold that defamatory statements in radio and television broadcasts are considered libel because of the permanency of the media.

Publishing an untrue statement of fact is not the same as publishing an opinion. The publication of opinions is usually not actionable. "My lawyer is lousy" is an opinion. Because defamation is defined as an untrue statement of fact, truth is an absolute defense to a charge of defamation.

In *New York Times Co. v. Sullivan* [376 U.S. 254, 84 S.Ct. 710 (1964)], the U.S. Supreme Court held that *public officials* cannot recover for defamation unless they can prove that the defendant acted with "actual malice." Actual malice means that the defendant made the false statement knowingly or with reckless disregard of its falsity. This requirement has since been extended to *public figure* plaintiffs such as movie stars, sports personalities, and other celebrities.

Misappropriation of the Right to Publicity

Each person has the exclusive legal right to control and profit from the commercial use of his or her name and personality during his or her lifetime. This is a valuable right, particularly to well-known persons such as sports figures and movie stars. Any attempt by another person to appropriate a living person's name or identity for commercial purposes is actionable. The wrongdoer is liable for the **tort of misappropriation of the right to publicity** (also called the *tort of appropriation*).

Police officers and firemen investigate an accident at an intersection in California.

In such cases, the plaintiff can (1) recover the unauthorized profits made by the offending party, and (2) obtain an injunction against further unauthorized use of his or her name or identity. Many states provide that the right to publicity survives a person's death and may be enforced by the deceased's heirs.

Invasion of the Right to Privacy

The law recognizes each person's right to live his or her life without being subjected to unwarranted and undesired publicity. Violation of this right constitutes the tort of **invasion of the right to privacy.** Examples of this tort are reading someone else's mail, wiretapping, and such. In contrast to defamation, the fact does not have to be untrue. Therefore, truth is not a defense to a charge of invasion of privacy. If the fact is public information, there is no claim to privacy. But a fact that was once public (e.g., commission of a crime) may become private after the passage of time.

Placing someone in a "false light" constitutes an invasion of privacy. For example, sending an objectionable telegram to a third party and signing another's name would place the purported sender in a false light in the eyes of the receiver. Falsely attributing beliefs or acts to another also can form the basis of a lawsuit.

Intentional Infliction of Emotional Distress

In some situations a victim might suffer mental or emotional distress without first being physically harmed. The Restatement (Second) of Torts provides that a person whose *extreme and outrageous conduct* intentionally or recklessly causes severe emotional distress to another is liable for that emotional distress. This is called the tort of **intentional infliction of emotional distress,** or the **tort of outrage.** The plaintiff must prove that the defendant's conduct was "so outrageous in character and so extreme in degree as to go beyond all possible bounds of decency, and to be regarded as atrocious and utterly intolerable in a civilized society." An indignity, an annoyance, rough language, or an occasional inconsiderate or unkind act does not constitute outrageous behavior. However, repeated annoyances or harassment coupled with threats are considered "outrageous."

Laws too gentle are seldom obeyed; too severe, seldom executed.

—Benjamin Franklin

The tort does not require any publication to a third party or physical contact between the plaintiff and defendant. For example, a credit collection agency making harassing telephone calls to a debtor every morning between 1:00 and 5:00 A.M. is outrageous conduct.

The mental distress suffered by the plaintiff must be severe. Many states require that this mental distress be manifested by some form of physical injury, discomfort, or illness, such as nausea, ulcers, headaches, or miscarriage. This requirement is intended to prevent false claims. Some states have abandoned this requirement. The courts have held that shame, humiliation, embarrassment, anger, fear, and worry constitute severe mental distress.

Liability for Frivolous Lawsuits

Entrepreneurs and others often believe they have a reason to sue someone to recover damages or other remedies. If the plaintiff has a reason to bring the lawsuit and does so, but the plaintiff does not win the lawsuit, he or she does not have to worry about being sued by the person whom he or she sued. But a losing plaintiff does have to worry about being sued by the defendant in a second lawsuit for **malicious prosecution** if certain elements are met.

In a lawsuit for malicious prosecution, the original defendant sues the original plaintiff. In this second lawsuit, which is a *civil* action for damages, the original defendant is the plaintiff and the original plaintiff is the defendant. To succeed in a malicious prosecution lawsuit, the courts require the plaintiff to prove all of the following:

- The plaintiff in the original lawsuit (now the defendant) instituted or was responsible for instituting the original lawsuit.
- There was no *probable cause* for the first lawsuit; that is, it was a frivolous lawsuit.
- The plaintiff in the original action brought it with *malice.* [Caution: This is a difficult element to prove.]
- The original lawsuit was terminated in favor of the original defendant (now the plaintiff).
- The current plaintiff suffered injury as a result of the original lawsuit.

The courts do not look favorably on malicious prosecution lawsuits because they think these inhibit the original plaintiff's incentive to sue.

CASE FOR DISCUSSION

Roach v. Stern

675 N.Y.S.2d 133, 1998 N.Y. App. Div. Lexis 7998 (1998) — Supreme Court, Appellate Division, New York

FACTS

Howard Stern is a famous television talk-show host who emcees an irreverent daily show on the radio. The show is syndicated by Infinity Broadcasting, Inc. (Infinity), and is listened to by millions of people across the country. Deborah Roach, a self-described topless dancer and cable-access television host, was a perennial guest on the Howard Stern radio show. She was famous for her stories about encounters with aliens. Roach died of a drug overdose at the age of 27. Roach's sister, Melissa Driscoll, had Roach's body cremated and gave a portion of the remains to Roach's close friend Chaunce Hayden. Driscoll said she did so with the understanding that Hayden would "preserve and honor said remains in an appropriate and private manner."

On July 18, 1995, Hayden brought a box containing Roach's cremated remains to Stern's radio show. Hayden said she did so as a memorial to Roach because "the only happiness Debbie had was the Howard Stern show." Thereafter, Stern, Hayden, and other participants in the broadcast played with Roach's ashes and made crude comments about the remains. The radio show was videotaped and later broadcast on a national cable television station. Roach's sister and brother sued Stern, Infinity, and Hayden to recover damages for intentional infliction of emotional distress. The trial court dismissed the complaint. The plaintiffs appealed.

ISSUE

Have the plaintiffs sufficiently pleaded a cause of action to recover damages for the intentional infliction of emotional distress?

COURT'S REASONING

The court stated that to impose liability for intentional infliction of emotional distress, "the conduct complained of must be so outrageous in character, and so extreme in degree, as to be beyond all possible bounds of decency, and to be regarded as atrocious, and utterly intolerable in a civilized community." The court noted that the element of outrageous conduct is rigorous and difficult to satisfy and that its purpose is to filter out trivial complaints and ensure that the claim of severe emotional distress is genuine. The court decided that a jury could reasonably conclude that the manner in which Roach's remains were handled for entertainment purposes went beyond the bounds of decent behavior. The court reinstated the plaintiffs' complaint.

DECISION AND REMEDY

The court held that the complaint and the facts of the case as pleaded sufficiently stated a cause of action to recover damages for intentional infliction of emotional distress. Reversed.

QUESTIONS

1. Should the tort of intentional infliction of emotional distress be recognized by the law? What difficulties arise in trying to apply this tort?
2. Was Stern's and the other participants' conduct on the radio show tasteless? Did it amount to "outrageous conduct" for which legal damages should be awarded?
3. If Stern and Infinity are found liable, will a chilling effect on future broadcasts result?

INTENTIONAL TORTS AGAINST PROPERTY

The two general categories of property are real property and personal property. *Real property* consists of land and anything permanently attached to that land. *Personal property* consists of things that are movable, such as automobiles, books, clothes, pets, and such. The law recognizes certain torts against real and personal property. These torts are discussed in the paragraphs that follow.

Trespass to Land

Interference with an owner's right to exclusive possession of land constitutes the tort of **trespass to land.** There does not have to be any interference with the owner's use or enjoyment of the land; the ownership itself is what counts. Actual harm to the property is not necessary.

Examples of trespass to land are entering another person's land without permission, remaining on the land of another after permission to do so has expired (e.g., a guest refuses to leave), or causing something or someone to enter another's land (e.g., one person builds a dam that causes another person's land to flood). A person who is pushed onto another's land or enters that land with good reason is not liable for trespass. For example, a person may enter another person's land to save a child or a pet from harm.

Trespass to and Conversion of Personal Property

The tort of **trespass to personal property** occurs whenever one person injures another person's personal property or interferes with that person's enjoyment of his or her personal property. The injured party can sue for damages. For example, breaking another's car window is trespass to personal property.

Depriving a true owner of the use and enjoyment of his or her personal property by taking over such property and exercising ownership rights over it constitutes the tort of **conversion of personal property.** Conversion also occurs when someone who originally is given possession of personal property fails to return it (e.g., fails to return a borrowed car). The rightful owner can sue to recover the property. If the property was lost or destroyed, the owner can sue to recover its value.

UNINTENTIONAL TORTS (NEGLIGENCE)

Under the doctrine of **unintentional tort,** commonly referred to as **negligence,** a person is liable for harm that is the *foreseeable consequence* of his or her actions. Negligence is defined as "the omission to do something which a reasonable man would do, or doing something which a prudent and reasonable man would not do." [*Blyth v. Birmingham Waterworks Co.*, 11 Exch. 781, 784 (1856)]

Negligence is the omission to do something which a reasonable man would do, or doing something which a prudent and reasonable man would not do.
—B. Alderson, *Blyth v. Birmingham Waterworks Co.* (1856)

Elements of Negligence

To be successful in a negligence lawsuit, the plaintiff must prove that (1) the defendant owed a *duty of care* to the plaintiff, (2) the defendant *breached* this duty of care, (3) the plaintiff suffered *injury*, and (4) the defendant's negligent act *caused* the plaintiff's injury. Each of these elements is discussed in the paragraphs that follow.

Duty of care. To determine whether a defendant is liable for negligence, it first must be ascertained whether the defendant owed a **duty of care** to the plaintiff. Duty of care refers to the obligation we all owe each other—the duty not to cause any unreasonable harm or risk of harm. For example, each person owes a duty to drive his or her car carefully, not to push or shove on escalators, not to leave skateboards on the sidewalk, and the like. Businesses owe a duty to make safe products, not to cause accidents, and so on.

The courts decide whether a duty of care is owed in specific cases by applying a **reasonable person standard.** Under this test, the courts attempt to determine how an *objective, careful, and conscientious person would have acted in the same circumstances*, and then measure the defendant's conduct against this standard. The defendant's subjective intent ("I did not mean to do it") is immaterial in asserting liability. Certain impairments do not affect the reasonable person standard. For instance, there is no reasonable alcoholics standard.

Every unjust decision is a reproach to the law or the judge who administers it. If the law should be in danger of doing injustice, then equity should be called in to remedy it. Equity was introduced to mitigate the rigour of the law.
—Lord Denning,
M. R. Re Vandervell's Trusts (1974)

Defendants with a specific expertise or competence are measured against a **reasonable professional standard.** This standard is applied in much the same way as the reasonable person standard. For example, a brain surgeon is measured against a reasonable brain surgeon standard rather than a lower reasonable doctor standard. Children are generally required to act as a *reasonable child* of similar age and experience would act.

Breach of duty. Once a court finds that the defendant actually owed the plaintiff a duty of care, it must determine whether the defendant breached this duty. A **breach of the duty of care** is the failure to exercise care. It is the failure to act as a reasonable person would act. A breach of this duty may consist of either an action (e.g., throwing a lit match on the ground in a forest and causing a fire) or a failure to act when there is a duty to act (e.g., a firefighter who refuses to put out a fire). Generally, passersby are not expected to rescue others gratuitously to save them from harm.

Injury to plaintiff. Even though a defendant's act might have breached a duty of care owed to the plaintiff, this breach is not actionable unless the plaintiff suffers **injury.** For example, a business's negligence causes an explosion and fire at its factory at night. No one is injured and there is no damage to the neighbor's property. The negligence is not actionable.

The damages recoverable depend on the effect of the injury on the plaintiff's life or profession. Now suppose two men injure their hands when a train door malfunctions. The first man is a professional basketball player. The second is a college professor. The first man can recover greater damages.

Causation. A person who commits a negligent act is not liable unless this act was the cause of the plaintiff's injuries. Courts have divided causation into two categories—*causation in fact* and *proximate cause*—and require each to be shown before the plaintiff may recover damages.

1. **Causation in fact:** The defendant's negligent act must be the **causation in fact,** or **actual cause,** of the plaintiff's injuries. For example, suppose a corporation negligently pollutes the plaintiff's drinking water. The plaintiff dies of a heart attack unrelated to the polluted water. Although the corporation has acted negligently, it is not liable for the plaintiff's death. There was a negligent act and an injury, but there was no *cause-and-effect* relationship

Ouch! The Coffee's Too Hot!

Studies have shown that people don't care about how good their coffee tastes if it is hot. So restaurants, coffee shops, and other sellers make their coffee hot. McDonald's, however, ended up in hot water for making its coffee *too* hot. Consider this case.

Stella Liebeck, an 81-year-old resident of Albuquerque, New Mexico, visited a drive-through window of a McDonald's restaurant with her grandson. Her grandson, the driver of the vehicle, placed the order. When it came, he handed the cup of hot coffee to Liebeck. As her grandson drove away from the drive-through window, Liebeck took the lid off the coffee cup she held in her lap. The coffee spilled on Liebeck, who suffered third-degree burns on her legs, groin, and buttocks. She required medical treatment, was hospitalized, and has permanent scars from the incident.

Liebeck sued McDonald's for selling coffee that was too hot and for failing to warn her of the danger of the hot coffee it served. McDonald's rejected Liebeck's pretrial offer to settle the case for $300,000 and went to trial.

At trial, McDonald's denied that it had been negligent and asserted that Liebeck's own negligence—opening a hot-coffee cup on her lap—caused her injuries. The jury heard evidence that McDonald's enforces a quality-control rule requiring its restaurants and franchises to serve coffee at 180 to 190 degrees Fahrenheit. Evidence showed that this was 10 to 30 degrees hotter than coffee served by competing restaurant chains, and approximately 40 to 50 degrees hotter than normal house-brewed coffee.

Based on this evidence, the jury concluded that McDonald's acted recklessly and awarded Liebeck $200,000 compensatory damages (reduced by $40,000 for her own negligence), and $2.7 million punitive damages. After the trial court judge reduced the amount of punitive damages to $480,000, the parties reached an out-of-court settlement for an undisclosed amount. Because of this case, McDonald's and other purveyors of coffee have reduced the temperature at which they sell coffee and have placed warnings on their coffee cups.

between them. If, instead, the plaintiff had died from the pollution, there would have been causation in fact, and the polluting corporation would have been liable. If two (or more) persons are liable for negligently causing the plaintiff's injuries, both (or all) can be held liable to the plaintiff if each of their acts is a substantial factor in causing the plaintiff's injuries.

2. **Proximate cause:** Under the law, a negligent party is not necessarily liable for all damages set in motion by his or her negligent act. Based on public policy, the law establishes a point along the damage chain after which the negligent party is no longer responsible for the consequences of his or her actions. This limitation on liability is referred to as **proximate cause,** or **legal cause.** The general test of proximate cause is *foreseeability*. A negligent party who is found to be the actual cause—but not the proximate cause—of the plaintiff's injuries is not liable to the plaintiff. Situations are examined on a case-by-case basis.

The landmark case establishing the doctrine of proximate cause is *Palsgraf v. Long Island Railroad Company* [248 N.Y. 339, 162 N.E. 99, 1928 N.Y. Lexis 1269 (1928)]. Helen Palsgraf was standing on a platform waiting for a passenger train. The Long Island Railroad Company owned and operated the trains and employed the station guards. As a man carrying a package wrapped in a newspaper tried to board the moving train, railroad guards tried to help him. In doing so, the package was dislodged from the man's arm, fell to the railroad tracks, and exploded. The package contained hidden fireworks. The explosion shook the railroad platform, causing a scale on the platform to fall on Palsgraf, injuring her. She sued the railroad for negligence. Justice Cardoza denied her recovery, finding that the railroad was not the proximate cause of her injuries.

Special Negligence Doctrines

SIDEBAR

Professional Malpractice
Professionals, including doctors, lawyers, architects, accountants, and others owe a duty of ordinary care in providing their services. This duty is known as the *reasonable professional standard.* A professional who breaches this duty of care is liable for the injury his or her negligence causes. This liability is commonly referred to as **professional malpractice.**

Consider these examples: A doctor who amputates a wrong leg is liable for *medical malpractice.* A lawyer who fails to file a document with the court on time, causing the client's case to be dismissed, is liable for *legal malpractice.* An accountant who fails to use reasonable care, knowledge, skill, and judgment when providing auditing and other accounting services to a client is liable for *accounting malpractice.*

Professionals who breach this duty are liable to their patients or clients. They also may be liable to some third parties.

The courts have developed many *special negligence doctrines.* The most important of these are discussed in the paragraphs that follow.

Negligent Infliction of Emotional Distress

Some jurisdictions have extended the tort of emotional distress to include the **negligent infliction of emotional distress.** The most common examples of this involve bystanders who witness the injury or death of a loved one that is caused by another's negligent conduct. Under this tort, the bystander, even though not personally physically injured, can sue the negligent party for his or her own mental suffering.

Generally, to be successful in this type of case, the plaintiff must prove that (1) a relative was killed or injured by the defendant, (2) the plaintiff suffered severe emotional distress, and (3) the plaintiff's mental distress resulted from a sensory and contemporaneous observance of the accident. Some states require that the plaintiff's mental distress be manifested by some physical injury; other states have eliminated this requirement.

Negligence Per Se

Statutes often establish duties that one person owes to another. Violation of a statute that proximately causes an injury is **negligence per se.** The plaintiff in such an action must prove that (1) a statute existed, (2) the statute was enacted to prevent the type of injury suffered, and (3) the plaintiff was within a class of persons that the statute meant to protect.

Consider this example: Most cities have an ordinance that places the responsibility for fixing public sidewalks in residential areas on the homeowners whose homes front the sidewalk. A homeowner is liable if he or she fails to repair a damaged sidewalk in front of his or her home and a pedestrian trips and is injured because of the damage. The injured party does not have to prove that the homeowner owed the duty, because the statute establishes that.

Res Ipsa Loquitur

If a defendant is in control of a situation in which a plaintiff has been injured and has superior knowledge of the circumstances surrounding the injury, the plaintiff might have difficulty proving the defendant's negligence. In such a situation, the law applies the doctrine of ***res ipsa loquitur*** (Latin for "the thing speaks for itself"). This doctrine raises a presumption of negligence and switches the burden to the defendant to prove that he or she was *not* negligent. *Res ipsa loquitur* applies in cases where the following elements are met:

1. The defendant had exclusive control of the instrumentality or situation that caused the plaintiff's injury.
2. The injury ordinarily would not have occurred "but for" someone's negligence.

CASE FOR DISCUSSION

James v. Meow Media, Inc.

300 F.3d 683, 2002 U.S.App. Lexis 16185 (2002) United States Court of Appeals, Sixth Circuit

BACKGROUND AND FACTS

Michael Carneal was a 14-year-old freshman student at Heath High School in Paducah, Kentucky. Carneal regularly played the violent interactive video and computer games "Doom," "Quake," "Castle Wolfenstein," "Rampage," "Nightmare Creatures," "Mech Warrior," "Resident Evil," and "Final Fantasy." These games involved the player shooting virtual opponents with computer guns and using other weapons. Carneal also watched videotaped movies, including one called "The Basketball Diaries," in which a high-school student protagonist dreams of killing his teacher and several of his fellow classmates. On December 1, 1997, Carneal brought a .22-caliber pistol and five shotguns into the lobby of Heath High School and shot several of his fellow students, killing three and wounding many others. The three students killed were Jessica James, Kayce Steger, and Nicole Hadley.

The parents of the three dead children ("James") sued the producers and distributors of the violent video games and movies that Carneal had watched previous to the shooting. The parents sued to recover damages for wrongful death, alleging that the defendants were negligent in producing and distributing such games and movies to Carneal. The U.S. district court applied Kentucky law and held that the defendants did not owe or breach a duty to the plaintiffs and therefore were not liable for negligence. The plaintiffs appealed.

ISSUE

Did the defendant video and movie producers and distributors breach a duty of care to the plaintiffs by selling and licensing violent video games and movies to Carneal, who killed the three children?

COURT'S REASONING

The court of appeals stated that the existence of a duty of care is determined by the "foreseeability" test and that this is a policy decision to be determined by the court. The court also stated that the court must act as a "filter" and dismiss cases lacking a duty of care. The court of appeals first noted, "Individuals are generally entitled to assume that third parties will not commit intentional criminal acts." The court then noted, however, "Carneal's reaction was not a normal reaction. Indeed, Carneal is not a normal person, but it is not utter craziness to predict that someone like Carneal is out there." The court applied its policy analysis as to foreseeability and held that the defendants did not owe a duty of care to the plaintiffs. The court of appeals stated, "It appears simply impossible to predict that these games, movies, and Internet sites (alone, or in what combinations) would incite a young person to violence. Carneal's reaction to the games and movies at issue here, assuming that his violent actions were such a reaction, was simply too idiosyncratic to expect the defendants to have anticipated it. We find that it is simply too far a leap from shooting characters on a video screen (an activity undertaken by millions) to shooting people in a classroom (an activity undertaken by a handful, at most) for Carneal's actions to have been reasonably foreseeable to the manufacturers of the media that Carneal played and viewed."

DECISION AND REMEDY

The court of appeals held that the defendant video game and movie producers and distributors did not breach a duty of care to the plaintiffs by selling and licensing violent video games and movies to Carneal, who murdered the three children.

QUESTIONS

1. How does the court define "foreseeability"? Did the court use a narrow, middle, or broad interpretation of foreseeability in deciding this case? Explain.
2. Do producers and distributors of video games and movies owe a duty of care to society not to produce and distribute violent games and movies?
3. What would have been the consequences for the video game and movie industries if the court had held in favor of the plaintiffs? Explain.

Exterior of two-story brick courthouse with weathered red fence, Appomattox, Virginia.

Consider this example: Haeran goes in for major surgery and is given anesthesia to put her to sleep during the operation. Sometime after the operation it is discovered that a surgical instrument had been left in Haeran during the operation. She suffers severe injury because of the left-in instrument. Haeran would be hard-pressed to identify which doctor or nurse had been careless and left the instrument in her body.

In this case, the court can apply the doctrine of *res ipsa loquitur* and place the presumption of negligence on the defendants. Any defendant who can prove he or she did not leave the instrument in Haeran escapes liability; any defendant who does not disprove his or her negligence is liable. Other typical *res ipsa loquitur* cases involve commercial airplane crashes, falling elevators, and the like.

Good Samaritan Laws

In the past, exposure to liability made many doctors, nurses, and other medical professionals reluctant to stop and render aid to victims in emergency situations, such as highway accidents. Almost all states have enacted **Good Samaritan laws** that relieve medical professionals from liability for injury caused by their ordinary negligence in such circumstances.

Good Samaritan laws protect medical professionals only from liability for their *ordinary negligence*, not for injuries caused by their gross negligence or reckless or intentional conduct. Most Good Samaritan laws protect licensed doctors and nurses and laypersons who have been certified in CPR. Good Samaritan statutes generally do not protect laypersons who are not trained in CPR—that is, they are liable for injuries caused by their ordinary negligence in rendering aid.

Consider this example: Sam is injured in an automobile accident and is unconscious in his automobile alongside the road. Doctor Pamela Heathcoat, who is driving by the scene of the accident, stops, pulls Sam from the burning wreckage, and administers first-aid. In doing so, Pamela negligently breaks Sam's shoulder. If Pamela's negligence is ordinary negligence, she is not liable to Sam because the Good Samaritan law protects her from liability. If Pamela was grossly negligent or reckless in administering aid to Sam, she is liable to him for the injuries she caused.

It is a question of fact for the jury to decide whether a doctor's conduct was ordinary negligence, gross negligence, or recklessness. If Cathy, a layperson not trained in CPR, had rendered aid to Sam and caused Sam injury because of her ordinary negligence, the Good Samaritan law would not protect her and she would be liable to Sam.

Dram Shop Acts

Many states have enacted **Dram Shop Acts** that make a tavern and bartender civilly liable for injuries caused to or by patrons who are served too much alcohol. The alcohol must be either served in sufficient quantity to make the patron intoxicated or served to an already intoxicated person. Both the tavern and the bartender are liable to third persons injured by the patron and for injuries the patron suffered. They also are liable for injuries caused by or to minors served by the tavern, regardless of whether the minor is intoxicated.

Guest Statutes

Many states have enacted **guest statutes** providing that if a driver voluntarily and without compensation gives a ride in a vehicle to another person (e.g., a hitchhiker), the driver is not liable to the passenger for injuries caused by the driver's ordinary negligence. If the passenger pays compensation to the driver, however, the driver owes a duty of ordinary care to the passenger and will be held liable. The driver is always liable to the passenger for wanton and gross negligence—for example, injuries caused because of excessive speed.

Law must be stable and yet it cannot stand still.
—Roscoe Pour, *Interpretation of Legal History* (1929)

Fireman's Rule

Under the **fireman's rule,** a firefighter who is injured while putting out a fire may not sue the party whose negligence caused the fire. This rule has been extended to police officers and other government workers. The bases for this rule are that (1) people might not call for help if they could be held liable; (2) firefighters, police officers, and other such workers receive special training for their jobs; and (3) these workers have special medical and retirement programs paid for by the public.

"Danger Invites Rescue" Doctrine

The law recognizes a **"danger invites rescue" doctrine.** Under this doctrine, a rescuer who is injured while going to someone's rescue can sue the person who caused the dangerous situation. For example, a passerby who is injured while trying to rescue children from a fire set by an arsonist can bring a civil suit against the arsonist.

Social Host Liability

Several states have adopted the **social host liability** rule. This rule provides that a social host is liable for injuries caused by a guest who is served alcohol at a social function (e.g., a birthday party, a wedding reception) and later causes injury because he or she is intoxicated. The injury may be to a third person or to the guest himself or herself. The alcohol served at the social function must be the cause of the injury. A few states have adopted statutes that relieve social hosts from such liability.

Liability of Landowners

Owners and renters of real property owe certain duties to protect visitors from injury while on the property. A landowner's and tenant's liability generally depends on the visitor's status. Visitors fall into the following two categories:

1. **Invitees and licensees:** An **invitee** is a person who has been expressly or impliedly invited onto the owner's premises for the *mutual benefit* of both parties (e.g., guests invited for dinner, the mail carrier, and customers of a business). A **licensee** is a person who, *for his or her own benefit,* enters the premises with the express or implied consent of the owner (e.g., Avon representative, encyclopedia salesperson, Jehovah's Witnesses). An owner owes a **duty of ordinary care** to invitees and licensees. An owner is liable if

he or she negligently causes injury to an invitee or a licensee. For example, a homeowner is liable if she leaves a garden hose across the walkway on which an invitee or a licensee trips and is injured.

2. **Trespassers:** A **trespasser** is a person who has no invitation, permission, or right to be on another's property. Burglars are a common type of trespasser. Generally, an owner does not owe a duty of ordinary care to a trespasser. For example, if a trespasser trips and injures himself on a bicycle the owner negligently left out, the owner is not liable. An owner, however, does owe a **duty not to willfully or wantonly injure** a trespasser. Thus, an owner cannot set traps to injure trespassers.

A few states have eliminated the invitee–licensee–trespasser distinction. These states hold that owners and renters owe a duty of ordinary care to all persons who enter the property.

Liability of Common Carriers and Innkeepers

No court has ever given, nor do we think ever can give, a definition of what constitutes a reasonable or an average man.
—Lord Goddard *C.J.R. v. McCarthy* (1954)

The common law holds common carriers and innkeepers to a higher standard of care than most other businesses. Common carriers and innkeepers owe a **duty of utmost care**—rather than a duty of ordinary care—to their passengers and guests. For example, innkeepers must provide security for their guests. The concept of utmost care is applied on a case-by-case basis. Obviously, a large hotel must provide greater security to guests than a "mom-and-pop" motel has to provide. Some states and cities have adopted specific statutes and ordinances relating to this duty.

Defenses Against Negligence

A defendant in a negligence lawsuit may raise several defenses to the imposition of liability. These defenses are discussed in the following paragraphs.

Superseding or Intervening Event

Under negligence, a person is liable only for foreseeable events. Therefore, an original negligent party can raise a **superseding,** or **intervening, event** as a defense to liability. For example, assume that an avid golfer negligently hits a spectator with a golf ball, knocking the spectator unconscious. While lying on the ground waiting for an ambulance to come, the spectator is struck by a bolt of lightning and killed. The golfer is liable for the injuries caused by the golf ball. He is not liable for the death of the spectator, however, because the lightning bolt was an unforeseen event.

Assumption of the Risk

If a plaintiff knows of and voluntarily enters into or participates in a risky activity that results in injury, the law recognizes that the plaintiff assumed, or took on, the risk involved. Thus, the defendant can raise the defense of **assumption of the risk** against the plaintiff. This defense assumes that the plaintiff (1) had knowledge of the specific risk, and (2) voluntarily assumed that risk. For example, under this theory, a race car driver assumes the risk of being injured or killed in a crash.

CASE FOR DISCUSSION

Cheong v. Antablin

68 Cal. Rptr.2d 859, 946 P.2d 817, 1997 Cal. Lexis 7662 (1997) Supreme Court of California

FACTS

On April 11, 1991, Wilkie Cheong and Drew R. Antablin, longtime friends and experienced skiers, skied together at Alpine Meadows, a resort near Tahoe City, California. While skiing, Antablin accidentally collided with Cheong, causing injury to him. Cheong sued Antablin to recover damages for negligent skiing. The trial court granted Antablin's motion for summary judgment, holding that the doctrine of assumption of risk barred Cheong's claim, and dismissed the lawsuit. The court of appeals affirmed. Cheong appealed to the California Supreme Court.

ISSUE

Does the doctrine of assumption of risk bar recovery?

COURT'S REASONING

As a general rule, persons have a duty to use due care to avoid injuring others. The supreme court held that this general rule does not apply to coparticipants in a sport where dangerous conditions or conduct are an inherent risk of the sport. The court stated: "Courts should not hold a sports participant liable to a coparticipant for ordinary careless conduct committed during the sport because in the heat of an active sporting event a participant's normal energetic conduct often includes accidentally careless behavior. Vigorous participation in such sporting events likely would be chilled if legal liability were to be imposed on a participant on the basis of his or her ordinary careless conduct." The court noted that the defense of assumption of risk does not apply where a sports participant intentionally injures another player or engages in reckless conduct outside the range of the ordinary activity involved in the sport. The court found that Antablin negligently caused the skiing collision and had not engaged in intentional or reckless conduct.

DECISION AND REMEDY

The state supreme court held that the doctrine of assumption of risk barred recovery in this case.

QUESTIONS

1. Do you think the law should recognize the doctrine of assumption of risk? Why or why not?
2. Should Cheong have sued Antablin? Discuss.
3. Should the doctrine of assumption of risk be applied as a defense when spectators are injured at professional sports events? Explain.

Contributory Negligence

Under the common law doctrine of **contributory negligence,** a plaintiff who is partially at fault for his or her own injury cannot recover against the negligent defendant. For example, suppose a driver who is driving faster than the speed limit negligently hits and injures a pedestrian who is jaywalking. Suppose the jury finds that the driver is 80 percent responsible for the accident and the jaywalker is 20 percent responsible. The pedestrian suffered $100,000 in injuries. Under the doctrine of contributory negligence, the pedestrian cannot recover any damages from the driver.

The doctrine of contributory negligence has one major exception: The defendant has a duty under the law to avoid the accident if at all possible. This rule is known as the **last clear chance rule.** For example, a driver who sees a pedestrian walking across the street against a "Don't Walk" sign must avoid hitting him or her if possible. When deciding cases involving this rule, the courts consider the attentiveness of the parties and the amount of time each has to respond to the situation.

Comparative Negligence

He who seeks equality must do equity.

—Joseph Story, *Equity Jurisprudence* (1836)

As seen, application of the doctrine of contributory negligence could reach an unfair result where a party only slightly at fault for his or her injuries could not recover from an otherwise negligent defendant. Many states have replaced the doctrine of contributory negligence with the doctrine of **comparative negligence.** Under this doctrine, damages are apportioned according to fault.

When the comparative negligence rule is applied to the previous example, the result is much fairer. The plaintiff–pedestrian can recover 80 percent of his or her damages (or $80,000) from the defendant–driver. This is an example of *pure comparative negligence*. Several states have adopted *partial comparative negligence*, which provides that a plaintiff must be less than 50 percent responsible for causing his or her own injuries to recover under comparative negligence; otherwise, contributory negligence applies.

Product Liability

In the landmark case *Greenmun v. Yuba Power Products, Inc.* [59 Cal.2d 57, 27 Cal.Rptr. 697, 377 P.2d 897, 1963 Cal. Lexis 140 (Cal. 1963)], the California Supreme Court adopted the doctrine of **strict liability** in tort as a basis for product liability actions. The doctrine of strict liability removes many of the difficulties for the plaintiff associated with other theories of product liability. In the remainder of this chapter, we will examine the scope of the strict liability doctrine.

Restatement of Torts

The doctrine of strict liability is not part of the Uniform Commercial Code (UCC). The most widely recognized articulation of the doctrine is found in Section 402A of the **Restatement (Second) of Torts,** which provides:

> I. One who sells any product in a defective condition unreasonably dangerous to the user or consumer or to his property is subject to liability for physical harm thereby caused to the ultimate user or consumer, or to his property, if
> A. the seller is engaged in the business of selling such a product, and
> B. it is expected to and does reach the user or consumer without substantial change in the condition in which it is sold.

II. The rule stated in Subsection (1) applies although
   A. the seller has exercised all possible care in the preparation and sale of his product, and
   B. the user or consumer has not bought the product from or entered into any contractual relation with the seller.

Liability Without Fault

Unlike negligence, strict liability does not require the injured person to prove that the defendant breached a duty of care. *Strict liability is imposed irrespective of fault.* A seller can be found strictly liable even though he or she has exercised all possible care in the preparation and sale of his or her product.

The doctrine of strict liability applies to sellers and lessors of products who are engaged in the business of selling and leasing products. Casual sales and transactions by nonmerchants are not covered. Thus, a person who sells a defective product to a neighbor in a casual sale is not strictly liable if the product causes injury.

Strict liability applies only to products, not services. In hybrid transactions involving both services and products, the dominant element of the transaction dictates whether strict liability applies. For example, in a medical operation that requires a blood transfusion, the operation would be the dominant element and strict liability would not apply. Strict liability may not be disclaimed.

SIDEBAR

"A manufacturer is strictly liable in tort when an article he places on the market, knowing that it is to be used without inspection for defects, proves to have a defect that causes injury to a human being."

—*Greenmun v. Yuba Power Products, Inc.* [59 Cal.2d 57, 27 Cal.Rptr. 697 1963 Cal. Lexis 140 (1963)]

All in the Chain of Distribution Are Liable

All parties in the **chain of distribution** of a defective product are strictly liable for the injuries caused by that product. Thus, all manufacturers, distributors, wholesalers, retailers, lessors, and subcomponent manufacturers may be sued under this doctrine. This view is based on public policy. Lawmakers presume that sellers and lessors will insure against the risk of a strict liability lawsuit and spread the cost to their consumers by raising the price of products.

Consider this example: Suppose a subcomponent manufacturer produces a defective tire and sells it to a truck manufacturer. The truck manufacturer places the defective tire on one of its new model trucks. The truck is distributed by a distributor to a retail dealer. Ultimately, the retail dealer sells the truck to a buyer. The defective tire causes an accident in which the buyer is injured. All of the parties in the tire's chain of distribution can be sued by the injured party. In this case, the liable parties are the subcomponent manufacturer, the truck manufacturer, the distributor, and the retailer.

A defendant who has not been negligent but who is made to pay a strict liability judgment can bring a separate action against the negligent party in the chain of distribution to recover the defendant's losses. In the preceding example, the retailer could sue the manufacturer to recover the strict liability judgment assessed against it. Exhibit 6.1 compares the doctrines of negligence and strict liability.

Parties Who Can Recover for Strict Liability

Because strict liability is a tort doctrine, privity of contract between the plaintiff and the defendant is not required. The doctrine applies even if the injured party had no contractual relations with the defendant. Under strict liability, sellers and lessors are liable to the ultimate user or consumer. Users include the purchaser or lessee, family members, guests, employees, customers, and persons who passively enjoy the benefits of the product (e.g., passengers in automobiles).

EXHIBIT 6.1 *Doctrines of negligence and strict liability compared.*

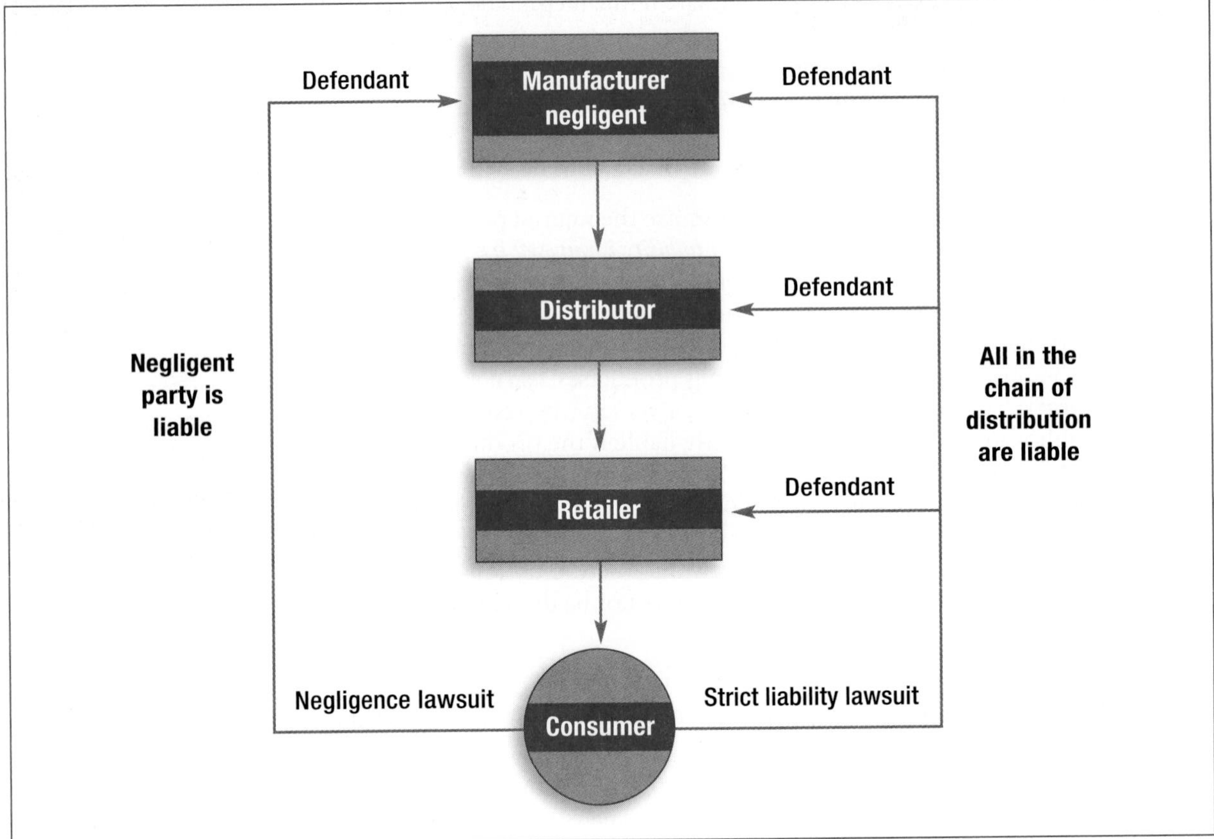

Most jurisdictions have judicially or statutorily extended the protection of strict liability to bystanders. The courts have stated that bystanders should be entitled to even greater protection than a consumer or user. This is because consumers and users have the chance to inspect for defects and to limit their purchases to articles manufactured by reputable manufacturers and sold by reputable retailers, whereas bystanders do not have the same opportunity.

Damages Recoverable for Strict Liability

The damages recoverable in a strict liability action vary by jurisdiction. Damages for personal injuries are recoverable in all jurisdictions that have adopted the doctrine of strict liability, although some jurisdictions limit the dollar amount of the award. Property damage is recoverable in most jurisdictions, but economic loss (e.g., lost income) is recoverable in only a few jurisdictions. Punitive damages are generally allowed if the plaintiff can prove that the defendant either intentionally injured him or her or acted with reckless disregard for his or her safety.

CASE FOR DISCUSSION

Shoshone Coca-Cola Bottling Co. v. Dolinski

420 P.2d 855, 1966 Nev. Lexis 260 (1967) — Supreme Court of Nevada

FACTS

Leo Dolinski purchased a bottle of "Squirt," a soft drink, from a vending machine at a Sea and Ski plant, his place of employment. Dolinski opened the bottle and consumed part of its contents. He immediately became ill. Upon examination, it was found that the bottle contained the decomposed body of a mouse, mouse hair, and mouse feces. Dolinski visited a doctor and was given medicine to counteract nausea. Dolinski suffered physical and mental distress from consuming the decomposed mouse and developed an aversion to soft drinks.

The Shoshone Coca-Cola Bottling Company (Shoshone) manufactured and distributed the Squirt bottle. Dolinski sued Shoshone, basing his lawsuit on the doctrine of strict liability. The state of Nevada had not previously recognized the doctrine of strict liability. However, the trial court adopted the doctrine of strict liability and the jury returned a verdict in favor of the plaintiff. Shoshone appealed.

ISSUE

Should the state of Nevada judicially adopt the doctrine of strict liability? If so, was there a defect in the manufacture of the Squirt bottle that caused the plaintiff's injuries?

COURT'S REASONING

In adopting the doctrine of strict liability, the court stated, "Public policy demands that one who places upon the market a bottled beverage in a condition dangerous for use must be held strictly liable to the ultimate user for injuries resulting from such use, although the seller has exercised all reasonable care."

DECISION AND REMEDY

The Supreme Court of Nevada adopted the doctrine of strict liability and held that the evidence supported the trial court's finding that there was a defect in manufacture. Affirmed.

QUESTIONS

1. Should the courts adopt the theory of strict liability? Why or why not?
2. Was it ethical for Shoshone to argue that it was not liable to Dolinski?
3. Should all in the chain of distribution of a defective product—even those parties who are not responsible for the defect—be held liable under the doctrine of strict liability? Or should liability be based only on fault?

ETHICAL PERSPECTIVE

GENERAL MOTORS HIT WITH BILLION-DOLLAR JUDGMENT

On Christmas Eve, Patricia Anderson was driving her Chevrolet Malibu automobile, which was manufactured by the General Motors Corporation (GM), home from church. Her four young children, ages 1 through 9, and a neighbor, were also in the car. The Chevy Malibu was stopped at a stoplight at 89th Place and Figueroa Street in Los Angeles when a drunken driver plowed his car into the back of the Malibu at 50 to 70 mph. The Malibu burst into flames as its gas tank ruptured and ignited. Although no one died in the crash, the occupants of the Malibu were severely burned. Many required substantial and multiple skin grafts.

The two injured women and four injured children sued GM for product liability. They alleged that the fuel tank of the Chevy Malibu was defectively designed and placed too close to the rear bumper. The accident victims produced evidence that showed that GM knew that the car's fuel-tank design was unsafe but had not changed the design because of cost. The plaintiffs produced GM memos that said it would cost GM $8.59 per vehicle to produce and install a safer fuel tank design, but that it would cost the company only an estimated $2.40 per car not to fix the cars and pay damages to injured victims.

After a 10-week trial, the jurors returned a verdict of $107 million in compensatory damages to the plaintiffs for injuries, disfigurement, and pain and suffering caused to them by the accident. The jury then tacked on $4.9 billion as punitive damages to punish GM. GM, the world's largest automobile company, reported annual earnings of $3 billion in 1998, the year of the verdict.

In its post-trial motions, GM argued that the award of damages, specifically the $4.8 billion of punitive damages, was the result of bias and prejudice of the jury, and asked the trial court judge to reduce the award of damages. This the trial court judge did do: He let the compensatory damages award stand but reduced the award of punitive damages to $1 billion. The revised award is equivalent to 2 percent of GM's net worth and 10 times the compensatory damages.

1. Should General Motors have designed the fuel-tank placement differently? Explain.
2. Was an award of punitive damages warranted in this case? Why or why not?

LEGAL TERMINOLOGY

Actual cause
Assault
Assumption of the risk
Battery
Breach of the duty of care
Causation in fact
Chain of distribution
Civil lawsuit
Comparative negligence
Contributory negligence
Conversion of personal property
"Danger invites rescue" doctrine
Defamation of character
Doctrine of transferred intent
Dram Shop Act
Duty not to willfully or wantonly injure
Duty of care
Duty of ordinary care
Duty of utmost care
False imprisonment
Fireman's rule
Good Samaritan laws
Guest statute
Injunction

Injury
Intentional infliction of emotional distress
Intentional tort
Intervening event
Invasion of the right to privacy
Invitee
Last clear chance rule
Legal cause
Libel
Licensee
Malicious prosecution
Merchant protection statute
Negligence *per se*
Negligent infliction of emotional distress
Professional malpractice
Proximate cause
Punitive damages
Reasonable person standard
Reasonable professional standard
Res ipsa loquitur
Restatement (Second) of Torts
Shopkeeper's privilege
Slander
Social host liability
Strict liability
Superseding event
Tort
Tort damages
Tort of misappropriation of the right to publicity
Tort of outrage
Transferred intent doctrine
Trespass to land
Trespass to personal property
Trespasser
Unintentional tort
Wrongful death action

chapter summary

TORTS AND PRODUCT LIABILITY

Intentional Torts Against Persons	
Assault	Threat of immediate harm or offensive contact, or any action that arouses reasonable apprehension of imminent harm.
Battery	The unauthorized and harmful or offensive physical contact with another person. If a person intends to injure one person but actually harms another person, the law transfers the perpetrator's intent from the target to the actual victim under the *doctrine of transferred intent.*
False Imprisonment	Intentional confinement or restraint of another person without authority or justification and without that person's consent.
Merchant Protection	These statutes permit businesses to stop, detain, and investigate suspected shoplifters (and not be held liable for false imprisonment) if the following requirements are met: 1. There are reasonable grounds for the suspicion. 2. Suspects are detained for only a reasonable time. 3. Investigations are conducted in a reasonable manner. *(continued)*

Defamation of Character	The defendant makes an untrue statement of fact about the plaintiff that is published to a third party. Truth is an absolute defense. Types of defamations: 1. *Slander:* oral defamation 2. *Libel:* written defamation
Public Figure Plaintiffs	Must prove the additional element of *malice.*
Misappropriation of the Right to Publicity	Appropriating another person's name or identity for commercial purposes without that person's consent. Also called *tort of appropriation.*
Invasion of Privacy	Unwarranted and undesired publicity of a private fact about a person. The fact does not have to be untrue. Truth is not a defense.
Intentional Infliction of Emotional Distress	Extreme and outrageous conduct intentionally or recklessly done that causes severe emotional distress. Some states require that the mental distress be manifested by physical injury. Also known as *tort of outrage.*
Malicious Prosecution	A successful defendant in a prior lawsuit can sue the plaintiff if the first lawsuit was frivolous.
Intentional Torts Against Property	
Trespass to Land	Interference with a landowner's right to exclusive possession of his or her land.
Trespass to Personal Property	Injury to another person's personal property or interference with that person's enjoyment of his or her property.
Conversion of Personal Property	Taking over another person's personal property and depriving him or her of the use and enjoyment of the property.
Unintentional Torts (Negligence)	
Definition of Negligence	The omission to do something which a reasonable man would do, or doing something which a prudent and reasonable man would not do.
Elements of Negligence	To establish negligence, the plaintiff must prove: 1. The defendant owed a *duty of care* to the plaintiff. 2. The defendant *breached this duty.* 3. The plaintiff suffered *injury.* 4. The defendant's negligent act *caused* the plaintiff's injury. Two types of causation must be shown: a. *Causation in fact* (or *actual cause*). The defendant's negligent act was the actual cause of the plaintiff's injury. b. *Proximate cause* (or *legal cause*). The defendant is liable only for the *foreseeable* consequences of his or her negligent act.

Special Negligence Doctrines	
Negligent Infliction of Emotional Distress	A person who witnesses a close relative's injury or death may sue the negligent party who caused the accident to recover damages for any emotional distress suffered by the bystander. To recover for *negligent infliction of emotional distress*, the plaintiff must prove: 1. A relative was killed or injured by the defendant. 2. The plaintiff suffered severe emotional distress. 3. The plaintiff's mental distress resulted from a sensory and contemporaneous observance of the accident.
Professional Malpractice	Doctors, lawyers, architects, accountants, and other professionals owe a duty of ordinary care in providing their services. They are judged by a *reasonable professional standard*. Professionals who breach this duty are liable to clients and some third parties for *professional malpractice*.
Negligence *Per Se*	A statute or ordinance establishes the duty of care. A violation of the statute or ordinance constitutes a breach of this duty of care.
Res Ipsa Loquitur	A presumption of negligence is established if the defendant had exclusive control of the instrumentality or situation that caused the plaintiff's injury and the injury would not have ordinarily occurred but for someone's negligence. The defendants may rebut this presumption.
Good Samaritan Laws	Relieve doctors and other medical professionals from liability for ordinary negligence when rendering medical aid in emergency situations.
Dram Shop Acts	State statutes that make taverns and bartenders liable for injuries caused to or by patrons who are served too much alcohol and cause injury to themselves or others.
Guest Statutes	Provide that a driver of a vehicle is not liable for ordinary negligence to passengers he or she gratuitously transports. The driver is liable for gross negligence.
Fireman's Rule	Firefighters, police officers, and other government employees who are injured in the performance of their duties cannot sue the person who negligently caused the dangerous situation that caused the injury.
"Danger Invites Rescue" Doctrine	A person who is injured while going to someone's rescue may sue the person who caused the dangerous situation.
Social Host Liability	Some states make social hosts liable for injuries caused by guests who are served alcohol at a social function and later cause injury because they are intoxicated.
Liability of Landowners	Landowners (and tenants) owe the following duties to persons who come upon their property: 1. *Invitees:* Duty of ordinary care 2. *Licensees:* Duty of ordinary care 3. *Trespassers:* Duty not to willfully and wantonly injure trespassers *(continued)*

Liability of Common Carriers and Innkeepers	Owe a *duty of utmost care* rather than the duty of ordinary care, to protect their passengers and patrons from injury.
Defenses Against Negligence	
Superseding Event	An intervening event, caused by another person, that caused the plaintiff's injuries and thus relieves the defendant from liability.
Assumption of the Risk	A defendant is not liable for the plaintiff's injuries if the plaintiff had knowledge of a specific risk and voluntarily assumed the risk.
Plaintiff Partially at Fault	States have adopted one of the following two rules that affect a defendant's liability if the plaintiff had been partially at fault for causing his or her own injuries: 1. *Contributory negligence.* A plaintiff cannot recover anything from the defendant. 2. *Comparative negligence.* Damages are apportioned according to the parties' fault. Also called *comparative fault.*
Product Liability	
Strict Liability in Tort	A manufacturer or seller who sells a defective product is liable to the ultimate user who is injured thereby. All in the chain of distribution are liable irrespective of fault. Sometimes called *vertical liability.*

WORKING THE WEB

WWW

Visit the Web sites listed below for more information about the topics covered in this chapter.

1. Find a state court case opinion relating to intentional torts. See for example, a state-based plaintiffs' trial lawyers association site: **www.wstla.org**, or, at the national level, the Association of Trial Lawyers of America: **www.atla.org**, or the ABA Tort and Insurance Practice Section: **www.abanet.org/tips/thebrief.html**.
2. Find a medical malpractice case. For the viewpoint of the defense, see **www.dri.org**. For the insurance industry's view, see **www.ircweb.org**.

Check the following site as a starting point for the questions below:
www.law.cornell.edu/topics/torts.html

3. Find a state court case that establishes the rule in your jurisdiction on Social Host Liability.
4. Find the statute in your jurisdiction that contains the Good Samaritan Rule.
5. Find the statute in your jurisdiction that contains the Innkeepers Liability Law.

CRITICAL LEGAL THINKING QUESTIONS

1. What is the legal purpose for allowing a person to sue for defamation of character?
2. Should the right to publicity be a protected right? Why or why not?
3. Should the tort of intentional infliction of emotional distress be recognized by the law? What difficulties arise in trying to apply this tort?
4. What are the elements necessary to prove negligence? Describe each element.
5. Explain the doctrine of proximate cause. Give an example of this doctrine's application.
6. Should the law recognize the doctrine of negligent infliction of emotional distress? Are the elements easy to meet?
7. Compare the doctrine of contributory negligence to the doctrine of comparative negligence.
8. What does the Good Samaritan law provide? Do you think this law serves a good purpose?
9. What does the doctrine of strict liability provide? Do you think this doctrine is fair?
10. What are punitive damages? What public policies are served by an award of punitive damages?

CASE FOR BRIEFING

Read Case 6 in Appendix A *(Braun v. Soldier of Fortune Magazine, Inc.)*. Review and brief the case using the *Critical Legal Thinking* "Briefing the Case" example described in Chapter 1.

CASES FOR DISCUSSION

6.1 *Manning v. Grimsley*

643 F.2d 20, 1981 U.S. App. Lexis 19782 (1981)
United States Court of Appeals, First Circuit

FACTS On September 16, 1975, the Baltimore Orioles professional baseball team was at Boston's Fenway Park to play the Boston Red Sox. Ross Grimsley was a pitcher for the visiting Baltimore club. During one period of the game, Grimsley was warming up in the bull pen, throwing pitches to a catcher. During this warmup, Boston spectators in the stands heckled Grimsley. After Grimsley had completed warming up and the catcher had left from behind the plate in the bull pen, Grimsley wound up as if he were going to throw the ball in his hand at the plate, then turned and threw the ball at one of the hecklers in the stand. The ball traveled at about 80 miles an hour, passed through a wire fence protecting the spectators, missed the heckler that Grimsley was aiming at, and hit another spectator, David Manning, Jr., causing injury. Manning sued Grimsley and the Baltimore Orioles.

ISSUE Are the defendants liable?

6.2 *Johnson v. Kmart Enterprises, Inc.*

297 N.W.2d 74, 1980 Wisc. App. Lexis 3197 (1980)
Court of Appeals of Wisconsin

FACTS At about 7:30 P.M. on September 8, 1976, Deborah A. Johnson entered a Kmart store located in Madison, Wisconsin, to purchase some diapers and several cans of motor oil. She took her young child along to enable her to purchase the correct-size diapers, carrying the child in an infant seat that the mother had purchased at Kmart 2 or 3 weeks previously. A large Kmart price tag was still attached to the infant seat. Johnson purchased the diapers and oil and some children's clothes. She was in a hurry to leave because it was 8:00 P.M., her child's feeding time, and she hurried through the checkout lane. She paid for the diapers, the oil, and the clothing.

Just after leaving the store, she heard someone ask her to stop. She turned around and saw a Kmart security officer. He showed her a badge and asked her to come back into the store, which she did. The man stated, "I have reason to believe that you have stolen this car seat." Johnson explained that she had purchased the seat previously. She demanded to see the manager, who was called to the scene. When Johnson pointed out that the seat had cat hairs, food crumbs, and milk stains on it, the man said, "I'm really sorry. There's been a terrible mistake. You can go." Johnson looked at the clock when she left, which read 8:20 P.M. Johnson sued Kmart for false imprisonment.

ISSUE Is Kmart liable?

6.3 *Karns v. Emerson Electric Co.*

817 F.2d 1452, 1987 U.S. App. Lexis 5608 (1987)
United States Court of Appeals, Tenth Circuit

FACTS The Emerson Electric Co. manufactures and sells a product called the Weed Eater Model XR-90. The Weed Eater is a multipurpose weed-trimming and brush-cutting device. It consists of a handheld gasoline-powered engine connected to a long drive shaft, at the end of which can be attached various tools for cutting weeds and brush. One such attachment is a 10-inch circular sawblade capable of cutting through growth up to 2 inches in diameter. When this sawblade is attached to the Weed Eater, a blade edge of approximately 270 degrees is exposed when in use.

The owner's manual contained the following warning: "Keep children away. All people and pets should be kept at a safe distance from the work area, at least 30 feet, especially when using the blade."

Donald Pearce, a 13-year-old boy, was helping his uncle clear an overgrown yard. The uncle was operating a Weed Eater XR-90 with the circular sawblade attachment. When Pearce stooped to pick up something off the ground about 6 to 10 feet behind and slightly to the left of where his uncle was operating the Weed Eater, the sawblade on the Weed Eater struck something near the ground. The Weed Eater kicked back to the left and cut off Pearce's right arm to the elbow. Pearce, through his mother, Charlotte Karns, sued Emerson to recover damages under strict liability.

ISSUE Is Emerson liable?

ETHICS CASE

6.4 *Luque v. McLean, Trustee*

104 Cal.Rptr.443, 501 P.2d 1163, 1972 Cal. Lexis 245 (1972)
Supreme Court of California

FACTS Celestino Luque lived with his cousins Harry and Laura Dunn in Millbrae, California. The Dunns purchased a rotary lawn mower from Rhoads Hardware. The lawn mower was manufactured by Air Capital Manufacturing Company and was distributed by Garehime Corporation. On December 4, 1965, neighbors asked Luque to mow their lawn. While Luque was cutting the lawn, he noticed a small carton in the path of the lawn mower. Luque left the lawn mower in a stationary position with its motor running and walked around the side of the lawn mower to remove the carton. As he did so, he suddenly slipped on the wet grass and fell backward. Luque's left hand entered the unguarded hole of the lawn mower and was caught in the revolving blade, which turns at 175 miles per hour and 100 revolutions per second. Luque's hand was severely mangled and lacerated. The word *Caution* was printed above the unguarded hole on the lawn mower.

Luque sued Rhoads Hardware, Air Capital, and Garehime Corporation for strict liability. The defendants argued that strict liability does not apply to *patent* (obvious) defects.

ISSUE Was it ethical for the defendants to argue that they were not liable for patent defects? Would patent defects ever be corrected if the defendants' contention were accepted by the court? Who wins?

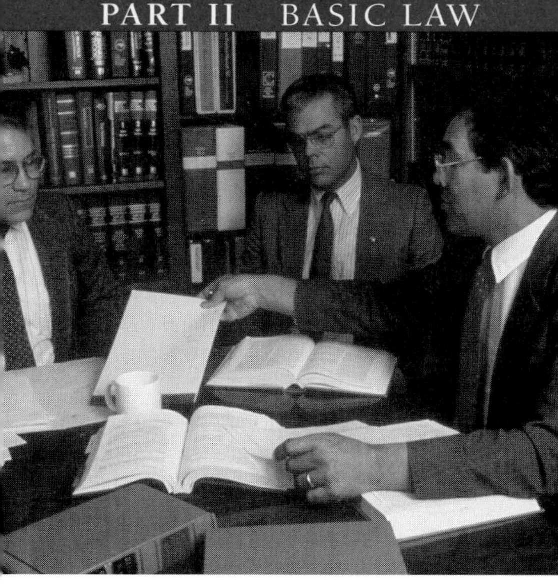

7 Contracts and E-Commerce

The movement of the progressive societies has hitherto been a movement from status to contract.

—SIR HENRY MAINE, *ANCIENT LAWS*, CH. 5

CHAPTER OBJECTIVES

After studying this chapter, you should be able to

1. List and describe the elements necessary to form a valid contract, including agreement, consideration, capacity, and lawful object.
2. Define sales and lease contracts governed by the Uniform Commercial Code (UCC).
3. Describe online contracts and the law that governs e-commerce.
4. Explain breach of contract and describe the different types of monetary damages that can be awarded for breach of contract.
5. Describe the different types of equitable remedies and explain the circumstances in which they would be awarded.

CHAPTER OUTLINE

- Parties to a Contract
- Requirements of a Contract
- Agreement
- Consideration
- Case for Discussion: *Wrench LLC v. Taco Bell*
- Capacity to Contract
- Case for Discussion: *Alden v. Presley*
- Lawful Object
- Statute of Frauds
- Case for Discussion: *Flood v. Fidelity & Guaranty*
- Assignment of Rights
- Third-Party Beneficiaries
- Performance
- Remedies
- Case for Discussion: *Lim v. The .TV Corporation*
- The UCC
- Legal Terminology
- Case for Discussion: *Brumfield v. Death Row Records, Inc.*
- Chapter Summary
- Internet Exercises and Cases

INTRODUCTION

Contracts are the basis of many of our daily activities. They provide the means for individuals and businesses to sell and otherwise transfer property, services, and other rights. The purchase of goods, such as books and automobiles, is based on sales contracts; the hiring of employees is based on service contracts; the use of software is subject to licensing agreements; and the lease of an apartment is based on a rental contract. The list is almost endless. Without enforceable contracts, commerce would collapse. Contracts are voluntarily entered into by parties. The terms of the contract become **private law** between the parties. The contract between parties is the law between them, and the courts are obliged to give legal effect to such contracts according to the true interests of the parties.

This chapter introduces you to the study of traditional contract law, commercial transactions governed by the Uniform Commercial Code (UCC), and online commerce. The discussion includes the definition of a contract, requirements for forming a contract, the performance of contracts, and remedies for breach of contracts.

Definition of and Parties to a Contract

> Freedom of contracts begins where equality of bargaining power begins.
>
> —Oliver Wendell Holmes, Jr. (1928)

A **contract** is an agreement that is enforceable by a court of law or equity. A simple and widely recognized definition of a contract is provided by the Restatement (Second) of Contracts: "A contract is a promise or a set of promises for the breach of which the law gives a remedy or the performance of which the law in some way recognizes a duty [Restatement (Second) of Contracts, § 1].

Parties to a Contract

Every contract involves at least two parties. The **offeror** is the party who makes an offer to enter into a contract. The **offeree** is the party to whom the offer is made (see Exhibit 7.1). In making an offer, the offeror promises to do—or to refrain from doing—something. The offeree then has the power to create a contract by accepting the offeror's offer. A contract is created if the offer is accepted. No contract is created if the offer is not accepted.

Requirements of a Contract

To be an enforceable contract, the following four basic requirements must be met:

1. **Agreement:** To have an enforceable contract, there must be an agreement between the parties.
2. **Consideration:** The promise must be supported by a bargained-for consideration that is legally sufficient.
3. **Contractual capacity:** The parties to a contract must have the capacity to contract.
4. **Lawful object:** The object of the contract must be lawful, or legal.

The following text discusses these requirements in greater detail.

EXHIBIT 7.1 *Parties to a contract.*

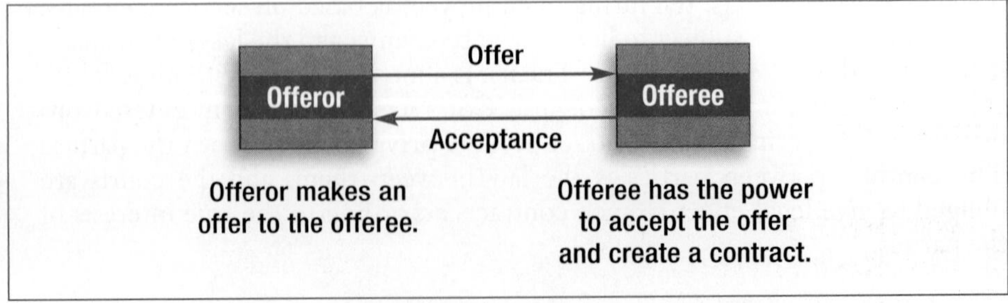

Evolution of the Modern Law of Contracts

The use of contracts goes back to ancient times. The common law of contracts developed in England around the 15th century. American contract law evolved from the English common law.

At first the United States adopted a *laissez-faire* approach to the law of contracts. The central theme of this theory was *freedom of contract.* The parties (such as consumers, shopkeepers, farmers, and traders) generally dealt with one another face-to-face, had equal knowledge and bargaining power, and had the opportunity to inspect the goods prior to sale. Contract terms were openly negotiated. There was little, if any, government regulation of the right to contract. This "pure" or **classical law of contracts** produced objective rules.

The Industrial Revolution changed many of the underlying assumptions of pure contract law. For example, as large corporations developed and gained control of crucial resources, the traditional balance of parties' bargaining power shifted: Large corporations now had the most power. Buyers often did not deal face-to-face with sellers, and there was not always an opportunity to inspect the goods prior to sale. Eventually sellers began using **form contracts** that offered their goods to buyers on a take-it-or-leave-it basis. Most contracts in the United States today are form contracts.

In recent years, the advent of the Web and the Internet has created a new breed of contracts. These include e-mail contracts, Web contracts, and other contracts pertaining to online commerce. Special contract rules have been developed to apply to **electronic commerce (e-commerce)**. Federal and state governments alike have enacted statutes intended to protect consumers, creditors, and others from unfair contracts. Today, under this **modern law of contracts,** there is substantial government regulation of the right to contract.

AGREEMENT

Agreement is the manifestation by two or more persons of the substance of a contract. It requires an *offer* and *acceptance.* The process of reaching an agreement usually proceeds as follows: Prior to entering into a contract, the parties may engage in preliminary negotiations about price, time of performance, and such. At some point during these negotiations, one party makes an **offer.** The offer sets forth the terms under which the offeror is willing to enter into the contract. The offeree has the power to create an agreement by accepting the offer.

A contract is a promise.

—William Paley

Requirements of the Offer

Section 24 of the Restatement (Second) of Contracts defines an *offer* as: "The manifestation of willingness to enter into a bargain, so made as to justify another person in understanding that his assent to that bargain is invited and will conclude it." To be effective:

1. The offeror must *objectively intend* to be bound by the offer.
2. The terms of the offer must be definite or reasonably *certain.*
3. The offer must be *communicated* to the offeree.

Consider the following examples: A question such as "Are you interested in selling your building for $2 million?" is not an offer. It is an invitation to make an offer or an invitation to negotiate. But the statement "I will buy your building for $2 million" is a valid offer because it indicates the offeror's present intent to contract.

Suppose the owner of Company A has lunch with the owner of Company B. In the course of their conversation, Company A's owner exclaims in frustration, "For $2 I'd sell the whole computer division!" A valid contract cannot result from that offer made in anger.

SIDEBAR

Option Contracts
An offeree can prevent the offeror from revoking his or her offer by paying the offeror compensation to keep the offer open for an agreed-upon period of time. This is called an **option contract,** in which the offeror agrees not to sell the property to anyone other than the offeree during the option period. The death or incompetency of either party does not terminate an option contract unless it is for the performance of a personal service. **Example:** Anne Mason offers to sell a piece of real estate to Harold Greenberg for $1 million. Mr. Greenberg wants time to make a decision, so he pays Ms. Mason $20,000 to keep her offer open to him for 6 months. At any time during the option period, Mr. Greenberg may exercise his option and pay Ms. Mason the $1 million purchase price. If he lets the option expire, however, Ms. Mason may keep the $20,000 and sell the property to someone else.

Termination of the Offer

A valid offer gives the offeree the power to accept the offer and thereby create a contract. This power, however, does not continue indefinitely. An offer can be terminated by the *action of the parties.*

Under the common law, an offeror may revoke (withdraw) an offer any time prior to its acceptance by the offeree. Generally, this is so even if the offeror promised to keep the offer open for a longer period of time. An offer is terminated if the offeree rejects it. Any subsequent attempt by the offeree to accept the offer is ineffective and is construed as a new offer that the original offeror (now the offeree) is free to accept or reject.

A **counteroffer** by the offeree simultaneously terminates the offeror's offer and creates a new offer. A counteroffer might be: "I think $250,000 is too high for the computers. I will pay you $200,000." With this, the original offer is terminated and the counteroffer is a new offer that the other is free to accept or reject.

Acceptance

Acceptance is a manifestation of assent by the offeree to the terms of the offer in a manner invited or required by the offer as measured by the objective theory of contracts. Generally (1) *unilateral contracts* can be accepted only by the offeree's performance of the required act, and (2) a *bilateral contract* can be accepted by an offeree who promises to perform (or, where permitted, by performance of) the requested act.

Only the offeree has the legal power to accept an offer and create a contract. Third persons usually do not have the power to accept an offer. If an offer is made individually to two or more persons, each has the power to accept the offer. Once an offeree accepts the offer, though, it terminates as to the other offerees. An offer that is made to two or more persons jointly must be accepted jointly. .

Express and Implied Contracts

An **actual contract** (as distinguished from a quasi-contract, discussed later in this chapter) may be either *express* or *implied-in-fact.*

1. **Express contracts** are stated in oral or written words. Examples of such contracts include an oral agreement to purchase a neighbor's bicycle and a written agreement to buy an automobile from a dealership.
2. **Implied-in-fact contracts** are implied from the conduct of the parties. Implied-in-fact contracts leave more room for questions than express contracts do. The following elements must be established to create an implied-in-fact contract:
   A. The plaintiff provided property or services to the defendant.

A Contract Is a Contract Is a Contract

Mighty Morphin Power Rangers was a phenomenal success as a television series. The Power Rangers battled to save the universe from all sorts of diabolical plots and bad guys. They also were featured in a profitable line of toys and garments bearing the Power Rangers' logo. The Power Rangers' name and logo are known to millions of children and their parents worldwide. The claim of ownership of the logo for the Power Rangers ended up in a battle itself, this time in a courtroom.

David Dees is a designer who works as d/b/a David Dees Illustration. Saban Entertainment, Inc. (Saban), which owns the copyright and trademark to Power Ranger figures and the name "Power Ranger," hired Dees as an independent contractor to design a logo for the Power Rangers. The contract signed by the parties was entitled "Work-for-Hire/Independent Contractor Agreement." The contract was drafted by Saban with the help of its attorneys; Dees signed the agreement without the representation of legal counsel.

Dees designed the logo currently used for the Power Rangers and, pursuant to the contract, was paid $250 to transfer his copyright ownership in the logo. Subsequently, Dees sued Saban to recover damages for copyright and trademark infringement. Saban defended, arguing that "a contract is a contract is a contract," and Dees was bound by the agreement he had signed.

The trial court agreed with Saban, finding that the "Work-for-Hire/Independent Contractor Agreement" was an enforceable contract between the parties and that Dees had transferred his ownership interests in the logo to Saban. Dees appealed. The court of appeals affirmed the judgment for Saban, stating, "The disputed agreement transferred plaintiff's copyright in the Mighty Morphin Power Rangers' logo with as much specificity as the law requires." The court found that "a contract is a contract is a contract," at least in this case. Dees' appeal to the U.S. Supreme Court was denied.

Dees, d/b/a David Dees Illustration v. Saban Entertainment, Inc. [131 F.3d 146, 1997 U.S. App. Lexis 39173 (1997)]

B. The plaintiff expected to be paid by the defendant for the property or services and did not provide the property or services gratuitously.
C. The defendant was given an opportunity to reject the property or services provided by the plaintiff but failed to do so.

Consideration

Consideration is a necessary element for a contract to exist. Consideration is defined as the thing of value given in exchange for a promise. Consideration can come in many forms. The most common types consist of either a tangible payment (e.g., money or property) or the performance of an act (e.g., providing legal services). Less-usual forms of consideration include the forbearance of a legal right (e.g., accepting an out-of-court settlement in exchange for dropping a lawsuit) and noneconomic forms of consideration (e.g., refraining from drinking, using tobacco, swearing, or playing cards or billiards for money for a specified time period).

Written contracts are presumed to be supported by consideration. This is a rebuttable presumption that may be overcome by sufficient evidence. A few states provide that contracts made under seal cannot be challenged for lack of consideration.

CASE FOR DISCUSSION

Wrench LLC v. Taco Bell Corporation

256 F.3d 446, 2001 U.S.App. Lexis 15097 (2003) — United States Court of Appeals, Sixth Circuit

FACTS

Thomas Rinks and Joseph Shields created the "Psycho Chihuahua" cartoon character, which they promote, market, and license through their company, Wrench LLC. The Psycho Chihuahua is a clever, feisty, cartoon-character dog with an attitude; a self-confident, edgy, cool dog. In June 1996, Rinks and Shields attended a licensing trade show in New York City, where they were approached by two Taco Bell employees, Rudy Pollak, a vice president, and Ed Alfaro, a creative services manager. Taco Bell owns and operates a nation-wide chain of fast food Mexican restaurants. Pollak and Alfaro expressed interest in the Psycho Chihuahua character for Taco Bell advertisements because they thought his character would appeal to Taco Bell's core consumers, males aged 18 to 24. Pollak and Alfaro obtained some Psycho Chihuahua materials to take back with them to Taco Bell's headquarters.

Later, Alfaro contacted Rinks and asked him to create art boards combining Psycho Chihuahua with the Taco Bell name and image. Rinks and Shields prepared art boards and sent them to Alfaro along with Psycho Chihuahua T-shirts, hats, and stickers. Alfaro showed these materials to Taco Bell's vice president of brand management as well as to Taco Bell's outside advertising agency. Alfaro tested the Psycho Chihuahua marketing concept with focus groups. Rinks suggested to Alfaro that instead of using the cartoon version of Psycho Chihuahua in its advertisements, Taco Bell should use a live Chihuahua dog manipulated by computer graphic imaging, who had the personality of Psycho Chihuahua and a love for Taco Bell food. In early March 1997, Rinks and Shields gave a formal presentation of this concept to Taco Bell's marketing department. One idea presented by Rinks and Shields was a commercial in which a male Chihuahua dog passed by a female Chihuahua dog in order to get to Taco Bell food. Taco Bell did not enter into an express contract with Wrench LLC, Rinks, or Shields.

On March 18, 1997, Taco Bell hired a new outside advertising agency, Chiat/Day. Taco Bell gave Chiat/Day materials received from Rinks and Shields regarding the Psycho Chihuahua. On June 2, 1997, Chiat/Day proposed using a Chihuahua in Taco Bell commercials. One commercial had a male Chihuahua passing up a female Chihuahua to get to a person seated on a bench eating Taco Bell food. Chiat/Day says that it conceived these ideas by itself. In July 1997, Taco Bell aired its first Chihuahua commercial in the United States, which became an instant success and the basis of its advertising. Taco Bell paid nothing to Wrench LLC, or to Rinks and Shields. Plaintiffs Wrench LLC, Rinks, and Shields sued defendant Taco Bell to recover damages for breach of an implied-in-fact contract. The district court granted summary judgment in favor of Taco Bell. Wrench LLC, Rinks, and Shields appealed.

ISSUE

Do the plaintiffs Wrench LLC, Rinks, and Shields state a cause of action for the breach of an implied-in-fact contract against Taco Bell?

COURT'S REASONING

The U.S. court of appeals held that although no specific dollar numbers were ever mentioned, Taco Bell understood that if it used the Psycho Chihuahua concept it would have to pay the plaintiffs for doing so. The court noted that the plaintiffs' state law implied-in-fact contract claim is for Taco Bell's breach of this promise to pay for the plaintiffs' creative work and ideas. The court of appeals stated that there was strong circumstantial evidence proving that Taco Bell used the plaintiffs' Psycho Chihuahua concept.

DECISION AND REMEDY

The court of appeals held that the plaintiffs had stated a proper cause of action against defendant Taco Bell for breach of an implied-in-fact contract. The court of appeals reversed the judgment of the district court and remanded the case for trial.

QUESTIONS

1. What does the doctrine of implied-in-fact contract provide? Explain.
2. Did Taco Bell act ethically in this case? Did Chiat/Day act ethically in this case?
3. Do you think there was an implied-in-fact contract in this case? If so, what damages should be awarded to the plaintiffs?

Gift Promises

Gift promises, also called **gratuitous promises,** are unenforceable because they lack consideration. To change a gift promise into an enforceable promise, the promisee must offer to do something in exchange—that is, provide consideration—for the promise. Suppose Mrs. Colby promised to give her son $10,000 and then rescinded the promise. The son would have no recourse because it was a gift promise that lacked consideration. If, however, Mrs. Colby promised her son $10,000 for getting an "A" in his business law course and the son performed as required, the contract would be enforceable. A completed gift promise cannot be rescinded for lack of consideration.

Capacity to Contract

Generally, the law presumes that the parties to a contract have the requisite **contractual capacity** to enter into the contract. Certain persons, however, do not have this capacity. They include minors, mentally incompetent persons, and intoxicated persons. The common law of contracts and many state statutes protect persons who lack contractual capacity from having contracts enforced against them. The party asserting incapacity or his or her guardian, conservator, or other legal representative bears the burden of proof.

> Contracts must not be the sports of an idle hour, mere matters of pleasantry and badinage, never intended by the parties to have any serious effect whatever.
>
> —Lord Stowell, *Dalrymple v. Dalrymple* (1811)

Minors

Minors do not always have the maturity, experience, or sophistication needed to enter into contracts with adults. States have enacted statutes that specify the *age of majority.* The most prevalent age of majority is 18 years for males and females alike. Any age below the statutory age of majority is called the **period of minority.**

To protect minors, the law recognizes the **infancy doctrine,** which allows minors to **disaffirm,** or **cancel,** most contracts they have entered into with adults. A minor's right to disaffirm a contract is based on public policy, with the reasoning that minors should be protected from unscrupulous behavior of adults.

Under the infancy doctrine, a minor has the option of choosing whether to enforce the contract. That is, the contract is **voidable** by a minor. The adult party is bound to the minor's decision. If both parties to the contract are minors, both parties have the right to disaffirm the contract.

A minor can expressly disaffirm a contract orally, in writing, or by the minor's conduct. No special formalities are required. The contract may be disaffirmed at any time prior to reaching the age of majority plus a "reasonable time." The designation of a reasonable time is determined on a case-by-case basis.

Minors are obligated to pay for the **necessaries of life** that they contract for. Otherwise, many adults would refuse to sell these items to them. There is no standard definition of a necessity of life, but items such as food, clothing, shelter, medical services, and the like are generally understood to fit this category. Goods and services such as automobiles, tools of trade, education, and vocational training also have been found to be necessities of life in some situations. The minor's age, lifestyle, and economic status in life influence what is considered necessary.

CASE FOR DISCUSSION

Alden v. Presley

637 S.W. 2d 862, 1982 Tenn. Lexis 340 (1982) Supreme Court of Tennessee

FACTS

Elvis Presley, a singer of great renown and a man of substantial wealth, became engaged to Ginger Alden. He was generous with the Alden family, paying for landscaping the lawn, installing a swimming pool, and making other gifts. When his fiancée's mother, Jo Laverne Alden, sought to divorce her husband, Presley promised to pay off the remaining mortgage indebtedness on the Alden home, which Mrs. Alden was to receive in the divorce settlement. On August 16, 1977, Presley died suddenly, leaving the mortgage unpaid. When the legal representative of Presley's estate refused to pay the $39,587 mortgage, Mrs. Alden brought an action to enforce Presley's promise. The trial court denied recovery. Mrs. Alden appealed.

ISSUE

Was Presley's promise to pay the mortgage enforceable?

COURT'S REASONING

Under contract law, gift promises are unenforceable because they lack consideration. The court found that plaintiff Alden had not given any consideration in exchange for Presley's promise. The court also found that the gift promise had not been completed by Presley. Therefore, the unexpected gift promise could not be enforced against Presley's estate.

DECISION

The supreme court held that Presley's promise was a gratuitous executory promise that was not supported by consideration. As such, it was unenforceable against Presley's estate. The court dismissed the case and assessed costs against the plaintiff.

QUESTIONS

1. Should gratuitous promises be enforced? Why or why not?
2. Was it unethical for the representative of Presley's estate to refuse to complete the gift? Did he have any other choice?
3. Does it make a difference if a gift promise is executed or executory? Explain.

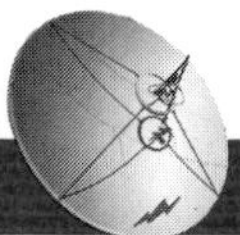

INFORMATION TECHNOLOGY

NONDISCLOSURE AGREEMENTS

NDAs have been around for a long time. A **nondisclosure agreement**—or **NDA,** as they are called—swears the signatory to secrecy about confidential ideas, trade secrets, and other nonpublic information revealed by the party proffering the NDA. Traditionally NDAs have been used by lawyers, investment bankers, and others involved in secret takeovers and other large corporate deals. Today, many entrepreneurs, particularly those in Internet and high-tech industries, are also using NDAs.

NDAs serve a purpose in that they protect people who have a great idea (or so they think) and want to share it with a potential partner, investor, lawyer, or investment banker, but want assurance that the recipient of the information will not steal or reveal the information to anyone else.

An NDA is an enforceable contract, so if someone violates it, the disclosing party can sue the breaching party for damages. Bill Gates of Microsoft requires plumbers and others who work on his house to sign NDAs. Sabeer Bhatia, founder of Hotmail, collected more than 400 NDAs in 2 years before selling his company to Microsoft for $400 million.

Although it may not be hard to get some people to sign NDAs, others balk. Some friends and relatives refuse to sign NDAs thrust on them because NDAs present an aura of distrust. Industry bigwigs—venture capitalists, securities analysts, and successful technology companies—routinely refuse to sign NDAs because they see too many similar ideas and do not want their tongues tied by any single one. NDAs will continue to increase in use, though.

Mentally Incompetent Persons

Mental incapacity may arise because of mental illness, brain damage, mental retardation, senility, and the like. The law protects people suffering from substantial mental incapacity from enforcement of contracts against them because these persons may not understand the consequences of their actions in entering into a contract.

Intoxicated Persons

Most states provide that contracts entered into by certain intoxicated persons are voidable by that person. The intoxication may occur because of alcohol or drug use. The contract is not voidable by the other party if that party had contractual capacity. Under the majority rule, the contract is voidable only if the person was so intoxicated when the contract was entered into that he or she was incapable of understanding or comprehending the nature of the transaction. In most states, this rule holds even if the intoxication was self-induced. A disaffirmed contract based on intoxication generally must be returned to the status quo.

LAWFUL OBJECT

As an essential element for the formation of a contract, the object of the contract must be a **lawful object.** A contract to perform an illegal act is called an **illegal contract.** Illegal contracts are void; they cannot be enforced by either party to the contract. Because illegal contracts are void, the parties cannot sue for nonperformance.

Further, if an illegal contract is executed, the court will generally leave the parties where it finds them. Most contracts are presumed to be lawful. The burden of proving that a contract is unlawful rests on the party who asserts its illegality.

Federal and state legislatures alike have enacted statutes prohibiting certain types of conduct. Contracts to perform an activity that is prohibited by statute are illegal contracts. These contracts include gambling contracts, contracts that provide for usurious rates of interest, and contracts that violate Sabbath laws and licensing statutes.

Illegality—Contracts Contrary to Public Policy

Certain contracts are illegal because they are **contracts contrary to public policy.** Although *public policy* eludes a precise definition, the courts have held contracts to be contrary to public policy if they have a negative impact on society or interfere with the public's safety and welfare.

Statute of Frauds—Writing Requirement

All states have enacted a **Statute of Frauds** that requires certain types of contracts to be in *writing*. This statute is intended to ensure that the terms of important contracts are not forgotten, misunderstood, or fabricated.

Generally, an *executory contract* that is not in writing—even though the Statute of Frauds requires it to be—is unenforceable by either party. (If the contract is valid in all other respects, however, it may be voluntarily performed by the parties.) The Statute of Frauds is usually raised by one party as a defense to enforcement of the contract by the other party. But if an oral contract that should have been in writing under the Statute of Frauds is already executed, neither party can seek to rescind the contract on the ground of noncompliance with the Statute of Frauds. Contracts that are required to be in writing under the Statute of Frauds are discussed in the following paragraphs.

Two lawyers shake hands to seal the deal outside the Los Angeles County Courthouse, California.

Contracts Involving Interests in Land

Any contract that transfers an ownership interest in **real property** must be in writing to be enforceable under the Statute of Frauds. Real property includes the land itself, buildings, trees, soil, minerals, timber, plants, crops, fixtures, and things permanently affixed to the land or buildings. Certain personal property that is permanently affixed to the real property—for example, built-in cabinets in a house—are *fixtures* that become part of the real property.

Other contracts that transfer an ownership interest in land must be in writing under the Statute of Frauds. For example, borrowers often give a lender an interest in real property as security for the repayment of a loan. This must be done through a written mortgage or **deed of trust.** A **lease** is the transfer of the right to use real property for a specified period of time. Most Statutes of Frauds require leases for a term of more than one year to be in writing.

CASE FOR DISCUSSION

Flood v. Fidelity & Guaranty Life Insurance Co.

394 So.2d 1311, 1981 La. App. Lexis 3538 (1981) **Court of Appeals of Louisiana**

FACTS

Ellen and Richard Alvin Flood, who were married in 1965, lived in a mobile home in Louisiana. Richard worked as a maintenance man and Ellen was employed at an insurance agency. Evidence at trial showed that Ellen was unhappy with her marriage. Ellen took out a life insurance policy on the life of her husband and named herself as beneficiary. The policy was issued by Fidelity & Guaranty Life Insurance Co. (Fidelity).

In June 1972, Richard became unexpectedly ill. He was taken to the hospital, where his condition improved. After a visit at the hospital from his wife, Richard died. Ellen was criminally charged with the murder of her husband by poisoning. Evidence showed that six medicine bottles at the couple's home, including Tylenol and paregoric bottles, contained arsenic. The court found that Ellen had fed Richard ice cubes laced with arsenic at the hospital.

Ellen was tried and convicted of the murder of her husband. As beneficiary of Richard's life insurance policy, Ellen requested Fidelity to pay her the benefits. Fidelity refused to pay the benefits and returned all premiums paid on the policy. This suit followed. The district court held in favor of Ellen Flood and awarded her the benefits of the life insurance policy. Fidelity appealed.

ISSUE

Was the life insurance policy an illegal contract that is void?

COURT'S REASONING

Louisiana follows the majority rule that holds, as a matter of public policy, that a beneficiary named in a life insurance policy is not entitled to the proceeds of the insurance if the beneficiary feloniously kills the insured. Applying this rule, the appellate court held that Ellen Flood could not recover the life insurance benefits from the policy she had taken out on her husband's life. The court stated: "Life insurance policies are procured because life is, indeed, precarious and uncertain. Our law does not and cannot sanction any scheme which has as its purpose the certain infliction of death for, inter alia, financial gain through receipt of the proceeds of life insurance. To sanction this policy in any way would surely shackle the spirit of the letter and life of our laws."

DECISION AND REMEDY

The appellate court held that the life insurance policy that Ellen Flood had taken out on the life of her husband was void based on public policy. Reversed.

QUESTIONS

1. Should Ellen Flood have been allowed to retain the insurance proceeds in this case?
2. Did Ellen Flood act unethically in this case? Did she act illegally?
3. What would be the economic consequences if persons could recover insurance proceeds for losses caused by their illegal activities (e.g., murder, arson)?

"Heads I Win, Tails You Lose"

Sometimes courts face a close question of whether a contract is illegal. Consider the following case.

R. D. Ryno Jr. owned Bavarian Motors, an automobile dealership in Fort Worth, Texas. On March 5, 1981, Lee Tyra discussed purchasing a 1980 BMW M-1 from Ryno for $125,000. Ryno then suggested a double-or-nothing coin flip, to which Tyra agreed. When Tyra won the coin flip, Ryno said, "It's yours," and handed Tyra the keys and German title to the car. Tyra drove away in the car. This suit ensued as to the ownership of the car. The trial court held in favor of Tyra. Ryno appealed. Who owns the car?

The appellate court held that Tyra, winner of the coin toss, owned the car. The appellate court reasoned as follows:

> Ryno complains that the trial court erred in granting the Tyra judgment because the judgment enforces a gambling contract. We find there was sufficient evidence to sustain the jury finding that Ryno intended to transfer to Tyra his ownership interest in the BMW at the time he delivered the documents, keys, and possession of the automobile to Tyra. We agree with appellant Ryno that his wager with Tyra was unenforceable. The trial court could not have compelled Ryno to honor his wager by delivering the BMW to Tyra. However, Ryno did deliver the BMW to Tyra and the facts incident to that delivery are sufficient to establish a transfer by gift of the BMW from Ryno to Tyra.

The appellate court found that there was an illegal contract and left the parties where it found them—that is, with Tyra in possession of the car. [*Ryno v. Tyra*, 752 S.W.2d 148, 1988 Tex. App. Lexis 1646 (Tex.App. 1988)]

One-Year Rule

According to the Statute of Frauds, an executory contract that cannot be performed by its own terms within one year of its formation must be in writing. This **one-year rule** is intended to prevent disputes about contract terms that otherwise may occur toward the end of a long-term contract. If performance of the contract is possible within the one-year period, the contract may be oral.

Contracts for the Sale of Goods

Statute of frauds: That unfortunate statute, the misguided application of which has been the cause of so many frauds.
—Bacon, V. C., *Morgan v. Worthington* (1878)

UCC Section 201 is the basic Statute of Frauds provision for sales contracts. It requires that contracts for the sale of goods costing $500 or more must be in writing to be enforceable. If the contract price of an original sales contract is below $500, it does not have to be in writing under the UCC Statute of Frauds, but if a modification of the contract increases the sales price to $500 or more, the modification has to be in writing to be enforceable [UCCB § 2-209(3)].

Formality of the Writing

Many written commercial contracts are long, detailed documents that have been negotiated by the parties and drafted and reviewed by their lawyers. Other written contracts are preprinted forms that are prepared in advance to be used in recurring situations.

To be legally binding, a written contract does not have to be either drafted by a lawyer or formally typed. Generally, the law only requires a writing containing the essential terms of the parties' agreement. Under this rule, any writing—letters,

ETHICAL PERSPECTIVE

UNCONSCIONABLE CONTRACT

The general rule of freedom of contract holds that if (1) the object of a contract is lawful and (2) the other elements for the formation of a contract are met, the courts will enforce a contract according to its terms. Although it is generally presumed that parties are capable of protecting their own interests when contracting, it is a fact of life that dominant parties sometimes take advantage of weaker parties. As a result, some otherwise lawful contracts are so oppressive or manifestly unfair that they are unjust.

To prevent the enforcement of such contracts, the courts developed the equitable doctrine of unconscionability, which is based on public policy. A contract found to be unconscionable under this doctrine is called an **unconscionable contract,** or a **contract of adhesion.**

The courts are given substantial discretion in determining whether a contract or contract clause is unconscionable. There is no single definition of *unconscionability.* The doctrine may not be used merely to save a contracting party from a bad bargain.

The following elements must be shown to prove that a contract or clause in a contract is unconscionable:

- The parties possessed severely unequal bargaining power.
- The dominant party unreasonably used its unequal bargaining power to obtain oppressive or manifestly unfair contract terms.
- The adhering party had no reasonable alternative.

Unconscionable contracts are sometimes found where there is a consumer contract that takes advantage of uneducated, poorer, or senior citizens who have been talked into an unfair contract. This often involves door-to-door sales and sales over the telephone.

If the court finds that a contract or contract clause is unconscionable, it may (1) refuse to enforce the contract, (2) refuse to enforce the unconscionable clause but enforce the remainder of the contract, or (3) limit the applicability of any unconscionable clause so as to avoid any unconscionable result. The appropriate remedy depends on the facts and circumstances of each case. Note that because unconscionability is a matter of law, the judge may opt to decide the case without a jury trial.

1. Explain the doctrine of unconscionability.
2. Does the doctrine of unconscionability promote ethics? Explain.

telegrams, invoices, sales receipts, handwritten agreements written on scraps of paper, and such—can be an enforceable contract.

Required Signature

The Statute of Frauds and the UCC require the written contract, whatever its form, to be signed by the party against whom the enforcement is sought. The signature of the person who is enforcing the contract is not necessary. Thus, a written contract may be enforceable against one party but not the other party.

A verbal contract isn't worth the paper it's written on.

—Samuel Goldwyn

Generally, the signature may appear anywhere on the writing. In addition, it does not have to be a person's full legal name. The person's last name, first name, nickname, initials, seal, stamp, engraving, or other symbol or mark (e.g., an X) that indicates the person's intent can be binding. The signature may be affixed by an authorized agent.

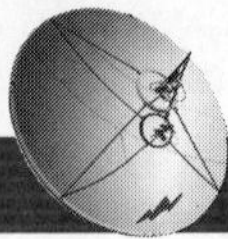

INFORMATION TECHNOLOGY

THE FEDERAL ELECTRONIC SIGNATURE ACT

In the world of pen-and-paper, it used to be, "Sign on the dotted line," "Put your John Hancock right here," or "Sign by the X." No more. In the e-commerce world, it is now, "What is your mother's maiden name?" "Slide your smart card in the sensor," or "Look into the iris scanner." But are electronic signatures sufficient to form an enforceable contract?

In 2000, the federal government enacted the **Electronic Signature in Global and National Commerce Act (E-Sign Act).** This federal statute has national reach.

ELECTRONIC SIGNATURE

One of the main features of the federal law is that it recognizes an electronic signature or e-signature. The Act gives an e-signature the same force and effect as a pen-inscribed signature on paper. The Act is technology-neutral, however, in that the law does not define or decide which technologies should be used to create a legally binding signature in cyberspace.

Loosely defined, a digital signature is some electronic method that identifies an individual. The challenge is to make sure that someone who uses a digital signature is the person he or she claims to be. The Act provides that a digital signature can be verified in one of three ways:

1. By something the signatory knows, such as a secret password, a pet's name, and so forth.
2. By something a person has, such as a smart card, which looks like a credit card and stores personal information.
3. By biometrics, which uses a device that digitally recognizes fingerprints or the retina or iris of the eye.

The verification of electronic signatures creates a need for the use of scanners and methods for verifying personal information.

WRITING REQUIREMENTS

The Act recognizes electronic contracts as meeting the writing requirement of the Statute of Frauds for most contracts. Statutes of Frauds are state laws that require certain types of contracts to be in writing. The federal act provides that electronically signed contracts cannot be denied effect because they are in electronic form or delivered electronically. The Act also provides that record retention requirements are satisfied if the records are stored electronically.

The federal law was passed with several provisions to protect consumers.

1. Consumers must consent to receiving electronic records and contracts.
2. To receive electronic records, consumers must be able to demonstrate that they have access to the electronic records.
3. Businesses must tell consumers that they have the right to receive hard-copy documents of the transaction.

The Act places the world of electronic commerce on par with the world of paper contracts in the United States.

ASSIGNMENT OF RIGHTS

In many cases, the parties to a contract can transfer their rights under the contract to other parties. The transfer of contractual rights is called an **assignment of rights** or just an **assignment.** The party who owes the duty of performance is called the *obligor.* The party owed a right under the contract is called the *obligee.* An obligee who transfers the right to receive performance is called an **assignor.** The party to whom the right has been transferred is called the **assignee.** The assignee

Fraud

Contracting parties must be careful not to be taken by **fraud.** Basically, if a deal sounds "too good to be true," it is a signal that the situation might be fraudulent. If there is fraud, the innocent party can get out of the contract and recover his or her losses from the perpetrator of the fraud. To prove fraud, the following elements must be shown:

1. The wrongdoer made a false representation of material fact.
2. The wrongdoer intended to deceive the innocent party.
3. The innocent party justifiably relied on the misrepresentation.
4. The innocent party was injured.

MATERIAL MISREPRESENTATION OF FACT

A misrepresentation may occur by words (oral or written) or by the conduct of the party. To be actionable as fraud, the misrepresentation must be of a past or existing material fact. This means that the misrepresentation must have been a significant factor in inducing the innocent party to enter into the contract. It does not have to be the sole factor. Statements of opinion or predictions about the future generally do not form the basis for fraud.

INTENT TO DECEIVE

To prove fraud, the person making the misrepresentation must have either had knowledge that the representation was false or made it without sufficient knowledge of the truth. This is called *scienter* ("guilty mind"). The misrepresentation must have been made with the intent to deceive the innocent party. Intent can be inferred from the circumstances.

RELIANCE ON THE MISREPRESENTATION

A misrepresentation is not actionable unless the innocent party to whom the misrepresentation was directed acted upon it. Further, an innocent party who acts in reliance on the misrepresentation must justify his or her reliance. Justifiable reliance generally is found unless the innocent party knew that the misrepresentation was false or was so extravagant as to be obviously false. For example, reliance on a statement such as, "This diamond ring is worth $10,000, but I'll sell it to you for $100" would not be justified.

INJURY TO THE INNOCENT PARTY

To recover damages, the innocent party must prove that the fraud caused economic injury. The measure of damages is the difference between the value of the property as represented and the actual value of the property. This measure of damages gives the innocent party the "benefit of the bargain." In the alternative, the buyer can rescind the contract and recover the purchase price.

can assign the right to yet another person (called a subsequent assignee, or subassignee). Exhibit 7.2 illustrates these relationships.

Suppose the owner of a clothing store purchases $5,000 worth of goods on credit from a manufacturer. Payment is due in 120 days. Assume that the manufacturer needs cash before that period expires, so he sells his right to collect the money to a factor for $4,000. If the store owner is given proper notice of the assignment, he must pay $5,000 to the factor. The manufacturer is the assignor and the factor is the assignee.

Generally, no formalities are required for a valid assignment of rights. Although the assignor often uses the word *assign*, other words or terms, such as *sell*, *transfer*, *convey*, and *give*, are sufficient to indicate an intent to transfer a contract right.

EXHIBIT 7.2 *Assignment of a right.*

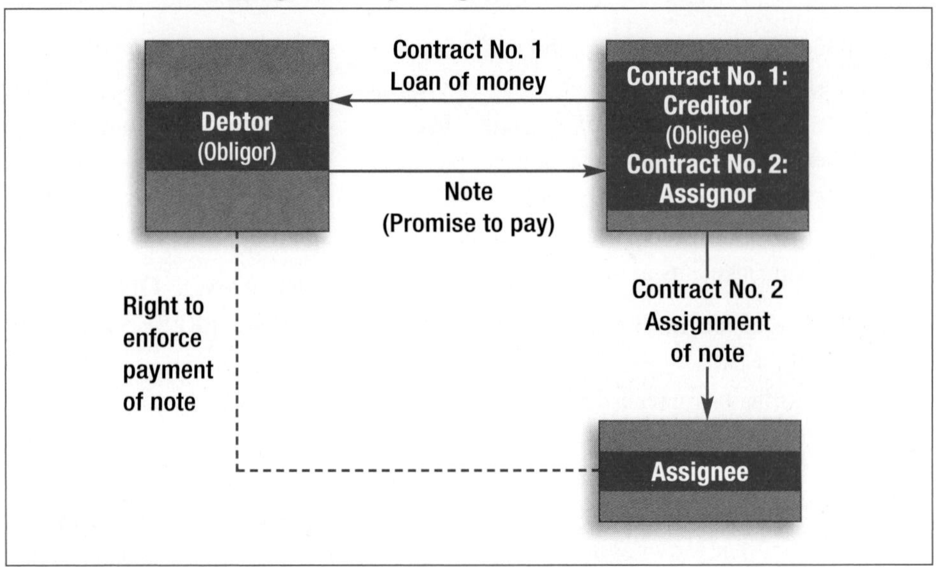

THIRD-PARTY BENEFICIARIES

Third parties sometimes claim rights under others' contracts. Such third parties are either *intended* or *incidental beneficiaries.* When the parties enter into a contract, they can agree that one of the party's performances should be rendered to or directly benefit a third party. Under such circumstances, the third party is called an **intended third-party beneficiary.** An intended third-party beneficiary can enforce the contract against the party who promised to render performance.

The beneficiary may be expressly named in the contract from which he or she is to benefit or may be identified by another means. For example, there is sufficient identification if a testator of a will leaves his estate to "all my children, equally."

When a person enters into a contract with the intent to confer a benefit or gift on an intended third party, the contract is called a **donee beneficiary** contract. A life insurance policy with a named beneficiary is an example of such a contract. The three persons involved in such a contract are:

1. The *promisee* (the contracting party who directs that the benefit be conferred on another)
2. The *promisor* (the contracting party who agrees to confer performance for the benefit of the third person)
3. The *donee beneficiary* (the third person on whom the benefit is to be conferred)

If the promisor fails to perform the contract, the donee beneficiary can sue the promisor directly. Consider this example: Brian Peterson hires a lawyer to draft his will. He directs the lawyer to leave all of his property to his best friend, Jeffrey Silverman. Assume that (1) Peterson dies, and (2) the lawyer's negligence in drafting the will causes it to be invalid. Consequently, Peterson's distant relatives instead of Silverman receive the property under the state's inheritance statute. Silverman can sue the lawyer for damages because he was the intended donee beneficiary of the will.

PERFORMANCE

In contracts, parties make certain promises to each other. These promises may be classified as *covenants* (or *conditions*). **Performance** may be classified as complete performance, substantial performance (minor breach), or inferior performance (material breach).

Covenants

A **covenant** is an unconditional promise to perform. Nonperformance of a covenant is a breach of contract that gives the other party the right to sue. For example, if Medcliff Corporation borrows $100,000 from a bank and signs a promissory note to repay this amount plus 10 percent interest in one year, this promise is a covenant. It is an unconditional promise to perform.

Conditions Precedent

If the contract requires the occurrence (or nonoccurrence) of an event before a party is obligated to perform a contractual duty, there is a **condition precedent.** The happening (or nonhappening) of the event triggers the contract or duty of performance. If the event does not occur, no duty to perform arises because there is a failure of condition.

Suppose X Company offers Joan Andrews a job as an industrial engineer upon her graduation from college. If Ms. Andrews graduates, the condition has been met. If the employer refuses to hire Ms. Andrews at that time, she can sue the employer for breach of contract. But if Ms. Andrews does not graduate, X Company is not obligated to hire her because there has been a failure of condition.

Complete Performance

Most contracts are discharged by the **complete** (or strict) **performance** of the contracting parties. Complete performance occurs when a party to a contract renders performance exactly as required by the contract. A fully performed contract is called an **executed contract.**

Tender of performance also discharges a party's contractual obligations. Tender is an unconditional and absolute offer by a contracting party to perform his or her obligations under the contract.

Suppose Ashley's Dress Shops, Inc., contracts to purchase dresses from a dress manufacturer for $25,000. Ashley's has performed its obligation under the contract once it tenders the $25,000 to the manufacturer. If the manufacturer fails to deliver the dresses, Ashley's can sue it for breach of contract.

SIDEBAR

Force Majeure Clauses The parties may agree in their contract that certain events will excuse nonperformance of the contract. These clauses are called **force majeure clauses.** Usually force majeure clauses excuse nonperformance caused by natural disasters such as floods, tornadoes, earthquakes, and such. Modern clauses often excuse nonperformance resulting from labor strikes, shortages of raw materials, and the like.

Substantial Performance Minor Breach

Substantial performance occurs when there has been a **minor breach of contract.** It occurs when a party to a contract renders performance that deviates only slightly from complete performance. The nonbreaching party may (1) convince the breaching party to elevate his or her performance to complete performance, or (2) deduct the cost to repair the defect from the contract price and remit the balance to the breaching party, or (3) sue the breaching party to recover the cost to repair the defect if the breaching party has already been paid.

Suppose Donald Trumble contracts with Big Apple Construction Co. to have Big Apple construct an office building for $50 million. The architectural plans call for installation of three-ply windows in the building. Big Apple constructs the building exactly to plan except that it installs two-ply windows. There has been substantial performance. It would cost $300,000 to install the correct windows. If Big Apple agrees to replace the windows, its performance is elevated to complete performance and Trumble must remit the entire contract price. But if Trumble has to hire someone else to replace the windows, he may deduct this cost of repair from the contract price and remit the difference to Big Apple.

Inferior Performance Material Breach

Men keep their agreements when it is an advantage to both parties not to break them.

—Solon (c. 600 B.C.)

A **material breach of contract** occurs when a party fails to perform certain express or implied obligations that impair or destroy the essence of the contract—**inferior performance.** Because there is no clear line between a minor breach and a material breach, determination is made on a case-by-case basis. Where there has been a material breach of a contract, the nonbreaching party has two choices:

1. The nonbreaching party may rescind the contract, seek restitution of any compensation paid under the contract to the breaching party, and be discharged from any further performance under the contract.
2. The nonbreaching party may treat the contract as being in effect and sue the breaching party to recover **damages.**

Suppose a university contracts with a general contractor to build a new three-story building with classroom space for 1,000 students. But the completed building can support the weight of only 500 students because the contractor used inferior materials. The defect cannot be repaired without rebuilding the entire structure. Because this is a material breach, the university may rescind the contract and require removal of the building. The university is discharged of any obligations under the contract and is free to employ another contractor to rebuild the building. Alternatively, the university could accept the building and deduct from the contract price the damages caused by the defect.

Remedies

The most common remedy for a breach of contract is an award of *monetary damages.* This is often called the "law remedy." But if a monetary award does not provide adequate relief, the court may order any one of several *equitable remedies,* including specific performance, injunction, reformation, and quasi-contract. Equitable remedies are based on the concept of fairness.

Monetary Damages

Monetary damages are of three types: compensatory, consequential, and liquid.

Compensatory damages. **Compensatory damages** are intended to compensate a nonbreaching party for the loss of the bargain. They place the nonbreaching party in the same position as if the contract has been fully performed by restoring the "benefit of the bargain."

CASE FOR DISCUSSION

Lim v. The .TV Corporation International

99 Cal.App.4th 684, 121 Cal.Rptr.2d 323, 2002 Cal.App. Lexis 4315 (2002) Supreme Court of California

FACTS

The island nation of Tuvalu was awarded the top-level domain name "tv." The country of Tuvalu controlled what parties could use domain names with the suffix "tv" on the Internet. For example, if a person named Jones acquired the suffix tv, her domain name on the Internet would be "jones.tv." Tuvalu hired The .TV Corporation International, a California corporation doing business under the name dotTV, to sell Internet names bearing the top-level domain name "tv." In April 2000, dotTV posted the name "golf.tv" for sale on its Web site, to be sold to the highest bidder. Je Ho Lim, a resident of South Korea, submitted the highest bid of $1,010 and authorized dotTV to charge his credit card for the amount of the bid. DotTV sent the following e-mail to Lim confirming the sale:

> *DotTV—The New Frontier on the Internet*
> *E-Mail Invoice for Domain Registration*
> *NAME: Je Ho Lim*
> *Congratulations!*
> *You have won the auction for the following domain name:*
> *DOMAIN NAME: -- -- golf*
> *SUBSCRIPTION LENGTH: 2 years, starts from activation date*
> *Amount (US$): $1,010 (first year registration fee)*
> *Please remember that the annual registration fee increases by 5% annually.*
> *You have the guaranteed right to renew the registration indefinitely.*
> *DotTV expects to charge your card and activate the registered domain name by May 15, 2000.*
> *See ya on the new frontier of the Internet!*
> *Lou Kerner CEO, dotTV Corporation* www.TV

Shortly thereafter, dotTV sent another e-mail to Lim that stated "we have decided to release you from your bid" and that Lim should "disregard" the prior e-mail because of "an e-mail error that occurred." Later, dotTV publicly offered the domain name "golf.tv" with a beginning bid of $1 million. DotTV claimed that its original e-mail to Lim concerned a different domain name "-- --golf" instead of "golf." Lim correctly countered that characters such as two dashes ("-- --") are not recognized on the Internet and therefore the name "-- --golf" is an invalid domain name. When dotTV refused to transfer the domain name "golf.tv" to Lim, Lim sued dotTV for breach of contract. The trial court dismissed Lim's case against dotTV. Lim appealed.

ISSUE

Did Lim properly state a cause of action for breach of contract against dotTV?

COURT'S REASONING

The court of appeal noted that there is a presumption that auctions are with reserve unless there is a contrary manifestation. The court stated that if dotTV's Web site announcement of the auction was an invitation to make an offer, then plaintiff Lim's bid was an offer, and that this offer was accepted by dotTV when it sent its confirmation e-mail to Lim. The court rejected dotTV's argument that Lim had purchased the domain name "-- --golf" and not "golf" because the name "-- --golf" was not a valid Internet domain name.

DECISION AND REMEDY

The court of appeal held that plaintiff Lim had properly pleaded a cause of action against defendant dotTV for breach of contract and reinstated Lim's case against dotTV.

QUESTIONS

1. Explain the difference between an auction with reserve and an auction without reserve. Which is presumed if there is no statement to the contrary?
2. Did dotTV act ethically in this case? Why do you think dotTV reneged on its e-mail confirmation to Lim?
3. Are Internet domain names valuable? How do you register an Internet domain name?

Exterior of Tippecanoe County Courthouse, Lafayette, Indiana.

Suppose Lederle Laboratories enters into a written contract to employ a manager for three years at a salary of $6,000 per month. Before work is to start, the manager is informed that he will not be needed. This is a material breach of contract.

Assume that the manager finds another job, but it pays only $5,000 a month. The manager may recover $1,000 per month for 36 months (total $36,000) from Lederle Laboratories as compensatory damages. These damages place the manager in the same situation as if the contract with Lederle had been performed.

Consequential damages. In addition to compensatory damages, a nonbreaching party sometimes can recover **consequential (special) damages** from the breaching party. Consequential damages are foreseeable damages that arise from circumstances outside the contract. To be liable for consequential damages, the breaching party must know or have reasons to know that the breach will cause special damages to the other party.

Consider this example: Suppose Soan–Allen Co., a wholesaler, enters into a contract to purchase 1,000 men's suits for $150 each from the Fabric Manufacturing Co., a manufacturer. Prior to contracting, the wholesaler tells the manufacturer that the suits will be resold to retailers for $225. The manufacturer breaches the contract by failing to manufacture the suits. The wholesaler cannot get the suits manufactured by anyone else in time to meet his contracts. He can recover $75,000 of lost profits on the resale contracts (1,000 suits × $75 profit) as consequential damages from the manufacturer because the manufacturer knew of this special damage to Soan–Allen Co. if it were to breach the contract.

Liquidated damages. Under certain circumstances, the parties to a contract may agree in advance to the amount of damages payable upon a breach of contract. These are called **liquidated damages.** To be lawful, the actual damages must be difficult or impracticable to determine, and the liquidated amount must be reasonable in the circumstances. An enforceable liquidated damage clause is an exclusive remedy even if actual damages are later determined to be different.

A liquidated damage clause is considered a **penalty** if actual damages are clearly determinable in advance or the liquidated damages are excessive or unconscionable. If a liquidated damage clause is found to be a penalty, it is unenforceable. The nonbreaching party may then recover actual damages.

Mitigation of Damages

If a contract has been breached, the law places a duty on the innocent nonbreaching party to take reasonable efforts to mitigate (i.e., avoid and reduce) the resulting damages. The extent of **mitigation of damages** required depends on the type of contract involved. For example, if an employer breaches an employment contract, the employee owes a duty to mitigate damages by trying to find substitute employment. The employee is required to accept only comparable

ETHICAL PERSPECTIVE

STATE FARM: NOT SUCH A GOOD NEIGHBOR

Most car drivers purchase automobile insurance to cover themselves from liability for accidents. Many drivers also purchase collision insurance, which means that the insurance covers the cost of repairing an insured's damaged automobile. Collision insurance policies routinely provide that replacement parts be of "like kind and quality" as the original damaged parts. But what if the replacement parts are "after-market" parts, that is, parts manufactured by companies other than the original automobile manufacturer? Do these generic parts qualify as "like kind and quality"? Many insureds (and their lawyers, of course) did not think so and sued their insurance company, State Farm Mutual Automobile Insurance Company, the largest insurance company in the United States, in a class-action lawsuit for breach of contract for including replacement parts in their vehicles without telling them.

The plaintiffs presented evidence that State Farm required body shops to use replacement parts made by after-market manufacturers and not by the automobile's original manufacturer. State Farm said it did this to save costs. For example, a replacement hood for a 1995 Pontiac Grand Am cost $307 from General Motors but only $154 from an after-market manufacturer.

The plaintiffs argued that the replacement parts were inferior to original parts, were less safe and had not been crash-tested, and therefore lowered the value of the automobile. The plaintiffs argued that State Farm forced body shops to use after-market parts to save it money at the expense of the insureds, and therefore that State Farm had breached its contract to provide replacement parts of "like kind and quality." The case went to trial in rural Marion, Illinois. After hearing the evidence, the jurors believed the plaintiffs and held that State Farm had breached its contract with the insureds.

As a remedy, the jury returned a verdict of $456 million against State Farm. In a further blow, the trial court judge held that State Farm had committed consumer fraud and tacked on an additional $730 million in punitive and other damages, bringing the total award to almost $1.2 billion. Each of the 4.7 million affected insureds would receive on average about $275 from State Farm. [*Lundy v. Farmers Group, Inc.* (2001)]

1. Should State Farm have disclosed to its insureds that it was requiring after-market parts to be installed to repair their insured automobiles?

employment. In determining the comparability of jobs, the courts consider factors such as compensation, rank, status, job description, and geographical location.

Equitable Remedies

Equitable remedies include specific performance, injunction, reformation, and quasi-contract.

Specific performance. An award of **specific performance** orders the breaching party to *perform* the acts promised in the contract. The courts have the discretion to award this remedy if the subject matter of the contract is unique. This remedy is available to enforce land contracts because every piece of real property is considered unique. Works of art, antiques, items of sentimental value, rare coins, stamps, heirlooms, and such also fit the requirement for uniqueness. Most other personal property does not. Specific performance of personal-service contracts is not granted because the courts would find it difficult or impracticable to supervise or monitor performance of the contract.

Injunction. An **injunction** is a court order that *prohibits* a person from doing a certain act. To obtain an injunction, the requesting party must show that he or she will suffer irreparable injury unless the injunction is issued.

Suppose a professional football team enters into a 5-year employment contract with a "superstar" quarterback. The quarterback breaches the contract and enters into a contract to play for a competing team. Here, the first team can seek an injunction to prevent the quarterback from playing for the other team.

Reformation. **Reformation** is an equitable doctrine that permits the court to *rewrite* a contract to express the parties' true intentions. For example, suppose a clerical error is made during the typing of the contract and both parties sign the contract without discovering the error. If a dispute later arises, the court can reform the contract to correct the clerical error to read what the parties originally intended.

Quasi-contract. A **quasi-contract** (also called *quantum meruit* or an *implied-in-law contract*) is an equitable doctrine that permits the *recovery* of compensation even though no enforceable contract exists between the parties because of lack of consideration, the Statute of Frauds has run out, or the like. Such contracts are imposed by law to prevent unjust enrichment. Under quasi-contract, a party can recover the reasonable value of the services or materials provided. For example, a physician who stops to render aid to an unconscious victim of an automobile accident may recover the reasonable value of his services from that person.

THE UNIFORM COMMERCIAL CODE (UCC)

One of the major frustrations of businesspersons conducting interstate business is that they are subject to the laws of each of the states in which they operate. To address this problem, in 1949 the National Conference of Commissioners on Uniform State Laws promulgated the **Uniform Commercial Code (UCC).** The UCC is a model act containing uniform rules that govern commercial transactions. To create this uniformity, individual states had to enact the UCC as their commercial law statute. In fact, they did, and every state except Louisiana (which has adopted only parts of the UCC) enacted the UCC as a commercial statute.

The UCC is divided into articles, each of which establishes uniform rules for a facet of commerce in the United States. The articles of the UCC are

Article 1 General provisions
Article 2 Sales
Article 2A Leases
Article 3 Negotiable instruments

Article 4	Bank deposits and collections
Article 4A	Wire transfers
Article 5	Letters of credit
Article 6	Bulk transfers
Article 7	Documents of title
Article 8	Investment securities
Article 9	Secured transactions

The UCC is continually being revised to reflect changes in modern commercial practices and technology. For example, Article 2A was drafted to govern leases of personal property, and Article 4A was added to regulate the use of wire transfers in the banking system. Articles 3 and 4, which cover the creation and transfer of negotiable instruments and the clearing of checks through the banking system, were amended substantially in 1990. Article 2, which covers the sale of goods, is currently in the initial stages of revision.

Article 2 (Sales) of the Uniform Commercial Code

Article 2 (Sales) of the Uniform Commercial Code applies to *transactions in goods*, that is, the sale of goods [UCC 2-102]. All states except Louisiana have adopted some version of Article 2 of the UCC. A "sale" consists of the passing of title from a seller to a buyer for a price [UCC 2-106(1)].

For example, the purchase of a book is a sale subject to Article 2. This is so whether the book was paid for by cash, check, credit card, or other form of consideration.

Article 2 establishes a uniform law covering the formation, performance, and default of sales contracts.

Goods are defined as tangible things that are movable at the time of their identification to the contract [UCC 2-105(1)]. Examples of goods are specially manufactured goods and the unborn young of animals.

Money and intangible items, such as stocks, bonds, and patents, are not tangible goods. Therefore, they are not subject to Article 2.

Real estate is not subject to Article 2 either, because it is not movable [UCC 2-105(1)]. Minerals, structures, growing crops, and other things that are severable from real estate may be classified as goods subject to Article 2, however. For example, the sale and removal of a chandelier in a house is a sale of goods subject to Article 2 because its removal would not materially harm the realty. However, the sale and removal of the furnace would be a sale of real property because its removal would cause material harm [UCC 2-107(2)].

Contracts for the provision of services—including legal services, medical services, dental services, and such—are not covered by Article 2. Sometimes, however, a sale involves both the provision of a service and a good in the same transaction. This is referred to as a *mixed sale*. Article 2 applies to mixed sales only if the goods are the predominant part of the transaction. The UCC provides no guidance for deciding cases based on mixed sales. Therefore, the courts decide these issues on a case-by-case basis.

Article 2A (Leases) of the Uniform Commercial Code

Personal property leases are a billion-dollar industry. Consumer rentals of automobiles or equipment and commercial leases of items such as aircraft and industrial machinery fall into this category.

Article 2A of the UCC was promulgated in 1987. This article, cited as **Uniform Commercial Code—Leases,** directly addresses personal property leases [UCC 2A-101]. It establishes a comprehensive, uniform law covering the formation, performance, and default of leases in goods [UCC 2A-102, 2A-103(h)].

Article 2A is similar to Article 2. In fact, many Article 2 provisions were changed to reflect leasing terminology and practices and carried over to Article 2A. Many states have adopted Article 2A, and many more are expected to do so in the future.

A lease is a transfer of the right to the possession and use of the named goods for a set term in return for certain consideration [UCC 2A-103(1)(i)(x)]. The leased goods can be anything from a hand tool leased to an individual for a few hours to a complex line of industrial equipment leased to a multinational corporation for a number of years.

In an ordinary lease, the **lessor** is the person who transfers the right of possession and use of goods under the lease [UCC 2A-103(1)(p)]. The **lessee** is the person who acquires the right to possession and use of goods under a lease [UCC 2A-103(1)(n)].

A **consumer lease** is one with a value of $25,000 or less between a lessor regularly engaged in the business of leasing or selling and a lessee who leases the goods primarily for a personal, family, or household purpose [UCC 2A-103(1)(e)].

A **finance lease** is a three-party transaction consisting of the lessor, the lessee, and the supplier (or vendor) [UCC 2A-103(1)(g)].

Consider this example: The Dow Chemical Company decides to use robotics to manufacture most of its products. It persuades Ingersoll–Rand to design the robotic equipment that will meet its needs. To finance the purchase of the equipment, Dow Chemical goes to Citibank, which purchases the robotics equipment from Ingersoll–Rand and leases it to Dow Chemical. Citibank is the lessor, Dow Chemical is the lessee, and Ingersoll–Rand is the supplier.

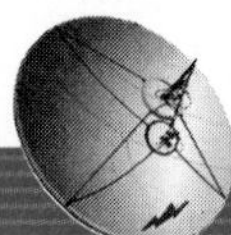

INFORMATION TECHNOLOGY

THE UNIFORM COMPUTER INFORMATION TRANSACTIONS ACT (UCITA)

In July 1999, after years of study and debate, the National Conference of Commissioners on Uniform State Laws (a group of lawyers, judges, and legal scholars) issued the **Uniform Computer Information Transactions Act (UCITA).** This is a model act that establishes a uniform and comprehensive set of rules that governs the creation, performance, and enforcement of computer information transactions. A computer information transaction is an agreement to create, transfer, or license computer information or information rights [UCITA § 102(a)(11)].

The UCITA does not become law until a state's legislature enacts it as a state statute. States have begun adopting the UCITA as their law for computer transactions and the licensing of informational rights.

State law and equity principles, including principal and agent law, fraud, duress, mistake, trade secret law, and other state laws, supplement the UCITA [UCITA § 114].

INTERNATIONAL PERSPECTIVE

U.N. CONVENTION ON CONTRACTS FOR THE INTERNATIONAL SALE OF GOODS (CISG)

Businesspersons who engage in international commerce face the daunting task of trying to comply with the laws of many nations. To ease this burden, more than 60 countries are signatories to the **United Nations Convention on Contracts for the International Sale of Goods (CISG).** This treaty took more than 50 years to negotiate and incorporates rules from all the major legal systems of the world.

The CISG establishes uniform rules for the formation and enforcement of contracts involving the international sale of goods. Many of its provisions are remarkably similar to the provisions of the American UCC. The CISG applies if the buyer and seller have their places of business in different countries and both nations are parties to the convention.

The contracting parties may agree to exclude (opt out of) the CISG and let other laws apply. The parties to any international contract can agree that the CISG controls, even if one or both of their countries are not signatories to the convention.

LEGAL TERMINOLOGY

Acceptance
Actual contract
Agreement
Article 2 (Sales) of the Uniform Commercial Code
Article 2A (Leases) of the Uniform Commercial Code
Assignee
Assignment of a right
Assignor
Cancellation
Classical law of contracts
Compensatory damages
Complete performance
Conditions precedent
Consequential damages
Consideration
Consumer lease
Contract
Contract of adhesion
Contracts contrary to public policy
Contractual capacity
Counteroffer
Covenant
Damages
Deed of trust
Disaffirmance
Donee beneficiary
Electronic commerce (e-commerce)
Electronic Signature in Global and National Commerce Act
Equitable remedies
Executed contract
Express contract
Finance lease
Force majeure clause
Form contracts
Fraud
Gift promise (gratuitous promise)
Illegal contract
Implied-in-fact contract
Infancy doctrine
Inferior performance
Injunction
Intended third-party beneficiary
Lawful object
Lease
Lessee
Lessor
Liquidated damages

CASE FOR DISCUSSION

Brumfield v. Death Row Records, Inc.

2003 Cal.App. Lexis 7843 (2003) Court of Appeal of California

FACTS

Ricardo E. Brown, Jr., known as "Kurupt," was an unknown teenage rap singer who lived with his father. In 1989, Lamont Brumfield, a promoter of young rappers, "discovered" Kurupt. Lamont introduced his brother, Kenneth Brumfield, who owned a music publishing business, to Kurupt. Beginning in 1990, Lamont produced demos for Kurupt, set up photo shoots, booked him to sing at many clubs, and paid for Kurupt's clothing, personal, and living expenses. Kurupt lived with Lamont after Kurupt's father kicked him out of the house. In 1991, Lamont obtained recording work for Kurupt with the rap group SOS. In November 1991, Kurupt signed an exclusive recording agreement with Lamont's company, an exclusive publishing agreement with Kenneth's company, and a management agreement with Kenneth for an initial term of three years with an additional option term. These contracts gave Kurupt 7% royalties on sales. The Brumfields spent at least $65,000 to support and promote Kurupt, often borrowing money from family and friends to do so.

Andre Young, known as Dr. Dre, invited Lamont, Kenneth, and Kurupt to a picnic where he introduced them to Marion Knight, the owner of Death Row Records, Inc. The Brumfields and Kurupt made it clear to Dr. Dre and Knight that the Brumfields had exclusive contracts with Kurupt. After Kurupt performed at the picnic, Dr. Dre invited Kurupt to his house to record songs for Dr. Dre's album "Chronic." In December 1992, "Chronic" was released by Death Row Records, Inc. and sold millions of albums. The Brumfields continued to promote Kurupt and to take care of his living expenses. When Dr. Dre invited Kurupt to go on tour to promote the "Chronic" album, Kurupt told the Brumfields that he was going to visit family in Philadelphia, but instead went on tour for four weeks. In 1993, Kurupt worked on another Death Row Records album. In May 1994, Kenneth exercised his option and renewed his management agreement with Kurupt. Despite the multimillion dollar profit of the "Chronic" album, the Brumfields were paid nothing by Death Row Records. At the end of 1994, Death Row moved Kurupt out of the condominium he shared with Lamont and into a house. While cleaning out the condominium, Lamont found papers showing that Death Row Records had paid Kurupt advances commencing in April 1993.

The Brumfields sued Death Row Records, Inc. and its owner Knight for damages for the tort of intentional interference with their contracts with Kurupt. The jury found in favor of the Brumfields and awarded them $14,344,000 in compensatory and punitive damages. The trial court judge reduced the award to $5,519,000, including $1.5 million in punitive damages to Lamont and $1 million in punitive damages to Kenneth. Defendants Death Row Records and Knight appealed this decision.

ISSUE

Did the defendants Marion Knight and Death Row Records, Inc. engage in the tort of intentional interference with the contracts that plaintiffs Lamont and Kenneth Brumfield had with rapper Kurupt?

COURT'S REASONING

The evidence showed that Kurupt had breached the contracts he had with the Brumfields and had earned approximately $1.5 million in royalties from Death Row Records for his work on the "Chronic" album and many other albums. The court of appeal held that there was evidence that Death Row Records and Knight had caused Kurupt to breach these contracts and were therefore liable for the tort of intentional interference with a contract. The court of appeal found that the necessary elements for the tort of intentional interference with a contract had been proven. There were valid contracts between the Brumfields and Kurupt, the defendants had knowledge of these contracts, the defendants intentionally induced Kurupt to breach these contracts, and such breach resulted in damages to the Brumfields.

DECISION AND REMEDY

The court of appeal held that defendants Death Row Records, Inc. and Marion Knight had committed the tort of intentionally interfering with the contracts that the Brumfields had with rapper Kurupt. The court of appeal upheld the award of $5,519,000 to the Brumfields, including $1.5 million in punitive damages to Lamont and $1 million punitive damages to Kenneth. Affirmed.

QUESTIONS

1. Should there be a tort of intentional interference with a contract? Why or why not? What public policy is served by this tort?
2. Did Marion Knight and Dr. Dre act ethically in this case? Did Kurupt act ethically in this case?
3. Will this decision make parties more apt to not interfere with other parties' contracts?

Material breach of contract
Minor
Minor breach of contract
Mitigation of damages
Modern law of contracts
Monetary damages
Necessaries of life
Nondisclosure agreement (NDA)
Offer
Offeree
Offeror
One-year rule
Option contract
Penalty
Performance
Private law
Quasi-contract (implied-in-law contract)
Real property
Reformation
Specific performance
Statute of Frauds
Substantial performance
Tender of performance
UCC Section 201 (Statute of Frauds)
Unconscionable contract
Uniform Commercial Code (UCC)
Uniform Computer Information Transactions Act (UCITA)
United Nations Convention on Contracts for the International Sale of Goods (CISG)
Voidable contract

chapter summary

CONTRACTS AND E-COMMERCE

Definition of and Parties to a Contract	
Definition	A promise or set of promises for the breach of which the law gives a remedy or the performance of which the law in some way recognizes a duty.
Parties to a Contract	1. *Offeror:* Party who makes an offer to enter into a contract. 2. *Offeree:* Party to whom the offer is made.
Requirements of a Contract	
Elements	1. Agreement 2. Consideration 3. Contractual capacity 4. Lawful object
Agreement	
Process of Agreement	1. *Offer:* Manifestations by one party of a willingness to enter into a contract. 2. *Offeror:* Party who makes an offer. 3. *Offeree:* Party to whom an offer is made. This party has the power to create an agreement by accepting the terms of the offer. *(continued)*

Termination of an Offer by Action of the Parties	1. *Revocation:* The offeror may *revoke* (withdraw) an offer any time prior to its acceptance by the offeree. 2. *Rejection:* An offer is terminated if the offeree rejects the offer by his or her words or conduct. 3. *Counteroffer:* A counteroffer by the offeree terminates the offeror's offer (and creates a new offer).
Acceptance	Manifestation of assent by the offeree to the terms of the offer. Acceptance of the offer by the offeree creates a contract.
Express and Implied Contracts	1. *Express contract:* A contract expressed in oral or written words. 2. *Implied-in-fact contract:* A contract implied from the conduct of the parties.
Consideration	
Consideration	Thing of value given in exchange for a promise. May be tangible or intangible property, performance of a service, forbearance of a legal right, or another thing of value.
Capacity to Contract	
Capacity to Contract	1. *Infancy doctrine:* Minors under the age of majority may *disaffirm* (cancel) most contracts they have entered into with adults. The contract is *voidable* by the minor but not by the adult. 2. *Mental incompetence:* Contracts by persons who are incompetent are *voidable* by the insane person but not by the competent party to the contract. 3. *Intoxicated persons:* Contracts by intoxicated persons are *voidable* by the intoxicated person but not by the competent party to the contract.
Lawful Object	
Illegal Contracts	An illegal contract is *void.* Therefore, the parties cannot sue for nonperformance. If the contract has been executed, the court will *leave the parties where it finds them.* 1. Contracts that violate statutes are illegal, void, and unenforceable. 2. Contracts that violate public policy are illegal, void, and unenforceable.
Unconscionable Contracts	*Unconscionable contracts:* Contracts that are oppressively unfair or unjust. Also called *contracts of adhesion.* 1. *Elements of unconscionable contracts:* a. The parties possessed severely unequal bargaining power. b. The dominant party unreasonably used its power to obtain oppressive or manifestly unfair contract terms. c. The adhering party had no reasonable alternative. 2. *Remedies for unconscionability:* Where a contract or contract clause is found to be unconscionable, the court may do one of the following: a. Refuse to enforce the contract. b. Refuse to enforce the unconscionable clause but enforce the remainder of the contract. c. Limit the applicability of any unconscionable clause so as to avoid any unconscionable result.

Statute of Frauds—Writing Requirement	
Writing Requirement	A state statute requires the following contracts to be in writing: 1. *Contracts involving the transfer of interests in real property*, including contracts for the sale of land, buildings, and items attached to land; mortgages; leases for a term of more than one year; and express easements. 2. Contracts that cannot be performed within one year of their formation *(one-year rule).* 3. *Contracts for the sale of goods* costing $500 or more (UCC 201).
Sufficiency of the Writing	1. *Formality of the writing:* A written contract does not have to be formal or drafted by a lawyer to be enforceable. Informal contracts, such as handwritten notes, letters, invoices, and the like, are enforceable contracts. 2. *Required signature:* The party against whom enforcement of the contract is sought must have signed the contract. The signature may be the person's full legal name, last name, first name, nickname, initials, or other symbol.
Electronic Signatures	*Electronic Signature in Global and National Commerce Act (E-Sign Act):* A federal statute that recognizes and gives electronic signatures—e-signatures—the same force and effect as a pen-inscribed signature on paper. The act is technology-neutral in that the law does not define or decide which technologies should be used to create a legally binding signature in cyberspace.
Assignment of Rights	
Form of Assignment	1. *Assignment:* Transfer of contractual rights by a party to a contract to a third person. 2. *Assignor.* Contract party who assigns the contractual rights. 3. *Assignee.* Third person to whom contract rights are assigned.
Third-Party Beneficiaries	
Intended Beneficiary	Third person who is owed performance under other parties' contract. 1. *Donee beneficiary:* Person who is to be rendered performance gratuitously under a contract. For example, a beneficiary of a life insurance policy. Donee beneficiary may sue the promisor for nonperformance.
Performance	
Covenants	Unconditional promises to perform. Nonperformance of a covenant is a breach of contract that gives the other party the right to sue.
Conditions Precedent	Requires the occurrence or nonoccurrence of an event before a party is obligated to perform. *(continued)*

Levels of Performance	1. *Complete performance:* A party renders performance exactly as required by the contract. That party's contractual duties are discharged. 2. *Substantial performance:* A party renders performance that deviates only slightly from complete performance. There is a *minor breach.* The non-breaching party may recover damages caused by the breach. 3. *Inferior performance:* A party fails to perform express or implied contractual duties that impair or destroy the essence of the contract. There is a *material breach.* The nonbreaching party may either (1) rescind the contract and recover restitution or (2) affirm the contract and recover damages.
Remedies	
Monetary Damages	1. *Compensatory damages:* Damages that compensate a nonbreaching party for loss of the contract. Restore the "benefit of the bargain" to the nonbreaching party as if the contract had been fully performed. 2. *Consequential damages:* Foreseeable damages that arise from circumstances outside the contract and of which the breaching party either knew or had reason to know. Also called *special damages.* 3. *Liquidated damages:* Damages payable upon breach of contract that are agreed on in advance by the contracting parties. Liquidated damages substitute for actual damages.
Mitigation of Damages	The duty the law places on a nonbreaching party to take reasonable efforts to avoid or reduce the damages resulting from a breach of contract. To mitigate a breach of an employment contract, the nonbreaching party must accept only "comparable" employment.
Equitable Remedies	*Equitable remedies* are available if the nonbreaching party cannot be adequately compensated by a legal remedy or to prevent unjust enrichment. 1. *Specific performance:* Court order that requires the breaching party to perform his or her contractual duties. Available only if the subject matter of the contract is *unique.* 2. *Injunction:* Court order that prohibits a person from doing a certain act. The requesting party must show that he or she will suffer irreparable injury if the injunction is not granted. 3. *Reformation:* Permits the court to rewrite a contract to express the parties' true intention. Available to correct clerical and mathematical errors. 4. *Quasi-contract:* Permits the court to order recovery of compensation even though no enforceable contract exists between the parties. Used to prevent unjust enrichment. Also called an *implied-in-law contract* or *quantum meruit.*

WORKING THE WEB

Visit the Web sites listed below for more information about the topics covered in this chapter.

1. Visit **cori.missouri.edu** to aid in drafting specific types of contracts and/or clauses. Test your ability by searching for employment agreements with non-competition clauses.
2. To review the basic elements of a contract, visit **www.freeadvice.com/law/518us.htm**.
3. For some tips on entering into contracts, see **www.itslegal.com/infonet/consumer/contracts.html**.
4. For a simplified explanation of the concept of consideration, see **www.nolo.com** and visit the encyclopedia section. Type in *consideration.*
5. Review the laws of your jurisdiction regarding minors and purchases of alcohol and tobacco; motor vehicles; renting an apartment.
6. Find your state statutes relating to usury. What is the maximum allowable interest rate?
7. Determine whether the following are provided in your jurisdiction. Find a leading case for: (a) Punitive damages; (b) Implied covenant of good faith and fair dealing; and (c) Intentional interference with contractual relations.

CRITICAL LEGAL THINKING QUESTIONS

1. Describe an offer and acceptance. When is a contract made?
2. What is an implied-in-fact contract? Why does the law recognize these contracts?
3. Explain a gift promise. Why are these contracts unenforceable?
4. What does the infancy doctrine provide? What public policy does this doctrine serve?
5. What does the Statute of Frauds provide? Why is the Statute of Frauds necessary?
6. What are the main provisions of the Electronic Signature Act? Why was this law enacted?
7. What is an unconscionable contract? Why does the law recognize this doctrine?
8. What are the differences among complete performance, substantial performance, and inferior performance of a contract?
9. What is an equitable remedy? Why does the law provide for equitable remedies?
10. What do Article 2 and Article 2A of the Uniform Commercial Code (UCC) provide? What is the difference between the common law of contracts and Articles 2 and 2A?

CASE FOR BRIEFING

Read Case 7 in Appendix A *(Carnival Leisure Industries, Ltd. v. Aubin)*. Review and brief the case using the *Critical Legal Thinking* "Briefing the Case" example described in Chapter 1.

CASES FOR DISCUSSION

7.1 *Bobby Floars Toyota, Inc. v. Smith*

269 S.E.2d 320, 1980 N.C. App. Lexis 3263 (1980)
Court of Appeals of North Carolina

FACTS *Infancy Doctrine.* Charles Edwards Smith, a minor, purchased an automobile from Bobby Floars Toyota on August 15, 1973. Smith executed a security agreement to finance part of the balance due on the purchase price, agreeing to pay off the balance in 30 monthly installments. On September 25, 1973, Smith turned 18, the age of majority. Smith made 10 monthly payments after turning 18. He then decided to disaffirm the contract and stopped making the payments. Smith claims that he may disaffirm the contract entered into when he was a minor. Toyota argues that Smith had ratified the contract since attaining the age of majority.

ISSUE Who is correct?

7.2 *Liz Claiborne, Inc. v. Avon Products, Inc.*

530 N.Y.S.2d 425, 1988 N.Y. App. Div. Lexis 6423 (1988)
Supreme Court of New York, Appellate Division

FACTS *Specific Performance.* Liz Claiborne, Inc. is a large maker of women's better sportswear in the United States and a well-known name in fashion, with sales of more than $1 billion a year. Claiborne distributes its products through 9,000 retail outlets in the United States. Avon Products, Inc. is a major producer of fragrances, toiletries, and cosmetics, with sales of more than $3 billion a year. Claiborne, which desired to promote its well-known name on perfumes and cosmetics, entered into a joint venture with Avon whereby Claiborne would make available its name, trademarks, and marketing experience and Avon would engage in the procurement and manufacture of the fragrances, toiletries, and cosmetics. The parties would equally share the financial requirements of the joint venture.

In 1986, its first year of operation, the joint venture had sales of more than $16 million. In the second year, sales increased to $26 million, making it one of the fastest-growing fragrance and cosmetic lines in the country. In 1987, Avon sought to "uncouple" the joint venture. Avon thereafter refused to procure and manufacture the line of fragrances and cosmetics for the joint venture. When Claiborne could not obtain the necessary fragrances and cosmetics from any other source for the fall/Christmas season, Claiborne sued Avon for breach of contract, seeking specific performance on the contract by Avon.

ISSUE Is specific performance an appropriate remedy in this case?

7.3 *Crisci v. Security Insurance Company of New Haven, Connecticut*

58 Cal.Rptr. 13, 426 P.2d 173, 1967 Cal. Lexis 313 (1967)
Supreme Court of California

FACTS Rosina Crisci owned an apartment building in which Mrs. DiMare was a tenant. One day while DiMare was descending a wooden staircase on the outside of the apartment building she fell through the staircase and was left hanging 15 feet above the ground until she was saved. Crisci had a $10,000 liability insurance policy on the building from the Security Insurance Company (Security) of New Haven, Connecticut. DiMare sued Crisci and Security for $400,000 for physical injuries and psychosis suffered from the fall. Prior to trial, DiMare agreed to take $10,000 in settlement of the case. Security refused this settlement offer. DiMare reduced her settlement offer to $9,000, of which Crisci offered to pay $2,500. Security again refused to settle the case. The case proceeded to trial and the jury awarded DiMare and her husband $110,000. Security paid $10,000 pursuant to the insurance contract, and Crisci had to pay the difference. Crisci, a widow of 70 years of age, had to sell her assets, became dependent on her relatives, declined in physical health, and suffered from hysteria and suicide attempts. Crisci sued Security for tort damages for breach of the implied covenant of good faith and fair dealing.

ISSUE Did Security act in bad faith?

ETHICS CASE

7.4 *Walgreen Co. v. Sara Creek Property Co.*

966 F.2d 273, 1992 U.S. App. Lexis 14847 (1992)
United States Court of Appeals, Seventh Circuit

FACTS Walgreen Company operated a pharmacy in the Southgate Mall in Milwaukee since 1951, when the mall opened. Its lease, signed in 1971 and carrying a 30-year term, contains an exclusive clause in which the landlord, Sara Creek Property Company, promised not to lease space in the mall to anyone else who wanted to operate a pharmacy or a store containing a pharmacy.

In 1990, after its anchor tenant went broke, Sara Creek informed Walgreen that it intended to lease the anchor tenant space to Phar-Mor Corporation. Phar-Mor, a "deep discount" chain, would occupy 100,000 square feet, of which 12,000 square feet would be occupied by a pharmacy the same size as Walgreen's. The entrances to the two stores would be within a few hundred feet of each other.

Walgreen sued Sara Creek for breach of contract and sought a permanent injunction against Sara Creek's leasing the anchor premises to Phar-Mor.

ISSUE Do the facts of this case justify issuing a permanent injunction? Did Sara Creek act ethically in not living up to the contract?

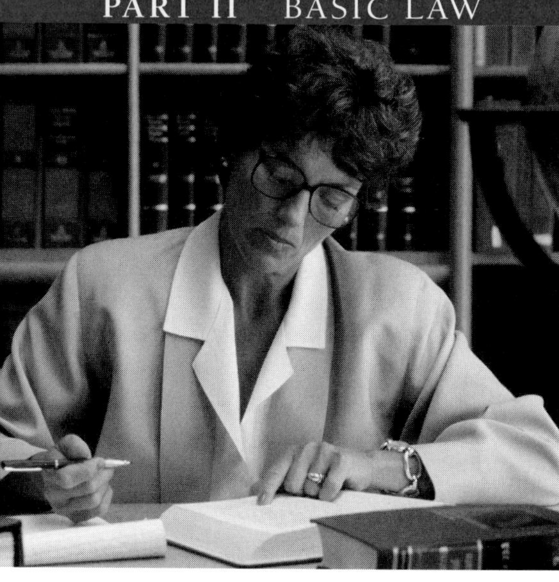

8 Real and Personal Property

Property and law are born and must die together.

—JEREMY BENTHAM, *PRINCIPLES OF THE CIVIL CODE*

CHAPTER OBJECTIVES

After studying this chapter, you should be able to

1. Define *personal property* and describe methods for acquiring ownership.
2. Describe bailments and explain the rights and duties of parties to bailments.
3. List and describe the types of real property.
4. Explain the different types of ownership rights in real property and explain how real property rights are transferred.
5. Describe the landlord–tenant relationship and explain the rights and obligations of the parties.

CHAPTER OUTLINE

- Introduction
- Personal Property
- Bailments
- Case for Discussion: *Sisters of Charity of the Incarnate Word v. Meaux*
- Real Property
- Freehold Estates
- Future Interests
- Concurrent Ownership
- Transfer of Ownership of Real Property
- Case for Discussion: *Cunningham v. Hastings*
- Case for Discussion: *Walker v. Ayres*
- Landlord–Tenant Relationship
- Land-Use Control
- Case for Discussion: *Guinnane v. San Francisco City Planning Commission*
- Legal Terminology
- Chapter Summary
- Internet Exercises and Cases

INTRODUCTION

Private ownership of property forms the foundation of our economic system. As such, a comprehensive body of law has been developed to protect property rights. The law protects the right of property owners to use, sell, dispose of, control, and prevent others from trespassing on their rights.

This chapter covers the topics of personal property, real property, landlord–tenant relationships, insurance, devising property through gift or inheritance, and protection of the environment.

PERSONAL PROPERTY

The two kinds of property are real property and personal property. Real property includes land and property that is permanently attached to it. For example, minerals, crops, timber, and buildings that are attached to land are generally considered real property. **Personal property** (sometimes referred to as goods or chattels) consists of everything that is not real property. Real property can become personal property if it is removed from the land. For example, a tree that is part of a forest is real property and a tree that is cut down is personal property.

Personal property that is permanently affixed to land or buildings is called a **fixture.** Such property, which includes things such as heating systems and storm windows, is categorized as real property. Unless otherwise agreed, fixtures remain with a building when it is sold. Personal property (e.g., furniture, pictures, and other easily portable household items) may be removed by the seller prior to sale.

Personal property can be either tangible or intangible. **Tangible property** includes physically defined property such as goods, animals, and minerals. **Intangible property** represents rights that cannot be reduced to physical form, such as stock certificates, certificates of deposit, bonds, and copyrights.

Gifts of Personal Property

A **gift** is a voluntary transfer of property without consideration. The lack of consideration is what distinguishes a gift from a purchase. The person making a gift is called the **donor.** The person who receives the gift is called the **donee.**

A gift made during a person's lifetime that is an irrevocable present transfer of ownership is a **gift *inter vivos*.** A **gift *causa mortis*** is a gift made in contemplation of death. A gift *causa mortis* is established when (1) the donor makes a gift in anticipation of approaching death from some existing sickness or peril, and (2) the donor dies from such sickness or peril without having revoked the gift. Gifts *causa mortis* can be revoked by the donor up until the time he or she dies. A gift *causa mortis* takes precedent over a prior conflicting will.

Suppose Sandy is a patient in the hospital. She is to have a major operation from which she may not recover. Prior to going into surgery, Sandy removes her diamond ring and gives it to her friend Pamela, stating, "In the event of my death, I want you to have this." This gift is a gift *causa mortis.* If Sandy dies from the operation, the gift is effective and Pamela owns the ring. If Sandy lives, the requisite condition for the gift (her death) has not occurred; therefore, the gift is not effective and Sandy can recover the ring from Pamela.

SIDEBAR

Uniform Gifts to Minors Acts

All states have adopted in whole or part the **Uniform Gift to Minors Act** or the **Revised Uniform Gift to Minors Act**. These laws establish procedures for adults to make irrevocable gifts of money and securities to minors. Gifts of money can be made by depositing the money in an account with a financial institution with the donor or another trustee (such as another adult or a bank) as custodian for the minor. Gifts of securities can be made by registering the securities in the name of a trustee as custodian for the minor. The laws give custodians broad discretionary powers to invest the money or securities for the benefit of the minor.

Mislaid, Lost, and Abandoned Property

Often, people find another person's personal property. Ownership rights to the property differ depending on whether the property is mislaid, lost, or abandoned. The following paragraphs discuss these legal rules.

Mislaid property. **Mislaid property** refers to property that the owner voluntarily places somewhere and then inadvertently forgets. The owner likely will return for the property upon realizing that it was misplaced.

The owner of the premises where the property is mislaid is entitled to take possession of the property against all except the rightful owner. This right is superior to the rights of the person who finds it. Such possession does not involve a change of title. Instead, the owner of the premises becomes an involuntary bailee of the property (bailments are discussed later in this chapter) and owes a duty to take reasonable care of the property until it is reclaimed by the owner.

As an example, suppose Felicity is on a business trip and stays in a hotel during her trip. Felicity accidentally leaves her diamond engagement ring in the hotel room she has stayed in and checks out of the hotel. The engagement ring is mislaid property, and the hotel has a duty to return it to Felicity, its rightful owner.

Lost property. **Lost property** refers to property that the owner negligently, carelessly, or inadvertently leaves somewhere. The finder obtains title to such property against the whole world except the true owner. The lost property must be returned to its rightful owner whether the finder discovers the loser's identity or the loser finds the finder. A finder who refuses to return the property is liable for the tort of conversion and the crime of larceny. Many states require the finder to conduct a reasonable search (e.g., place advertisements in newspapers) to find the rightful owner.

As an example, if a commuter finds a laptop computer on the floor of a subway station in New York City, the computer is considered lost property. The finder can claim title to the computer against the whole world except the true owner. If the true owner discovers that the finder has her computer, she may recover it from the finder. If there is identification of the owner on the computer (e.g., name, address, and/or telephone number), the finder owes a duty to contact the rightful owner and give the computer back.

"While we're waiting for His Honor, may I offer the jury a selection of hand-dipped Swiss chocolates, compliments of my client?"

Abandoned property. **Abandoned property** refers to (1) property that an owner discards with the intent to relinquish his or her rights in it, or (2) mislaid or lost property that the owner gives up any further attempts to locate. Anyone who

Estray Statutes

Most states have enacted **estray statutes** that permit a finder of *mislaid* or *lost* property to clear title to the property if

1. The finder reports the found property to the appropriate government agency and then turns over possession of the property to this agency.
2. Either the finder or the government agency posts notices and publishes advertisements describing the lost property, and
3. A specified time (usually a year or a number of years) has passed without the rightful owner's reclaiming the property.

Many state estray statutes require that the government receive a portion of the value of the property. Some statutes provide that title cannot be acquired in found property that is the result of illegal activity. For example, title has been denied to finders of property and money deemed to have been used for illegal drug purchases.

ETHICAL PERSPECTIVE

HONEST CITIZEN

Consider the following case: While hunting on unposted and unoccupied property in Oceola Township, Michigan, Duane Willsmore noticed an area with branches arranged in a crisscross pattern. When he kicked aside the branches and sod, he found a watertight suitcase in a freshly dug hole. Willsmore informed the Michigan state police of his find. A state trooper and Willsmore together pried open the suitcase and discovered $383,840 in cash. The state police took custody of the money, which was deposited in an interest-bearing account.

Michigan's estray statute provided that the finder and the township in which the property was found must share the value of the property if the finder publishes the required notices and the true owner does not claim the property within one year. Willsmore published the required notices and brought a declaratory judgment action seeking the determination of ownership of the money. After one year had gone by and the rightful owner had not claimed the briefcase, the court ordered that Willsmore and the Township of Oceola were equal one-half owners of the briefcase and its contents. [*Willsmore v. Township of Oceola, Michigan*, 308 N.W.2d 796, 1981 Mich. App. Lexis 2993 (Mich. App. 1981)]

1. Did Duane Willsmore act honestly in this case?
2. How many people do you think would have done what Willsmore did?

finds abandoned property acquires title to it. The title is good against the whole world, including the original owner. For example, property left at a garbage dump is abandoned property. It belongs to the first person who claims it.

BAILMENTS

A **bailment** occurs when the owner of personal property delivers his or her property to another person to be held, stored, or delivered, or for some other purpose. In a bailment, the owner of the property is the **bailor** and the party to whom the property is delivered for safekeeping, storage, or delivery (e.g., warehouse or common carrier) is the **bailee** (see Exhibit 8.1).

> Only a ghost can exist without material property.
> —Ayn Rand, *Atlas Shrugged*

A bailment is different from a sale or a gift because title to the goods does not transfer to the bailee. Instead, the bailee must follow the bailor's directions concerning the goods. For example, suppose Hudson Corp. is relocating its offices and hires American Van Lines to move its office furniture and equipment to the new location. American Van Lines (the bailee) must follow Hudson's (the bailor) instructions regarding delivery. The law of bailments establishes the rights, duties, and liabilities of parties to a bailment.

EXHIBIT 8.1 *Parties to a bailment.*

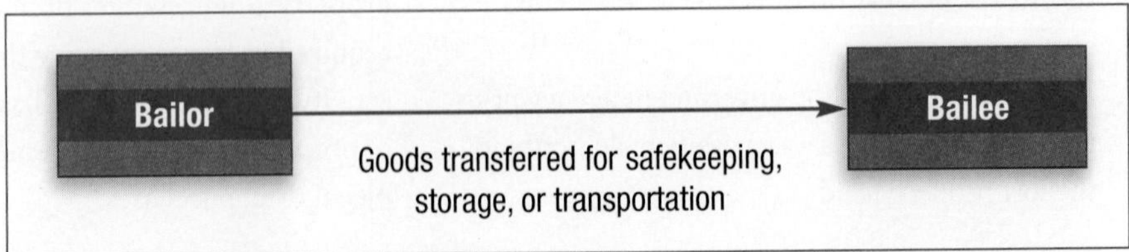

CASE FOR DISCUSSION

Sisters of Charity of the Incarnate Word v. Meaux

122 S.W.3d 428, 2003 Tex. App. Lexis 10189 (2003) **Court of Appeals of Texas**

FACTS

The Sisters of Charity of the Incarnate Word, d/b/a St. Elizabeth Hospital of Beaumont, operates a health and wellness center. Phil Meaux was a paying member of the health center. The rules of the health center, which Meaux had been given, state, "The Health & Wellness Center is not responsible for lost or stolen items." A sign stating "We cannot assure the safety of your valuables" was posted at the check-in desk. The health center furnished a lock and key to each member, but it had a master key to open lockers in case a member forgot or lost his key. On January 19, 2000, Meaux went to the Health & Wellness Center and placed his clothes, an expensive Rolex watch, and a money clip with $400 cash in the locker assigned him. Upon returning from swimming Meaux discovered that his locker had been pried open, and his watch and money had been stolen by some unknown person. Meaux sued the Sisters of Charity, alleging that a bailment had been created between him and the Sisters and that the Sisters, as bailee, were negligent and therefore liable to him for the value of his stolen property. The trial court held in favor of Meaux and awarded him $19,500 as the value of the stolen property, plus interest and attorney's fees. The Sisters of Charity appealed.

ISSUE

Was a bailment created between Meaux and the Sisters of Charity?

COURT'S REASONING

The court of appeals stated that in order to create a bailment, there must be delivery of personal property by one person (the bailor) to another (the bailee) in trust for a specific purpose. If there is a bailment, the bailee owes a duty to exercise ordinary care over the goods and is therefore responsible for their loss if the bailee is negligent. The court of appeals held that no bailment was created between Meaux and the Sisters of Charity. Instead, the court of appeals held that a landlord–tenant relationship had been created between Meaux and the Sisters of Charity. In a landlord–tenant agreement, the landlord does not possess dominion and control over the lessee's property, and is therefore not responsible for the loss of the lessee's property. The court stated, "There is no evidence of a bailment agreement."

DECISION AND REMEDY

The court of appeals held that a landlord–tenant agreement, and not a bailment, had been created between Meaux and the Sisters of Charity. The court held that the Sisters of Charity was not liable for Meaux's loss. The court of appeals reversed the trial court's judgment in favor of Meaux and rendered a decision in favor of the Sisters of Charity.

QUESTIONS

1. What is the difference between a bailment and a landlord–tenant relationship? Explain.
2. Did Meaux act ethically in arguing that a bailment had been created in this case?
3. Do you think the fact that the Sisters of Charity had a public rule that it was "not responsible" for the loss of items had much bearing on the outcome of this case?

Mutual-Benefit Bailments

Mutual-benefit bailments are bailments that *benefit both parties.* The bailee owes a **duty of reasonable care,** or duty of ordinary care, to protect the bailed goods. This means that the bailee is liable for any goods that are lost, damaged, or destroyed because of his or her negligence.

Property is an instrument of humanity. Humanity is not an instrument of property.
—Woodrow Wilson

Suppose ABC Garment Co. delivers goods to Lowell, Inc., a commercial warehouseman, for storage. A fee is charged for this service. ABC Garment Co. receives the benefit of having its goods stored, and Lowell, Inc., receives the benefit of being paid compensation for storing the goods. In this example, Lowell, Inc. (the bailee) owes a duty of ordinary care to protect the goods.

Innkeepers

An **innkeeper** is the owner of a facility that provides lodging to the public for compensation (e.g., a hotel or motel). Under the common law, innkeepers are held to a strict liability standard regarding loss caused to the personal property of transient guests. Permanent lodgers are not subject to this rule.

Almost all states, however, have enacted **innkeepers statutes** that change the common law and limit the liability of innkeepers. These statutes allow innkeepers to avoid liability for loss caused to guests' property if a safe is provided in which the guests' valuable property may be kept, and the guests are aware of the safe's availability. Most state laws also allow innkeepers to limit the dollar amount of their liability by notifying their guests of this limit (e.g., by posting a notice on each guest room door). This limitation on liability does not apply if the loss is caused by the innkeeper's negligence.

As an example, Hospitality Hotel Inc. operates a hotel. The hotel is located in a state that has an innkeepers statute that (1) eliminates a hotel's liability for guests' property not placed in a safe located at the hotel's registration desk, and (2) limits a hotel's liability to $500 for any guest's property stored in the hotel's safe. The hotel has proper notices posted at the registration counter and in guests' rooms notifying guests of these limitations on liability. Suppose Gian, a guest at the hotel, leaves expensive jewelry and cameras in his room when he temporarily leaves the hotel. Upon return, Gian's jewelry and cameras have been stolen. Because of the innkeeper statute, the hotel is not liable for Gian's loss. Suppose instead that Gian had taken his items to the hotel's registration desk and had the hotel place them in the hotel's safe. If the items had been stolen from the hotel's safe, the innkeepers statute would limit the hotel's liability to $500.

Real Property

Property and ownership rights in real property play an important part in this country's society and economy. Individuals and families own or rent houses, farmers and ranchers own farmland and ranches, and businesses own or lease commercial and office buildings. Real property includes the following:

1. **Land and buildings. Land** is the most common form of real property. A landowner usually purchases the **surface rights** to the land—that is, the right to occupy the land. The owner may use, enjoy, and develop the property as he or she sees fit, subject to any applicable government regulations. **Buildings** constructed on land—such as houses, apartment buildings, manufacturing plants, and office buildings—are real property. Things such as radio towers, bridges, and the like are considered real property as well.

2. **Subsurface rights.** The owner of land possesses subsurface rights or **mineral rights,** to the earth located beneath the surface of the land. These rights can be valuable. For example, gold, uranium, oil, or natural gas may lie beneath the surface of land. Theoretically, mineral rights extend to the center of the earth. In reality, mines and oil wells usually extend only several miles into the earth. Subsurface rights may be sold separately from surface rights.

3. **Plant life and vegetation.** Plant life and vegetation growing on the surface of land are considered real property. This includes natural plant life (e.g., trees) and cultivated plant life (e.g., crops). When land is sold, any plant life growing on the land is included unless the parties agree otherwise. Plant life that is severed from the land is considered personal property.

4. **Fixtures.** Certain personal property is associated so closely with real property that it becomes part of the realty. These items are called fixtures. For example, kitchen cabinets, carpeting, and doorknobs are fixtures, but throw rugs and furniture are personal property. Unless otherwise provided, if a building is sold, the fixtures are included in the sale. If the sale agreement is silent as to whether an item is a fixture, the courts make their determinations on the basis of whether the item can be removed without causing substantial damage to the realty.

Freehold Estates

A person's ownership right in real property is called an **estate in land,** or simply **estate.** An estate is defined as the bundle of *legal rights* that the owner has to possess, use, and enjoy the property. The type of estate that an owner possesses is determined from the deed, will, lease, or other document that transferred the ownership rights to him or her.

A **freehold estate** is one in which the owner has a *present possessory interest* in the real property; that is, the owner may use and enjoy the property as he or she sees fit, subject to any applicable government regulation or private restraint. The two types of freehold estates are **estates in fee** and *life estates.*

Estates in Fee

A **fee simple absolute** (or **fee simple**) is the highest form of ownership of real property because it grants the owner the fullest bundle of legal rights that a person can hold in real property. It is the type of ownership that most people connect with "owning" real property. A fee simple owner has the right to exclusively possess and use his or her property to the extent that the owner has not transferred any interest in the property (e.g., by lease).

A **fee simple defeasible,** or **qualified fee,** grants the owner all the incidents of a fee simple absolute except that it may be taken away if a specified *condition* occurs or does not occur. For example, a conveyance of property to a church "as long as the land is used as a church or for church purposes" creates a qualified fee. The church has all of the rights of a fee simple absolute owner except that its ownership rights are terminated if the property is no longer used for church purposes.

Life Estate

A **life estate** is an interest in real property that lasts for the life of a specified person, usually the grantee. For example, a conveyance of real property "to Anna for her life" creates a life estate. A life estate also may be measured by the life of a third

SIDEBAR

Air Rights: Value in the Heavens

Common law provided that the owners of real property owned that property from the center of the earth to the heavens. This rule has been eroded by modern legal restrictions such as **land-use control** laws, **environmental protection** laws, and **air navigation requirements**. Even today, however, the owners of land may sell or lease air space parcels above their land. An **air-space parcel** is a three-dimensional cube of air above the surface of the earth. Air-space parcels are valuable property rights, particularly in densely populated metropolitan areas where building property is scarce. For example, many developments have been built in air-space parcels in New York City. The most notable are Madison Square Garden and Two Penn Plaza, which were built in air-space parcels above Penn Station.

party (e.g., "to Anna for the life of Benjamin"). This is called an **estate *pour autre vie*.** A life estate may be defeasible (e.g., "to John for his life, but only if the party continues to occupy this residence"). Upon the death of the named person, the life estate terminates and the property reverts to the grantor or the grantor's estate or other designated person.

The right of property has not made poverty, but it has powerfully contributed to make wealth.
—J. R. McCulloch

A **life tenant** is treated as the owner of the property during the duration of the life estate. He or she has the right to possess and use the property except to the extent that it would cause permanent *waste* of the property. A life tenant may sell, transfer, or mortgage his or her estate in the land. The mortgage, however, cannot exceed the duration of the life estate. A life tenant is obligated to keep the property in repair and to pay property taxes.

Future Interests

A person may be given the right to possess property in the *future* rather than in the present. This right is called a **future interest.** The two forms of future interests are *reversion* and *remainder.*

Reversion

A **reversion** is a right of possession that returns to the grantor after the expiration of a limited or contingent estate. Reversions do not have to be expressly stated because they arise automatically by law. For example, if a grantor conveys property "to M. R. Harrington for life," the grantor has retained a reversion in the property. That is, when Harrington dies, the property reverts to the grantor or, if he or she is not living, then to his or her estate.

Remainder

If the right of possession returns to a *third party* upon the expiration of a limited or contingent estate, it is called a **remainder.** The person who is entitled to the future interest is called a remainderman. For example, a conveyance of property "to Joe for life, remainder to Meredith" is a vested remainder; the only contingency to Meredith's possessory interest is Joe's death.

Concurrent Ownership

Two or more persons may own a piece of real property. This is called **co-ownership** or **concurrent ownership.** The following forms of co-ownership are recognized: *joint tenancy, tenancy in common, tenancy by the entirety, community property, condominium,* and *cooperative.* These are summarized in Table 8.1.

Joint Tenancy

To create a **joint tenancy,** words that clearly show a person's intent to create a joint tenancy must be used. Language such as "Marsha Leest and James Leest, as joint tenants" is usually sufficient. The most distinguishing feature of a joint tenancy is the co-owners' **right of survivorship.** This means that upon the death of one of the co-owners, or joint tenants, the deceased person's interest in the property au-

TABLE 8.1 *Summary of concurrent ownership.*

Form of Ownership	Right of Survivorship	May Tenant Unilaterally Transfer His or Her Interest?
Joint tenancy	Yes, deceased tenant's interest automatically passes to co-tenants.	Yes, tenant may transfer his or her interest without the consent of co-tenants. Transfer severs joint tenancy.
Tenancy in common	No, deceased tenant's interest passes to his or her estate.	Yes, tenant may transfer his or her interest without the consent of co-tenants. Transfer does not sever tenancy in common.
Tenancy by the entirety	Yes, deceased tenant's interest automatically passes to his or her spouse.	No, neither spouse may transfer his or her interest without the other spouse's consent.
Community property	Yes, when a spouse dies, the surviving spouse automatically receives one-half of the community property. The other half passes to the heirs of the deceased spouse as directed by a valid will or by state intestate statute if there is no will.	No, neither spouse may transfer his or her interest without the other spouse's consent.

tomatically passes to the surviving joint tenants. Any contrary provision in the deceased's will is ineffective.

Consider this example: Jones, one of four people who own a piece of property in joint tenancy, executes a will leaving all of his property to a university. Jones dies. The surviving joint tenants—not the university—acquire his interest in the piece of property. Each joint tenant has a right to sell or transfer his or her interest in the property, but such conveyance terminates the joint tenancy. The parties then become tenants in common.

Tenancy in Common

In a **tenancy in common,** the interests of a surviving tenant in common pass to the deceased tenant's estate and not to the co-tenants. A tenancy in common may be created by express words, such as "Iran Cespedes and Joy Park, as tenants in common." Unless otherwise agreed, a tenant in common can sell, give, devise, or otherwise transfer his or her interest in the property without the consent of the other co-owners.

Consider this example: Lopez, one of four tenants in common who own a piece of property, has a will that leaves all of his property to his granddaughter. When Lopez dies, the granddaughter receives his interest in the tenancy in common, and the granddaughter becomes a tenant in common with the three other owners.

Tenancy by the Entirety

Tenancy by the entirety is a form of co-ownership of real property that can be used only by married couples. This type of tenancy must be created by express words, such as "Harold Jones and Maude Jones, husband and wife, as tenants by the entireties." A surviving spouse has the right of survivorship.

Tenancy by the entirety is distinguished from a joint tenancy in that neither spouse may sell or transfer his or her interest in the property without the other spouse's consent. Only about half of the states recognize a tenancy by the entirety.

Community Property

Ten states—Alaska, Arizona, California, Idaho, Louisiana, Nevada, New Mexico, Texas, Washington, and Wisconsin—recognize a form of co-ownership known as **community property.** This method of co-ownership applies only to married couples and is based on the notion that a husband and wife should share equally in the fruits of the marital partnership.

Under these laws, each spouse owns an equal one-half share of the income of both spouses and the assets acquired during the marriage regardless of who earns the income. Property that is acquired through gift or inheritance either before or during marriage remains separate property.

When a spouse dies, the surviving spouse automatically receives one-half of the community property. The other half passes to the heirs of the deceased spouse as directed by will or by state intestate statute if there is no will.

For example, a husband and wife have community property assets of $1.5 million and the wife dies with a will. The husband automatically has a right to receive $750,000 of the community property. The remaining $750,000 passes as directed by the wife's will. Any separate property owned by the wife, such as jewelry she inherited, also passes in accordance with her will. Her husband has no vested interest in that property.

During the marriage, neither spouse can sell, transfer, or gift community property without the consent of the other spouse. Upon a divorce, each spouse has a right to one-half of the community property.

The location of the real property determines whether community property law applies. For example, if a married couple who lives in a noncommunity property state purchases real property located in a community property state, community property laws apply to that property.

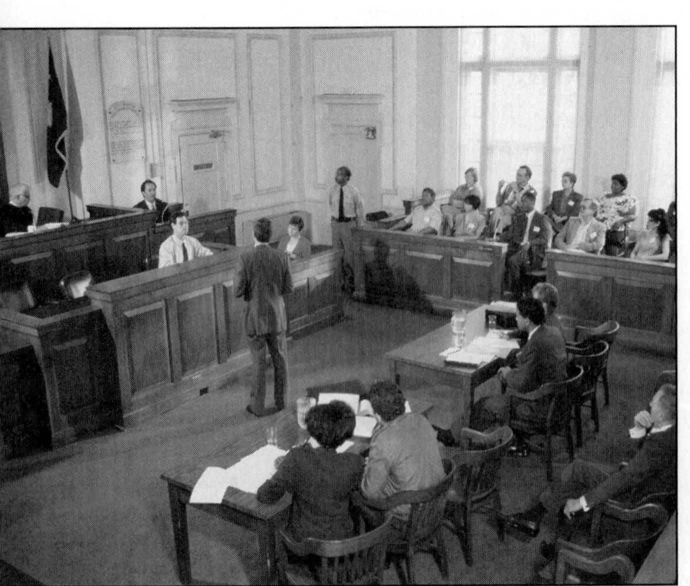

A courtroom scene with a trial in progress.

Condominiums

Condominiums are a common form of ownership in multiple-dwelling buildings. Purchasers of a condominium (1) have title to their individual units, and (2) own the common areas (e.g., hallways, elevators, parking areas, and recreational facilities) as tenants in common with the other owners. Owners may sell or mortgage their units without the permission of the other owners. Owners are assessed monthly fees for the maintenance of common areas. In addition to dwelling units,

Recording Statutes

Every state has a **recording statute** that provides that copies of deeds and other documents concerning interests in real property (e.g., mortgages, liens, easements) may be filed in a government office where they become public records open to viewing by the public. Recording statutes are intended to prevent fraud and to establish certainty in the ownership and transfer of property. Instruments usually are filed in the *county recorder's office* of the county in which the real property is located. A fee is charged to record an instrument.

Persons interested in purchasing the property or lending on the property check these records to determine if the grantor or borrower actually owns the property and whether any other parties (e.g., lienholders, mortgagees, easement holders) have an interest in the property. The recordation of a deed is not required to pass title from the grantor to the grantee. Recording the deed gives **constructive notice** to the world of the owner's interest in the property.

A party who is concerned about his or her ownership rights in a parcel of real property can bring a **quiet title** action to have a court determine the extent of those rights. Public notice of the hearing must be given so that anyone claiming an interest in the property may appear and be heard. After the hearing, the judge declares who has title to the property—that is, the court "quiets title" by its decision.

the condominium form of ownership is offered for office buildings, boat docks, and such.

Cooperative

A **cooperative** is a form of co-ownership of a multiple-dwelling building in which a corporation owns the building and the residents own shares in the corporation. Each cooperative owner then leases a unit in the building from the corporation under a renewable, long-term, proprietary lease. Individual residents may not secure loans with the units they occupy. The corporation may borrow money on a blanket mortgage, and each shareholder is jointly and severally liable on the loan. Usually, cooperative owners may not sell their shares or sublease their units without the approval of the other owners.

Good fences make good neighbors.
—Robert Frost,
"Mending Wall"

TRANSFER OF OWNERSHIP OF REAL PROPERTY

Ownership of real property may be transferred from one person to another. Title to real property may be transferred by sale, tax sale, gift, will, or inheritance. A **deed** is used to convey real property by sale or gift. The seller or donor is called the **grantor.** The buyer or recipient is called the **grantee.** A deed may be used to transfer a fee simple absolute interest in real property or any lesser estate (e.g., life estate).

State laws recognize different types of deeds that provide differing degrees of protection to grantees. A **warranty deed** contains the greatest number of warranties and provides the most protection to grantees. A **quitclaim deed** provides the least amount of protection because the grantor conveys only whatever interest he or she has in the property.

CASE FOR DISCUSSION

Cunningham v. Hastings

556 N.E.2d 12, 1990 Ind. App. Lexis 764 (1990) — Court of Appeals of Indiana

FACTS

On August 30, 1984, Warren R. Hastings and Joan L. Cunningham, who were unmarried, purchased a house together. Hastings paid a $45,000 down payment toward the purchase price out of his own funds. The deed referred to Hastings and Cunningham as "joint tenants with the right of survivorship." Hastings and Cunningham occupied the property jointly. After their relationship ended, Hastings took sole possession of the property. Cunningham filed a complaint seeking partition of the real estate. Based on its determination that the property could not be split, the trial court ordered it to be sold. The trial court further ordered that $45,000 of the sale proceeds be paid to Hastings to reimburse him for his down payment, and the remainder of the proceeds be divided equally between Hastings and Cunningham. Cunningham appealed, alleging that Hastings should not have been given credit for the down payment.

ISSUE

Is Cunningham entitled to an equal share of the proceeds of the sale of the real estate?

COURT'S REASONING

The court commented that, "*the determination of the parties' interests in the present case is simple: There are only two parties involved in the joint tenancy. Once a joint tenancy relationship is found to exist between two people in a partition action, it is axiomatic that each person owns a one-half interest.*" The court stated, "*Regardless of who provided the money to purchase the land, the creation of a joint tenancy relationship entitles each party to an equal share of the proceeds of the sale upon partition.*"

DECISION AND REMEDY

The court of appeals held that Cunningham was entitled to an equal share of the proceeds of the sale because she and Hastings owned the property as joint tenants. The court ordered that the entire proceeds of the sale be divided equally between Cunningham and Hastings.

QUESTIONS

1. Should the law recognize so many different forms of ownership of real property? Do you think most people understand the legal consequences of taking title in the various forms?
2. Did Cunningham act ethically in demanding one-half the value of the down payment even though she did not contribute to it?
3. Could Hastings have protected the $45,000 he paid for the down payment? If so, how could he have done it?

Sale of Real Estate

A sale or conveyance is the most common method for transferring ownership rights in real property. Under the Statute of Frauds, an agreement for the sale of real property must be in writing to be enforceable. The seller delivers a deed to the buyer and the buyer pays the purchase price at the closing or settlement.

Marketable Title

Marketable title means that the title is free from any encumbrances, defects in title, or other defects that are not disclosed but would affect the value of the property. A buyer of real property can purchase title insurance from a title insurance company. The title insurance policy lists any defects in the title of the property, if any, and ensures against unlisted defects in title.

The title insurer must reimburse the insured for any losses caused by undiscovered defects in the title. Each time a property is transferred, a new title insurance policy must be obtained.

> Without that sense of security which property gives, the land would still be uncultivated.
>
> —Francois Quesnay

Adverse Possession

In most states, a person who wrongfully possesses someone else's real property obtains title to that property if certain statutory requirements are met. This is called **adverse possession.** Property owned by federal and state governments are not subject to adverse possession.

Under this doctrine, the transfer of the property is involuntary and does not require delivery of a deed. To obtain title under adverse possession, the wrongful possession must be:

- **For a statutorily prescribed period of time:** In most states, this period is between 10 and 20 years.
- **Open, visible, and notorious:** The adverse possessor must occupy the property so as to put the owner on notice of the possession.
- **Actual and exclusive:** The adverse possessor must physically occupy the premises. The planting of crops, grazing of animals, or building of a structure on the land constitutes physical occupancy.
- **Continuous and peaceful:** The occupancy must be uninterrupted for the required statutory period. Any break in normal occupancy terminates the adverse possession. This means that the adverse possessor may leave the property to go to work, to the store, on a vacation, and such. The adverse possessor cannot take the property by force from an owner.
- **Hostile and adverse:** The possessor must occupy the property without the express or implied permission of the owner. Thus, a lessee cannot claim title to property under adverse possession.

If the elements of adverse possession are met, the adverse possessor acquires clear title to the land. But title is acquired only as to the property actually possessed and occupied during the statutory period, and not the entire tract. For example, an adverse possessor who occupies one acre of a 200,000-acre ranch for the statutory period of time acquires title to only the one acre.

ETHICAL PERSPECTIVE

MODERN-DAY SQUATTERS

Edward and Mary Shaughnessey purchased a 16-acre tract in St. Louis county in 1954. Subsequently, they subdivided 12 acres into 18 lots offered for sale and retained possession of the remaining 4-acre tract. In 1967, Charles and Elaine Witt purchased lot 12, which is adjacent to the 4-acre tract. The Witts constructed and moved into a house on their lot. In 1968, they cleared an area of land that ran the length of their property and extended 40 feet onto the 4-acre tract. The Witts constructed a pool and a deck, planted a garden, made a playground for their children, set up a dog run, and built a fence along the edge of the property line, which included the now-disputed property. Neither the Witts nor the Shaughnesseys realized that the Witts had encroached on the Shaughnesseys' property.

In February 1988, the Shaughnesseys sold the 4-acre tract to Thomas and Rosanne Miller. When a survey showed the encroachment, the Millers demanded that the Witts remove the pool and cease using the property. When the Witts refused to do so, the Millers sued to quiet title. The Witts defended, arguing that they had obtained title to the disputed property by adverse possession.

The court of appeals agreed with the Witts. The court held that the Witts had proven the necessary elements for adverse possession under state law. The Witts' occupation of the land was open and notorious, actual and exclusive, hostile and adverse, continuous and peaceful, and had been for over the statutory period of 10 years. The court issued an order quieting title to the disputed property in the Witts' favor. [*Witt v. Miller,* 845 S.W.2d 665, 1993 Mo. App. Lexis 20 (Mo.App. 1993)]

1. Did the Millers act ethically in trying to stop use of the land parcel by people who had occupied it for 20 years?
2. Did the Witts act ethically in claiming title to someone else's land? Should they be allowed to benefit from their own mistake?

Easements

An **easement** is an interest in land that gives the holder the right to make limited use of another's property without taking anything from it. Easements may be expressly created by **grant** (where an owner gives another party an easement across his or her property) or reservation (where an owner sells land that he or she owns but reserves an easement on the land). Easements also may be implied by (1) *implication*, where an owner subdivides a piece of property with a well, path, road, or other beneficial appurtenant that serves the entire parcel, or by (2) *necessity*, for example, where "landlocked" property has an implied easement across surrounding property to enter and exit the landlocked property. Easements can also be created by *prescription*, that is, adverse possession.

Typical easements are common driveways, party walls, and rights-of-way. There are two types of easements: easements appurtenant and easements in gross.

1. **Easements appurtenant:** An **easement appurtenant** is created when the owner of one piece of land is given an easement over an adjacent piece of land. The land over which the easement is granted is called the **servient estate.** The land that benefits from the easement is called the **dominant estate.** Adjacent land is defined as two estates that are in proximity to each other, but do not necessarily abut each other. An appurtenant easement runs with the land. For example, if an owner sells the dominant estate, the new

Walker v. Ayres

1993 Del. Lexis 105 (1993) Supreme Court of Delaware

FACTS

Elizabeth Star Ayres and Clara Louise Quillen own in fee simple absolute a tract of land in Sussex County known as Bluff Point. The tract is surrounded on three sides by Rehoboth Bay and is landlocked on the fourth side by Walker's land. At one time, the two tracts in question were held by a common owner. In 1878, Bluff Point was sold in fee simple absolute apart from the other holdings, thereby landlocking the parcel. A narrow dirt road, which traverses Walker's land, connects Bluff Point to a public road and is its only means of access. Ayres and Quillen sought an easement to use this road, and Walker objected. This lawsuit ensued. The trial court granted an easement. Walker appealed.

ISSUE

Should Ayres' and Quillen's estate be granted an easement against Walker's estate?

COURT'S REASONING

The supreme court held that an easement appurtenant had been created between two adjacent parcels of property. The court held that the easement was created by implication in 1878 when Bluff Point was separated from the rest of the holdings and landlocked at that time. The court also held that an easement was created by necessity because Bluff Point was landlocked and its only access was over Walker's property. The court found that water access, even if a reasonable substitute for land access, was not feasible because of the shallowness of the water surrounding Bluff Point.

DECISION AND REMEDY

The supreme court held that an easement had been created. Affirmed.

QUESTIONS

1. Should easements be recognized by the law? Why or why not?
2. Did Walker act ethically in denying the easement? Did Ayres and Quillen act ethically in seeking to use Walker's property?
3. Does an easement increase or decrease the value of the servient estate? Of the dominant estate?

owner acquires the benefit of the easement. If an owner sells the servient estate, the buyer purchases the property subject to the easement.

2. **Easements in gross:** An **easement in gross** authorizes a person who does not own adjacent land the right to use another's land. An easement in gross is a personal right because it does not depend on the easement holder's owning adjacent land. Thus, there is no dominant estate. Examples of easements in gross include those granted to run power, telephone, and cable television lines across an owner's property. Commercial easements in gross are transferable, but ordinary, noncommercial easements in gross are not. Thus, if a farmer grants a hunter the right to hunt pheasant on his farm, it does not mean that other hunters are permitted to hunt on the farmer's property.

Laws are always useful to persons of property, and hurtful to those who have none.
—Jean Jacques Rousseau

The easement holder owes a duty to maintain and repair the easement. The owner of the estate can use the property as long as it does not interfere with the easement. For example, if a piece of property is subject to an easement for an underground pipeline, the owner of the property could graze cattle or plant crops on the land above the easement, subject to the easement holder's right to repair the pipeline.

Landlord–Tenant Relationship

Landlord–tenant relationships are common in the United States because (1) more than half of the population rent their homes, and (2) many businesses lease office space, stores, manufacturing facilities, and other commercial property. The parties to the relationship have certain legal rights and duties governed by a mixture of real estate and contract law.

A landlord–tenant relationship is created when the owner of a freehold estate (i.e., an estate in fee or a life estate) transfers a right to exclusively and temporarily possess the owner's property. The tenant receives a **nonfreehold estate** in the property—that is, the tenant has a right to possession of the property but not title to the property.

Types of Tenancy

The tenant's interest in the property is called a **leasehold estate,** or **leasehold.** The owner who transfers the leasehold estate is called the **landlord,** or lessor. The party to whom the leasehold estate is transferred is called the **tenant,** or lessee. *Tenancies* are of four types:

1. **Tenancy for years:** A **tenancy for years** is created when the landlord and the tenant agree on a specific duration for the lease. Any lease for a stated period—no matter how long or short—is called a tenancy for years. Examples of these arrangements include office space leased in a high-rise office building on a 30-year lease and a cabin leased for the summer. A tenancy for years terminates automatically, without notice, upon expiration of the stated term.

2. **Periodic tenancy:** A **periodic tenancy** is created when a lease specifies intervals at which payments are due but does not specify the duration of the lease. A lease that states, "Rent is due on the first day of the month" establishes a periodic tenancy. Many such leases are created by implication. A periodic tenancy may be

terminated by either party at the end of any payment interval, but adequate notice of the termination must be given. At common law, the notice period equaled the length of the payment period. Therefore, a month-to-month tenancy requires a one-month notice of termination.

3. **Tenancy at will:** A lease that may be terminated at any time by either party is termed a **tenancy at will.** A tenancy at will may be created expressly (e.g., "to tenant as long as landlord wishes") but more likely is created by implication. Most states have enacted statutes requiring minimum advance notice for the termination of a tenancy at will. The death of either party terminates a tenancy at will.

4. **Tenancy at sufferance:** A **tenancy at sufferance** is created when a tenant retains possession of the property after the expiration of another tenancy or a life estate without the owner's consent. That is, the owner suffers the *wrongful possession* of his or her property by the holdover tenant. This is not really a true tenancy but merely the possession of property without right. Technically, a tenant at sufferance is a trespasser. A tenant at sufferance is liable for the payment of rent during the period of sufferance. To evict a holdover tenant, most states require an owner to go through certain legal proceedings, called **eviction proceedings** or **unlawful detainer actions.** A few states allow owners to use self-help to evict a holdover tenant if force is not used.

The right of property enables an industrious man to reap where he has sown.

—Unknown

The Lease

The rental agreement between the landlord and the tenant is called the lease. Leases generally can be either oral or written, except that most statutes of frauds require written leases for periods of time longer than one year. The lease must contain the essential terms of the parties' agreement. The lease is often a form contract prepared by the landlord and presented to the tenant. This is particularly true of residential leases. Other leases are negotiated between the parties. For example, a bank's lease of a branch office would be negotiated with the owner of the building.

Implied Warranty of Habitability

The courts of many jurisdictions hold that an **implied warranty of habitability** applies to residential leases for their duration. This warranty provides that the leased premises must be fit, safe, and suitable for ordinary residential use. For example, unchecked rodent infestation, leaking roofs, and unworkable bathroom facilities have been held to breach the implied warranty of habitability. On the other hand, a small crack in the wall or some paint peeling from a door does not breach this warranty.

If the landlord's failure to maintain or repair the leased premises affects the tenant's use or enjoyment of the premises, state statutes and judicial decisions provide various remedies. Generally, the tenant may (1) withhold from his or her rent the amount by which the defect reduced the value of the premises to him or her, (2) repair the defect and deduct the cost of repairs from the rent due for the leased premises, (3) cancel the lease if the failure to repair constitutes constructive eviction, or (4) sue for damages for the amount the landlord's failure to repair the defect reduced the value of the leasehold.

Land-Use Control

Although the United States has the most advanced private-property system in the world, ownership and possession of real estate are not free of government regulation. Pursuant to constitutional authority, federal, state, and local governments have enacted myriad laws that regulate ownership, possession, and use of real property. These laws are collectively referred to as **land-use control.**

Most counties and municipalities have enacted zoning ordinances to regulate land use. **Zoning ordinances** (1) establish use districts within the municipality (i.e., areas usually are designated residential, commercial, or industrial), (2) restrict the height, size, and location of buildings on a building site, and (3) establish aesthetic requirements or limitations for the exterior of buildings.

A zoning commission usually formulates zoning ordinances, conducts public hearings, and makes recommendations to the city council, which must vote to enact an ordinance. Once enacted, the zoning ordinance commission enforces the zoning ordinance. If landowners believe that a zoning ordinance is illegal or that it has been applied unlawfully to them or their property, they may institute a court proceeding seeking judicial review of the ordinance or its application.

An owner who wishes to use his or her property for a use different from that permitted under a current zoning ordinance may seek relief from the ordinance by obtaining a **variance.** To do this, the landowner must prove that the ordinance causes an undue hardship by preventing him or her from making a reasonable return on the land as zoned. Variances tend to be difficult to obtain.

Zoning laws act prospectively; that is, uses and buildings that already exist in the zoned area are permitted to continue even though they do not fit within new zoning ordinances. Such uses are called **nonconforming uses.** For example, if a new zoning ordinance is enacted making an area a residential zone, an existing funeral parlor is a nonconforming use.

Government Regulation Versus Compensable "Taking" of Real Property

The government may use its power of **eminent domain** to acquire private property for public purposes. However, the Due Process Clause of the U.S. Constitution (and state constitutions where applicable) requires the government to allow the owner to make a case for keeping the property. The **Just Compensation Clause** of the Constitution mandates that the government must compensate the property owner (and possibly others, such as lessees) when it exercises the power of eminent domain. Anyone who is not satisfied with the compensation offered by the government can bring an action to have the court determine the compensation to be paid. Often, the government's action is not considered a "taking" even if it causes economic losses to property owners and others.

Consider this example: Assume that ITT acquired a large piece of property with the intention of erecting a commercial building at some future time. Now suppose the government wants to build a new highway that passes through property owned by ITT. The government can use its power of eminent domain to acquire the property. There has been a "taking," so the government must pay ITT just compensation. Suppose, instead, that the government enacts a zoning law that affects ITT's property by restricting building in the area to single-family housing. Although ITT would suffer a substantial economic loss, the zoning law, nevertheless, would probably not constitute a "taking" that required the payment of compensation.

CASE FOR DISCUSSION

Guinnane v. San Francisco City Planning Commission

209 Cal.App.3d. 732, 257 Cal.Rptr. 742, 1989 Cal. App. Lexis 377 (1989) California Court of Appeal

FACTS

In 1979, Roy Guinnane purchased four vacant lots located in Edgehill Way in San Francisco. In July 1980, the city of San Francisco designated an area as "Edgehill Woods." Guinnane's property was located in that area. In 1982, the city enacted a Municipal Code that gave the San Francisco Planning Commission authority to exercise its discretionary review power over proposed development in the Edgehill Woods area, including authority to decide whether the development matched the character of surrounding properties. Guinnane filed an application for a building permit to construct a four-story, 6,000-square-foot house with five bedrooms, five baths, and parking for two cars on one of his lots. Pursuant to the city's Municipal Code, the San Francisco Planning Commission disapproved the application because the proposed structure was "not in character" with other homes in the neighborhood. The board of permit appeals agreed. Guinnane appealed.

ISSUE

Is the aesthetic zoning by the city of San Francisco lawful?

COURT'S REASONING

The appellate court held that the planning commission acted within its discretion in finding that Guinnane's proposed building was "not in character" with other homes in the area. The court stated that the basic standard guiding the San Francisco Planning Commission in discharging its function is the "promotion of the public health, safety, peace, morals, comfort, convenience, and general welfare." In particular, the Commission is directed to "protect the character and stability of residential areas." Under the San Francisco Municipal Code, the Planning Commission may exercise its discretion in deciding whether to approve any application; and in doing so, it may consider the effect of the proposed project upon the surrounding properties.

DECISION AND REMEDY

The appellate court held that San Francisco's aesthetic zoning ordinance was lawful. The court found that the ordinance was enacted pursuant to the city's "police power" to protect its residents' health, safety, and welfare. The appellate court affirmed the trial court's judgment.

QUESTIONS

1. Should a city be given zoning authority over the aesthetics of an area? Why or why not?
2. Is it ethical for a property owner to build a structure that does not comport with the character of the area?
3. Are businesses helped or harmed by zoning ordinances?

LEGAL TERMINOLOGY

Abandoned property
Adverse possession
Air navigation requirements
Air-space parcel
Bailee
Bailment
Bailor
Buildings
Community property
Concurrent ownership
Condominium
Constructive notice
Cooperative
Co-ownership
Deed
Dominent estate
Duty of ordinary care
Duty of reasonable care
Easement
Easement appurtenant
Easement in gross
Eminent domain
Environmental protection
Estate (or estate in land)
Estate *pour autre vie*
Estates in fee
Estray statute
Eviction proceedings
Fee simple absolute (fee simple)
Fee simple defeasible (qualified fee)
Fixture
Freehold estate
Future interest
Gift *causa mortis*
Gift *inter vivos*
Grant
Grantee
Grantor
Implied warranty of habitability
Innkeeper
Innkeeper statutes
Intangible property
Joint tenancy
Just Compensation Clause
Land
Landlord
Land-use control
Leasehold estate (leasehold)
Life estate
Life tenant
Lost property
Marketable title
Mineral rights
Mislaid property
Mutual-benefit bailment
Nonconforming uses
Nonfreehold estate
Periodic tenancy
Personal property
Plant life and vegetation
Qualified fee
Quiet title
Quitclaim deed
Real property
Recording statute
Remainder
Reversion
Revised Uniform Gift to Minors Act
Right of survivorship
Servient estate
Strict liability standard
Subsurface rights
Surface rights
Tangible property
Tenancy in common
Tenancy by the entirety
Tenancy at sufferance
Tenancy at will
Tenancy for years
Tenant/lessee
Uniform Gifts to Minors Act
Unlawful detainer actions
Variance
Warranty deed
Zoning ordinance

chapter summary

REAL AND PERSONAL PROPERTY

Personal Property	
Definition	Everything that is not real property; sometimes referred to as *goods* or *chattels*.
Types of Personal Property	1. *Tangible property:* Physically defined property such as goods, animals, and minerals. 2. *Intangible property:* Rights that cannot be reduced to physical form, such as stock certificates, bonds, and copyrights.
Types of Gifts	1. Gifts *inter vivos:* Gifts made during a donor's lifetime that are irrevocable present transfers of ownership. 2. Gifts *causa mortis:* Gifts that are made in anticipation of death.
Mislaid, Lost, and Abandoned Property	1. *Mislaid property:* Personal property that an owner voluntarily places somewhere and then inadvertently forgets. The owner of the premises where the property is mislaid does not acquire title to the property but has the right of possession against all except the rightful owner. The rightful owner can reclaim the property. 2. *Lost property:* Personal property that an owner leaves somewhere because of negligence or carelessness. The finder obtains title to the property against the whole world except the true owner. The rightful owner can reclaim the property. 3. *Estray statutes:* State statutes that permit a finder of mislaid or lost property to obtain title to the property. To obtain clear title, the finder must: a. Report the find to the appropriate government agency and turn over possession of the property to the agency. b. Post and publish required notices. c. Wait the statutorily required time (e.g., one year) without the rightful owner claiming the property. 4. *Abandoned property:* Personal property that an owner has discarded, or mislaid or lost property that the owner gives up any further attempt to locate. The finder acquires title to the property. The prior owner cannot reclaim the property.
Bailments	
Description	Occurs when the owner of personal property delivers the property to another person to be held, stored, or delivered, or for some other purpose.
Parties	1. *Bailor:* Owner of the property. 2. *Bailee:* Party to whom the property is delivered.
Mutual-Benefit Bailment	Bailment for the mutual benefit of the bailor and the bailee. 1. Arises when both parties benefit from the bailment. This includes commercial bailments. 2. The bailee owes a *duty of reasonable care* (or *ordinary care*).

(continued)

Real Property	
Nature of Real Property	*Real property* is immovable. It includes land, buildings, subsurface rights, air rights, plant life, and fixtures.
Freehold Estates	
Definition	Estates where the owner has a present possessory interest in the real property.
Estate in Fee	1. *Fee simple absolute* (or *fee simple*): Highest form of ownership. 2. *Fee simple defeasible* (or *qualified fee*): Estate that ends if a specified condition occurs.
Life Estate	An interest in real property that lasts for the life of a specified person; called an *estate pour autre vie* if the time is measured by the life of a third person.
Future Interests	
Definition	Right to possess real property in the future rather than currently.
Reversion	Right to possession that returns to the grantor after the expiration of a limited or contingent estate.
Remainder	Right to possession that goes to a third person after the expiration of a limited or contingent estate; the third person is called a *remainderman.*
Concurrent Ownership	
Definition	Where two or more persons jointly own real property.
Joint Tenancy	Owners may transfer their interests without the consent of co-owners; transfer severs the joint tenancy. Under the *right of survivorship*, the interest of a deceased owner passes to his or her co-owners.
Tenancy in Common	Owners may transfer their interests without the consent of co-owners; transfer does not sever the tenancy in common. Interest of a deceased owner passes to his or her estate.
Tenancy by the Entirety	Form of co-ownership that can be used only by a married couple; neither spouse may transfer his or her interest without the other spouse's consent. A surviving spouse has the right of survivorship.
Community Property	Form of co-ownership that applies only to a married couple; neither spouse may transfer his or her interest without the other spouse's consent. When a spouse dies, the surviving spouse automatically receives one-half of the community property.
Condominium	Owners have title to their individual units and own the common areas as tenants in common; owners may transfer their interests without the consent of other owners.
Cooperative	A corporation owns the building, and the residents own shares of the corporation. Usually, owners may not transfer their shares without the approval of the other owners.

Transfer of Ownership of Real Property	
Sale of Real Estate	An owner sells his or her property to another for consideration.
Marketable Title	A title free of encumbrances, defects in the title, or other defects.
Deed	Instrument used to convey real property by sale or gift. 1. *Warranty deed:* Provides the most protection to the grantee because the grantor makes warranties against defect in title. 2. *Quitclaim deed:* Provides least amount of protection to the grantee because the grantor transfers only the interest he or she had in the property.
Recording Statutes	Permit copies of deeds and other documents concerning interests in real property (e.g., mortgages, liens) to be filed in a government office where they become public record. Puts third parties on notice of recorded interests.
Adverse Possession	A person who occupies another's property acquires title to the property if the occupation has been: 1. For a statutory period of time (in many states, 10 to 20 years) 2. Open, visible, and notorious 3. Actual and exclusive 4. Continuous and peaceful 5. Hostile and adverse
Easement	An interest in land that gives the holder the right to make limited use of another's property without taking anything from it (e.g., driveways, party walls).
Landlord–Tenant Relationship	
Definition	A contract created when an owner of a freehold estate transfers a right to another to exclusively and temporarily possess the owner's property.
Types of Tenancy	1. *Tenancy for years:* Tenancy for a specified period of time. 2. *Periodic tenancy:* Tenancy for a period of time determined by the payment interval. 3. *Tenancy at will:* Tenancy that may be terminated at any time by either party. 4. *Tenancy at sufferance:* Tenancy created by the wrongful possession of property.
Lease	The rental agreement between the landlord and the tenant that contains the essential terms of the parties' agreement.
Land-Use Control	
Public Regulation of Land Use	*Zoning ordinances:* Laws adopted by local governments that restrict use of property, set building standards, and establish architectural requirements. 1. *Variance:* Permits an owner to make a nonzoned use of his or her property; requires permission from a zoning board. 2. *Nonconforming use:* A nonzoned use that is permitted (grandfathered in) when an area is rezoned.

WORKING THE WEB

Visit the Web sites below for more information about the topics covered in this chapter.

1. Find your state's law on bailments relating to parking lots. See "The Parking Lot Cases Revisited: Confusion at or About the Gate," 40 Santa Clara L. Rev. 27 (1999) by William V. Vetter.
2. Review your state's laws on innkeeper liability for lost or stolen property of hotel guests. What is the statutory limitation on losses?
3. Many states have statutes regarding lost or abandoned property. For example, see Washington State's statute, Title 63 RCW, Personal Property.
4. Although most real estate law is local law, there are important federal controls on certain types of transactions. See 42 USC, Chapter 45—Federal Fair Housing Act.
5. There is an ongoing and vigorous debate about governmental authority to regulate land use without paying compensation to the property owner. Read the cited law review for an overview of the taking clause of the Fifth Amendment and related issues: "Windfalls or Windmills: The Right of a Property Owner to Challenge Land Use Regulations," at **www.law.fsu.edu/journals/landuse/Vol131/ABRA.html.**
6. Is your state one that has adopted the Uniform Landlord–Tenant Act? See **www.law.cornell.edu/uniform/vol7.html#lndtn.** For a general overview, see **www.law.cornell.edu/topics/landlord_tenant.html.**

CRITICAL LEGAL THINKING QUESTIONS

1. Describe personal property. How does this differ from real property?
2. What does an estray statute provide? What public policy underlies an estray statute?
3. How does a bailment occur? Who are the parties to a bailment? How is liability for lost or damaged goods assessed?
4. What is a fee simple absolute (or fee simple) estate? How does this differ from a life estate?
5. Describe the differences between joint tenancy, tenancy in common, and tenancy by the entirety.
6. What is the purpose of a recording statute?
7. Describe the doctrine of adverse possession. Why does the law recognize this doctrine?
8. What is an easement? Describe the difference between an express easement and an implied easement.
9. Describe the differences between tenancy for years, periodic tenancy, tenancy at will, and tenancy by sufferance.
10. Are land-use control laws necessary? What purpose do they serve?

CASE FOR BRIEFING

Read Case 8 in Appendix A (*The Wackenhut Corporation and Delta Airlines, Inc. v. Lippert*). Review and brief the case using the *Critical Legal Thinking* "Briefing the Case" example described in Chapter 1.

8.1 *Naab v. Nolan*

327 S.E.2d 151, 1985 W.Va. Lexis 476 (1985)
Supreme Court of Appeals of West Virginia

FACTS In 1973, Joseph and Helen Naab purchased a tract of land in a subdivision of Williamstown, West Virginia. At the time of purchase, the property had both a house and a small concrete garage. Evidence showed that the garage had been erected sometime prior to 1952 by one of the Naabs' predecessors in title. In 1975, Roger and Cynthia Nolan purchased a lot contiguous to that owned by the Naabs. The following year, the Nolans had their property surveyed. The survey indicated that one corner of the Naabs' garage encroached 1.22 feet onto the Nolans' property and the other corner encroached 0.91 feet over the property line. The Nolans requested that the Naabs remove the garage from their property. When the Naabs refused, the lawsuit ensued.

ISSUE Who wins?

8.2 *Hill v. Pinelawn Memorial Park, Inc.*

282 S.E.2d 779, 1981 N.C. Lexis 1326 (1981)
Supreme Court of North Carolina

FACTS On October 13, 1972, Johnnie H. Hill and his wife, Clara Mae, entered into an installment sales contract with Pinelawn Memorial Park (Pinelawn) to purchase a mausoleum crypt. They made it clear they wanted to buy crypt "D," which faced eastward toward Kinston. The Hills paid a $1,035 down payment and continued to make $33.02 monthly payments.

On February 13, 1974, William C. Shackleford and his wife, Jennie L., entered into an agreement with Pinelawn to purchase crypt D. They paid a $1,406 down payment and two annual installments of $912. The Hills were first put on notice of the second contract when they visited Pinelawn in February 1977 and saw the Shackleford name on crypt D. The Hills then tendered full payment to Pinelawn for crypt D. On April 25, 1977, the Hills sued Pinelawn and the Shacklefords. They demanded specific performance on the contract and the deed to crypt D. Upon being served with summons, the Shacklefords discovered that they had no deed to the crypt and demanded one from Pinelawn. Pinelawn delivered them a deed dated August 18, 1977, which the Shacklefords recorded in the County Register on September 9, 1977.

ISSUE Who wins crypt D?

8.3 *Love v. Monarch Apartments*

771 P.2d 79, 1989 Kan. App. Lexis 219 (1989)
Court of Appeals of Kansas

FACTS Sharon Love entered into a written lease agreement with Monarch Apartments for apartment 4 at 441 Winfield in Topeka, Kansas. Shortly after moving in, she experienced serious problems with termites. Her walls swelled, clouds of dirt came out, and when she checked on her children one night, she saw termites flying around the room. She complained to Monarch, which arranged for the apartment to be fumigated.

When the termite problem persisted, Monarch moved Love and her children to apartment 2. Upon moving in, Love noticed that roaches crawled over the walls, ceilings, and floors of the apartment. She complained, and Monarch called an exterminator, who sprayed the apartment. When the roach problem persisted, Love vacated the premises.

ISSUE Did Love lawfully terminate the lease?

ETHICS CASE

8.4 *Souders v. Johnson*

501 So.2d 745, 1987 Fla. App. Lexis 6579 (1987)
Court of Appeals of Florida

FACTS When Dr. Arthur M. Edwards died, leaving a will disposing of his property, he left the villa-type condominium in which he lived, its "contents," and $10,000 to his stepson, Ronald W. Souders. Edwards left the residual of his estate to other named legatees. In administering the estate, certain stock certificates, passbook savings accounts, and other bank statements were found in Edwards' condominium. Souders claimed that these items belonged to him because they were "contents" of the condominium. The other legatees opposed Souders' claim, alleging that the disputed property was intangible property and not part of the contents of the condominium.

The value of the property was as follows: condominium, $138,000; furniture in condominium, $4,000; stocks, $377,000; and passbook and other bank accounts, $124,000.

ISSUE Who is entitled to the stocks and bank accounts? Do you think Souders acted ethically in this case?

9 Family Law

I take thee to be my wedded husband, to have and to hold from this day forward, for better for worse, for richer for poorer, in sickness and in health, to love and cherish, till death us do part, according to God's holy ordinance; and thereto I give thee my troth. —THE BOOK OF COMMON PRAYER (1662)

CHAPTER OBJECTIVES

After studying this chapter, you should be able to

1. Define *marriage* and enumerate the legal requirements of marriage.
2. Explain adoption and describe how adoption proceedings work.
3. Define *divorce* and *no-fault divorce*, and describe divorce proceedings.
4. Describe how assets are distributed upon the termination of marriage and explain the requirements for awarding spousal support.
5. Explain child custody, visitation rights, joint custody of children, and child support.

CHAPTER OUTLINE

- Introduction
- Premarriage Issues
- Marriage
- Case for Discussion: *Baker v. State of Vermont*
- Parents and Children
- Adoption
- Marriage Termination
- Child Custody
- Case for Discussion: *Giha v. Giha*
- Financial Consideration Associated with the Termination of a Marriage
- Prenuptial Agreements
- Legal Terminology
- Chapter Summary
- Internet Exercises and Cases

Introduction

Family law and domestic relations is a broad area of the law, involving marriage, prenuptial agreements, dissolution of marriage, division of property upon dissolution of marriage, spousal and child support, child custody, child and spousal abuse, and other family law issues. This chapter covers in detail the family law and domestic relations issues.

Premarriage Issues

Prior to marriage, several legal issues may arise. The first concerns the period of engagement and the second, promises to marry.

Engagement

As a prelude to getting married, many couples go through a period of time known as **engagement.** The engagement begins when one party proposes marriage to the other. If the second party, most often the female, accepts, the female typically is given an engagement ring (usually a diamond ring). The engagement period runs until the wedding is held or the engagement is broken off. If the couple get married, they often exchange wedding rings at the marriage ceremony.

Law cannot stand aside from the social changes around it.
—William J. Brennan, Jr.

Sometimes the engagement is broken off prior to the wedding. Then the issue becomes: Who gets the engagement ring if the engagement is broken off? Some states follow a **fault rule,** which works as follows:

- If the prospective groom breaks off the engagement, the prospective bride gets to keep the engagement ring.
- If the prospective bride breaks off the engagement, she must return the engagement ring to the prospective groom.

The fault rule is sometimes difficult to apply. Questions often arise as to who broke off the engagement, and then a trial may be necessary to decide the issue.

The modern rule and trend is to abandon the fault rule and adopt an **objective rule:** If the engagement is broken off, the prospective bride must give back the engagement ring irrespective as to who broke off the engagement. This objective rule is clear and usually avoids litigation unless the female refuses to return the ring.

Promise to Marry

In the 19th century, many courts recognized an action for breach of a **promise to marry.** This usually would occur if a man proposed marriage, the woman accepted, and then the man backed out before the marriage took place. The lawsuit was based on a breach-of-contract theory. Today, most courts do not recognize a breach of promise-to-marry lawsuit. The denial of such lawsuits is based on current social norms. If the potential groom backs out late, after many of the items for the pending marriage were purchased or contracted for (e.g., flowers, rental of a reception hall), he may be responsible for paying these costs, however.

MARRIAGE

Each state has marriage laws that recognize a legal union between a man and a woman. **Marriage** confers certain legal rights and duties upon the spouses, as well as upon the children born of the marriage. A couple wishing to marry must meet the legal requirements established by the state in which they are to be married. The following paragraphs discuss the legal rights and duties of spouses.

Marriage Requirements

State law establishes certain requirements that must be met before two people can be married. Most states require that the parties be a man and a woman. The parties must be of a certain age (usually 18 years of age). States will permit younger persons to be married if they have the consent of their parents or if they are emancipated from their parents. **Emancipation** means that the person is not supported by his or her parents and provides for himself or herself.

Same-Sex Marriages

Many couples of the same sex cohabit as if they are married couples. These same-sex couples have fought legal battles in many states to have the law changed to recognize **same-sex marriage.** Several states have provided that gay partners can enter into "civil unions" that grant gay partners rights similar to those of heterosexual marriage partners.

Under the Full Faith and Credit Clause of the U.S. Constitution, states are required to recognize and give full faith and credit to the laws of other states. Thus, if one or a few states were to legally recognize same-sex marriages, homosexual couples would go to these states to get married, then return to their home state and demand that their marriage be recognized. Many states have adopted statutes stating that no same-sex marriages would be legally recognized.

In 1996, the federal Congress enacted the **Defense of Marriage Act (DOMA),** [28 U.S.C. § 1738C], which provides that a legal marriage is only between a man and a woman and bars same-sex couples from enjoying federal benefits (e.g., social security benefits due the spouse of a married couple). This federal act also provides that states cannot be forced to recognize same-sex marriages performed in other states. The battle for the recognition of same-sex marriages will continue to be waged in federal and state legislatures and courts.

All states provide that persons under a certain age, such as 14 or 15 years of age, cannot be married. States also prohibit marriages between persons who are closely related, usually by blood. For example, a brother could not marry his sister or half-sister. Cousins may marry in some states. Another requirement of marriage is that neither party is currently married to someone else.

In order to be legally married, certain legal procedures must be followed. State law requires that the parties obtain a **marriage license** issued by the state. Marriage licenses usually are obtained at the county clerk's office. Some states require that the parties take a blood test prior to obtaining a license. This is to determine if the parties have certain diseases, particularly sexually transmitted diseases.

Most states require that, in addition to a marriage license, there must be some sort of **marriage ceremony.** This ceremony usually is held in front of a justice of the peace or similar government officer, or at a church, temple, or synagogue, in front of a minister, priest, or rabbi. At the ceremony, the parties exchange wedding vows, in which they make a public statement that they will take each other as wife and husband.

After the wedding ceremony, the marriage license is recorded. Some states require a waiting period between the time the marriage license is obtained and when the wedding ceremony takes place.

The Manitou County Courthouse in Missouri.

Financial Support

Most states require a spouse to financially support the other spouse and their children during their marriage. This includes providing for the necessities

CASE FOR DISCUSSION

Baker v. State of Vermont

744 A.2d 864, 1999 Vt. Lexis 406 (1999) Supreme Court of Vermont

FACTS

The plaintiffs are three same-sex couples who have lived together in committed relationships for periods ranging from four to twenty-five years. Two of the couples have raised children together. Each couple applied for a marriage license from their respective town clerks in the Vermont towns that they lived in, and each was refused a marriage license because the town clerk determined that same-sex couples were ineligible to marry under Vermont law that permitted opposite-sex couples to marry. The plaintiffs filed this lawsuit against the State of Vermont and the three towns, seeking declaratory judgment that the refusal to issue the plaintiffs marriage licenses violated the Vermont Constitution. The Vermont trial court upheld the state's and the towns' decision to refuse to grant marriage licenses to the plaintiffs. The plaintiffs appealed to the Vermont Supreme Court.

ISSUE

May the State of Vermont exclude same-sex couples from the benefits and protections that its laws provide to opposite-sex married couples?

COURT'S REASONING

Although the court noted that the issue arouses deeply felt religious, moral, and political beliefs, the court stated that it had a constitutional responsibility to consider the legal merits of this controversial issue. The Common Benefits Clause of the Vermont Constitution reads in pertinent part, "That government is, or ought to be, instituted for the common benefit, protection, and security of the people, nation, or community, and not for the particular emolument or advantage of any single person, family, or set of persons, who are a part of that community."

The Vermont Supreme Court held that same-sex partners may not be deprived of the benefits and protections afforded persons of opposite-sex marriages. The court stated, "We hold that the State is constitutionally required to extend to same-sex couples the common benefits and protections that flow from marriage under Vermont law. Whether this ultimately takes the form of inclusion within marriage laws themselves or a parallel 'domestic partnership' system or some equivalent statutory alternative, rests with the Legislature."

DECISION AND REMEDY

The Vermont Supreme Court held that the state's and the towns' refusal to grant marriage licenses to same-sex couples violated the Common Benefits Clause of the Vermont Constitution. The supreme court directed the legislature to develop state laws that grant parity of state benefits and protections to opposite-sex and same-sex couples.

In 2000, the Vermont legislature enacted a state law that provided for the granting of licenses for "civil unions" between same-sex partners. The law conferred on same-sex couples all of the rights and benefits of marriage that state law granted to opposite-sex partners.

QUESTIONS

1. Do you think the drafters of the Common Benefits Clause of the Vermont Constitution envisioned the modern issues that the clause would be called upon to address? Explain.
2. Should a supreme court justice's moral beliefs affect how she or he votes on a case? Explain.
3. Will same-sex couples from other states that do not permit same-sex civil unions (or marriages) go to Vermont and similar states to be joined in a civil union (or marriage)?

Common Law Marriage

Several states recognize a form of marriage called **common law marriage.** A common law marriage is one in which the parties have not obtained a valid marriage license, nor have they participated in a legal marriage ceremony. Instead, a common law marriage is recognized if the following requirements are met: (1) The parties are eligible to marry; (2) the parties voluntarily intend to be husband and wife; (3) the parties live together; and (4) the parties hold themselves out as husband and wife.

There are several misconceptions about common law marriages. First, cohabitation is not sufficient in and of itself to establish a common law marriage. Second, the length of time the parties live together is not sufficient alone to establish a common law marriage. For example, couples who immediately live together and intend a common law marriage have one, whereas couples who live together a long time but do not intend a common law marriage do not have one.

When a state recognizes a common law marriage and the necessary requirements are met to establish one, the couple has a legal and formal marriage. All the rights and duties of a normal licensed marriage apply. As such, a court decree of divorce must be obtained to end a common law marriage. States that do not recognize common law marriages must give full faith and credit to and recognize a common law marriage from states that permit common law marriages.

such as food, shelter, clothing, and medical care. A spouse is obligated only up to the level he or she is able to provide. In some states this duty exists even if the spouses are living apart. The spouses are free to agree on additional duties in separate contracts. Contracts to provide sex violate public policy and therefore are illegal.

Spousal Abuse

All states have laws that prohibit **spousal abuse.** Many cases of spousal abuse go unreported, however. In the case of spousal abuse, a court may order the offending party to serve jail time and attend educational programs. A court also may issue a **restraining order** that orders the offending party to refrain from seeing the other party and from coming within a certain distance of the other party. In addition, state and local governments and charitable organizations have established shelters, counseling, hotlines, and other assistance for victims of spousal abuse.

Parents and Children

In many instances, marriage produces children. Couples who have children have certain legal rights and duties that develop from their parental status.

Parents' Rights and Duties

Parents have the obligation to provide food, shelter, clothing, medical care, and other necessities to their children until the child reaches the age of 18 or until emancipation. A child becomes emancipated if he or she leaves the parents and voluntarily lives on his or her own. The law imposes certain duties on parents as well. For example, a parent must see to it that the child attends school up until 16 or 18 years of age, depending on the state, unless the child is home-schooled.

SIDEBAR

Interspousal Immunity

The common law adopted a doctrine called **interspousal immunity,** which provided that a spouse could not sue the other spouse for torts. This doctrine has been abolished in most states to permit a spouse to sue the other spouse for intentional torts, such as assault and battery. In addition, a number of states permit a spouse to sue the other spouse for knowingly exposing him or her to AIDS, herpes, or other sexually transmitted diseases.

Interspousal immunity provides that a spouse may not be required to testify against the other spouse in court. The spouse may voluntarily testify, however.

SIDEBAR

Liability for Children's Wrongful Acts
Generally, parents are not liable for their child's negligent acts. For example, if a child negligently injures another child while they are playing, the parents of the child who caused the injury are not liable. Parents are liable if their negligence caused their child's act. For example, if a parent lets a child who does not have a driver's license drive an automobile and the child-driver injures someone, the parents are liable.

About half of the states have enacted child liability statutes that make the parents financially liable for the intentional torts of their children. This liability is usually limited to a specified dollar amount, such as $5,000.

Parents may be legally responsible for a child beyond the age of majority if the child has a disability.

Parents also have the right to control the behavior of a child. Parents have the right to select the schools for their children and the religion they will practice. Parents have the right to use corporal punishment (physical punishment) as long as it does not rise to the level of child abuse. For example, mild slapping or spanking is legally permitted. A parent's refusal to obtain medical care for a child can be punished as a crime.

Paternity Actions

If there is any question as to who the father of a child is, a **paternity action** may be filed in court to determine the true identity of the father. The majority of these actions are filed by a mother against a man whom the mother claims to be the father of the child. This often is done to seek financial assistance from the father for the child's upbringing.

Paternity lawsuits are sometimes brought by the government where the mother is receiving welfare payments. In these cases, the government seeks to recover the financial assistance payments made to the mother and to establish the father's financial responsibility in the future. Sometimes a paternity action is brought by a male to prove that he is not the father of a child.

Sometimes a father will bring a paternity action to establish that he is the biological father of a child. This is usually done when the father seeks to obtain legal rights, such as custody or visitation rights, concerning the child. Most states have a **father's registry** where a male may register as the father of a child. A registered father must be notified of planned adoption of the child so he may appear and oppose the adoption.

In most states, the law presumes that the husband of a wife who bears a child is the legal father of the child. In about half of the states, a husband who believes that he is not the father can bring a lawsuit to prove that he is not. The other half of the states do not permit such actions.

A male can be proven to be or not to be the father of a child through DNA testing. A male may prove that he is not the father of a child if he had no access to

Child Abuse

The law prohibits parents from physically abusing their children. Doctors, day-care workers, schoolteachers, and others have a legal duty to report suspected cases of **child abuse** to state authorities. The state will investigate suspected cases of child abuse and may remove the child temporarily from the abusive parents. In severe or continuing cases of child abuse, the state may remove the child permanently from abusive parents and put the child up for adoption. The state must obtain a court order to do so, however. A hearing will be held, at which the parents will have a right to be heard and present evidence on their behalf. Child abuse also may occur if a parent emotionally abuses a child—for example, if a parent verbally abuses a child continually.

Child neglect occurs when a parent fails to provide a child with the necessities of life or other basic needs. The state may remove a child, either temporarily or permanently, from situations of child neglect.

Surrogacy

A relatively new area of the law has to do with reproductive medicine. This includes the areas of **surrogacy** and fertilized embryos. Several cases highlight the legal questions that arise.

The first case is the famous Baby M case [*In re Baby M*, 109 N.J. 396, 537 A.2d 1227, 1988 N.J. Lexis 1 (N.J. 1988)]. In that case, William and Elizabeth Stern contracted with Mary Beth Whitehead. Ms. Whitehead was artificially inseminated with Mr. Stern's sperm and agreed to give the baby to the Sterns when it was born, at which time the Sterns would adopt the baby. Ms. Whitehead was compensated $10,000 by the Sterns.

When the baby was born, Ms. Whitehead decided to keep the baby. The Sterns sued Ms. Whitehead for breach of contract. The New Jersey Supreme Court held that the **surrogacy contract** violated public policy and could not be enforced because it represented baby selling. The court decided, however, that it was in the child's best interests to place the baby in the Sterns' custody but awarded visitation rights to Ms. Whitehead.

In the second case, *Anna J. v. Mark C.* [286 Cal.Rptr 369, 1991 Cal. App. Lexis 1162 (Cal. 1991)], a contract was executed whereby a fertilized embryo formed from the husband's sperm and the wife's egg was implanted in the womb of a surrogate mother. When the nonbiological surrogate mother refused to turn over the baby to the biological parents, the biological parents sued. In this case, the court enforced the contract and ruled in favor of the biological parents. The court held that the surrogate mother had no legal rights concerning the child she had borne.

As these cases suggest, surrogate parenting is an unsettled area of the law. As medical science expands, so must the law in delineating the rights and duties of biological and surrogate parents of children born using advanced medical technology.

the mother at the time of pregnancy, or that he is impotent or has had a vasectomy prior to the pregnancy.

Adoption

Adoption occurs when persons become the legal parents of a child who is not their biological child. The process for adoption is complicated and is regulated by state law. Basically, the procedure for adoption consists of the following requirements being met:

- All procedures of the state law for adoption are met.
- The biological parents' legal rights as parents are terminated by legal decree or death.
- A court formally approves the adoption.

The two main ways by which persons can become adoptive parents are *agency adoptions* and *independent adoptions.*

Agency Adoption

An **agency adoption** occurs when parents adopt a child from a social service organization of the state. The state often obtains jurisdiction over children who are born out of wedlock and whose biological parents give up the child for adoption by terminating their parental rights. The state also may obtain jurisdiction over a child if the child has been permanently removed from parents who are judged unsuitable to be parents, or where parents are deceased and no relative wants or qualifies to become the child's parent.

In the past, the identity of the biological parents of adopted children was kept confidential in an agency adoption. Currently, many states allow for disclosure of the identity of the biological parents in certain circumstances. Usually, the court will notify the other side—either the child or the biological parent—that the other wishes to meet with them. If both sides consent, the meeting will be arranged.

In many cases today, **open-adoption** procedures are being used. In these cases, the biological and adoptive parents are introduced prior to the adoption. The biological parents may screen the prospective adoptive parents to assure that the adoptive parents are suitable for the child. In many instances, the adoptive and biological parents remain in contact with each other and the biological parents are given visitation rights to see the child.

SIDEBAR

Foster Care

Traditionally, children who became the legal responsibility of the state were placed in government-operated orphanages. Charitable and religious organizations also operate private orphanages. Today, the primary means of caring for children under the state's jurisdiction is to place children in **foster care.** This is usually a temporary arrangement. The state pays the foster family for the care given to the foster child. This temporary arrangement will be terminated if the child is returned to his or her biological parents, or if the child is legally adopted. Sometimes the foster parents will legally adopt a child who has been placed in their care.

Independent Adoption

An **independent adoption** occurs when there is a private arrangement between the biological and adoptive parents. Often, an intermediary, such as a lawyer, doctor, or private adoption agency, introduces the two parties. The biological parents and the adoptive parents enter into a private arrangement for adoption of the child. Adoptive parents usually pay intermediaries a fee for their services, as well as paying the costs of the adoption.

Many divorced people who have children remarry. Often, a new stepparent formally adopts the child or children of his or her new spouse. To do so, the other biological parent of the child must relinquish his or her legal rights concerning the child. This can be done voluntarily, or by order of the court if it is in the best interests of the child.

Court Approval of Adoptions

In both agency adoptions and independent adoptions, the court must approve the adoption before it is legal. The court will consider the home environment, financial resources, and family stability of the adoptive parents, as well as their religious beliefs, ages, and other factors. The decision of the court will be based on the best interests of the child. Although preference is usually given to couples, single parents can adopt children. States vary as to whether they permit homosexual couples to adopt children.

Once the court approves an adoption, the adoptive couple is subject to a probation period, which is usually six months or one year. During this time, government social workers will investigate whether the adoptive parents are properly caring for the adopted child. If they are not, the court can remove the child from the adoptive parents.

Marriage Termination

Once a state has recognized the marital status of a couple, only the state can terminate this marital status. This is so even if the partners separate and live apart from one another. As long as they are married, they continue to have certain legal rights and duties to one another. The law recognizes two methods for legally terminating a marriage: (1) *annulment*, and (2) *divorce*.

Annulment

An **annulment** is an order of the court declaring that a marriage did not exist. The order invalidates the marriage. Annulments are rarely granted now that most states recognize no-fault divorces.

Certain grounds must be asserted to obtain a legal annulment. One ground is that the parties lacked capacity to consent. Examples are: (1) one of the parties was a minor and had not obtained his or her parents' consent to marry, (2) one of the parties was mentally incapacitated at the time of marriage, (3) a party was intoxicated at the time of the marriage, or (4) the marriage was never consummated. Marriage can also be annulled if the parties are too closely related to one another or there was bigamy (one of the parties was already married). A marriage can also be annulled if there was duress or fraud leading to the marriage (e.g., one of the parties declared that he or she could conceive children when the person knew in fact that he or she could not).

Many annulments are sought because of a person's religion. For example, a Roman Catholic cannot be remarried in the church if he or she is divorced. An annulment would allow for a subsequent marriage in the church. A person may also be required to go through a procedure to seek an annulment from the church. A legal annulment and a religious annulment are two separate and distinct procedures.

The law considers children born of a marriage that is annulled to be legitimate. When a marriage is annulled, issues of child support, child custody, spousal support, and property settlement must be agreed upon by the couple or decided by the court.

Our legal system faces no theoretical dilemma but a single continuous problem: how to apply to ever changing conditions the never changing principles of freedom.

—Earl Warren

Divorce

The most common option used by married partners to terminate their marriage is divorce. **Divorce** is a legal proceeding whereby the court issues a decree that legally orders a marriage terminated.

No-fault divorce. Traditionally, a married person who sought a divorce had to prove that the other person was *at fault* for causing a major problem with continuing the marriage. Grounds for granting a divorce consisted of adultery, physical or emotional abuse, abandonment, substance or alcohol abuse, or insanity.

Beginning in the 1960s, states began to recognize **no-fault divorce.** A spouse wishing to obtain a divorce merely had to assert **irreconcilable differences** with his or her spouse. In a no-fault divorce, neither party is blamed for the divorce. Today, every state recognizes no-fault divorce. A spouse may still decide to assert that the other party was at fault for causing the divorce in those states that consider fault when deciding how to divide marital assets and award spousal support.

Divorce proceedings. A divorce proceeding is commenced by a spouse filing a **petition for divorce** with the proper state court. The petition must contain required information, such as the names of the spouses, date and place of marriage, names of minor children, and the reason for the divorce. The petition must be served on the other spouse. This spouse then has a certain period of time (usually 20 to 30 days) to file an answer to the petition.

If the spouses do not reach a settlement of the issues involved in the divorce—such as property division, custody of the children, spousal and child support—the case will go to trial. The parties are permitted to conduct discovery, which includes taking depositions and obtaining the production of documents. If the case goes to trial, each side is permitted to call witnesses, including expert witnesses (e.g., financial experts) to testify on his or her behalf. Both parties are also allowed to introduce evidence that will support their claims.

Many states require a certain waiting period from the date a divorce petition is filed to the date the court grants a divorce. A typical waiting period is 6 months. The public policy for this waiting period is to give the parties time for reconciliation. After the waiting period has passed, a court will enter a **decree of divorce** terminating the marriage. The parties are then free to marry again. The decree of divorce may be granted even if the other issues concerning the divorce, such as the division of property or support payments, have not yet been settled or tried.

Most of the disputes in the world arise from words.

—Lord Mansfield, *Morgan v. Jones* (1773)

If there is a showing that one partner is likely to injure the other, a court may issue a restraining order. This places limitations on the ability of the dangerous partner to go near the other partner.

Pro se divorce. In a ***pro se* divorce,** the parties do not have to hire lawyers to represent them but may represent themselves in the divorce proceeding. Most states permit pro se—commonly called "do-it-yourself"—divorces. If there are substantial assets at stake in the divorce, or other complicated issues involving child custody, child support, or spousal support, the parties usually hire lawyers to represent them in the divorce proceeding.

Negotiation and settlement. Approximately 90 percent of divorce cases are settled between the parties prior to trial. The parties often engage in negotiations to try to settle a divorce lawsuit in order to save the time and expense of a trial and to reach an agreement acceptable to each side. These negotiations are usually conducted between the parties with the assistance of each of their attorneys.

Some divorcing parties use mediation to try to reach a settlement of the issues involved in terminating their marriage. Some states have mandatory mediation before divorcing couples can use the court to try the case. In **mediation,** a neutral third party—often an attorney, a retired judge, or other party—acts as a mediator between the parties. A mediator is not empowered to make a decision but, instead, acts as a go-between and facilitator to try to help the parties reach an acceptable settlement of the issues. Mediation is often successful because it forces the parties to consider all facets of the case, even the position of the opposing side.

If a settlement is reached, a **settlement agreement** will be drafted, usually by the attorneys. After being signed by the parties, the settlement agreement will be presented to the court. The court will accept the terms of the settlement agreement if the judge believes that the settlement is fair and that the rights of the parties and minor children are properly taken care of. If a case is not settled, the case will then go to trial.

Child Custody

When a couple terminates their marriage, and they have children, the issue of who is legally and physically responsible for raising the children must be decided, either by settlement or by the court. The legal term **custody** is used to describe who has legal responsibility for raising a child. **Child custody** is often the most litigated issue of a divorcing couple.

CASE FOR DISCUSSION

Giha v. Giha

609 A.2d 945, 1992 R.I. Lexis 133 (1992) — Supreme Court of Rhode Island

FACTS

On October 7, 1987, Nagib Giha (Husband) filed a complaint for divorce from Nelly Giha (Wife) on the grounds of irreconcilable differences. On May 20, 1988, the parties reached an agreement for the disposition of their property that provided they would divide equally the net proceeds from the sale of their marital assets. They had to wait a statutory waiting period before the divorce was final.

On December 25, 1988, Husband learned that he had won $2.4 million in the Massachusetts Megabucks state lottery. Husband kept this fact secret. After the waiting period was over, the family court entered its final judgment, severing the parties' marriage on April 27, 1989. Husband claimed his lottery prize on October 6, 1989.

In December 1990, after learning of the lottery winnings, Wife sued to recover the lottery prize. She alleged that the lottery prize was a marital asset because Husband had won it before their divorce was final. The trial court dismissed her complaint. Wife appealed.

ISSUE

Was the $2.4 million lottery prize personal property of the marital estate?

COURT'S REASONING

The court held that the marital agreement did not sever either the matrimonial or economic ties between the husband and the wife. Because the parties' marriage remained in effect during the statutory waiting period, so did the property rights of each spouse during that period. The court concluded that the lottery prize was a marital asset.

DECISION AND REMEDY

The appellate court held that the parties remained husband and wife until the entry of final judgment of divorce in April 1989. Therefore, the lottery prize was a marital asset. Reversed and remanded.

QUESTIONS

1. Should a spouse's lottery winnings be considered separate property? Why or why not?
2. Why does the law require a statutory period of time to pass before a divorce is final?
3. Did Husband act ethically in this case?

Factors for Determining Child Custody

Traditionally, the court almost always granted custody of a child to the mother. Today, with fathers taking a more active role in childrearing, and with many mothers working, this is not always the case.

In child custody disputes, where both parents want custody of a child, the courts will determine what is in the *best interests of the child* in awarding custody. Some of the factors that a court will consider are:

- The ability of each parent to provide for the emotional needs of the child.
- The ability of each parent to provide for the needs of the child, such as education.
- The ability of each parent to provide a stable environment for the child.
- The ability of each parent to provide for the special needs of a child if the child has a disability or requires special care.
- The desire of each parent to provide for the needs of the child.
- The wishes of the child. This factor is given more weight the older the child is.
- The religion of each parent.
- Other factors the court deems relevant.

The foundation of justice is good faith.

—Cicero

The awarding of custody to a **custodial parent** is not permanent. Custody may be altered by the court if circumstances change.

The parent who is awarded custody has **legal custody** of the child. This usually includes physical custody of the child. The custodial parent has the right to make day-to-day decisions and major decisions concerning the child's education, religion, and other such matters.

The court will not award custody to a parent, and sometimes not to either parent, if it is in the child's best interest not to be awarded to a parent, or there has been child abuse, or because of other such extenuating circumstances. In such cases, the court may award custody to other relatives, such as grandparents, or place the child in a foster home.

Visitation Rights

If the parents do not have joint custody of a child, the **noncustodial parent** is usually awarded **visitation rights.** This means that the noncustodial parent is given the right to visit the child for limited periods of time as determined by a settlement agreement or by the court.

If the court is concerned about the safety of a child, the court may grant only supervised visitation rights to a noncustodial parent. This means that a court-appointed person must be present during the noncustodial parent's visitation with the child. This is usually done if there has been a history of child abuse or there is a strong possibility that the noncustodial parent may kidnap the child.

Joint Custody

Most states now permit joint custody of a child. **Joint custody** means that both parents are responsible for making major decisions concerning the child, such as his or her education, religion, and other major matters.

Parents are sometimes awarded **joint physical custody** of the child as well. This means that the child spends a certain portion of time being raised by each parent. For example, the child may spend every other week with each parent, or the weekdays with one parent and the weekends with another parent. These arrangements are awarded only if the child's best interests are served, such as the child remains in the same school while in the physical custody of each parent.

Guardian *Ad Litem*

In some situations where a child custody battle is particularly contentious, the court may appoint a guardian *ad litem*. A **guardian *ad litem*** is usually an attorney who is appointed to represent the interests of a child in a child custody matter.

Financial Considerations Associated with the Termination of a Marriage

When a marriage is terminated, there are certain financial ramifications. The marital assets and debts must be divided, and child support payments and spousal support payments may be awarded. These issues are discussed in the following paragraphs.

Property has its duties as well as its rights.

—Benjamin Disraeli

Division of Assets

Upon termination of a marriage, the parties may own certain assets, including property owned prior to marriage, gifts and inheritances received during marriage, and assets purchased with income earned during marriage. In most cases, the parties reach a settlement as to how these assets are to be divided. If no settlement agreement is reached, the court will order the division of assets.

Separate Property

In most states, each spouse's separate property will be awarded to the spouse who owns the separate property. **Separate property** includes property owned by a spouse prior to the marriage, as well as inheritances and gifts received during the marriage. In most states, upon termination of a marriage, each spouse is awarded his or her separate property.

However, if separate property is commingled with marital property during the course of the marriage, or the owner of the separate property changes title to the separate property by placing the other spouse's name on the title to the property (e.g., real estate), the separate property is then considered a marital asset.

Marital Property

Marital property consists of property acquired during the course of the marriage using income earned during the marriage, and separate property that has been converted to marital property.

There are two major legal theories that different states adhere to when dividing marital assets upon the termination of a marriage. These are the theories of *equitable distribution* and *community property*.

Equitable distribution. In states that follow the rule of **equitable distribution,** the court may order the *fair distribution* of property. The fair distribution of property does not necessarily mean the equal distribution of property. In determining the fair distribution of property, the court may consider factors such as:

- Length of the marriage.
- Occupation of each spouse.
- Standard of living during the marriage.
- Wealth and income-earning ability of each spouse.
- Which party is awarded custody of the children.
- Health of the individuals.
- Other factors relevant to the case.

In most states, the house is usually awarded to the parent who is granted custody of the children. A court may order the house to be sold and the proceeds divided fairly between the individuals.

Community property. Under the doctrine of **community property,** all property acquired during the marriage using income earned during the marriage is considered marital property. It does not matter which spouse earned the income, or which spouse earned the higher income. Money placed in pension funds, stock options, the value of businesses, the value of professional licenses, and such are considered community property.

The very definition of a good award is that it gives dissatisfaction to both parties.

—M. R. Plumer, *Goodman v. Sayers* (1820)

In community-property states, marital property is divided *equally* between the individuals. This does not necessarily mean that each piece of property is sold and the proceeds divided equally between the individuals. Usually each asset of the marital property is valued using appraisers and expert witnesses. The court then awards the property to the spouses. If one spouse is awarded the house, the other spouse is awarded other property of equal value.

Division of Debts

Individuals often have debts that must be divided upon termination of the marriage. How these debts are divided depends on the type of debt and on state law. In most states, each spouse is personally liable for his or her own premarital debts and the other spouse is not liable for these debts. This is because the debt was incurred prior to the marriage. Student loans are a good example of these types of debts.

Debts that are incurred during the marriage for necessities and other joint needs, including but not limited to shelter, clothing, automobiles, medical expenses, and such, are **joint marital debts** and are the joint responsibility of each spouse. The court may equally distribute these debts upon termination of the marriage. Spouses are jointly liable for taxes incurred during their marriage. If a debt is not paid by the spouse to whom the court has distributed the debt, the third-party creditor may recover payment of the debt from the other spouse, however. This individual's only recourse is to recover the amount paid from his or her prior spouse.

Upon the termination of a marriage, it is wise for the individuals to notify prior creditors that they will no longer be responsible for the other's debts. This is particularly true if the individuals have joint credit cards.

Child Support

The noncustodial parent is obligated to contribute to the financial support of his or her natural and adopted children. This includes the child's costs for food, shel-

Family Support Act

In the past, many noncustodial parents failed to pay child support when due. This often required long and expensive legal procedures by the custodial parent to obtain child support payments. To remedy this situation, the federal government enacted the **Family Support Act.** This federal law, effective in 1994, provides that all original or modified child support orders require automatic wage withholding from a noncustodial parent's income. The Family Support Act was designed primarily to prevent noncustodial parents from failing to pay required support payments.

Assume that a court order requires a noncustodial parent to pay 25 percent of his or her gross monthly income for child support. In this case, the court will order that noncustodial parent's employer to deduct this amount from that parent's income and send a check in this amount to the custodial parent. The noncustodial parent receives a check for the remainder of his or her income.

ter, clothing, medical expenses, and other necessities of life. This payment is called **child support.** The custodial and noncustodial parents may agree to the amount of child support. If they do not, the court will determine the amount of child support to be paid.

In awarding child support, the court may consider several factors, including the number of children, needs of the children, net income of the parents, standard of living of the child prior to termination of the marriage, any special medical or other needs of the children, and other factors the court deems relevant. The duty to pay child support usually continues until a child reaches the age of majority or graduates from high school, or emancipates himself or herself by voluntary choosing to live on his or her own.

To help in the determination of child support, about half of the states have adopted a formula for computing the amount of child support. These formulas are usually based on a percentage of the noncustodial parent's income. A court is permitted to deviate from the formula if a child has special needs, such as if the child has a disability or requires special educational assistance.

An award of child support may be *modified* if conditions change. For example, an award of child support may be decreased if the noncustodial parent loses his or her job. The amount of child support may be modified if the child's needs change, such as if the child needs special care because of a disability. The parent wishing to obtain modification of child support must petition the court to change the award of child support.

Spousal Support

In some cases where a marriage is terminated, a court may award **spousal support**—also called **alimony**—to one of the individuals. The parties may agree to the amount of alimony to be paid. If an agreement is not reached, the court will determine if the payment of alimony is warranted and, if so, the amount of alimony to be paid. In the past, alimony has usually been awarded to the female. Today, with the female often earning more than the male, the male has been awarded alimony in some cases.

Alimony is usually awarded for a specific period of time. This is called **temporary alimony** or **rehabilitation alimony.** This alimony is designed to provide the receiving individual with payment for a limited time during which the individual can obtain the education or job skills necessary to enter the job force. Alimony is also awarded in cases where a parent, usually the female, is needed to care for a disabled child and must remain at home to care for the child. The amount of alimony is based on the needs of the individual who will receive the alimony and the income and ability of the other individual to pay.

Spousal support payments usually terminate if the former spouse dies, remarries, or otherwise becomes self-sufficient. Spousal support awards may be modified by the court if circumstances change. This usually occurs if the paying individual loses his or her job or income decreases, or if the receiving individual's income increases. A party wishing to have a spousal support award changed must petition the court to *modify* the award of spousal support.

The award of **permanent alimony**—sometimes called **lifetime alimony**—is usually awarded only if the individual to receive the alimony is of an older age and if that individual has been a homemaker who has little opportunity to obtain job skills to enter the workplace. Permanent alimony must be paid until the individual receiving it dies or remarries.

Prenuptial Agreements

The law relating to public policy cannot remain immutable, it must change with the passage of time. The wind of change blows on it.
—L. J. Danckwerts
Nagle v. Feilden (1966)

In today's society, many spouses sign prenuptial agreements in advance of their marriage. **Prenuptial agreements**—also called **premarital agreements**—are contracts that specify how property will be distributed upon termination of the marriage or death of a spouse. To be enforced, a prenuptial agreement must be in writing.

Prenuptial agreements are often used where both parties to a marriage have their own careers and have accumulated assets prior to the marriage, or one of the spouses has significant assets prior to the marriage. Prenuptial agreements also are often used where there are children from a prior marriage and the agreement guarantees that these children will receive a certain share of the assets of the remarrying spouse if he or she dies or the marriage is terminated.

To be enforceable, each party must make full disclosure of all his or her assets and liabilities, and each party should be represented by his or her own attorney. Prenuptial agreements must be voluntarily entered into without threats or undue pressure. They must provide for the fair distribution of assets and must not be unconscionable. Generally, courts will enforce a properly negotiated prenuptial agreement even if the agreement provides for an unequal distribution of assets and eliminates financial support of a spouse in case the marriage is terminated.

Courts will not enforce a prenuptial agreement in the following circumstances:

- One of the parties was not represented by an attorney.
- One of the parties failed to make full disclosure of his or her assets and liabilities.
- The agreement was entered into at the "last moment" immediately prior to the marriage.
- The terms of the agreement are unfair or unconscionable.
- The agreement violates public policy. For example, a party is forced to live on government assistance if the agreement is enforced.

Sometimes the parties enter into an agreement during the marriage, setting forth the distribution of property upon death or termination of the marriage. This is called an **antenuptial agreement.** The courts apply the same standards for enforceability as they apply to prenuptial agreements.

Palimony

Often, heterosexual couples live together without being married. Usually they do so out of convenience, or because one or both partners do not want to get married. If the parties separate, there is no divorce proceeding. If the partners have been cohabiting for years, however, one partner may claim an interest in the other partner's property.

Absent an express contract, a cohabiting partner may assert *implied contract* rights to the property of the other. California, in the case of *Marvin v. Marvin* [557 P.2d 106, 134 Cal.Rptr. 815, 1976 Cal. Lexis 377 (California 1976)], found that a contract for the division of property and provision of spousal support payments may be implied from a cohabitation agreement. The nonlegal term **palimony** has been applied to describe such rights.

Because of the possibility of palimony claims, many partners to cohabitation arrangements enter into a **cohabitation agreement** specifying how the partners' property will be distributed upon separation of the partners or one of the partner's death.

LEGAL TERMINOLOGY

Adoption
Agency adoption
Alimony
Annulment
Antenuptial agreement
Child abuse
Child custody
Child neglect
Child support
Cohabitation agreement
Common law marriage
Community property
Custodial parent
Custody
Decree of divorce
Defense of Marriage Act (DOMA)
Divorce
Emancipation
Engagement
Equitable distribution
Family Support Act
Father's registry
Fault rule
Foster care
Guardian *ad litem*
Independent adoption
Interspousal immunity
Irreconcilable differences
Joint custody
Joint marital debts
Joint physical custody
Legal custody
Lifetime alimony
Marital property
Marriage
Marriage ceremony
Marriage license
Mediation
No-fault divorce
Noncustodial parent
Objective rule
Open adoption
Palimony
Paternity action
Permanent alimony
Petition for divorce
Premarital agreements
Prenuptial agreements
Promise to marry
Pro se divorce
Rehabilitation alimony
Restraining order
Same-sex marriage
Separate property

Settlement agreement
Spousal abuse
Spousal support
Surrogacy
Surrogacy contract
Temporary alimony
Visitation rights

chapter summary

FAMILY LAW

Premarriage Issues	
Engagement	Begins when a male proposes marriage to a female. If the female accepts, the male usually gives her an engagement ring. 1. *Fault rule:* If the prospective groom breaks off the engagement, the prospective bride may keep the ring. If the prospective bride breaks off the engagement, the prospective groom may get the ring back. 2. *Objective rule:* If the engagement is broken off by either party, the prospective groom gets the ring back.
Promise to Marry	Today, courts do not recognize a lawsuit for breach of a promise to marry.
Marriage	
Marriage	Each state has laws that recognize a legal union of a man and woman.
Marriage Requirements	State law establishes certain requirements that must be met before two people can be married. 1. *Age:* The parties must be a certain age. States permit younger persons to marry if they have the consent of their parents. 2. *Marriage license:* State law requires that the parties to be married obtain a marriage license issued by the state. 3. *Marriage ceremony:* Most states require some sort of marriage ceremony in front of a government officer or a minister, priest, or rabbi.
Same-Sex Marriage	Most states do not permit marriages of two people of the same sex.
Common Law Marriages	Several states recognize a common law marriage, in which the parties have not obtained a valid license or participated in a legal marriage ceremony. The parties must be eligible to marry, intend to be husband and wife, have voluntarily lived together, and hold themselves out as husband and wife.
Parents and Children	
Children	If parents have children, they have an obligation to provide food, shelter, clothing, medical care, and other necessities of life until the child reaches the age of 18 or until the child becomes emancipated.
Emancipation	A child becomes emancipated if he or she voluntarily leaves the parents and lives on his or her own.

Paternity	1. *Paternity:* A male who is the father of a child. 2. *Paternity action:* Action that may be filed in court to determine whether a male is the father of a child. 3. *Father's registry:* A registry kept by the state where a male may register as the father of a child.
Surrogacy	*Surrogacy contract:* A contract in which a female agrees to bear a child from the sperm of a male and agrees to give the baby to the father and his wife when the child is born. The sperm is usually inserted in the surrogate mother by artificial insemination.
Adoption	
Definition	A legal entity that occurs when persons become legal parents of a child who is not their biological child.
Agency Adoption	Occurs when parents adopt a child from a social service organization of the state.
Independent Adoption	Occurs when there is a private arrangement between the biological and adoptive parents.
Court Approval	In both agency adoptions and independent adoptions, the court must approve the adoption before it is legal.
Foster Care	Temporary placement of a child in a foster home to be cared for until the child is returned to his or her biological parents or is legally adopted.
Marriage Termination	
Termination of a Marriage	The state can terminate the marital status of a couple if a proper legal proceeding is brought.
Annulment	An order of the court declaring that a marriage did not exist. Certain grounds must be asserted and proven to obtain an annulment. Annulments are quite rare.
Divorce	A legal proceeding that terminates a marriage. The court issues a decree that legally orders a marriage terminated.
Petition for Divorce	A document that is filed with the court by the party seeking a divorce. The petition must be served on the other spouse.
No-Fault Divorce	Every state recognizes no-fault divorce. A spouse seeking to obtain a divorce merely has to assert that he or she has "irreconcilable differences" with his or her spouse.
Waiting Period	Many states require a certain waiting period (e.g., 6 months) from the date a petition for divorce is filed to the date the divorce is granted by the court. *(continued)*

Pro Se Divorce	Occurs when a party does not hire a lawyer and represents himself or herself in the divorce proceeding; commonly called "do-it-yourself" divorce.
Settlement	Most divorce cases do not go to trial but, instead, are settled through a process of negotiation. After an agreement is reached, a *settlement agreement* that sets forth the terms of the settlement is drafted and signed by both parties.
Mediation	A process whereby a neutral third party, often a lawyer or a retired judge, acts as a *mediator* to assist the parties in reaching a settlement.
Child Custody	
Custody	Upon termination of a marriage, the parties may agree, or if not, the court will determine, who gets custody of children of the marriage. The court will award custody of the child based on the "best interests" of the child.
Custodial Parent	The parent awarded *legal custody* also is usually awarded *physical custody* of the child. The custodial parent has the right to make day-to-day decisions and major decisions concerning the child's education, religion, and other such matters.
Visitation Rights	The noncustodial parent is usually granted the right to visit the child for limited periods of time by agreement between the parents or by order of the court.
Joint Custody	Sometimes the parties agree on or the court awards joint custody of a child. This means that both parents are responsible for making major decisions concerning the child. It also may include *joint physical custody*, where the child spends a certain amount of time with each parent.
Division of Property	
Separate Property	Includes property owned by a spouse prior to marriage, as well as inheritances and gifts received during marriage. In most states, each spouse is awarded his or her separate property upon termination of the marriage.
Marital Property	Consists of property acquired during the course of a marriage using income earned during the marriage. States follow one of two major doctrines in dividing marital property upon the termination of a marriage: 1. *Equitable distribution:* The court will order the *fair distribution* of the marital property. This does not necessarily mean equal distribution of the property. 2. *Community property:* All property acquired during the marriage using income earned during the marriage is divided *equally* between the parties.
Division of Debts	
Premarital Debts	In most states, each spouse is liable for his or her own premarital debts upon the termination of the marriage.

Joint Marital Debts	Debts incurred during marriage for necessities and other joint needs are the joint responsibility of each spouse. The court may distribute these debts fairly upon the termination of the marriage.
Child Support	
Requirements	The noncustodial parent is obligated to contribute money to pay for the financial support of his or her natural and adopted children. The amount may be agreed upon by the parties, but if not, the amount will be determined by the court.
Family Support Act	This federal statute provides that the amount of child support will be withheld from the noncustodial parent's income by his or her employer.
Spousal Support	
Definition	A portion of one individual's income that is paid to the other individual after termination of their marriage. This amount may be agreed upon by the parties or determined by the court. Also called *alimony.*
Temporary Alimony	Alimony that is awarded for a limited period of time until the individual receiving the alimony can acquire the education or job skills necessary to enter the job market. Also called *rehabilitation alimony.*
Permanent Alimony	Alimony that is often awarded to an individual of an older age who has been a homemaker and has little opportunity to obtain education or job skills necessary to enter the job market. Also called *lifetime alimony.*
Prenuptial Agreements	
Prenuptial Agreement	An agreement entered into by spouses in advance of their marriage whereby they agree how their property will be distributed upon termination of their marriage or death of a spouse. Also known as a *premarital agreement.*
Antenuptial Agreement	An agreement entered into by spouses during their marriage whereby they agree how their property will be distributed upon the termination of their marriage or the death of a spouse.

WORKING THE WEB

Visit the Web sites below for more information about the topics covered in this chapter.

1. Go to **www.google.com**. Type in "family law—divorce" and find a Web site of a law firm specializing in divorce legal services in your state. Does the site explain the procedures for obtaining a divorce in your state?
2. See **www.lawyerment.com.my/family/divorce.shtml.** What are the requirements for obtaining a divorce in Malaysia by mutual consent? How long does it take to obtain a divorce?
3. Go to **www.acf.dhhs.gov/programs/cse.** Go to the link "States." Find your state on the map and click on it. Find one issue related to the payment of child support in your state and report your findings.
4. Go to **www.mishpat.net/law/family-law/adoption.** Click on "Adoption," then click on "Adoption Resources." Find an adoption agency. Is this a government agency or a private adoption service?
5. Visit **www.legalconsumerguide.com.** Go to "Fact Sheet" on the Child Citizenship Act of 2000. What are the provisions of the Act?

CRITICAL LEGAL THINKING QUESTIONS

1. Define *engagement*. Who owns the engagement ring if an engagement is broken if the *fault rule* is applied? What if the *objective rule* is applied?
2. Define *marriage*. What are the requirements for a marriage? Should same-sex marriages be permitted?
3. What is a paternity action? What is a father's registry? What is a surrogacy contract?
4. Define *annulment*. What are the requirements to obtain an annulment?
5. Define *divorce*. What is a no-fault divorce?
6. What is child custody? What factors does the court consider in awarding child custody? What is joint custody?
7. Describe separate property. Describe marital property. How is property divided upon termination of a marriage using the *equitable distribution* doctrine? Using the *community property* doctrine?
8. What is child support? What factors does the court consider in awarding child support?
9. What is spousal support? Explain the difference between temporary alimony and permanent alimony.
10. What is a prenuptial agreement? What is necessary to make a prenuptial agreement enforceable?

CASE FOR BRIEFING

Read Case 9 in Appendix A (*Troxel v. Granville*). Review and brief the case using the *Critical Legal Thinking* "Briefing the Case" example described in Chapter 1.

9.1 *Neville v. Neville*

734 So.2d 352, 1999 Miss. App. Lexis 68 (1999)
Court of Appeals of Mississippi

FACTS George Neville and Tina Neville were married in 1988. At the time, George was 31 years old and a practicing attorney; Tina was a 23-year-old medical student. After 7 years, Tina became a licensed physician. In 1995, George filed for divorce from Tina because she was having an adulterous affair with a doctor. At the time of the divorce, George was earning $55,000 per year practicing law; Tina was earning $165,000 per year as a physician.

The divorce was filed in Mississippi where the couple lived. Mississippi follows the doctrine of equitable distribution. George sought to have Tina's medical license and medical practice valued as an ongoing business, and he claimed a portion of the value. The court refused George's request and instead applied the doctrine of equitable distribution and awarded him rehabilitative alimony of $1,400 per month for 120 months. The aggregate amount of the alimony was $168,000. George appealed this award, alleging on appeal that Tina's medical license and practice should be valued and he should receive a portion of this value.

ISSUE Under the doctrine of equitable distribution, was the trial court's award fair, or should George win on appeal?

9.2 *Johnston v. Johnston*

649 N.E.2d 799, 1995 Mass. App. Lexis 429 (1995)
Appeal Court of Massachusetts

FACTS Ronald R. and Edith Johnston were married in 1967 and had three sons ranging from ages 12 to 16 when the parties separated in 1986. Edith filed for divorce the same year. The Johnstons owned a primary residence worth $186,000 with no mortgage on it. Ronald was a successful entrepreneur. He owned Depot Distributors, Inc., a business involved in selling and installing bathroom cabinets. He also owned several other businesses. Ronald's income was $543,382 in 1985, $820,439 in 1986, $1,919,713 in 1987, and $1,462,712 in 1988. Ronald invested much of his income in commercial and residential real estate, which was held in his name only. At the time of the divorce trial in 1991, the real estate was valued at $11,790,000 and was subject to mortgages of $4,966,343.

After their separation, Ronald engaged in certain transfers of property and distributions of property, in violation of the court's order, that obfuscated his income and net worth. The trial court judge therefore accepted Edith's appraisals of the value of the real estate. The trial court judge applied the equitable distribution doctrine of Massachusetts and awarded Edith real estate totaling $2,446,000, the family residence, and alimony of $1,200 per month. The trial court judge awarded Ronald real estate valued at $9,314,000 subject to mortgages of $4,966,343, for a net value of $4,347,657. The judge characterized this as a roughly 60–40 split of the real estate (i.e., 60 percent for Ronald and 40 percent for Edith). Ronald appealed the split of real estate and the award of alimony as violating the equitable distribution doctrine.

ISSUE Under the doctrine of equitable distribution, was the trial court's award fair, or should Ronald win on appeal?

9.3 *Schweinberg v. Click*

627 So.2d 548, 1993 Fla. App. Lexis 11660 (1993)
Court of Appeal of Florida

FACTS Randolph J. Schweinberg and Sandra Faye Click were married on January 26, 1973. On March 12, 1986, Sandra Click moved out of the couple's home, and the couple was divorced on December 2, 1986. At the time of the divorce, the couple had two minor children, Randolph II and Russell. Randolph II has cerebral palsy and walks with difficulty. The children lived with Randolph after Sandra moved out. Randolph was a sergeant in the United States Air Force stationed in South Carolina; he considered Florida his permanent home, however.

In the divorce proceeding, the court awarded custody of the two minor children to Randolph. The two children were doing well in school, and the court found that Randolph II needed the emotional support provided by his brother Russell. Sandra was permitted visitation rights to see the children. Sandra later remarried to a man who had previously been convicted of lewd and lascivious behavior on a female child and was under court supervision for 15 years.

On December 19, 1991, Sandra petitioned the court to modify the custody order to grant her custody of the two minor children. The trial court granted the petition and awarded custody to Sandra. Randolph appealed the trial court's decision.

ISSUE Under the best interests test, should Randolph or Sandra be awarded custody of the two minor children?

ETHICS CASE

9.4 *Chadwick v. Janecka, Warden, Delaware County Prison, Pennsylvania*

312 F.3d 597, 2002 U.S.App. LEXIS 25263 (2002)
United States Court of Appeals, Third Circuit

FACTS In 1992, Mrs. Barbara Chadwick filed for divorce in Pennsylvania from Mr. H. Beatty Chadwick. During an equitable distribution conference in 1993, Mr. Chadwick informed the divorce court that he transferred more than $2.5 million of the marital estate to pay an alleged debt he owed to Maison Blanche, Ltd., a Gibraltar partnership. It was later discovered that the principals of Maison Blanche had transferred $995,726 to a bank account in Switzerland in Mr. Chadwick's name and had purchased $869,106 of insurance annuity contracts in Mr. Chadwick's name. Mr. Chadwick redeemed these annuity contracts and received the money. In addition, $550,000 in stock certificates in Mr. Chadwick's name had been "lost."

The divorce court ordered Mr. Chadwick to return the $2,502,000 to an account under the jurisdiction of the court. When Mr. Chadwick refused, the court held Mr. Chadwick in civil contempt of court and ordered him jailed. During a 7-year period of incarceration, Mr. Chadwick applied 14 times to be released from prison, each request being denied. Mr. Chadwick filed another request to be released from prison, alleging that he should be released because it is unlikely that he will comply with the divorce court's order to turn over the money and that, therefore, the civil contempt order has lost its coercive effect. The district court agreed, and granted Mr. Chadwick's petition to be released from prison. The government appealed the case to the U.S. Court of Appeals.

ISSUE Did Mr. Chadwick act ethically in this case? Should Mr. Chadwick be released from prison?

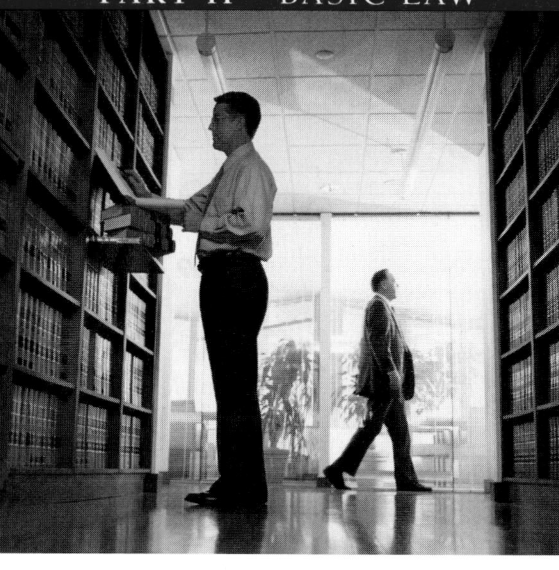

10 Wills, Trusts, and Estates

When you have told someone you have left him a legacy, the only decent thing to do is to die at once.

—SAMUEL BUTLER (1835–1902)

CHAPTER OBJECTIVES

After studying this chapter, you should be able to

1. List and describe the requirements for making a will.
2. Explain specific and general devises under a will.
3. Explain how property is distributed under intestacy statutes if a person dies without a will.
4. Define a *living trust* and explain its benefits.
5. Define a *living will* and *health care proxy.*

CHAPTER OUTLINE

- Introduction
- Wills
- Special Types of Wills
- Types of Testamentary Gifts
- Case for Discussion: *In the Matter of the Estate of Reed*
- Case for Discussion: *Opperman v. Anderson*
- Special Issues Concerning Wills
- Intestate Succession
- Probate
- Case for Discussion: *Robison v. Graham*
- Trusts
- Legal Terminology
- Chapter Summary
- Internet Exercises and Cases

INTRODUCTION

Wills and trusts are a means of transferring property. Wills transfer property upon a person's death. A person who dies without a will is said to have died **intestate.** In this case, the deceased's property is distributed to relatives according to state statute. The property escheats to the state if there are no relatives. Trusts are used to transfer property that is to be held and managed for the benefit of another person. Trusts are created during one's lifetime, but they may be worded to become effective upon the trustor's death. This chapter covers wills, trusts, and estates.

WILLS

A **will** is a declaration of how a person wants his or her property to be distributed upon his or her death. It is a *testamentary* deposition of property. The person who makes the will is called the **testator** or **testatrix.** The persons designated in the will to receive the testator's property are called **beneficiaries.**

Requirements for Making a Will

Every state has a **Statute of Wills** that establishes the requirements for making a valid will in that state. These requirements are:

- **Testamentary capacity:** The testator must have been of legal age and "sound mind" when the will was made. The courts determine **testamentary capacity** on a case-by-case basis. The legal age for executing a will is set by state statute.
- **Writing:** Wills must be in writing to be valid (except for dying declarations, discussed later in this chapter). The writing may be formal or informal. Although most wills are typewritten, they can be handwritten (see the discussion of holographic wills). The writing may be on legal paper, scratch paper, envelopes, napkins, or other paper. A will may incorporate additional documents by reference.
- **Testator's signature:** Wills must be signed.

Most jurisdictions require the testator's signature to appear at the end of the will. This is to prevent fraud that could occur if someone were to add provisions to the will below the testator's signature. Generally, courts have held that initials ("R.K.H."), a nickname ("Buffy"), title ("mother"), or even an "X" is a valid signature on a will if it can be proven that the testator intended it to be his or her signature.

"After probate, family members will receive duplicate videos."

Attestation by Witnesses

Wills must be attested to by mentally competent witnesses. Although state law varies, most states require two or three witnesses for **attestation.** The witnesses do not have to reside in the jurisdiction in which the testator is domiciled. Most jurisdictions stipulate that interested parties (e.g., a beneficiary under the will or the testator's attorney) cannot be witnesses. If an interested party has attested to a will, state law either voids any clauses that benefit such person or voids the entire will.

Witnesses usually sign the will following the signature of the testator. This is called the *attestation clause*. Most jurisdictions require that each witness attest to the will in the presence of the other witnesses.

A will that meets the requirements of the Statute of Wills is called a **formal will.** A sample will is shown as Exhibit 10.1.

Changing a Will

A will cannot be amended by merely striking out existing provisions and adding new ones. The legal way to change an existing will is through a **codicil.** A codicil is a separate document that must be executed with the same formalities as a will. In addition, it must incorporate by reference the will it is amending. The codicil and the will then are read as one instrument.

EXHIBIT 10.1 *Sample will.*

Last Will and Testament of Florence Winthorpe Blueblood

I, FLORENCE WINTHORPE BLUEBLOOD, presently residing at Boston, County of Suffolk, Massachusetts, being of sound and disposing mind and memory, hereby make, publish, and declare this to be my Last Will and Testament.

FIRST. I hereby revoke any and all Wills and Codicils previously made by me.

SECOND. I direct that my just debts and funeral expenses be paid out of my Estate as soon as practicable after my death.

THIRD. I am presently married to Theodore Hannah Blueblood III.

FOURTH. I hereby nominate and appoint my husband as the Personal Representative of this my Last Will and Testament. If he is unable to serve as Personal Representative, then I nominate and appoint Mildred Yardly Winthorpe as Personal Representative of this my Last Will and Testament. I direct that no bond or other security be required to be posted by my Personal Representative.

FIFTH. I hereby nominate and appoint my husband as Guardian of the person and property of my minor children. In the event that he is unable to serve as Guardian, then I nominate and appoint Mildred Yardly Winthorpe Guardian of the person and property of my minor children. I direct that no bond or other security be required to be posted by any Guardian herein.

SIXTH. I give my Personal Representative authority to exercise all the powers, rights, duties, and immunities conferred upon fiduciaries under law with full power to sell, mortgage, lease, invest, or reinvest all or any part of my Estate on such terms as he or she deems best.

SEVENTH. I hereby give, devise, and bequeath my entire estate to my husband, except for the following specific bequests:

I give my wedding ring to my daughter, Hillary Smythe Blueblood.

I give my baseball card collection to my son, Theodore Hannah Blueblood IV.

In the event that either my above-named daughter or son predeceases me, then and in that event, I give, devise, and bequeath my deceased daughter's or son's bequest to my husband.

EIGHTH. In the event that my husband shall predecease me, then and in that event, I give, devise and bequeath my entire estate, with the exception of the bequests in paragraph SEVENTH, to my beloved children or grandchildren surviving me, per stirpes.

NINTH. In the event I am not survived by my husband or any children or grandchildren, then and in that event, I give, devise, and bequeath my entire estate to Harvard University.

IN WITNESS WHEREOF, I Florence Winthorpe Blueblood, the Testatrix, sign my name to this Last Will and Testament this 3rd day of January, 2005.

____

(Signature)

Signed, sealed, published and declared by the above-named Testatrix, as and for her Last Will and Testament, in the presence of us, who at her request, in her presence and in the presence of one another, have hereunto subscribed our names as attesting witnesses, the day and year last written above.

Witness	*Address*

Queen Anne–style brick Talbot County Courthouse, completed 1892, in Talbot, Georgia.

Revoking a Will

A will may be revoked by acts of the testator. A will is revoked if the testator intentionally burns, tears, obliterates, or otherwise destroys it. A properly executed *subsequent will* revokes a prior will if it specifically states that it is the testator's intention to do so. If the second will does not expressly revoke the prior will, the wills are read together. If any will provisions are inconsistent, the provision in the second will controls.

Wills can be revoked by operation of law. For example, divorce or annulment revokes disposition of property to the former spouse under the will. The remainder of the will is valid. The birth of a child after a will has been executed does not revoke the will but does entitle the child to receive his or her share of the parents' estate as determined by state statute.

Special Types of Wills

The law recognizes some types of wills that do not meet all of the requirements discussed above. Two special types of wills admitted by the courts are holographic wills and noncupative wills.

Holographic Wills

Holographic wills are entirely handwritten and signed by the testator. The writing may be in ink, pencil, crayon, or some other writing instrument. Many states recognize the validity of such wills even though they are not witnessed.

Noncupative Wills

Noncupative wills are oral wills made before witnesses. These wills are usually valid only if they are made during the testator's last illness. They sometimes are called *deathbed wills* or *dying declarations.*

Types of Testamentary Gifts

A gift of real estate by will is called a **devise.** A gift of personal property by will is called a **bequest** or **legacy.** Gifts in wills can be *specific, general,* or *residuary:*

- **Specific gifts:** Specifically named pieces of property, such as a ring, a boat, or a piece of real estate.
- **General gifts:** Gifts that do not identify the specific property from which the gift is to be made, such as a cash amount that can come from any source in the decedent's estate.
- **Residuary gifts:** Established by a *residuary clause* in the will. The clause might state, for example, "I give my daughter the rest, remainder, and residual of my estate." This means that any portion of the estate left after the debts, taxes, and specific and general gifts have been paid belongs to the decedent's daughter.

CASE FOR DISCUSSION

In the Matter of the Estate of Reed

672 P.2d 829, 1983 Wyo. Lexis 389 (1983) — Supreme Court of Wyoming

FACTS

Robert G. Reed died on March 2, 1982. On April 23, 1982, the court appointed coadministrators of Reed's estate, finding that he died intestate. On October 29, 1982, Margaret F. Buckley filed a petition for probate of a will, alleging that a tape recording found by the police in Reed's home was a valid will of the deceased. The tape recording was found in a sealed envelope on which Reed had written, "To be played in the event of my death." The trial court refused to admit the tape recording into probate. Buckley appealed.

ISSUE

Is a tape-recorded statement a holographic will that can be admitted into probate?

COURT'S REASONING

Appellant contends that the tape recording should be admitted to probate as a form of holographic will. Appellant Buckley reasoned that the tape recorder should be a method of "writing" that conforms with the holographic will statute. The supreme court stated that the Wyoming statutes are clear and unambiguous in their description of a holographic will. A holographic will must be entirely in the handwriting of the decedent. Handwriting is not an ambiguous word. The court stated, "We are not aware of any definition of handwriting that includes voice print, nor do we know of any authority that has held that handwriting includes voice prints. It seems to be stating the obvious that a voice print is not writing."

DECISION AND REMEDY

The state supreme court held that a tape recording did not meet the requirements for a holographic will under the Wyoming statute. The supreme court affirmed the decision of the trial court denying the probate of the tape recording.

QUESTIONS

1. Should tape recordings be admitted into probate? Why or why not?
2. Did Buckley act ethically in trying to probate the tape recording as a will?
3. What were the economic consequences of this decision?

A person who inherits property under a will or an intestacy statute takes the property subject to all of the outstanding claims against it (e.g., liens, mortgages). A person can *renounce* an inheritance—and often does—when the liens or mortgages against the property exceed the value of the property.

Ademption

If a testator leaves a specific gift of property to a beneficiary but the property is no longer in the estate of the testator when he or she dies, the beneficiary receives nothing. This is called the doctrine of **ademption.**

Abatement

The good of man is in the will, and the evil too.

—Epictetus

If the testator's estate is not large enough to pay all of the devises and bequests, the doctrine of **abatement** applies. The doctrine works as follows:

- If a will provides for both general and residuary gifts, the residuary gifts are abated first (i.e., paid last). Suppose a testator executes a will when he owns $500,000 of property that leaves (1) $100,000 to the Red Cross, (2) $100,000 to a university, and (3) the residue to his niece. When the testator dies, his estate is worth only $225,000. Here the Red Cross and the university receive $100,000 each and the niece receives $25,000.
- If a will provides for only general gifts, the reductions are proportionate. Suppose a testator's will leaves $75,000 to each of two beneficiaries but the estate is worth only $100,000. Each beneficiary would receive $50,000.

Per Stirpes and Per Capita Distribution

A testator's will may state that property is to be left to his or her **lineal descendents** (children, grandchildren, great-grandchildren, etc.) either *per stirpes* or *per capita*. The difference between these two methods is as follows:

- **Per stirpes distribution:** The lineal descendants inherit by representation of their parent; that is, they split what their deceased parent would have received. If their parent is not deceased, they receive nothing.
- **Per capita distribution:** The lineal descendants equally share the property of the estate without regard to degree of relationship to the testator. That is, children of the testator share equally with grandchildren, great-grandchildren, and so forth.

Suppose Anne dies without a surviving spouse and she had three children: Bart, Beth, and Bruce. Bart, who survives his mother, has no children. Beth has one child, Carla, and they both survive Anne. Bruce, who predeceased his mother, had two children, Clayton and Cathy; and Cathy, who predeceased Anne, had two children, Deborah and Dominic, both of whom survive Anne.

If Anne leaves her estate to her lineal descendants *per stirpes*, Bart and Beth each get one-third, Carla receives nothing because Beth is alive, Clayton gets one-sixth, and Deborah and Dominic both get one-twelfth. Exhibit 10.2 illustrates this per-stirpes example graphically.

But if Anne leaves her estate to her lineal descendants *per capita*, all of the surviving issue—Bart, Beth, Carla, Clayton, Deborah, and Dominic—share equally in the estate. They each get one-sixth of Anne's estate. Exhibit 10.3 illustrates the per-capita distribution for this example.

CASE FOR DISCUSSION

Opperman v. Anderson

782 S.W.2d 8, 1989 Tex. App. Lexis 3175 (1989) — Court of Appeals of Texas

FACTS

On September 26, 1983, Ethel M. Ramchissel executed a will that made the following bequests: (1) one-half of the stock she owned in Pabst Brewing Company (Pabst) to Mary Lee Anderson, (2) all of the stock she owned in Houston Natural Gas Corporation (Houston Natural Gas) to Ethel Baker and others (Baker), and (3) the residue and remainder of her estate to Boysville, Inc. In response to an offer by G. Heilman Brewing Company to purchase Pabst, Ramchissel sold all of her Pabst stock for cash. She placed the proceeds in a separate bank account to which no other funds have been added. Pursuant to a merger agreement between Internorth, Inc., and Houston Natural Gas, Ramchissel converted her shares in Houston Natural Gas to cash. The proceeds were placed in another bank account, to which no other funds have been added. When Ramchissel died on April 4, 1987, her will was admitted into probate. The probate court awarded the money in the two bank accounts to Anderson and Baker, respectively. This appeal ensued.

ISSUE

Were the bequests to Anderson and Baker specific bequests that were adeemed when the stock was sold and therefore Anderson and Baker receive nothing?

COURT'S REASONING

Ademption is the doctrine by which a specific bequest becomes inoperative because of the disappearance of its subject matter from a testator's estate during his lifetime. A specific bequest is one comprised of specific articles of the testator's estate. The court concluded that Ramchissel clearly intended the gifts of stock to Anderson and Baker be specific bequests subject to ademption. The court found that ademption occurred when the specific shares of stock described were sold prior to the testatrix's death.

DECISION AND REMEDY

The court of appeals held that the bequests of stock at issue in this case were specific bequests that were adeemed when the stock was converted to cash. Therefore, the cash proceeds of these stock sales pass pursuant to the residuary clause of Ramchissel's will, and not to Anderson and Baker. The court of appeals reversed the trial court's decision that had awarded the two bank accounts to Anderson and Baker, respectively.

QUESTIONS

1. Should the doctrine of ademption be recognized by law? What other solution would there be?
2. Do you think the result reached in this case was fair or what Ramchissel intended?
3. Explain the difference between ademption and abatement.

EXHIBIT 10.2 *Per stirpes distribution.*

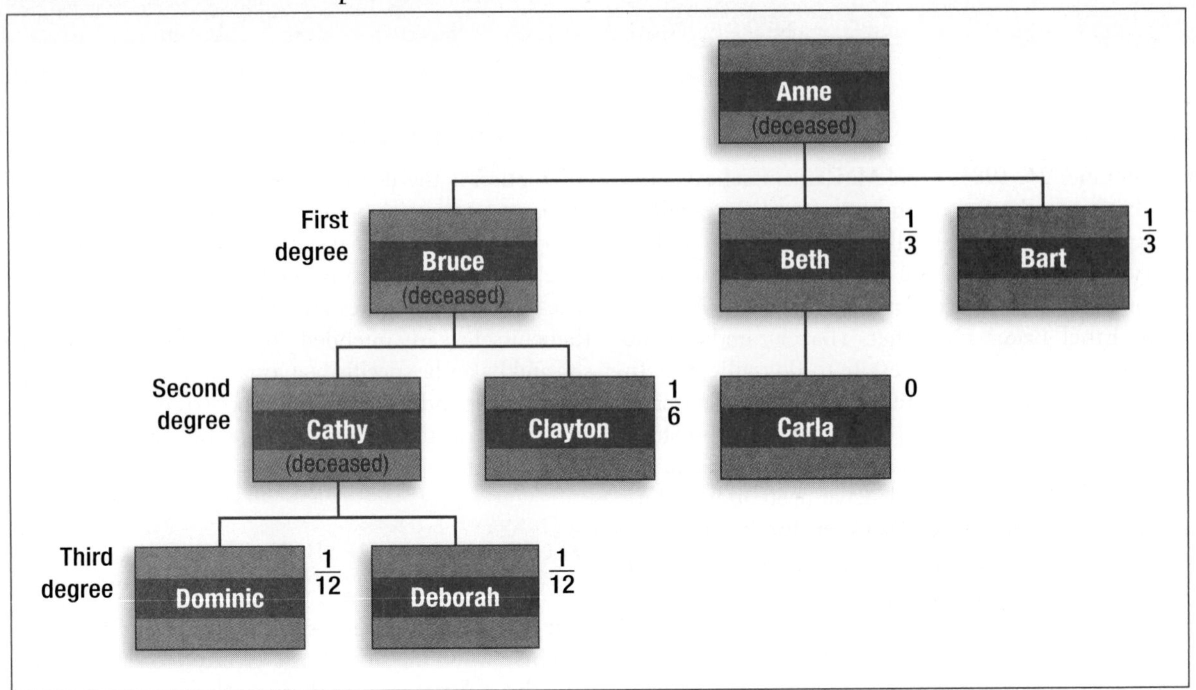

EXHIBIT 10.3 *Per capita distribution.*

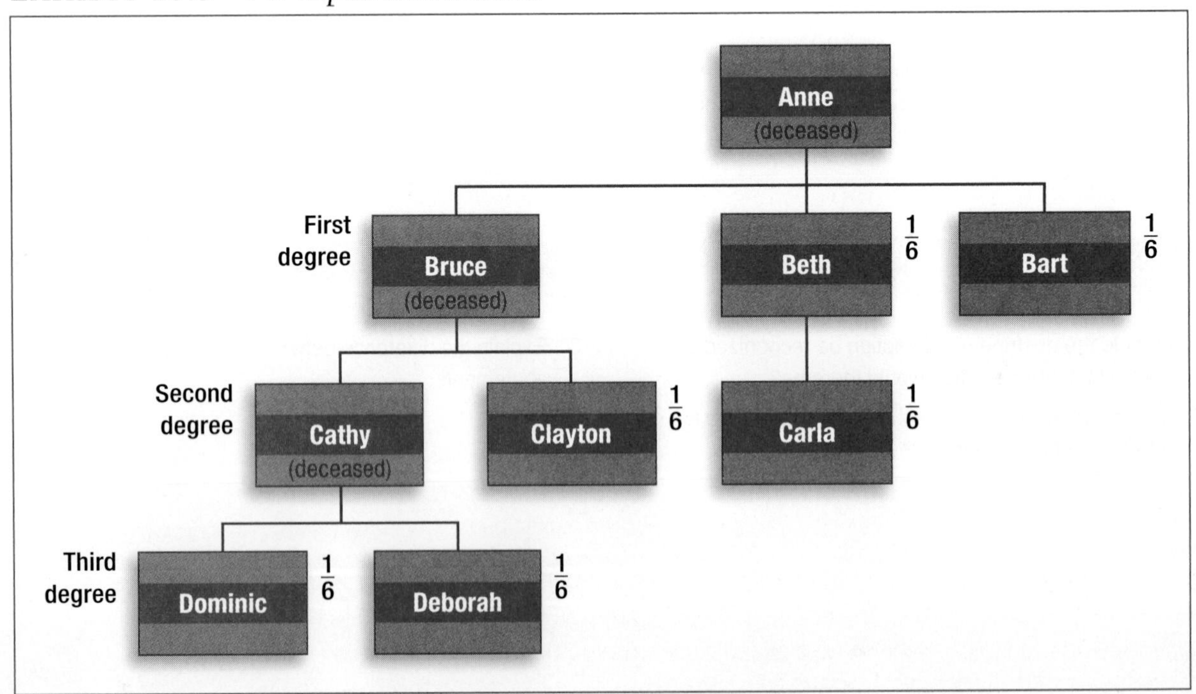

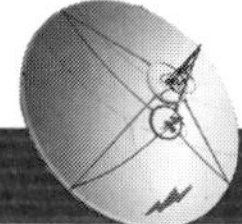

INFORMATION TECHNOLOGY

VIDEOTAPED AND ELECTRONIC WILLS

Many acrimonious will contests involve written wills. The contestors allege such things as mental incapacity of the testator at the time the will was made, undue influence, fraud, or duress. Although the written will speaks for itself, the mental capacity of the testator and the voluntariness of his or her actions cannot be determined from the writing alone.

If a challenge to the validity of a will has merit, it, of course, should be resolved. But some will contests are based on unfounded allegations. After all, the testator is not there to defend his or her testamentary wishes.

To prevent unwarranted will contests, a testator can use a videotaped or electronically recorded will to supplement a written will. Videotaping the reading and signing of a will can withstand challenges by disgruntled relatives and alleged heirs.

A written will should be prepared to comply with the state's Statute of Wills. The video should begin with the testator reciting the will verbatim. Next the lawyer should ask the testator questions to demonstrate the testator's sound mind and understanding of the implications of his or her actions. The last segment on the film should be the execution ceremony—signing of the will by the testator and attestation by the witnesses.

With the testator's actions crystallized on videotape, a judge or jury will be able to determine the testator's mental capacity at the time the will was made and the voluntariness of his or her testamentary gifts. In addition, fraudulent competing wills will crumble in the face of such proof.

Special Issues Concerning Wills

Some unique issues in wills involve simultaneous deaths, joint and mutual wills, and undue influence.

Simultaneous Deaths

Sometimes people who would inherit property from each other incur **simultaneous death.** If it is impossible to determine who died first, the question becomes one of inheritance. The **Uniform Simultaneous Death Act** provides that each deceased person's property is distributed as if he or she had survived the other.

Suppose a husband and wife who have no children make wills leaving their entire estate to each other. The husband and wife are killed simultaneously in an airplane crash. Here, the husband's property would go to his relatives and the wife's property would go to her relatives.

Uniform Simultaneous Death Act
An act that provides that if people who would inherit property from each other die simultaneously, each person's property is distributed as though he or she had survived.

Joint and Mutual Wills

If two or more testators execute the same instrument as their will, the document is called a **joint will.** A joint will may be held invalid as to one testator but not the other(s).

Mutual wills, or **reciprocal wills,** are developed when two or more testators execute separate wills that make testamentary dispositions of their property to each other on the condition that the survivor leave the remaining property on his or her

SIDEBAR

Undue Influence
Occurs where one person takes advantage of another person's mental, emotional, or physical weakness and unduly persuades that person to make a will; the persuasion by the wrongdoer must overcome the free will of the testator. Undue influence is difficult to prove. It may be inferred from the facts and circumstances surrounding the making of a will.

SIDEBAR

Murder Disqualification Rule
Most states, by statute or court decision, provide that a person who murders another person cannot inherit the victim's property. This rule, often called the **murder disqualification doctrine**, is based on the public policy that a person should not benefit from his or her wrongdoing.

death as agreed by the testators. The wills usually are separate instruments with reciprocal terms. Because of their contractual nature, mutual wills cannot be revoked unilaterally after one of the parties has died.

Undue Influence

A will may be found to be invalid if it was made as a result of **undue influence** on the testator. Undue influence can be inferred from the facts and circumstances surrounding the making of the will. For example, if an 85-year-old woman leaves all of her property to the lawyer who drafted her will and ignores her blood relatives, the court is likely to presume undue influence.

Undue influence is difficult to prove by direct evidence, but it may be proved by circumstantial evidence. The elements that courts examine to find the presence of undue influence include the following.

- The benefactor and beneficiary are involved in a relationship of confidence and trust.
- The will contains substantial benefit to the beneficiary.
- The beneficiary caused or assisted in effecting execution of the will.
- There was an opportunity to exert influence.
- The will contains an unnatural disposition of the testator's property.
- The bequests constitute a change from a former will.
- The testator was highly susceptible to the undue influence.

Intestate Succession

People often accumulate sizeable estates. They therefore should have a proper will designating who is to receive his or her property when he or she dies. If a person dies without a will, or his or her will fails for some legal reason, the property is distributed to his or her relatives pursuant to the state's **intestacy statute.**

Relatives who receive property under these statutes are called **heirs.** Although intestacy statutes differ from state to state, the general rule is that the deceased's real property is distributed according to the intestacy statute of the state where the deceased had his or her permanent residence.

Intestacy statutes usually leave the deceased's property to his or her heirs in this order: spouse, children, lineal heirs (e.g., grandchildren, parents, brothers and sisters), collateral heirs (e.g., aunts, uncles, nieces, nephews), and other next of kin (e.g., cousins). If the deceased has no surviving relatives, the deceased's property **escheats** (goes) to the state. In-laws do not inherit under most intestacy statutes. If a child dies before his or her parents, the child's spouse does not receive the inheritance.

To avoid the distribution of an estate as provided in an intestacy statute, a person should have a properly written, signed, and witnessed will that distributes the estate property as the testator wishes.

Probate

When a person dies, his or her property must be collected, debts and taxes paid, and the remainder of the estate distributed to the beneficiaries of the will or the heirs under the state intestacy statute. This process is called **settlement** of the es-

CASE FOR DISCUSSION

Robison v. Graham

799 P. 2d 610, 1990 Okla. Lexis 104 (1990) **Supreme Court of Oklahoma**

FACTS

Mary Kay Graham (Mary) and William Clyde Graham (Clyde) were married in 1942. On March 3, 1973, Mary and Clyde executed a mutual and joint will in which they left all of each other's property to the survivor, with the survivor agreeing to leave half of the remaining property to Kathryn Robison and the other half in trust to William Lee Robison. Mary and Clyde agreed not to revoke, alter, or amend the will except by mutual written consent.

The will was not revoked prior to Mary's death on April 15, 1979. In May 1981, Clyde married Stella E. Berry (Stella), at which time he placed his property in joint tenancy with Stella and executed a new will. The new will revoked his prior one and designated Stella as the beneficiary of the remainder of his estate. The marriage lasted until Clyde's death in 1985.

Stella introduced the new will to probate. The beneficiaries of the mutual will sued, alleging breach of the mutual will. The trial court held in favor of the original beneficiaries. The court of appeals reversed. The original beneficiaries appealed.

ISSUE

Is the mutual will enforceable?

COURT'S REASONING

The Supreme Court of Oklahoma held that in the present case, proof of a mutually binding contract to devise property was within the four corners of the will executed by Clyde and Mary. The language clearly expressed the intent of Clyde and Mary to make a binding and irrevocable contract concerning the disposition of their property. Clyde offered Mary's will for probate and took the estate subject to its terms.

The court stated that according to the specific agreement of the parties to the mutual will, the survivor agreed not to revoke, alter, or amend the will, carried with it an implicit agreement by the survivor to see to it that the testamentary intent expressed in the mutual will be carried out and to make no disposition of the estate property inconsistent with that intent. It is undisputed that the property that was the subject of the contractual will was intact at Clyde's death even though the legal title was in his surviving spouse, Stella. The court held that Clyde breached the contractual will by revoking it and executing subsequent wills.

DECISION AND REMEDY

The state supreme court held that Clyde breached the mutual will that he had made with Mary. The supreme court vacated the judgment of the court of appeals and imposed a constructive trust on Clyde's estate in favor of the beneficiaries of the mutual will.

QUESTIONS

1. Should mutual wills be enforced? Why or why not?
2. Did Clyde act ethically?
3. Why are mutual wills made? Explain.

The Right to Die and Living Wills

Technological breakthroughs have greatly increased the lifespan of human beings. This same technology, however, permits life to be sustained long after a person is "brain dead." Some people say they have a right to refuse such treatment. Others argue that human life must be preserved at all costs. The U.S. Supreme Court was called upon to decide the **right-to-die** issue in the case of Nancy Cruzan.

In 1983, an automobile accident left Cruzan, a 25-year-old Missouri woman, in an irreversible coma. Four years later, Cruzan's parents petitioned a state court judge to permit the hospital to withdraw the artificial feeding tube that had been keeping Cruzan alive. The judge agreed.

But Missouri's attorney general intervened and asked an appellate court to reverse the lower court's decision. The appellate court sided with the attorney general.

In reviewing the Missouri court's decision, eight of the nine justices of the U.S. Supreme Court acknowledged that the right to refuse medical treatment is a personal liberty protected by the U.S. Constitution. But the Court also recognized that the states have an interest in preserving life. This interest can be expressed through a requirement for clear and convincing proof that the patient did not want to be sustained by artificial means. A Missouri judge finally permitted the family to have Cruzan's tubes withdrawn. She died shortly afterward.

The clear message of the Supreme Court's opinion is that people who do not want their lives prolonged indefinitely by artificial means should sign a **living will** that stipulates their wishes before catastrophe strikes and they become unable to express it themselves because of an illness or an accident.

Those who have a living will could state which life-saving measures they do and do not want. Alternatively, they could state that they want any such treatments withdrawn if doctors determine that there is no hope of a meaningful recovery. The living will provides clear and convincing proof of a patient's wishes with respect to medical treatment.

Exhibit 10.4 is an example of a living will and health-care proxy.

Cruzan v. Director, Missouri Department of Health [497 U.S. 261, 110 S.Ct. 2841, 1990 U.S. Lexis 3301 (1990)]

SIDEBAR

Uniform Probate Code

The **Uniform Probate Code (UPC)** was promulgated to establish consistent rules for the creation of wills, the administration of estates, and the resolution of conflicts in settling estates. These rules provide a speedy, efficient, and less expensive method for settling estates than many existing state laws. Only about one-third of the states have adopted all or part of the UPC.

tate or **probate.** The process and procedures for settling an estate are governed by state statute. A specialized state court, called the probate court, usually supervises the administration and settlement of an estate.

A *personal representative* must be appointed to administer the estate during its settlement phase. If the testator's will names the personal representative, that person is called an **executor** or **executrix.** If no one is named or if the decedent dies intestate, the court will appoint an **administrator** or **administratrix.** Usually, this party is a relative of the deceased or a bank. An attorney is usually appointed to help administer the estate and to complete the probate.

TRUSTS

A **trust** is a legal arrangement under which one person—the **settlor, trustor,** or **transferor**—delivers and transfers legal title to property to another person, the **trustee**, to be held and used for the benefit of a third person, the beneficiary. The property held in trust is called the **trust corpus** or **trust res.** The trustee has **legal title** to the trust corpus, and the beneficiary has **equitable title.** Unlike wills, trusts are not public documents, so property can be transferred in privacy. Exhibit 10.5 shows the parties to a trust.

EXHIBIT 10.4 *Sample living will and health-care proxy.*

Living Will and Health-Care Proxy

I. Living Will Including Statement Concerning Right to Die

Death is as much a reality as birth, growth, maturity and old age—it is the one certainty of life. If the time comes when I, John Doe, can no longer take part in decisions for my own future, let this statement stand as an expression of my wishes and directions to my Health Care Agent and others while I am still of sound mind. I intend, without otherwise limiting the absolute authority granted to my Health Care Agent in this instrument, that this instrument be binding upon my Health Care Agent.

If the situation should arise in which there is no reasonable expectation of my recovery from extreme physical or mental disability, including, but not limited to, a circumstance where there is no reasonable expectation that I will recover consciousness, commonly referred to as "brain dead," I direct that I be allowed to die and not be kept alive by medications, artificial means, including but not limited to artificial nutrition and hydration, or "heroic measures." Without limiting the generality of the foregoing, I hereby consent in such situation to an order not to attempt cardiopulmonary resuscitation. I do, however, ask that medication be mercifully administered to me to alleviate suffering even though this may shorten my remaining life and retard my consciousness.

II. Health Care Proxy

I hereby appoint my spouse, Jane Doe, to be my Health Care Agent to make any and all health care decisions in accordance with my wishes and instructions as stated above and as otherwise known to her. In the event the person I appoint above is unable, unwilling or unavailable to act as my Health Care Agent, I hereby appoint my twin brother, Jack Doe, as my Health Care Agent.

This health care proxy shall take effect in the event that I become unable to make my own health care decisions. I hereby revoke any prior health care proxy given by me to the extent it purports to confer the authority herein granted. I understand that, unless I revoke it, this health care proxy will remain in effect indefinitely.

Although I do not know today the exact circumstances that will exist when my Health Care Agent is called upon to make a decision or decisions on my behalf, I have selected my Health Care Agent with the confidence that such person understands my feelings in these matters and will make the decision I will want made considering the circumstances as they exist at the time. It is my intention, therefore, that the decision of my Health Care Agent be taken as a final and binding decision of mine, and will be the conclusive interpretation of the wishes I have made known in this document.

III. Waiver and Indemnity

To the extent permitted by law, I, for myself and for my heirs, executors, legal representatives and assigns, hereby release and discharge and agree to indemnify and hold harmless my Health Care Agent from and against any claim or liability whatsoever resulting from or arising out of my Health Care Agent's reliance on my wishes and directions as expressed herein. To induce any third party to act hereunder, I hereby agree that any third party receiving a duly executed copy or facsimile of this instrument may act hereunder, and that revocation or termination by me hereof shall be ineffective as to such third party unless and until actual notice or knowledge of such revocation shall have been received by such third party, and, to the extent permitted by law, I, for myself and for my heirs, executors, legal representatives and assigns, hereby release and discharge and agree to indemnify and hold harmless any such third party from and against any claims or liability whatsoever that may arise against such third party by reason of such third party having relied on the provisions of this instrument.

I understand the full import of this directive and I am emotionally and mentally competent to make this directive.

Signed ______________________________

The declarant has been personally known to me and I believe him or her to be of sound mind.

Witness ______________________________

Witness ______________________________

EXHIBIT 10.5 *Parties to a trust.*

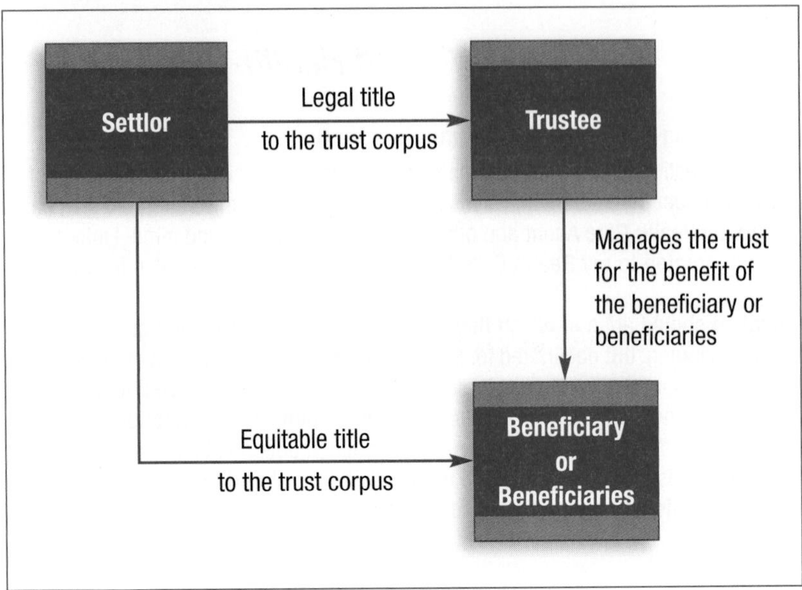

Trusts often provide that any trust income is to be paid to a person called the **income beneficiary.** The person to receive the trust corpus upon termination of the trust is called the **remainderman.** The income beneficiary and the remainderman can be the same person or different persons. The designated beneficiary can be any identifiable person, animal (such as a pet), charitable organization, or other institution or cause that the settlor chooses. An entire class of persons—for example, "my grandchildren"—can be named.

> An honest man's word is as good as his bond.
>
> —Don Quixote

A trust can allow the trustee to invade (use) the trust corpus for certain purposes that can be specifically named (e.g., "for the beneficiary's college education"). The trust agreement usually specifies how the receipts and expenses of the trust are to be divided between the income beneficiary and the remainderman.

Generally, the trustee has broad management powers over the trust property. This means that the trustee can invest the trust property to preserve its capital and make it productive. The trustee must follow any restrictions on investments contained in the trust agreement or state statute.

Express Trusts

Express trusts are created voluntarily by the settlor. These usually are written, and the agreement is called a *trust instrument* or *trust agreement.*

Express trusts fall into two categories.

1. ***Inter vivos*** **trusts or living trusts:** created while the settlor is alive. The settlor transfers legal title of property to a named trustee to hold, administer, and manage for the benefit of named beneficiaries.
2. **Testamentary trusts:** created by will. The trust comes into existence when the settlor dies. If the will that establishes the trust is found to be invalid, the trust is also invalid.

Implied Trusts

Implied trusts are those imposed by law or by conduct of the parties. These trusts are divided into two categories: *constructive trusts* and *resulting trusts.*

A **constructive trust** is an equitable trust imposed by law to avoid fraud, unjust enrichment, and injustice. In constructive trust arrangements, the holder of the actual title to property (the trustee) holds the property in trust for its rightful owner.

Suppose Thad and Kaye are partners. Assume that Kaye embezzles partnership funds and uses the stolen funds to purchase a piece of real estate. In this case, the court can impose a constructive trust under which Kaye (who holds actual title to the land) is considered a trustee who is holding the property in trust for Thad, its rightful owner.

A **resulting trust** is created by the conduct of the parties. Consider this example: Henry is purchasing a piece of real estate but cannot attend the closing. He asks his brother, Gregory, to attend the closing and take title to the property until he can return. In this case, Gregory holds the title to the property as trustee for Henry until he returns.

Special Types of Trusts

Trusts may be created for special purposes. Three types of special trusts are fairly common:

1. **Charitable trusts:** created for the benefit of a segment of society or society in general. An example is a trust created for the construction and maintenance of a public park.
2. **Spendthrift trusts:** designed to prevent a beneficiary's personal creditors from reaching his or her trust interest. All control over the trust is removed from the beneficiary. Personal creditors still can go after trust income that is paid to the beneficiary, however.
3. **Totten trusts:** created when a person deposits money in a bank account in his or her own name and holds it as a trustee for the benefit of another person. A totten trust is a tentative trust because (1) the trustee can add or withdraw funds from the account, and (2) the trust can be revoked at any time prior to his or her death or prior to completing delivery of the funds to the beneficiary.

Termination of a Trust

A trust is irrevocable unless the settlor reserves the right to revoke it. Most trusts fall into the first category.

Usually, a trust either contains a specific termination date or provides that it will terminate upon the happening of an event (e.g., when the remainderman reaches a certain age). Upon termination, the trust corpus is distributed as provided in the trust agreement.

Living Trusts

Living trusts have become a popular method for holding property during a person's lifetime and distributing the property upon that person's death. A living trust works as follows. During his or her life, a person establishes a living trust, which is a legal entity. A living trust is also referred to as a **grantor's trust,** a **revocable trust,** or an *inter vivos trust.* The person who creates the trust is called the *grantor* or *settlor* (also the *trustor*).

To fund a living trust, the grantor transfers title to his property to the trust. Bank accounts, stock certificates, real estate, personal property, intangible property, and other property owned by the grantor must be retitled to the trust's name. For example, the grantor must execute deeds transferring title to real estate to the trust. Once property is transferred to the trust, the trust is considered *funded.* A living trust is revocable during the grantor's lifetime. Thus, a grantor can later change his mind and undo the trust and retake title of the property in his own name.

The living trust will name a *trustee* who is responsible for maintaining, investing, buying, or selling trust assets. The trustee is usually the grantor. Thus, the grantor who establishes the trust does not lose control of the property placed in the trust and may manage and invest trust assets during his lifetime. The trust should name a *successor trustee* to replace the grantor-trustee if the grantor becomes incapacitated or too ill to manage the trust.

A living trust names *beneficiaries* who are entitled to receive income from the trust while it is in existence, and to receive the property of the trust when the grantor dies. Usually the grantor is the beneficiary who receives the income from the trust during his lifetime. Upon the death of the grantor, assets of the trust are distributed to the beneficiaries named in the trust. The designated trustee has the fiduciary duties of identifying assets, paying creditors, paying income and estate taxes, transferring assets to named beneficiaries, and rendering an accounting.

The primary purpose of using a living trust is to avoid probate associated with using a will. If a person dies with a will, the will must be probated so the deceased's assets can be properly distributed according to the will. A probate judge is named to oversee the probate process, and all documents, including the will, are public record. A living trust, on the other hand, is private. When the grantor dies, the assets are owned by the living trust and therefore are not subject to probate proceedings. In addition, if real property is owned in more than one state and a will is used, then ancillary probate must be conducted in each of the other states in which the real property is located. If a living trust is used, ancillary probate is avoided.

A **pour-over will** is necessary to distribute any property acquired in the name of the grantor after the living trust was established or any property that was not transferred to the trust in the first place. The pour-over will transfers this property to the trust upon the grantor's death, which is then distributed to the named beneficiaries of the trust. A pour-over will is subject to probate and is therefore public. A pour-over will is usually created at the same time that the living trust is established.

Living trusts often are promoted for claimed benefits that do not exist. The true facts are that a living trust

- Does not reduce estate taxes any more than a will does.
- Does not reduce the grantor's income taxes. All the income earned by the trust is attributed to the grantor, who must pay income taxes on the earnings just as if the trust did not exist.
- Does not avoid creditors. Thus, creditors can obtain liens against property in the trust.
- Is subject to property division upon divorce.
- Is usually not cheaper than a will. Both require payments to lawyers and usually to accountants and other professionals to draft and probate a will or draft and manage the living trust.

- Does not avoid controversies upon the grantor's death. Like wills, living trusts can be challenged for lack of capacity, undue influence, duress, and other legal grounds.

The Federal Trade Commission (FTC), a federal government agency that protects consumer rights, has warned against "mills" that sell boilerplate one-fits-all living trusts. A living trust is a legitimate planning tool for many people. A person should seek professional advice from, and have the living trust, pour-over will, and other necessary documents drafted by, an attorney.

LEGAL TERMINOLOGY

Abatement
Ademption
Administrator or administratrix
Attestation
Beneficiary
Bequest (legacy)
Charitable trust
Codicil
Constructive trust
Devise
Equitable title
Escheat
Executor or executrix
Express trust
Formal will
General gifts
Grantor's trust
Heirs
Holographic will
Implied trust
Income beneficiary
Inter vivos (living) trusts
Intestacy statute
Intestate
Intestate succession
Joint will
Legacy
Legal title
Lineal descendants
Living trust
Living will
Murder disqualification doctrine
Mutual will
Noncupative will
Per capita distribution
Per stirpes distribution
Pour-over will
Probate (settlement of the estate)
Reciprocal will
Remainderman
Residuary gifts
Resulting trust
Revocable trust
Right to die
Settlement
Settlor
Simultaneous deaths
Specific gifts
Spendthrift trust
Statute of Wills
Testamentary capacity
Testamentary trust
Testator or testatrix
Totten trust
Transferor
Trust
Trust corpus (trust res.)
Trustee
Trustor
Undue influence
Uniform Probate Code (UPC)
Uniform Simultaneous Death Act
Will

chapter summary

WILLS, TRUSTS, AND ESTATES

Wills	
Definition	A declaration of how a person wants his or her property to be distributed upon his or her death.
Parties to a Will	1. *Testator or testatrix:* Person who makes a will. 2. *Beneficiary:* Person designated in the will to receive the testator's property. There may be multiple beneficiaries. 3. *Executor or executrix:* Person named in a will to administer the testator's estate during settlement of the estate.
Requirements for Making a Will	1. *Statute of Wills:* A state statute that establishes the requirements for making a valid will. 2. The normal requirements for making a will are: a. *Testamentary capacity* (legal age and "sound mind") b. *In writing* c. *Testator's signature* d. *Attestation by witnesses* (mentally competent and uninterested)
Changing a Will	1. *Codicil:* A legal way to change an existing will. 2. Must be executed with the same formalities as a will.
Special Types of Wills	
Holographic Will	A will that is entirely handwritten and signed by the testator. Most states recognize the validity of these wills even though they are not witnessed.
Noncupative Will	Oral will made by dying person before witnesses. Many states recognize these oral wills. Also called a *deathbed will* or a *dying declaration.*
Types of Testamentary Gifts	
Specific Gift	Gift of a specifically mentioned piece of property (e.g., a ring).
General Gift	Gift that does not identify the specific property from which the gift is to be made (e.g., gift of cash).
Residuary Gift	Gift of the remainder of the testator's estate after the debts, taxes, and specific and general gifts have been paid.
Ademption	A situation in which a specific gift of property is no longer in the estate when the testator dies, so the beneficiary of that gift receives nothing.
Abatement	A situation in which the testator's estate is insufficient to pay the stated gifts and the gifts are abated (reduced) in the following order: (1) residuary gifts, then (2) general gifts proportionately.

Per Stirpes Distribution	Lineal descendants inherit by representation of their parent; they split what their deceased parent would have received.
Per Capita Distribution	Lineal descendants equally share the property of the estate without regard to degree of relationship to testator.
Special Issues Concerning Wills	
Simultaneous Deaths	The Uniform Simultaneous Death Act provides that if people who would inherit property from each other die simultaneously, each deceased person's property is distributed as if he or she had survived the other.
Joint Will	Two or more testators execute the same instrument as their will.
Mutual or Reciprocal Will	Two or more testators execute separate wills that leave property in favor of the other on condition that the survivor leave the remaining property upon his or her death as agreed by the testators.
Undue Influence	A will may be found to be invalid if it was made under undue influence, in which one person takes advantage of another person's mental, emotional, or physical weakness and unduly persuades that person to make a will.
Murder Disqualification	A person who murders another person cannot inherit the victim's property.
Intestate Succession	1. *Intestacy statute:* State statute that stipulates how a deceased's property will be distributed if he or she dies without leaving a will or if the will fails for some legal reason. 2. *Heirs:* Relatives who receive property under an intestacy statute. 3. *Escheat:* If no heirs exist, the deceased's property goes to the state, under intestacy statutes.
Probate	
Definition	Legal process of settling a deceased person's estate.
Administrator or Administratrix	Person named to administer the estate of a deceased person who dies intestate. An administrator also is named if an executor is not named in a will or the executor cannot or does not serve.
Trusts	
Definition	A legal arrangement whereby one person delivers and transfers legal title to property to another person to be held and used for the benefit of a third person.
Trust Corpus or Trust Res.	The property that is held in trust. *(continued)*

Parties	1. *Settlor:* Person who establishes a trust; also called a *trustor* or *transferor.* 2. *Trustee:* Person to whom *legal title* of the trust assets is transferred; responsible for managing the trust assets as established by the trust and law. 3. *Beneficiary:* Person for whose benefit a trust is created; holds *equitable title* to the trust assets. There can be multiple beneficiaries, including: a. *Income beneficiary:* Person to whom trust income is to be paid. b. *Remainderman:* Person who is entitled to receive the trust corpus upon termination of the trust.
Express Trusts	Voluntarily created by the settlor. Two types: 1. Inter vivos *trust:* Created while the settlor is alive; also called a *living trust.* 2. *Testamentary trust:* Created by will and comes into existence when the settlor dies.
Implied Trusts	Imposed by law or from the conduct of the parties. Two types: 1. *Constructive trust:* Equitable trust imposed by law to avoid fraud, unjust enrichment, and injustice. 2. *Resulting trust:* Trust created from the conduct of the parties.
Special Types of Trusts	1. *Charitable trust:* Created for the benefit of a segment of society or society in general. 2. *Spendthrift trust:* A trust whereby the creditors of the beneficiary cannot recover the trust's assets to satisfy debts owed to them by the beneficiary. 3. *Totten trust:* Created when a person deposits money in a bank account in his or her own name and holds it as a trust for the benefit of another person.

WORKING THE WEB

Visit the Web sites listed below for more information about the topics covered in this chapter.

1. Estate planning is more than just distribution of decedents' property. Review the issues presented by the Kansas Elder Law Network on Aging, Legal, Senior Citizens, Resources, and Awards at **www.keln.org.**
2. Review the requirements of Maryland state law with regard to probate at **www.registers.state.md.us/html/pamphlet2.html.** Compare with your state's procedure. Does it follow the Uniform Probate Code? See State Laws at **www.law.cornell.edu/statutes.html#state.**
3. For an overview of trusts, including a link to the draft Uniform Trust Act, see **www.law.cornell.edu/topics/estates_trusts.html.** Note the historical purposes of a trust. Why are trusts permitted by law?

CRITICAL LEGAL THINKING QUESTIONS

1. Define a *will.* What purposes does a will serve?
2. Describe the requirements for making a valid will. Why are the requirements so stringent?
3. Define the following types of special wills: (1) holographic will, and (2) noncupative will.
4. Describe the following types of testamentary gifts: (1) specific gifts, (2) general gifts, and (3) residuary gifts.
5. Explain the difference between the doctrines of *ademption* and *abatement.*
6. Describe how a testator's property is left pursuant to *per stirpes* distribution and pursuant to *per capita* distribution.
7. Describe the doctrine of *undue influence.* Is it difficult to prove?
8. Define *intestate succession.* What is an intestate statute?
9. Define a *trust.* Who are the parties to a trust?
10. What is a living will and health-care proxy? Is it a good idea for people to have these?

CASE FOR BRIEFING

Read Case 10 in Appendix A *(In re Estate of Vallerius).* Review and brief the case using the *Critical Legal Thinking* "Briefing the Case" example described in Chapter 1.

10.1 *In the Matter of the Estate of Jansa*

670 S.W.2d 767, 1984 Tex. App. Lexis 5503 (1984)
Court of Appeals of Texas

FACTS On or about June 10, 1959, Martha Jansa executed a will naming her two sons as executors of her will and leaving all of her property to them. The will was properly signed and attested to by witnesses. Thereafter, Martha died. When Martha's safe deposit box at a bank was opened, the original of this will was discovered along with two other instruments that were dated after the will. One was a handwritten document that left her home to her grandson, with the remainder of her estate to her two sons; this document was not signed. The second document was a typed version of the handwritten one; this document was signed by Martha but was not attested to by witnesses.

ISSUE Which of the three documents should be admitted to probate?

10.2 *In re Estate of Potter*

469 So.2d 957, 1985 Fla. App. Lexis 14338 (1985)
Court of Appeals of Florida

FACTS Mrs. Mildred D. Potter executed a will providing that her residence in Pompano Beach, Florida, was to go to her daughter and an equivalent amount of cash to her son upon her death. Evidence showed that Mrs. Potter's intent was to treat the daughter and son equally in the distribution of her estate. When she died, her will was admitted into probate. At the time, she still possessed her home in Pompano Beach. Unfortunately, assets were insufficient to pay Mrs. Potter's son the equivalent amount of cash.

ISSUE Can the son share in the value of the house so that his inheritance is equal to his sister's?

10.3 *Chapman v. Chapman*

577 A.2d 775, 1990 Me. Lexis 192 (1990)
Supreme Judicial Court of Maine

FACTS Hazel Chapman Kidik executed a will that provided "I give, devise, and bequeath to Wilhelmina K. Chapman my house at 7 Winsteria Road, West Yarmouth, Massachusetts and the contents therein if she should survive me." The will provided for several other specific devises and stipulated the residue of the estate should be divided equally among her niece Cynthia, her nephew Douglas, and Douglas's former wife, Wilhelmina. In the summer of 1986, Kidik sold her house in West Yarmouth and received back a mortgage deed securing a $65,000 promissory note from the buyer. Kidik died in September 1986. Kidik's will was admitted into probate.

ISSUE Does Wilhelmina have the right to receive the $65,000 note?

ETHICS CASE

10.4 *Jones v. Jones*

718 S.W.2d 416, 1986 Tex. App. Lexis 8929 (1986)
Court of Appeals of Texas

FACTS In 1967, Homer and Edna Jones, husband and wife, executed a joint will that provided, "We will and give to our survivor, whether it be Homer Jones or Edna Jones, all property and estate of which the first of us that dies may be seized and possessed. If we should both die in a common catastrophe, or upon the death of our survivor, we will and give all property and estate then remaining to our children, Leonida Jones Eschman, daughter, Sylvia Marie Jones, daughter, and Grady V. Jones, son, share and share alike."

Homer died in 1975, and Edna Jones received his entire estate under the 1967 will. In 1977, Edna executed a new will that left a substantially larger portion of the estate to her daughter, Sylvia Marie Jones, than to the other two children. Edna Jones died in 1982. Edna's daughter introduced the 1977 will for probate. The other two children introduced the 1967 will for probate.

ISSUE Did Edna act ethically in this case? Who wins?

PART III

Advanced Law

- Chapter 11 Business Organizations
- Chapter 12 Agency, Employment, and Equal Opportunity Law
- Chapter 13 Credit, Suretyship, and Bankruptcy
- Chapter 14 Intellectual Property and Internet Law
- Chapter 15 Administrative Law and Consumer, Investor, and Environmental Protection

Part III covers many advanced areas of substantive law. The topic of Chapter 11 is business organizations, including sole proprietorships, partnerships, limited liability companies, and corporations. Chapter 12 focuses on agency law, employment laws, and equal opportunity in employment law. Chapter 13 covers the laws of credit, suretyship, and bankruptcy. Chapter 14 is devoted to the intellectual property law, including patents, copyrights, and trademarks, plus the expanding area of domain names and Internet law. Chapter 15 covers government regulation, including consumer, investor, and environmental-protection laws.

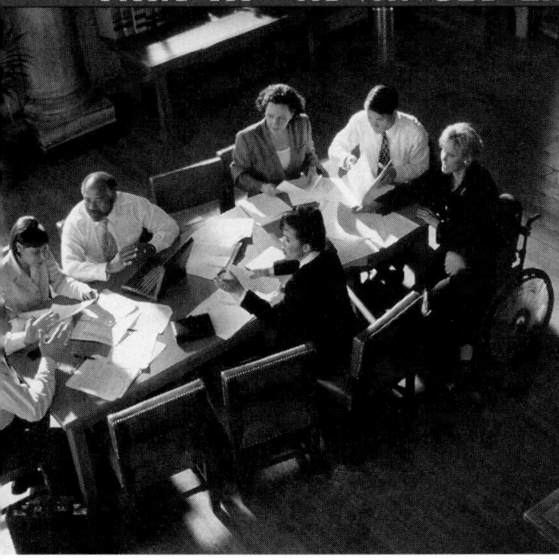

11 Business Organizations

The biggest corporation, like the humblest private citizen, must be held to strict compliance with the will of the people. —THEODORE ROOSEVELT, 1902

CHAPTER OBJECTIVES

After studying this chapter, you should be able to

1. Define a *sole proprietorship* and describe the liability of a sole proprietor.
2. Define *general partnership* and describe the liability of general partners.
3. Define *limited partnership*, *limited liability partnership*, and *limited liability company*, and describe the liability of their owners.
4. Define *corporation* and explain the process of forming a corporation.
5. Explain the functions and liability of corporate directors, officers, and shareholders.

CHAPTER OUTLINE

- Introduction
- Sole Proprietorship
- General Partnership
- Limited Partnership
- Limited Liability Partnership (LLP)
- Limited Liability Company (LLC)
- Corporation
- Case for Discussion: *Kinney Shoe Corp. v. Polan*
- Franchise
- Licensing
- Legal Terminology
- Case for Discussion: *Martin v. McDonald's Corporation*
- Chapter Summary
- Internet Exercises and Cases

INTRODUCTION

A person who wants to start a business must decide whether the business should operate as one of the major forms of business organization—*sole proprietorship, general partnership, limited partnership, limited liability partnership, limited liability company*, and *corporation*—or under some other available legal business form. These are called **business organizations.** The selection depends on many factors, including the ease and cost of formation, capital requirements of the business, flexibility of management decisions, government restrictions, extent of personal liability, tax considerations, and the like. This chapter covers forms of business, including sole proprietorships, general partnerships, limited partnerships, limited liability partnerships, limited liability companies, and corporations.

Sole Proprietorship

SIDEBAR

"Doing Business As"
A sole proprietorship can operate under the name of the sole proprietor or a *trade name.* For example, the author of this book can operate a sole proprietorship under the name "Henry R. Cheeseman" or under a trade name such as "The Big Cheese." Operating under a trade name is commonly designated as a **d.b.a. (doing business as)** (e.g., Henry R. Cheeseman, doing business as "The Big Cheese").

Most states require all businesses that operate under a trade name to file a **fictitious business name statement** (or certificate of trade name) with the appropriate government agency. The statement must contain the name and address of the applicant, the trade name, and the address of the business. Most states also require that notice of the trade name be published in a newspaper of general circulation serving the area in which the applicant does business.

Sole proprietorships are the simplest form of business organization. The owner, called a **sole proprietor,** is the business; there is no separate legal entity. Sole proprietorships are the most common form of business organization in the United States. Many small businesses—and a few large ones—operate this way.

Operating a business as a sole proprietorship has several major advantages:

1. Forming a sole proprietorship is easy and is relatively inexpensive.
2. The owner has a right to make all management decisions concerning the business, including those involving hiring and firing employees.
3. The sole proprietor owns all of the business and has the right to receive all of the business's profits.
4. A sole proprietorship can be easily transferred or sold if and when the owner desires to do so; no other approval (such as from partners or shareholders) is necessary.

This business form has disadvantages, too; among them: (1) the sole proprietor's access to capital is limited to personal funds plus any loans he or she can obtain, and (2) the sole proprietor is legally responsible for the business's contracts and the torts he or she or any of his or her employees commit in the course of employment.

Creation of a Sole Proprietorship

It is easy to create a sole proprietorship. There are no formalities, and no federal or state government approval is required. Some local governments require all businesses, including sole proprietorships, to obtain a license to do business within the city. If no other form of business organization is chosen, the business is a sole proprietorship by default.

Personal Liability of Sole Proprietors

The sole proprietor bears the entire risk of loss of the business; that is, the owner will lose his or her entire capital contribution if the business fails. In addition, the sole proprietor has **unlimited personal liability** (see Exhibit 11.1). Therefore, creditors may recover claims against the business from the sole proprietor's personal assets (e.g., home, automobile, and bank accounts).

Suppose Ken Smith opens a clothing store called The Rap Shop and operates it as a sole proprietorship. Smith files the proper statement and publishes the necessary notice of use of the trade name. He contributes $25,000 of his personal funds to the business and borrows $100,000 in the name of the business from a bank. Assume that after several months Smith closes the business because it was unsuccessful. At the time it is closed, the business has no assets, owes the bank $100,000, and owes rent, trade credit, and other debts of $25,000. Here, Smith is personally liable to pay the bank and all of the debts from his personal assets.

General Partnership

General, or ordinary, partnerships have been recognized since ancient times. The English common law of partnerships governed early U.S. partnerships. The individual states expanded the body of partnership law.

EXHIBIT 11.1 *Sole proprietorship.*

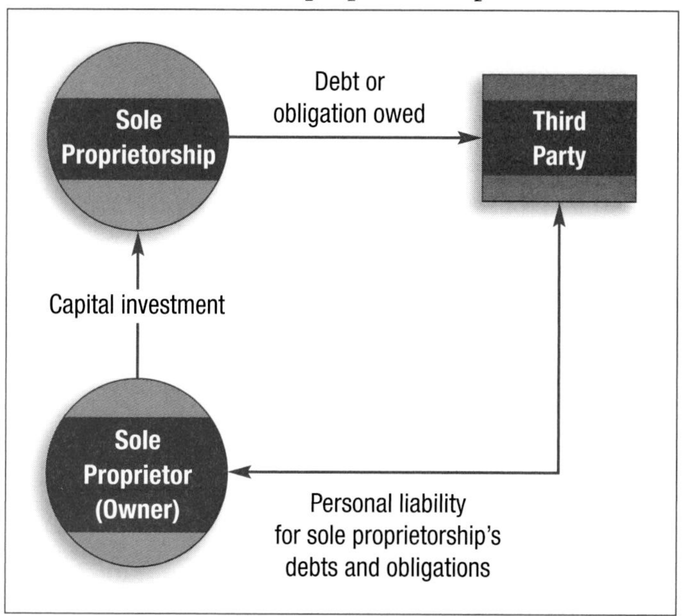

A **general partnership,** or **partnership,** is a voluntary association of two or more persons for carrying on a business as co-owners for profit. The formation of a partnership creates certain rights and duties among partners and with third parties. These rights and duties are established in the **partnership agreement** and by law. **General partners,** or **partners,** are personally liable for the debts and obligations of the partnership (see Exhibit 11.2).

Formation of a Partnership

A business must meet four criteria to qualify as a partnership under the Uniform Partnership Act [UPA § 6(1)]. It must be

1. an association of two or more persons
2. carrying on a business
3. as co-owners
4. for profit

The partner of my partner is not my partner.

—Legal Maxim

Partnerships are voluntary associations of two or more persons. All partners must agree to the participation of each co-partner. A person cannot be forced to be a partner or to accept another person as a partner. The UPA definition of "person" includes natural persons, partnerships (including limited partnerships), corporations, and other associations. A business—trade, occupation, or profession—must be carried on. The organization or venture must have a profit motive to qualify as a partnership, even though the business does not actually have to make a profit.

A general partnership may be formed with little or no formality. Co-ownership of a business is essential to create a partnership. The most important factor in determining co-ownership is whether the parties share the business's profits and management responsibility.

Receipt of a share of business profits is prima facie evidence of a partnership because nonpartners usually are not given the right to share in the business's profits.

EXHIBIT 11.2 *General partnership.*

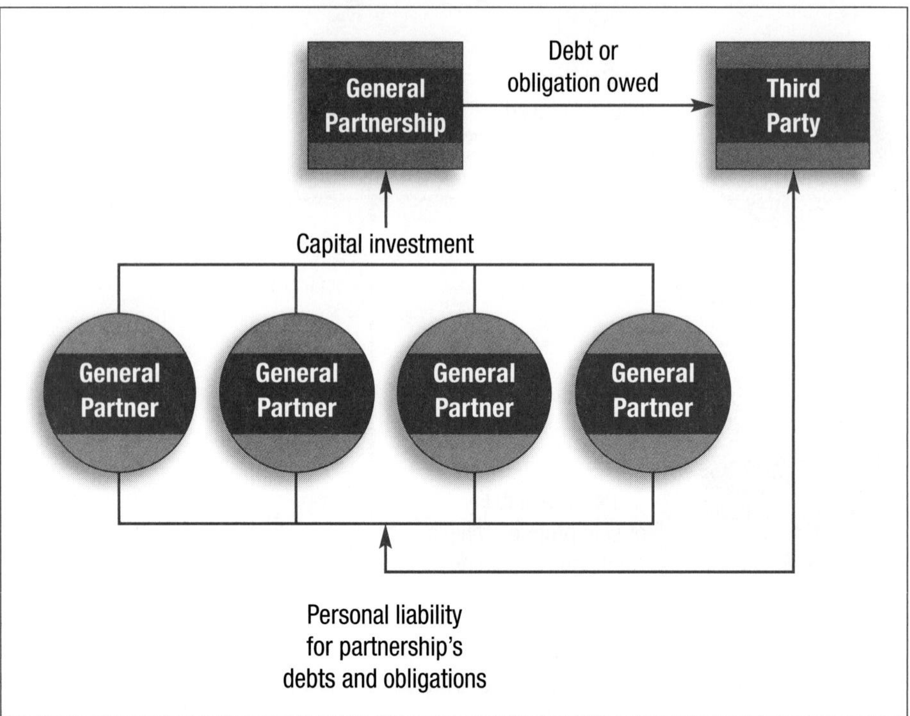

SIDEBAR

Uniform Partnership Act

In 1914, the National Conference of Commissioners on Uniform State Laws (a group of lawyers, judges, and legal scholars) promulgated the **Uniform Partnership Act (UPA),** which codifies partnership law. Its goal was to establish consistent partnership law that would be uniform throughout the United States. The UPA has been adopted in whole or in part by 48 states, the District of Columbia, Guam, and the Virgin Islands.

The UPA covers most problems that arise in the formation, operation, and dissolution of ordinary partnerships.

The UPA adopted the **entity theory** of partnership, which considers partnerships as separate legal entities. As such, partnerships can hold title to personal and real property, transact business in the partnership name, and the like.

No inference of the existence of a partnership is drawn if profits are received in payment of (1) a debt owed to a creditor in installments or otherwise, (2) wages owed to an employee, (3) rent owed to a landlord, (4) an annuity owed to a widow, widower, or representative of a deceased partner, (5) interest owed on a loan, or (6) consideration for the sale of goodwill of a business [UPA § 7]. An agreement to share losses of a business is strong evidence of a partnership.

The right to participate in the management of a business is important evidence for determining the existence of a partnership, but it is not conclusive evidence because the right to participate in management is sometimes given to employees, creditors, and others. If a person is given the right to share in profits, losses, and management of a business, it is compelling evidence of the existence of a partnership.

The Partnership Agreement

The agreement to form a partnership may be oral, written, or implied from the conduct of the parties. It may even be created inadvertently. No formalities are necessary, although a few states require general partnerships to file certificates of partnership with an appropriate government agency. Partnerships that exist for more than one year or are authorized to deal in real estate must be in writing under the Statute of Frauds.

It is good practice for partners to put their partnership agreement in writing. A written document is important evidence of the terms of the agreement, particularly if a dispute arises among the partners.

A written partnership agreement is called a partnership agreement or **articles of partnership.** The partners can agree to almost any terms in their partnership agreement, except terms that are illegal. The articles of partnership can be short and simple or long and complex. If the agreement fails to provide for an essential term or contingency, the provisions of the UPA control. Thus, the UPA acts as a gap-filling device to the partners' agreement.

Contract Liability

As a legal entity, a partnership must act through its agents, that is, its partners. Contracts entered into with suppliers, customers, lenders, or others on the partnership's behalf are binding on the partnership.

Under the UPA, partners have **joint liability** for the contracts and debts of the partnership [UPA § 15(b)]. This means that a third party who sues to recover on a partnership contract or debt must name all of the partners in the lawsuit. If the lawsuit is successful, the plaintiff can collect the entire amount of the judgment against any or all of the partners. If the third party's suit does not name all of the partners, the judgment cannot be collected against any of the partners or the partnership assets. Similarly, releasing any partner from the lawsuit releases them all. A partner who is made to pay more than his or her proportionate share of contract liability may seek **indemnification** from the partnership and from those partners who have not paid their share of the loss.

It is when merchants dispute about their own laws that they invoke the law.

—J. Brett,
Robinsone v. Mollett (1875)

Tort Liability

While acting on partnership business, a partner or an employee of the partnership may commit a tort that causes injury to a third person. This tort could be caused by a negligent act, a breach of trust (such as embezzlement from a customer's account), a breach of fiduciary duty, defamation, fraud, or other intentional tort. The partnership is liable if the act is committed while the person is acting within the ordinary course of partnership business or with the authority of his or her copartners.

Under the UPA, partners have **joint and several liability** for torts and breaches of trust [UPA § 15(a)]. This is so even if a partner did not participate in the commission of the act. This type of liability permits a third party to sue one or more of the partners separately. Judgment can be collected only against the partners who are sued. The partnership and partners who are made to pay **tort liability** may seek indemnification from the partner who committed the wrongful act. A release of one partner does not discharge the liability of other partners.

Suppose Nicole, Jim, and Maureen form a partnership. Assume that Jim, while on partnership business, causes an automobile accident that injures Kurt, a pedestrian. Kurt suffers $100,000 in injuries. Kurt, at his option, can sue Nicole, Jim, or Maureen separately, or any two of them, or all of them.

Dissolution of Partnerships

The duration of a partnership can be for a fixed term (e.g., five years) or until a particular undertaking is accomplished (e.g., until a real estate development is completed), or it can be for an unspecified term. A partnership with a fixed duration is called a **partnership for a term.** A partnership with no fixed duration is called a **partnership at will.**

Although a partner has the *power* to withdraw and dissolve the partnership at any time, he or she may not have the *right* to do so. For example, a partner who withdraws from a partnership before expiration of the term stated in the partnership agreement does not have the right to do so. The partner's action causes a

Liability of General Partners

Jose Peña and Joseph Antenucci were both medical doctors who were partners in a medical practice. Both doctors treated Elaine Zuckerman during her pregnancy. Her son, Daniel Zuckerman, was born with severe physical problems. Elaine, as Daniel's mother and natural guardian, brought a medical malpractice suit against both doctors. The jury found that Peña was guilty of medical malpractice but that Antenucci was not. The amount of the verdict totaled $4 million. The trial court entered judgment against Peña but not against Antenucci. The plaintiffs have made a posttrial motion for judgment against both defendants.

Is Antenucci jointly and severally liable for the medical malpractice of his partner, Peña? The court said yes. The court noted that a partnership is liable for the tortious act of a partner, and a partner is jointly and severally liable for tortious acts chargeable to the partnership. When a tort is committed by the partnership, the wrong is imputable to all of the partners jointly and severally. Therefore, even though the jury found that defendant Antenucci was not guilty of malpractice in his treatment of the patient, but that defendant Peña, his partner, *was* guilty of malpractice in his treatment of the patient, they were then both jointly and severally liable for the malpractice committed by defendant Peña by operation of law.

Zuckerman v. Antenucci, 478 N.Y.S.2d 578, 1984 N.Y. misc. Lexis 3283 (N.Y. 1984)

wrongful dissolution of the partnership. The partner is liable for damages caused by the wrongful dissolution of the partnership.

Limited Partnership

Limited partnerships are statutory creations that have been used since the Middle Ages. They include both general (manager) and limited (investor) partners. Today, all states have enacted statutes that provide for the creation of limited partnerships. In most states these partnerships are called **limited partnerships** or **special partnerships.** Limited partnerships are used for business ventures such as investing in real estate, drilling oil and gas wells, investing in movie productions, and the like.

General and Limited Partners

Limited partnerships have two types of partners: (1) general partners, who invest capital, manage the business, and are personally liable for partnership debts and (2) **limited partners,** who invest capital but do not participate in management and are not personally liable for partnership debts beyond their capital contribution (see Exhibit 11.3).

A limited partnership must have at least one or more general partners and one or more limited partners [RULPA § 101(7)]. There are no restrictions on the number of general or limited partners allowed in a limited partnership. Any person may be a general or limited partner. This includes natural persons, partnerships, limited partnerships, trusts, estates, associations, and corporations. A person may be both a general and a limited partner in the same limited partnership.

EXHIBIT 11.3 *Limited partnership.*

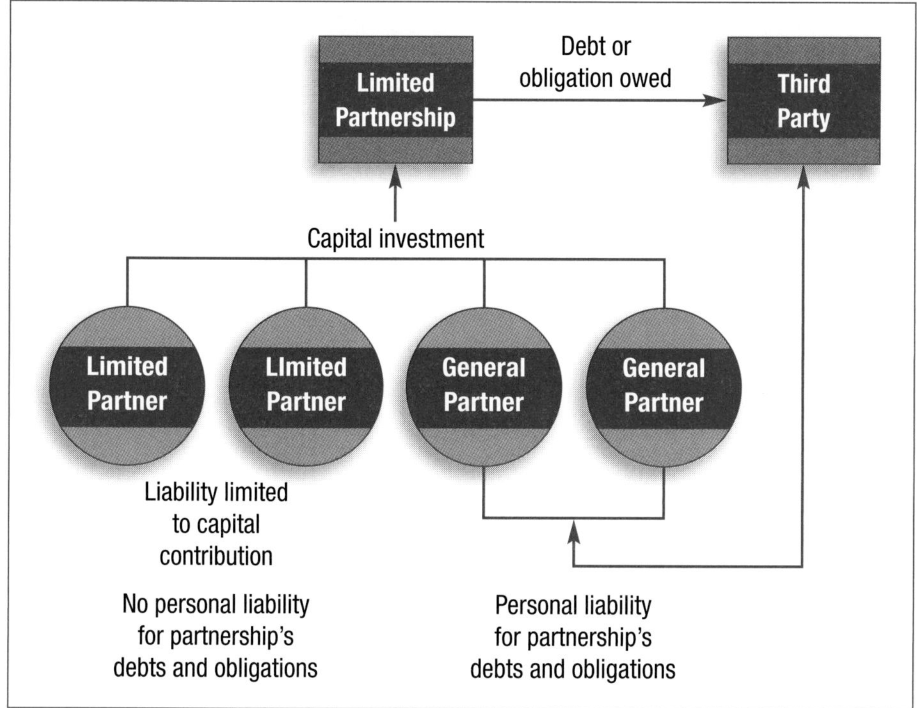

Formation of Limited Partnerships

The creation of a limited partnership is formal and requires public disclosure. The entity must comply with the statutory requirements of the Revised Uniform Limited Partnership Act or other state statutes.

Under the RULPA, two or more persons must execute and sign a **certificate of limited partnership** [RULPA §§ 201 and 206]. The certificate must contain the following information:

1. Name of the limited partnership
2. General character of the business
3. Address of the principal place of business, and the name and address of the agent to receive service of legal process
4. Name and business address of each general and limited partner
5. The latest date upon which the limited partnership is to dissolve
6. Amount of cash, property, or services (and description of property or services) contributed by each partner, and any contributions of cash, property, or services promised to be made in the future
7. Any other matters that the general partners determine to include.

The certificate of limited partnership must be filed with the secretary of state of the appropriate state and, if required by state law, with the county recorder in the county or counties in which the limited partnership carries on business. The limited partnership is formed when the certificate of limited partnership is filed.

SIDEBAR

Revised Uniform Limited Partnership Act

In 1916 the National Conference of Commissioners on Uniform State Laws, a group composed of lawyers, judges, and legal scholars, promulgated the **Uniform Limited Partnership Act (ULPA).** The ULPA contains a set of provisions for the formation, operation, and dissolution of limited partnerships. Most states originally enacted this law. In 1976, the National Conference on Uniform State Laws promulgated the **Revised Uniform Limited Partnership Act (RULPA)** which provides a more modern comprehensive law for the formation, operation, and dissolution of limited partnerships. This law supersedes the ULPA in the states that have adopted it. The RULPA provides the basic foundation for our discussion of limited partnership law.

SIDEBAR

Written Agreements
It is good practice to have a written partnership agreement that sets forth in detail the rights and duties of the partners. This will reduce later disputes and lawsuits.

Limited Partnership Agreement

Although not required by law, the partners of a limited partnership often draft and execute a **limited partnership agreement,** also called the **articles of limited partnership,** that sets forth the rights and duties of the general and limited partners, terms and conditions regarding the operation, termination, and dissolution of the partnership, and so on. Where there is no such agreement, the certificate of limited partnership serves as the articles of limited partnership.

The limited partnership agreement may specify how profits and losses from the limited partnership are to be allocated among the general and limited partners. If there is no such agreement, the RULPA provides that profits and losses from a limited partnership are shared on the basis of the value of the partner's capital contribution [RULPA § 503]. A limited partner is not liable for losses beyond his or her capital contribution.

In addition, it is good practice to establish voting rights in the limited partnership agreement or certificate of limited partnership. The limited partnership agreement can provide which transactions must be approved by which partners (i.e., general, limited, or both). General and limited partners may be given unequal voting rights.

Facade of family court building on the Benjamin Franklin Parkway, Philadelphia.

Liability of General and Limited Partners

The general partners of a limited partnership have *unlimited liability* for the debts and obligations of the limited partnership. This liability extends to debts that cannot be satisfied with the existing capital of the limited partnership. Generally limited partners are liable only for the debts and obligations of the limited partnership up to their capital contributions.

As a trade-off for *limited liability*, limited partners give up their right to participate in the control and management of the limited partnership. This means, in part, that limited partners have no right to bind the partnership to contracts or other obligations. Under the RULPA, a limited partner is liable as a general partner if his or her participation in the control of the business is substantially the same as that of a general partner, but the limited partner is liable only to persons who reasonably believed him or her to be a general partner [RULPA § 303(a)].

Limited Liability Partnership (LLP)

Many states have enacted legislation to permit the creation of **limited liability partnerships (LLPs).** An LLP does not have to have a general partner who is personally liable for the debts and obligations of the partnership. Instead, *all* partners are limited partners who stand to lose only their capital contribution if the partnership fails. None of the partners is personally liable for the debts and obligations of the partnership beyond his or her capital contribution (see Exhibit 11.4).

Limited Partner Liable on Personal Guarantee

Many small businesses, including limited partnerships, borrow money from banks or obtain an extension of credit from suppliers. Often these lenders require owners of small businesses to personally guarantee the loan to the business; otherwise the extensions of credit will not be made.

Consider the following case: Linnane Magnavox Home Entertainment Center (Linnane Magnavox) was a limited partnership that was organized under the laws of Kansas. Paul T. Linnane was the sole general partner, and Richard Gale Stover was the limited partner. Stover was the silent partner who provided the capital for the partnership. Stover took no part in the day-to-day management or control of the partnership.

In November 1977, Linnane Magnavox entered into a contract with General Electric Credit Corporation (GE Credit) whereby GE Credit would provide financing to the partnership. GE Credit refused to grant credit to the undercapitalized partnership unless Stover signed as the guarantor of the credit. It was not until Stover furnished his personal financial statements to GE Credit and personally signed the credit agreement as a guarantor that it extended credit to the partnership. When Linnane Magnavox defaulted on the debt and Paul Linnane was adjudicated bankrupt, GE Credit sued Stover to recover on the debt. The trial court held in favor of GE Credit. Stover appealed.

Is Richard Gale Stover, the limited partner, personally liable for Linnane Magnavox's debt to GE Credit? The court of appeals held that defendant Stover was liable to pay the debts of Linnane Magnavox to GE Credit. The court stated: "Stover had every reason to know that his unqualified signature on the documents would bind his personal credit as that of the general partner." The court held the limited partner Stover to his word.

General Electric Credit Corporation v. Stover, 708 S.W.2d 355, 1986 Mo. App. Lexis 3931 (Mo. 1986).

LLPs enjoy the **flow-through tax benefit** of other types of partnerships; that is, no tax is paid at the partnership level and all profits and losses are reported on the individual partners' income tax returns.

Articles of Partnership

LLPs must be created formally by filing **articles of limited liability partnership** with the secretary of state of the state in which the LLP is organized. This is a public document. The LLP is a **domestic LLP** in the state in which it is organized. The limited liability partnership law of the state governs the operation of the LLP. An LLP may do business in other states, however. To do so, the LLP must register as a **foreign LLP** in any state in which it wants to conduct business.

Limited Liability Company (LLC)

A majority of states have approved a new form of business entity called a **limited liability company (LLC).** An LLC is an unincorporated business entity that combines the most favorable attributes of general partnerships, limited partnerships, and corporations. An LLC may elect to be taxed as a partnership, the owners can manage the business, and the owners have limited liability. Many entrepreneurs who begin new businesses choose the LLC as their legal form for conducting business.

EXHIBIT 11.4 *Limited liability partnership (LLP).*

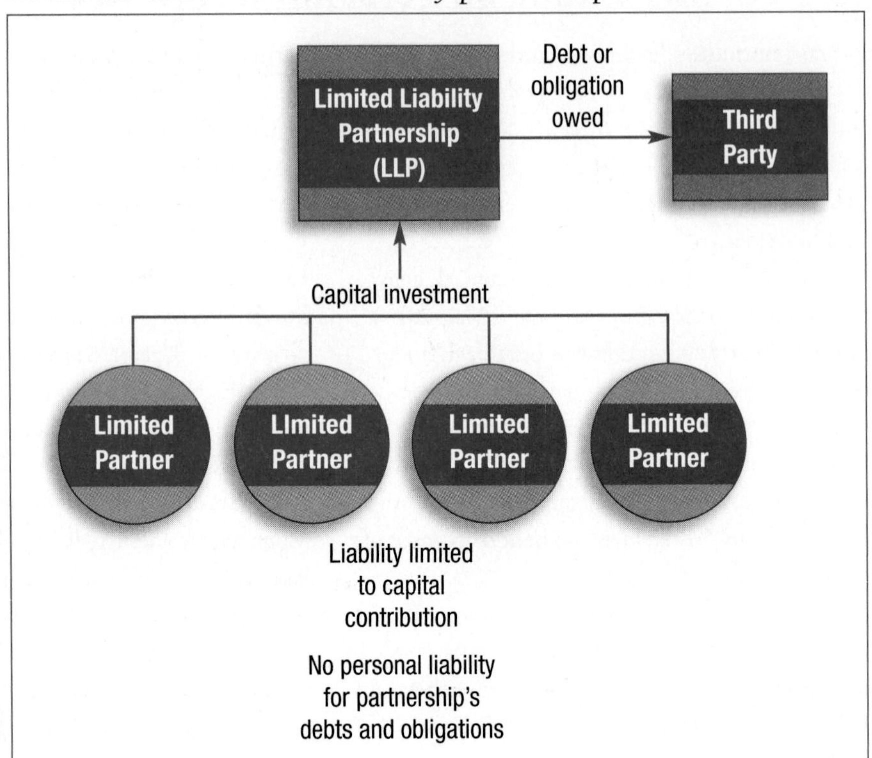

SIDEBAR

Uniform Limited Liability Company Act In 1995, the National Conference of Commissioners on Uniform State Laws (a group of lawyers, judges, and legal scholars) issued the **Uniform Limited Liability Company Act (ULLCA).** The ULLCA codifies limited liability company law. Its goal is to establish comprehensive LLC law that is uniform throughout the United States. The ULLCA covers most problems that arise in the formation, operation, and termination of LLCs. The ULLCA is not law unless a state adopts it as its LLC statute. Most states have adopted all or part of the ULLCA as their limited liability company law.

Limited liability companies can be created only pursuant to the laws of the state in which the LLC is being organized. These statutes, commonly referred to as **limited liability company codes,** regulate the formation, operation, and dissolution of LLCs.

Formation of an LLC

Forming an LLC is similar to organizing a corporation. Two or more persons (which include individuals, partnerships, corporations, and associations) may form an LLC for any lawful purpose. To form an LLC, **articles of organization** must be filed with the appropriate state office, usually the secretary of state's office (see Exhibit 11.5). The articles of organization must state the LLC's name, duration, and other information required by statute or that the organizers deem important to include. The name of an LLC must contain the words *Limited Liability Company* or the abbreviation *L.L.C.* or *L.C.*

Members of an LLC may enter into an **operating agreement** that regulates the affairs of the company and the conduct of its business and governs relations among the members, managers, and company [ULLCA § 103(a)]. The operating agreement may be amended by the approval of all members unless otherwise provided in the agreement. The operating agreement and amendments may be oral but usually are written.

The Check-the-Box Regulations have default rules that provide that eligible entities, such as an LLC, are treated as partnerships with flow-through taxation unless an election is made to be taxed as a corporation. This election is made by filing Form 8832 with the IRS and must be signed by all owners or a manager who is given authority to sign such an election. The Check-the-Box Regulations make it easier for LLCs to obtain partnership taxation status for federal income tax purposes. Most states automatically apply the federal classification rules for state income tax purposes, although a few do not.

Accounting Firms Operating as LLPs

Prior to the advent of the limited liability partnership (LLP) form of doing business, accounting firms operated as general partnerships. As such, the general partners were personally liable for the debt and obligations of the general partnership. In large accounting firms, this personal liability was rarely imposed because the general partnership usually carried sufficient liability insurance to cover most awards to third-party plaintiffs in negligence tort actions.

Beginning in the early 1980s, large accounting firms were hit with many large court judgments. These cases were brought in conjunction with the failure of large corporations that accountants had audited. Many of these corporations failed because of fraud by their major owners and officers. The shareholders and creditors of these failed companies sued the auditors, alleging that the auditors had been negligent in not catching the fraud. Many juries agreed and awarded large sums against the accounting firms. Sometimes the accounting firm's liability insurance was not enough to cover the judgment, thus imposing personal liability on the partners.

In the 1990s, state legislatures created a new form of business, the limited liability partnership (LLP). This entity was created particularly for accountants, lawyers, and other professionals to offer their services under an umbrella of limited liability. The partners of an LLP have limited liability up to their capital contribution; the partners do not have personal liability for the debts and liabilities of the LLP, however.

Once LLPs were permitted by law, all of the big accounting firms changed their status from general partnerships to LLPs. The signs and letterheads of the accounting firms prominently announce that the accounting firm is an "LLP." Many law firms also have changed to LLP status. The LLP form of business has transformed how accountants, lawyers, and other professionals offer their services.

Members' Limited Liability

The owners of LLCs are usually called **members.** The general rule is that members are not personally liable to third parties for the debts, obligations, and liabilities of an LLC beyond their capital contribution. Members are said to have **limited liability** (see Exhibit 11.6). The debts, obligations, and liabilities of an LLC, whether arising from contracts, torts, or otherwise, are solely those of the LLC [ULLCA § 303(a)].

Consider this example: Jasmin, Shan-Yi, and Vanessa form an LLC and each contributes $25,000 in capital. The LLC operates for a period of time during which it borrows money from banks and purchases goods on credit from suppliers. After some time, the LLC experiences financial difficulty and goes out of business. If the LLC fails with $500,000 in debts, each of the members will lose her capital contribution of $25,000 but will not be personally liable for the rest of the unpaid debts of the LLC.

Corporation: An ingenious device for obtaining individual profit without individual responsibility.
—Ambrose Bierce, *The Devil's Dictionary* (1911)

CORPORATIONS

Corporations are the dominant form of business organization in the United States, generating more than 85 percent of the country's gross business receipts. Corporations range in size from one owner to thousands of owners. Owners of corporations are called **shareholders.** Exhibit 11.7 depicts the hierarchy of a corporation.

EXHIBIT 11.5 *Sample LLC articles of organization.*

ARTICLES OF ORGANIZATION
FOR FLORIDA LIMITED LIABILITY COMPANY

ARTICLE I – NAME

The name of the Limited Liability Company is

iCitrusSystems.com

ARTICLE II – ADDRESS

The mailing address and street address of the principal office of the Limited Liability Company is

3000 Dade Boulevard

Suite 200

Miami Beach, Florida 33139

ARTICLE III – DURATION

The period of duration for the Limited Liability Company shall be

50 years

ARTICLE IV – MANAGEMENT

The Limited Liability Company is to be managed by a manager and the name and address of such manager is

Susan Escobar

1000 Collins Avenue

Miami Beach, Florida 33141

Thomas Blandford

Pam Rosales

A corporation is a separate **legal entity** (or *legal person*) for most purposes. Corporations are treated, in effect, as artificial persons created by the state who can sue or be sued in their own names, enter into and enforce contracts, hold title to and transfer property, and be found civilly and criminally liable for violations of law. Corporations cannot be put in prison, so the normal criminal penalty is the assessment of a fine, loss of a license, or other sanction.

EXHIBIT 11.6 *Limited liability company (LLC).*

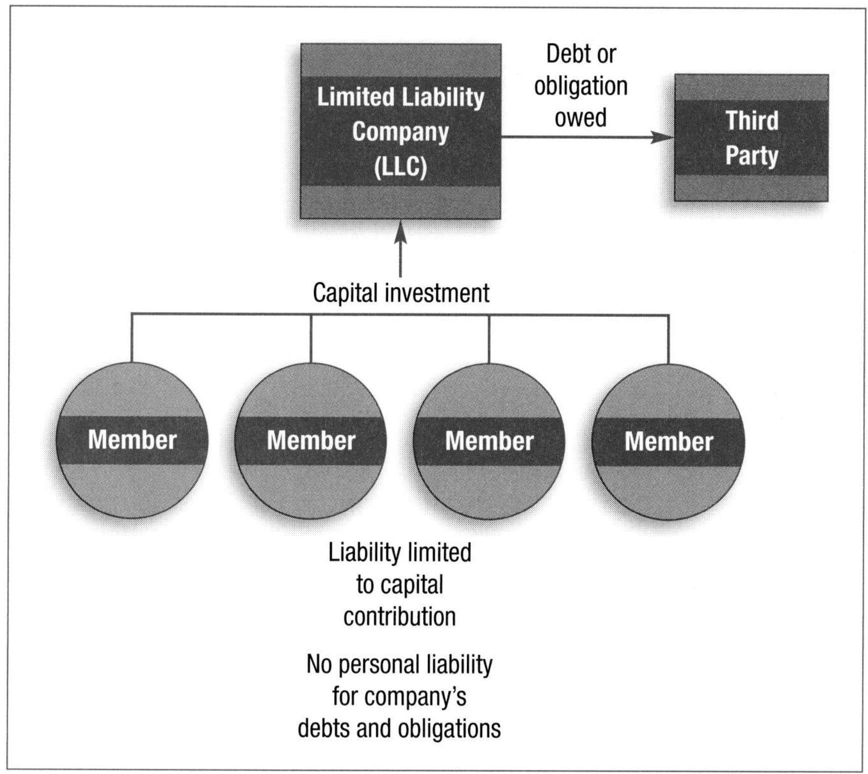

EXHIBIT 11.7 *Hierarchy of a corporation.*

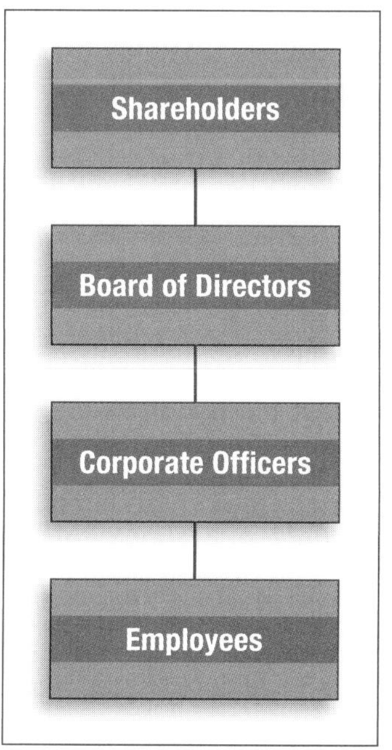

Commerce never really flourishes so much as when it is delivered from the guardianship of legislators and ministers.
—William Godwin

DreamWorks SKG, LLC

In 1995, Steven Spielberg, Jeffrey Katzenberg, and David Geffen formed DreamWorks SKG, a major movie and recording production company. Spielberg's fame and money came from directing films; Katzenberg was a leading executive at Disney; and Geffen built and sold Geffen Records. These multimillionaire multimedia giants combined their talents to form a formidable entertainment company.

Interestingly, DreamWorks was hatched as a Delaware limited liability company, or LLC. The organizers chose an LLC because it is taxed as a partnership and the profits (or losses) flow directly to the owners, but like a corporation, the owners are protected from personal liability beyond their capital contributions.

DreamWorks issued several classes of stock, or interests. The three principals put up $100 million ($33.3 million each) for SKG stock, which grants the principals 100 percent voting control and 67 percent of the firm's profits.

DreamWorks raised the other $900 million of its $1 billion capital from other investors, who received a third of future profits. The other investors were issued the following classes of stock:

Class	Investment
A	*Outside investors.* Class A stock was sold to big investors with more than $20 million to invest. Microsoft's co-founder, Paul Allen, purchased $500 million of Class A stock. Class A investors got seats on the board of directors.
S	*Outside investors.* Class S stock was issued for smallish, "strategic" investments with other companies for cross-marketing purposes.
E	*Employees.* Employees were granted the right to participate in an employee stock purchase plan.

Corporations have the following unique characteristics:

- **Limited liability of shareholders:** As separate legal entities, corporations are liable for their own contracts and debts. Generally, the shareholders have only limited liability. They are liable only to the extent of their capital contributions.
- **Free transferability of shares:** Corporate shares are freely transferable by the shareholder, by sale, assignment, pledge, or gift, unless they are issued pursuant to certain exemptions from securities registration. Shareholders may agree among themselves on restrictions on the transfer of shares. National securities markets, such as the New York Stock Exchange, the American Stock Exchange, and NASDAQ, have been developed for the organized sale of securities.
- **Perpetual existence:** Corporations exist in perpetuity unless a specific duration is stated in the corporation's **articles of incorporation.** The existence of a corporation can be voluntarily terminated by the shareholders.

  Corporations may be involuntarily terminated by the corporation's creditors if an involuntary petition for bankruptcy against the corporation is granted. The death, insanity, or bankruptcy of a shareholder, a director, or an officer of the corporation does not affect its existence.
- **Centralized management:** The **board of directors** makes policy decisions concerning the operation of the corporation. Members of the board of directors are elected by the shareholders. The directors, in turn, appoint

corporate **officers** to run the corporation's day-to-day operations. Together, the directors and the officers form the corporate "management."

Classifications of Corporations

A private, for-profit corporation is a **domestic corporation** in the state in which it is incorporated. It is a **foreign corporation** in all other states and jurisdictions. Suppose a corporation is incorporated in Texas and does business in Montana. The corporation is a domestic corporation in Texas and a foreign corporation in Montana. An **alien corporation** is a corporation that is incorporated in another country.

Incorporation Procedure

Corporations are creatures of statute. Thus, the organizers of the corporation must comply with the state's **incorporation** statute to form a corporation. Although relatively similar, the procedure for incorporating a corporation varies somewhat from state to state.

Selecting a state for incorporation. A corporation can be incorporated in only one state even though it can do business in all other states in which it qualifies to do business. In choosing a state for incorporation, the incorporators, directors, and/or shareholders must consider the corporations law of the states under consideration.

For the sake of convenience, most corporations (particularly small ones) choose as the state for incorporation the state in which the corporation will be doing most of its business. Large corporations generally opt to incorporate in the state with the laws that are most favorable to the corporation's internal operations.

Articles of incorporation. The basic governing document of the corporation is called the *articles of incorporation*, or **corporate charter.** It must be drafted and filed with, and approved by, the state before the corporation can be officially incorporated. Under the RMBCA, the articles of incorporation must include [RMBCA § 2.02(a)]:

1. The name of the corporation
2. The number of shares the corporation is authorized to issue
3. The address of the corporation's initial registered office and the name of the initial registered agent
4. The name and address of each incorporator.

The articles of incorporation also may include provisions concerning (1) the period of duration, which may be perpetual, (2) the purpose or purposes for which the corporation is organized, (3) limitation or regulation of the powers of the corporation, (4) regulation of the affairs of the corporation, and (5) any provision that otherwise would be contained in the corporation's bylaws.

The RMBCA provides that corporate existence begins when the articles of incorporation are filed. The secretary of state's filing of the articles of incorporation is *conclusive proof* that the incorporators satisfied all conditions of incorporation. The corollary to this rule is that failure to file articles of incorporation is conclusive proof of the nonexistence of the corporation.

SIDEBAR

Revised Model Business Corporation Act

The Committee on Corporate Laws of the American Bar Association drafted the **Model Business Corporation Act (MBCA)** in 1950. The model act was intended to provide a uniform law regulating the formation, operation, and termination of corporations. In 1984, the committee completely revised the MBCA and issued the **Revised Model Business Corporation Act (RMBCA).** Certain provisions of the RMBCA have been amended since 1984. The RMBCA arranged the provisions of the act more logically, revised the language of the Act to be more consistent, and made substantial changes in the provisions of the model act. Many states have adopted all or part of the RMBCA as their **corporation codes.** The RMBCA serves as the basis for our discussion of corporations law in this book.

The articles of incorporation can be amended to contain any provision that could have been lawfully included in the original document. After the amendment is approved by the shareholders, the corporation must file **articles of amendment** with the secretary of state [RMBCA § 10.06]. Exhibit 11.8 illustrates a sample articles of incorporation.

Selecting a corporate name. When starting a new corporation, the organizers must choose a name for the entity. To ensure that the name selected is not already being used by another business, the organizers should take the following steps [RMBCA § 4.01]:

> Commercial law lies within a narrow compass, and is far purer and freer from defects than any other part of the system.
> —Henry Peter Brougham

- Choose a name (and alternative names) for the corporation. The name must contain the words *corporation, company, incorporated,* or *limited,* or an abbreviation of one of these words (i.e., *Corp., Co., Inc., Ltd.*).
- Make sure that the name chosen does not contain any word or phrase that indicates or implies that the corporation is organized for any purpose other than those stated in the articles of incorporation. For example, a corporate name cannot contain the word *bank* if it is not authorized to conduct the business of banking.
- Determine whether the name selected is federally trademarked by another company and is therefore unavailable for use.
- Determine whether the chosen name is similar to other non-trademarked names and therefore unavailable for use.
- Determine whether the name selected is available as a domain name on the Internet. If the domain name is already owned by another person or business, the new corporation cannot use this domain name to conduct e-commerce over the Internet. Therefore, it is advisable to select another corporate name.

Corporate bylaws. In addition to the articles of incorporation, corporations are governed by **corporate bylaws.** Either the incorporators or the initial directors can adopt the bylaws of the corporation. The bylaws are much more detailed than are the articles of incorporation. Bylaws may contain any provision for managing the business and affairs of the corporation that is not inconsistent with law or the articles of incorporation [RMBCA § 2.06]. They do not have to be filed with any government official. The bylaws are binding on the directors, officers, and shareholders of the corporation.

The bylaws govern the internal management structure of the corporation. Typically, they specify the time and place of the annual shareholders' meeting, how special meetings of shareholders are called, the time and place of annual and monthly board of directors' meetings, how special meetings of the board of directors are called, the notice required for meetings, the quorum necessary to hold a shareholders' or board of directors' meeting, the vote necessary to enact a corporate matter, the corporate officers and their duties, the committees of the board of directors and their duties, where the records of the corporation are to be kept, directors' and shareholders' inspection rights of corporate records, the procedure for transferring shares of the corporation, and such.

The board of directors has the authority to amend the bylaws unless the articles of incorporation reserve that right for the shareholders. The shareholders of the corporation have the absolute right to amend the bylaws even though the by-

EXHIBIT 11.8 *Sample articles of incorporation.*

ARTICLES OF INCORPORATION
OF
THE BIG CHEESE CORPORATION

ONE: The name of this corporation is:

THE BIG CHEESE CORPORATION

TWO: The purpose of this corporation is to engage in any lawful act or activity for which a corporation may be organized under the General Corporation Law of California other than the banking business, the trust company business, or the practice of a profession permitted to be incorporated by the California Corporations Code.

THREE: The name and address in this state of the corporation's initial agent for service of process is:

Nikki Nguyen, Esq. 1000 Main Street, Suite 800
Los Angeles, California 90010

FOUR: This corporation is authorized to issue only one class of shares which shall be designated common stock. The total number of shares it is authorized to issue is 1,000,000 shares.

FIVE: The names and addresses of the persons who are appointed to act as the initial directors of this corporation are:

Shou-Yi Kang	100 Maple Street	Los Angeles, California 90005
Frederick Richards	200 Spruce Road	Los Angeles, California 90006
Jessie Qlan	300 Palm Drive	Los Angeles, California 90007
Richard Eastin	400 Willow Lane	Los Angeles, California 90008

SIX: The liability of the directors of the corporation from monetary damages shall be eliminated to the fullest extent possible under California law.

SEVEN: The corporation is authorized to provide indemnification of agents (as defined in Section 317 of the Corporations Code) for breach of duty to the corporation and its stockholders through bylaw provisions or through agreements with the agents, or both, in excess of the indemnification otherwise permitted by Section 317 of the Corporations Code, subject to the limits on such excess indemnification set forth in Section 204 of the Corporations Code.

IN WITNESS WHEREOF, the undersigned, being all the persons named above as the initial directors, have executed these Articles of Incorporation.

____________________ ____________________

____________________ ____________________

____________________ ____________________

Dated: January 1, 2005

laws also may be amended by the board of directors. Sample provisions of corporate bylaws are set forth in Exhibit 11.9

Organizational meeting. An **organizational meeting** of the initial directors of the corporation must be held after the articles of incorporation are filed. At this meeting the directors must adopt the bylaws, elect corporate officers, and transact other business that may come before the meeting [RMBCA § 2.05]. The latter category

EXHIBIT 11.9 *Sample provisions from corporate bylaws.*

BYLAWS OF
THE BIG CHEESE CORPORATION

ARTICLE I Offices

Section 1. Principal Executive Office. The corporation's principal executive office shall be fixed and located at such place as the Board of Directors (herein called the "Board") shall determine. The Board is granted full power and authority to change said principal executive office from one location to another.

Section 2. Other Offices. Branch or subordinate offices may be established at any time by the Board at any place or places.

ARTICLE II Shareholders

Section 1. Annual Meetings. The annual meetings of shareholders shall be held on such date and at such time as may be fixed by the Board. At such meetings, directors shall be elected and any other proper business may be transacted.

Section 2. Special Meetings. Special meetings of the shareholders may be called at any time by the Board, the Chairman of the Board, the President, or by the holders of shares entitled to cast not less than ten percent of the votes at such meeting. Upon request in writing to the Chairman of the Board, the President, any Vice President or the Secretary by any person (other than the Board) entitled to call a special meeting of shareholders, the officer forthwith shall cause notice to be given to the shareholders entitled to vote that a meeting will be held at a time requested by the person or persons calling the meeting, not less than thirty-five nor more than sixty days after the receipt of the request. If the notice is not given within twenty days after receipt of the request, the persons entitled to call the meeting may give the notice.

Section 3. Quorum. A majority of the shares entitled to vote, represented in person or by proxy, shall constitute a quorum at any meeting of shareholders. If a quorum is present, the affirmative vote of a majority of the shares represented and voting at the meeting (which shares voting affirmatively also constitute at least a majority of the required quorum) shall be the act of the shareholders, unless the vote of a greater number or voting by classes is required by law or by the Articles, except as provided in the following sentence. The shareholders present at a duly called or held meeting at which a quorum is present may continue to do business until adjournment, notwithstanding the withdrawal of enough shareholders to leave less than a quorum, if any action taken (other than adjournment) is approved by at least a majority of the shares required to constitute a quorum.

ARTICLE III Directors

Section 1. Election and Term of Office. The directors shall be elected at each annual meeting of the shareholders, but if any such annual meeting is not held or the directors are not elected thereat, the directors may be elected at any special meeting of shareholders held for that purpose. Each director shall hold office until the next annual meeting and until a successor has been elected and qualified.

Section 2. Quorum. A majority of the authorized number of directors constitutes a quorum of the Board for the transaction of business. Every act or decision done or made by a majority of the directors present at a meeting duly held at which a quorum is present shall be regarded as the act of the Board, unless a greater number be required by law or by the Articles. A meeting at which a quorum is initially present may continue to transact business notwithstanding the withdrawal of directors, if any action taken is approved by at least a majority of the required quorum for such meeting.

Section 3. Participation in Meetings by Conference Telephone. Members of the Board may participate in a meeting through use of conference telephone or similar communications equipment, so long as all members participating in such meeting can hear one another.

Section 4. Action Without Meeting. Any action required or permitted to be taken by the Board may be taken without a meeting if all members of the Board shall individually or collectively consent in writing to such action. Such consent or consents shall have the same effect as a unanimous vote of the Board and shall be filed with the minutes of the proceedings or the Board.

S Corporations

Corporations are separate legal entities. As such, they generally must pay corporate income taxes to federal and state governments. If a corporation distributes its profits to shareholders in the form of dividends, shareholders must pay personal income tax on the dividends. This *double taxation* of corporations is one of the major disadvantages of doing business in the corporate form. Some corporations and their shareholders can avoid double taxation by electing to be an S Corporation.

In 1982, Congress enacted the **Subchapter S Revision Act.** The act divided all corporations into two groups: **S Corporations,** which are those that elect to be taxed under Subchapter S, and **C Corporations,** which are all other corporations [26 U.S.C. §§ 6242 et seq.].

If a corporation elects to be taxed as an S Corporation, it pays no federal income tax at the corporate level. As in a partnership, the corporation's income or loss flows to the shareholders' individual income tax returns. Thus, this election is particularly advantageous if (1) the corporation is expected to have losses that can be offset against other income of the shareholders, or (2) the corporation is expected to make profits and the shareholders' income tax brackets are lower than the corporation's. Profits are taxed to the shareholders even if the income is not distributed. The shares retain other attributes of the corporate form, including limited liability.

Corporations that meet the following criteria can elect to be taxed as S Corporations:

1. The corporation must be a domestic corporation.
2. The corporation cannot be a member of an affiliated group.
3. The corporation can have no more than 75 shareholders.
4. Shareholders must be individuals, estates, or certain trusts. Corporations and partnerships cannot be shareholders.
5. Shareholders must be citizens or residents of the United States. Nonresident aliens cannot be shareholders.
6. The corporation cannot have more than one class of stock. Shareholders do not have to have equal voting rights.
7. No more than 20 percent of the corporation's income can be from passive investment income.

An S Corporation election is made by filing Form 2553 with the Internal Revenue Service. The election can be rescinded by shareholders who collectively own at least a majority of the shares of the corporation. However, if the election is rescinded, another S Corporation election cannot be made for five years.

includes matters such as accepting share subscriptions, approving the form of the stock certificate, authorizing issuance of the shares, ratifying or adopting promoters' contracts, selecting a bank, choosing an auditor, forming committees of the board of directors, fixing the salaries of officers, hiring employees, authorizing the filing of applications for government licenses to transact the business of the corporation, and empowering corporate officers to enter into contracts on behalf of the corporation.

Shareholders

Common stock is an equity security that represents the residual value of the corporation. Common stock has no preferences. That is, creditors and preferred shareholders must receive their required interest and dividend payments before common shareholders receive anything. Common stock does not have a fixed maturity date. If the corporation is liquidated, the creditors and preferred shareholders are paid the value of their interests first, and the common shareholders are paid the value of their interest (if any) last. Corporations may issue different classes of common stock [RMBCA § 6.01 (a) and (b)].

Persons who own common stock are called **common stockholders.** A common stockholder's investment in the corporation is represented by a **common stock certificate.** Common stockholders have the right to elect directors and to vote on mergers and other important matters. In return for their investment, common stockholders receive **dividends** declared by the board of directors.

A corporation's shareholders *own* the corporation. Nevertheless, they are not agents of the corporation (i.e., they cannot bind the corporation to any contracts), and the only management duties they have are the right to vote on matters such as the election of directors and the approval of fundamental changes in the corporation.

Disregard of the Corporate Entity

Shareholders of a corporation generally have limited liability (i.e., they are liable for the debts and obligations of the corporation only to the extent of their capital contribution). But if a shareholder or shareholders dominate a corporation and misuse it for improper purposes, a court of equity can *disregard the corporate entity* and hold the shareholders of a corporation personally liable for the corporation's debts and obligations. This doctrine is commonly referred to as **piercing the corporate veil.** It is often resorted to by unpaid creditors who are trying to collect from shareholders a debt owed by the corporation. The piercing the corporate veil doctrine is also called the *alter-ego doctrine* because the corporation has become the alter ego of the shareholder.

The notion that a business is clothed with a public interest and has been devoted to the public use is little more than a fiction intended to beautify what is disagreeable to the sufferers.

—Justice Holmes, *Tyson & Bro-United Theatre Ticket Officers v. Banton* (1927)

Courts will pierce the corporate veil if the corporation has been formed without sufficient capital (called *thin capitalization*), or if the corporation and its shareholders have not maintained separateness (e.g., commingling of personal and corporate assets, failure to hold required shareholders' meetings, failure to maintain corporate records and books). The courts examine this doctrine on a case-by-case basis.

Board of Directors

The board of directors of a corporation is responsible for formulating the policy decisions affecting the management, supervision, and control of the operation of the corporation [RMBCA § 8.01]. Such policy decisions include deciding the business or businesses in which the corporation should be engaged, selecting and removing the top officers of the corporation, determining the capital structure of the corporation, declaring dividends, and the like.

Typically, a board of directors is composed of inside directors and outside directors. An **inside director** is a person who is also an officer of the corporation. For example, the president of a corporation often sits as a director of the corporation. An **outside director** is a person who sits on the board of directors of a corporation but is not an officer of that corporation. Outside directors often are officers and directors of other corporations, bankers, lawyers, professors, and others. Outside directors usually are selected for their business knowledge and expertise.

The directors can act only as a board. They cannot act individually on the corporation's behalf. Every director has the right to participate in any meeting of the board of directors. Each director has one vote. Directors cannot vote by proxy.

CASE FOR DISCUSSION

Kinney Shoe Corp. v. Polan

939 F2d 209, 1991 U.S. App. Lexis 15304 (1991) **United States Court of Appeals, Fourth Circuit**

FACTS

In 1984, Lincoln M. Polan formed Industrial Realty Company (Industrial), a West Virginia corporation. Polan was the sole shareholder of Industrial. Although a certificate of incorporation was issued, no organizational meeting was held and no officers were elected. Industrial issued no stock certificates because nothing was ever paid in to the corporation. Other corporate formalities were not observed. Polan, on behalf of Industrial, signed a lease to sublease commercial space in a building controlled by Kinney Shoe Corporation (Kinney). The first rental payment to Kinney was made out of Polan's personal funds, and no further payments were made on the lease. Kinney filed suit against Industrial and obtained a judgment of $66,400 for unpaid rent. When the amount was unpaid by Industrial, Kinney sued Polan individually and sought to pierce the corporate veil to collect from Polan. The district court held for Polan. Kinney appealed.

ISSUE

Is Polan personally liable for Industrial's debts?

COURT'S REASONING

The court of appeals found that Industrial's corporate veil should be pierced because the corporation was undercapitalized, corporate formalities were not observed, and Polan commingled his funds with those of the corporation. The court stated that Polan tried to limit his liability by "setting up a paper curtain constructed of nothing more than Industrial's certificate of incorporation." The court allowed Kinney to pierce the corporate veil to reach the responsible party and produce an equitable result.

DECISION AND REMEDY

The court of appeals pierced the corporate veil and held Polan personally liable for Industrial's debt to Kinney. Reversed.

QUESTIONS

1. Is the doctrine of piercing the corporate veil needed? Should parties like Kinney bear the risk of dealing with corporations like Industrial?
2. Is it ethical for persons to form corporations to avoid personal liability? Should this be allowed?
3. What is the risk if corporate formalities are not observed? Explain.

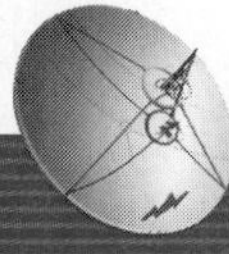

INFORMATION TECHNOLOGY

DELAWARE AMENDS CORPORATION CODE TO RECOGNIZE ELECTRONIC COMMUNICATIONS

The state of Delaware leads the nation as the site for incorporation of the United States' largest corporations. This is the result of the Delaware corporation code itself, as well as the expertise of the Delaware courts in resolving corporate disputes. To keep this leadership position, in 2000 the state legislature amended the Delaware General Corporation law to recognize evolving electronic technology. The major changes to the law are:

- Delivery of notices to stockholders may be made electronically if the stockholder consents to the delivery of notice in this form.
- Proxy solicitation for shareholder votes may be made by electronic transmission.
- The shareholder list of a corporation that must be made available during the 10 days prior to a stockholder meeting may be made available either at the principal place of business of the corporation or by posting the list on an electronic network.
- Stockholders who are not physically present at a meeting may be deemed present, participate in, and vote at the meeting by electronic communication; a meeting may be held solely by electronic communication without a physical location.
- The election of directors of the corporation may be held by electronic transmission.
- Directors' actions by unanimous consent may be taken by electronic transmission.

The use of electronic transmissions, electronic networks, and communication by email will make the operation and administration of corporate affairs more efficient in Delaware. Other states are expected to amend their corporation codes to recognize the importance of electronic communications.

Regular meetings of the board of directors are held at the times and places established in the bylaws. Such meetings can be held without notice. The board can call **special meetings** as provided in the bylaws [RMBCA § 8.20(a)]. They usually are convened for reasons such as issuing new shares, considering proposals to merge with other corporations, adopting maneuvers to defend against hostile takeover attempts, and the like.

The board of directors may act without a meeting if all of the directors sign written consents that set forth the actions taken. Such consent has the effect of a unanimous vote. The RMBCA permits meetings of the board to be held via conference calls.

Corporate Officers

The board of directors has the authority to appoint the **officers** of the corporation. The officers are elected by the board of directors at such time and by such manner as prescribed in the corporation's bylaws. The directors can delegate certain management authority to the officers of the corporation.

At minimum, most corporations have the following officers: (1) a president, (2) one or more vice presidents, (3) a secretary, and (4) a treasurer. The bylaws or the board of directors can authorize duly appointed officers the power to appoint assistant officers. The same individual may simultaneously hold more than one office in the corporation [RMBCA § 8.40]. The duties of each officer are specified in the bylaws of the corporation.

ETHICAL PERSPECTIVE

DIRECTORS' AND OFFICERS' DUTY OF LOYALTY

The **duty of loyalty** requires directors and officers to subordinate their personal interests to those of the corporation and its shareholders. If a director or an officer breaches his or her duty of loyalty and makes a secret profit on a transaction, the corporation can sue the director or officer to recover the secret profit. Justice Benjamin Cardozo defined this duty of loyalty as follows:

> [A corporate director or officer] owes loyalty and allegiance to the corporation—a loyalty that is undivided and an allegiance that is influenced by no consideration other than the welfare of the corporation. Any adverse interest of a director [or officer] will be subjected to scrutiny rigid and uncompromising. He may not profit at the expense of his corporation and in conflict with its rights; he may not for personal gain divert unto himself the opportunities that in equity and fairness belong to the corporation.
>
> Many forms of conduct permissible in a workaday world for those acting at arm's length are forbidden to those bound by fiduciary ties. Not honesty alone, but the punctilio of an honor the most sensitive, is then the standard of behavior. As to this there has developed a tradition that is unbending and inveterate.
>
> ["Punctilio" means a careful observance to detail; "inveterate" means firmly established. Justice Cardozo's opinions are known for their beauty and precision of language.]

Meinhard v. Salmon, 164 N.E. 545, 1928 N.Y. Lexis 830 (N.Y.App. 1928)

Officers of the corporation have such authority as may be provided in the bylaws of the corporation or as determined by resolution of the board of directors.

Duty of Care

The **duty of care** requires corporate directors and officers to use *care and diligence* when acting on behalf of the corporation. To meet this duty, the directors and officers must discharge their duties (1) in good faith, (2) with the care that an *ordinary prudent person* in a like position would use under similar circumstances, and (3) in a manner he or she reasonably believes to be in the best interests of the corporation [RMBCA §§ 8.30(a) and 8.42(a)].

> The law does not permit the stockholders to create a sterilized board of directors.
>
> —J. Collins, *Manson v. Curtis* (1918)

A director or an officer who breaches this duty of care is personally liable to the corporation and its shareholders for any damages caused by the breach. Such breaches, which are normally caused by **negligence,** often involve a director's or officer's failure to (1) make a reasonable investigation of a corporate matter, (2) attend board meetings on a regular basis, (3) properly supervise a subordinate who causes a loss to the corporation through embezzlement and such, or (4) keep adequately informed about corporate affairs. Breaches are examined by the courts on a case-by-case basis.

The determination of whether a corporate director or officer has met his or her duty of care is measured as of the time the decision is made. The benefit of hindsight is not a factor. Therefore, the directors and officers are not liable to the corporation or its shareholders for honest mistakes of judgment. This is called the **business judgment rule.**

The Sarbanes-Oxley Act of 2002

During the late 1990s and early 2000s, the U.S. economy was wracked by a number of business and accounting scandals. Companies such as Enron, Tyco, and WorldCom engaged in fraudulent conduct, leading to the conviction of corporate officers of financial crimes. Many of these companies went bankrupt, causing huge losses to their shareholders, employees, and creditors. Accounting firms were caught conspiring to conceal this fraudulent conduct. Boards of directors were complacent, not keeping a watchful eye over the conduct of officers and employees.

In response, Congress enacted the federal **Sarbanes-Oxley Act of 2002**. This act established far-reaching new rules regarding corporate governance. The goals of the Sarbanes-Oxley Act are to improve corporate governance rules, eliminate conflicts of interest, and instill confidence in investors and the public that management will run public companies in the best interests of all constituents. Although the Sarbanes-Oxley Act applies only to public companies, private companies and nonprofit organizations will be influenced by the act's accounting and corporate governance rules.

A summary of important provisions of the Sarbanes-Oxley Act follows.

CEO and CFO Certification

The CEO and CFO of a public company must file a statement accompanying each annual and quarterly report, certifying that the signing officer has reviewed the report, that based on the officer's knowledge the report does not contain any untrue statement of a material fact or omit to state a material fact that would make the statement misleading, and that the financial statement and disclosures fairly present, in all material aspects, the operation and financial condition of the company. A knowing and willful violation is punishable for up to 20 years in prison and a fine of not more than $5 million.

Reimbursement of Bonuses and Incentive Pay

If a public company is required to restate its financial statements because of material noncompliance with financial reporting requirements, the CEO and CFO must reimburse the company for any bonuses, incentive pay, or securities trading profits made because of the noncompliance.

Prohibition on Personal Loans

The act prohibits public companies from making personal loans to its directors or executive officers.

Tampering with Evidence

The act makes it a crime for any person knowingly to alter, destroy, mutilate, conceal, or create any document to impair, impede, influence, or obstruct any federal investigation. A violation is punishable by up to 20 years in prison and a monetary fine.

Bar from Acting as an Officer or a Director

The Securities and Exchange Commission (SEC) may issue an order prohibiting any person who has committed securities fraud from acting as an officer or a director of a public company.

Off-Balance-Sheet Items

Annual and quarterly reports of public companies must disclose material off-balance-sheet transactions and relationships with other entities that may have a material effect on the financial condition of the company.

Audit Committee

A public company must have an audit committee. Members of the audit committee must be members of the board of directors and must be independent—that is, not employed by or receiving compensation from the company or any of its subsidiaries for services other than as a board member and member of the audit committee. The audit committee is responsible for the appointment, payment of compensation, and oversight of public accounting firms employed to audit the company. The audit committee must preapprove all audit and permissible nonaudit services to be performed by a public accounting firm.

Internal Control Procedures of Public Companies The act requires public companies to establish and maintain adequate internal controls and procedures for financial reporting. The act requires public companies to prepare an assessment of the effectiveness of their internal quality controls at the end of each fiscal year.

INTERNATIONAL PERSPECTIVE

THE MULTINATIONAL CORPORATION

Today, corporations have expanded overseas by setting up subsidiary corporations under the laws of other countries. These international networks, or **multinational corporations,** are made up of companies of different nationalities that constitute a single economic unit connected by shareholding, managerial control, or contractual agreement.

The simplest international operating structure is one that subcontracts with independent firms in the host country to carry out sales or purchases. "National multinational" firms that establish wholly owned branches and subsidiaries overseas are somewhat more complex. "International multinational" firms are even more complicated. They are made up of two or more parents from different countries that co-own operating businesses in two or more countries.

The Ford Motor Company is an example of a national multinational firm. Organized in the United States at the beginning of the 20th century, Ford has always viewed the entire world as its market. The company's policy is for the American parent to own and control all of its overseas subsidiaries. Ford's European subsidiaries are all owned entirely by the American parent. The Mitsubishi Group is another example of this organizational format. It is actually made up of several Japanese companies that use joint directors' meetings to coordinate their activities in Japan and overseas.

The Royal Dutch/Shell Group is an example of an international multinational corporation. In 1907, the Dutch and British parents each formed a wholly owned holding company in their respective countries. Each then transferred the ownership of the operating subsidiary to the holding company and exchanged shares in the holding companies. The Dutch parent held 60 percent of each holding company, and the British parent held 40 percent. In addition, the management and operation of the two companies were organized to function as a single economic unit. Unilever, Dunlop Pirelli, and VFW/Fokker also operate under an international multinational umbrella.

Suppose, after conducting considerable research and investigation, the directors of a major automobile company decide to produce a large and expensive automobile. When the car is introduced to the public for sale, few of the automobiles are sold because of the public's interest in buying smaller, less expensive automobiles. Because this was an honest mistake of judgment on the part of corporate management, the judgment is shielded by the business judgment rule.

FRANCHISE

A **franchise** is established when one party (the franchisor or licensor) licenses another party (the franchisee or licensee) to use the franchisor's trade name, trademarks, commercial symbols, patents, copyrights, and other property in the distribution and selling of goods and services. Generally, the franchisor and the franchisee are established as separate corporations. The term *franchise* refers to both the agreement between the parties and the franchise outlet.

Franchising has several advantages, including the following:

1. The franchisor can reach lucrative new markets.
2. The franchisee has access to the franchisor's knowledge and resources while running an independent business.
3. Consumers are assured of uniform product quality.

A typical franchise arrangement is illustrated in Exhibit 11.10.

A prospective franchisee must apply to the franchisor for a franchise. The application often requires detailed information about the applicant's previous employment, financial and educational history, credit status, and so on. If an applicant is approved, the parties enter into a **franchise agreement** that sets forth the terms and conditions of the franchise.

Franchisors and franchisees are liable for their own *contracts*. The same is true of *tort liability*. For example, if a person is injured by a franchisee's negligence, the franchisee is liable.

EXHIBIT 11.10 *Parties to a typical franchise arrangement.*

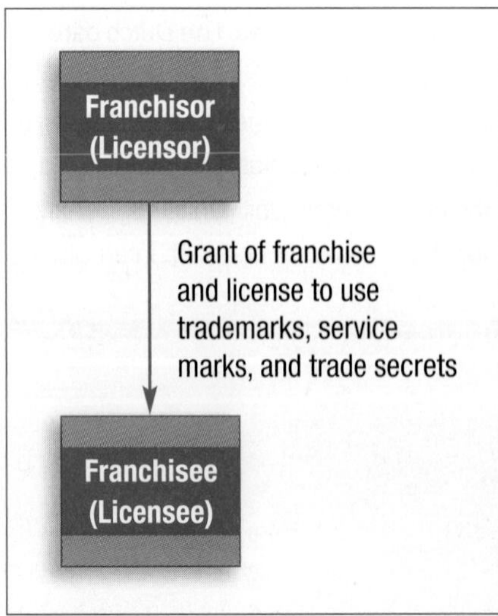

CASE FOR DISCUSSION

Martin v. McDonald's Corporation

572 N.E.2d 1073, 1991 Ill. App. Lexis 715 (1991) — **Appellate Court of Illinois**

FACTS

McDonald's Corporation (McDonald's) is a franchisor that licenses franchisees to operate fastfood restaurants and to use McDonald's trademarks and service marks. One such franchise, which was located in Oak Forest, Illinois, was owned and operated by McDonald's Restaurants of Illinois, the franchisee.

Recognizing the threat of armed robbery at its franchises, especially in the time period immediately after closing, McDonald's established an entire corporate division to deal with security problems at franchises. McDonald's prepared a manual for restaurant security operations and required its franchisees to adhere to these procedures.

Jim Carlson was McDonald's regional security manager in the area in which the Oak Forest franchise was located. Carlson visited the Oak Forest franchise on October 31, 1979, to inform the manager of security procedures. He specifically mentioned these rules: (1) No one should throw garbage out the back door after dark, and (2) trash and grease were to be taken out the side glass door at least one hour prior to closing. During his inspection, Carlson noted that the locks had to be changed at the restaurant and an alarm system had to be installed for the back door. Carlson never followed up to determine whether these security measures had been taken.

On the evening of Nov. 29, 1979, a six-woman crew, all teenagers, was working to clean up and close the Oak Forest restaurant. Laura Martin, Therese Dudek, and Maureen Kincaid were members of that crew. A person later identified as Peter Logan appeared at the back of the restaurant with a gun. He ordered the crew to open the safe and get him the money, and then ordered them into the refrigerator. In the course of moving the crew into the refrigerator, Logan shot and killed Martin and assaulted Dudek and Kincaid. Dudek and Kincaid suffered severe emotional distress from the assault.

Evidence showed that Logan had entered the restaurant through the back door. Trial testimony proved that the work crew used the back door exclusively, both before and after dark, and emptied garbage and grease through the back door all day and all night. In addition, there was evidence that the latch on the back door did not work properly. Evidence also showed that the crew had not been instructed about the use of the back door after dark and had never received copies of McDonald's security manual, and that the required warning about not using the back door after dark had not been posted at the restaurant.

Martin's parents, Dudek, and Kincaid sued McDonald's to recover damages for negligence. The trial court awarded damages of $1,003,445 to the Martins for the wrongful death of their daughter, and awarded $125,000 each to Dudek and Kincaid. McDonald's appealed.

ISSUE

Is McDonald's liable for negligence?

COURT'S REASONING

The appellate court held that McDonald's had voluntarily assumed a duty to the crew at the Oak Forest franchise by establishing and requiring the franchisee to implement certain security measures and by obligating itself to inspect the restaurant to see that the required security measures were implemented. The court held that McDonald's was liable for its own negligence due to the failure of security measures and the failure of its employee, Carlson, to follow up to determine that the security deficiencies at the Oak Forest franchise had been corrected. The appellate court held that there was ample evidence for the jury to determine that McDonald's had breached its assumed duty to the plaintiffs.

DECISION AND REMEDY

The appellate court held that McDonald's was negligent for not following up and making sure that the security deficiencies it had found at the Oak Forest franchise had been corrected. Affirmed.

QUESTIONS

1. Should businesses be held liable for criminal actions of others? Why or why not?
2. Should McDonald's have denied liability in this case?
3. What is the benefit to a franchisor to establish and require its franchisees to adhere to security rules? Is there any potential detriment? Explain.

Licensing

Licensing is an arrangement whereby a party that owns rights to intellectual property—such as software, a novel, or animated characters—contracts with another party to allow that party to use the licensed rights. In a license, the rights are not sold but merely "rented" to the licensee for a limited purpose or duration. The party that grants the license is the **licensor.** The party who receives the license is the **licensee.**

For example, the Walt Disney Company licenses many of its cartoon and animated characters, such as Mickey Mouse and Mulan, to other companies to place on childrens' apparel or toys. Another example would be Microsoft Corporation, which licenses the use of its software to computer users for limited use.

Licensing is currently a very important business model. It will become even more important as intellectual property owners expand worldwide.

LEGAL TERMINOLOGY

Alien corporation
Articles of amendment
Articles of limited liability partnership
Articles of incorporation
Articles of organization
Articles of limited partnership
Articles of partnership
Board of directors
Business judgment rule
Business organizations
C Corporation
Certificate of limited partnership
Common stock
Common stock certificate
Common stockholders
Corporate bylaws
Corporate charter
Corporation
Corporation codes
Dividends
"Doing business as" (d.b.a.)
Domestic corporation
Domestic LLP
Duty of care
Duty of loyalty
Entity theory
Fictitious business name statement
Flow-through tax benefit
Foreign corporation
Foreign LLP
Franchise
Franchise agreement
Free transferability of shares
General partners
General partnership
Incorporation
Indemnification
Inside director
Joint and several liability
Joint liability
Legal entity (legal person)
Licensee
Licensing
Licensor
Limited liability company (LLC)
Limited liability company codes
Limited liability partnership (LLP)
Limited partners
Limited partnership
Limited partnership agreement
Members

Model Business Corporation Act (MBCA)
Multinational corporation
Negligence
Officers (of corporation)
Operating agreement
Organizational meeting
Outside director
Partners
Partnership
Partnership agreement (articles of partnership)
Partnership at will
Partnership for a term
Perpetual existence
Personal guarantee
Piercing the corporate veil
Regular meeting of board of directors
Revised Model Business Corporation Act (RMBCA)
Revised Uniform Limited Partnership Act (RULPA)
Sarbanes-Oxley Act of 2002
S Corporation
Shareholders
Sole proprietor
Sole proprietorship
Special meetings of board of directors
Special partnerships
State of incorporation
Subchapter S Revision Act
Tort liability
Uniform Limited Liability Company Act (ULLCA)
Uniform Limited Partnership Act (ULPA)
Uniform Partnership Act (UPA)
Unlimited personal liability
Wrongful dissolution

chapter summary

BUSINESS ORGANIZATIONS	
Sole Proprietorship	
Definition	A form of business in which the owner and the business are one; the business is not a separate legal entity.
Business Name	A sole proprietorship can operate under the name of the sole proprietor or a *trade name*. Operating under a trade name is commonly designated as a *d.b.a. (doing business as)*. If a trade name is used, a *fictitious business name statement* must be filed with the appropriate state government office.
Liability	The sole proprietor is personally liable for the debts and obligations of the sole proprietorship.
General Partnership	
Definition	An association of two or more persons to carry on as co-owners of a business for profit [UPA § 6(1)].
Uniform Partnership Act (UPA)	Model act that codifies partnership law; most states have adopted all or part of the UPA. *(continued)*

Entity Theory of Partnerships	A theory that holds that partnerships are *separate legal entities* that can hold title to personal and real property, transact business in the partnership name, and the like.
Taxation of Partnerships	Partnerships do not pay federal income taxes; the income and losses of partnerships flow onto individual partners' federal income tax returns.
Partnership Agreement	Agreement establishing a general partnership; sets forth terms of the partnership. It is good practice to have a written partnership agreement that partners sign.
Partners' Contract Authority	A contract entered into by a partner with a third party on behalf of a partnership is binding on the partnership.
Tort Liability	1. *Tort:* Occurs when a partner causes injury to a third party by his or her negligent act, breach of trust, breach of fiduciary duty, or intentional tort. 2. *Partnership liability:* The partnership is liable to third persons who are injured by torts committed by a partner while he or she is acting within the ordinary course of partnership business. 3. *Joint and several liability of partners:* Partners are *personally liable* for torts committed by partners acting on partnership business. This liability is *joint and several,* which means that the plaintiff can sue *one or more* of the partners separately. If successful, the plaintiff can recover the entire amount of the judgment from any or all of the defendant–partners.
Dissolution of Partnerships	Change in the relation of the partners caused by any partner ceasing to be associated in carrying on the business [UPA § 29].
Wrongful Dissolution	Occurs when a partner withdraws from a partnership without having the *right* to do so at the time. The partner is liable for damages caused by the wrongful dissolution of the partnership.
Limited Partnership	
Definition	A special form of partnership that has both limited and general partners. 1. *General partners:* Partners in a limited partnership who invest capital, manage the business, and are personally liable for partnership debts. 2. *Limited partners:* Partners in a limited partnership who invest capital but do not participate in management and are not personally liable for partnership debts beyond their capital contributions.
Uniform Limited Partnership Act (ULPA)	A 1916 model act that contains a uniform set of provisions for the formation, operation, and dissolution of limited partnerships.
Revised Uniform Limited Partnership Act (RULPA)	A 1976 revision of the ULPA that provides a more modern comprehensive law for the formation, operation, and dissolution of limited partnerships.
Formation of Limited Partnerships	1. *Certificate of limited partnership:* A document that two or more persons must execute and sign that establishes a limited partnership. The certificate of limited partnership must be filed with the secretary of state of the appropriate state.

	2. *Limited partnership agreement:* A document that sets forth the rights and duties of general and limited partners; the terms and conditions regarding the operation, termination, and dissolution of the partnerships; and so on.
Liability of General and Limited Partners	1. *General partners:* General partners of a limited partnership have *unlimited personal liability* for the debts and obligations of the limited partnership. 2. *Limited partners:* Limited partners of a limited partnership are liable for the debts and obligations of the limited partnership only up to their capital contributions. 3. *Limited partners and management:* Limited partners have no right to participate in management of the partnership. A limited partner is *liable as a general partner* if his or her participation in control of the business is substantially the same as that of a general partner, but the limited partner is liable only to persons who reasonably believed him or her to be a general partner.
Limited Liability Partnership (LLP)	
Definition	A newer form of business in which there does not have to be a general partner who is personally liable for debts and obligations of the partnership. All partners are limited partners and stand to lose only their capital contribution if the partnership fails. LLPs are formed by accountants and other professionals as allowed by LLP law.
Partners	Owners of an LLP.
Articles of Partnership	A document that the partners of an LLP must execute, sign, and file with the secretary of state of the appropriate state to form an LLP.
Taxation	An LLP does not pay federal income taxes unless it elects to do so. If an LLP is taxed as a partnership, the income and losses of the LLP flow onto individual partners' federal income tax returns.
Limited Liability Company (LLC)	
Definition	A special form of unincorporated business entity that combines the tax benefits of a partnership with the limited personal liability attribute of a corporation.
Members	Owners of an LLC.
Articles of Organization	A document that owners of an LLC must execute, sign, and file with the secretary of state of the appropriate state to form an LLC.
Operating Agreement	An agreement entered into among members that governs the affairs and business of the LLC and the relations among members, managers, and the LLC.
Taxation	An LLC does not pay federal income taxes unless it elects to do so. If an LLC is taxed as a partnership, the income and losses of the LLC flow onto individual members' federal income tax returns. *(continued)*

Corporations	
Definition	A legal entity created pursuant to the laws of the state of incorporation. A corporation is a separate legal entity—an *artificial person*—that can own property, sue and be sued, enter into contracts, and such.
Characteristics of Corporations	1. *Limited liability of shareholders:* Shareholders are liable for the debts and obligations of the corporation only to the extent of their capital contributions. 2. *Free transferability of shares:* Shares of a corporation are freely transferable by the shareholders unless they are expressly restricted. 3. *Perpetual existence:* Corporations exist in perpetuity unless a specific duration is stated in the corporation's articles of incorporation. 4. *Centralized management:* The *board of directors* of the corporation makes policy decisions of the corporation. Corporate *officers* appointed by the board of directors run the corporation's day-to-day operations. Together, the directors and officers form the corporation's management.
Business Corporation Acts	1. *Model Business Corporation Act (MBCA):* A model act drafted in 1950 that was intended to provide a uniform law for the regulation of corporations. 2. *Revised Model Business Corporation Act (RMBCA):* A revision of the MBCA promulgated in 1984 that arranged the provisions of the model act more logically, revised the language to be more consistent, and made substantial changes that modernized the provisions of the act.
Classifications of Corporations	1. *Domestic corporation:* A corporation in the state in which it is incorporated. 2. *Foreign corporation:* A corporation in any state other than the one in which it is incorporated. A domestic corporation often transacts business in states other than its state of incorporation; hence, it is a foreign corporation in these other states. A foreign corporation must obtain a *certificate of authority* from these other states in order to transact intrastate business in those states. 3. *Alien corporation:* A corporation that is incorporated in another country. Alien corporations are treated as foreign corporations for most purposes.
Procedure	*Incorporation:* The process of incorporating (forming) a new corporation.
Selecting a State of Incorporation	A corporation can be incorporated in only one state, although it can conduct business in other states.
Articles of Incorporation	1. The basic governing document of a corporation; must be filed with the secretary of state of the state of incorporation. It is a public document, also called the *corporate charter.* 2. The corporation code of each state sets out the information that must be included in the articles of incorporation. Additional information may be included in the articles of incorporation as deemed necessary or desirable by the incorporators.
Corporate Bylaws	A detailed set of rules adopted by the board of directors after the corporation is formed, containing provisions for managing the business and affairs of the corporation. This document does not have to be filed with the secretary of state.

Organizational Meeting	A meeting that must be held by the initial directors of the corporation after the articles of incorporation are filed. At this meeting, the directors adopt the bylaws, elect corporate officers, ratify promoters' contracts, adopt a corporate seal, and transact such other business as may come before the meeting.
Common Stock	A type of equity security that represents the *residual value* of the corporation. Common stock has no preferences, and its shareholders are paid dividends and assets upon liquidation only after creditors and preferred shareholders have been paid. 1. *Common stockholder:* A person who owns common stock. 2. *Common stock certificate:* A document that represents the common shareholders' investment in the corporation.
Liability of Shareholders	1. Shareholders of corporations generally have *limited liability;* that is, they are liable for the debts and obligations of the corporation only to the *extent of their capital contribution* to the corporation. 2. Shareholders may be found *personally liable* for the debts and obligations of the corporation under the doctrine called *piercing the corporate veil* (also called the *alter-ego doctrine*). Courts can *disregard the corporate entity* and hold shareholders personally liable for the debts and obligations of the corporation if (a) the corporation has been formed without sufficient capital (*thin capitalization*) or (b) separateness has not been maintained between the corporation and its shareholders (e.g., commingling of personal and corporate assets, failure to hold required shareholders' meetings, and such).
Board of Directors	A panel of decision makers for the corporation, the members of which are elected by the shareholders. 1. The directors of a corporation are responsible for formulating the *policy* decisions affecting the corporation, such as deciding what businesses to engage in, determining the capital structure of the corporation, selecting and removing top officers of the corporation, and the like. 2. *Inside director:* A member of the board of directors who is also an officer of the corporation. 3. *Outside director:* A member of the board of directors who is not an officer of the corporation.
Meetings of the Board of Directors	1. *Regular meeting:* A meeting of the board of directors held at a time and place scheduled in the bylaws. 2. *Special meeting:* A meeting of the board of directors convened to discuss an important or emergency matter, such as a proposed merger, a hostile takeover attempt, and such. 3. *Written consents:* The board of directors may act without a meeting if all of the directors sign written consents that set forth the action taken. *(continued)*

Officers	Employees of the corporation who are appointed by the board of directors to manage the *day-to-day operations* of the corporation.
Duty of Loyalty	A duty that directors and officers have not to act adversely to the interests of the corporation and to subordinate their personal interests to those of the corporation and its shareholders.
Duty of Care	A duty that corporate directors and officers have to use care and diligence when acting on behalf of the corporation. This duty is discharged if they perform their duties (a) in good faith, (b) with the care that an *ordinary prudent person* in a like position would use under similar circumstances, and (c) in a manner they reasonably believe to be in the best interests of the corporation. 1. *Negligence:* Failure of a corporate director or officer to exercise this duty of care when conducting the corporation's business. 2. *Business judgment rule:* Directors and officers are not liable to the corporation or its shareholders for honest mistakes of judgment.
Franchise	
Definition	Established when one party licenses another party to use the franchisor's trade name, trademarks, commercial symbols, patents, copyrights, and other property in the distribution and selling of goods and services. Often, the franchisee is given a geographical territory to serve.
Parties	1. *Franchisor:* The party who does the licensing in a franchise arrangement. Also called the *licensor.* 2. *Franchisee:* The party who is licensed by the franchisor in a franchise arrangement. Also called the *licensee.*
Licensing	
Definition	Established when an owner of intellectual property grants another party the limited right to use the intellectual property.
Parties	1. *Licensor:* The party who owns the intellectual property and grants the license. 2. *Licensee:* The party who is granted the license.

WORKING THE WEB

Visit the Web sites listed below for more information about the topics covered in this chapter.

1. Review the materials at **smallbiz.biz.findlaw.com/planning/index.html?planning/wa.** Compare with the text discussion of partnerships. Can you see why lawyers generally advise business clients *not* to do business in a partnership form?
2. A large, rambling, and self-consciously offbeat site is the "Lectric Law Library," **www.lectlaw.com/bus.html.** There you will find a business law section with numerous items of interest, including an overview of (business) partnership law with links to key primary and secondary sources.
3. A checklist of questions about partnership can be found at **www.nolo.com/ lawcenter/faqs/detail.cfm/objectID/D2C7200B-28A8-49FB-9EA5E2B7E7F15CB5.** Use it as a self-test.
4. Study the provisions of the Uniform Limited Partnership Act at **www.law.upenn.edu/bll/ulc/ulpa/final2001.htm.**
5. Check your state statute on LLPs. Are they permitted in your jurisdiction? Are there any limitations on the types of businesses allowed to operate as an LLP? See the Legal Information Institute's Law About . . . Partnership page at **www.law.cornell.edu/topics/partnership.html.**
6. Review business associations at **jurist.law.pitt.edu/sg_bus.htm** to determine why the LLC is an increasingly popular form of doing business.
7. Check your state statute on LLCs. How many persons are required to form an LLC? Try **www.4inc.com/llcfaq.htm**.
8. For an overview of partnerships and LLCs in the context of a state law, see "Florida's New Partnership Law" at **www.law.fsu.edu/journals/lawreview/issues/232/larson.html.**
9. Create a hypothetical corporation by preparing articles of incorporation, bylaws, and a shareholder agreement, using forms suitable for your state. For a list of state corporation statutes, see **www.law.cornell.edu/topics/state_statutes.html#corporations.**
10. Prepare minutes of the organizational meeting for your newly formed corporation. See Findlaw's Compilation of State Corporation and Business Forms at **www.findlaw.com/11stategov/indexcorp.html.**
11. Using your state's database of corporations, find the last filed annual report of a local corporation and determine who the officers are and who is designated as the registered agent for service of process. See also the Legal Information Institute's Corporate Law Page at **www.law.cornell.edu/topics/corporations.html.** See also the Corporate Library at **www.thecorporatelibrary.com.**
12. Assume you have decided to form a nonprofit corporation. What other steps do you need to take to properly create such an entity? See U.S. Incorporation and Nonprofits Online Directory; Charities, Secretary of State, Corporations Division, Foundation Directories, UCC, Trademarks 1996 at **www.internet-prospector.org/secstate.html.**

13. Find your state statute on indemnification for corporate officers and directors. Why do you think that this concept was included in the statute? See **www.law.cornell.edu/topics/corporations.html** for an overview of corporations law with links to key primary and secondary sources.
14. Review a sample indemnification agreement at **www.lawvantage.com/description/corporate_law/director_and_officer_benefits_incentives_and_indemnification/summaries/CODO1000S.shtml.**
15. For more coverage on directors' and officers' liability, see **www.griffincom.com/docont.htm.** For a lengthy list of topics, see **guide.lp.findlaw.com/01topics/08corp/index.html.**
16. For a quick overview of corporate law, see **www.nolo.com/category/sb_home.html.**
17. Go to **lawcrawler.findlaw.com.** Type in the search terms *piercing the corporate veil.* Note how many articles are written from the perspective of an attorney representing a small business owner against claims seeking personal assets.
18. For socially responsible investing information, see **www.socialinvest.org.**

CRITICAL LEGAL THINKING QUESTIONS

1. Define a *sole proprietorship.* Describe the tort and contract liability of a sole proprietor for the debts and obligations of the sole proprietorship.
2. Define a *general partnership.* Describe the liability of general partners for the debts and obligations of the general partnership.
3. Define a *limited partnership.* Describe the liability of general partners versus limited partners for the debts and obligations of the limited partnership.
4. Define a *limited liability partnership* (LLP). What is the liability exposure of the partners of an LLP?
5. Define a *limited liability company* (LLC). What is the liability exposure of the member–owners of an LLC?
6. Define a *corporation.* What are the major attributes of a corporation? What is the liability exposure of shareholders for the debts and obligations of the corporation?
7. Describe the articles of incorporation, bylaws, and minutes of a corporation.
8. Define an *S corporation.* What requirements must be met for a corporation to qualify to be an S corporation?
9. Explain an officer's and a director's duty of care to the corporation. Explain how the business judgment rule protects officers and directors from liability.
10. Define a *franchise.* Describe the tort and contract liability of the franchisor and franchisee.

CASE FOR BRIEFING

Read Case 11 in Appendix A *(United States v. WRW Corporation).* Review and brief the case using the *Critical Legal Thinking* "Briefing the Case" example described in Chapter 1.

11.1 *National Lumber Company v. Advance Development Corp.*

732 S.W.2d 840 840, 1987 Ark. Lexis 2225 (1987)
Supreme Court of Arkansas

FACTS Pat McGowan, Val Somers, and Brent Robertson were general partners of Vermont Place, a limited partnership formed on January 20, 1984, for the purpose of constructing duplexes on an undeveloped tract of land in Fort Smith, Arkansas. The general partners appointed McGowan and his company, Advance Development Corporation, to develop the project, including contracting with material men, mechanics, and other suppliers. None of the limited partners took part in the management or control of the partnership.

On September 3, 1984, Somers and Robertson discovered that McGowan had not been paying the suppliers. They removed McGowan from the partnership and took over the project. The suppliers sued the partnership to recover the money owed them. The partnership assets were not sufficient to pay all of their claims.

ISSUE Who is liable to the suppliers?

11.2 *Singer v. Microhard.com, LLC et al.*

Hypothetical

FACTS Harold, Jasmine, Caesar, and Yuan form "Microhard.com, LLC," a limited liability company, to sell computer hardware and software over the Internet. Microhard.com, LLC hires Heather, a recent graduate of the University of Chicago and a brilliant software designer, as an employee. Heather's job is to design and develop software that will execute a computer command when the computer user thinks of the next command he or she wants to execute on the computer.

Using Heather's research, Microhard.com, LLC develops the "Third Eye" software program that does this. Microhard.com, LLC sends Heather to the annual Comdex Computer Show in Las Vegas, Nevada, to unveil this revolutionary software. Heather goes to Las Vegas and while there rents an automobile to get from the hotel to the computer show and to meet interested buyers at different locations in Las Vegas. While Heather is driving from her hotel to the site of the Comdex Computer Show, she negligently causes an accident and runs over Harold Singer, a pedestrian. Singer, who suffers severe personal injuries, sues Microhard.com, LLC; Heather; Harold; Jasmine; Caesar; and Yuan to recover monetary damages for his injuries.

ISSUE Who is liable?

11.3 *Billy v. USM Corp.*

412 N.E.2d 934, 432 N.Y.S.2d 879, 1980 N.Y. Lexis 2638 (1980)
Court of Appeals of New York

FACTS Joseph M. Billy was an employee of the USM Corporation. USM is a publicly held corporation. On October 21, 1976, Billy was at work when a 4,600-pound ram from a vertical boring mill broke loose and crushed him to death. Billy's widow brought suit against USM, alleging that the accident was caused by certain defects in the manufacture and design of the vertical boring mill and in the two moving parts directly involved in the accident, a metal lifting arm and the 4,600-pound ram.

ISSUE If Mrs. Billy's suit is successful, can the shareholders of USM Corporation be held personally liable for any judgment against USM?

ETHICS CASE

11.4 *Chelsea Industries, Inc. v. Gaffney*

449 N.E.2d 320, 1983 Mass. Lexis 1413 (1983)
Supreme Judicial Court of Massachusetts

FACTS Lawrence Gaffney was the president and general manager of Ideal Tape Co. Ideal, a subsidiary of Chelsea Industries, Inc., was engaged in the business of manufacturing pressure-sensitive tape. In 1975, Gaffney recruited three other Ideal executives to join him in starting a tape-manufacturing business. The four men remained at Ideal for the two years it took them to plan the new enterprise. During this time they used their positions at Ideal to travel around the country to gather business ideas, recruit potential customers, and purchase equipment for their business. At no time did they reveal to Chelsea their intention to open a competing business. In November 1977, the new business was incorporated as Action Manufacturing Co. When executives at Chelsea discovered the existence of the new venture, Chelsea sued them for damages.

ISSUE Who wins?

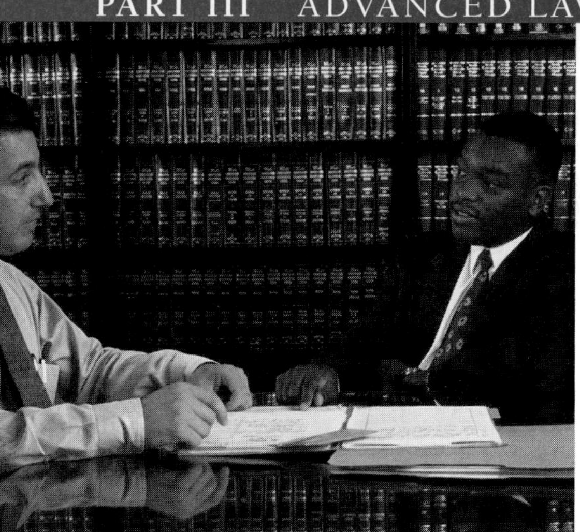

12 Agency, Employment, and Equal Opportunity Law

Let every eye negotiate for itself and trust no agent. —WILLIAM SHAKESPEARE, *MUCH ADO ABOUT NOTHING*

CHAPTER OBJECTIVES

After studying this chapter, you should be able to

1. Define *agency* and explain the liability of principals and agents.
2. Describe Title VII and the protection it affords against discrimination in the workplace based on race, national origin, color, sex, and religion.
3. Define *sexual harassment* and examine the protections against the creation of hostile work environments.
4. Describe the protections afforded by the Age Discrimination in Employment Act and the Americans with Disabilities Act.
5. Describe the process of forming a union, engaging collective bargaining, and the rights of the parties during strikes and picketing.

CHAPTER OUTLINE

- Introduction
- Agency
- Case for Discussion: *Holiday Inns, Inc. v. Shelburne*
- Independent Contractor
- Workers' Compensation
- OSHA
- Case for Discussion: *Smith v. Workers' Compensation Appeals Board*
- Title VII of the Civil Rights Act of 1964
- Case for Discussion: *NAACP v. Town of Harrison*
- Case for Discussion: *Harris v. Forklift Systems*
- ADEA
- ADA
- Labor Union Law
- Legal Terminology
- Chapter Summary
- Internet Exercises and Cases

INTRODUCTION

If businesspeople had to personally conduct all of their business, the scope of their activities would be severely curtailed. Partnerships would not be able to operate; corporations could not act through managers and employees; and sole proprietorships would not be able to hire employees. The use of agents (or agency), which allows one person to act on behalf of another, solves this problem. Agency is governed by a large body of common law, known as *agency law*.

The U.S. Congress has created many federal laws that protect job applicants and employees from discrimination in employment. Title VII of the Civil Rights Act of 1964 protects against employment discrimination based on race, national origin, color, sex, and religion. The Age Discrimination in Employment Act prohibits certain age discrimination, and the Americans with Disabilities Act protects individuals with disabilities from being discriminated against by employers.

The Occupational Safety and Health Act and workers' compensation laws impose worker safety rules and guarantee payment to workers injured on the job. Federal labor laws guarantee workers the right to form and join labor unions, to engage in collective bargaining with their employer concerning wages and other benefits of employment, and to engage in strikes and picketing.

Employment law is a burgeoning area of the law. This chapter covers agency law, employment law, equal opportunity in employment laws, worker safety laws, and labor laws.

AGENCY

It has been uniformly laid down in this Court, as far back as we can remember, that good faith is the basis of all mercantile transactions.

—J. Buller, *Salomons v. Nissen* (1788)

Agency relationships are formed by the mutual consent of a principal and an agent. Section 1(1) of the Restatement (Second) of Agency defines *agency* as a **fiduciary relationship** "which results from the manifestation of consent by one person to another that the other shall act in his behalf and subject to his control, and consent by the other so to act." The Restatement (Second) of Agency is the reference source of the rules of agency. A party who employs another person to act on his or her behalf is called a **principal.** A party who agrees to act on behalf of another is called an **agent.** The **principal–agent relationship** is commonly referred to as an **agency.** This relationship is depicted in Exhibit 12.1.

Persons Who Can Initiate an Agency Relationship

Any person who has the capacity to contract can appoint an agent to act on his or her behalf. Generally, persons who lack contractual capacity, such as insane persons and minors, cannot appoint an agent. However, the court can appoint a legal guardian or other representative to handle the affairs of insane persons, minors, and others who lack capacity to contract. With court approval, these representatives can enter into enforceable contracts on behalf of the persons they represent.

An agency can be created only to accomplish a lawful purpose. Agency contracts that are created for illegal purposes or are against public policy are void and unenforceable. For example, a principal cannot hire an agent to kill another person.

Some agency relationships are prohibited by law. For example, unlicensed agents cannot be hired to perform the duties of certain licensed professionals (e.g., doctors and lawyers).

EXHIBIT 12.1 *The principal–agent relationship.*

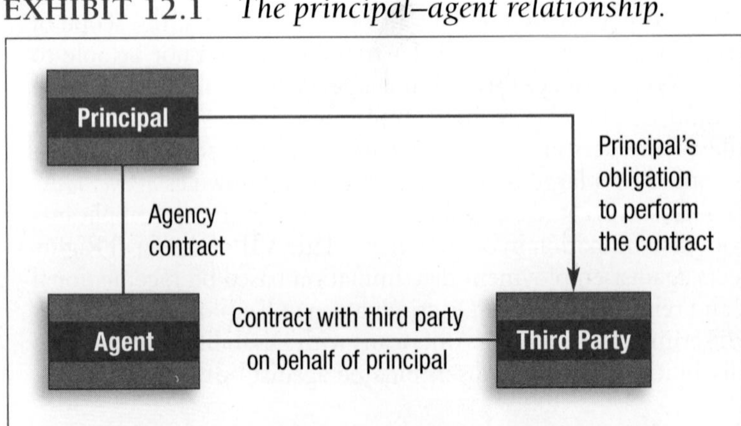

Kinds of Employment Relationships

Businesses usually have three kinds of employment relationships: (1) employer–employee relationships; (2) principal–agent relationships; and (3) principal–independent contractor relationships.

Employer–Employee Relationship

An **employer–employee relationship** exists when an employer hires an employee to perform some form of physical service. For example, a welder on General Motors Corporation's assembly line is employed in an employer–employee relationship because he performs a physical task.

An employee is not an agent unless he or she is specifically empowered to enter into contracts on the principal employer's behalf. Employees may enter into only the contracts that are within the scope of their employment. The welder in the previous example is not an agent because he cannot enter into contracts on behalf of General Motors Corporation. If the company empowers him to enter into contracts, he becomes an agent.

Principal–Agent Relationship

A principal–agent relationship is formed when an employer hires an employee and gives that employee authority to act and enter into contracts on his or her behalf. The extent of this authority is governed by an express agreement between the parties and implied from the circumstances of the agency. For example, the president of a corporation usually has the authority to enter into major contracts on the corporation's behalf, but a supervisor on the corporation's assembly line may have the authority to purchase only the supplies necessary to keep the line running.

Principal–Independent Contractor Relationship

Principals often employ outsiders—persons and businesses who are not employees—to perform certain tasks on their behalf. These persons and businesses are called **independent contractors.** Types of professions and trades that commonly act as independent contractors include doctors, dentists, stockbrokers, architects, certified public accountants, real estate brokers, and plumbers.

TABLE 12.1 *Summary of employment relationships.*

Types of Relationship	Description
Employer–employee	The employer has the right to control the physical conduct of the employee.
Principal–agent	The agent has the authority to act on behalf of the principal as authorized by the principal and implied from the agency. An employee is often the agent of his employer.
Principal–independent contractor	The principal has no control over the details of the independent contractor's conduct. An independent contractor is usually not an agent of the principal.

Employment-At-Will

Employees who are offered express employment contracts for a definite term cannot be discharged in violation of the contract. Most employees, however, do not have employment contracts. They are considered at-will employees.

Under common law, an at-will employee could be discharged by an employer at any time for any reason. Today, there are many statutory, contract, public policy, and tort exceptions to the at-will doctrine. These exceptions are:

- *Statutory exception.* Federal and state statutes that restrict the **employment-at-will** doctrine include federal labor laws that prohibit employers from discharging employee-members of labor unions in violation of labor laws or collective bargaining agreements. Title VII and other federal and state antidiscrimination laws that prohibit employers from engaging in race, sex, religious, age, disability, or other forms of discrimination are additional examples of such laws.
- *Contract exception.* The courts have held that an **implied-in-fact contract** can be created between an employer and an employee. Implied-in-fact contracts develop from the conduct of the parties. For example, a company bulletin, handbook, or personnel policy might mention that employees who do their jobs properly will not be discharged. This can be construed as an implied promise that an employee can be discharged only for good cause. An employee who is discharged in violation of an implied-in-fact contract can sue the employer for breach of contract.
- *Public policy exception.* The most used common-law exception to the employment-at-will doctrine is the **public policy exception.** This rule states that an employee cannot be discharged if such discharge violates the public policy of the jurisdiction. Examples of violations of public policy are discharging an employee for serving as a juror, refusing to do an act in violation of the law (e.g., refusing to engage in dumping of toxic wastes in violation of environmental protection laws), and refusing to distribute defective products.

An employee who has been wrongfully discharged can sue his or her employer for damages and other remedies (reinstatement, back pay, and such). Punitive damages may be recovered if the employer has engaged in fraud or other intentional conduct.

A principal can authorize an independent contractor to enter into contracts. Principals are bound by the authorized contracts of their independent contractors. For example, if a client authorizes an attorney to settle a case within a certain dollar amount and the attorney does so, the settlement agreement is binding.

Table 12.1 provides a summary of the several employment relationships.

Formation of the Agency Relationship

An agency and the resulting authority of an agent can arise in any of these four ways: (1) express agency, (2) implied agency, (3) apparent agency, and (4) agency by ratification. Each of these types of agencies is discussed in the paragraphs that follow.

Express Agency

The most common form of agency is **express agency.** In an express agency, the agent has the authority to contract or otherwise act on the principal's behalf as expressly stated in the agency agreement. In addition, the agent may possess certain implied or apparent authority to act on the principal's behalf (as discussed later in this chapter).

Express agency occurs when a principal and an agent expressly agree to enter into an agency agreement with each other. Express agency contracts can be either oral or written unless the Statute of Frauds stipulates that they must be written. For example, in most states a real estate broker's contract to sell real estate must be in writing.

If the principal and agent enter into an **exclusive agency contract,** the principal cannot employ any agent other than the exclusive agent. If the principal does so, the exclusive agent can recover damages from the principal. If an agency is not an exclusive agency, the principal can employ more than one agent to try to accomplish a stated purpose. When multiple agents are employed, the agencies with all of the agents terminate when any one of the agents accomplishes the stated purpose.

A **power of attorney** is one of the most formal types of express agency agreements. It is often used to give an agent the power to sign legal documents, such as deeds to real estate, on behalf of the principal. The two kinds of powers of attorney are (1) **general power of attorney,** which confers broad powers on the agent to act in any matters on the principal's behalf; and (2) **special power of attorney,** which limits the agent to acts specifically enumerated in an agreement. The agent is called an **attorney-in-fact** even though he or she does not have to be a lawyer. Powers of attorney must be written, and usually they must be notarized. A general power of attorney is shown in Exhibit 12.2.

It is difficult to imagine any grounds, other than our own personal economic predilections, for saying that the contract of employment is any the less an appropriate subject of legislation than are scores of others, in dealing with which this Court has held that legislatures may curtail individual freedom in the public interest.

—Justice Stone
Morehead v. New York (1936)

Implied Agency

In many situations, a principal and an agent do not expressly create an agency. Instead, the agency is implied from the conduct of the parties. This type of agency is referred to as **implied agency.** The extent of the agent's authority is determined from the facts and circumstances of the particular situation. Implied authority can be conferred by (1) industry custom, (2) prior dealing between the parties, (3) the agent's position, and (4) the acts deemed necessary to carry out the agent's duties. The court may deem other factors relevant as well. Implied authority cannot conflict with express authority or with stated limitations on express authority.

Often, even an express agency agreement does not provide enough detail to cover all contingencies that may arise in the future regarding performance of the agency. In this case, the agent possesses certain implied authority to act. This implied authority is sometimes referred to as **incidental authority.** Certain emergency situations may arise in the course of an agency. If the agent cannot contact the principal for instructions, the agent has implied emergency powers to take all actions reasonably necessary to protect the principal's property and rights.

Apparent Agency

Apparent agency, or **agency by estoppel,** arises when a principal creates the appearance of an agency that in actuality does not exist. Where an apparent agency is established, the principal is estopped from denying the agency relationship and is bound to contracts entered into by the apparent agent while acting within the scope of the apparent agency. Note that it is the principal's actions—not the agent's—that create an apparent agency.

Suppose Georgia-Pacific, Inc., interviews Albert Iorio for a sales representative position. Mr. Iorio, accompanied by Jane Franklin, the national sales manager, visits retail stores located in the open sales territory. While visiting one store, Jane tells the store manager, "I wish I had more sales reps like Albert." Nevertheless,

EXHIBIT 12.2 *Sample general power of attorney.*

POWER OF ATTORNEY

Know All Men by These Presents: That ____ the undersigned (jointly and severally, if more than one) hereby make, constitute and appoint ____

My true and lawful Attorney for me and in my name, place and stead and for my use and benefit:

(a) To ask, demand, sue for, recover, collect and receive each and every sum of money, debt, account, legacy, bequest, interest, dividend, annuity and demand (which now is or hereafter shall become due, owing or payable) belonging to or claimed by me, and to use and take any lawful means for the recovery thereof by legal process or otherwise, and to execute and deliver a satisfaction or release therefor, together with the right and powers to compromise or compound any claim or demand;

(b) To exercise any or all of the following powers as to real property, any interest therein and/or any building thereon: To contract for, purchase, receive and take possession thereof and of evidence of title thereto; to lease the same for any term or purpose, including leases for business, residence, and oil and/or mineral development; to sell, exchange, grant or convey the same with or without warranty; and to mortgage, transfer in trust, or otherwise encumber or hypothecate the same to secure payment of a negotiable or non-negotiable note or performance of any obligation or agreement;

(c) To exercise any or all of the following powers as to all kinds of personal property and goods, wares and merchandise, chosen in action and other property in possession or in action: To contract for, buy, sell, exchange, transfer and in any legal manner deal in and with the same and to mortgage, transfer in trust, or otherwise encumber or hypothecate the same to secure payment of a negotiable or non-negotiable note or performance of any obligation or agreement;

(d) To borrow money and to execute and deliver negotiable or non-negotiable notes therefor with or without security, and to loan money and receive negotiable or non-negotiable notes therefor with such security as said Attorney shall deem proper;

(e) To create, amend, supplement and terminate any trust and to instruct and advise the trustee of any trust wherein I am or may be trustor or beneficiary; to represent and vote stock, exercise stock rights, accept and deal with any dividend, distribution or bonus, join in any corporate financing reorganization, merger, liquidation, consolidation or other action and the extension, compromise, conversion, adjustment, enforcement or foreclosure, singly or in conjunction with others of any corporate stock, bond, note, debenture or other security; to compound, compromise, adjust, settle and satisfy any obligation secured or unsecured, owing by or to me and to give or accept any property and/or money whether or not equal to or less in value than the amount owing in payment, settlement or satisfaction thereof;

(f) To transact business of any kind or class and as my act and deed to sign, execute, acknowledge and deliver any deed, lease, assignment of lease covenant, indenture, indemnity, agreement, mortgage, deed of trust, assignment of mortgage or of the beneficial interest under deed of trust, extension or renewal of any obligation, subordination or waiver of priority, hypothecation, bottomry, charter-party, bill of lading, bill of sale, bill, bond, note, whether negotiable or non-negotiable, receipt, evidence of debt, full or partial release or satisfaction of mortgage, judgment and other debt, request for partial or full reconveyance of deed of trust and such other instruments in writing of any kind or class as may be necessary or proper in the premises.

Giving and Granting unto my said Attorney full power and authority to do and perform all and every act and thing whatsoever, requisite, necessary or appropriate to be done in and about the premises as fully to all intents, and purposes as I might or could do it personally present, hereby ratifying all that my said Attorney shall lawfully do or cause to be done by virtue of these presents. The powers and authority hereby conferred upon my said Attorney shall be applicable to all real and personal property or interests therein now owned or hereafter required by me and whenever situated.

My said Attorney is empowered hereby to determine in said Attorney's sole discretion the time when, purpose for and manner in which any power herein conferred upon said Attorney shall be exercised, and the conditions, provisions and covenants of any instrument or document which may be executed by said Attorney pursuant hereto and in the acquisition or disposition of real or personal property, my said Attorney shall have exclusive power to fix the terms thereof for cash, credit and/or property, and if on credit with or without security.

The undersigned, if a married person, hereby further authorizes and empowers my said Attorney, as my duly authorized agent, to join in my behalf, in the execution of any instrument by which any community real property or any interest therein, now owned or hereafter acquired by my spouse and myself, or either of us, is sold, leased, encumbered, or conveyed.

When the context so requires, the masculine gender includes the feminine and/or neuter, and the singular number includes the plural.

Witness my hand this ________ day of ________________________ 20______

STATE OF CALIFORNIA, COUNTY OF ____________________________ SS. ____________________

On ____________________ before me, the undersigned, a Notary Public in and for said State personally appeared ________________________

____

personally known to me (or proved to me on the basis of satisfactory evidence) to be the person ________________ whose name ________________ subscribed to the within instrument and acknowledge that ________________ executed the same.

WITNESS my hand and official seal.

Signature ____

Name *(Typed or Printed)* ________________________________ *(This area for official seal)*

Albert is not hired. If Albert later enters into contracts with the store on behalf of Georgia-Pacific and Jane has not controverted the impression of Albert she left with the store manager, the company will be bound to the contract.

Agency by Ratification

Agency by ratification occurs when (1) a person misrepresents himself or herself as another's agent when in fact he or she is not, and (2) the purported principal ratifies (accepts) the unauthorized act. In such cases, the principal is bound to perform and the agent is relieved of any liability for misrepresentation.

As an example, Bill Levine sees a house for sale and thinks his friend Sherry Maxwell would want it. Bill enters into a contract to purchase the house from the seller and signs the contract "Bill Levine, agent for Sherry Maxwell." Because Bill is not Sherry Maxwell's agent, she is not bound to the contract. However, if Sherry agrees to purchase the house, there is an agency by ratification. The ratification "relates back" to the moment Bill Levine entered into the contract. Upon ratification of the contract, Sherry Maxwell is obligated to purchase the house.

Contract Liability to Third Parties

A principal who authorizes an agent to enter into a contract with a third party is liable on the contract. Thus, the third party can enforce the contract and recover damages if the principal fails to perform it.

By what justice can an association of citizens be held together when there is no equality among the citizens?

—Cicero

The agent also can be held liable on the contract in certain circumstances. Imposition of such liability depends upon whether the agency is classified as (1) fully disclosed, (2) partially disclosed, or (3) undisclosed.

Fully Disclosed Agency

A **fully disclosed agency** results if the third party entering into the contract knows (1) that the agent is acting as an agent for a principal, and (2) the actual identity of the principal. The third party has the requisite knowledge if the principal's identity is disclosed to the third party by either the agent or some other source.

In a fully disclosed agency, the contract is between the principal and the third party. Thus, the principal, who is called a fully disclosed principal, is liable on the contract. The agent, however, is not liable on the contract because the third party relied on the principal's credit and reputation when the contract was made. An agent is liable on the contract if he or she guarantees that the principal will perform the contract.

Partially Disclosed Agency

A **partially disclosed agency** occurs if the agent discloses his or her agency status but does not reveal the principal's identity and the third party does not know the principal's identity from another source. The nondisclosure may be because (1) the principal instructs the agent not to disclose his or her identity to the third party, or (2) the agent forgets to tell the third party the principal's identity. In this kind of agency, the principal is called a partially disclosed principal.

In a partially disclosed agency, both the principal and the agent are liable on third-party contracts. This is because the third party must rely on the agent's reputation, integrity, and credit because the principal is unidentified. If the agent is made to pay the contract, the agent can sue the principal for indemnification. The third party and the agent can agree to relieve the agent's liability.

CASE FOR DISCUSSION

Holiday Inns, Inc. v. Shelburne

576 So.2d 322, 1991 Fla.App. Lexis 585 (1991) **District Court of Appeals of Florida**

FACTS

Holiday Inns, Inc. (Holiday Inns) is a franchisor that licenses franchisees to operate hotels using its trademarks and service marks. Holiday Inns licensed Hospitality Venture to operate a franchised hotel in Fort Pierce, Florida. The Rodeo Bar was located in the hotel.

The Fort Pierce Holiday Inn and Rodeo Bar did not have sufficient parking, so security guards posted in the Holiday Inn parking lot required Rodeo Bar patrons to park in vacant lots that surrounded the hotel but that were not owned by the hotel. The main duty of the guards was to keep the parking lot open for hotel guests. Two unarmed security guards were on duty on the night in question. One guard was drinking on the job, and the other was an untrained temporary fill-in.

The record disclosed that although the Rodeo Bar had a capacity of 240 people, the bar regularly admitted 270 to 300 people, with 50 to 75 people waiting outside. Fights occurred all the time in the bar and the parking lots, and often there were three or four fights a night. Police reports involving 58 offenses, including several weapons charges and battery and assault charges, had been filed during the previous 18 months.

On the night in question, the two groups involved in the altercation did not leave the Rodeo Bar until closing time. According to the record, these individuals exchanged remarks as they moved toward their respective vehicles in the vacant parking lots adjacent to the Holiday Inn. Ultimately, a fight erupted. The evidence shows that during the course of physical combat, Lester Carter of one group shot David Rice, Scott Turner, and Robert Shelburne of the other group. Rice died from his injuries.

Rice's heirs, Turner, and Shelburne sued the franchisee, Hospitality Venture, and the franchisor, Holiday Inns, for damages. The trial court found Hospitality Ventures negligent for not providing sufficient security to prevent the foreseeable incident that took the life of Rice and injured Turner and Shelburne. The court also found that Hospitality Venture was the apparent agent of Holiday Inns, and therefore Holiday Inns was vicariously liable for its franchisee's tortious conduct. Turner was awarded $3,825,000 for his injuries, Shelburne received $1 million, and Rice's interests were awarded $1 million. Hospitality Venture and Holiday Inns appealed.

ISSUE

Are the franchisee and the franchisor liable?

COURT'S REASONING

A franchisee is always liable for its own tortious conduct. A franchisor may be held liable for the tortious conduct of a franchisee if the franchisee is the "apparent agent" of the franchisor. This "apparent agency" occurs when the franchisor misleads the public into believing that the franchise is really owned and operated by the franchisor, even though it is not. Here, the court held that Holiday Inns led the public into believing that its franchisees were part of Holiday Inns' system and not independently owned businesses. The court held that Holiday Inns' reservation system, as well as the signs at the Fort Pierce franchise hotel, gave this appearance to the public. Therefore, Holiday Inns is vicariously liable for the tortious conduct of its franchisee.

DECISION AND REMEDY

The court of appeals held that the franchisee was negligent, and that the franchisee was the apparent agent of the franchisor. The court affirmed the trial court's judgment that found the defendants liable to the plaintiffs.

QUESTIONS

1. What does the doctrine of apparent agency provide? How does it differ from actual agency?
2. Did Hospitality Venture act ethically in denying liability? Did Holiday Inns act ethically in denying liability?
3. Why do you think the plaintiffs included Holiday Inns as a defendant in their lawsuit? Do you think the damages that were awarded were warranted?

Undisclosed Agency

An **undisclosed agency** occurs when the third party is unaware of either the existence of an agency or the principal's identity. The principal is called an undisclosed principal. Undisclosed agencies are lawful. They often are used when the principal thinks the terms of the contract would be changed if his or her identity were known. For example, a wealthy person may use an undisclosed agency to purchase property if he thinks the seller would raise the price of the property if his identity were revealed.

In an undisclosed agency, both the principal and the agent are liable on the contract with the third party. This is because the agent, by not divulging that he or she is acting as an agent, becomes a principal to the contract. The third party relies on the reputation and credit of the agent in entering into the contract. If the principal fails to perform the contract, the third party can recover against the principal or the agent. If the agent is made to pay the contract, he or she can recover indemnification from the principal.

Agent Exceeding the Scope of Authority

An agent who enters into a contract on behalf of another party impliedly warrants that he or she has the authority to do so. This is called the agent's **implied warranty of authority.** If the agent exceeds the scope of his or her authority, the principal is not liable on the contract unless the principal ratifies it. The agent, however, is liable to the third party for breaching the implied warranty of authority. To recover, the third party must show (1) reliance on the agent's representation, and (2) ignorance of the agent's lack of status.

Suppose Sam, Sara, Satchel, Samantha, and Simone form a rock band called SSSSex. SSSSex is just a voluntary association without any legal status. Sam enters into a contract with Rocky's Musical Instruments to purchase instruments and equipment for the band on credit and signs the contract, "Sam for SSSSex." When SSSSex fails to pay the debt, Rocky's can sue Sam and recover. Sam must pay the debt because he breached his implied warranty of authority when he acted as an agent for a nonexistent principal; that is, the purported principal was not a legal entity upon which liability could be imposed.

Tort Liability to Third Parties

The principal and the agent are each personally liable for their own tortious conduct. The principal is liable for the tortious conduct of an agent who is acting within the scope of his or her authority. The agent, however, is liable for the tortious conduct of the principal only if he or she directly or indirectly participates in or aids and abets the principal's conduct.

The courts have applied a broad and flexible standard in interpreting scope of authority in the context of employment. Although other factors also may be considered, the courts rely on the following factors to determine whether an agent's conduct occurred within the scope of his or her employment:

- Was the act specifically requested or authorized by the principal?
- Was it the kind of act that the agent was employed to perform?
- Did the act occur substantially within the time period of employment authorized by the principal?

SIDEBAR

Signing Properly as an Agent

The agent's signature on a contract entered into on the principal's behalf is important. It can establish the agent's status and, therefore, his or her liability. For instance, in a fully disclosed agency the agent's signature must clearly indicate that he or she is acting as an agent for a specifically identified principal. Examples of proper signatures are "Allison Adams, agent for Peter Perceival," "Peter Perceival, by Allison Adams, agent," and "Peter Perceival, by Allison Adams."

An agent who is authorized to sign a contract for a fully disclosed principal but fails to properly do so can be held personally liable on the contract. For example, in the prior example a partially disclosed agency would be created if the contract were signed "Allison Adams, agent." If Adams merely signed the contract "Allison Adams," the agency would be an undisclosed agency. In both of these instances the agent is liable on the contract.

- Did the act occur substantially within the location of employment authorized by the employer?
- Was the agent advancing the principal's purpose when the act occurred?

Where liability is found, tort remedies are available to the injured party. These remedies include recovery for medical expenses, lost wages, pain and suffering, emotional distress, and, in some cases, punitive damages. The three main sources of tort liability for principals and agents are misrepresentation, intentional torts, and negligence.

Misrepresentation

Intentional misrepresentations are also known as **fraud** or **deceit.** They occur when an agent makes statements that he or she knows are not true. An **innocent misrepresentation** occurs when an agent negligently makes a misrepresentation to a third party.

A judge should not stand in judgment over a person whom he likes or dislikes.

—*Talmud*

A principal is liable for the intentional and innocent misrepresentations made by an agent acting within the scope of employment. The third party can either (1) rescind the contract with the principal and recover any consideration paid, or (2) affirm the contract and recover damages.

Assume that (1) a car salesman is employed to sell the principal's car, and (2) the principal tells the agent that the car was repaired after it was involved in a major accident. If the agent intentionally tells the buyer that the car was never involved in an accident, the agent has made an intentional misrepresentation. Both the principal and the agent are liable for this misrepresentation.

Intentional Torts

Intentional torts include assault, battery, false imprisonment, and other willful conduct that causes injury to another person. A principal is not liable for the intentional torts of agents and employees that are committed outside the principal's scope of business. For example, if an employee attends a sporting event after working hours and gets into a fight with another spectator at the event, the employer is not liable.

However, a principal is liable under the doctrine of vicarious liability for intentional torts of agents and employees committed within the agent's scope of employment. The courts generally apply one of the following tests in determining whether an agent's intentional tort was committed within the agent's scope of employment.

Motivation test. Under the **motivation test,** if the agent's motivation in committing the intentional tort is to promote the principal's business, the principal is liable for any injury caused by the tort. But if the agent's motivation in committing the intentional tort was personal, the principal is not liable even if the tort took place during business hours or on business premises. For example, a principal is not liable if his agent was motivated by jealousy to beat up someone on the job who dated her boyfriend.

Work-related test. Some jurisdictions have rejected the motivation test as too narrow. These jurisdictions apply the **work-related test** instead. Under this test, if an agent commits an intentional tort within a work-related time or space—for example, during working hours or on the principal's premises—the principal is liable for any injuries caused by the agent's intentional torts. Under this test, the agent's motivation is immaterial.

Negligence

Principals are liable for the negligent conduct of agents acting within the scope of their employment. This liability is based on the common law doctrine of **respondeat superior** ("let the master answer"), which, in turn, is based on the legal theory of **vicarious liability** (liability without fault). The principal is liable because of his or her employment contract with the negligent agent, not because the principal was personally at fault.

This doctrine rests on the principle that if someone (i.e., the principal) expects to derive certain benefits from acting through another (i.e., an agent), the principal also should bear the liability for injuries caused to third persons by the negligent conduct of an agent who is acting within the scope of his or her employment.

> Morality cannot be legislated, but behavior can be regulated. Judicial decrees may not change the heart, but they can restrain the heartless.
> —Martin Luther King, Jr.

Frolic and detour. Agents sometimes do things during the course of their employment to further their own interests rather than the principal's. For example, an agent might take a detour to run a personal errand while on assignment for the principal. This is commonly referred to as a **frolic and detour.** Negligence actions stemming from frolic and detour are examined on a case-by-case basis. Agents always are personally liable for their tortious conduct in such situations. Principals generally are relieved of liability if the agent's frolic and detour is substantial. If the deviation is minor, however, the principal is liable for the injuries caused by the agent's tortious conduct.

Consider these examples: A salesperson stops home for lunch while on an assignment for his principal. While leaving his home, the agent hits and injures a pedestrian with her automobile. The principal is liable if the agent's home was not too far out of the way from the agent's assignment. But the principal would not be liable if an agent who is supposed to be on assignment in Los Angeles flies to San Francisco to meet a friend and is involved in an accident. The facts and circumstances of each case determine its outcome.

The "coming and going" rule. Under the common law, a principal generally is not liable for injuries caused by its agents and employees while they are on their way to or from work. This **"coming and going" rule** applies even if the principal supplies the agent's automobile or other transportation or pays for gasoline, repairs, and other automobile operating expenses. This rule is quite logical. Because principals do not control where their agents and employees live, they should not be liable for tortious conduct of agents on their way to and from work.

Dual-purpose mission. Sometimes principals request that agents run errands or conduct other acts on their behalf while the agent or employee is on personal business. In this case, the agent is on a **dual-purpose mission.** That is, he or she is acting partly for himself or herself and partly for the principal. Most jurisdictions hold both the principal and the agent liable if the agent injures someone while on such a mission.

Suppose a principal asks an employee to drop off a package at a client's office on the employee's way home. If the employee negligently injures a pedestrian while on this dual-purpose mission, the principal is liable to the pedestrian.

Minimum Wage and Overtime Pay

The **Fair Labor Standards Act (FLSA)** establishes minimum wage and overtime pay requirements for workers. Managerial, administrative, and professional employees are exempt from the Act's wage and hour provisions. As outlined below, the FLSA requires employers to pay covered workers at least the minimum wage for their regular work hours. Overtime pay is also mandated.

- **Minimum wage.** The minimum wage is set by Congress and can be changed. The Department of Labor permits employers to pay less than the minimum wage to students and apprentices. An employer may reduce minimum wages by an amount equal to the reasonable cost of food and lodging provided to employees.
- **Overtime pay.** Under the FLSA, an employer cannot require nonexempt employees to work more than 40 hours per week unless they are paid one-and-a-half times their regular pay for each hour worked in excess of 40 hours. Each week is treated separately. For example, if an employee works 50 hours one week and 30 hours the next, the employer owes the employee 10 hours of overtime pay.

29 U.S.C. 201 et seq.

Termination of an Agency and Employment Contract

An agency contract is similar to other contracts in that it can be terminated either by an act of the parties or by operation of law. These different methods of termination are discussed next. Note that once an agency relationship is terminated, the agent no longer can represent the principal or bind the principal to contracts.

Termination by Acts of the Parties

The parties to an agency contract can terminate an agency contract by agreement or by their actions. The four methods of termination of an agency relationship by acts of the parties are:

1. **Mutual agreement.** As with any contract, the parties to an agency contract can mutually agree to terminate their agreement. By doing so, the parties relieve each other of any further rights, duties, obligations, or powers provided for in the agency contract. Either party can propose the termination of an agency contract.

2. **Lapse of time.** Agency contracts are often written for a specific period of time. The agency terminates when the specified time period elapses. Suppose, for example, that the principal and agent enter into an agency contract "beginning January 1, 2002, and ending December 31, 2005." The agency automatically terminates on December 31, 2005. If the agency contract does not set forth a specific termination date, the agency terminates after a reasonable time has elapsed. The courts often look to the custom of an industry in determining the reasonable time for termination of the agency.

3. **Purpose achieved.** A principal can employ an agent for the time it takes to accomplish a certain task, purpose, or result. Such agencies automatically terminate once they are completed. Suppose a principal employs a licensed real estate

broker to sell his house. The agency terminates when the house is sold and the principal pays the broker the agreed-upon compensation.

4. **Occurrence of a specified event.** An agency contract can specify that the agency exists until a specified event occurs. The agency terminates when the specified event happens. For example, if a principal employs an agent to take care of her dog until she returns from a trip, the agency terminates when the principal returns from the trip.

Wrongful Termination of an Agency or Employment Contract

Generally, agency and employment contracts that do not specify a definite time for their termination can be terminated at will by either the principal or the agent without liability to the other party. When a principal terminates an agency contract, it is called a **revocation of authority.** When an agent terminates an agency, it is called a **renunciation of authority.**

Justice is the end of government. It is the end of civil society. It ever has been, and ever will be pursued, until it is obtained, or until liberty be lost in the pursuit.

—James Madison

Unless an agency is irrevocable, both the principal and the agent have an individual power to unilaterally terminate any agency contract. Note that having the *power* to terminate an agency agreement is not the same as having the *right* to terminate it. The unilateral termination of an agency contract may be wrongful. If the principal's or agent's termination of an agency contract breaches the contract, the other party can sue for damages for **wrongful termination.**

Consider this example: A principal employs a licensed real estate agent to sell his house. The agency contract gives the agent an exclusive listing for three months. After one month, the principal unilaterally terminates the agency. The principal has the power to do so, and the agent can no longer act on behalf of the principal. Because the principal did not have the right to terminate the contract, however, the agent can sue him and recover damages (i.e., lost commission) for wrongful termination.

Independent Contractor

Section 2 of the Restatement (Second) of Agency defines an independent contractor as "a person who contracts with another to do something for him who is not controlled by the other nor subject to the other's right to control with respect to his physical conduct in the performance of the undertaking." Independent contractors usually work for a number of clients, have their own offices, hire employees, and control the performance of their work.

Merely labeling someone an "independent contractor" is not enough. The crucial factor in determining whether someone is an employee or an independent contractor is the *degree of control* that the employer has over the agent. Critical factors in determining independent contractor status include:

- Whether the worker is engaged in a distinct occupation or an independently established business
- The length of time the agent has been employed by the principal
- The amount of time that the agent works for the principal
- Whether the principal supplies the tools and equipment used in the work
- The method of payment, whether by time or by the job
- The degree of skill necessary to complete the task

- Whether the worker hires employees to assist him or her
- Whether the employer has the right to control the manner and means of accomplishing the desired result

If an examination of these factors shows that the principal asserts little control, the person is an independent contractor. Substantial control indicates an employer–employee relationship.

Liability of Independent Contractor and Principal

Independent contractors are personally liable for their own torts. Generally, a principal is not liable for the torts of its independent contractors. The rationale behind this rule is that principals do not control the means by which the results are accomplished. Nevertheless, this rule has several exceptions:

- **Nondelegable duties:** Certain duties may not be delegated. For example, railroads owe a duty to maintain safe railroad crossings. They cannot escape this liability by assigning the task to an independent contractor.
- **Special risks:** Principals cannot avoid strict liability for dangerous activities assigned to independent contractors. For example, the use of explosives,

Principal Liable for Repo Man's Tort

Yvonne Sanchez borrowed money from MBank El Paso (MBank) to purchase an automobile. She gave MBank a security interest in the vehicle to secure the loan. Thus, the automobile became collateral for the loan. The bank could repossess the collateral—the automobile—if Sanchez did not repay the loan. When Sanchez defaulted on the loan, MBank hired El Paso Recovery Service, an independent contractor, to repossess the automobile.

The two men who were dispatched to Sanchez's house found the car parked in the driveway and hooked it to a tow truck. Sanchez demanded that they cease their efforts and leave the premises, but the men nonetheless continued with the repossession. Before the men could tow the automobile into the street, Sanchez jumped into the car, locked the doors, and refused to leave. The men towed the car at a high rate of speed to the repossession yard. They parked the car in the fenced repossession yard, with Sanchez inside, and padlocked the gate. Sanchez was left in the repossession lot with a Doberman Pinscher guard dog loose in the yard. Later, she was rescued by the police. The law prohibits the repossession of a vehicle if a breach of peace would occur. Sanchez filed suit against MBank, alleging that it was liable for the tortious conduct of El Paso Recovery Service. The trial court granted summary judgment to MBank, but the court of appeals reversed. MBank appealed.

The supreme court of Texas held that MBank, the principal, was liable for the tortious conduct of El Paso Recovery Service, an independent contractor. The court held that the act of repossessing an automobile from a defaulting debtor is an inherently dangerous activity and a nondelegable duty. The court concluded that El Paso Recovery Service had breached the peace in repossessing the car from Sanchez and caused her physical and emotional harm. The court held that MBank, the principal, could not escape liability by hiring an independent contractor to do this task. The court found MBank liable to Sanchez.

MBank El Paso, N.A. v. Sanchez, 836 S.W.2d 151, 1992 Tex. Lexis 97 (1992)

ETHICAL PERSPECTIVE

MICROSOFT VIOLATES EMPLOYMENT LAW

Microsoft Corporation is the world's largest provider of computer operating systems, software programs, and Internet browsers. In addition to having regular employees, Microsoft used the services of other workers classified as *independent contractors* (called *freelancers*) and temporary agency employees (called *temps*). Most of these special employees worked full time for Microsoft doing jobs that were identical to jobs performed by Microsoft's regular employees. Microsoft paid the special employees by check as outside workers.

In 1990, the IRS conducted an employment tax examination and determined that Microsoft had misclassified these special workers as independent contractors and that the workers in these positions should be reclassified as "employees" for federal tax purposes. The IRS used the following factors to reach the conclusion that the special workers were Microsoft employees rather than independent contractors:

- The party that has the right to control the manner and means by which the service or product is produced
- The degree of skill required
- The source of the instrumentalities and tools
- The location of the work
- The duration of the relationship between the parties
- The extent of the hiring party's discretion over when and how long to work
- The hiring party's role in hiring and paying assistants
- Whether the work is part of the regular business of the hiring party

The IRS applied these factors to both the freelancers and the temps who worked at Microsoft and found both groups to be employees of Microsoft. But that was not the end of the story. Plaintiff Donna Vizcaino and other freelancers sued Microsoft in a class-action lawsuit alleging that they were denied employment benefits, especially employee stock options, that were paid to regular employees. Microsoft contributed 3 percent of an employee's salary to the stock option plan.

The court of appeals agreed with the plaintiffs, citing the Internal Revenue Code that requires such stock-option plans to be available to all employees. Thus, Microsoft's attempt to define certain full-time employees as freelancers and temps was rebuffed by the courts.

1. Did Microsoft act ethically in this case?
2. Why did Microsoft classify these employees as "freelancers" and "temps"?

Vizcaino v. United States District Court for the Western District of Washington, 173 F.3d 713, 1999 U.S. App. Lexis 9057 (9th Cir. 1999)

clearing land by fire, crop dusting, and such involve special risks that are shared by the principal.

- **Negligence in the selection of an independent contractor:** A principal who hires an unqualified or known dangerous person as an independent contractor is liable if that person injures someone while on the job.

WORKERS' COMPENSATION

Many types of employment are dangerous, and each year many workers are injured on the job. At common law, employees who were injured on the job could sue their employer for negligence. This time-consuming process placed the employee at odds with his or her employer. In addition, there was no guarantee that the employee would win the case. Ultimately, many injured workers—or the heirs of deceased workers—were left uncompensated.

Workers' compensation acts were enacted in response to the unfairness of that result. These acts create an administrative procedure for workers to receive compensation for injuries that occur on the job. First, the injured worker files a claim with the appropriate state government agency (often called the workers' compensation board or commission). Next, that entity determines the legitimacy of the claim. If the worker disagrees with the agency's findings, he or she may appeal the decision through the state court system. Workers' compensation benefits are paid according to preset limits established by statute or regulation. The amounts that are recoverable vary from state to state.

Employment-Related Injury

To be compensable under workers' compensation, the claimant must prove that the injury arose out of and in the course of his or her employment—an **employment-related injury.** An accident that occurs while an employee is actively working is clearly within the scope of this rule. Accidents that occur at a company cafeteria or while on a business lunch for an employer are covered. Accidents that happen while the employee is at an off-premises restaurant during his or her personal lunch hour are not covered. Many workers' compensation acts include stress as a compensable work-related injury.

Exclusive Remedy

Workers' compensation is an **exclusive remedy.** Thus, workers cannot sue their employers in court for damages. The one exception to this rule is: If an employer intentionally injures a worker, the worker can collect workers' compensation benefits and sue the employer. Workers' compensation acts do not bar injured workers from suing responsible third parties to recover damages.

Occupational Safety and Health Act

In 1970, Congress enacted the **Occupational Safety and Health Act** [29 U.S.C. §§ 651–678] to promote safety in the workplace. Virtually all private employers are within the scope of the act, but federal, state, and local governments are exempted. Industries regulated by other federal safety legislation also are exempt. The Act also established the **Occupational Safety and Health Administration (OSHA),** a federal administrative agency within the Department of Labor. The act imposes record-keeping and reporting requirements on employers and requires them to post notices in the workplace informing employees of their rights under the Act.

Specific and General Duty Standards

OSHA is empowered to administer the Act and adopt rules and regulations to interpret and enforce it. OSHA has adopted thousands of regulations to enforce the safety standards established by the Act. These include the following:

- **Specific duty standards:** Many of the OSHA standards address safety problems of a specific-duty nature. For example, OSHA standards establish safety requirements for equipment (e.g., safety guards), set maximum

CASE FOR DISCUSSION

Smith v. Workers' Compensation Appeals Board

236 Cal.Rptr. 248, 1987 Cal. App. Lexis 1587 (1987) — Court of Appeal of California

FACTS

Ronald Wayne Smith was employed by Modesto High School as a temporary math instructor. In addition, he coached the girls' baseball and basketball teams. The contract under which he was employed stated that he "may be required to devote a reasonable amount of time to other duties" in addition to instructional duties. The teachers in the school system were evaluated once a year regarding both instructional duties and noninstructional duties, including "sponsorship or the supervision of out-of-classroom student activities."

The high school's math club holds an annual end-of-year outing. For the 1983–84 school year, a picnic was scheduled for June 7, 1984, at the Modesto Reservoir. The students invited their math teachers, including Smith, to attend. The food was paid for by math club members' dues. Smith attended the picnic with his wife and three children. One of the students brought along a windsurfer. Smith watched the students as they used it before and after the picnic. When Smith tried it himself, he fell and was seriously injured. He died shortly thereafter. Mrs. Smith filed a claim for workers' compensation benefits, which was objected to by the employer. The workers' compensation judge denied benefits. The Workers' Compensation Appeals Board affirmed. Mrs. Smith appealed.

ISSUE

Was Smith engaged in employment-related activities when the accident occurred?

COURT'S REASONING

The court of appeal held that the decedent believed that his participation in the math club picnic was expected by his employer and that this belief was objectively reasonable. The court stated, "The school was more than minimally involved in the picnic." Teachers were encouraged to involve themselves in extracurricular activities of the school, thus conferring the benefit of better teacher–student relationships. The court noted that teachers were evaluated on whether they shared equally in the sponsorship or the supervision of out-of-classroom student activities. The court concluded that the decedent's engagement in the recreational activities was causally connected to his employment.

DECISION

The court of appeal held that the decedent's accident was causally connected to his employment for purposes of awarding workers' compensation benefits to his heirs. Reversed and remanded.

QUESTIONS

1. Should workers' compensation benefits be awarded only for accidents that occur at the job site? Why or why not?
2. Did the employer act ethically in objecting to the payment of benefits in this case?
3. How costly is workers' compensation for business? Do you think that many fraudulent workers' compensation claims are filed?

exposure levels to hazardous chemicals, regulate the location of machinery, establish safety procedures for employees, and the like.

- **General duty standards:** The Act imposes a general duty on an employer to provide a work environment "free from recognized hazards that are causing or are likely to cause death or serious physical harm to his employees." This is so even if no specific regulation applies to the situation.

OSHA is empowered to inspect places of employment for health hazards and safety violations. If a violation is found, OSHA can issue a *written citation* that requires the employer to abate or correct the situation. Contested citations are reviewed by the Occupational Safety and Health Review Commission. Its decision is appealable to the federal circuit court of appeals. Employers who violate the Act, OSHA rules and regulations, or OSHA citations are subject to both civil and criminal penalties.

Title VII of the Civil Rights Act of 1964

After substantial debate, Congress enacted the **Civil Rights Act of 1964. Title VII** of that Act, entitled the **Fair Employment Practices Act,** was intended to eliminate job discrimination based on the following *protected classes:* (1) *race,* (2) *color,* (3) *religion,* (4) *sex,* and (5) *national origin* [42 U.S.C. §§ 2000e et seq.]. As amended by the **Equal Employment Opportunity Act of 1972,** Section 703(a)(2) of Title VII provides in pertinent part that

> It shall be an unlawful employment practice for an employer
>
> (1) to fail or refuse to hire or to discharge any individual, or otherwise to discriminate against any individual with respect to his compensation, terms, conditions, or privileges of employment, because of such individual's race, color, religion, sex, or national origin; or
>
> (2) to limit, segregate, or classify his employees or applicants for employment in any way which would deprive or tend to deprive any individual of employment opportunities or otherwise adversely affect his status as an employee, because of such individual's race, color, religion, sex, or national origin.

Racial discrimination in any form and in any degree has no justifiable part whatever in our democratic way of life. It is unattractive in any setting but it is utterly revolting among a free people who have embraced the principles set forth in the Constitution of the United States.
—J. Murphy
Korematsu v. U.S. (1944)

Scope of Coverage of Title VII

Title VII prohibits **discrimination** in hiring, decisions regarding promotion or demotion, payment of compensation and fringe benefits, availability of job training and apprenticeship opportunities, referral systems for employment, decisions regarding dismissal, work rules, and any other "term, condition, or privilege" of employment. Any employee of covered employers, including undocumented aliens, may bring actions for employment discrimination under Title VII.

Race, Color, and National Origin Discrimination

Title VII of the Civil Rights Act of 1964 was enacted primarily to prohibit **employment discrimination** based on *race, color,* and *national origin. Race* refers to broad categories such as Black, Caucasian, Asian, and American Indian. *Color* refers to the color of a person's skin. *National origin* refers to the country of a person's ancestors or cultural characteristics.

CASE FOR DISCUSSION

National Association for the Advancement of Colored People, Newark Branch v. Town of Harrison, New Jersey

907 F.2d 1408, 1990 U.S. App. Lexis 11793 (1990) United States Court of Appeals, Third Circuit

FACTS

The town of Harrison, New Jersey (Harrison), followed a policy of hiring only town residents as town employees for as long as any townspeople could remember. In 1978, New Jersey adopted an Act Concerning Residency Requirements for Municipal and County Employees that permitted towns, cities, and counties in the state to require that their employees be bona fide residents of the local government unit. Pursuant to this statute, Harrison adopted Ordinance 747, which stipulated that "all officers and employees of the Town shall, as a condition of employment, be bona fide residents of the Town."

Although Harrison is a small industrial community located in Hudson County, New Jersey, it is clearly aligned with Essex County to the west and is considered an extension of the city of Newark, which it abuts. Adjacent counties are within an easy commute of Harrison. Only 0.2 percent of Harrison's population is Black. None of the 51 police officers, 55 firefighters, or 80 nonuniformed employees of the town are Black. Several Blacks who were members of the National Association for the Advancement of Colored People (NAACP), Newark Branch applied for employment with Harrison but were rejected because they did not meet the residency requirement. The NAACP sued Harrison for employment discrimination. Harrison countered that its employment rule was neutral and did not discriminate.

ISSUE

Does the residency requirement of the town of Harrison violate Title VII of the Civil Rights Act of 1964?

COURT'S REASONING

The district court noted that Harrison's geographical location and transportation facilities allowed the town to be viewed as a functional component of the city of Newark and a part of Essex County. Newark's population is approximately 60 percent Black. Essex County's civilian labor force is 33.3 percent Black. Of the persons employed by private industry, 22.1 percent are Black. Because so few Black persons live in Harrison, most of these persons must have commuted from elsewhere in the labor market that serves Harrison. The court held that the otherwise socially neutral employment rule caused an adverse impact on Blacks.

DECISION AND REMEDY

The district court held that the plaintiffs had established that the ordinance constituted disparate impact race discrimination in violation of Title VII of the Civil Rights Act of 1964. The court issued an injunction against enforcement of the ordinance.

QUESTIONS

1. Would the same residency requirement rule cause disparate impact discrimination if it were adopted by New York City or Los Angeles?
2. Did the town of Harrison act ethically when it adopted the residency requirement?
3. Could a private business impose a residency requirement on its employees?

Sex Discrimination

Although the prohibition against **sex discrimination** applies equally to men and women, the overwhelming majority of Title VII sex discrimination cases are brought by women. An example of such discrimination is the old airline practice of ignoring the marital status of male flight attendants but hiring only single female flight attendants.

Sexual Harassment

In the modern work environment, co-workers sometimes become sexually interested or involved with each other voluntarily. On other occasions, though, a co-worker's sexual advances are not welcome.

Refusing to hire or promote someone unless he or she has sex with the manager or supervisor is sex discrimination that violates Title VII. Other forms of conduct, such as lewd remarks, touching, intimidation, posting pinups, and other verbal or physical conduct of a sexual nature, constitute **sexual harassment** and violate Title VII. To determine what conduct creates a hostile work environment, the U.S. Supreme Court stated [*Harris v. Forklift Systems, Inc.*, 510 U.S. 17, 114 So.Ct. 367, 1993 U.S. Lexis 7155 (1993)]:

> We can say that whether an environment is "hostile" or "abusive" can be determined only by looking at all the circumstances. These may include the frequency of the discriminatory conduct; its severity; whether it is physically threatening or humiliating, or a mere offensive utterance; and whether it unreasonably interferes with an employee's work performance.

Exhibit 12.3 sets forth an employer's policies against sexual harassment.

Religious Discrimination

Title VII prohibits employment discrimination based on a person's religion. Religions include traditional religions, other religions that recognize a supreme being, and religions based on ethical or spiritual tenets. Many **religious discrimination** cases involve a conflict between an employer's work rule and an employee's religious beliefs (e.g., when an employee is required to work on his or her religious holiday).

Rights matter most when they are claimed by unpopular minorities.
—J. Michael Kirby

The right of an employee to practice his or her religion is not absolute. Under Title VII, an employer is under a duty to *reasonably accommodate* the religious observances, practices, or beliefs of its employees if it does not cause an **undue hardship** on the employer. The courts must apply these general standards to specific fact situations. In making their decisions, the courts must consider factors such as the number of employees of the employer, the importance of the employee's position, and the availability of alternative workers.

Bona Fide Occupational Qualification (BFOQ)

Discrimination based on protected classes (other than race or color) is permitted if it is shown to be a **bona fide occupational qualification (BFOQ).** To be legal, a BFOQ must be both *job-related* and a *business necessity.* For example, allowing only women to be locker-room attendants in a women's gym is a valid BFOQ, but prohibiting males from being managers or instructors at the same gym would not be a BFOQ.

EXHIBIT 12.3 *Policies against sexual harassment.*

Many businesses have taken steps to prevent sexual harassment in the workplace. For example, some businesses have explicitly adopted policies (see below) forbidding sexual harassment, implemented procedures for reporting incidents of sexual harassment, and conducted training programs to sensitize managers and employees about the issue.

Statement of Prohibited Conduct

The management of Company considers the following conduct to illustrate some of the conduct that violates Company's Sexual Harassment Policy:

A. Physical assaults of a sexual nature, such as

1. Rape, sexual battery, molestation, or attempts to commit these assaults.
2. Intentional physical conduct that is sexual in nature, such as touching, pinching, patting, grabbing, brushing against another employee's body, or poking another employee's body.

B. Unwanted sexual advances, propositions, or other sexual comments, such as

1. Sexually oriented gestures, noises, remarks, jokes, or comments about a person's sexuality or sexual experience directed at or made in the presence of any employee who indicates or has indicated in any way that such conduct is unwelcome in his or her presence.
2. Preferential treatment or promises of preferential treatment to an employee for submitting to sexual conduct, including soliciting or attempting to solicit any employee to engage in sexual activity for compensation or reward.
3. Subjecting, or threats of subjecting, an employee to unwelcome sexual attention or conduct or intentionally making performance of the employee's job more difficult because of the employee's sex.

C. Sexual or discriminatory displays or publications anywhere in Company's workplace by Company employees, such as

1. Displaying pictures, posters, calendars, graffiti, objects, promotional materials, reading materials, or other materials that are sexually suggestive, sexually demeaning, or pornographic, or bringing into Company's work environment or possessing any such material to read, display, or view at work.

   A picture will be presumed to be sexually suggestive if it depicts a person of either sex who is not fully clothed or in clothes that are not suited to or ordinarily accepted for the accomplishment of routine work in and around the workplace and who is posed for the obvious purpose of displaying or drawing attention to private portions of his or her body.
2. Reading or otherwise publicizing in the work environment materials that are in any way sexually revealing, sexually suggestive, sexually demeaning, or pornographic.
3. Displaying signs or other materials purporting to segregate an employee by sex in any area of the workplace (other than restrooms and similar semi-private lockers/changing rooms).

Age Discrimination in Employment Act (ADEA)

In the past, some employers discriminated against employees and prospective employees based on their age. For example, employers often refused to hire older workers. The **Age Discrimination in Employment Act (ADEA),** which prohibits certain **age discrimination** practices, was enacted in 1967 [29 U.S.C. §§ 621–634].

CASE FOR DISCUSSION

Harris v. Forklift Systems, Inc.

510 U.S. 17, 114 S.Ct. 367, 1993 U.S. Lexis 7155 (1993) **Supreme Court of the United States**

FACTS

Teresa Harris worked as a manager at Forklift Systems, Inc. (Forklift), an equipment rental company, from April 1985 until October 1987. Charles Hardy was Forklift's president. Throughout Harris's time at Forklift, Hardy often insulted her because of her gender and made her the target of unwanted sexual innuendoes. Hardy told Harris on several occasions, in the presence of other employees, "You're a woman, what do you know" and "We need a man as the rental manager"; at least once, he told her she was "a dumb ass woman." Again in front of others, he suggested that the two of them "go to the Holiday Inn to negotiate Harris's raise." Hardy occasionally asked Harris and other female employees to get coins from his front pants pocket. He threw objects on the ground in front of Harris and other women and asked them to pick the objects up. He made several innuendoes about Harris's and other women's clothing.

In mid-August 1987, Harris complained to Hardy about his conduct. Hardy said he was surprised that Harris was offended, claimed he was only joking, and apologized. He also promised he would stop, and based on this assurance, Harris stayed on the job. But in early September, Hardy began anew: While Harris was arranging a deal with one of Forklift's customers, he asked her, again in front of other employees, "What did you do, promise the guy. . . some [sex] Saturday night?" On October 1, Harris collected her paycheck and quit.

Harris then sued Forklift, claiming that Hardy's conduct had created an abusive work environment for her because of her gender. The district court held that because Harris had not suffered severe psychological injury, she could not recover. The court of appeals affirmed. Harris appealed to the U.S. Supreme Court.

ISSUE

Must conduct, to be actionable as abusive work environment harassment, seriously affect the victim's psychological well-being?

COURT'S REASONING

The Supreme Court stated, "A discriminatorily abusive work environment, even one that does not seriously affect employees' psychological well-being, can and often will detract from employees' job performance, discourage employees from remaining on the job, or keep them from advancing in their careers." The Supreme Court held that even without regard to these tangible effects, the very fact that the discriminatory conduct was so severe or pervasive that it created a work environment abusive to employees because of their race, gender, religion, or national origin offends Title VII's broad rule of workplace equality. The Court stated that as long as the work environment would reasonably be perceived, and is perceived, as hostile or abusive, there is no need for it also to be psychologically injurious.

DECISION AND REMEDY

The Supreme Court held that Title VII does not require a victim to prove that the challenged conduct seriously affected her psychological well-being. The case was remanded to the district court for trial. On remand, the district court awarded Harris $151,435 plus interest, attorney's fees, and costs. The court also issued an injunction against conduct that would create a hostile work environment.

QUESTIONS

1. Should an employer be held liable for sexual harassment committed by one of its employees?
2. What penalty should be assessed against Hardy for his conduct?
3. How can businesses eliminate sexual harassment on the job?

The ADEA prohibits age discrimination in all employment decisions, including hiring, promotions, payment of compensation, and other terms and conditions of employment. Originally, ADEA prohibited employment discrimination against persons between 40 and 65 years of age. In 1978, its coverage was extended to persons up to 70 years of age. Further amendments completely eliminated an age ceiling, so ADEA now applies to employees who are age 40 and older.

Americans with Disabilities Act (ADA)

The **Americans with Disabilities Act (ADA),** signed into law on July 26, 1990 [42 U.S.C. §§ 1201 et seq.], is the most comprehensive piece of civil rights legislation since the Civil Rights Act of 1964. The ADA imposes obligations on employers and providers of public transportation, telecommunications, and public accommodations to accommodate individuals with disabilities.

Title I of the ADA prohibits employment discrimination against qualified individuals with disabilities in regard to job application procedures, hiring, compensation, training, promotion, and termination. It requires an employer to make reasonable accommodations to individuals with disabilities that do not cause undue hardship to the employer. **Reasonable accommodations** may include making facilities readily accessible to individuals with disabilities, providing part-time or modified work schedules, acquiring equipment or devices, modifying examination and training materials, and providing qualified readers or interpreters.

Employers are not obligated to provide accommodations that would impose an **undue burden,** or actions that would require significant difficulty or expense. The courts consider factors such as the nature and cost of accommodation, the employer's overall financial resources, and the employer's type of operation. Obviously, what may be a significant difficulty or expense for a small employer may not be an undue hardship for a large employer.

Family and Medical Leave Act

In February 1993, Congress enacted the **Family and Medical Leave Act.** This law guarantees workers unpaid time off from work for medical emergencies. The Act, which applies to companies with 50 or more workers as well as federal, state, and local governments, covers about half of the nation's workforce. To be covered by the Act, an employee must have worked for the employer for at least one year and have performed more than 1,250 hours of service during the previous 12-month period.

Covered employers are required to provide up to 12 weeks of unpaid leave during any 12-month period as a result of the

1. Birth of, and care for, a son or daughter
2. Placement of a child for adoption or in foster care
3. Serious health condition that makes the employee unable to perform his or her duties
4. Care for a spouse, child, or parent with a serious health problem

An eligible employee who takes leave must, upon returning to work, be restored to either the same or an equivalent position with equivalent employment benefits and pay. The restored employee is not entitled to the accrual of seniority during the leave period, however. A covered employer may deny restoration to a salaried employee who is among the highest-paid 10 percent of that employer's employees if the denial is necessary to prevent "substantial and grievous economic injury" to the employer's operations.

Labor Union Law

Section 7 of the **National Labor Relations Act** (NLRA) [29 U.S.C. §§ 101–110 and 113–115] gives employees the right to join together and form a union. The group that the union is seeking to represent—called the **appropriate bargaining unit** or bargaining unit—must be defined before the union can petition for an election. This group can be the employees of a single company or plant, a group within a single company (e.g., maintenance workers at all of a company's plants), or an entire industry (e.g., nurses at all hospitals in the country). Managers and professional employees may not belong to unions formed by employees whom they manage.

Collective Bargaining

Strong, responsible unions are essential to industrial fair play. Without them the labor bargain is wholly one-sided.
—Louis D. Brandeis

Once a union has been elected, the employer and the union discuss the terms of employment of union members and try to negotiate a contract that embodies these terms. The act of negotiating is called **collective bargaining,** and the resulting contract is called a collective bargaining agreement. The employer and the union must negotiate with each other in good faith. Among other things, this prohibits making take-it-or-leave-it proposals.

Strikes and Picketing

The NLRA gives union management the right to recommend that the union call a **strike** if a collective bargaining agreement cannot be reached. Before there can be a strike, though, a majority vote of the union's members must agree to the action.

Striking union members often engage in **picketing** in support of their strike. Picketing usually takes the form of the striking employees and union representatives walking in front of the employer's premises carrying signs announcing their strike. It is used to put pressure on an employer to settle a strike. The right to picket is implied from the NLRA.

Picketing is lawful unless it (1) is accompanied by violence, (2) obstructs customers from entering the employer's place of business, (3) prevents nonstriking employees from entering the employer's premises, or (4) prevents pickups and deliveries at the employer's place of business. An employer may seek an injunction against unlawful picketing.

Illegal strikes. Several types of strikes have been held to be illegal and are not protected by federal labor law. Illegal strikes are:

- **Violent strikes:** Striking employees cause substantial damage to property of the employer or a third party. Courts usually tolerate a certain amount of isolated violence before finding that the entire strike is illegal.
- **Sit-down strikes:** Striking employees continue to occupy the employer's premises. Such strikes are illegal because they deny the employer's statutory right to continue its operations during the strike.
- **Partial or intermittent strikes:** Employees strike part of the day or workweek and work the other part. This type of strike is illegal because it interferes with the employer's right to operate its facilities at full operation.
- **Wildcat strikes:** Individual union members go on strike without proper authorization from the union. The courts have recognized that a wildcat strike becomes lawful if it is quickly ratified by the union.

- **Strikes during the 60-day cooling-off period:** Strikes begin during the mandatory 60-day cooling-off period. This time is designed to give the employer and the union time to negotiate a settlement of the union grievances and avoid a strike. Any strike without a proper 60-day notice is illegal.
- **Strikes in violation of a no-strike clause:** Strikes take place in violation of a negotiated no-strike clause, under which an employer gives economic benefits to the union and, in exchange, the union agrees that no strike will be called for a set time.

Illegal strikers may be discharged by the employer with no rights to reinstatement.

Crossover and replacement workers. Individual members of a union do not have to honor a strike and may continue to work for the employer. They may (1) choose not to strike or (2) return to work after joining the strikers for a time. Employees who choose either of these options are known as **crossover workers.**

Once a strike begins, the employer may continue operations by using management personnel and hiring **replacement workers** to take the place of the striking employees. Replacement workers can be hired on either a temporary or permanent basis. If replacement workers are given permanent status, they do not have to be dismissed when the strike is over.

Management and union may be likened to that serpent of the fables who on one body had two heads that fighting with poisoned fangs, killed themselves.

—Peter Drucker

LEGAL TERMINOLOGY

Age discrimination
Age Discrimination in Employment Act
Agency
Agency by estoppel
Agency by ratification
Agent
Americans with Disabilities Act (ADA)
Apparent agency
Appropriate bargaining unit
Attorney-in-fact
Bona fide occupational qualification (BFOQ)
Civil Rights Act of 1964
Collective bargaining
"Coming and going" rule
Crossover workers
Deceit
Discrimination
Dual-purpose mission
Employer–employee relationship
Employment-at-will
Employment discrimination
Employment-related injury
Equal Employment Opportunity Act of 1972
Exclusive agency contract
Exclusive remedy
Express agency
Fair Employment Practices Act
Fair Labor Standards Act (FLSA)
Family and Medical Leave Act
Fiduciary relationship
Fraud
Frolic and detour
Fully disclosed agency
General duty standards
General power of attorney
Implied agency
Implied warranty of authority
Incidental authority
Implied-in-fact contract
Independent contractor
Innocent misrepresentation
Intentional misrepresentation
Intentional tort
Motivation test
National Labor Relations Act
National origin discrimination
Negligence

Occupational Safety and Health Act
Occupational Safety and Health Administration (OSHA)
Partial (intermittent) strike
Partially disclosed agency
Picketing
Power of attorney
Principal
Principal–agent relationship
Principal–independent contractor relationship
Public policy exception
Reasonable accommodations
Religious discrimination
Renunciation of authority
Replacement workers
Respondeat superior
Revocation of authority
Sex discrimination
Sexual harassment
Sit-down strike
Special power of attorney
Specific duty standards
Strike
Title VII of Civil Rights Act of 1964
Undisclosed agency
Undue burden
Undue hardship
Vicarious liability
Violent strike
Wildcat strike
Worker's compensation acts
Work-related test
Wrongful termination (of an agency)

chapter summary

AGENCY, EMPLOYMENT, AND EQUAL OPPORTUNITY LAW

The Nature of Agency	
Definition	A fiduciary relationship that results from the manifestation of consent by one person to act on behalf of another person with that person's consent.
Parties	1. *Principal:* Party who employs another person to act on his or her behalf. 2. *Agent:* Party who agrees to act on behalf of another person.
Kinds of Employment Relationships	
Employer–Employee Relationship	An employer hires an employee to perform some form of physical service. An employee is not an agent unless the principal authorizes him or her to enter into contracts on the principal's behalf.
Principal–Agent Relationship	An employer hires an employee and authorizes the employee to enter into contracts on the employer's behalf.
Principal–Independent Contractor Relationship	Principal employs a person who is not an employee of the principal. The independent contractor has authority only to enter into contracts authorized by the principal.
Formation of the Agency Relationship	
Express Agency	Is agreed to in words by principal and agent. The agency contract may be oral or written unless the Statute of Frauds requires it to be in writing.

Implied Agency	Is inferred from the conduct of the parties.
Apparent Agency	Arises when a principal creates an appearance of an agency that in actuality does not exist. Also called *agency by estoppel* or *ostensible agency.*
Agency by Ratification	Occurs when a person misrepresents himself or herself as another's agent when he or she is not and the purported principal ratifies (accepts) the unauthorized act.
Contract Liability to Third Parties	
Fully Disclosed Agency	The third party entering into the contract knows that the agent is acting for a principal and knows the identity of the principal. The principal is liable on the contract; the agent is not liable on the contract.
Partially Disclosed Agency	The third party knows that the agent is acting for a principal but does not know the identity of the principal. Both the principal and the agent are liable on the contract.
Undisclosed Agency	The third party does not know that the agent is acting for a principal. Both the principal and the agent are liable on the contract.
Tort Liability to Third Parties	
Misrepresentation	Principals are liable for intentional and innocent misrepresentation made by agents acting within the scope of their employment.
Negligence	Principals are liable for the negligent conduct of agents acting within the scope of their employment. Special negligence doctrines include: 1. *Frolic and detour:* Principals are generally relieved of liability if the agent's negligent act occurred on a substantial frolic and detour from the scope of employment. 2. *"Coming and going" rule:* Principals are not liable if the agent's tortious conduct occurred while on the way to or from work. 3. *Dual-purpose mission:* If the agent is acting on his or her own behalf and on behalf of the principal, the principal is generally liable for the agent's tortious conduct.
Intentional Torts	States apply one of the following rules: 1. *Motivation test:* The principal is liable if the agent's intentional tort was committed to promote the principal's business. 2. *Work-related test:* The principal is liable if the agent's intentional tort was committed within a work-related time or space. Agents are personally liable for their own tortious conduct. *(continued)*

Independent Contractor	
Liability for Independent Contractor's Torts	Generally, principals are not liable for the tortious conduct of independent contractors. Exceptions to the rule are for: 1. *Nondelegable duties.* 2. *Special risks.* 3. *Negligence in selecting an independent contractor.* Independent contractors are personally liable for their own torts.
Termination of an Agency and Employment Contract	
Termination by Acts of the Parties	The following *acts of the parties* terminate agency contracts: 1. *Mutual agreement.* 2. *Lapse of time.* 3. *Purpose achieved.* 4. *Occurrence of a specified event.*
Wrongful Termination of an Agency Contract	If an agency is for an agreed-upon term or purpose, the *unilateral termination* of the agency contract by either the principal or the agent constitutes the *wrongful termination* of the agency. The breaching party is liable to the other party for damages caused by the breach.
Workers' Compensation	
Workers' Compensation Acts	State statutes that create an administrative procedure for workers to receive payments for job-related injuries. 1. *Workers' compensation insurance:* Most states require employers to carry private or government-sponsored workers' compensation insurance. Some states permit employers to self-insure.
Employment-Related Injury	To be compensable under workers' compensation, the claimant must prove that the injury arose out of and in the course of his or her employment.
Exclusive Remedy	Workers' compensation is an exclusive remedy. Thus, workers cannot sue their employers to recover damages for job-related injuries.
Occupational Safety and Health Act	
Occupational Safety and Health Act	Federal statute that requires employers to provide safe working conditions.
Occupational Safety and Health Administration (OSHA)	Federal administrative agency that administers and enforces the Occupational Safety and Health Act.
Specific and General Duty Standards	1. *Specific duty standards:* Safety standards for specific equipment (e.g., lathe) or industry (e.g., mining). 2. *General duty standards:* Impose a general duty on employers to provide safe working conditions.

Title VII of the Civil Rights Act of 1964	
Description	Federal statute that prohibits job discrimination based on the (1) race, (2) color, (3) religion, (4) sex, or (5) national origin of the job applicant.
Scope of Coverage of Title VII	Decisions regarding hiring; promotion; demotion; payment of salaries, wages, and fringe benefits; job training and apprenticeships; work rules; or any other "term, condition, or privilege of employment."
Protected Classes	Employment discrimination based on the following protected classes is forbidden by Title VII: 1. *Race:* Broad class based on common physical characteristics 2. *Color:* Skin color 3. *National origin:* A person's national heritage 4. *Sex:* Male or female 5. *Religion:* Discrimination solely because of a person's religious beliefs or practices. An employer has a duty to *reasonably accommodate* an employee's religious beliefs if it does not cause an *undue hardship* on the employer.
Sexual Harassment	Lewd remarks, touching, intimidation, posting pinups, and other verbal or physical conduct of a sexual nature that occurs on the job. Sexual harassment that creates a *hostile work environment* violates Title VII [*Harris v. Forklift Systems, Inc.*, 510 U.S. 17, 114 S.Ct. 367, 1993 U.S. Lexis, 7155 (1993)].
Age Discrimination in Employment Act (ADEA)	
Description	Federal statute that prohibits employment discrimination against applicants and employees who are 40 years of age and older.
Americans with Disabilities Act (ADA)	
Description	Federal law that imposes obligations on employers and providers of public transportation, telecommunications, and public accommodations to accommodate individuals with disabilities.
Title I of ADA	Federal law that prohibits employment discrimination against qualified individuals with disabilities. Requires employers to make *reasonable accommodations* that do not cause *undue hardship* to the employer to accommodate employees with disabilities.
Labor Union Law	
Organizing a Union	1. *Section 7 of the NLRA:* Gives employees the right to join together and form a union. 2. *Appropriate bargaining unit:* Group of employees that a union is seeking to represent. *(continued)*

Collective Bargaining	Process whereby the union and the employer negotiate the terms and conditions of employment for the covered employee union members. A collective bargaining agreement is the contract resulting from collective bargaining.
Strikes	A strike is a cessation of work by union members in order to obtain economic benefits, to correct an unfair labor practice, or to preserve their work. The NLRA gives union employees the right to strike.
Picketing	Striking employees and union organizers walking around the employer's premises, usually carrying signs, notifying the public of their grievance against the employer. *Illegal picketing:* Picketing accompanied by violence or obstructing customers, nonstriking workers, or suppliers from entering the employer's premises.
Crossover Workers	Individual members of a union who do not honor a strike and continue to work for the employer.
Replacement Workers	Once a strike begins, the employer may hire replacement workers to take the place of striking employees.

WORKING THE WEB

Visit the Web sites listed below for more information about the topics covered in this chapter.

1. Visit Nolo Press at **www.nolo.com/category/ic_home.html** to find general information regarding the classification of independent contractor versus employee.
2. One way to create an agency is to execute a power of attorney. See **smallbiz.biz.findlaw.com/bookshelf/sblg/sblgchp13_f.html** for information, and **consumer.pub.findlaw.com/nllg/forms/128.html** for a form.
3. For an outline of agency liability issues see **www.terry.uga.edu/~bboehmer/ls470/transparencies/principalagent/index.htm.**
4. Review the case *Gupta v. Florida Board of Regents* (5/17/2000, No. 98-5392) on the Cornell Discrimination Web site at **www.law.cornell.edu/topics/employment_discrimination.html.** According to the 11th Circuit Court of Appeals, is it sexual harassment to make comments to co-workers such as "You are looking very beautiful"?
5. For a discussion of the courts' definition of *disability*, see **www.law.ua.edu/lawreview/tucker521.htm.**
6. The National Labor Relations Board Web site: **www.nlrb.gov** is packed with useful information.
7. Visit the Web site of one of the largest labor unions at **www.aflcio.org/home.htm.**

CRITICAL LEGAL THINKING QUESTIONS

1. Define an *agency*. What purpose does an agency serve?
2. Define an *independent contractor*. What factors does a court look at in determining whether an independent contractor status exists?
3. Explain the tort liability of a principal and an agent. Explain the tort liability of a principal and an independent contractor.
4. Describe workers' compensation laws. What are the public purposes for these laws?
5. Describe occupational safety laws. What are the public purposes for these laws?
6. What are the protected classes under Title VII of the Civil Rights Act of 1964?
7. Describe the protections afforded by the Family and Medical Leave Act. Why did Congress pass this act?
8. Define *sexual harassment*. Give some examples of sexual harassment.
9. Describe the protections afforded by the Americans with Disabilities Act (ADA).
10. What functions are served by federal labor union laws?

CASE FOR BRIEFING

Read Case 12 in Appendix A *(Robinson v. Jacksonville Shipyards, Inc.)*. Review and brief the case using the *Critical Legal Thinking* "Briefing the Case" example described in Chapter 1.

CASES FOR DISCUSSION

12.1 *Grinder v. Bryans Road Building & Supply Co., Inc.*

453, 1981 Md. Lexis 246 (1981)
Court of Appeals of Maryland

FACTS G. Elvin Grinder of Marbury, Maryland, was a building contractor who, prior to May 1, 1973, did business as an individual and traded as "Grinder Construction." Grinder maintained an open account, on his individual credit, with Bryans Road Building & Supply Co., Inc. Grinder purchased materials and supplies from Bryans on credit and later paid the invoices.

On May 1, 1973, G. Elvin Grinder Construction, Inc., a Maryland corporation, was formed with Grinder personally owning 52 percent of the stock of the corporation. Grinder did not inform Bryans that he had incorporated, and continued to purchase supplies on credit from Bryans under the name "Grinder Construction."

In May 1978, after certain invoices were not paid by Grinder, Bryans sued Grinder personally to recover. Grinder asserted that the debts were owed by the corporation. Bryans amended its complaint to include the corporation as a defendant.

ISSUE Who is liable to Bryans?

12.2 *Largey v. Intrastate Radiotelephone, Inc.*

186 Cal. Rptr. 520, 1982 Cal. App. Lexis 2049 (1982)
Court of Appeal of California

FACTS Intrastate Radiotelephone, Inc., a public utility, supplies radiotelephone utility service to the general public for radiotelephones, pocket pagers, and beepers. Robert Kranhold, an employee of Intrastate, was authorized to use his personal vehicle on company business. On the morning of March 9, 1976, when Kranhold was driving his vehicle to Intrastate's main office, he negligently struck a motorcycle driven by Michael S. Largey, causing severe and permanent injuries to Largey. The accident occurred at the intersection where Intrastate's main office is located.

Evidence showed that Kranhold acted as a consultant to Intrastate, worked both in and out of Intrastate's offices, had no set hours of work, often attended meetings at Intrastate's offices, and went to Intrastate's office to pick up things or drop off things. Largey sued Intrastate for damages.

ISSUE Is Intrastate liable?

12.3 *Huddleston v. Roger Dean Chevrolet, Inc.*

845 F.2d 900, 1988 U.S. App. Lexis 6823 (1988)
United States Court of Appeals, Eleventh Circuit

FACTS Shirley Huddleston became the first female sales representative of Roger Dean Chevrolet, Inc. (RDC) in West Palm Beach, Florida. Shortly after she began working at RDC, Philip Geraci, a fellow sales representative, and other male employees began making derogatory comments to and about her, expelled gas in her presence, called her a bitch and a whore, and such. Many of these remarks were made in front of customers. The sales manager of RDC participated in the harassment. On several occasions, Huddleston complained about this conduct to RDC's general manager.

ISSUE Was Title VII violated?

ETHICS CASE

12.4 *Dothard, Director, Department of Public Safety of Alabama v. Rawlinson*

433 U.S. 321, 97 S.Ct. 2720, 1977 U.S. Lexis 143 (1977)
Supreme Court of the United States

FACTS Dianne Rawlinson, 22 years old, was a college graduate whose major course of study was correctional psychology. After graduation, she applied for a position as a correctional counselor (prison guard) with the Alabama Board of Corrections. Her application was rejected because she failed to meet the minimum 120-pound weight requirement of an Alabama statute that also established a height minimum of 5 feet 2 inches. In addition, the Alabama Board of Corrections adopted Administrative Regulation 204, which established gender criteria for assigning correctional counselors to maximum-security prisons for "contact positions." These are correctional counselor positions that require continual close physical proximity to inmates. Under this rule, Rawlinson did not qualify for contact positions with male prisoners in Alabama maximum-security prisons. Rawlinson brought this class action lawsuit against Dothard, who was the director of the Department of Public Safety of Alabama.

ISSUE Does either the height–weight requirement or the contact position rule constitute a bona fide occupational qualification that justifies the sexual discrimination in this case? Does society owe a duty of social responsibility to protect women from dangerous job positions? Or is this "romantic paternalism"?

13 Credit, Suretyship, and Bankruptcy

Creditors have better memories than debtors. —BENJAMIN FRANKLIN, *POOR RICHARD'S ALMANACK* (1758)

CHAPTER OBJECTIVES

After studying this chapter, you should be able to

1. Distinguish between unsecured and secured credit.
2. Describe security interests in real and personal property.
3. Define and distinguish between surety and guaranty contracts.
4. Explain Chapter 7 liquidation bankruptcy and Chapter 13 consumer debt adjustment bankruptcy.
5. Describe how a business is reorganized in Chapter 11 bankruptcy.

CHAPTER OUTLINE

- Unsecured and Secured Credit
- Security Interests in Real Property
- Security Interests in Personal Property
- Case for Discussion: *In Re Greenbelt Cooperative, Inc.*
- Surety and Guaranty Arrangements
- Federal Bankruptcy Law
- Case for Discussion: *General Motors Acceptance Corporation v. Daniels*
- Chapter 7 Bankruptcy
- Case for Discussion: *In Re Witwer*
- Case for Discussion: *Kawaauhau v. Geiger*
- Chapter 13 Bankruptcy
- Chapter 11 Bankruptcy
- Legal Terminology
- Chapter Summary
- Internet Exercises and Cases

INTRODUCTION

The American economy is a credit economy. Consumers borrow money to make major purchases (e.g., homes, automobiles, and appliances) and use credit cards (e.g., VISA and MasterCard) to purchase goods and services at restaurants, clothing stores, and the like. Businesses use **credit** to purchase equipment, supplies, and other goods and services. In a credit transaction, the **borrower** is the **debtor** and the **lender** is the **creditor.**

Because lenders are reluctant to lend large sums of money simply on the borrower's promise to repay, many of them take a *security interest* either in the item purchased or some other property of the debtor. The property in which the security interest is taken is called **collateral.** If the debtor does not pay the debt, the creditor can foreclose on and recover the collateral.

On occasion, borrowers become overextended and are unable to meet their debt obligations. The founders of our country thought the plight of debtors was so important that they included a provision in the U.S. Constitution giving Congress the authority to establish uniform bankruptcy laws. The goal of federal bankruptcy law is to give debtors, both individuals and businesses, a "fresh start" by relieving them from legal responsibility for some past debts.

The information in this chapter covers unsecured and secured credit, suretyship, bankruptcy, and reorganization.

Unsecured and Secured Credit

Credit may be extended on either an *unsecured* or a *secured* basis. The following paragraphs discuss these types of credit.

Unsecured Credit

Unsecured credit does not require any security (collateral) to protect the payment of the debt. Instead, the creditor relies on the debtor's promise to repay the principal (plus any interest) when it is due. If the debtor fails to make the payments, the creditor may bring legal action and obtain a judgment against him or her. If the debtor is *judgment-proof* (i.e., has little or no property or no income that can be garnished), the creditor may never collect.

Klondike Bar's Unsecured Claim Melts

Generally, a creditor would rather be a secured creditor than an unsecured creditor because of the extra protection and priority status the secured position gives the creditor. The following case shows why.

Sunstate Dairy & Food Products Co. (Sunstate) distributed dairy products in Florida. It had the following two debts among its other debts:

1. On November 19, 1990, Sunstate borrowed money from Barclays Business Credit, Inc. (Barclays) and signed a security agreement granting Barclays a continuing security interest in and lien upon substantially all of Sunstate's personal property, including all of Sunstate's inventory, equipment, accounts receivable, and general intangibles then existing or thereafter acquired. Barclays perfected its security interest by filing a financing statement with the proper state government authorities.
2. On February 14, 1992, Sunstate purchased $49,512 of Klondike ice cream bars from Isaly Klondike Company (Klondike) on credit. Klondike did not take a security interest in the ice cream bars.

On February 19, 1992, Sunstate filed for bankruptcy. At that time, Sunstate owed Barclays $10,050,766, and $47,731 of unpaid-for Klondike bars remaining in Sunstate's possession. Barclays and Klondike fought over the Klondike bars. Klondike filed a motion with the court seeking to reclaim the Klondike bars. Barclays sought to enforce its security agreement against Sunstate and recover the Klondike bars in Sunstate's possession.

The court sided with Barclays because it was a secured creditor with a perfected security interest. The court found that Klondike, as an unsecured creditor, had no legal right to reclaim the Klondike bars. Klondike was merely one of many unsecured general creditors that would receive but pennies on the dollar in Sunstate's bankruptcy. Klondike learned a costly lesson: It is better to be a **secured creditor** than an **unsecured creditor.**

In the Matter of Sunstate Dairy & Food Products Co., 145 B.R. 341, 1992 Banks. Lexis 1496 (Bk.M.D. Fla.)

Secured Credit

To minimize the risk associated with extending unsecured credit, a creditor may require a security interest in the debtor's property (collateral). The collateral secures payment of the loan. This type of credit is called **secured credit.** Security interests may be taken in real, personal, intangible, and other property.

If the debtor fails to make the payments when due, the creditor may repossess the collateral to recover the outstanding amount. Generally, if the sale of the collateral is insufficient to repay the amount of the loan (plus any interest), the creditor may bring a lawsuit against the debtor to recover a **deficiency judgment** for the difference. Some states prohibit or limit deficiency judgments with respect to certain types of loans.

Security Interests in Real Property

Owners of real estate can create security interests in their property. This occurs if the owner borrows money from a lender and pledges real estate as security for repayment of the loan. Security interests in real estate are discussed in the following paragraphs.

Small debts are like small shot; they are rattling on every side, and can scarcely be escaped without a wound; great debts are like cannon; of loud noise, but little danger.

—Samuel Johnson

Mortgages

A person who owns a piece of real property has an ownership interest in that property. This interest is generally described in a writing known as a *deed.* A property owner who borrows money from a creditor may use this interest as collateral for repayment of the loan. This type of collateral arrangement, known as a **mortgage,** is a *two-party instrument.* The *owner-debtor* is the **mortgagor,** and the *creditor* is the **mortgagee.** The parties to a mortgage are illustrated in Exhibit 13.1.

Suppose General Electric purchases a manufacturing plant for $10 million, pays $2 million cash as a down payment, and borrows the remaining $8 million from City Bank. To secure the loan, City Bank requires General Electric to give it a mortgage on the plant. If General Electric defaults on the loan, the bank may take action under state law to foreclose on the property.

Notes and Deeds of Trust

Some state laws provide for the use of a *deed of trust* and **note** in place of a mortgage. The note is the instrument that evidences the borrower's debt to the lender; the **deed of trust** is the instrument that gives the creditor a security interest in the debtor's property that is pledged as collateral.

EXHIBIT 13.1 *Parties to a mortgage.*

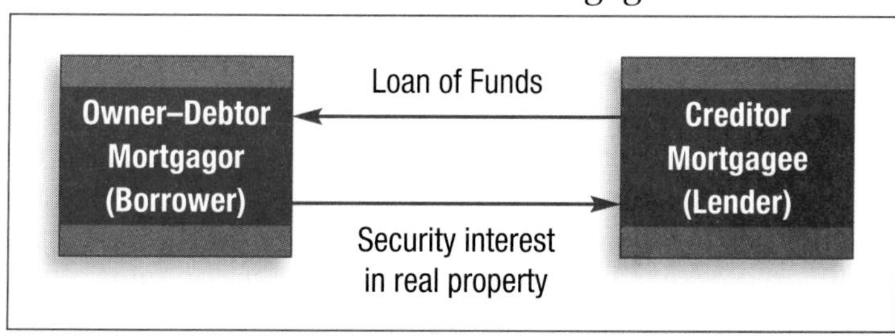

EXHIBIT 13.2 *Parties to a note and deed of trust.*

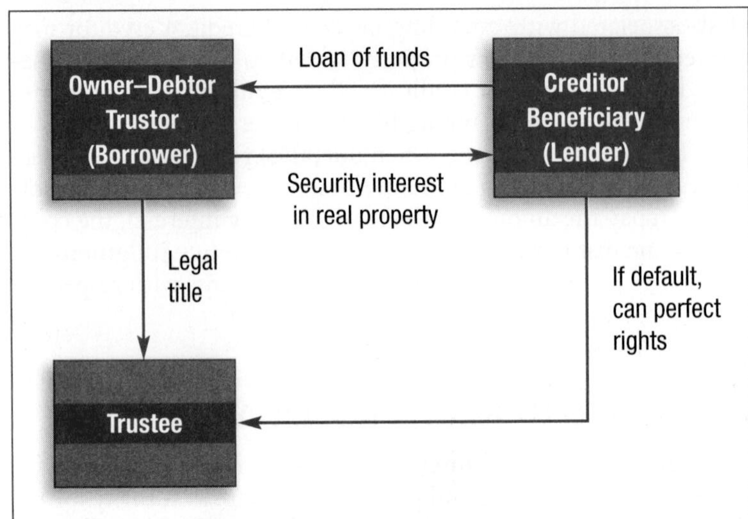

A deed of trust is a *three-party instrument.* Under it, legal title to the real property is placed with a **trustee** (usually a trust corporation) until the amount borrowed has been paid. The *owner–debtor* is called the **trustor.** Although legal title is vested in the trustee, the trustor has full legal rights to possession of the real property. The *creditor* is called the **beneficiary.** Exhibit 13.2 illustrates the relationship between the parties.

Recording Statutes

Most states have enacted **recording statutes** that require the mortgage or deed of trust to be recorded in the county recorder's office of the county in which the real property is located. This record gives potential lenders or purchasers of real property the ability to determine whether there are any existing liens (mortgages) on the property.

The nonrecordation of a mortgage or deed of trust does not affect either the legality of the instrument between the mortgagor and the mortgagee or the rights and obligations of the parties. In other words, the mortgagor is obligated to pay the amount of the mortgage according to the terms of the mortgage even if the document is not recorded. However, an improperly recorded document is not effective against either (1) subsequent purchasers of the real property, or (2) other mortgagees or lienholders who have no notice of the prior mortgages.

Suppose Debbie Brown purchases a house for $100,000. She borrows $75,000 from Country Bank and gives the bank a mortgage on the house for this amount. Country Bank fails to record the mortgage. Brown contracts to sell the house to Edward Johnson. He reviews the recordings and finds no mortgage against the property. Johnson pays $125,000 cash to Brown for the house. Brown defaults on her loan from Country Bank. In this case, Country Bank cannot foreclose because it failed to record the mortgage. Johnson owns the house free of Country Bank's mortgage. The bank's only recourse is to sue Brown to recover the amount of the loan (if she can be found).

Foreclosure

If a mortgagor defaults on a mortgage, the mortgagee can declare the entire debt due and payable immediately. This right can be enforced through a procedure called **foreclosure.**

All states permit *foreclosure sales.* Under this method, the debtor's default may trigger a legal court action for foreclosure. Any party having an interest in the property—including owners of the property and other mortgagees or lienholders—must be named as a defendant. If the mortgagee's case is successful, the court will issue a judgment that orders the real property to be sold at a judicial sale. The procedures for a foreclosure action and sale are mandated by state statute. Any surplus must be paid to the mortgagor.

Most states permit foreclosure by *power of sale*, although this must be expressly conferred in the mortgage or deed of trust. Under a power of sale, the procedure for that sale is contained in the mortgage or deed of trust itself. No court action is necessary. Some states have enacted statutes that establish the procedure for conducting the sale. Such a sale must be by auction for the highest price obtainable. Any surplus must be paid to the mortgagor.

> I will pay you some, and, as most debtors do, promise you infinitely.
>
> —William Shakespeare, *Henry IV*, Pt. II

Deficiency Judgments

Some states permit the mortgagee to bring a separate legal action to recover a deficiency from the mortgagor. If the mortgagee is successful, the court will award a deficiency judgment that entitles the mortgagee to recover the amount of the judgment from the mortgagor's property.

Several states have enacted statutes that prohibit deficiency judgments regarding certain types of mortgages, such as those on residential property. These statutes are called **antideficiency statutes.**

Consider this example: Kaye buys a house in San Francisco, puts $100,000 down, and borrows $300,000 of the purchase price from a bank, which takes a deed of trust on the property to secure the loan. Suppose that Kaye defaults, and when the bank forecloses on the property, it is worth only $240,000. The bank cannot recover the $60,000 deficiency from Kaye because California has an antideficiency statute.

Material Person's Liens

Owners of real property often hire contractors and laborers (e.g., painters, plumbers, roofers, bricklayers, furnace installers, and the like) to make improvements to that property. The contractors and laborers expend the time to provide their services as well as money to provide the materials for the improvements. Their investments are protected by state statutes that permit them to file a **material person's lien** (sometimes called a mechanic's lien) against the improved real property.

When a lien is properly filed, the real property to which the improvements have been made becomes security for the payment of these services and materials. In essence, the lienholder has the equivalent of a mortgage on the property. If the owner defaults, the lienholder may foreclose on the lien, sell the property, and satisfy the debt plus interest and costs out of the proceeds of the sale. Any surplus must be paid to the owner–debtor.

Generally, the lien must be foreclosed on during a specific period of time (commonly 6 months to 2 years) from the date the lien is filed. Material person's liens are usually subject to the debtor's right of redemption.

Security Interests in Personal Property

Article 9 of the Uniform Commercial Code governs secured transactions in personal property. Article 9 has been adopted in one form or another by all states except Louisiana. Although there may be some variance between the states, most of the basics of Article 9 are the same.

When a creditor extends credit to a debtor and takes a security interest in some personal property of the debtor, the transaction is called a **secured transaction.** The **secured party** is the seller, lender, or other party in whose favor there is a security interest, including a party to whom accounts or chattel paper have been sold [UCC 9-105(1)].

Exhibit 13.3 illustrates a two-party secured transaction. These transactions occur, for example, when a seller sells goods to a buyer on credit and retains a security interest in the goods.

A *three-party secured transaction* is illustrated in Exhibit 13.4. This type of situation occurs where a seller sells goods to a buyer who has obtained financing from a third-party lender (e.g., bank) who takes a security interest in the goods sold.

EXHIBIT 13.3 *Two-party secured transaction.*

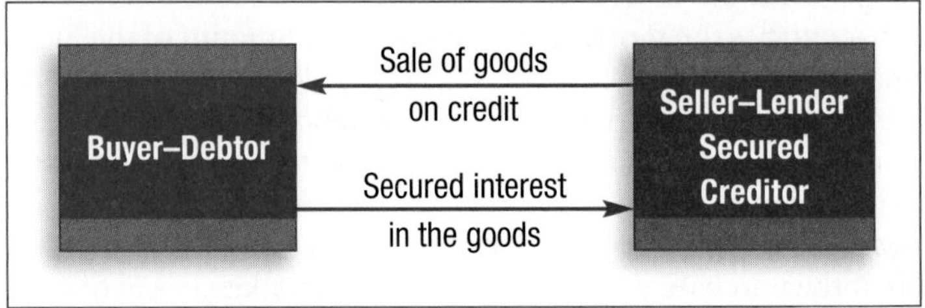

EXHIBIT 13.4 *Three-party secured transaction.*

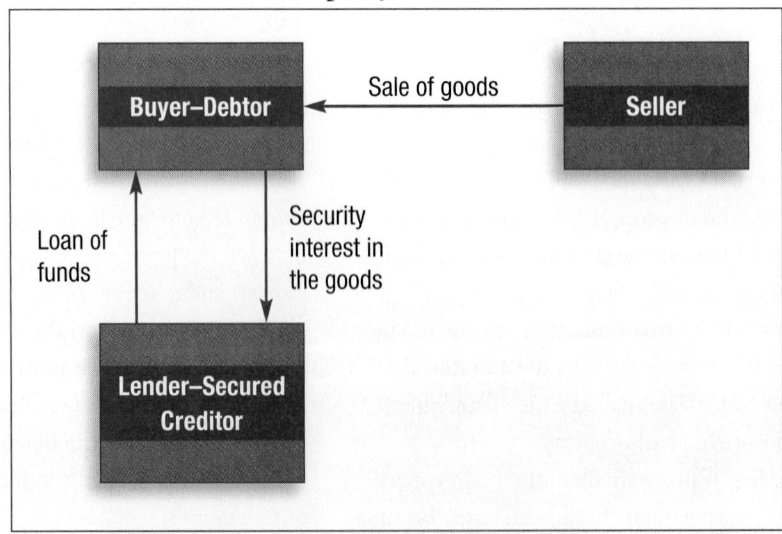

Written Security Agreement

Unless the creditor has possession of the collateral, there must be a written security agreement. To be valid, a written **security agreement** must (1) clearly describe the collateral so that it can be readily identified, (2) contain the debtor's promise to repay the creditor, including terms of repayment (e.g., the interest rate, time of payment), (3) set forth the creditor's rights upon the debtor's default, and (4) be signed by the debtor [UCC 9-203(1)].

Suppose Ashley borrows $1,000 from Chris and gives Chris her gold ring as security for the loan. This agreement does not have to be in writing because the creditor is in possession of the collateral. This oral security agreement is enforceable. If Ashley retained possession of the ring, however, a written security interest describing the collateral (the ring) signed by Ashley would be required.

Perfection by Filing a Financing Statement

Often, the creditor's physical possession of the collateral is impractical because it would deprive the debtor of use of the collateral (e.g., farm equipment, industrial machinery, and consumer goods). At other times, it is simply impossible (e.g., accounts receivable). Filing a **financing statement** in the appropriate government office is the most common method of perfecting a creditor's security interest in such collateral. The person who files the financing statement should request the filing officer to note on his or her copy of the document the file number, date, and hour of filing [UCC 9-402(1)]. A financing statement covering fixtures is called a *fixture filing.*

Debt rolls a man over and over, binding him hand and foot, and letting him hang upon the fatal mesh until the long-legged interest devours him.

—Henry Ward Beecher

Financing statements are available for review by the public. They serve as constructive notice to the world that the creditor claims an interest in the property. Financing statements are effective for 5 years from the date of filing. A *continuation statement* may be filed up to 6 months prior to the expiration of the financing statement's five-year term. Such statements are effective for a new 5-year term. Succeeding continuation statements may be filed [UCC 9-403(2) and (3)].

To be enforceable, the financing statement must contain (1) the debtor's name and mailing address, (2) the name and address of the secured party from whom information concerning the security interest can be obtained, and (3) a statement (preferably exactly as shown in the security agreement) indicating the types, or describing the items, of collateral. The secured party can file the security agreement as a financing statement [UCC 9-402(1)].

State law specifies where the financing statement must be filed. The UCC provides that a state may choose either the secretary of state or the county clerk in the county of the debtor's residence or, if the debtor is not a resident of the state, in the county where the goods are kept or other county office, or both. Most states require financing statements covering farm equipment, farm products, accounts, and consumer goods to be filed with the county clerk [UCC 9-401].

Perfection by Possession of Collateral

No financing statement has to be filed if the creditor has physical **possession of the collateral.** The rationale behind this rule is that if someone other than the debtor is in possession of the property, a potential creditor is on notice that another may claim an interest in the debtor's property. A secured creditor who holds the debtor's property as collateral must use reasonable care in its custody and preservation [UCC 9-207].

CASE FOR DISCUSSION

In Re Greenbelt Cooperative, Inc.

124 B.R. 465, 1991 Bankr. Lexis 233 (1991) United States Bankruptcy Court, Maryland

FACTS

Greenbelt Cooperative, Inc. (Greenbelt) was a consumer-owned cooperative engaged in the retail furniture business. It engaged in the business under the trade name SCAN, and it was well known among consumers by that name. On May 4, 1987, Greenbelt executed an Equipment Lease and Security Agreement with Raymond Leasing Corporation (Raymond) to lease forklifts and other items. At the conclusion of the lease term, Greenbelt could purchase the equipment for $1. On July 6, 1987, Raymond filed a financing statement covering the equipment in the proper state government office. Raymond listed "SCAN Furniture" as the debtor on the financing statement. On December 4, 1988, Greenbelt filed for bankruptcy. The bankruptcy trustee made a motion to avoid Raymond's claimed security interest in the equipment.

ISSUE

Did Raymond properly identify the debtor on the financing statement?

COURT'S REASONING

For a financing statement to be effective, the UCC requires that it be filed under the legal name of the debtor or under a name that is substantially similar to the legal name of the debtor so that it would not mislead a reasonably diligent creditor searching the financing records. The court held that a filing under SCAN Furniture would not be found by those looking for security interests in the assets of Greenbelt Cooperative, Inc. Consequently, Raymond's financing statement was not sufficient to perfect its security interests in Greenbelt's assets.

DECISION AND REMEDY

The bankruptcy court held that Raymond failed to identify the actual debtor in its financing statement. The court voided Raymond's lien on the equipment.

QUESTIONS

1. Should creditors searching financing records be required to search for financing statements filed under the debtor's trade names as well as its legal name?
2. Did the bankruptcy trustee act ethically in avoiding the secured creditor's security interest?
3. Was the filing of the financing statement under the wrong name an error that could easily have been prevented?

Super-Priority Liens

If a worker in the ordinary course of business furnishes services or materials to someone with respect to goods and receives a lien on the goods by statute or rule of law, this **artisan's lien** or **mechanic's lien** prevails over all other security interests in the goods unless a statutory lien provides otherwise. Thus, such liens are often called *super-priority liens* [UCC 9-310].

Suppose Janice borrows money from First Bank to purchase an automobile. First Bank has a purchase money security interest in the car and files a financing statement. The automobile is involved in an accident and Janice takes the car to Joe's Repair Shop (Joe's) to be repaired. Joe's retains a mechanic's lien in the car for the amount of the repair work. When the repair work is completed, Janice refuses to pay. She also defaults on her payments to First Bank. If the car is sold to satisfy the liens, the mechanic's lien is paid in full from the proceeds before First Bank is paid anything.

Surety and Guaranty Arrangements

Sometimes a creditor refuses to extend credit to a debtor unless a third person agrees to become liable on the debt. The third person's credit becomes the security for the credit extended to the debtor. This relationship may be either a surety or a guaranty arrangement. Each of these arrangements is discussed in the following paragraphs.

Surety Arrangement

In a strict **surety arrangement,** a third person—known as the **surety** or **codebtor**—promises to be liable for the payment of another person's debt. A person who acts as a surety is commonly called an **accommodation party** or **cosigner.** Along with the principal debtor, the surety is primarily liable for paying the principal debtor's debt when it is due. The principal debtor does not have to be in default on the debt, and the creditor does not have to have exhausted all its remedies against the principal debtor before seeking payment from the surety.

Debt is the prolific mother of folly and of crime.

—Benjamin Disraeli

Guaranty Arrangement

In a **guaranty arrangement,** a third person—the **guarantor**—agrees to pay the debt of the principal debtor if the debtor defaults and does not pay the debt when it is due. In this type of arrangement, the guarantor is secondarily liable on the debt. In other words, the guarantor is obligated to pay the debt only if the principal debtor defaults and the creditor has attempted unsuccessfully to collect the debt from the debtor.

Federal Bankruptcy Law

Article I, Section 8, clause 4 of the U.S. Constitution provides that "The Congress shall have the power . . . to establish . . . uniform laws on the subject of bankruptcies throughout the United States." Congress enacted the original Bankruptcy Act in 1878. The law was completely revised by the **Bankruptcy Reform Act of 1978** [11 U.S.C. §§ 101-1330]. The 1978 Act established the requirements and procedures for filing bankruptcy.

CASE FOR DISCUSSION

General Motors Acceptance Corporation v. Daniels

492 A.2d 1306, 1985 Md. Lexis 596 (1985) Court of Appeals of Maryland

FACTS

In June 1981, John Daniels agreed to purchase a used automobile from Lindsay Cadillac Company (Lindsay Cadillac). Because John had a poor credit rating, his brother, Seymour, agreed to cosign with him. General Motors Acceptance Corporation (GMAC), a company engaged in the business of financing automobiles, agreed to finance the purchase. On June 23, 1981, Seymour accompanied John to Lindsay Cadillac. John signed the contract on the line designated "Buyer." Seymour signed the contract on the line designated "Co-Buyer." In May 1982, GMAC declared the contract in default. After attempting to locate the automobile for several months, GMAC brought this action against the Daniels brothers. Because service of process was never effected upon John, the case proceeded to trial against only Seymour. The trial court found that Seymour had entered into a guaranty contract and that Seymour was not liable because GMAC had not yet proceeded against John. GMAC appealed.

ISSUE

Was the contract Seymour signed a guaranty or surety contract?

COURT'S REASONING

If the contract Seymour signed was a guaranty contract, he would have been only secondarily liable on his brother's loan. This situation was not true in this case, however, because Seymour signed the contract on the line on the contract designated "Co-Buyer." The contract clearly stated that all buyers agreed to be jointly and severally liable for the purchase of the vehicle. Seymour executed the same contract as his brother, thereby making himself a party to the original contract. These facts establish the existence of a surety contract upon which Seymour became primarily liable.

DECISION AND REMEDY

The court of appeals held that Seymour signed a surety contract and thus agreed to be primarily liable with his brother John for the purchase of the automobile. GMAC was therefore not required to proceed against John in the first instance. The court of appeals reversed the decision of the trial court, and held that Seymour was liable as a surety co-buyer to GMAC for his brother John's car loan.

QUESTIONS

1. What purposes do guaranty and surety contracts serve? Explain.
2. Did Seymour act ethically in trying to avoid liability for his brother's loan?
3. As a lender, would you rather have a third party sign as a surety or guarantor?

Several years later, Congress enacted the **Bankruptcy Amendments and Federal Judgeship Act of 1984.** This Act made bankruptcy courts part of the federal district court system and attached a bankruptcy court to each district court. Bankruptcy courts have exclusive jurisdiction to hear bankruptcy cases. Bankruptcy judges are appointed by the President for 14-year terms.

"Fresh Start"

The primary purpose of federal bankruptcy law is to discharge the debtor from burdensome debts. The law gives debtors a **fresh start** by freeing them from legal responsibility for past debts by (1) protecting debtors from abusive activities by creditors in collecting debts, (2) preventing certain creditors from obtaining an unfair advantage over other creditors, (3) protecting creditors from actions of the debtor that would diminish the value of the bankruptcy estate, (4) providing for the speedy, efficient, and equitable distribution of the debtor's nonexempt property to claim holders, and (5) preserving existing business relations.

It is the policy of the law that the debtor be just before he be generous.

—J. Finch,
Hearn 45 St. Corp. v. Jano (1940)

Types of Bankruptcy

The Bankruptcy Code is divided into chapters. The most common forms of bankruptcy are provided by the following chapters: Chapter 7 (liquidation), Chapter 11 (reorganization), and Chapter 13 (consumer debt adjustment). The remaining chapters of the Bankruptcy Code govern the bankruptcies of municipalities, stockbrokers, and railroads.

Chapter 7 Liquidation Bankruptcy

Chapter 7 liquidation bankruptcy (also called *straight bankruptcy*) is the most familiar form of bankruptcy. In this type of proceeding, the debtor's nonexempt property is sold for cash, the cash is distributed to the creditors, and any unpaid debts are **discharged.** Any entity, including person, individual partnership, and corporation, may be a debtor in a Chapter 7 proceeding.

Filing a Petition

A Chapter 7 bankruptcy is commenced when a **petition** is filed with the bankruptcy court. The petition may be filed by either the debtor (voluntary) or by one or more creditors (involuntary). **Voluntary petitions** only have to state that the debtor has debts; insolvency (i.e., that debts exceed assets) need not be declared. The petition must include the following schedules:

1. A list of secured and unsecured creditors, including their addresses and the amount of debt owed to each,
2. A list of all property owned by the debtor, including property claimed to be exempt by the debtor,
3. A statement of the financial affairs of the debtor,
4. A list of the debtor's current income and expenses.

The petition must be signed and sworn to under oath. Married couples may file a joint petition.

An **involuntary petition** can be filed against any debtors who can file a voluntary petition. An involuntary petition must allege that the debtor is not paying his or her debts as they become due.

Automatic Stay

The filing of a voluntary or an involuntary petition automatically stays—that is, suspends—certain action by creditors against the debtor or the debtor's property. This is called an **automatic stay.** The stay, which applies to collection efforts of secured and unsecured creditors alike, is designed to prevent a scramble of the debtor's assets in a variety of court proceedings. The following creditor actions are stayed:

Beggars can never be bankrupts.
—Thomas Fuller

1. Instituting or maintaining legal actions to collect prepetition debts.
2. Enforcing judgments obtained against the debtor.
3. Obtaining, perfecting, or enforcing liens against property of the debtor.
4. Attempting to set off debts owed by the creditor to the debtor against the creditor's claims in bankruptcy.
5. Nonjudicial collection efforts, such as self-help activities (e.g., repossession of a car).

Property of the Bankruptcy Estate

The **bankruptcy estate** is created upon the commencement of a Chapter 7 proceeding. It includes all the debtor's legal and equitable interests in real, personal, tangible, and intangible property, wherever located, that exist when the petition is filed. The debtor's separate and community property are included in the estate.

Property acquired after the petition does not become part of the bankruptcy estate. The only exceptions are gifts, inheritances, life insurance proceeds, and property from divorce settlements that the debtor is entitled to receive within 180 days after the petition is filed. Earnings from property of the estate—such as rents, dividends, and interest payments—are property of the estate.

Exempt Property

Because the Bankruptcy Code is not designed to make the debtor a pauper, certain property is exempt from the bankruptcy estate. The debtor may retain **exempt property.**

The Bankruptcy Code establishes a *federal* exemption scheme (see Exhibit 13.5).

State Law Exemptions

The Bankruptcy Code also permits states to enact their own exemptions. States that do so may (1) give debtors the option of choosing between federal and state exemptions or (2) require debtors to follow state law. The exemptions available under state law are often quite liberal. For example, homestead exemptions are often higher under state law than under the federal exemption scheme. Many states require the debtor to file a **Declaration of Homestead** prior to bankruptcy. This document is usually filed in the county recorder's office in the county in which the property is located.

Voidable Transfers

The Bankruptcy Code prevents debtors from making unusual payments or transfers of property on the eve of bankruptcy that would unfairly benefit the debtor or some creditors at the expense of others. Voidable transactions include:

EXHIBIT 13.5 *Federal exemptions from the bankruptcy estate.*

1. Interest up to $17,425 in equity in property used as a residence and burial plots (called the "homestead exemption")
2. Interest up to $2,775 in value in one motor vehicle
3. Interest up to $450 per item in household goods and furnishings, wearing apparel, appliances, books, animals, crops, or musical instruments, up to an aggregate value of $9,300 for all items
4. Interest in jewelry up to $1,150
5. Interest in any property the debtor chooses (including cash) up to $925, plus up to $8,725 of any unused portion of the $17,425 homestead exemption
6. Interest up to $1,750 in value in implements, tools, or professional books used in the debtor's trade
7. Any unmatured life insurance policy owned by the debtor
8. Professionally prescribed health aids
9. Many government benefits, regardless of value, including Social Security benefits, unemployment compensation, veteran's benefits, disability benefits, and public assistance benefits
10. Certain rights to receive income, including alimony and support payments, certain pension benefits, profit sharing, and annuity payments
11. Interests in wrongful death benefits, life insurance proceeds, and personal injury awards (up to $17,425)

- **Preferential transfers to insiders:** The Bankruptcy Code provides that preferential transfers and liens made to "insiders" within one year of the filing of the petition in bankruptcy may be avoided by the court. **Insiders** are defined as relatives, partners, partnerships, officers and directors of a corporation, corporations, and others who have a relationship with the debtor. To avoid a transfer to an insider within a one-year period, the trustee must prove that the debtor was insolvent at the time of the transfer.
- **Preferential liens:** Debtors sometimes attempt to favor certain unsecured creditors on the eve of bankruptcy by giving them a secured interest in property. This type of interest is called a **preferential lien.** Preferential liens occur when (1) the debtor gives the creditor a secured interest in property within 90 days of petition, (2) the secured interest is given for a preexisting debt, and (3) the creditor would receive more because of this lien than it would as an unsecured creditor in liquidation.

Debtors are liars.

—George Herbert

Priority of Distribution

Under Chapter 7, the nonexempt property of the bankruptcy estate must be distributed to the debtor's secured and unsecured creditors. The statutory priority of distribution is discussed in the following paragraphs.

Secured creditors. The claim of a secured creditor to the debtor's property has priority over the claims of unsecured creditors. The secured creditor may (1) accept the collateral in full satisfaction of the debt, (2) foreclose on the collateral and

CASE FOR DISCUSSION

In Re Witwer

148 B.R. 930, 1992 Bankr. Lexis 1926 (1992) **United States Bankruptcy Court, Central District of California**

FACTS

Dr. James J. Witwer is the sole stockholder, sole employee, and president of James J. Witwer, M.D., Inc., a California corporation under which he practices medicine. He is also the sole beneficiary of the corporation's retirement plan, which was established in 1970. On October 21, 1991, Witwer filed a voluntary petition for relief under Chapter 7 (liquidation). At the time, the value of the assets in his retirement plan was $1.8 million. California law exempted retirement plans from a debtor's bankruptcy estate. When Witwer claimed that his retirement plan was exempt from the bankruptcy estate, several creditors filed objections.

ISSUE

Is Witwer's retirement plan exempt from the bankruptcy estate?

COURT'S REASONING

Under California law, the assets of a retirement plan are entirely exempt if the plan was designed and used for retirement purposes. The bankruptcy court found that the retirement plan established by Witwer fit this exemption. The court stated that although "Allowing the debtor to retain over $1.8 million in retirement benefits in bankruptcy while being discharged from debts legitimately owed to creditors seems fundamentally unfair," under the law Witwer's retirement plan was beyond the reach of his creditors.

DECISION AND REMEDY

The bankruptcy court held that Witwer's retirement plan is fully exempt from his bankruptcy estate.

QUESTIONS

1. Do you think bankruptcy law was intended to reach the result in this case?
2. Was it ethical for the debtor to declare bankruptcy and wipe out his unsecured creditors while retaining $1.8 million in his retirement account?
3. Should businesspeople establish and fund retirement programs?

use the proceeds to pay the debt, or (3) allow the trustee to retain the collateral, dispose of it at a sale, and remit the proceeds of the sale to him or her. If the value of the collateral exceeds the secured interest, the excess becomes available to satisfy the claims of the debtor's unsecured creditors. Before the excess funds are released, however, the secured creditor is allowed to deduct reasonable fees and costs resulting from the default. If the value of the collateral is less than the secured interest, the secured creditor becomes an unsecured creditor to the difference.

Unsecured creditors. The Bankruptcy Code stipulates that unsecured claims are to be satisfied out of the bankruptcy estate in the order of their statutory priority. The statutory priority of an unsecured claim is as follows.

1. Fees and expenses of administrating the estate, including court costs, trustee fees, attorneys' fees, appraisal fees, and other costs of administration.
2. In an involuntary bankruptcy, secured claims of "gap" creditors who sold goods or services on credit to the debtor in the ordinary course of the debtor's business between the date of the filing of the petition and the date of the appointment of the trustee or issuance of the order for relief (whichever occurred first).
3. Unsecured claims for wages, salary, or commissions earned by the debtor's employees within 90 days immediately preceding the filing of the petition, up to $4,000 per employee; any claim exceeding $4,000 is treated as a claim of a general unsecured creditor (item 9 below).
4. Unsecured claims for contributions to employee benefit plans based on services performed within 180 days immediately preceding the filing of the petition, up to $4,000 per employee.
5. Farm producers and fishermen against debtors who operate grain storage facilities or fish produce storage or processing facilities, up to $4,000 per claim.
6. Unsecured claims for cash deposited by a consumer with the debtor prior to the filing of the petition in connection with the purchase, lease, or rental of property or the purchase of services that were not delivered or provided by the debtor, up to $1,800 per claim.
7. Debts owed for child support, paternity, alimony, and spousal support.
8. Certain tax obligations owed by the debtor to federal, state, and local governmental units.
9. Claims of general unsecured creditors.
10. If there is any balance remaining after the allowed claims of the creditors are satisfied, it is returned to the debtor.

Each class must be paid in full before any lower class is paid anything. If a class cannot be paid in full, the claims of that class are paid *pro rata* (proportionately).

Discharge

After the property is distributed to satisfy the allowed claims, the remaining unpaid claims are discharged (i.e., the debtor is no longer legally responsible for them). Only individuals may be granted a discharge. Discharge is not available to partnerships and corporations. These entities must liquidate under state law before or upon completion of the Chapter 7 proceeding. A debtor can be granted a discharge in a Chapter 7 proceeding only once every 6 years.

SIDEBAR

Discharge of Student Loans

In the past, many students who borrowed a lot of money in student loans sought to avoid paying back their loans by filing a voluntary petition for bankruptcy immediately on leaving college. Section 523(a)(8) of the Bankruptcy Code was enacted to prevent this practice. For any bankruptcy case commenced after October 7, 1998, Section 523(a)(8)(A) mandates that student loans can be discharged in bankruptcy only if nondischarge would cause an "undue hardship" to the debtor and his or her dependents. [Higher Education Amendments of 1998, P. L. 105-244]. Undue hardship is construed strictly and would include not being able to pay for food or shelter for the debtor or the debtor's family. Cosigners (e.g., parents who guarantee their child's student loan) must also meet the heightened undue hardship test to discharge their obligation.

CASE FOR DISCUSSION

Kawaauhau v. Geiger

523 U.S. 57, 118 S.Ct. 974, 1998 U.S. Lexis 1595 (1998) Supreme Court of the United States

FACTS

Margaret Kawaauhau sought treatment from Dr. Paul Geiger for a foot injury. Geiger examined Kawaauhau and admitted her to the hospital to attend to the risks of infection. Although Geiger knew that intravenous penicillin would have been the more effective treatment, he prescribed oral penicillin, explaining that he thought that his patient wished to minimize the cost of her treatment. Geiger then departed on a business trip, leaving Kawaauhau in the care of other physicians. When Geiger returned, he discontinued all antibiotics because he believed that the infection had subsided. Kawaauhau's condition deteriorated over the next few days, requiring the amputation of her right leg below the knee. Kawaauhau and her husband sued Geiger for medical malpractice. The jury found Geiger liable and awarded the Kawaauhaus $355,000 in damages. Geiger, who carried no malpractice insurance, filed for bankruptcy in an attempt to discharge the judgment. The bankruptcy court denied discharge, and the district court agreed. The court of appeals reversed and allowed discharge, and the Kawaauhaus appealed to the U.S. Supreme Court.

ISSUE

Is a debt arising from a medical malpractice judgment that is attributable to negligence or reckless conduct dischargeable in bankruptcy?

COURT'S REASONING

Section 523(a)(6) of the Bankruptcy Code provides that a debt "for willful and malicious injury by the debtor to another" is not dischargeable. The question before the U.S. Supreme Court is whether a debt arising from a medical malpractice judgment, attributable to negligent or reckless conduct, falls within this statutory exception. The Supreme Court held that the exception that prohibits willful and malicious acts from being discharged in bankruptcy does not apply to debts arising from negligent or reckless conduct. Therefore, the Kawaauhaus' medical malpractice judgment against Dr. Geiger in this case can be discharged in Dr. Geiger's bankruptcy proceeding.

DECISION AND REMEDY

The U.S. Supreme Court ruled that a medical malpractice judgment based on negligent or reckless conduct—and not intentional conduct—is dischargeable in bankruptcy. The Supreme Court affirmed the judgment of the court of appeals allowing the discharge of the medical malpractice judgment.

QUESTIONS

1. What public policy is promoted by denying discharge for "willful" injurious conduct? Do you think Geiger's conduct was willful?
2. Was it ethical for Geiger to avoid liability to the Kawaauhaus by declaring bankruptcy?
3. What purpose is served by allowing individuals and businesses to declare bankruptcy? What are the business implications of bankruptcy laws?

Chapter 13 Consumer Debt Adjustment

Chapter 13 bankruptcy, which is called a **consumer debt adjustment,** is a rehabilitation form of bankruptcy for natural persons. Chapter 13 permits the court to supervise the debtor's plan for the payment of unpaid debts by installments.

The debtor has several advantages under Chapter 13. These include avoiding the stigma of Chapter 7 liquidation, retaining more property than is exempt under Chapter 7, and incurring less expense and less complication than a Chapter 7 proceeding. The creditors have advantages, too: They may recover a greater percentage of the debts owed them than they would under a Chapter 7 proceeding.

Filing the Petition

A Chapter 13 proceeding can be initiated only by the voluntary filing of a petition by a debtor who alleges that he or she is (1) insolvent, or (2) unable to pay his or her debts when they become due. The petition must state that the debtor desires to effect an extension or composition of debts, or both. An **extension** provides for a longer period of time for the debtor to pay his or her debts. A **composition** provides for a reduction of debts. Only individuals (including sole proprietors) with regular income who owe individually (or with their spouse) noncontingent, liquidated, unsecured debts of less than $250,000 and secured debts of less than $750,000 may file such a petition.

Plan of Payment

The debtor's plan of payment must be filed within 15 days of filing the petition. The debtor must file information about his or her finances, including a budget of estimated income and expenses during the period of the plan. The plan period cannot exceed 3 years unless the court approves a longer period (of up to 5 years). During the plan period, the debtor retains possession of his or her property, may acquire new property and incur debts, and so on. The debtor must begin making the planned installment payments to the trustee within 30 days after the plan is filed.

A trifling debt makes a man your debtor, a large one makes him your enemy.

—Seneca

Discharge

The court will grant an order discharging the debtor from all unpaid debts covered by the plan after all the payments required under the plan are completed. All debts are dischargeable under Chapter 13 except alimony and child support and priority debts such as trustee fees. Dischargeable debts include student loans, fraudulently incurred debts, and debts arising from malicious or willful injury from drunken driving. Thus, a Chapter 13 **discharge** may be more beneficial to a debtor than a Chapter 7 liquidation discharge.

Chapter 11 Reorganization Bankruptcy

Chapter 11 of the Bankruptcy Code provides a method for reorganizing the debtor's financial affairs under the supervision of the Bankruptcy Court. Its goal is to reorganize the debtor with a new capital structure so that it will emerge from bankruptcy as a viable concern. This option, which is referred to as **reorganization bankruptcy,** is often in the best interests of the debtor and its creditors.

SIDEBAR

Sarbanes-Oxley Act Imposes Criminal Penalties for Bankruptcy Fraud

When Congress enacted the Sarbanes-Oxley Act of 2002 to revise the corporate governance rules in this country, Congress included Section 802 in the Act to address the issue of hiding fraud that led to bankruptcies. Section 802 makes it a crime for anyone knowingly to alter, destroy, mutilate, conceal, cover up, falsify, or make a false entry in any record, document, or tangible object with the intent to impede, obstruct, or influence the investigation or proper administration of any matter in any bankruptcy case, or in relation to or in contemplation of a bankruptcy filing. A violation is punishable by a fine or imprisonment for not more than 20 years, or both.

Reorganization Proceeding

Chapter 11 is available to individuals, partnerships, corporations, nonincorporated associations, and railroads. It is not available to banks, savings and loan associations, credit unions, insurance companies, stockbrokers, or commodities brokers. The majority of Chapter 11 proceedings are filed by corporations. A Chapter 11 petition may be filed voluntarily by the debtor or involuntarily by its creditors.

Plan of Reorganization

The debtor has the exclusive right to file a **plan of reorganization** with the Bankruptcy Court within the first 120 days after the date of the order for relief. The debtor also has the right to obtain creditor approval of the plan within the first 180 days after the date of the order. After that, any party of interest (i.e., a trustee, a creditor, or an equity holder) may propose a plan. The court has discretion to extend the 120- and 180-day periods in complex cases.

The plan of reorganization sets forth the debtor's proposed new capital structure. In a Chapter 11 proceeding, creditors have claims and equity holders have interests. The plan must designate the different classes of claims and interests. The reorganization plan may propose altering the rights of creditors and equity holders. For example, it might require claims and interests to be reduced, the conversion of unsecured creditors to equity holders, the sale of assets, or the like. The final step is **confirmation of the plan of reorganization** by the court.

Executory Contracts

Under the Bankruptcy Code, the debtor-in-possession (or trustee) is given the authority to assume or reject **executory contracts** (i.e., contracts that are not fully performed by both sides). In general, unfavorable executory contracts will be rejected and favorable executory contracts will be assumed. For example, a debtor-in-possession may reject an unfavorable lease. Court approval is necessary to reject an executory contract. Executory contracts may also be rejected in Chapter 7 and Chapter 13 proceedings.

LEGAL TERMINOLOGY

Accommodation party
Antideficiency statute
Article 9 of the Uniform Commercial Code
Artisan's liens
Automatic stay
Bankruptcy Amendments and Federal Judgeship Act of 1984
Bankruptcy estate
Bankruptcy Reform Act of 1978
Beneficiary
Borrower
Chapter 7 liquidation bankruptcy
Chapter 11 reorganization bankruptcy
Chapter 13 consumer debt adjustment bankruptcy
Codebtor
Collateral
Composition
Confirmation of plan of reorganization
Consumer debt adjustment
Cosigner
Credit
Creditor

Kmart Emerges from Bankruptcy

The Kmart Corporation was founded in 1899 and became one of the most successful retailers in America. The company offered goods for sale at low prices and was famous for its spontaneous "Blue Light Special" sales offered to consumers while they were in Kmart stores. Kmart's business model consisted of building stores bigger than its competitors and offering for sale goods that it purchased at volume discounts from vendors. By 2000, Kmart had more than 2,100 stores nationwide.

Kmart's strategy worked for most of the twentieth century, until more formidable competition appeared—Wal-Mart and Target stores. Wal-Mart's larger warehouse stores and lower prices stole customers from Kmart. And Target offered more trendy brand names than Kmart. Kmart fought back but eventually lost the battle to these competitors. Kmart's shelves became emptier as many vendors refused to deliver goods to Kmart unless they were paid in cash.

In 2002, Kmart filed for Chapter 11 bankruptcy. It was the largest bankruptcy filed by a retailer in America. Once under the protection of the federal bankruptcy laws, Kmart used the executory contract rule, shed more than 300 leases on its worst-performing stores, and closed these stores. Kmart also used its bankruptcy reorganization to discharge billions of dollars of unpaid unsecured credit owed to creditors.

Kmart is a good example of how a financially troubled company can use Chapter 11 reorganization bankruptcy to rid itself of problem debts and obligations and have a "fresh start." Kmart emerged from bankruptcy with a leaner balance sheet and the ability to make a profit again. Once out of bankruptcy, creditors and vendors again sold goods to Kmart.

Creditor–beneficiary
Debtor
Declaration of Homestead
Deed of trust
Deficiency judgment
Discharge
Executory contract
Exempt property
Extension
Financing statement
Foreclosure
Fresh start
Guarantor
Guaranty arrangement
Insiders
Involuntary petition (for bankruptcy)
Lender
Material person's lien
Mechanic's lien
Mortgage
Mortgagee
Mortgagor
Note
Petition
Plan of reorganization
Possession of the collateral
Preferential lien
Prepackaged filing
Recording statute
Reorganization bankruptcy
Secured credit
Secured creditor
Secured party
Secured transaction
Security agreement
Surety
Surety arrangement
Trustee
Trustor
Unsecured credit
Unsecured creditor
Voidable transfer
Voluntary petition (for bankruptcy)

chapter summary

CREDIT, SURETYSHIP, AND BANKRUPTCY

Types of Credit	
Unsecured Credit	1. Credit that does not require any security (collateral) to protect the payment of the loan. 2. *Recovery of unpaid loan:* If the debtor does not pay the loan, the creditor may bring a legal action and obtain a *judgment* against the debtor. The debtor is called *judgment-proof* if he or she has no money to pay the judgment.
Secured Credit	1. Credit that requires security (collateral) that secures the payment of the loan. 2. *Collateral:* The property that is pledged as security for the loan.
Security Interests in Real Property	
Mortgage	1. *Mortgage:* The instrument that represents a security interest in real property. 2. *Mortgagor:* The owner–debtor who pledges his or her real property as security for a loan. 3. *Mortgagee:* The creditor who holds a security interest in the owner–debtor's real property.
Note and Deed of Trust	Some states use a note and deed of trust as an alternative to a mortgage. 1. *Note:* The instrument that evidences the debt. 2. *Deed of trust:* The instrument that gives the creditor a security interest in the owner–debtor's real property.
Recording Statutes	Permits copies of deeds and other documents concerning interests in real property (e.g., mortgages, liens) to be filed in a government office where they become public record. Puts third parties on notice of recorded interests.
Foreclosure	Method whereby if a mortgagor defaults on the payment on a mortgage, the mortgagee can declare the entire debt due and proceed to acquire title to the property that is collateral for the loan.
Deficiency Judgment	If, after foreclosure of the property, there is a deficiency owing, the mortgagee can sue the mortgagor to recover the amount of the deficiency.
Antideficiency Statute	Some states have enacted an antideficiency statute that prohibits a mortgagee from recovering a deficiency owed on a loan.
Material Person's Lien	Lien that is given by law to contractors and laborers on real property they make improvement on until the amount they are owed is paid.
Security Interests in Personal Property	
Article 9 of the UCC	An article of the Uniform Commercial Code that governs secured transactions in personal property.

Secured Transactions	Transactions that are created when a creditor makes a loan to a debtor in exchange for the debtor's pledge of personal property as security. 1. *Two-party secured transaction:* Seller sells goods to a buyer on credit and retains a security interest in the goods. 2. *Three-party secured transaction:* A seller sells goods to a buyer who has obtained financing from a third-party lender (e.g., bank) who takes a security interest in the goods sold. 3. A written security agreement is required.
Perfection of a Security Interest	Establishes the right of the secured creditor against other creditors who claim an interest in the collateral. The UCC provides the following two methods of perfecting a security interest. 1. *Perfection by filing a financing statement:* The creditor files a *financing statement* with the appropriate government recording office. This statement puts the world on notice of the creditor's security interest in the property. This method is the most common form of perfecting a security interest. 2. *Perfection by possession of collateral:* If the creditor has physical possession of the collateral, no financing statement has to be filed. This method is the least common form of perfecting a security interest.
Surety and Guaranty Arrangements	
Conditions	Both occur when a creditor refuses to extend credit to a debtor without further security and a third person agrees to provide that security by agreeing to become liable on the debt.
Surety Arrangement	A third party—called the *surety* or *codebtor*—promises to be liable for another person's debt. The surety is *primarily liable* for payment of the debt when it is due, along with the principal debtor. The creditor does not have to attempt to collect the debt from the principal debtor before demanding payment from the surety.
Guaranty Arrangement	A third party—called the *guarantor*—agrees to pay the debt of the principal debtor if the debtor *defaults* and does not pay the debt when it is due. The guarantor is *secondarily liable* and has to pay the debt only if the creditor has attempted unsuccessfully to collect the debt from the debtor.
Federal Bankruptcy Law	
Bankruptcy	1. *Bankruptcy Reform Act of 1978:* Federal statute that established the requirements and procedures for filing bankruptcy. 2. *Bankruptcy courts:* Have exclusive jurisdiction to hear bankruptcy cases. A bankruptcy court is attached to each federal district court. Bankruptcy judges are appointed for 14-year terms.
"Fresh Start"	The purpose of a bankruptcy is to discharge the debtor from burdensome debts. *(continued)*

Chapter 7 Liquidation Bankruptcy	
Description	The debtor's nonexempt property is sold for cash, the cash is distributed to the creditors, and any unpaid debts are discharged.
Bankruptcy Procedure	1. *Filing a petition:* The filing of a petition commences a bankruptcy case. a. *Voluntary petition:* Filed by the debtor. b. *Involuntary petition:* Filed by a creditor or creditors.
Automatic Stay	The filing of a bankruptcy petition *stays* (suspends) certain legal actions against the debtor or the debtor's property. A secured creditor may petition the court for a *relief from stay* in situations involving depreciating assets and the creditor is not adequately protected during the bankruptcy proceeding.
Property of the Bankruptcy Estate	*Bankruptcy estate* includes: 1. All the debtor's legal and equitable interests in real, personal, tangible, and intangible property at the time the petition is filed. 2. Gifts, inheritances, life insurance proceeds, and property from divorce settlements that the debtor is entitled to receive within 180 days after the petition is filed.
Exempt Property	The Bankruptcy Code permits the debtor to retain certain property that does not become part of the bankruptcy estate. Exemptions are stipulated in federal and state law.
Voidable Transfers	The following transfers and preferences are voidable by the trustee: 1. *Preferential transfer to an insider within one year before bankruptcy:* The transferee must be an "insider" (e.g., relative, business associate) and the creditor insolvent. 2. *Preferential liens within 90 days before bankruptcy:* Transfer must be for an antecedent debt, and the creditor would receive more because of this lien than he or she would as an unsecured creditor in bankruptcy.
Priority of Distribution	Nonexempt property of the bankruptcy estate is distributed to the creditors in the following statutory priority: 1. *Secured creditors:* Either a secured creditor obtains the collateral or the collateral is sold and the secured creditor is paid. If the value of the collateral exceeds the secured interest, the excess becomes available to pay other creditors. If the value of the collateral is less than the secured interest, the secured creditor becomes an unsecured creditor to the difference. 2. *Unsecured creditors:* Unsecured creditors are paid in priority established by the Bankruptcy Code. Each class must be paid in full before any lower class is paid anything. If a class cannot be paid in full, the claims of that class are paid pro rata (proportionately).
Discharge	After the nonexempt property is distributed, the remaining unpaid claims of the debtor are *discharged;* the debtor's legal obligation to pay these unpaid debts is terminated. Discharge is available only to individuals.

Discharge of Student Loans	A student loan may be discharged after it is due only if nondischarge would cause an *undue hardship* on the debtor or his or her family.
Chapter 13 Consumer Debt Adjustment	
Description	A rehabilitation form of bankruptcy that permits bankruptcy courts to supervise the debtor's plan for the repayment of unpaid debts by installment. Called *consumer debt adjustment* or *Chapter 13 bankruptcy*.
The Plan of Payment	The debtor must file a plan of payment. The plan period cannot exceed 3 years unless the court approves a longer period (of up to 5 years). A plan may be modified if the debtor's circumstances materially change. A permanent *trustee* will be appointed by the court. The debtor makes payments to the trustee, who is responsible for remitting payments to the creditors.
Discharge	The court will grant an order discharging the debtor from all unpaid debts covered by the plan only after all the payments required under the plan are completed. The court can grant the debtor a *hardship discharge* even if the debtor does not complete the payments called for by the plan if (1) the failure to make the payments was caused by an unforeseeable circumstance, (2) the creditors have been paid as much as they would have been paid in a Chapter 7 liquidation proceeding, and (3) it is not practical to modify the plan.
Chapter 11 Reorganization Bankruptcy	
Description	Provides a method for reorganizing the debtor's financial affairs under the supervision of the bankruptcy court.
Plan of Reorganization	Sets forth the debtor's proposed new capital structure. The debtor has the exclusive right to file a plan within the first 120 days after the date of the order for relief.
Executory Contracts	The debtor-in-possession (or trustee) may assume or reject executory contracts. A special procedure has been established for rejecting union collective bargaining agreements.
Confirmation of a Plan	A plan of reorganization must be confirmed by the bankruptcy court before it becomes effective.

WORKING THE WEB

Visit the Web sites listed below for more information about the topics covered in this chapter.

1. For an overview of the pervasiveness and importance of credit in the United States and the world economy, see **www.equifax.com.**
2. For a definition and examples of suretyship, see **www.lectlaw.com/def2/s208.htm.**
3. Using the Cornell site at **www.law.cornell.edu/topics/secured_transactions.html,** find which part of the UCC provides for secured transactions.
4. Check on current statistics on the level of bankruptcies filed at **www.abiworld.org/stats/newstatsfront.html** and InterNet Bankruptcy Library—Worldwide Troubled Company Resources and Daily Source of Bankruptcy News at **www.bankrupt.com.**
5. What is the amount of your state's homestead exemption? More theory may be found in "The Outer Boundaries of the Bankruptcy Estate" at **www.law.emory.edu/ELJ/volumes/fall98/plank.html.**
6. The FTC has practical advice for debtors at **www.ftc.gov/bcp/conline/pubs/credit/kneedeep.htm.**
7. See for yourself the plight of commercial debt relief companies that promise more than they can deliver at **www.ftc.gov/os/1998/9803/watson.fin.htm.**

CRITICAL LEGAL THINKING QUESTIONS

1. What is the difference between secured credit and unsecured credit? As a creditor, which is preferable?
2. Describe a mortgage and the parties to a mortgage. Describe a note and deed of trust and the parties to a note and deed of trust.
3. What is a recording statute? What protection does a recording statute provide?
4. Describe Article 9 of the Uniform Commercial Code. What is a secured transaction? What is a financing statement?
5. Explain the difference between a surety arrangement and a guaranty arrangement.
6. What does the bankruptcy doctrine of "fresh start" provide? What public policy is served by bankruptcy laws?
7. Describe Chapter 7 liquidation bankruptcy. What is the property of the bankruptcy estate?
8. Describe the concept of *discharge*. Is any party hurt by a bankruptcy discharge?
9. Describe Chapter 13 consumer debt adjustment bankruptcy. When is discharge granted?
10. Describe Chapter 11 reorganization bankruptcy. What does a plan of reorganization do?

CASE FOR BRIEFING

Read Case 13 in Appendix A *(Dewsnup v. Timm)*. Review and brief the case using the *Critical Legal Thinking* "Briefing the Case" example described in Chapter 1.

13.1 *S & D Petroleum Company, Inc. v. Tamsett*

534 N.Y.S.2d 800, 1988 N.Y. App. Div. Lexis 11258 (1988)
Supreme Court of New York, Appellate Division

FACTS In 1984, C&H Trucking, Inc. (C&H), borrowed $19,747.56 from S&D Petroleum Company, Inc. (S&D). S&D hired Clifton M. Tamsett to prepare a security agreement naming C&H as the debtor and giving S&D a security interest in a 1984 Mack truck. The security agreement prepared by Tamsett declared that the collateral also secured

> *any other indebtedness or liability of the debtor to the secured party direct or indirect, absolute or contingent, due or to become due, now existing or hereafter arising, including all future advances or loans which may be made at the option of the secured party.*

Tamsett failed to file a financing statement or the executed agreement with the appropriate government office. C&H subsequently paid off the original debt, and S&D continued to extend new credit to C&H. In March 1986, when C&H owed S&D more than $17,000, S&D learned that (1) C&H was insolvent, (2) the Mack truck had been sold, and (3) Tamsett had failed to file the security agreement.

ISSUE Does S&D have a security interest in the Mack truck? Is Tamsett liable to S&D?

13.2 *In Re Tabala*

11 B.R. 405, 1981 Bankr. Lexis 3663 (1981)
United States Bankruptcy Court, Southern District of New York

FACTS In November 1974, Peter and Geraldine Tabala (Debtors), husband and wife, purchased a house in Clarkstown, New York. In November 1976, they purchased an ice cream business from Carvel Corp. for $70,000 with a loan obtained from People's National Bank. In addition, the Carvel Corporation extended trade credit to Debtors. On October 23, 1978, Debtors conveyed their residence to their three daughters, ages 9, 19, and 20, for no consideration. Debtors continued to reside in the house and to pay maintenance expenses and real estate taxes due on the property. On the date of transfer Debtors owed obligations in excess of $100,000. On March 28, 1980, Debtors filed a petition for Chapter 7 bankruptcy. The bankruptcy trustee moved to set aside the Debtors' conveyance of their home to their daughters as a fraudulent transfer.

ISSUE Who wins?

13.3 *In Re Air Florida System, Inc.*

105 B.R. 137, 1989 Bankr. Lexis 1629 (1989)
United States Bankruptcy Court, Southern District of Florida

FACTS Air Florida System, Inc. (Air Florida), an airline company, filed a voluntary petition to reorganize under Chapter 11 of the Bankruptcy Code. Within 90 days prior to commencement of the case, Air Florida paid $13,575 to Compania Panamena de Aviacion, S.A. (COPA), in payment of an antecedent debt. This payment enabled COPA to receive more than it would have received if Air Florida were liquidated under Chapter 7.

ISSUE Is the payment to COPA an avoidable preferential transfer?

ETHICS CASE

13.4 *Forsyth County Memorial Hospital Authority, Inc. v. Lynch*

346 S.E.2d 212, 1986 N.C. App. Lexis 2432 (1986)
Court of Appeals of North Carolina

FACTS On February 26, 1982, Jessie Lynch became seriously ill and needed medical attention. Her sister, Ethel Sales, took her to the Forsyth Memorial Hospital in North Carolina for treatment. Lynch was admitted for hospitalization. Sales signed Lynch's admission form, which included the following section:

> *The undersigned, in consideration of hospital services being rendered or to be rendered by Forsyth County Memorial Hospital Authority, Inc., in Winston-Salem, N.C., to the above patient, does hereby guarantee payment to Forsyth County Hospital Authority, Inc., on demand all charges for said services and incidentals incurred on behalf of such patient.*

Lynch received the care and services rendered by the hospital until her discharge more than 30 days later. The total bill during her hospitalization amounted to $7,977. When Lynch refused to pay the bill, the hospital instituted an action against Lynch and Sales to recover the unpaid amount.

ISSUE Is Sales liable? Did Sales act ethically in denying liability? Did she have a choice when she signed the contract?

14 Intellectual Property and Internet Law

The Congress shall have the power . . . To promote the Progress of Science and useful Arts, by securing for limited Times to Authors and Inventors the exclusive Right to their respective Writings and Discoveries.

—ARTICLE I, SECTION 8, CLAUSE 8, U.S. CONSTITUTION

CHAPTER OBJECTIVES

After studying this chapter, you should be able to

1. Describe the business tort of misappropriating a trade secret.
2. Describe how an invention can be patented under federal patent laws and the penalties for patent infringement.
3. List the writings that can be copyrighted and describe the penalties of copyright infringement.
4. Define trademarks and service marks, and describe the penalties for trademark infringement.
5. Describe the protection of domain names and explain the coverage of state and federal Internet laws.

CHAPTER OUTLINE

- Introduction
- Trade Secrets
- Patents
- Copyrights
- Case for Discussion: *Newton v. Beastie Boys*
- Trademarks
- The Internet
- Case for Discussion: *E. & J. Gallo Winery v. Spider Webs Ltd.*
- Legal Terminology
- Chapter Summary
- Internet Exercises and Cases

INTRODUCTION

The U.S. economy is based on the freedom of ownership of property. **Intellectual property rights** have value to businesses and individuals alike. This is particularly the case in the modern era of the Information Age, computers, and the Internet.

Trade secrets form the basis of many successful businesses, which are protected from misappropriation. Federal law provides protections for intellectual property rights, such as patents, copyrights, and trademarks. Anyone who infringes on these rights may be stopped from doing so and is liable for damages. Computers and computer software are accorded special protection from infringement. In addition, the area of Internet law, e-commerce, and domain names is exploding in use.

This chapter covers trade secrets, patents, copyrights, trademarks, domain names, Internet law, and e-commerce.

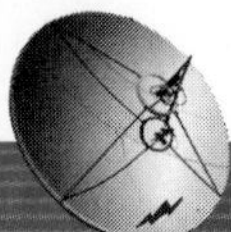

INFORMATION TECHNOLOGY

ECONOMIC ESPIONAGE ACT

Stealing trade secrets exposes the offender to a civil lawsuit by the injured party to recover economic damages. In addition, the enactment by Congress of the federal **Economic Espionage Act** of 1996 [18 U.S.C. 1831–1839] makes it a federal crime to steal another's trade secrets.

Under the Espionage Act it is a federal crime for any person to convert a trade secret to his or her benefit or for the benefit of others, knowing or intending that the act would cause injury to the owner of the trade secret. Under the Espionage Act, the definition of *trade secret* is broad and parallels the definition used under the civil laws of misappropriating a trade secret.

One of the major reasons for passing the Espionage Act was to address the ease of stealing trade secrets through espionage and using the Internet. For example, hundreds of pages of confidential information can be downloaded onto an electronic storage device, placed in someone's pocket, and taken from the legal owner. In addition, computer hackers can hack into a company's computers and steal customer lists, databases, formulas, and other trade secrets. The Espionage Act adds an important weapon to address and penalize computer and Internet espionage.

The Espionage Act provides for severe criminal penalties. An organization can be fined up to $5 million per criminal act and $10 million if the criminal act was committed to benefit a foreign government. The Act imposes prison terms on individuals of up to 15 years per criminal violation, which can be increased to 25 years per violation if the criminal act was done with the intent to benefit a foreign government.

TRADE SECRETS

Many businesses are successful because their **trade secrets** set them apart from their competitors. Trade secrets may be product formulas, patterns, designs, compilations of data, customer lists, or other business secrets. Many trade secrets either do not qualify to be—or simply are not—patented, copyrighted, or trademarked. Many states have adopted the **Uniform Trade Secrets Act** to give statutory protection to trade secrets.

State unfair competition laws allow the owner of a trade secret to bring a lawsuit for *misappropriation* against anyone who steals a trade secret. To be actionable, the defendant (often an employee of the owner or a competitor) must have obtained the trade secret through unlawful means such as theft, bribery, or industrial espionage. No tort has occurred if there is no misappropriation. For example, a competitor can lawfully discover a trade secret by performing reverse engineering (i.e., taking apart and examining a rival's product).

The owner of a trade secret is obliged to take all reasonable precautions to prevent the secret from being discovered by others. These precautions include fencing in buildings, placing locks on doors, hiring security guards, and the like. If the owner fails to take such actions, the secret is not subject to protection under state unfair competition laws.

Generally, a successful plaintiff in a trade secret action can:

1. recover the profits made by the offender from the use of the trade secret,
2. recover for damages, and
3. obtain an injunction prohibiting the offender from divulging or using the trade secret.

PATENTS

To receive a **patent,** the invention must be *novel*, *useful*, and *nonobvious*. In addition, only certain subject matters can be patented. Patentable subject matter includes (1) machines, (2) processes, (3) compositions of matter, (4) improvements to existing machines, processes, or compositions of matter, (5) designs for an article of manufacture, (6) asexually reproduced plants, and (7) living material invented by a person. Abstractions and scientific principles cannot be patented unless they are part of the tangible environment. For example, Einstein's theory of relativity ($E = MC^2$) cannot be patented.

U.S. Patent and Trademark Office: www.uspto.gov

In 1995, in order to bring the U.S. patent system in harmony with the systems of the majority of other developed nations, Congress made the following important changes in U.S. patent law.

1. Patents for inventions are valid for *20 years* (instead of the previous term of 17 years). Design patents are valid for 14 years.
2. The patent term begins to run from the date the patent application is *filed* (instead of when the patent is issued, as was previously the case).

After the patent period runs out, the invention or design enters the *public domain*, which means that anyone can produce and sell the invention without paying the prior patent holder.

The United States follows the *first-to-invent rule* rather than the *first-to-file rule* followed by some other countries. Thus, in the United States the first person to invent an item or process is given patent protection over another party who was first to file a patent application.

Federal Patent Statute

Pursuant to the express authority granted in the U.S. Constitution, Congress enacted the **Federal Patent Statute of 1952** [35 U.S.C. §§ 10 et seq.]. This law is intended to provide an incentive for inventors to invent and make their inventions public and to protect patented inventions from infringement. Federal patent law is exclusive; there are no state patent laws. The U.S. Court of Appeals for the Federal Circuit in Washington, DC was created in 1982 to hear patent appeals. The court was established to promote uniformity in patent law.

Patent applicants must file a *patent application* containing a written description of the invention with the **U.S. Patent and Trademark Office (PTO)** in Washington, DC. If a patent is granted, the invention is assigned a patent number. Patent holders usually affix the word *Patent* or *Pat.* and the patent number to the patented article. If a patent application is filed but a patent has not yet been issued, the applicant usually places the words *patent pending* on the article. Any party can challenge either the issuance of a patent or the validity of an existing patent.

American Inventors Protection Act

In 1999, Congress enacted the **American Inventors Protection Act.** This statute does the following:

- Permits an inventor to file a *provisional application* with the PTO, pending the preparation and filing of a final and complete patent application. This part of the law grants "provisional rights" to an inventor for 3 months, pending the filing of a final application.
- Requires the PTO to issue a patent within 3 years after the filing of a patent application unless the applicant engages in dilatory activities.

INFORMATION TECHNOLOGY

AMAZON.COM LOSES ITS ONE-CLICK PATENT

Amazon.com, Inc., enables customers to find and purchase books, music, videos, consumer electronics, games, toys, gifts, and other items over the Internet by using its Web site, www.amazon.com. As an early entrant into this market, Amazon.com became a leader in electronic commerce.

Amazon.com devised a method that enabled online customers to purchase selected items with a single click of a computer mouse button. Customers who had previously registered their name, address, and credit card number with Amazon.com could complete purchases by clicking an instant "buy" button. This ordering system was implemented by Amazon.com in September 1997. On September 21, 1997, Amazon.com applied for a patent for its one-click ordering system, and on September 28, 1998, the U.S. PTO granted patent No. 5,960,411 (411 patent) to Amazon.com. This was designated the 1-clik® ordering system by Amazon.com.

While Amazon.com's patent application was pending, other online retailers began offering similar one-click ordering systems. One was Barnesandnoble.com, which operates a Web site that sells books, software, music, videos, and other items.

On October 21, 1999, Amazon.com sued Barnesandnoble.com, alleging patent infringement, and sought an injunction against Barnesandnoble.com from using its 1-click ordering system. Barnesandnoble.com defended, asserting that a one-click ordering system was obvious and, therefore, did not meet the required "nonobvious" test of federal patent law for an invention to qualify for a patent.

After examining the evidence, the U.S. district court decided that Amazon.com's 1-clik system was nonobvious when it was invented in 1997 and upheld Amazon.com's patent. Barnesandnoble.com appealed to the Federal Court of Appeals, arguing that Amazon.com's 1-clik ordering system was not novel or nonobvious as required by patent law. Barnesandnoble.com cited evidence that one-click ordering systems existed in the *prior art* before Amazon.com filed for its patent. The Federal Court of Appeals relied on these prior art references and reversed the trial court's decision. The court of appeals allowed Barnesandnoble.com to use its "Express Lane" one-click ordering system.

Amazon.com, Inc., v. Barnesandnoble.com, Inc., 239 F.3d 1343, 2001 U.S. App. Lexis 2163 (Fed. Cir. 2001).

ETHICAL PERSPECTIVE

INVENTOR WIPES FORD'S AND CHRYSLER'S WINDSHIELDS CLEAN

In 1967, Robert Kearns, a professor at Wayne State University in Detroit, Michigan, patented his design for the electronic intermittent-speed windshield wiper for automobiles and other vehicles. He peddled his invention around to many automobile manufacturers but never reached a licensing deal with any of them. In 1969, automobile manufacturers began producing cars using Kearns's intermittent-speed windshield wiper invention. Virtually all cars sold in the United States today now have these wipers as standard equipment. Kearns filed patent infringement lawsuits against virtually all automobile manufacturers.

The Ford case went to trial first. Ford alleged that Kearns's patents were not valid because of obviousness and prior art. The jury disagreed with Ford, decided that Kearns's patents were valid, and ordered Ford to pay $5.2 million, plus interest, for patent infringement. In 1990, Ford settled by paying Kearns $10.2 million and agreeing to drop all appeals. This represented 50¢ per Ford vehicle that used the wiper system.

In the Chrysler case, Kearns fired his lawyers and represented himself. Kearns won a second victory: In 1991, the jury found that Chrysler had infringed Kearns's patents and awarded him $11.3 million. Kearns received over $21 million from Chrysler, which amounted to 90¢ for every vehicle sold by Chrysler with the wiper system.

In 1993 and 1994, courts dismissed Kearns's lawsuits against 23 automobile manufacturers, including General Motors, Porsche, Nissan, Toyota, and Honda, because Kearns failed to comply with court orders to disclose documents. Thus ended Kearns's legal battle with the automobile industry.

1. Do you think that intermittent-speed windshield wipers were obvious when Kearns invented them?
2. Did the automobile manufacturers that used Kearns' invention without paying him act ethically? Explain.

Patent Infringement

Patent holders own exclusive rights to use and exploit their patent. **Patent infringement** occurs when someone makes unauthorized use of another's patent. In a suit for patent infringement, a successful plaintiff can recover:

1. Money damages equal to a reasonable royalty rate on the sale of the infringed articles
2. Other damages caused by the infringement (such as loss of customers)
3. An order requiring the destruction of the infringing article
4. An injunction preventing the infringer from such action in the future.

The court has the discretion to award up to treble damages if the infringement was intentional.

> The patent system added the fuel of interest to the fire of genius.
>
> —Abraham Lincoln

Public-Use Doctrine

Under the **one-year "on sale" doctrine,** also known as the **public-use doctrine,** a patent may not be granted if the invention was used by the public for more than one year prior to filing of the patent application. This doctrine forces inventors to file their patent applications at the proper time. For example, suppose Cindy Parsons invents a new invention on January 1. She allows the public to use this invention and does not file a patent application until February of the following year. She has lost the right to patent her invention.

U.S. Copyright Office:
www.loc.gov/copyright

Copyrights

Only **tangible writings**—writings that can be physically seen—are subject to **copyright** registration and protection. The term *writing* has been broadly defined to include books, periodicals, and newspapers; lectures, sermons, and addresses; musical compositions; plays, motion pictures, and radio and television productions; maps; works of art, including paintings, drawings, sculpture, jewelry, glassware, tapestry, and lithographs; architectural drawings and models; photographs, including prints, slides, and filmstrips; greeting cards and picture postcards; photoplays, including feature films, cartoons, newsreels, travelogues, and training films, and sound recordings published in the form of tapes, cassettes, compact discs, and phonograph albums.

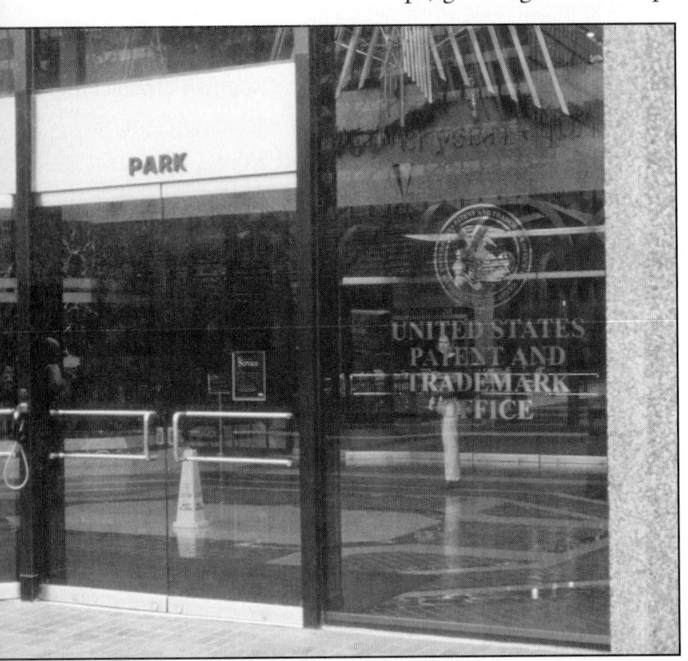

Exterior of the U.S. Patent and Trademark Office, Washington, D.C.

Registration of Copyrights

To be protected under federal copyright law, a work must be the original work of the author. A copyright is created when an author produces her work. For example, when a student writes a term paper for her class, she owns a copyright to her work.

Published and unpublished works may be registered with the **U.S. Copyright Office** in Washington, DC. Registration is permissive and voluntary and can be effected at any time during the term of the copyright.

In 1989, the United States signed the **Berne Convention,** an international copyright treaty. This law eliminated the need to place the symbol © or the word "Copyright" or "copr." on the copyrighted work.

The **Sonny Bono Copyright Term Extension Act of 1998** (CTEA) granted individuals copyright protection for their life plus 70 years. For example, if an author writes a novel at age 25 and she dies when she is 85, the copyright on her novel applies for the remaining 60 years of her life, and her heirs have copyright protection for an additional 70 years beyond the author's life. Copyrights owned by businesses are protected for 95 years from the year of first publication or for 120 years from the year of creation, whichever is shorter. After the copyright period runs out, the work enters the *public domain*, which means that anyone can publish the work without paying the prior copyright holder.

Federal Copyright Revision Act

Congress enacted a federal copyright law pursuant to an express grant of authority in the U.S. Constitution. This law protects the work of authors and other creative persons from the unauthorized use of their copyrighted materials and provides a financial incentive for authors to write, thereby increasing the number of creative works available in society. The **Copyright Revision Act of 1976** governs copyright law [17 U.S.C. §§ 101 et seq.].

Federal copyright law is exclusive; there are no state copyright laws. Published and unpublished works may be copyrighted and registered with the U.S. Copyright Office in Washington, DC.

Copyright Infringement

Copyright infringement occurs when a party copies a substantial and material part of the plaintiff's copyrighted work without permission. The copying does not have to be either word-for-word or the entire work. A successful plaintiff can recover (1) the profit made by the infringer from the copyright infringement, (2) damages suffered by the plaintiff, (3) an order requiring the impoundment and destruction of the infringing works, and (4) an injunction preventing the infringer from doing so in the future. The court, at its discretion, can award statutory damages up to $150,000 for willful infringement in lieu of actual damages.

Exterior of the Red Bluff County Courthouse, Sacramento, California.

Fair-Use Doctrine

The copyright holder's rights in the work are not absolute. The law permits certain limited unauthorized use of copyrighted materials under the **fair-use doctrine.** The following uses are protected under this doctrine:

1. Quotation of the copyrighted work for review or criticism or in a scholarly or technical work
2. Use in a parody or satire
3. Brief quotation in a news report
4. Reproduction by a teacher or student of a small part of the work to illustrate a lesson
5. Incidental reproduction of a work in a newsreel or broadcast of an event being reported
6. Reproduction of a work in a legislative or judicial proceeding.

The copyright holder cannot recover for copyright infringement where fair use is found.

INFORMATION TECHNOLOGY

COPYRIGHTING SOFTWARE

In 1980, Congress enacted the **Computer Software Copyright Act** [17 U.S.C. § 101], which amended the Copyright Act of 1976. The 1980 amendments include computer programs in the list of tangible items protected by copyright law. The creator of a copyrightable software program obtains automatic copyright protection. The Register of Copyright is authorized to accept and record any document pertaining to computer software and to issue a **certificate of recordation** to the recorder.

Congress passed the **Semiconductor Chip Protection Act of 1984** to provide greater protection of electronic hardware components [17 U.S.C. §§ 901–914]. This law protects masks that are used to create computer chips. A *mask* is an original layout of micro-electronic components that is used to create a semiconductor chip. This act is sometimes referred to as the "Mask Work Act." Notice on the work is optional, but when used must contain the words *Mask Work* or the symbol "M" or (M) and the name of the owner.

CASE FOR DISCUSSION

Newton v. Beastie Boys

349 F.3d 591, 2003 U.S. App. Lexis 22635 (2003) United States Court of Appeals, Ninth Circuit

FACTS

James W. Newton, Jr., is an accomplished avant-garde jazz composer and flutist. In 1978, Newton wrote a composition for the song "Choir," a piece for flute and voice that incorporated elements of African American gospel music. Newton owns the copyright to the composition "Choir." In 1992, the Beastie Boys, a rap and hip-hop group, used six seconds of Newton's "Choir" composition in their song "Pass the Mic" without obtaining a license from Newton to do so. Newton sued the Beastie Boys for copyright infringement. The Beastie Boys defended, arguing that their use of six seconds of Newton's song was fair use. The district court found that the Beastie Boys' use of Newton's composition was *de minimis* and therefore fair use. The district court granted summary judgment in favor of the Beastie Boys, and Newton appealed.

ISSUE

Does the incorporation of a short segment of a copyrighted musical composition into a new musical recording constitute fair use, or is it copyright infringement?

COURT'S REASONING

The court of appeals noted that the dispute between Newton and the Beastie Boys centers around the copyright implications of the practice of "sampling," a practice now common to many types of popular music. Sampling entails the incorporation of short segments of prior sound recordings into new recordings. The court of appeals held that the unauthorized use of a copyrighted work is actionable if there is substantial copying. The court noted that *de minimis* copying is not actionable and constitutes fair use. The court found that the sampled portion of Newton's composition comprised a six-second, three-note sequence from his four-and-a-half minute "Choir." The court of appeals held that the Beastie Boys' use of this small segment in their "Pass the Mic" song was *de minimis* and therefore constituted fair use and not copyright infringement.

DECISION AND REMEDY

The court of appeals held that the Beastie Boys' *de minimis* sampling of Newton's "Choir" composition constituted fair use and not copyright infringement. The court of appeals affirmed the district court's grant of summary judgment in favor of the Beastie Boys.

QUESTIONS

1. Should sampling be allowed as fair use? Why or why not?
2. Did the Beastie Boys act ethically when they used part of Newton's "Choir" composition in their song?
3. Has the use of sampling become a big part of today's music recordings? Why do you think recording artists engage in sampling?

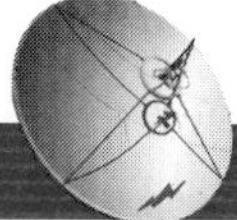

INFORMATION TECHNOLOGY

DIGITAL MILLENNIUM COPYRIGHT ACT

The Internet makes it easier for people to copy and distribute copyrighted work illegally. To combat this, software and entertainment companies developed "wrappers" and encryption technology to protect their copyrighted works from unauthorized access. Not to be outdone, software pirates and other Internet users devised ways to crack these wrappers and protection devices. Software and entertainment companies lobbied Congress to enact legislation that made illegal the cracking of their wrappers and selling of technology to do so. In 1998, Congress responded by enacting the **Digital Millennium Copyright Act (DMCA)** [17 U.S.C. 1201], which does the following:

- Prohibits unauthorized *access* to copyrighted *digital works* by circumventing the wrapper or encryption technology that protects the intellectual property. This "black-box" protection prohibits simply accessing the protected information and does not require that the accessed information be misused.
- Prohibits the manufacture and distribution of technologies, products, or services designed primarily for the purpose of circumventing wrappers or encryption technology protecting digital works. However, multipurpose devices that can be used in ways other than cracking wrappers or encryption technology can be manufactured and sold without violating the DMCA.

The DMCA imposes civil and criminal penalties. A successful plaintiff in a civil action can recover actual damages from first-time offenders and treble damages from repeat offenders, costs and attorney's fees, an order for the destruction of illegal products and devices, and an injunction against future violations by the offender. As an alternative to actual damages, a plaintiff can recover statutory damages of up to $25,000 per act of circumvention. The following criminal penalties can be accessed for willful violations committed for "commercial advantage" or "private financial gain": First-time violators can be fined up to $500,000 and imprisoned for up to 5 years; subsequent violators can be fined up to $1 million and imprisoned for up to 10 years.

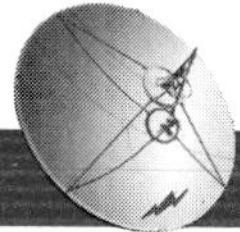

INFORMATION TECHNOLOGY

NET ACT: CRIMINAL COPYRIGHT INFRINGEMENT

In 1997, Congress enacted the **No Electronic Theft Act (NET Act),** which criminalizes certain copyright infringement. The NET Act prohibits any person from willfully infringing a copyright for the purpose of either commercial advantage or financial gain, or by reproduction or distribution even without commercial advantage or financial gain, including by electronic means, where the retail value of the copyrighted work exceeds $1,000. Criminal penalties for violating the act include imprisonment for up to one year and fines of up to $100,000.

The NET Act adds a new law for the federal government to attack copyright infringement and curb digital piracy.

Trademarks

> The law in respect to literature ought to remain upon the same footing as that which regards the profits of mechanical inventions and chemical discoveries.
> —William Wordsworth

An applicant can register a mark if (1) it was in use in commerce (e.g., actually used in the sale of goods or services) or (2) the applicant verifies a bona fide intention to use the mark in commerce and actually does so within 6 months of its registration. Failure to do so during this period causes loss of the mark to the registrant. A party other than the registrant can submit an opposition to a proposed registration of a mark or the cancellation of a previously registered mark.

Distinctiveness of a Mark

To qualify for federal protection, there must be **distinctiveness of a mark** or the mark must have acquired a **secondary meaning.** For example, marks such as *Xerox* and *Acura* are *distinctive.* A term such as *English Leather,* which literally means leather processed in England, has taken on a secondary meaning as a trademark for an aftershave lotion. For example, Nike, Inc. has trademarked its name *Nike,* its *swoosh* symbol, and its *Just Do It* slogan. Words that are *descriptive* but have no secondary meaning cannot be trademarked. For example, the word *cola* alone could not be trademarked. Exhibit 14.1 is the Prentice Hall logo with trademark.

Marks That Can Be Trademarked

The following types of **marks** can be trademarked:

- **Trademarks:** A **trademark** is a distinctive mark, symbol, name, word, motto, or device that identifies the *goods* of a particular business. For example, the words *Xerox, Coca-Cola,* and *IBM* are trademarks.
- **Service marks:** A **service mark** is used to distinguish the *services* of the holder from those of its competitors. The trade names *United Airlines, Marriott Hotels,* and *Weight Watchers* are examples of service marks.
- **Certification marks:** A **certification mark** is a mark used to certify that goods and services are of a certain quality or originate from particular geographical areas—for example, wines from the *Napa Valley* of California or *Florida* oranges. The owner of the mark is usually a nonprofit corporation that licenses producers that meet certain standards or conditions to use the mark.
- **Collective marks:** A **collective mark** is a mark used by cooperatives, associations, and fraternal organizations. An example is *Boy Scouts of America.*

The following marks cannot be registered: (1) the flag or coat of arms of the United States, any state, municipality, or foreign nation, (2) marks that are im-

EXHIBIT 14.1 *Prentice Hall logo with trademark.*

Pearson Prentice Hall™ is a trademark of Pearson Education, Inc.

Federal Lanham Trademark Act

Trademark law is intended to (1) protect the owner's investment and goodwill in a mark and (2) prevent consumers from being confused as to the origin of goods and services. In 1946, Congress enacted the **Lanham Trademark Act** to provide federal protection to trademarks, service marks, and other marks [15 U.S.C. §§ 1114 et seq.]. Congress passed the **Trademark Law Revision Act of 1988,** which amended trademark law in several respects. The amendments made it easier to register a trademark but harder to maintain it. States may also enact trademark laws.

Trademarks are registered with the U.S. Patent and Trademark Office in Washington, DC. The original registration of a mark is valid for 10 years and can be renewed for an unlimited number of 10-year periods. The registration of a trademark, which is given nationwide effect, serves as constructive notice that the mark is the registrant's personal property. The registrant is entitled to use the registered trademark symbol ® in connection with a registered trademark or service mark. Use of the symbol is not mandatory. Note that the frequently used notations "TM" and "SM" have no legal significance.

moral or scandalous, (3) geographical names standing alone (e.g., "South"), (4) surnames standing alone (note that a surname can be registered if it is accompanied by a picture or fanciful name, such as *Smith Brothers' Cough Drops*, and (5) any mark that resembles a mark already registered with the federal Patent and Trademark Office.

Trademark Infringement

The owner of a mark can sue a third party for the unauthorized use of a mark. To succeed in a **trademark infringement** case, the owner must prove that (1) the defendant infringed the plaintiff's mark by using it in an unauthorized manner, and (2) such use is likely to cause confusion, mistake, or deception of the public as to the origin of the goods or services. A successful plaintiff can recover:

1. The profits made by the infringer by the unauthorized use of the mark
2. Damages caused to the plaintiff's business and reputation
3. An order requiring the defendant to destroy all goods containing the unauthorized mark
4. An injunction preventing the defendant from such infringement in the future.

The court has discretion to award up to treble damages where intentional infringement is found.

Generic Names

Most companies promote their trademarks and service marks to increase the public's awareness of the availability and quality of their products and services. At some point in time, however, the public may begin to treat the mark as a common name to denote the type of product or service being sold, rather than as the trademark or trade name of an individual seller. A trademark that becomes a common term for a product line or type of service is called a **generic name.** Once that happens, the term loses its protection under federal trademark law because it has become *descriptive* rather than *distinctive* (see Exhibit 14.2).

SIDEBAR

Loss of Trademark
Nestlè Company, Inc., lost its trademark on the term "Toll House" for its chocolate chip cookies when a court ruled that the term had become generic because the public had come to associate the name Toll House with chocolate chip cookies in general, not only those sold by Nestlè.

Nestlè Company, Inc. v. Chester's Market, Inc. 571 F.Supp. 763 (D.Conn. 1983)

EXHIBIT 14.2 *Corporations strive to protect their copyrights and trademarks.*

There are two R's in Xerox.

One is right in the middle.

But the really important one is the one you probably never notice.

It's the little R in a circle—like the one you see at the bottom of this ad—that tells you that Xerox is a registered trademark.

And it reminds you that our name—which is also our trademark—should only be used in connection with the products and services of our corporation.

Including everything from Xerox copiers to information processors to electronic printers.

So as you can see, our trademark is a very valuable one.

To us. And to you, too.

Because it ensures that when you ask for something you can be sure of what you're going to get.

Of course, we don't expect you to use the second R every time you use our name.

But we do hope you'll give it a second thought.

XEROX

XEROX® is a trademark of XEROX CORPORATION.

Reprinted with permission of Xerox Corporation.

THE INTERNET

The **Internet,** or Net, is a collection of millions of computers that provide a network of electronic connections between the computers. The Internet was initiated in 1969 by the U.S. Department of Defense to create electronic communications for military and national defense purposes. Building on this start, in the 1980s the National Science Foundation, the federal government's main scientific and technical agency, established the Net to facilitate high-speed communications among research centers at academic and research institutions around the world.

Eventually, individuals and businesses began using the Internet for communicating information and data. In 1980, fewer than 250 computers were hooked to the Internet. Growth was rapid in the late 1990s and into the early 2000s, and today several hundred million computers are connected to the Internet. The Internet's evolution helped usher in the Information Age of today. Use of the Internet and the World Wide Web has required courts to apply existing laws to new technologies, as well as spurring the federal Congress and state legislatures to enact new laws to govern modern means of communication and the conduct of electronic business.

> Through the use of chat rooms, any person with a phone line can become a town crier with a voice that resonates farther than it could from any soapbox. Through the use of Web pages, mail exploders, and newsgroups, the same individual can become a pamphleteer.
>
> —Justice Stevens
> *Reno v. American Civil Liberties Union*

World Wide Web

The **World Wide Web** consists of millions of computers that support a standard set of rules for the exchange of information called *hypertext transfer protocol* (HTTP). Web-based documents are formatted using common coding languages such as *hypertext markup language* (HTML) and Java. Businesses and individuals can hook up to the Web by registering with a server such as America Online (AOL) or other servers.

Individuals and businesses can have their own Web sites. A Web site is composed of electronic documents known as Web pages. The Web sites and pages are stored on servers throughout the world, which are operated by **Internet Service Providers (ISPs).** They are viewed by using Web browsing software such as Microsoft Internet Explorer and Netscape Navigator. Each Web site has a unique online address. Web pages can contain a full range of multimedia content, including text, images, video, sound, and animation. Web pages can include references, called *hyperlinks*, or *links*, to other Web pages or sites.

The Web has made it extremely attractive to conduct commercial activities online. Companies such as Amazon.com and eBay are e-commerce powerhouses that sell all sorts of goods and services. Existing companies such as Wal-Mart, Merrill Lynch, and Dell Computers sell their goods and services online as well. E-commerce over the Web will continue to grow dramatically each year.

Electronic Mail

Electronic mail, or **email,** is one of the most widely used applications for communication over the Internet. Using email, individuals can instantaneously communicate in electronic writing with one another around the world. Each person can have his or her own email address, which identifies the user by a unique address. Email will continue to grow in use in the future as it replaces some telephone and paper correspondence and increases communication between persons.

Domain Names

Each Web site is identified by a unique Internet **domain name.** For example, the domain name for the publisher of this book is **www.prenhall.com.** Some of the top-level suffixes for domain names are *com* for commercial use, *net* for networks, *org* for organizations, and *edu* for educational institutions.

Domain names can be registered. The first step in registering a domain name is determining whether any other party already owns the name. For this purpose, InterNIC maintains a "Whois" database that contains the domain names that have been registered. The InterNIC Web site is located online at **internic.net.** Domain names can also be registered at Network Solutions, Inc.'s Web site, which is located at **www.networksolutions.com**, as well as at other sites. An applicant must complete a registration form, which can be done online. It costs less than $50 to register a domain for one year, and the fee may be paid by credit card online.

The most commonly used top-level extensions for domain names are listed in Exhibit 14.3.

EXHIBIT 14.3 *Top-level extensions for domain names.*

- ***.com*** This extension represents the word *commercial* and is the most widely used extension in the world. Most businesses prefer a .com domain name because it is a highly recognized business symbol.
- ***.net*** This extension represents the word *network,* and it is most commonly used by Internet service providers, Web-hosting companies, and other businesses that are directly involved in the infrastructure of the Internet. Some businesses also choose domain names with a .net extension.
- ***.org*** This extension represents the word *organization* and is primarily used by nonprofit groups and trade associations.
- ***.info*** This extension signifies a "resource" Web site. It is an unrestricted global name that may be used by businesses, individuals, and organizations.
- ***.biz*** This extension is used for small-business Web sites.
- ***.us*** This extension is for U.S. Web sites. Many businesses choose this relatively new extension.
- ***.cc*** This extension was originally the country code for Coco Keeling Islands, but it is now unrestricted and may be registered by anyone from any country. It is often registered by businesses.
- ***.bz*** This extension was originally the country code for Belize, but it is now unrestricted and may be registered by anyone from any country. It is commonly used by small businesses.
- ***.name*** This new extension is for individuals, who can use it to register personalized domain names.
- ***.museum*** This extension enables museums, museum associations, and museum professionals to register their own Web sites.
- ***.coop*** This extension represents the word *cooperative* and may be used by cooperative associations around the world.
- ***.aero*** This extension is exclusively reserved for the aviation community. It enables organizations and individuals to reserve Web sites.
- ***.pro*** This extension is available to professionals, such as doctors, lawyers, consultants, and other professionals.
- ***.edu*** This extension is for educational institutions.

CASE FOR DISCUSSION

E. & J. Gallo Winery v. Spider Webs Ltd.

286 F.3d 270, 2002 U.S. App. Lexis 5928 (2002) United States Court of Appeals, Fifth Circuit

FACTS

Ernest and Julio Gallo Winery (Gallo) is a famous maker of wines that is located in California. The company registered the trademark "Ernest & Julio Gallo" in 1964 with the United States Patent and Trademark Office. The company has spent over $500 million promoting its brand name and has sold more than four billion bottles of wine. Its name has taken on a secondary meaning as a famous trademark name. In 1999, Steve, Pierce, and Fred Thumann created Spider Webs Ltd., a limited partnership, to register Internet domain names. Spider Webs registered more than 2,000 Internet domain names, including *ernestandjuliogallo.com*. Spider Webs is in the business of selling its domain names. Gallo filed suit against Spider Webs Ltd. and the Thumanns, alleging violation of the federal Anticybersquatting Consumer Protection Act (ACPA). The district court held in favor of Gallo and ordered Spider Webs to transfer the domain name ernestandjuliogallo.com to Gallo. Spider Webs Ltd. appealed.

ISSUE

Did Spider Webs Ltd. and the Thumanns act in bad faith in registering the Internet domain name ernestandjuliogallo.com?

COURT'S REASONING

Spider Webs does not appeal the holdings that Gallo had a valid registration in its mark, that the mark is famous and distinctive, and that the domain name registered by Spider Webs is identical or confusingly similar to Gallo's mark. However, Spider Webs argues that it did not act with a "bad faith intent to profit," as required by the ACPA.

The court of appeals turned to consider the listed bad-faith factors as they apply to this case. The court found that Spider Webs had no intellectual property rights or trademark in the name "ernestandjuliogallo," aside from its registered domain name. The domain name did not contain the name of Spider Webs or any of the other defendants. Spider Webs had no "prior use" or any current use of the domain name in connection with the bona fide offering of goods or services, and Spider Webs' use was commercial. Additionally, there is uncontradicted evidence that Spider Webs was engaged in commerce in the selling of domain names and that they hoped to sell this domain name some day. The court stated that the ACPA was passed to address situations just like this one.

The court found that Gallo's mark was distinctive and famous. The court further found that Gallo registered the mark, which is a family name, 38 years ago, and that "Gallo" has clearly become associated with wine in the United States. The court stated, "The circumstances of this case all indicate that Spider Webs knew Gallo had a famous mark in which Gallo had built up goodwill, and that they hoped to profit from this by registering ernestandjuliogallo.com and waiting for Gallo to contact them so they could 'assist' Gallo."

DECISION AND REMEDY

The court of appeals held that the name Ernest and Julio Gallo was a famous trademark name and that Spider Webs Ltd. and the Thumanns acted in bad faith when they registered the Internet domain name ernestandjuliogallo.com. The court of appeals upheld the district court's decision, ordering the defendants to transfer the domain name to plaintiff E. & J. Gallo Winery.

QUESTIONS

1. Should Congress have enacted the ACPA? Is it really consumers who are being protected? Explain.
2. Did the defendants act ethically in registering so many Internet domain names? What was the defendants' motive?
3. How valuable is a company's trademark name? Does the ACPA protect that value? Explain.

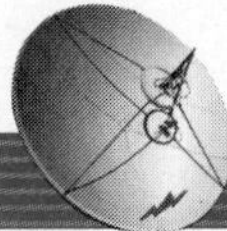

INFORMATION TECHNOLOGY

ANTICYBERSQUATTING ACT PASSED BY CONGRESS

In November 1999, the U.S. Congress enacted, and the president signed, the **Anticybersquatting Consumer Protection Act** [15 U.S.C. § 1125(d)]. The Act was specifically aimed at cybersquatters who register Internet domain names of famous companies and people and hold them "hostage" by demanding "ransom payments" from the famous company or person. In the past, trademark law was of little help, either because the famous person's name was not trademarked or because, even if the name was trademarked, trademark law required distribution of goods or services to find infringement and most cybersquatters did not distribute goods or services but merely sat on the Internet domain name.

The new Act has two fundamental requirements: (1) The name must be famous and (2) The domain name was registered in bad faith. Thus, the law prohibits the act of cybersquatting itself if it is done in *bad faith.*

The first issue in applying the statute is whether the domain name is someone else's famous name. Trademarked names qualify; nontrademarked names—such as those of famous actors, actresses, singers, sports stars, politicians, and such—also are protected. In determining bad faith, the law provides that courts may consider the extent to which the domain name resembles the holder's name or the famous person's name, whether goods or services are sold under the name, the holder's offer to sell or transfer the name, and whether the holder has acquired multiple Internet domain names of famous companies and persons.

The Act provides for the issuance of cease-and-desist orders and injunctions by the court. In addition, the law adds monetary penalties: A plaintiff has the option of seeking statutory damages of between $1,000 and $300,000 in lieu of proving damages. The Anticybersquatting Consumer Protection Act gives owners of trademarks and persons with famous names a new weapon to attack the kidnapping of Internet domain names by cyberpirates.

For example, the Academy Award–winning Actress Julia Roberts won back the domain name *juliaroberts.com* after it had been registered in bad faith by another party. The musician Sting was not so lucky because the word *sting* is generic, allowing someone else to register and keep the domain name *sting.com.*

LEGAL TERMINOLOGY

American Inventors Protection Act
Anticybersquatting Consumer Protection Act
Berne Convention
Certificate of recordation
Certification mark
Collective mark
Computer Software Copyright Act
Copyright
Copyright infringement
Copyright Revision Act of 1976
Digital Millennium Copyright Act (DMCA)
Distinctiveness of a mark
Domain name
Economic Espionage Act
Electronic mail (email)
Fair-use doctrine
Federal Patent Statute of 1952
Generic name
Intellectual property rights
Internet (Net)
Internet Sevice Provider (ISP)
Lanham Trademark Act
Mark

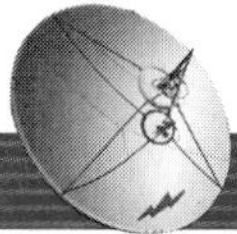

INFORMATION TECHNOLOGY

ARMANI OUTMANEUVERED FOR DOMAIN NAME

G.A. Modefine S.A. is the owner of the famous "Armani" trademark under which it produces and sells upscale and high-priced apparel. The Armani label is recognized worldwide. But Modefine was surprised when it tried to register for the domain name armani.com and found that it had already been taken. Modefine brought an arbitration action in the **World Intellectual Property Organization (WIPO),** an international arbitration and mediation center, against the domain name owner to recover the armani.com domain name. To win, Modefine had to prove that the domain name was identical or confusingly similar to its trademark, that the owner who registered the name did not have a legitimate interest in the name, and that the owner registered the name in bad faith.

The person who owned the domain name, Anand Ramnath Mani, appeared at the proceeding and defended his ownership rights. The arbitrator found that Modefine's trademark and Mr. Mani's domain name were identical, but held that Mr. Mani had a legitimate claim to the domain name. The arbitrator wrote that it is "common practice for people to register domain names which are based upon initials and a name, acronyms or otherwise variants of their full names." The court rejected Modefine's claim that Mr. Mani's offer to sell the name for $1,935 constituted bad faith. The arbitrator ruled against Modefine and permitted Mr. Mani to own the domain name armani.com.

G.A. Modefine S.A. v. A.R. Mani, WIPO, No. D2001-0537 (2001)

No Electronic Theft Act (NET Act)
Patent
Patent infringement
Public-use doctrine
Secondary meaning
Semiconductor Chip Protection Act
Service mark
Sonny Bono Copyright Term Extension Act (CTEA)
Tangible writing
Trade secret
Trademark
Trademark infringement
Trademark Law Revision Act of 1988
Uniform Trade Secrets Act
U.S. Copyright Office
U.S. Patent and Trademark Office (PTO)
World Intellectual Property Organization (WIPO)
World Wide Web

chapter summary

INTELLECTUAL PROPERTY AND INTERNET LAW

Trade Secrets

Definition	A *trade secret* is a product formula, pattern, design, compilation of data, customer list, or other business secret that makes a business successful. The owner of a trade secret must take reasonable precautions to prevent its trade secret from being discovered by others.
Misappropriation	Obtaining another's trade secret through unlawful means such as theft, bribery, or espionage is a tort. A successful plaintiff can recover profits, damages, and an injunction against the offender.
Economic Espionage Act	This federal statute makes it a crime for any person to convert a trade secret for his or another's benefit, knowing or intending to cause injury to the owners of the trade secret.

Patents

Scope	Patent law is exclusively federal law; there are no state patent laws. Patentable subject matter includes inventions such as machines; processes; compositions of matter; improvements to existing machines, processes, or compositions of matter; designs for articles of manufacture; asexually reproduced plants; and living matter invented by an individual.
Criteria	To be patented, an invention must be: (a) novel, (b) useful, and (c) nonobvious.
Patent Application	An application containing a written description of the invention must be filed with the *U.S. Patent and Trademark Office* in Washington, DC.
Term	Patents are valid for 20 years.
Public-Use Doctrine	A patent may not be granted if the invention was used by the public for more than one year prior to the filing of the patent application.
Patent Infringement	The patent holder may recover damages and other remedies against a person who makes unauthorized use of another's patent.
American Inventors Protection Act	This federal statute does the following: 1. Permits an inventor to file a *provisional application* with the U.S. Patent and Trademark Office 3 months pending the filing of a final patent application. 2. Requires the PTO to issue a patent within 3 years after the filing of a patent application.
Patent Appeal	The *United States Court of Appeals for the Federal Circuit* in Washington, DC, hears patent appeals.

Copyrights	
Scope	Copyright law is exclusively federal law; there are no state copyright laws. Only tangible writings can be copyrighted. These include books, newspapers, addresses, musical compositions, motion pictures, works of art, architectural plans, greeting cards, photographs, sound recordings, computer programs, and mask works fixed in semiconductor chips.
Requirements for Copyright	The writing must be the original work of the author.
Copyright Registration	Copyright registration is permissive and voluntary. Published and unpublished works may be registered with the U.S. Copyright Office in Washington, DC. Registration itself does not create the copyright.
Term	Copyrights are for the following terms: 1. *Individual holder:* Life of the author plus 70 years. 2. *Corporate holder:* Either (1) 120 years from the date of creation, or (2) 95 years from the date of publication, whichever is shorter.
Copyright Infringement	The copyright holder may recover damages and other remedies against a person who copies a substantial and material part of a copyrighted work without the holder's permission.
Fair-Use Doctrine	This law permits use of copyrighted material without the consent of the copyright holder for limited uses (e.g., scholarly work, parody or satire, or brief quotation in news reports).
Digital Millennium Copyright Act (DMCA)	This federal statute enacted in 1998 provides civil and criminal penalties that 1. Prohibit the manufacture and distribution of technologies, products, or services designed primarily for the purpose of circumventing wrappers or encryption protection. 2. Prohibit unauthorized *access* to copyrighted digital works by circumventing the wrapper or encryption technology that protects the intellectual property.
No Electronic Theft Act (NET Act)	This federal statute makes it a crime for a person to willfully infringe a copyright work exceeding $1,000 in retail value.
Trademarks	
Mark	Trade name, symbol, word, logo, design, or device that distinguishes the owner's good or services. Marks are often referred to collectively as *trademarks.*
Types of Marks	1. *Trademark:* Identifies goods of a particular business. 2. *Service mark:* Identifies services of a particular business. 3. *Certification mark:* Certifies that goods or services are of a certain quality or origin. 4. *Collective mark:* Used by cooperatives, associations, and fraternal organizations. *(continued)*

Requirements for a Trademark	The mark must either 1. be *distinctive*, or 2. have acquired a *secondary meaning*. The mark must have been used in commerce or the holder must intend to use the mark in commerce and actually do so within six months after registering the mark.
Trademark Registration	Marks are registered with the U.S. Patent and Trademark Office in Washington, DC.
Term	The original registration of a mark is valid for 10 years and can be renewed for an unlimited number of 10-year periods.
Trademark Infringement	The mark holder may recover damages and other remedies from a person who makes unauthorized use of another's registered mark.
Generic Name	A mark that becomes a common term for a product line or type of service loses its protection under federal trademark law.
The Internet	
Internet	A collection of millions of computers that provide a network of electronic connections between computers.
World Wide Web	An electronic connection of computers that support a standard set of rules for the exchange of information called hypertext transfer protocol (HTTP).
Electronic Mail (email)	Electronic written communication between individuals using computers connected to the Internet.
Domain Name	A unique name that identifies an individual's or company's Web site.
Anticybersquatting Consumer Protection Act	A federal statute that permits a court to issue cease-and-desist orders and injunctions and to award monetary damages against anyone who has registered a domain name (1) of a famous name (2) in bad faith.

WORKING THE WEB

www

Visit the Web sites listed below for more information about the topics covered in this chapter.

1. The site **www.uspto.gov** contains information about the federal trademark registration system. Find your analogous state trademark site. See also Marksonline, the free trademark search and domain name search, at **www.marksonline.com.**
2. The site **www.uspto.gov** contains information about the federal copyright registration system. Does the most recent copyright law require authors to use the copyright notice on printed material in order to protect it from infringement?
3. What is the current duration of a U.S. patent? What was the duration of a U.S. patent under previous law and why was it changed? See information on patents at **www.uspto.gov.**
4. Visit **www.wipo.int** and outline the process for international registration of a patent.
5. For a discussion of the Federal Dilution Act featuring Barbie, Elvis, and Coca-Cola, see **cyber.law.harvard.edu/property/respect/antibarbie.html.**
6. Domain name dispute resolution procedures are presented in great detail at **lweb.law.harvard.edu/udrp/library.html.** Check this site for everything from an overview to sample pleading forms.

CRITICAL LEGAL THINKING QUESTIONS

1. What is a *trade secret?* How long can a trade secret be legally protected?
2. Describe a *patent.* How is a patent obtained? How long is a patent valid? What is the public policy behind granting patents?
3. Explain patent infringement. What remedies are available for patent infringement?
4. Describe a *copyright.* How is a copyright obtained? How long is a copyright valid?
5. Explain copyright infringement. What remedies are available for copyright infringement?
6. What is the *fairness doctrine?* What public policy underlies the fairness doctrine?
7. Describe a *trademark.* How long is a trademark valid?
8. What is a *generic name?* What public policy underlies the generic name doctrine?
9. What is a *domain name?* What protections are provided by the Anticybersquatting Consumer Protection Act?
10. What are the main prohibitions of the Digital Millennium Copyright Act? Why was this act passed?

CASE FOR BRIEFING

Read Case 14 in Appendix A *(Feist Publications, Inc. v. Rural Telephone Service Co., Inc.)*. Reviw and brief the case using the *Critical Legal Thinking* "Briefing the Case" example described in Chapter 1.

14.1 *Acuson Corp. v. Aloka Co., Ltd.*

257 Cal.Rptr. 368, 1989 Cal. App. Lexis 317 (1989)
Court of Appeal of California

FACTS Acuson Corporation, a Delaware corporation, and Aloka Co., Ltd., a Japanese company, are competitors that both manufacture ultrasonic imaging equipment, a widely used medical diagnostic tool. The device uses soundwaves to produce moving images of the inside of a patient's body, which a computer processes into an image that is displayed on a video monitor. Acuson's unit provides finer resolution than Aloka's unit. Both companies have sold many units to hospitals and medical centers.

In November 1985, Aloka decided to purchase an Acuson unit. Aloka had another company make the actual purchase because it was concerned that Acuson would not sell the unit to a competitor. After the unit was shipped to Tokyo, Aloka's engineers partially dismantled the Acuson unit. They recorded their observations in notebooks. When Acuson discovered that Aloka had purchased one of its units, it sued Aloka, seeking an injunction and return of the unit.

ISSUE Is Aloka liable for misappropriation of a trade secret?

14.2 *The Coca-Cola Company v. Net*

Hypothetical

FACTS Francis Net, a freshman in college and computer expert, browses Web sites for hours each day. One day she thinks to herself, "I can make money registering domain names and selling them for a fortune." She recently has seen an advertisement for Classic Coke, a cola drink produced and marketed by the Coca-Cola Company. The Coca-Cola Company has a famous trademark on the term *Classic Coke* and has spent millions of dollars advertising this brand and making the term famous throughout the United States and the world. Francis goes to the Web site www.networksolutions.com, an Internet domain name registration service, to see if the Internet domain name classiccoke.com has been taken. She discovers that it is available, so she immediately registers the Internet domain name classiccoke.com for herself and pays the $70 registration fee with her credit card.

Coca-Cola Company decides to register the Internet domain name classiccoke.com but discovers that Francis Net has already registered it. Coca-Cola contacts Francis, who demands $500,000 for the name. Coca-Cola Company sues her to prevent Francis from using the Internet domain name "classiccoke.com" and to recover it from her under the federal Anticybersquatting Consumer Protection Act.

ISSUE Who wins?

14.3 *Roux Laboratories, Inc. v. Clairol, Inc.*

427 F.2d 823, 1970 C.C.P.A. Lexis 344
United States Court of Customs and Patent Appeals

FACTS Clairol Incorporated manufactures and distributes hair tinting, dyeing, and coloring preparations. In 1956, Clairol embarked on an extensive advertising campaign to promote the sale of its "Miss Clairol" hair-color preparations that included advertisements in national magazines, on outdoor billboards, on radio and television, in mailing pieces, and on point-of-sale display materials to be used by retailers and beauty salons. The advertisements prominently displayed the slogans "Hair Color So Natural Only Her Hairdresser Knows for Sure" and "Does She or Doesn't She?" Clairol registered these slogans as trademarks. During the next decade Clairol spent more than $22 million for advertising materials, resulting in more than a billion separate audio and visual impressions using the slogans. Roux Laboratories, Inc., a manufacturer of hair-coloring products and a competitor of Clairol's, filed an opposition to Clairol's registration of the slogans as trademarks.

ISSUE Do the slogans qualify for trademark protection?

ETHICS CASE

14.4 *Exxon Oil Company v. BluePeace.org*

Hypothetical

FACTS BluePeace.org is a new environmentalist group that has decided that expounding its environmental causes over the Internet is the best and most efficient way to spend its time and money to advance its environmental causes. To draw attention to its Web sites, BluePeace.org comes up with catchy Internet domain names. One is macyswearus.org; another is *exxonvaldezesseals.org*; and another is *generalmotorscrashesdummies.org*. The macyswearus.org Web site first shows beautiful women dressed in mink coats sold by Macy's Department Stores and then goes into graphic photos of minks being slaughtered and skinned and made into the coats. The exxonvaldezesseals.org Web site first shows a beautiful pristine bay in Alaska with the Exxon Valdez oil tanker quietly sailing through the waters, and then shows photos of the ship breaking open and spewing forth oil, and then seals that are gooed with oil suffocating and dying on the shoreline. The Web site generalmotorscrashes dummies.org shows a General Motors automobile involved in normal crash tests with dummies, followed by photographs of automobile accident scenes where people and children lie bleeding and dying after accidents involving General Motors automobiles.

Macy's Department Stores, the Exxon Oil Company, and the General Motors Corporation sue BluePeace.org for violating the federal Anticybersquatting Consumer Protection Act.

ISSUE Who wins? Has BluePeace.org acted unethically in this case?

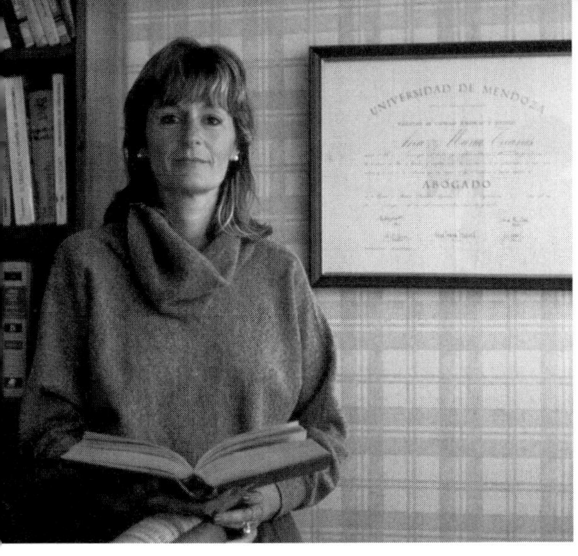

15 Administrative Law, Consumer, Investor, and Environmental Protection

I should regret to find that the law was powerless to enforce the most elementary principles of commercial morality. —LORD HERSHELL, *REDDAWAY V. BANHAM* (1896)

CHAPTER OBJECTIVES

After studying this chapter, you should be able to

1. Describe government regulation of business.
2. Define *administrative law* and explain the functions of administrative agencies.
3. Describe consumer protection laws that protect consumers from unsafe products, foods, cosmetics, and packaging and from deceptive practices.
4. Explain how securities laws protect investors from fraud.
5. List and describe environmental laws that protect the environment from pollution.

CHAPTER OUTLINE

- Introduction
- Administrative Law
- Consumer Protection
- Case for Discussion: *Federal Trade Commission v. Colgate-Palmolive Co.*
- Investor Protection
- Case for Discussion: *Securities and Exchange Commission v. Edwards*
- Environmental Protection
- Case for Discussion: *Tennessee Valley Authority v. Hill, Secretary of the Interior*
- Legal Terminology
- Chapter Summary
- Internet Exercises and Cases

INTRODUCTION

Federal and state governments enact laws that regulate business. The executive and legislative branches of government have created numerous administrative agencies to assist in implementing and enforcing these laws. This chapter discusses administrative law and the administrative agencies that regulate three vital areas: consumer protection, investor protection, and environmental protection.

ADMINISTRATIVE LAW

Congress and the executive branch of government have created more than 100 federal **administrative agencies.** These agencies are intended to provide resources and expertise in dealing with complex commercial organizations and businesses. In addition, state governments have created many state administrative agencies. Thousands of *rules and regulations* regulating business operations have been adopted and enforced by federal and state administrative agencies. Since the 1960s, the number of administrative agencies, and the regulations they produce, have increased substantially. Because of their importance, administrative agencies are informally referred to as the *fourth branch of government.*

Administrative law is a combination of *substantive* and *procedural* law. Each federal administrative agency is empowered to administer a particular statute or statutes. For example, the federal Securities and Exchange Commission (SEC) is authorized to enforce the Securities Act of 1933 and the Securities Exchange Act of 1934; the federal Food and Drug Administration (FDA) is empowered to enforce the Federal Food, Drug, and Cosmetics Act; and the federal Environmental Protection Agency (EPA) is authorized to enforce federal environmental protection laws. These statutes are the *substantive law* that is enforced by the particular agency.

People say law, but they mean wealth.

—Ralph Waldo Emerson

The government's recordkeeping and reporting requirements form a large part of administrative law. Other government regulations concern proper business purpose and conduct, entry restrictions into an industry, government rate setting, and the like.

Proponents of government regulation argue that it is needed to protect consumers and others from unethical and deceptive business practices. Opponents say that the time and compliance and enforcement costs outweigh the benefits of regulation. The debate rages on, but one fact is certain: Government regulation will continue to affect business operations.

General Government Regulation

Most government regulation, which is **general government regulation,** applies to many businesses and industries collectively. For example, the National Labor Relations Board (NLRB) is empowered to regulate the formation and operation of labor unions in most industries, the Occupational Safety and Health Administration (OSHA) is authorized to formulate and enact safety and health standards for the workplace, and the Consumer Product Safety Commission (CPSC) is empowered to establish mandatory safety standards for products sold in this country.

Specific Government Regulation

Congress and the executive branch created some administrative agencies to monitor certain regulated industries in **specific government regulation.** The Federal Communications Commission (FCC) regulates the operation of television and radio stations, the Interstate Commerce Commission (ICC) regulates railroads; the Federal Aviation Administration (FAA) regulates commercial airlines; and the Office of the Comptroller of the Currency (OCC) regulates national banks. Although a detailed discussion of these agencies and the laws they administer is beyond the scope of this book, it is important to know that they exist.

Delegation of Powers

Because the U.S. Constitution does not stipulate that administrative agencies are a separate branch of the government, they must be created by the legislative or executive branch. When an administrative agency is created, it is delegated certain powers. The agency has only the legislative, judicial, and executive powers that are delegated to it. This is called the **delegation doctrine.**

Thus, an agency can adopt a rule or regulation (a legislative function), prosecute a violation of the statute or rule (an executive function), and adjudicate the dispute (a judicial function). The courts have generally upheld this combined power of administrative agencies as being constitutional. If an administrative agency acts outside the scope of its delegated powers, it is an unconstitutional act.

Administrative Agencies

Administrative agencies are generally established with the goal of creating a body of professionals who are experts in a particular field. These experts have delegated authority to regulate an individual industry or a specific area of commerce.

Administrative agencies are created by federal, state, and local governments. They range from large, complex federal agencies, such as the Department of Homeland Security, to local zoning boards. Many administrative agencies are given the authority to adopt **rules and regulations** that enforce and interpret statutory law. (The rule-making power of administrative agencies is discussed later in this chapter.)

Good government is an empire of laws.

—John Adams

Federal administrative agencies. The most pervasive government regulations have developed from the statutes enforced by and the rules and regulations adopted by **federal administrative agencies.** The majority of federal administrative agencies—including the Department of Justice, the Department of Housing and Urban Development, the Department of Labor, the Department of Transportation, and the Department of Commerce—are part of the executive branch of government.

Congress has established many federal administrative agencies. These agencies are independent of the executive branch and have broad regulatory powers over key areas of the national economy. Many of these independent agencies are discussed elsewhere in this book.

State administrative agencies. All states have created administrative agencies to enforce and interpret state law. For example, most states have a corporations department to enforce state corporations law; a banking department to regulate the operation of banks; fish and game departments; and workers' compensation boards. **State administrative agencies** also have a profound effect on business. Local governments and municipalities create administrative agencies, such as zoning commissions, to administer local law.

Licensing Powers of Administrative Agencies

Statutes often require the issuance of a government **license** before a person can enter certain types of industries (e.g., banking, television and radio broadcasting, commercial aviation) or professions (e.g., doctors, lawyers, dentists, certified public accountants, contractors). Most administrative agencies have the power to determine whether to grant licenses to applicants.

Applicants usually must submit detailed applications to the appropriate administrative agency. In addition, the agency usually accepts written comments from interested parties and holds hearings on the matter. The administrative agency's decision is subject to judicial review. However, the courts generally defer to the expertise of administrative agencies in licensing matters.

Administrative Procedure Act

In 1946, Congress enacted the **Administrative Procedure Act (APA)** [5 U.S.C. §§ 551 et seq.]. This Act establishes certain administrative procedures that federal administrative agencies must follow in conducting their affairs. For example, the APA establishes notice and hearing requirements, rules for conducting agency adjudicative actions, and procedures for rule making. Most states have enacted administrative procedural acts that govern state administrative agencies.

Administrative law judges (ALJs) preside over administrative proceedings. They decide questions of law and fact concerning the case. There is no jury. The ALJ is an employee of the administrative agency. Both the administrative agency and the respondent may be represented by counsel. Witnesses may be examined and cross-examined, evidence may be introduced, objections may be made, and such.

The ALJ's decision is issued in the form of an **order**. The order must state the reasons for the ALJ's decision.

The order becomes final if it is not appealed. An appeal consists of a review by the agency. The agency review can result in new findings of fact and law. Further appeal can be made to the appropriate federal court (in federal agency actions) or state court (in state agency actions).

Consumer Protection

Things are seldom what they seem.
Skim milk masquerades as cream.
—William S. Gilbert,
H.M.S. Pinafore

Originally, sales transactions in this country were guided by the principle of ***caveat emptor*** ("let the buyer beware"). To promote product safety and prohibit abusive, unfair, and deceptive selling practices, federal and state governments have enacted a variety of statutes to regulate the behavior of businesses that deal with consumers. These laws are collectively referred to as **consumer protection laws.** Several of the major consumer protection laws are discussed in the following paragraphs.

Federal Food, Drug, and Cosmetic Act

The federal **Food, Drug, and Cosmetic Act (FDCA)** was enacted in 1938 [21 U.S.C. § 301]. This Act, as amended, regulates the testing, manufacture, distribution, and sale of foods, drugs, cosmetics, and medicinal products and devices in the United States. The Food and Drug Administration (FDA) is the federal administrative agency empowered to enforce the FDCA.

Before certain food additives, drugs, cosmetics, and medicinal devices can be sold to the public, they must receive FDA approval. An applicant must submit an application to the FDA that contains relevant information about the safety and uses of the product. The FDA, after considering the evidence, will either approve or deny the application.

The FDA can seek search warrants and conduct inspections; obtain orders for the seizure, recall, and condemnation of products; and seek injunctions to halt and prosecute suspected criminal violations of the U.S. Department of Justice regulations.

Regulation of Food

The FDCA prohibits the shipment, distribution, or sale of **adulterated food**. Food is deemed adulterated if it consists in whole or in part of any "filthy, putrid, or de-

Do-Not-Call Registry

Two federal administrative agencies—the **Federal Trade Commission (FTC)** and the **Federal Communications Commission (FCC)**—are accorded hero status by consumers for creating the **"Do-Not-Call" Registry,** on which consumers can place their names and free themselves from most unsolicited commercial telephone calls. The FTC and FCC found their authority to adopt their coordinated do-not-call rules in several federal statutes. The first is the *Telephone Consumer Protection Act of 1991*, which authorized the FCC to establish a national database of consumers who objected to receiving commercial sales calls. The second is the *Telemarketing and Consumer Fraud and Abuse Prevention Act of 1994*, which authorized the FTC to prohibit sales calls that a reasonable consumer would consider abusive to his or her privacy. And just to wrap things up, after the Do-Not-Call Registry was put in place, in 2003 Congress enacted *An Act to Ratify the Authority of the Federal Trade Commission to Establish a Do-Not-Call Registry.*

In 2003, the FTC and FCC promulgated administrative rules that created the Do-Not-Call Registry. A person can place themselves on the registry by calling toll-free 1-888-382-1222 or registering online at *www.donotcall.gov*. Both wire-connected phones and wireless cell phones can be registered. Telemarketers have three months from the date on which a consumer signs up for the registry to remove the customer's phone number from their sales call list. Registration remains valid for five years, and can be renewed. Charitable and political organizations are exempt from the registry. Also, there is an "established business relationship" exception that allows businesses to call customers for 10 months after they sell or lease goods or services to that person or conduct a financial transaction with that person. The Do-Not-Call Registry allows consumers to designate specific companies not to call them, including those who otherwise qualify for the established business relationship exemption.

Telemarketers, who claimed they would lose substantial business and have to fire millions of workers, sued to have the Do-Not-Call Registry declared unconstitutional as a violation of their constitutional right to free speech. A U.S. district court in Colorado agreed with the telemarketers. On appeal, however, the U.S. Court of Appeals for the Tenth Circuit reversed, holding that the do-not-call rules did not violate telemarketers' free speech rights. The court of appeals justified its decision by finding that the Do-Not-Call Registry

- Restricts only core commercial speech (i.e., sales calls)
- Targets speech that invades the privacy of the home, a personal sanctuary
- Is an opt-in program that puts the choice on whether to restrict commercial calls in the hands of consumers
- Furthers the government's interest in combating fraudulent and abusive telemarketing

The court of appeals held that the do-not-call registry was narrowly tailored and did not prevent marketers from reaching consumers by direct mail, advertisements, and other lawful methods. The court upheld the lawfulness of the charitable and political organizations exception and the established business relationship exception. In reaching its decision, the court stated "The do-not-call registry is a valid commercial speech regulation because it directly advances the government's important interests in safeguarding personal privacy and reducing the danger of telemarketing abuse without burdening an excessive amount of speech. The Do-Not-Call Registry lets consumers avoid unwanted sales pitches that invade the home via telephone."

Mainstream Marketing Services, Inc. v. Federal Trade Commission, 358 F.3d 1228, 2004 U.S. App. Lexis 2564 (2004)

SIDEBAR

Food and Drug Administration
The federal **Food and Drug Administration (FDA)** is the federal administrative agency charged with enforcing federal laws that regulate the safety of foods, drugs, cosmetics, and medicinal products and devices.

composed substance" or if it is otherwise "unfit for food." Note that food does not have to be entirely pure to be distributed or sold; it only has to be unadulterated.

The FDCA also prohibits **false and misleading labeling** of food products. In addition, it mandates affirmative disclosure of information on food labels, including the name of the food, the name and place of the manufacturer, and a statement of ingredients. A manufacturer may be held liable for deceptive labeling or packaging.

Regulation of Drugs

The FDCA gives the FDA the authority to regulate the testing, manufacture, distribution, and sale of **drugs.** The **Drug Amendment to the FDCA,** enacted in 1962, gives the FDA broad powers to license new drugs in the United States. After a new drug application is filed, the FDA holds a hearing and investigates the merits of the application. This process can take many years. The FDA may withdraw approval of any previously licensed drug.

This law requires all users of prescription and nonprescription drugs to receive proper directions for use (including the method and duration of use) and adequate warnings about any related side effects. The manufacture, distribution, or sale of adulterated or misbranded drugs is prohibited.

Regulation of Cosmetics

The FDA's definition of **cosmetics** includes substances and preparations for cleansing, altering the appearance of, and promoting the attractiveness of a person. Eye shadow and other facial makeup products are examples of cosmetics subject to FDA regulation. Ordinary household soap is expressly exempted from this definition.

The FDA has issued regulations that require cosmetics to be labeled, to disclose ingredients, and to contain warnings if they are carcinogenic (cancer-causing) or otherwise dangerous to a person's health. The manufacture, distribution, or sale of adulterated or misbranded cosmetics is prohibited. The FDA may remove from commerce any cosmetics that contain unsubstantiated claims of preserving youth, increasing virility, growing hair, and such.

Food Labeling

In late 1990, Congress passed a sweeping truth-in-labeling law called the **Nutrition Labeling and Education Act.** The statute requires food manufacturers and processors to provide more nutritional information on virtually all foods and bars them from making scientifically unsubstantiated health claims.

The new law requires the more than 20,000 food labels found on grocery store shelves to disclose the number of calories derived from fat and the amount of dietary fiber, saturated fat, cholesterol, and a variety of other substances. The law applies to packaged foods as well as fruit, vegetables, and raw seafood. Meat, poultry, and egg products, which are regulated by the Department of Agriculture, are exempt from the Act, as are restaurant food and prepared dishes sold in supermarkets or delicatessens.

The FDA announced final regulations to implement the Act. The regulations require food processors to provide uniform information about serving sizes and nutrients on labels of the food products they sell and establish standard definitions for *light, low fat, natural,* and other terms routinely bandied about by food processors.

A Hidden Source of Protein in Peanut Butter

You take a big bite of a peanut butter sandwich and savor the taste. It has been processed by a food manufacturer and inspected by the federal government, so you think it is pure peanut butter. Not necessarily. Under federal FDA guidelines, peanut butter may contain up to 30 insect fragments per 3½ ounces and still be considered "safe" for human consumption.

The FDA has set ceilings, or "action levels," for certain contaminants, or "defects," as the FDA likes to call them, for various foods. Several of these action levels are

Golden raisins—35 fly eggs per 8 ounces
Popcorn—two rodent hairs per pound
Shelled peanuts—20 insects per 100 pounds
Canned mushrooms—20 maggots per 3½ ounces
Tomato juice—10 fly eggs per 3½ ounces

The FDA can mount inspections and raids to enforce its action levels. If it finds that the federal tolerance system has been violated, it can seize the offending food and destroy it at the owner's expense.

The courts have upheld the presence of some contamination in food as lawful under the federal Food, Drug, and Cosmetic Act. For example, in one case the court found that 28 insect parts in 9 pounds of butter did not violate the act. The court stated, "Few foods contain no natural or unavoidable defects. Even with modern technology, all defects in foods cannot be eliminated."

United States v. Capital City Foods, Inc., 345 F. Supp. 277, 1972 U.S. Dist. Lexis (Dist N.D. 1972)

In April 1991, the FDA had U.S. marshals seize 24,000 half-gallon cartons of "Citrus Hill Fresh Choice" orange juice, which is made by mammoth food processor Procter & Gamble (P&G). After trying for a year to get P&G to remove the word *fresh* from the carton—the product is made from concentrate and is pasteurized—the FDA finally got tough. P&G gave in after 2 days and agreed to remove the word *fresh* from its Citrus Hill products.

Product Safety

In 1972, Congress enacted the **Consumer Product Safety Act (CPSA)** [U.S.C. § 2051] and created the **Consumer Product Safety Commission (CPSC).** The CPSC is an independent federal regulatory agency empowered to (1) adopt rules and regulations to interpret and enforce the CPSA, (2) conduct research on the safety of consumer products, and (3) collect data regarding injuries caused by consumer products.

Because the CPSC regulates potentially dangerous consumer products, it issues product safety standards for consumer products that pose an unreasonable risk of injury. If a consumer product is found to be imminently hazardous—that is, its use can cause an unreasonable risk of death or serious injury or illness—the manufacturer can be required to recall, repair, or replace the product or take other corrective action. Alternatively, the CPSC can seek injunctions, bring actions to seize hazardous consumer products, seek civil penalties for knowing violations of the Act or of CPSA rules, and seek criminal penalties for knowing and willful violations of the Act or of CPSC rules. A private party can sue for an injunction to prevent violations of the Act or of CPSC rules and regulations.

Certain consumer products, including motor vehicles, boats, aircraft, and firearms, are regulated by other government agencies.

SIDEBAR

Consumer Product Safety Commission (CPSC)
An independent federal regulatory agency empowered to (1) adopt rules and regulations to interpret and enforce the Consumer Product Safety Act, (2) conduct research on safety, and (3) collect data regarding injuries.

INTERNATIONAL PERSPECTIVE

UNITED NATIONS BIOSAFETY PROTOCOL FOR GENETICALLY ALTERED FOODS

Many food processors in the United States and across the world genetically modify some foods by adding genes from other organisms to help crops grow faster or ward off pests. In the past, food processors did not notify consumers that they were purchasing genetically modified agricultural products. Although the companies insist that genetically altered foods are safe, consumers and many countries began to demand that such foods be clearly labeled so that buyers could decide for themselves.

The most concerned countries in the world regarding this issue were in Europe. Led by Germany, many European countries wanted to require genetically engineered food products to be labeled as such and be transported separately from non-altered agricultural products. Some European countries wanted genetically altered foods to be banned completely. The United States, a major exporter of agricultural products and the leader in the development of biotech foods, argued that these countries were using this issue to erect trade barriers to keep U.S.-produced food products out of their countries in violation of international trade treaties and conventions administered by the World Trade Organization (WTO) that had reduced or eliminated many international trade restrictions.

In January 2000, a compromise was reached when 138 countries, including the United States, agreed to the United Nations–sponsored **Biosafety Protocol.** After much negotiation, the countries agreed that all genetically engineered foods would be clearly labeled with the phrase "May contain living modified organisms." This allows consumers to decide on their own whether to purchase such altered food products. In addition, the boxes and containers in which such goods are shipped must also be clearly marked as containing genetically altered food products.

Safety Labeling

The federal **Fair Packaging and Labeling Act** [15 U.S.C. §§ 1451 et seq.] requires the labels on consumer goods to identify the product; the manufacturer, processor, or packager of the product and its address; the net quantity of the contents of the package; and the quantity of each serving if the number of servings is stated. The label must use simple and clear language that a consumer can understand. This Act is administered by the Federal Trade Commission (FTC) and the Department of Health and Human Services.

> No workman without tools, no lawyer without fools.
>
> —Benjamin Franklin

Many children suffer serious injury or death when they open household products and inhale, ingest, or otherwise mishandle dangerous products. The federal **Poison Prevention Packaging Act** [15 U.S.C. § 1471] is intended to prevent this problem by requiring manufacturers to provide "childproof" containers and packages for all household products.

Unfair and Deceptive Practices

The **Federal Trade Commission Act (FTC Act)** was enacted in 1914 [15 U.S.C. §§ 41–51]. The Federal Trade Commission (FTC) was created the following year. The FTC is empowered to enforce the FTC Act as well as other federal consumer protection statutes.

Section 5 of the FTC Act, as amended, prohibits *unfair and deceptive practices.* It has been used extensively to regulate business conduct. This section gives the

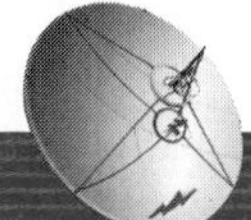

INFORMATION TECHNOLOGY

ANTI-SPAM STATUTE

Americans are being bombarded in their e-mail accounts by "**spam**"—unsolicited commercial advertising. Spammers try to sell you literally anything. In 2003, spam accounted for over 75 percent of all business e-mail traffic. In addition, many spam messages are fraudulent and deceptive, including misleading headers in the message's subject line. It takes time and money to sort through, review, and discard unwanted spam.

In 2003, Congress enacted the federal **Controlling the Assault of Non-Solicited Pornography and Marketing Act,** called the **CAN-SPAM Act.** The Act (1) prohibits spammers from using falsified headers in e-mail messages and (2) requires spammers who send sexually oriented email to properly label it as such. The Federal Trade Commission (FTC), a federal administrative agency, is empowered to enforce the CAN-SPAM Act.

In effect, the CAN-SPAM Act does not can spam, but instead approves businesses to spam as long as they do not lie. Spam that is not sexually oriented does not even have to be labeled as spam. The act expressly provides that victims of spam do not have the right to bring civil lawsuits against spammers. The CAN-SPAM Act does not regulate spam sent internationally from other countries. In essence, the CAN-SPAM Act is too weak to help consumers ward off the spam that deluges them on a daily basis.

In 2004, the FTC adopted a rule that requires that sexually explicit spam e-mail to contain a warning on the subject line reading "SEXUALLY-EXPLICIT." The FTC rule also prohibits the messages themselves from containing graphic material. The graphic material can appear only after the recipient has opened the e-mail.

FTC the authority to bring an administrative proceeding to attack a deceptive or unfair practice. If, after a public administrative hearing, the FTC finds a violation of Section 5, it may issue a cease-and-desist order, an affirmative disclosure to consumers, corrective advertising, or the like. The FTC may sue in state or federal court to issue compensation on behalf of consumers. The decision of the FTC may be appealed to federal court.

False and deceptive advertising violates Section 5. Advertising is false and deceptive under Section 5 if it (1) contains misinformation or omits important information that is likely to mislead a "reasonable consumer" or (2) makes an unsubstantiated claim (e.g., "This product is 33 percent better than our competitor's"). Proof of actual deception is not required. Statements of opinion and "sales talk" (e.g., "This is a great car") do not constitute false and deceptive advertising.

He will lie, sin, with such volubility that you would think truth were a fool.

—William Shakespeare, *All's Well That Ends Well*

Bait and switch is another type of deceptive advertising under Section 5. It occurs when a seller advertises the availability of a low-cost discounted item (the "bait") to attract customers to its store. Once the customers are in the store, however, the seller pressures them to purchase more expensive merchandise (the "switch"). The FTC states that a bait and switch occurs if the seller refuses to show consumers the advertised merchandise, discourages employees from selling the advertised merchandise, or fails to have adequate quantities of the merchandise available.

CASE FOR DISCUSSION

Federal Trade Commission v. Colgate–Palmolive Co.

380 U.S. 374, 85 S.Ct. 1035, 1965 U.S. Lexis 2300 (1965) Supreme Court of the United States

FACTS

The Colgate–Palmolive Co. (Colgate) manufactures and sells a shaving cream called "Rapid Shave." Colgate hired Ted Bates & Company (Bates), an advertising agency, to prepare television commercials designed to show that Rapid Shave could shave the toughest beards. With Colgate's consent, Bates prepared a television commercial that included the "sandpaper test." The announcer informed the audience, "To prove Rapid Shave's super-moisturizing power, we put it right from the can onto this tough, dry sandpaper. And off in a stroke."

While the announcer was speaking, Rapid Shave was applied to a substance that appeared to be sandpaper and immediately a razor was shown shaving the substance clean. Evidence showed that the substance resembling sandpaper was in fact a simulated prop or "mock-up" made of Plexiglas to which sand had been glued. The Federal Trade Commission (FTC) issued a complaint against Colgate and Bates, alleging a violation of Section 5 of the Federal Trade Commission Act. The FTC held against the defendants. The court of appeals reversed. The FTC appealed to the U.S. Supreme Court.

ISSUE

Did the defendants engage in false and deceptive advertising in violation of Section 5 of the Federal Trade Commission Act?

COURT'S REASONING

The U.S. Supreme Court agreed with the FTC that the undisclosed use of Plexiglas in the commercial was a material deceptive practice. The Supreme Court stated that if it becomes impossible or impracticable to show simulated demonstrations on television in a truthful manner, this indicates that television is not a medium that lends itself to this type of commercial. The Court stated, "All methods of advertising do not equally favor every seller. If the inherent limitations of a method do not permit its use in the way a seller desires, the seller cannot by material misrepresentation compensate for those limitations."

DECISION AND REMEDY

The U.S. Supreme Court held that Colgate and Bates had engaged in false and deceptive advertising. Reversed and remanded.

QUESTIONS

1. Does the government owe a duty to protect consumers from false and misleading business practices? Explain.
2. Did Colgate and Bates act ethically in this case? Do you think the viewing public believed the commercial?
3. Can you think of any advertisement or commercial you think is misleading? Explain.

INVESTOR PROTECTION

Prior to the 1920s and 1930s, the securities markets in this country were not regulated by the federal government. Securities were sold to investors with little, if any, disclosure. Fraud in these transactions was common.

Following the stock market crash of 1929, Congress enacted a series of statutes designed to regulate securities markets. The Securities Act of 1933 requires disclosure by companies and others who wish to issue securities to the public. The Securities Exchange Act of 1934 was enacted to prevent fraud in the subsequent trading of securities, including insider trading.

These federal and state statutes are designed to (1) require disclosure of information to investors and (2) prevent fraud.

The Securities and Exchange Commission (SEC)

The Securities Exchange Act of 1934 created the **Securities and Exchange Commission (SEC)** and empowered it to administer federal securities laws. The SEC is an administrative agency composed of five members who are appointed by the president. The major responsibilities of the SEC are:

Like a gun that fires at the muzzle and kicks over at the breach, a cheating transaction hurts the cheater as much as the man cheated.

—Henry Ward Beecher

1. Adopting rules (also called regulations) that further the purpose of the federal securities statutes. These rules have the force of law.
2. Investigating alleged securities violations and bringing enforcement actions against suspected violators. This may include a recommendation of criminal prosecution. Criminal prosecutions of violations of federal securities laws are brought by the U.S. Department of Justice.
3. Regulating the activities of securities brokers and advisors. This includes registering brokers and advisors and taking enforcement action against those who violate securities laws.

Issuance of Securities

The Securities Act of 1933 primarily regulates the *issuance* of securities by a corporation, a general or limited partnership, an unincorporated association, or an individual. The party selling the securities to the public is called the **issuer**. The issuer may be a relatively new company selling securities to the public through an **initial public offering (IPO),** or it may be an established company (e.g., Microsoft Corporation) selling new securities to the public.

Section 5 of the Securities Act of 1933 requires securities offered to the public through the use of the mails or any facility of interstate commerce to be *registered* with the SEC by means of a registration statement and an accompanying prospectus.

If securities that should be registered with the SEC are not registered and are sold to the public, this violates the 1933 Act. Investors can sue and recover damages. The U.S. government can impose criminal penalties on any person who willfully violates the 1933 Act.

Registration Statement

A covered issuer must file a written **registration statement** with the SEC. The issuer's lawyer normally prepares the statement, with the help of the issuer's management, accountants, and underwriters.

A registration statement must contain descriptions of (1) securities being offered for sale, (2) the registrant's business, (3) the management of the registrant, including compensation, stock options and benefits, and material transactions with the registrant, (4) pending litigation, (5) how the proceeds from the offering will be used, (6) government regulation, (7) the degree of competition in the industry, and (8) any special risk factors. In addition, the registration statement must be accompanied by financial statements as certified by certified public accountants.

Registration statements usually become effective 20 business days after they are filed, unless the SEC requires additional information to be disclosed. A new 20-day period begins each time the registration statement is amended. At the registrant's request, the SEC may "accelerate" the **effective date** (i.e., not require the registrant to wait 20 days after the last amendment is filed).

The SEC does not pass judgment upon the merits of the securities offered. It decides only whether the issuer has met the disclosure requirements.

Prospectus

The **prospectus** is a written disclosure document that must be submitted to the SEC along with the registration statement. The prospectus is used as a selling tool by the issuer. It is provided to prospective investors to enable them to evaluate the financial risk of the investment.

A prospectus must contain the following language in capital letters and boldface (usually red) type:

> THESE SECURITIES HAVE NOT BEEN APPROVED OR DISAPPROVED BY THE SECURITIES AND EXCHANGE COMMISSION OR ANY STATE SECURITIES COMMISSION NOR HAS THE SECURITIES AND EXCHANGE COMMISSION OR ANY STATE SECURITIES COMMISSION PASSED UPON THE ACCURACY OR ADEQUACY OF THIS PROSPECTUS. ANY REPRESENTATION TO THE CONTRARY IS A CRIMINAL OFFENSE.

Insider Trading

Congress enacted the Securities Exchange Act of 1934 to regulate and prevent fraud in the *subsequent trading* of securities after they have been issued. Subsequent trading would include purchasing or selling securities over an organized exchange (e.g., the New York Stock Exchange), in the open market, or even in individual sales.

> There are some frauds so well conducted that it would be stupidity not to be deceived by them.
>
> —C.C. Colton

Section 10(b) of the 1934 Act and **Rule 10b-5** adopted by the SEC prohibit fraud and deceptive practices in the purchase or sale of securities. Investors who are defrauded can sue and recover damages. The U.S. government can impose criminal penalties on persons who violate Section 10(b) and Rule 10b-5. One of the most important practices prohibited by Section 10(b) and Rule 10b-5 is **insider trading.** Insider trading occurs when a company employee (e.g., an executive or any employee) or company advisor (e.g., certified public accountant or lawyer) uses material nonpublic information to make a profit by trading in the securities of the company. This practice is considered illegal because it allows **insiders** to take advantage of the investing public.

For example, suppose the Widget Corporation has its annual audit done by its outside CPAs. Peter is one of the CPAs who conducts the audit. The audit discloses that the Widget Corporation's profits have doubled since last year, and Peter rightfully discloses this fact to Martha, Widget Corporation's chief financial officer (CFO). This earnings information is definitely material, and it is nonpublic until the corporation publicly announces its earnings in two days. Prior to the earnings

CASE FOR DISCUSSION

Securities and Exchange Commission v. Edwards

124 S.Ct. 892, 2004 U.S. Lexis 659 (2004) Supreme Court of the United States

FACTS

Charles Edwards was the Chairman, Chief Executive Officer (CEO), and sole shareholder of ETS Payphones, Inc. (ETS). ETS sold payphones to the public via independent distributors. The payphones were sold to buyers in a package deal for $7,000 consisting of a payphone site lease, a 5-year leaseback by ETS, and an agreement whereby ETS would install the equipment at the site, arrange for connection and long-distance telephone service, collect coin revenues, and maintain and repair the payphones. Under the ETS contract, each payphone investor was guaranteed to receive $82 per month on his or her investment. ETS guaranteed to refund the full purchase price at the end of the lease. ETS enrolled more than 10,000 people in the payphone program who together invested over $300 million.

In actuality, the payphone did not generate enough revenues for ETS to make the guaranteed monthly payments. After ETS defaulted on hundreds of millions of dollars of payments to investors, it filed for bankruptcy. The SEC brought a civil action against Edwards and ETS, alleging that the defendants had failed to register the payphone sale-and-leaseback arrangement with the SEC as a "security" prior to selling them to the public and committed securities fraud. The U.S. district court held that the payphone arrangement constituted a "security" and was therefore subject to federal securities laws. The U.S. Court of Appeals reversed, finding no security because the sale-and-leaseback provided for a fixed rate of return rather than capital appreciation or participation in the earnings of the enterprise. The SEC appealed to the U.S. Supreme Court.

ISSUE

Is the payphone sale-and-leaseback arrangement that guaranteed a fixed rate of return a security and therefore subject to federal securities laws?

COURT'S REASONING

The U.S. Supreme Court mocked ETS' promotional brochure that stated "Opportunity doesn't always knock, sometimes it rings" by stating "And sometimes it hangs up." The Supreme Court stated that is exactly what Edwards and ETS did to the 10,000 investors who lost $300 million on the payphone investment scheme. The Supreme Court held that Congress, by enacting federal securities laws, intended to regulate investments in whatever form they are made and by whatever name they are called. The Court stated: "There is no reason to distinguish between promises of fixed returns and promises of variable returns. In both cases, the investing public is attracted by representations of investment income. Moreover, investments pitched as low risk (such as those offering a guaranteed fixed return) are particularly attractive to individuals more vulnerable to investment fraud, including older and less sophisticated investors." The Court noted that under the reading that respondent Edwards advanced, unscrupulous marketers of investments could evade the securities laws by picking a fixed rate of return to promise.

DECISION AND REMEDY

The U.S. Supreme Court held that an investment arrangement that offers a fixed rate of return is a security subject to the provisions of federal securities laws. The Supreme Court reversed the decision of the court of appeals and remanded the case for further proceedings based on violations of securities laws and securities fraud.

QUESTIONS

1. If a financial arrangement that guaranteed a fixed rate of return was not found to be a security, what would be the result for society? Explain.
2. Did Edwards act ethically in this case? Is there any evidence that he acted fraudulently? Explain.
3. If Edwards had to disclose the truth about his and ETS' investment scheme, would many people have invested? Explain.

information being made public, Peter and Martha buy stock in Widget Corporation at $100 per share. After the earnings information is made public, the stock of Widget Corporation increases to $150 per share. Both Peter and Martha are liable for insider trading in violation of Section 10(b) and Rule 10b-5.

SIDEBAR

Environmental Protection Agency
In 1970, Congress created the **Environmental Protection Agency (EPA)** to coordinate the implementation and enforcement of the federal environmental protection laws. The EPA has broad rule-making powers to adopt regulations to advance the laws that it is empowered to administer. The agency also has adjudicative powers to hold hearings, make decisions, and order remedies for violations of federal environmental laws. In addition, the EPA can initiate judicial proceedings in court against suspected violators of federal environmental laws.

Environmental Protection

In producing and consuming products, businesses and consumers generate air pollution, water pollution, and hazardous and toxic wastes that cause harm to the environment and to human health. Although environmental protection has been a concern ever since medieval England enacted laws regulating the burning of soft coal, pollution has now reached alarming levels in this country and the world.

In the 1970s, the federal government began enacting statutes to protect our nation's air and water from pollution, to regulate hazardous wastes, and to protect wildlife. In many instances, states enacted their own environmental laws that now coexist with federal law. These laws provide both civil and criminal penalties. **Environmental protection** is one of the most important issues facing business and society today.

Environmental Impact Statement

The federal **National Environmental Policy Act (NEPA)** became effective January 1, 1970 [42 U.S.C. §§ 4321 et seq.]. The **Council on Environmental Quality** was created under this Act. The NEPA mandates that the federal government consider the "adverse impact" on the environment of proposed legislation, rule making, or other federal government action before the action is implemented.

The NEPA and rules adopted thereunder require that an **Environmental Impact Statement (EIS)** must be prepared for all proposed legislation or major federal action that significantly affects the quality of the human environment. The purpose of the EIS is to provide enough information about the environment to enable the federal government to determine the feasibility of the project. The EIS is also used as evidence in court whenever a federal action is challenged as violating the NEPA or other federal environmental protection laws. Examples of actions that require an EIS include proposals to build a new federally funded highway, to license nuclear plants, and the like.

Once an EIS is prepared, it is subject to public review, and the public has 30 days in which to submit comments to the EPA. After the comments have been received and reviewed, the EPA will issue an order that states whether the proposed federal action may proceed. Decisions of the EPA are appealable to the appropriate U.S. court of appeals.

Most states and many local governments have enacted laws that require an EIS to be prepared regarding proposed state and local government action as well as private development.

"My lawyer finally got me on the endangered-species list!"

Clean Air Act

The **Clean Air Act** was enacted in 1963 to assist states in dealing with air pollution. The Act was amended in 1970 and 1977 and, more recently, by the Clean Air Act Amendments of 1990 [42 U.S.C. §§ 7401 et seq.]. The Clean Air Act, as amended, provides comprehensive regulation of air quality in this country.

The Clean Air Act directs the EPA to establish **national ambient air quality standards (NAAQS)** for certain pollutants. These standards are set at two different levels: primary (to protect human beings) and secondary (to protect vegetation, matter, climate, visibility, and economic values). Specific standards have been established for carbon monoxide, nitrogen oxide, sulfur oxide, ozone, lead, and particulate matter.

Although the EPA establishes air quality standards, the states are responsible for their enforcement. Each state is required to prepare a *state implementation plan (SIP)* that sets out how the state plans to meet the federal standards. The EPA has divided each state into *air quality control regions (AQCRs)*. Each region is monitored to ensure compliance.

Air Pollution

One of the major problems facing this country is **air pollution.** Air pollution is caused both by mobile sources (such as automobiles) and by stationary sources (such as public utilities, manufacturing facilities, and households).

Automobile and other vehicle emissions are one of the major sources of air pollution in this country. In an effort to control emissions from these **mobile sources,** the Clean Air Act requires air pollution controls to be installed on motor vehicles. Emission standards have been set for automobiles, trucks, buses, motorcycles, and airplanes. The Clean Air Act requires new automobiles and light-duty trucks to meet air quality control standards. In addition, the Act authorizes the EPA to regulate air pollution caused by fuel and fuel additives.

Substantial amounts of air pollution are emitted by **stationary sources** (e.g., industrial plants, oil refineries, public utilities). The Clean Air Act requires states to identify major stationary sources and develop plans to reduce air pollution from these sources.

Discourage litigation. Persuade your neighbors to compromise whenever you can. Point out to them how the nominal winner is often a real loser—in fees, and expenses, and waste of time. As a peacemaker the lawyer has a superior opportunity of being a good man. There will still be business enough.

—Abraham Lincoln

Toxic Air Pollutants

Section 112 of the Clean Air Act requires the EPA to identify **toxic air pollutants** that cause serious illness or death to humans [42 U.S.C. § 7412(b)]. So far, more than 200 chemicals have been listed as toxic, including asbestos, mercury, vinyl chloride, benzene, beryllium, and radionuclides.

The Act requires the EPA to establish standards for these chemicals and requires stationary sources to install equipment and technology to control emissions of toxic substances. EPA standards for toxic substances are set without regard to economic or technological feasibility.

Water Pollution

Water pollution affects human health, recreation, agriculture, and business. Pollution of waterways by industry and humans has caused severe ecological and environmental problems, including water sources that are unsafe for drinking water,

Indoor Air Pollution: A Frontier for Environmental Litigation

According to officials at the EPA, the air inside some buildings may be 100 times more polluted than outside air. Doctors increasingly attribute a wide range of symptoms to **indoor air pollution,** or **sick building syndrome.**

Indoor air pollution has two primary causes. In an effort to reduce dependence on foreign oil, many recently constructed office buildings were overly insulated and built with sealed windows and no outside air ducts. As a result, no fresh air enters many workplaces. This absence of fresh air can cause headaches, fatigue, and dizziness among workers.

The other chief cause of sick building syndrome, which is believed to affect up to one-third of U.S. office buildings, is hazardous chemicals and construction materials. In the office, these include everything from asbestos to noxious fumes emitted from copy machines, carbonless paper, and cleaning fluids. In the home, radon, an odorless gas that is emitted from the natural breakdown of uranium in soil, poses a particularly widespread danger. Radon gas damages and may destroy lung tissue. The costs of eliminating these conditions can be colossal.

Experts predict that sick building syndrome is likely to spawn a flood of litigation, and that a wide range of parties will be sued. Manufacturers, employers, home sellers, builders, engineers, and architects will increasingly be forced to defend themselves against tort and breach-of-contract actions filed by homeowners, employees, and others affected by indoor air pollution. Insurance companies will undoubtedly be drawn into costly lawsuits stemming from indoor air pollution.

fish, birds, and animals. The federal government has enacted a comprehensive scheme of statutes and regulations to prevent and control water pollution.

Clean Water Act. In 1948, Congress enacted the **Federal Water Pollution Control Act (FWPCA)** to regulate water pollution. This act was amended several times before it was updated by the Clean Water Act of 1972, the Clean Water Act of 1977, and the Water Quality Act of 1987. The FWPCA, as amended, is simply referred to as the **Clean Water Act** [33 U.S.C. §§ 1251 et seq.]. This Act is administered by the EPA.

Pursuant to the Clean Water Act, the EPA has established water quality standards that define which bodies of water can be used for public drinking water, recreation (such as swimming), propagation of fish and wildlife, and agricultural and industrial uses.

The Clean Water Act authorizes the EPA to establish water pollution control standards for **point sources of water pollution** (i.e., mines, manufacturing plants, paper mills, electric utility plants, municipal sewage plants, and other stationary sources of water pollution). The EPA issues guidelines as to the best available technologies. Dischargers of pollutants are required to keep records, maintain monitoring equipment, and keep samples of discharges.

States are primarily responsible for enforcing the provisions of the Clean Water Act and EPA regulations adopted thereunder.

Thermal Pollution

The Clean Water Act expressly forbids **thermal pollution** because the discharge of heated waters or materials into the nation's waterways may upset the ecological balance; decrease the oxygen content of water; and harm fish, birds, and animals

Superfund

In 1980, Congress enacted the **Comprehensive Environmental Response, Compensation, and Liability Act (CERCLA),** which is commonly called **Superfund** [42 U.S.C. § 9601 et seq.]. The Act, which was significantly amended in 1986, is administered by the EPA. The Act gave the federal government a mandate to deal with hazardous wastes that have been spilled, stored, or abandoned. The Superfund provides for the creation of a government fund to finance the cleanup of hazardous waste sites (hence the name *Superfund*). The fund is financed through taxes on chemicals, feedstocks, motor fuels, and other products that contain hazardous substances.

The Superfund requires the EPA to (1) identify sites in the United States where hazardous wastes have been disposed, stored, abandoned, or spilled, and (2) rank these sites regarding the severity of the risk. When it ranks the sites the EPA considers factors such as the types of hazardous waste, toxicity of the wastes, types of pollution (air, water, land, or other pollution) caused by the wastes, number of people potentially affected by the risk, and other factors. The hazardous waste sites with the highest ranking are put on a National Priority List. The sites on this list receive first consideration for cleanup. The EPA has the authority to cleanup hazardous priority or non-priority sites quickly to prevent fire, explosion, contamination of drinking water, or other imminent danger.

The EPA can order a responsible party to cleanup a hazardous waste site. If that party fails to do so, the EPA can cleanup the site and recover the cost of the cleanup. The Superfund imposes strict liability—that is, liability without fault. The EPA can recover the cost of the cleanup from (1) the generator who deposited the wastes, (2) the transporter of the wastes to the site, (3) the owner of the site at the time of the disposal, and (4) the current owner and operator of the site. The Superfund permits states and private parties who cleanup hazardous waste sites to seek reimbursement from the fund.

that use the waterways [33 U.S.C. § 1254(t)]. Sources of thermal pollution (such as electric utility companies and manufacturing plants) are subject to the provisions of the Clean Water Act and regulations adopted by the EPA.

Wetlands

Wetlands are defined as areas that are inundated or saturated by surface water or ground water that support vegetation typically adapted for life in saturated soil conditions. Wetlands include swamps, marshes, bogs, and similar areas that support birds, animals, and vegetative life. The Clean Water Act forbids the filling or dredging of wetlands unless a permit has been obtained from the **Army Corps of Engineers (Corps).** The Corps is empowered to adopt regulations and conduct administrative proceedings to enforce the Act.

There is far too much law for those who can afford it and far too little for those who cannot.

—Derek Bo

Hazardous Waste

Wastes, which often contain hazardous substances that can harm the environment or pose a danger to human health, are generated by agriculture, mining, industry, other businesses, and households. Wastes consist of garbage, sewage, industrial discharges, old equipment, and such. The mishandling and disposal of **hazardous wastes** can cause air, water, and **land pollution.**

In 1976, Congress enacted the **Resource Conservation and Recovery Act (RCRA)** [42 U.S.C. § 6901 et seq.], which regulates the disposal of new hazardous

Environmental Protection

Those who hike the Appalachian Trail into Sunfish Pond, New Jersey, and camp or sleep there, or run the Allagash in Maine, or climb the Guadalupes in West Texas, or who canoe and portage the Quentico Superior in Minnesota, certainly should have standing to defend those natural wonders before courts or agencies, though they live 3,000 miles away. Then there will be assurances that all of the forms of life will stand before the court—the pileated woodpecker as well as the coyote and bear, the lemmings as well as the trout in the streams. Those inarticulate members of the ecological group cannot speak. But those people who have so frequented the place as to know its values and wonders will be able to speak for the entire ecological community.

Justice Douglas, Dissenting Opinion *Sierra Club v. Morton, Secretary of the Interior*, 405 U.S. 727, 92 S.Ct. 1361, 1972 U.S. Lexis 118 (1972)

wastes. This Act, which has been amended several times, authorizes the EPA to regulate facilities that generate, treat, store, transport, and dispose of hazardous wastes. States have primary responsibility for implementing the standards established by the Act and EPA regulations.

The Act defines hazardous waste as a solid waste that may cause or significantly contribute to an increase in mortality or serious illness or pose a hazard to human health or the environment if improperly managed. The EPA has designated substances that are toxic, radioactive, or corrosive or that ignite as hazardous and can add to the list of hazardous wastes as needed. The EPA also establishes standards and procedures for the safe treatment, storage, disposal, and transportation of hazardous wastes. Under the Act, the EPA is authorized to regulate underground storage facilities, such as underground gasoline tanks.

Endangered Species and Wildlife Protection

Many species of animals are endangered or threatened with extinction. The reduction of certain species of wildlife may be caused by environmental pollution, real estate development, or hunting. The **Endangered Species Act** was enacted in 1973 [16 U.S.C. §§ 1531 et seq.]. The Act, as amended, protects *endangered* and *threatened* species of animals. The Secretary of the Interior is empowered to declare a form of wildlife as *endangered* or *threatened.* The Act requires the EPA and the Department of Commerce to designate *critical habitats* for each endangered and threatened species. Real estate and other development in these areas is prohibited or severely limited. The Secretary of Commerce is empowered to enforce the provisions of the Act as to marine species.

In addition, the Endangered Species Act, which applies to both government and private persons, prohibits the *taking* of any endangered species. *Taking* is defined as an act intended to "harass, harm, pursue, hunt, shoot, wound, kill, trap, capture, or collect" an endangered animal.

Numerous other federal laws protect wildlife. These include (1) the Migratory Bird Treaty Act, (2) the Bald Eagle Protection Act, (3) the Wild Free-Roaming Horses and Burros Act, (4) the Marine Mammal Protection Act, (5) the Migratory Bird Conservation Act, (6) the Fishery Conservation and Management Act, (7) the Fish and Wildlife Coordination Act, and (8) the National Wildlife Refuge System. Many states have enacted statutes that protect and preserve wildlife.

Tennessee Valley Authority v. Hill, Secretary of the Interior

437 U.S. 153, 98 S.Ct. 2279, 1978 U.S. Lexis 33 (1978) — **Supreme Court of the United States**

FACTS

The Tennessee Valley Authority (TVA) is a wholly owned public corporation of the United States that operates a series of dams, reservoirs, and water projects that provide electric power, irrigation, and flood control to areas in several southern states. In 1967, with appropriations from Congress, the TVA began construction of the Tellico Dam on the Little Tennessee River. When completed, the dam would impound water covering 16,500 acres, thereby converting the river's shallow, fast-flowing waters into a deep reservoir over 30 miles in length. Construction of the dam continued until 1977, when it was completed.

In 1973, a University of Tennessee ichthyologist found a previously unknown species of perch called the *Percina (Imostoma) Tansai*—or "snail darter"—in the Little Tennessee River. After further investigation, it was determined that approximately 10,000 to 15,000 of these 3-inch, tannish-colored fish existed in the river's waters that would be flooded by the operation of the Tellico Dam. The snail darter was not found anywhere else in the world. It feeds exclusively on snails and requires substantial oxygen, both supplied by the fast-moving waters of the Little Tennessee River. Impounding of the water behind the Tellico Dam would destroy the snail darter's food and oxygen supplies, thereby causing its extinction. Evidence was introduced showing that the TVA could not, at that time, successfully transplant the snail darter to any other habitat.

Also in 1973, Congress enacted the Endangered Species Act (Act). The Act authorizes the secretary of the interior (Secretary) to declare species of animal life *endangered* and to identify the *critical habitat* of these creatures. When a species or its habitat is so listed, Section 7 of the Act mandates that the Secretary take such action as is necessary to ensure that actions of the federal government do not jeopardize the continued existence of such endangered species. The Secretary declared the snail darter an endangered species and the area that would be affected by the dam its critical habitat.

Congress continued to appropriate funds for the construction of the dam, which was completed at a cost of over $100 million. In 1976, a regional association of biological scientists, a Tennessee conservation group, and several individuals filed an action seeking to enjoin the TVA from closing the gates of the dam and impounding the water in the reservoir on the grounds that those actions would violate Section 7 of the Act by causing the extinction of the snail darter. The district court held in favor of the TVA. The court of appeals reversed and remanded with instructions to the district court to issue a permanent injunction halting the operation of the Tellico Dam. The TVA appealed to the U.S. Supreme Court.

ISSUE

Would the TVA be in violation of the Endangered Species Act if it were to operate the Tellico Dam?

COURT'S REASONING

The Supreme Court noted that it may seem curious to some that the survival of a relatively small number of 3-inch fish among all the countless millions of species extant would require the permanent halting of a virtually completed dam for which Congress has expended more than $100 million. The Court concluded, however, that the explicit provisions of the Endangered Species Act required precisely this result. One would be hard-pressed to find a statutory provision whose terms were any plainer than those in Section 7 of the Endangered Species Act. Its very words affirmatively command all federal agencies to ensure that actions authorized, funded, or carried out by them do not jeopardize the continued existence of an endangered species or result in the destruction or modification of habitat of such species. This language admits no exception. The Court stated, "Examination of the language, history, and structure of the legislation under review here indicates beyond doubt that Congress intended endangered species to be afforded the highest of priorities."

DECISION AND REMEDY

The Supreme Court held that the Endangered Species Act prohibited the impoundment of the Little Tennessee River by the Tellico Dam. Affirmed.

Note Eventually, after substantial research and investigation, it was determined that the snail darter could live in another habitat that was found for it. After the snail darter species was removed, at government expense, to this new location, the TVA was permitted to close the gates of the Tellico Dam and begin its operation.

QUESTIONS

1. Should the law protect endangered species? Why or why not?
2. Did the TVA act ethically in this case by completing construction of the dam?
3. Do you think the cost of constructing the Tellico Dam ($100 million) should have been considered by the Court in reaching its decision?

LEGAL TERMINOLOGY

Administrative agencies
Administrative law
Administrative law judge (ALJ)
Administrative Procedure Act (APA)
Adulterated food
Air pollution
Army Corps of Engineers (Corps)
Bait and switch
Biosafety Protocol
Caveat emptor
Clean Air Act
Clean Water Act
Comprehensive Environmental Response, Compensation, and Liability Act (CERCLA)
Consumer Product Safety Act
Consumer Product Safety Commission (CPSC)
Controlling the Assault of Non-Solicited Pornography and Marketing Act (CAN-SPAM Act)
Consumer protection laws
Cosmetics
Council on Environmental Quality
Delegation doctrine
"Do-Not-Call" Registry
Drug Amendment to the FDCA
Drugs
Effective date
Endangered Species Act
Environmental Impact Statement (EIS)
Environmental protection
Environmental Protection Agency (EPA)
Exclusive economic zone (EEZ)
Fair Packaging and Labeling Act
False and deceptive labeling
False and misleading advertising
Federal administrative agencies
Federal Trade Commission (FTC)
Federal Trade Commission Act (FTC Act)
Federal Water Pollution Control Act (FWPCA)
Food and Drug Administration (FDA)
Food, Drug, and Cosmetic Act (FDCA)
General government regulation
Hazardous wastes
Indoor air pollution
Initial public offering (IPO)
Insider
Insider trading
Issuer
Land pollution
License
Mobile sources of air pollution
National ambient air quality standards (NAAQS)
National Environmental Policy Act (NEPA)
Nutrition Labeling and Education Act
Order
Point sources of water pollution
Poison Prevention Packaging Act
Prospectus
Registration statement
Resource Conservation and Recovery Act (RCRA)
Rule 10b-5
Section 5 of the Federal Trade Commission Act
Section 10(b) of the Securities Exchange Act of 1934
Securities Act of 1933
Securities and Exchange Commission (SEC)
Securities Exchange Act of 1934
Sick building syndrome
Spam
Specific government regulation
State administrative agencies
Stationary sources of air pollution
SuperFund
Thermal pollution
Toxic air pollutants
Water pollution
Wetlands

chapter summary

ADMINISTRATIVE LAW, CONSUMER, INVESTOR, AND ENVIRONMENTAL PROTECTION

Administrative Law	
Government Regulation of Business	1. *General government regulation:* Applies to many industries (e.g., antidiscrimination laws). 2. *Specific government regulation:* Applies to a specific industry (e.g., banking laws).
Administrative Agencies	1. *Administrative agencies:* Created by federal and state legislative and executive branches. Consist of professionals having an area of expertise in a certain area of commerce, who interpret and apply designated statutes. 2. *Administrative rules and regulations:* Administrative agencies are empowered to adopt rules and regulations that interpret and advance the laws they enforce. 3. *Administrative Procedure Act:* Act that establishes procedures (i.e., notice, hearing, and such) to be followed by federal agencies in conducting their affairs. States have enacted their own procedural acts to govern state agencies.
Consumer Protection	
Regulation of Food, Drugs, and Cosmetics	1. *Federal Food, Drug, and Cosmetic Act (FDCA):* Federal statute that regulates the testing, manufacture, distribution, and sale of foods, food additives, drugs, cosmetics, and medicinal products. 2. *Federal Food and Drug Administration (FDA):* Federal administrative agency empowered to interpret and enforce the FDCA and other federal consumer protection laws. 3. *Powers of the FDA:* To approve or deny applications by private companies to distribute drugs, food additives, and medicinal devices to the public. 4. The FDA prohibits the shipment, distribution, or sale of *adulterated* or *misbranded* food, drugs, cosmetics, or medicinal devices. 5. *Nutrition Labeling and Education Act:* Federal statute that requires food manufacturers and processors to provide nutritional information on foods. 6. *United Nations Biosafety Protocol for Genetically Altered Foods:* A United Nations–sponsored protocol that require signatory countries to place the label "May contain living modified organisms" on all genetically engineered foods.
Product Safety	*Consumer Product Safety Act (CPSA):* Federal statute that regulates the safety of consumer products. It created the Consumer Product Safety Commission, an administrative agency that is empowered to 1. interpret and enforce the Consumer Product Safety Act, 2. conduct research on safety, and 3. collect data regarding injuries.
Unfair and Deceptive Practices	1. *Section 5 of the Federal Trade Commission Act (FTC Act):* Federal statute that prohibits unfair and deceptive practices, including false and deceptive advertising, abusive sales tactics, consumer fraud, and other unfair business practices. *(continued)*

	2. *The Federal Trade Commission (FTC):* Federal administrative agency empowered to enforce the FTC Act and other federal consumer protection statutes.
Investor Protection	
Securities Regulation	1. *The Securities and Exchange Commission (SEC):* Federal administrative agency empowered to administer federal securities laws. The SEC can adopt rules and regulations to interpret and implement federal securities.
Issuance of Securities	1. *The Securities Act of 1933:* Federal statute that primarily regulates the *issuance* of securities by corporations, partnerships, associations, and individuals. 2. *Registration statement:* Document that an issuer of securities files with the SEC to register its securities. It must contain information about the issuer, the securities to be issued, and other relevant information. 3. *Prospectus:* A written disclosure document that is submitted to the SEC with the registration statement. It is distributed to prospective investors to enable them to evaluate the financial risk of the investment.
Trading in Securities	1. *The Securities Exchange Act of 1934:* Federal statute that primarily regulates the *trading* of securities. 2. *Section 10(b):* A provision of the 1934 act that prohibits the use of manipulative and deceptive devices in the purchase or sale of securities in contravention of the rules and regulations prescribed by the SEC. 3. *Rule 10b-5:* A rule adopted by the SEC to clarify the reach of Section 10(b) against deceptive and fraudulent activities. 4. *Insider trading:* Occurs when a company employee or advisor uses material nonpublic information to make a profit by trading in the securities of the company.
Environmental Protection	
Environmental Protection	1. *Environmental protection laws:* Federal and state governments have enacted environmental protection statutes to control pollution and to penalize those who violate these statutes. 2. *The Environmental Protection Agency (EPA):* Federal administrative agency created in 1970 that is empowered to implement and enforce federal environmental protection statutes. The EPA can adopt regulations to interpret and enforce the laws it is authorized to administer. 3. *National Environmental Policy Act (NEPA):* Federal statute that mandates that the federal government consider the *adverse impact* a federal government action would have on the environment before the action is implemented. 4. *Environmental Impact Statement (EIS):* A document that must be prepared for all proposed legislation or major federal action that significantly affects the quality of the human environment. The EIS must (1) describe the affected environment, (2) describe the impact of the proposed federal action on the environment, (3) identify and discuss alternatives to the proposed action, (4) list the resources that will be committed to the action, and (5) contain a cost–benefit analysis of the proposed action and alternative actions.

Air Pollution	
Air Pollution	1. Pollution caused by factories, homes, vehicles, and the like that affects the air. 2. *Clean Air Act:* Federal statute enacted in 1963 and amended several times that regulates air pollution. 3. *National Ambient Air Quality Standards (NAAQS):* Standards for certain pollutants set by the EPA that protect (1) human beings (*primary*) and (2) vegetation matter, climate, visibility, and economic values (*secondary*). 4. *Stationary sources of air pollution:* Sources of air pollution such as industrial plants, oil refineries, and public utilities. Stationary sources are required to install pollution control equipment. 5. *Mobile sources of air pollutions:* Sources of air pollution such as automobiles, trucks, buses, motorcycles, and airplanes. The Clean Air Act requires air pollution controls to be installed on automobiles and other sources of mobile air pollution.
Water Pollution	
Water Pollution	1. Pollution of lakes, rivers, oceans, and other bodies of water. 2. *The Federal Water Pollution Control Act (FWPCA) of 1948:* Federal statute that regulates water pollution. As amended, it is now called the Clean Water Act. 3. *Point sources of water pollution:* Sources of water pollution such as paper mills, manufacturing plants, electric utility plants, and sewage plants. Point sources are required to install pollution control equipment. 4. *Thermal pollution:* Heated water or material discharged into waterways that upsets the ecological balance and decreases the oxygen content. Thermal pollution is subject to the provisions of the Clean Water Act. 5. *Wetlands:* Areas that are inundated or saturated by surface or groundwater and support vegetation typically adapted for life in such conditions. The Clean Water Act forbids the filling or dredging of wetlands unless a permit has been obtained from the *Army Corps of Engineers.*
Hazardous Waste	
Hazardous Waste	1. Solid waste that may cause or significantly contribute to an increase in mortality or serious illness, or pose a hazard to human health or the environment if improperly managed. 2. *Resource Conservation and Recovery Act:* Federal statute that authorizes the EPA to regulate facilities that generate, treat, store, transport, and dispose of hazardous wastes. 3. *Comprehensive Environmental Response, Compensation, and Liability Act (CERCLA):* Federal statute that gives the federal government a mandate to deal with hazardous wastes that have been spilled, stored, or abandoned. Commonly called Superfund: a. CERCLA requires the EPA to identify sites in the United States where hazardous wastes have been disposed, stored, spilled, or abandoned, and to rank these sites regarding the severity of the risk. *(continued)*

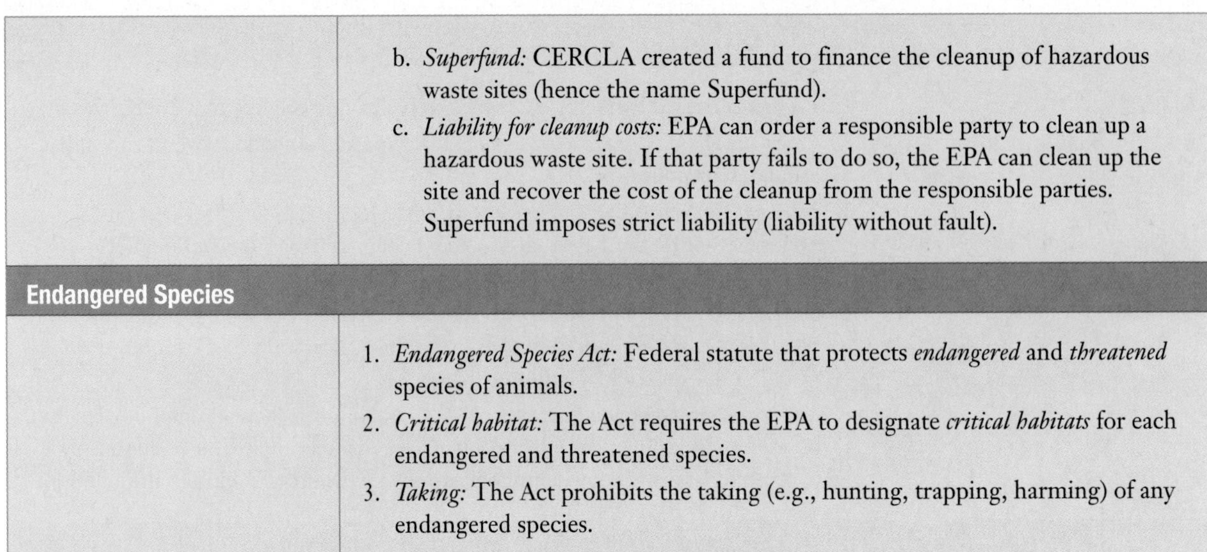

	b. *Superfund:* CERCLA created a fund to finance the cleanup of hazardous waste sites (hence the name Superfund). c. *Liability for cleanup costs:* EPA can order a responsible party to clean up a hazardous waste site. If that party fails to do so, the EPA can clean up the site and recover the cost of the cleanup from the responsible parties. Superfund imposes strict liability (liability without fault).
Endangered Species	
	1. *Endangered Species Act:* Federal statute that protects *endangered* and *threatened* species of animals. 2. *Critical habitat:* The Act requires the EPA to designate *critical habitats* for each endangered and threatened species. 3. *Taking:* The Act prohibits the taking (e.g., hunting, trapping, harming) of any endangered species.

WORKING THE WEB

www

Visit the Web sites listed below for more information about the topics covered in this chapter.

1. Check the Consumer Product Safety Commission site for information on window blinds and/or batteries for notebook computers. See U.S. Consumer Product Safety Commission at **www.cpsc.gov.**
2. Go to the Association of Trial Lawyers of America's Web site and find out what the trial lawyers have to say about products liability cases in the "Civil Justice Fact Sheets." Visit the Association of Trial Lawyers of America at **www.atla.org.**
3. Find out what "Made in the U.S.A." means, according to the FTC Web site. See the U.S. Federal Trade Commission at **www.ftc.gov.**
4. Review the FDA Enforcement Reports for a detailed list of recent violators. Are any of your favorite foods listed? See the U.S. Food & Drug Administration at **www.fda.gov.**
5. Go to the FTC site and find the "Top Ten Dot Cons" at **www.ftc.gov/bcp/menucredit.htm.** See also **www.law.cornell.edu/topics/consumer_credit.html** for an overview of consumer credit law with links to key primary and secondary sources.
6. Find the EPA Superfund toxic waste cleanup sites in your state. See U.S. Environmental Protection Agency at **www.epa.gov.**
7. Compare the positions of Greenpeace, the Sierra Club, and others on drilling in the Arctic National Wildlife Refuge at the following Web sites:
   Greenpeace: **www.greenpeace.org**
   National Audubon Society: **www.audubon.org**
   Natural Resources Defense Council: **www.nrdc.org**
   Sierra Club: **www.sierraclub.org**
   Earth Watch Institute: **www.earthwatch.org**
   World Environmental Law: **www.hg.org/environ.html**
8. Compare your state's environmental laws to the federal controls in the area of water and air pollution. For an overview of land-use law with links to key primary and secondary sources, see "Law About . . . Land Use" at **www.law.cornell.edu/topics/land_use.html.**
9. Is your state home to any of the animals protected by the Endangered Species Act? If so, which ones? See the Earth Justice Legal Defense Fund at **www.earthjustice.org** and the Environmental Defense Fund at **www.edf.org.**

CRITICAL LEGAL THINKING QUESTIONS

1. Describe the difference between general government regulations and specific government regulations.
2. Describe the federal government's regulation of foods, drugs, and cosmetics. Does this regulation serve a useful purpose?
3. What does the United Nations Biosafety Protocol for Genetically Altered Foods provide? Do you think this protocol is necessary?

4. What does the Consumer Product Safety Act regulate? Does this regulation serve a useful purpose?
5. Define an *unfair and deceptive practice* prohibited by Section 5 of the Federal Trade Commission Act. What is a bait and switch?
6. What is air pollution? Do you think current federal and state laws are doing enough to regulate air pollution?
7. What is water pollution? Do you think current federal and state laws are doing enough to regulate water pollution?
8. What does the Superfund Act provide? What is the public policy behind this Act?
9. Describe the protections afforded by the Endangered Species Act. What are the arguments for and against this Act?

CASE FOR BRIEFING

Read Case 15 in Appendix A *(FMC Corporation v. United States Department of Commerce).* Review and brief the case using the *Critical Legal Thinking* "Briefing the Case" example described in Chapter 1.

15.1 *United States v. Gel Spice Co., Inc.*

601 F.Supp. 1205, 1984 U.S. Dist. Lexis 21041 (1984)
United States District Court, Eastern District of New York

FACTS Barry Engel owned and operated Gel Spice Co., Inc., which specialized in the importation and packaging of various food spices for resale. All of the spices Gel Spice imported were unloaded at a pier in New York City and taken to a warehouse on McDonald Avenue. Storage and repackaging of the spices took place in the warehouse. Between July 1976 and January 1979, the McDonald Avenue warehouse was inspected four times by investigators from the FDA. The investigators found live rats in bags of basil leaves, rodent droppings in boxes of chili peppers, and mammalian urine in bags of sesame seeds. The investigators produced additional evidence that showed that spices packaged and sold from the warehouse contained insects, rodent excreta pellets, rodent hair, and rodent urine. The FDA brought criminal charges against Engel and Gel Spice.

ISSUE Are they guilty?

15.2 *United States v. Reserve Mining Co.*

8 Envir. Rep. Cases 1978 (1976)
United States District Court, Minnesota

FACTS The Reserve Mining Company (Reserve) owns and operates a mine in Minnesota that is located on the shores of Lake Superior and produces hazardous waste. In 1947, Reserve obtained a permit from the state of Minnesota to dump its wastes into Lake Superior. The permits prohibited discharges that would "result in any clouding or discoloration of the water outside the specific discharge zone" or "result in any material adverse effects on public water supplies." Reserve discharged its wastes into Lake Superior for years, until the amounts reached 67,000 tons per day in the early 1970s. Evidence showed that the discharges caused discoloration of surface waters outside the zone of discharge and contained carcinogens that adversely affected public water supplies. The United States sued Reserve for engaging in unlawful water pollution.

ISSUE Who wins?

15.3 *United States v. Hoflin*

880 F.2d 1033, 1989 U.S. App. Lexis 10169 (1989)
United States Court of Appeals, Ninth Circuit

FACTS Douglas Hoflin was director of the Public Works Department for Ocean Shores, Washington. From 1975 to 1982, the department purchased 3,500 gallons of paint for road maintenance. As painting jobs were finished, the 55-gallon drums that had contained the paint were returned to the department's yard. Paint contains hazardous substances such as lead. When 14 of the drums were discovered still to contain unused paint, Hoflin instructed employees to haul the paint drums to the city's sewage treatment plant and bury them. The employees took the drums, dug a hole on the grounds of the treatment plant, and dumped the drums in it. Some of the drums were rusted and leaking. The hole was not deep enough, so the employees crushed the drums with a front-end loader to make them fit. The refuse was then covered with sand.

Almost two years later, one of the city's employees reported the incident to state authorities, who referred the matter to the EPA. Investigation showed that the paint had contaminated the soil. The United States brought criminal charges against Hoflin for aiding and abetting the illegal dumping of hazardous waste.

ISSUE Who wins?

ETHICS CASE

15.4 *United States v. Carpenter*

484 U.S. 19, 108 S.Ct. 316, 1987 U.S. Lexis 4815 (1987)
Supreme Court of the United States

FACTS R. Foster Winans, a reporter for the *Wall Street Journal*, was one of the writers of the "Heard on the Street" column, a widely read and influential column in the *Journal*. This column frequently included articles that discussed the prospects of companies listed on national and regional stock exchanges and the over-the-counter market. David Carpenter worked as a news clerk at the *Journal*. The *Journal* had a conflict of interest policy that prohibited employees from using non-public information learned on the job for their personal benefit. Winans and Carpenter were aware of this policy.

Kenneth P. Felis and Peter Brant were stockbrokers at the brokerage house of Kidder Peabody. Winans agreed to provide Felis and Brant with information that was to appear in the "Heard" column in advance of its publication in the *Journal.* Generally, Winans would provide this information to the brokers the day before it was to appear in the *Journal.* Carpenter served as a messenger between the parties. Based on this advance information, the brokers bought and sold securities of companies discussed in the "Heard" column. During 1983 and 1984, prepublication trades of approximately 27 "Heard" columns netted profits of almost $690,000. The parties used telephones to transfer information. The *Wall Street Journal* is distributed by mail to many of its subscribers.

Eventually, Kidder Peabody noticed a correlation between the "Heard" column and trading by the brokers. After an SEC investigation, criminal charges were brought against defendants Winans, Carpenter, and Felis in U.S. district court. Brant became the government's key witness. Winans and Felis were convicted of conspiracy to commit securities, mail, and wire fraud. Carpenter was convicted of aiding and abetting the commission of securities, mail, and wire fraud. The defendants appealed their convictions.

ISSUE Can the defendants be held criminally liable for conspiring to violate, and aiding and abetting the violation of, Section 10(b) and Rule 10b-5 of securities law? Did Winans act ethically in this case? Did Brant act ethically by turning government's witness?

APPENDIX A

Cases

CASE 1

HARRIS V. FORKLIFT SYSTEMS, INC.
510 U.S. 17, 114 S.Ct. 367, 1993 U.S. Lexis 7155 (1993)
United States Supreme Court
O'Connor, Justice

Teresa Harris worked as a manager at Forklift Systems, Inc., an equipment rental company, from April 1985 until October 1987. Charles Hardy was Forklift's president. Throughout Harris's time at Forklift, Hardy often insulted her because of her gender and often made her the target of unwanted sexual innuendos. Hardy told Harris on several occasions, in the presence of other employees, "You're a woman, what do you know" and "We need a man as the rental manager"; at least once, he told her she was "a dumb-ass woman." Again in front of others, he suggested that the two of them "go to the Holiday Inn to negotiate Harris's raise." Hardy occasionally asked Harris and other female employees to get coins from his front pants pocket. He threw objects on the ground in front of Harris and other women, and asked them to pick the objects up. He made sexual innuendos about Harris's and other women's clothing.

In mid-August 1987, Harris complained to Hardy about his conduct. Hardy said he was surprised that Harris was offended, claimed he was only joking, and apologized. He also promised he would stop and based on this assurance, Harris stayed on the job. But in early September, Hardy began anew: While Harris was arranging a deal with one of Forklift's customers, he asked her, again in front of other employees, "What did you do, promise the guy some sex Saturday night?" On October 1, Harris collected her paycheck and quit.

Harris then sued Forklift, claiming that Hardy's conduct had created an abusive work environment for her because of her gender. The United States District Court for the Middle District of Tennessee found this to be "a close case," but held that Hardy's conduct did not create an abusive environment. The court found that some of Hardy's comments "offended Harris, and would offend the reasonable woman," but that they were not "so severe as to be expected to seriously affect Harris's psychological well-being." A reasonable woman manager under like circumstances would have been offended by Hardy, but his conduct would not have risen to the level of interfering with that person's work performance. The United States Court of Appeals for the Sixth Circuit affirmed in a brief unpublished decision.

We granted certiorari to resolve a conflict among the Circuits on whether conduct, to be actionable as "abusive work environment" harassment, must "seriously affect an employee's psychological well-being" or lead the plaintiff to "suffer injury."

Title VII of the Civil Rights Act of 1964 makes it "an unlawful employment practice for an employer . . . to discriminate against any individual with respect to his compensation, terms, conditions, or privileges of employment, because of such individual's race, color, religion, sex, or national origin" [42 U.S.C. §2000e-2(a)(1)].

When the workplace is permeated with discriminatory intimidation, ridicule, and insult that is sufficiently severe or pervasive to alter the conditions of the victim's employment and create an abusive working environment, Title VII is violated. This standard takes a middle path between making actionable any conduct that is merely offensive and requiring the conduct to cause a tangible psychological injury. Mere utterance of an epithet which engenders offensive feelings in an employee does not sufficiently affect the conditions of employment to implicate Title VII. Conduct that is not severe or pervasive enough to create an objectively hostile or abusive work environment—an environment that a reasonable person would find hostile or abusive—is beyond Title VII's purview. Likewise, if the victim does not subjectively perceive the environment to be abusive, the conduct has not actually altered the conditions of the victim's employment, and there is no Title VII violation.

But Title VII comes into play before the harassing conduct leads to a nervous breakdown. A discriminatorily abusive work environment, even one that does not seriously affect employees' psychological well-being, can and often will detract from employees' job performance, discourage employees from remaining on the job, or keep them from advancing in their careers. Moreover, even without regard to these tangible effects, the very fact that the discriminatory conduct was so severe or pervasive that it created a work environment abusive to employees because of their race, gender, religion, or national origin offends Title VII's broad rule of workplace equality.

We therefore believe the district court erred in relying on whether the conduct "seriously affected plaintiff's psychological well-being" or led her to "suffer injury." Such an inquiry may needlessly focus the factfinder's attention on concrete psychological harm, an element Title VII does not require. So long as the environment would reasonably be perceived, and is perceived, as hostile or abusive, there is no need for it also to be psychologically injurious. This is not, and by its nature cannot be, a mathematically precise test. But we can say that whether an environment is "hostile" or "abusive" can be determined only by looking at all the circumstances.

We therefore reverse the judgment of the Court of Appeals, and remand the case for further proceedings consistent with this opinion.

CASE 2

ANHEUSER-BUSCH, INC. V. SCHMOKE, MAYOR OF BALTIMORE CITY

63 F.3d 1305, 1995 U.S. App. Lexis 24515 (1995)
United States Court of Appeals, Fourth Circuit
Niemeyer, Circuit Judge

In January 1994, Baltimore exercised the authority granted it by the state and enacted Ordinance 288 prohibiting the outdoor advertising of alcoholic beverages in certain locations in Baltimore City. It also includes an exception permitting such advertising in certain commercially and industrially zoned areas of the City. By its terms, the ordinance was to become effective February 5, 1994. Before enacting the ordinance, the Baltimore City Council conducted public hearings, receiving testimony and previously conducted studies detailing the adverse effects of alcohol consumption on minors and the correlation between underage drinking and the advertising of alcoholic beverages.

The City Council found that alcoholic beverages are the second most heavily advertised products in America (after cigarettes), and that outdoor billboards are a "unique and distinguishable" medium of advertising that subjects the public to involuntary and unavoidable forms of solicitation. The City Council noted that children are exposed to the advertising of alcoholic beverages "simply by walking to school or playing in their neighborhood" and that children's "attitudes favorable to alcohol are significantly related to their exposure to alcohol advertisements." Attempting to tailor its ban, the City Council allowed advertising of alcoholic beverages in commercial and industrial areas, stating that it was "narrowly focus[ing] its efforts on those advertisements which most directly affect minors where they live, attend school, attend church and engage in recreational activities."

On January 14, 1994, several weeks before the ordinance was to become effective, Anheuser-Busch, Inc., filed suit in federal court, facially challenging the constitutionality of the ordinance under the First Amendment. Anheuser-Busch is the nation's largest brewer of beers and malt beverages, producing approximately 15 different brands, including Budweiser, Michelob, and Busch. It advertises in all media, including outdoor billboards and displays. In addition to contending that there is no correlation between alcoholic beverage advertising and underage drinking, Anheuser-Busch asserts that the purpose of its advertising is "to solidify brand loyalty and increase market share by shifting adult beer drinkers from other brands to the advertised brand of beer."

Following a hearing, the district court issued an opinion upholding the constitutionality of the ordinance [*Anheuser-Busch, Inc. v. Mayor and City Council*, 855 F.Supp. 811 (D.Md.1994)]. The court held the ordinance constitutional after concluding that it "directly advances the City's asserted interest in promoting the welfare and temperance of minors" and is "narrowly tailored" to that end.

On appeal, Anheuser-Busch argues that the ordinance is unconstitutional on its face because (1) it does not directly and materially advance the government's interest in promoting temperance of minors and (2) it is not narrowly tailored to serve that purpose. They also argue that, as applied, the ordinance would impermissibly restrict their noncommercial speech.

We find that it was reasonable for the Baltimore City Council to have concluded that Ordinance 288's regulation of the outdoor advertising of alcoholic beverages directly and materially advances Baltimore's interest in promoting the welfare and temperance of minors. The City Council found that outdoor advertising is a unique and distinct medium which subjects the public to involuntary and unavoidable solicitation, and that children, simply by walking to school or playing in their neighborhood, are exposed daily to this advertising. The City Council pointed to its legislative finding that the majority of research studies show a definite correlation between alcoholic beverage advertising and underage drinking.

We simply do not believe that the liquor industry spends a billion dollars a year on advertising solely to acquire an added market share at the expense of competitors. We hold, as a matter of law, that prohibitions against the advertising of alcoholic beverages are reasonably related to reducing the sale and consumption of those beverages and their attendant problems. The entire economy of the industries that bring these challenges is based on the belief that advertising increases sales.

It is readily acknowledged that limitations on outdoor advertising of alcoholic beverages designed to protect minors also reduce the opportunities for adults to receive advertised information. And adults, who constitute a majority of the population, are the object of the government's legislation. But it also appears that no less restrictive means may be available to advance the government's interest. Anheuser-Busch argues that Baltimore could just as effectively advance its goal of promoting the welfare and temperance of minors by increasing enforcement of existing laws prohibiting sales to, and possession of alcoholic beverages by, minors, or by implementing and encouraging educational programs on the dangers of alcohol. These approaches might indeed prove beneficial in reducing underage drinking, but they do not provide an alternative to the approach selected by the City of curbing the enticement to consume alcoholic beverages. In the face of a problem as significant as that which the City seeks to address, the City must be given some reasonable latitude.

The problem of underage drinking is a most serious one that contributes significantly to a variety of social problems. Baltimore was faced with statistics showing that fully one-half of all deaths of minors were alcohol-related, and 40 to 50 percent of juveniles who drowned or had diving accidents had consumed alcohol immediately prior to the incident. The City Council found that alcohol is overwhelmingly and consistently the most widely used "drug" at all adolescent age levels. It pointed to data which showed that over half of all twelfth graders, 40 percent of tenth graders, and over a quarter of eighth graders reported that they had consumed alcohol within the past 30 days. Widespread underage drinking was also found to be a major factor in crime. One-third of all juvenile males arrested said they had consumed alcohol within the previous 72 hours, and nearly 40 percent of all youths in adult correctional facilities reported drinking alcohol before committing their crimes.

Through outdoor advertising, children are involuntarily and unavoidably confronted daily with the advertised message. Billboards are "seen without the exercise of choice or volition," and viewers have the message "thrust upon them by all the arts and devices that skill can produce." The City argues that the only means to address this problem is to ban such advertising in locations where children generally walk and play. Such a ban still permits adults to receive advertising messages and information from signs in commercial areas of the City and through the numerous other media to which adults are constantly exposed.

In summary, Baltimore City's regulation of stationary outdoor "advertising that advertises alcoholic beverages" in certain locations directly and materially advances a substantial governmental interest in promoting the welfare and temperance of minors who are involuntarily and unavoidably exposed to such advertisements. While the means selected of limiting the location of such outdoor advertising is not a perfect "fit" with the governmental objective, it nevertheless falls well within the range tolerated by the First Amendment for the regulation of commercial speech.

For the reasons stated, we affirm the judgment of the district court, upholding Baltimore City Ordinance 288 against a facial constitutional challenge under the First Amendment. AFFIRMED.

CASE 3

GNAZZO V. G.D. SEARLE & CO.

973 F.2d 136, 1992 U.S. App. Lexis 19453 (1992)
United States Court of Appeals, Second Circuit
Pierce, Circuit Judge

On November 11, 1974, Gnazzo had a CU-7 intrauterine device (IUD) inserted in her uterus for contraceptive purposes. The IUD was developed, marketed, and sold by G.D. Searle & Co. (Searle). When Gnazzo's deposition was taken, she stated that her doctor had informed her that "the insertion would hurt, but not for long," and that she "would have uncomfortable and probably painful periods of the first three to four months." On October 11, 1975, Gnazzo found it necessary to return to her physician due to excessive pain and cramping. During this visit she was informed by her doctor that he thought she had Pelvic

Inflammatory Disease (PID). She recalled that he stated that the infection was possibly caused by venereal disease or the use of the IUD. The PID was treated with antibiotics and cleared up shortly thereafter. Less than one year later, Gnazzo was again treated for an IUD-associated infection. This infection was also treated with antibiotics. Gnazzo continued using the IUD until it was finally removed in December of 1977.

Following a laparoscopy in March of 1989, Gnazzo was informed by a fertility specialist that she was infertile because of PID-induced adhesions resulting from her prior IUD use. Subsequent to this determination, and at the request of her then-attorneys, Gnazzo completed a questionnaire dated May 11, 1989. In response to the question, "when and why did you first suspect that your IUD had caused you any harm?", Gnazzo responded "sometime in 1981" and explained: "I was married in April 1981 so I stopped using birth control so I could get pregnant—nothing ever happened (of course) then I started hearing and reading about how damaging IUDs could be. I figured that was the problem, however, my marriage started to crumble so I never pursued the issue."

On May 4, 1990, Gnazzo initiated the underlying action against Searle. In an amended complaint, she alleged that she had suffered injuries as a result of her use of the IUD developed by Searle. Searle argued, inter alia, that Gnazzo knew in 1981 that she had suffered harm caused by her IUD. Gnazzo contended that her cause of action against Searle accrued only when she learned from the fertility specialist that the IUD had caused her PID and subsequent infertility.

In a ruling dated September 18, 1991, the district court granted Searle's motion for summary judgment on the ground that Gnazzo's claim was time-barred by the applicable statute of limitations. In reaching this result, the court determined that Connecticut law provided no support for Gnazzo's contention that she should not have been expected to file her action until she was told of her infertility and the IUD's causal connection. This appeal followed.

On appeal, Gnazzo contends that the district court improperly granted Searle's motion for summary judgment because a genuine issue of material fact exists as to when she discovered, or reasonably should have discovered, her injuries and their causal connection to the defendant's alleged wrongful conduct. Summary judgment is appropriate when there is no genuine issue as to any material fact and the moving party is entitled to judgment as a matter of law. We consider the record in the light most favorable to the non-movant. However, the non-movant "may not rest upon the mere allegations of denials of her pleading, but must set forth specific facts showing that there is a genuine issue for trial."

Under Connecticut law, a product liability claim must be brought within "three years from the date when the injury is first sustained or discovered or in the exercise of reasonable care should have been discovered." In Connecticut, a cause of action accrues when a plaintiff suffers actionable harm. Actionable harm occurs when the plaintiff discovers or should discover, through the exercise of reasonable care, that he or she has been injured and that the defendant's conduct caused such injury.

Gnazzo contends that "the mere occurrence of a pelvic infection or difficulty in becoming pregnant does not necessarily result in notice to the plaintiff of a cause of action." Thus, she maintains that her cause of action did not accrue until 1989 when the fertility specialist informed her both that she was infertile and that this condition resulted from her previous use of the IUD.

Under Connecticut law, however, "the statute of limitations begins to run when the plaintiff discovers some form of actionable harm, not the fullest manifestation thereof." Therefore, as Gnazzo's responses to the questionnaire indicate, she suspected "sometime in 1981" that the IUD had caused her harm because she had been experiencing trouble becoming pregnant and had "started hearing and reading about how damaging IUDs could be and had figured that was the problem." Thus, by her own admission, Gnazzo had recognized, or should have recognized, the critical link between her injury and the defendant's causal connection to it. In other words, she had "discovered or should have discovered through the exercise of reasonable care, that she had been injured and that Searle's conduct caused such injury." However, as Gnazzo acknowledged in the questionnaire, she did not pursue the "issue" at the time because of her marital problems. Thus, even when viewed in the light most favorable to Gnazzo, the non-moving party, we are constrained to find that she knew by 1981 that she had "some form of actionable harm." Consequently, by the time she commenced her action in 1990, Gnazzo was time-barred by the Connecticut statute of limitations.

Since we have determined that Gnazzo's cause of action commenced in 1981, we need not address Searle's additional contention that Gnazzo's awareness in 1975 of her PID and her purported knowledge of its causal connection to the IUD commenced the running of the Connecticut statute of limitations at that time.

We are sympathetic to Gnazzo's situation and mindful that the unavoidable result we reach in this case is harsh. Nevertheless, we are equally aware that "it is within the Connecticut General Assembly's constitutional authority to decide when claims for injury are to be brought. Where a plaintiff has failed to comply with this requirement, a court may not entertain the suit." The judgment of the district court is AFFIRMED.

CASE 4

SCHALK V. TEXAS
823 S.W.2d 633, 1991 Tex.Crim.App. Lexis 201 (1991)
Court of Criminal Appeals of Texas
Miller, Judge

Appellants Schalk and Leonard are former employees of Texas Instruments (hereafter TI). Both men have doctoral degrees and specialized in the area of speech research at TI. Schalk resigned his position with TI in April 1983 to join a newly developed company, Voice Control Systems (hereafter VCS). In February 1985, Leonard resigned from TI and joined VCS. Several TI employees eventually joined the ranks of VCS. Speech research was the main thrust of the research and development performed by VCS. In fact, VCS was a competitor of TI in this field. In April 1985, Sam Kuzbary, then employed with VCS and a former TI employee, noticed some information which he believed to be proprietary to TI stored in the memory of the computer he was using at VCS. Kuzbary contacted TI and agreed to serve as "informant" for them.

He then searched the premises of VCS and photographed materials which he recognized from his employment with TI. A TI internal investigation revealed that a few hours prior to Schalk's and Leonard's departures from TI, each appellant, utilizing TI computers, copied the entire contents of the directories respectively assigned to them. This information included computer programs which TI claimed to be its trade secrets. Officials of TI then contacted the Dallas District Attorney's office. A search of the premises of VCS resulted in the seizure of computer tapes containing the alleged TI trade secret programs from appellants' offices. Appellants were arrested.

We granted review to consider, first, whether the evidence was sufficient to establish that the computer programs named in the indictments were trade secrets, and second, to determine whether the items listed in the search warrant were sufficiently described so as to preclude a general exploratory search.

Having determined that computer programs are proper subjects for trade secret litigation under Texas civil and criminal law, we now look to the case *sub judice* to determine whether the programs which appellants copied and took with them to VCS are trade secrets as defined by §31.05 of the Penal Code.

§31.05 Theft of trade secrets:

(a) For the purposes of this section:

(4) "Trade secret" means the whole or any part of any scientific or technical information, design, process, procedure, formula, or improvement that has value and that the owner has taken measures to prevent from becoming available to persons other than those selected by the owner to have access for limited purposes.

Appellants claimed on appeal that the programs did not meet the statutory trade secrets criteria because they alleged their former employer TI failed to take "measures to prevent [the information] from becoming available to persons other than those selected by the owner." We note, as did the court of appeals, that the statute sets no standards for degree of sufficiency of the "measures" taken. Specifically, appellants pointed to considerable disclosure of speech research information, citing the "academic environment" of the laboratory in which they worked as encouraging the sharing of information, rather than maintaining secrecy. Appellants also claimed that TI policy favored protection of its research and development efforts through the patent process, as opposed to trade secret designation. Further, appellants allege that the programs that are the subject of the instant case were not listed in the TI register of trade secrets and that TI was lax in implementing its standard procedures with regard to notifying employees of trade secrets within the company. The precise issue before us in the case *sub judice* is one of the first impressions in Texas, to wit: what constitutes requisite "measures" to protect trade secret status?

We now determine whether the information disclosed with TI's permission or encouragement, such as published articles, seminar papers, speeches given at public meetings, information provided to government agencies, etc., was so extensive as to destroy any trade secret status that may have existed regarding the computer software which is the subject of the instant indictments. It is axiomatic that the core element of a trade secret must be that it remain a secret. However, absolute secrecy is not required.

A trade secret can exist in a combination of characteristics and components, each of which, by itself, is in the public domain, but the unified process and operation of which, in unique combination, affords a competitive advantage and is a protectable secret. We find based on the record in this case that the limited disclosure made by TI in regard to the speech research lab activities merely described the application and configuration of certain elements of the software but did not reveal the actual composition of the programs. The measures used by TI to secure its premises to prevent unauthorized personnel from admission to or exposure to its proprietary research data were reasonable under the circumstances.

We need not decide today whether any one of the preventive measures listed, standing alone, is factually sufficient to support trade secret status. We do find that the combination of employment agreements, strict plant security, restricted computer access, the nonauthorization of disclosure of the subject programs and the general nondisclosure of those programs by TI and its employees served to support trade secret status of the computer programs that are the subject of the instant indictments. Appellants neither requested nor received permission to copy the files containing these programs. The unauthorized copying of the article representing a trade secret constitutes an offense under V.T.C.A. Penal Code §31.05(b)(2).

Therefore we AFFIRM the court of appeals' ruling that the subject programs are trade secrets.

CASE 5

LEE V. WEISMAN

120 L.Ed. 2d 467, 505 U.S. 577, 112 S.Ct. 2649,
1992 U.S. Lexis 4364 (1992)
Supreme Court of the United States
Kennedy, Justice

Deborah Weisman graduated from Nathan Bishop Middle School, a public school in Providence, at a formal ceremony in June 1989. She was about 14 years old. For many years it has been the policy of the Providence school committee and the Superintendent of Schools to permit principals to invite members of the clergy to give invocations and benedictions at middle school and high school graduations. Many, but not all, of the principals elected to include prayers as part of the graduation ceremonies. Acting for himself and his daughter, Deborah's father, Daniel Weisman, objected to any prayers at Deborah's middle school graduation, but to no avail. The school principal, petitioner Robert E. Lee, invited a rabbi to deliver prayers at the graduation exercises for Deborah's class. Rabbi Leslie Gutterman, of the Temple Beth El in Providence, accepted.

It has been the custom of Providence school officials to provide invited clergy with a pamphlet entitled "Guidelines for Civic Occasions," prepared by the National Conference of Christians and Jews. The Guidelines recommended that public prayers at nonsectarian civic ceremonies be composed with "inclusiveness and sensitivity," though they acknowledge that "prayer of any kind may be inappropriate on some civic occasions." The principal gave Rabbi Gutterman the pamphlet before the graduation and advised him the invocation and benediction should be non-sectarian.

Deborah's graduation was held on the premises of Nathan Bishop Middle School on June 29, 1989. Four days before the ceremony, Daniel Weisman, in his individual capacity as a Providence taxpayer and as next friend of Deborah, sought a temporary restraining order in the United States District Court for the District of Rhode Island to prohibit school offices from including an invocation or benediction in the graduation ceremony. The court denied the motion for lack of adequate time to consider it. Deborah and her family attended the graduation, where the prayers were recited. In July 1989, Daniel Weisman filed an amended complaint seeking a permanent injunction barring petitioners, various officials of the Providence public schools, from inviting the clergy to deliver invocations and benedictions at future graduations.

The case was submitted on stipulated facts. The district court held that petitioners' practice of including invocations and benedictions in public school graduations violated the Establishment Clause of the First Amendment, and it enjoined petitioners from continuing the practice. The court applied the three-part Establishment Clause test. Under that test, to satisfy the Establishment Clause a governmental practice must (1) reflect a clearly secular purpose, (2) have a primary effect that neither advances nor inhibits religion, and (3) avoid excessive government entanglement with religion. On appeal, the United States Court of Appeals for the First Circuit affirmed.

These dominant facts mark and control the confines of our decision: State officials direct the performance of a formal religious exercise at promotional and graduation ceremonies for secondary schools. Even for those students who object to the religious exercise, their attendance and participation in the state-sponsored religious activity are in a fair and real sense obligatory, though the school district does not require attendance as a condition for receipt of the diploma.

The controlling precedents as they relate to prayer and religious exercise in primary and secondary public schools compel the holding here that the policy of the city of Providence is an unconstitutional one. It is beyond dispute that, at a minimum, the Constitution guarantees that government may not coerce anyone to support or participate in religion or its exercise, or otherwise act in a way which "establishes a state religion or religious faith, or tends to do so."

We are asked to recognize the existence of a practice of nonsectarian prayer within the embrace of what is known as the Judeo-Christian tradition, prayer which is more acceptable than one which, for example, makes explicit references to the God of Israel, or to Jesus Christ, or to a patron saint. If common ground can be defined which permits once conflicting faiths to express the shared conviction that there is an ethic and a morality which transcend human invention, the sense of community and purpose sought by all decent societies might be advanced. But though the First Amendment does not allow the government to stifle prayers which aspire to these ends, neither does it permit the government to undertake that task for itself.

The sole question presented is whether a religious exercise may be conducted at a graduation ceremony in circumstances where, as we have found, young graduates who object are induced to conform. No holding by this Court suggests that a school can persuade or compel a student to participate in a religious exercise. That is being done here, and it is forbidden by the Establishment Clause of the First Amendment.

For the reasons we have stated, the judgment of the court of appeals is AFFIRMED.

Scalia, Justice (joined by Rehnquist, White, and Thomas) dissenting, expressed the view that (1) the establishment of religion clause should not have been interpreted so as to invalidate a long-standing American tradition of nonsectarian prayer at public school graduations, (2) graduation invocations and benedictions involve no psychological coercion of students to participate in religious exercises, (3) the only coercion that is forbidden by the establishment of religion clause is that which is backed by a threat of penalty, and (4) the middle school principal did not direct or control the content of the prayers in question, and thus there was no pervasive government involvement with religious activity.

CASE 6

BRAUN V. SOLDIER OF FORTUNE MAGAZINE, INC.

968 F.2d 1110, 1992 U.S. App. Lexis 18556 (1992)
United States Court of Appeals, Eleventh Circuit
Anderson, Circuit Judge

In January 1985, Michael Savage submitted a personal service advertisement to *Soldier of Fortune* (SOF). After several conversations between Savage and SOF's advertising manager, Joan Steel, the following advertisement ran in the June 1985 through March 1986 issues of SOF:

GUN FOR HIRE: 37-year-old professional mercenary desires jobs. Vietnam Veteran. Discrete [*sic*] and very private. Body guard, courier, and other special skills. All jobs considered. Phone (615) 436-9785 (days) or (615) 436-4335 (nights), or write: Rt. 2, Box 682 Village Loop Road, Gatlinburg, TN 37738.

Savage testified that, when he placed the ad, he had no intention of obtaining anything but legitimate jobs. Nonetheless, Savage stated that the overwhelming majority of the 30 to 40 phone calls a week he received in response to his ad sought his participation in criminal activity such as murder, assault, and kidnapping. The ad also generated at least one legitimate job as a bodyguard, which Savage accepted.

In late 1984 or early 1985, Bruce Gastwirth began seeking to murder his business partner, Richard Braun. Gastwirth enlisted the aid of another business associate, John Horton Moore, and together they arranged for at least three attempts on Braun's life, all of which were unsuccessful. Responding to Savage's SOF ad, Gastwirth and Moore contacted him in August 1985 to discuss plans to murder Braun. On August 26, 1985, Savage, Moore, and another individual, Sean Trevor Doutre, went to Braun's suburban Atlanta home. As Braun and his 16-year-old son Michael were driving down the driveway, Doutre stepped in front of Braun's car and fired several shots into the car with a MAC 11 automatic pistol. The shots hit Michael in the thigh and wounded Braun as well. Braun managed to roll out of the car, but Doutre walked over to Braun and killed him by firing two more shots into the back of his head as he lay on the ground.

On March 31, 1988, appellees Michael and Ian Braun filed this diversity against appellants in the United States District Court for the Middle District of Alabama, seeking damages for the wrongful death of their father. Michael Braun also filed a separate action seeking recovery for the personal injuries he received at the time of his father's death. The district court consolidated these related matters.

Trial began on December 3, 1990. Appellees contended that under Georgia law, SOF was liable for their injuries because SOF negligently published a personal service advertisement that created an unreasonable risk of the solicitation and commission of violent criminal activity, including murder. To show that SOF knew of the likelihood that criminal activity would result from placing an ad like Savage's, appellees introduced evidence of newspaper and magazine articles published prior to Braun's murder which described links between SOF and personal service ads and a number of criminal convictions including murder, kidnapping, assault, extortion, and attempts thereof. Appellees also presented evidence that, prior to SOF's acceptance of Savage's ad, law enforcement officials had contacted SOF staffers on two separate occasions in connection with investigations of crimes.

In his trial testimony, SOF president Robert K. Brown denied having any knowledge of criminal activity associated with SOF's personal service ads at any time prior to Braun's murder in August 1985. Both Jim Graves, a former managing editor of SOF, and Joan Steel, the advertising manager who accepted Savage's advertisement, similarly testified that they were not aware of other crimes connected with SOF ads prior to running Savage's ad. Steel further testified that she had understood the "Gun for Hire" in Savage's ad to refer to a "bodyguard or protection service-type thing," rather than to any illegal activity.

The jury returned a verdict in favor of appellee and awarded compensatory damages on the wrongful death claim in the amount of $2,000,000. The jury also awarded appellee Michael Braun $375,000 in compensatory damages and $10,000,000 in punitive damages for his personal injury claim.

To prevail in an action for negligence in Georgia, a party must establish the following elements:

(1) A legal duty to conform to a standard of conduct raised by the law for the protection of others against unreasonable risks of harm, (2) a breach of this standard, (3) a legally attributable causal connection between the conduct and the resulting injury, and (4) some loss or damage flowing to the plaintiff's legally protected interest as a result of the alleged breach of the legal duty. To the extent that SOF denies that a publisher owes any duty to the public when it publishes personal service ads, its position is clearly inconsistent with Georgia law. We believe, however, that the crux of SOF's argument is not that it had no duty to the public, but that, as a matter of law, there is a risk to the public when a publisher prints an "unreasonable" advertisement if the ad openly solicits criminal activity.

SOF further argues that imposing liability on publishers for the advertisements they print indirectly threatens core, noncommercial speech to which the Constitution accords its full protection. Supreme Court cases discussing the limitations the First Amendment places on state defamation law indicate that there is no constitutional infirmity in Georgia law holding publishers liable under a negligence standard with respect to the commercial advertisements they print. Past Supreme Court decisions indicate, however, that the negligence standard that the First Amendment permits is a "modified" negligence standard. The Court's decisions suggest that Georgia law may impose tort liability on publishers for injury caused by the advertisements they print only if the ad on its face, without the need to investigate, makes it apparent that there is a substantial danger of harm to the public.

We conclude that the First Amendment permits a state to impose upon a publisher liability for compensatory damages for negligently publishing a commercial advertisement where the ad on its face, and without the need for investigation, makes it apparent that there is a substantial danger of harm to the public. The absence of a duty requiring publishers to investigate the advertisements they print and the requirement that the substance of the ad itself must warn the publisher of a substantial danger of harm to the public guarantee that the burden placed on publishers will not impermissibly chill protected commercial speech.

Our review of the language of Savage's ad persuades us that SOF had a legal duty to refrain from publishing it. Savage's advertisement (1) emphasized the term "Gun for Hire," (2) described Savage as a "professional mercenary," (3) stressed Savage's willingness to keep his assignments confidential and "very private," (4) listed legitimate jobs involving the use of a gun—bodyguard and courier—followed by a reference to Savage's "other special skills," and (5) concluded by stating that Savage would consider "all jobs." The ad's combination of sinister terms makes it apparent that there was a substantial danger of harm to the public. The ad expressly solicits all jobs requiring the use of a gun. When the list of legitimate jobs—i.e., bodyguard and courier—is followed by "other special skills" and "all jobs considered," the implication is clear that the advertiser would consider illegal jobs. We agree with the district court that "the language of this advertisement is such that, even though couched in terms not explicitly offering criminal services, the publisher could recognize the offer of criminal activity as readily as its readers obviously did." We find that the jury had ample grounds for finding that SOF's publication of Savage's ad was the proximate cause of Braun's injuries.

For the foregoing reasons, we AFFIRM the district court's judgment.

CASE 7

CARNIVAL LEISURE INDUSTRIES, LTD. V. AUBIN

938 F.2d 624, 1991 U.S. App. Lexis 18704 (1991)
United States Court of Appeals, Fifth Circuit
Garwood, Circuit Judge

During a January 1987 visit to the Bahamas, George J. Aubin, a Texas resident, visited Cable Beach Hotel and Casino (the Casino), which was owned and operated by Carnival Leisure Industries, Ltd. (Carnival Leisure). While gambling at the Casino, Aubin received markers or chips from the Casino and the Casino received drafts drawn on Aubin's bank accounts in Texas. Aubin spent all of the markers provided on gambling, although he could also have spent them on food, beverages, souvenirs, or lodging at the Casino. Aubin ultimately gambled and lost $25,000, having given the Casino the same amount in bank drafts.

Carnival Leisure was unable to cash the bank drafts because Aubin had subsequently directed his bank to stop payment. Carnival Leisure sued Aubin in the United States District Court for the Southern District of Texas to enforce the debt. The district court granted Carnival Leisure's motion of summary judgment against Aubin in the amount of $25,000 and attorneys' fees and costs. Carnival Leisure claimed that the debt was enforceable under Texas law because public policy had changed and now favored enforcement of gambling debts. The district court agreed. Aubin raises on appeal only the issue of whether public policy in Texas continues to prevent the enforcement of gambling debts.

Carnival Leisure claims, however, that since 1973 the public policy of Texas toward gambling and the legality of gambling debts has changed. Although gambling is generally proscribed in Texas, there has been an exception for the "social" gambler since 1973. The Texas legislature enacted the Bingo Enabling Act in 1981, the Texas Racing Act in 1986, and the Charitable Raffle Enabling Act in 1989. Provisions were added to the Texas Penal Code excepting these three activities from its general proscription against gambling.

The enactment of statutes legalizing some forms of gambling admittedly evidences some dissipation or narrowing of public disapproval of gambling. However, such statutes hardly introduce a judicially cognizable change in public policy with respect to gambling generally. The social gambling permitted is confined to private places where no one receives any benefit other than his personal winnings and all participants are subject to the same risks, a categorically vastly different kind of activity from the sort involved here. The racing, bingo, and raffling exceptions are narrow, strictly regulated exceptions to a broad public policy in Texas against most forms of gambling. Further, the kind of gambling engaged in here is not of the sort permitted by any of these exceptions.

Even if gambling legislation in Texas were evidence sufficient to warrant judicial notice of a shift in public policy with respect to legalized gambling, such a shift would not be inconsistent with a continued public policy disfavoring gambling on credit. Although Aubin could have used the loaned markers for nongambling purposes at the Casino, it is undisputed that they were in fact used exclusively for gambling. Aubin's gambling debt therefore fits squarely within the terms of the public policy of Texas prohibiting enforcement of gambling debts owed to gambling participants incurred for the purposes of gambling.

We hold that the public policy in Texas against gambling on credit prevents enforcement of a debt incurred for the purpose of gambling and provided by a participant in the gambling activity. The district court's grant of summary judgment in favor of Carnival Leisure is accordingly REVERSED and this case is remanded to the district court for further proceedings consistent with this opinion.

CASE 8

THE WACKENHUT CORPORATION AND DELTA AIRLINES, INC. V. LIPPERT

609 So.2d 1304, 1992 Fla. Lexis 2016
Supreme Court of Florida
Grimes, Judge

While on her way to board a Delta Airlines flight from West Palm Beach to New York, Felice Lippert took a handbag containing approximately $431,000 worth of jewelry through a security checkpoint at Palm Beach International Airport. The security checkpoint was operated by The Wackenhut Corporation. The checkpoint consisted of a magnetometer scan of baggage and other carry-on items as well as a scan of the person which occurs as the person walks through a specially designed archway. Mrs. Lippert placed her bag on the conveyor belt as required and she walked through the archway. The archway magnetometer alarm sounded and Mrs. Lippert was briefly inspected by Wackenhut personnel. After being cleared by Wackenhut, Mrs. Lippert discovered her handbag with the jewelry was missing.

Mrs. Lippert sued Delta and Wackenhut for the value of her jewelry on a theory of negligence. Delta and Wackenhut asserted Delta's limitations of liability as their affirmative defense. The limitations of liability are expressed by reference on the back of Delta's ticket and in full in a governmentally required tariff which is posted according to federal regulations. The limitation contained in the tariff provides that:

> DL shall be liable for the loss, damage to, or delay in the delivery of a fare paying passenger's baggage, or other property (including carry on baggage, if tendered to DL's in flight personnel for storage during flight or otherwise delivered into the custody of DL). Such liability, if any, for the loss, damage, or delay in the delivery of a fare paying passenger's baggage or other property (whether checked or otherwise delivered into the custody of DL), shall be limited to an amount equal to the value of the property, plus consequential damages, if any, and shall not exceed the maximum limitation of USD $1250 for all liability for each fare paying passenger (unless the passenger elects to pay for higher liability). DL is not responsible for jewelry, cash, camera equipment, or other similar valuable items contained in checked or unchecked baggage, unless excess valuation has been purchased. These items should be carried by the passenger.

The trial court initially entered partial summary judgment for Delta and Wackenhut, upholding the limitation on liability to the maximum amount of $1,250. A new judge was assigned to the case by the time of trial. The jury returned a verdict for the plaintiff in the amount of $431,609, apportioning damages with Delta 65 percent liable and Wackenhut 35 percent liable. The trial court vacated the earlier partial summary judgment and entered final judgment for the plaintiff in the amount of $431,609. Delta and Wackenhut appealed the final judgment, arguing that the partial summary judgment should have been given its natural effect in limiting liability to $1,250.

The district court of appeal held that the limitation on liability contained in the ticket and the tariff did not apply under the facts of the case. The court also found that a bailment for the mutual benefit of both the passenger and the airline had been created when Mrs. Lippert relinquished possession of her valuables to go through the X-ray machine. Therefore, the trial court was correct in applying the ordinary negligence standard. However, the court felt that the defendants had been unduly prejudiced by the judge's assurances throughout the pretrial proceedings and the trial that the potential judgment could not exceed $1,250. Thus, the case was remanded for a new trial with the proviso that the limitation of liability would not apply.

On petition for review in this Court, Delta and Wackenhut argue for the $1,250 limitation. In addition, they contend that, because the airport security check was mandated by law, they were gratuitous bailees, who could only be held liable if grossly negligent. Mrs. Lippert cross-petitions to review the granting of a new trial.

Mrs. Lippert seems to argue that under the emphasized portion of section 1 of her ticket, quoted above, an article only becomes baggage, and therefore triggers the limitation on liability, when it reaches the cargo compartment or the cabin of the aircraft. However, this interpretation would lead to the dubious conclusion that passengers' property in transit to the airplane after being delivered to the airline at the check-in point where tickets are purchased should not be considered baggage. The phrase in the ticket's definition of baggage—"whether checked in the cargo compartment or carried in the cabin"—is more realistically construed as emphasizing that, for purposes of Delta's contract with its passengers, there is no difference between "carry-on" and "checked" baggage. Thus, the ticket's references to the cargo compartment and the cabin are merely descriptive of the words "checked" or "carried," and there can be no doubt that Mrs. Lippert's handbag was a passenger's "article or other property acceptable for transportation whether checked or carried." We believe that a ticketed passenger's property, destined for an airplane and in transit between the airport's security checkpoint and the actual airplane, constitutes "baggage" as defined by the ticket.

We hold that the $1,250 baggage limitation of liability was applicable to the loss of Mrs. Lippert's handbag while it was in the possession of Delta's agent at the airport security checkpoint. While we find the $1,250 liability limitation applicable in this case, we decline to answer the certified question because it does not precisely track the language of the tariff. We agree with the district court of appeal that the bailment created when Mrs. Lippert surrendered her handbag for inspection was for the mutual benefit of the passenger and the airline, and we adopt the court's reasoning in this respect. Our disposition of the baggage liability limitation issue renders the cross-petition moot. Because the case was tried under the proper standard of care, there is no need for a retrial. We quash the decision below to the extent that it is inconsistent with our opinion and remand the case for entry of a judgment in favor of Mrs. Lippert for $1,250.

CASE 9

TROXEL V. GRANVILLE

530 U.S. 57, 120 S.Ct. 2054, 2000 U.S. Lexis 3767 (2000)
Supreme Court of the United States
O'Connor, Justice

Section 26.10.160(3) of the Revised Code of Washington permits "[a]ny person" to petition a superior court for visitation rights "at any time," and authorizes that court to grant such visitation rights whenever "visitation may serve the best interest of the child." Petitioners Jenifer and Gary Troxel petitioned a Washington Superior Court for the right to visit their grandchildren, Isabelle and Natalie Troxel. Respondent Tommie Granville, mother of Isabelle and Natalie, opposed the petition. The case ultimately reached the Washington Supreme Court, which held that §26.10.160(3) unconstitutionally interferes with the fundamental right of parents to rear their children.

Tommie Granville and Brad Troxel shared a relationship that ended in June 1991. The two never married, but they had two daughters, Isabelle and Natalie. Jenifer and Gary Troxel are Brad's parents, and thus the paternal grandparents of Isabelle and Natalie. After Tommie and Brad separated in 1991, Brad lived with his parents and regularly brought his daughters to his parents' home for weekend visitation. Brad committed suicide in May 1993. Although the Troxels at first continued to see Isabelle and Natalie on a regular basis after their son's death, Tommie Granville informed the Troxels in October 1993 that she wished to limit their visitation with her daughters to one short visit per month.

In December 1993, the Troxels commenced the present action by filing, in the Washington Superior Court for Skagit County, a petition to obtain visitation rights with Isabelle and Natalie. In 1995, the Superior Court issued an oral ruling and entered a visitation decree ordering visitation one weekend per month, one week during the summer, and four hours on both of the petitioning grandparents' birthdays. Granville appealed, during which time she married Kelly Wynn.

Approximately nine months after the Court entered its order, Granville's husband formally adopted Isabelle and Natalie.

The Washington Court of Appeals reversed the lower court's visitation order and dismissed the Troxels' petition for visitation. The Washington Supreme Court granted the Troxels' petition for review and affirmed. The court rested its decision on the Federal Constitution, holding that §26.10.160(3) unconstitutionally infringes on the fundamental right of parents to rear their children.

The Fourteenth Amendment provides that no State shall "deprive any person of life, liberty, or property, without due process of law."

The liberty interest at issue in this case—the interest of parents in the care, custody, and control of their children—is perhaps the oldest of the fundamental liberty interests recognized by this Court. More than 75 years ago, in *Meyer v. Nebraska*, 262 U.S. 390, 399, 401, 43 S.Ct. 625 (1923), we held that the "liberty" protected by the Due Process Clause includes the right of parents to "establish a home and bring up children" and "to control the education of their own." In subsequent cases also, we have recognized the fundamental right of parents to make decisions concerning the care, custody, and control of their children. In light of this extensive precedent, it cannot now be doubted that the Due Process Clause of the Fourteenth Amendment protects the fundamental right of parents to make decisions concerning the care, custody, and control of their children.

The Troxels did not allege, and no court has found, that Granville was an unfit parent. That aspect of the case is important, for there is a presumption that fit parents act in the best interests of their children. Accordingly, so long as a parent adequately cares for his or her children (*i.e.*, is fit), there will normally be no reason for the State to inject itself into the private realm of the family to further question the ability of that parent to make the best decisions concerning the rearing of that parent's children.

We therefore hold that the application of § 26.10.160(3) to Granville and her family violated her due process right to make decisions concerning the care, custody, and control of her daughters. Accordingly, the judgment of the Washington Supreme Court is affirmed. It is so ordered.

CASE 10

IN RE ESTATE OF VALLERIUS

629 N.E.2d 1185, 1994 Ill. App. Lexis 267 (1994)
Appellate Court of Illinois
Lewis, Presiding Judge

On December 22, 1987, Douglas White murdered his grandmother, Adella G. Vallerius. On the same day, at the same time, and in the same house, Douglas's brother, Craig White, murdered his grandmother's friend, Carroll Pieper. Douglas was convicted of Mrs. Vallerius's murder. Craig entered a negotiated plea of guilty to, and was convicted of, the murder of Carroll Pieper. Craig testified for the state in Douglas's murder trial as part of his negotiated guilty plea.

Mrs. Vallerius died testate, naming Douglas and Craig as her sole beneficiaries. Mrs. Vallerius's only heir was her daughter Renie White, Douglas and Craig's mother. On January 11, 1988, Mrs. Vallerius's will was admitted to probate. In compliance with the terms of the will, Douglas White and Dennis Johnson were appointed legal representatives of Mrs. Vallerius's estate. About 2-1/2 months after Mrs. Vallerius was murdered, on March 7, 1988, Renie White died, intestate, of natural causes. She left as her only heirs her two sons, Douglas and Craig.

On March 12, 1990, the appellees, Peter M. Vallerius, Glenna F. Giacoletto, Lawrence Joe Davis, Helen L. Vallerius, Gail Kadavi, Iione V. Henry, Janis Murray, Terrie L. Illies, and Duffy Joe Vallerius, filed a petition to intervene and to consolidate the estates of Mrs. Vallerius and Renie White and an "Objection to Distribution" in the estate of Mrs. Vallerius, wherein they alleged that "Douglas Keith White and Craig Steven White, having intentionally and unjustifiably caused the death of Adella G. Vallerius, cannot lawfully receive any property, benefit or other interest" by reason of her death, through the estate of Mrs. Vallerius or through the estate of Renie White.

After an evidentiary hearing on the appellees' objection to distribution, the court entered an order granting the appellees' request. The trial court found that the issue in the case was whether Douglas and Craig could receive any property or interest by reason of the death of Mrs. Vallerius, whether through her estate or through the estate of Renie White. The court determined that, under both statute and common law, the public policy of Illinois has long been to prevent wrongdoers from profiting from intentionally committed wrongful acts. The court further found that the petitioner-objectors (appellees herein) had sustained their burden of proof, by clear and convincing evidence, that Douglas and Craig intentionally caused the death of their grandmother, Mrs. Vallerius.

Appellants argue that the law does not preclude a murderer from inheriting property from a person other than the victim. The obvious intent of the law is that persons like Douglas and Craig White must not profit from their brutal murder of their grandmother. The fact that there is an intervening estate should not expurgate the wrong of the murderer.

The appellants argue that Craig cannot be held accountable for Douglas' murder of Mrs. Vallerius, since Craig did not actually swing the sledgehammer that killed Mrs. Vallerius but only killed Carroll Pieper after Douglas killed Mrs. Vallerius. Appellants argue that even though Craig "may have borne criminal responsibility for the actions of Douglas White under the criminal accountability statute," Craig cannot be denied his right of inheritance from his mother.

Craig White cannot be permitted to receive any benefit by reason of the death of Mrs. Vallerius, whether through her estate directly or indirectly through the estate of her daughter, Renie White. If we were to allow Craig White to receive any property, benefit, or interest from the estate of Renie White, our decision would directly contravene the state's unambiguous mandate that he not receive any property by reason of his grandmother's death in any capacity or by any circumstance.

CASE 11

UNITED STATES V. WRW CORPORATION

986 F.2d 138, 1993 U.S. App. Lexis 2307 (1993)
United States Court of Appeals, Sixth Circuit
Peck, Judge

In 1985, civil penalties totaling $90,350 were assessed against WRW Corporation (WRW), a Kentucky corporation, for serious violations of safety standards under the Federal Mine Safety and Health Act (the Act) which resulted in the deaths of two miners. Following the imposition of civil penalties, WRW liquidated its assets and went out of business.

Three individual defendants, who were the sole shareholders, officers, and directors of WRW, were later indicted and convicted for willful violations of mandatory health and safety standards under the Act. Roger Richardson, Noah Woolum, and William Woolum each served prison sentences and paid criminal fines. After his release from prison, Roger Richardson filed for bankruptcy under Chapter 7 of the Bankruptcy Code.

The United States (the Government) brought this action in May of 1988 against WRW and Roger Richardson, Noah Woolum, and William Woolum to recover the civil penalties previously imposed against WRW. The district court denied the individual defendants' motion to dismiss and granted summary judgment to the Government piercing the corporate veil under state law and holding the individual defendants liable for the civil penalties assessed against WRW. For the reasons discussed herein, we affirm.

PIERCING THE CORPORATE VEIL

Having determined that the imposition of a $90,350 sanction upon the defendants does not violate principles of double jeopardy, we turn to the defendants' argument that the district court erred in holding the individual defendants liable for the penalty by piercing the corporate veil of WRW under Kentucky law.

The district court held that it was appropriate to pierce WRW's corporate veil under either an equity theory or an alter ego theory, both of which are recognized under Kentucky law. Under either theory, the following factors must be considered when determining whether to pierce the corporate veil: (1) undercapitalization; (2) a failure to observe the formalities of corporate existence; (3) nonpayment or overpayment of dividends; (4) a siphoning off of funds by dominant shareholders; and (5) the majority shareholders having guaranteed corporate liabilities in their individual capacities.

The court first found that WRW was undercapitalized because it was incorporated with only $3,000 of capital, which the record indicates was insufficient to pay normal expenses associated with the operation of a coal mine. The district court next found that WRW failed to observe corporate formalities, noting that no bylaws were produced by the defendants, and all corporate actions taken by the individual defendants were without corporation authorization. Finally, although WRW never distributed any dividends to the individual defendants, and there was no evidence that the individual defendants siphoned off corporate funds, these factors alone do not mitigate against piercing the corporate veil in this case because WRW was never sufficiently capitalized and operated at a loss during its two years of active existence.

In addition to holding that the equities of this case support piercing the corporate veil, the district court held that the corporate veil should be pierced under the "alter ego" theory, because WRW and the defendants did not have separate personalities. In light of the lack of observance of corporate formalities or distinction between the individual defendants and the corporation, we agree with the district court's conclusion that "there was a complete merger of ownership and control of WRW with the individual Defendants."

The specific factual findings made by the district court amply support piercing the corporate veil of WRW and holding the individual defendants liable for the penalty assessed against the corporate entity. For all of the foregoing reasons, judgment of the district court is AFFIRMED.

CASE 12

ROBINSON V. JACKSONVILLE SHIPYARDS, INC.

760 F.Supp. 1486, 1991 U.S. Dist. Lexis 4678 (1991)
United States District Court, Middle District of Florida
Melton, District Judge

Plaintiff Lois Robinson (Robinson) is a female employee of Jacksonville Shipyards, Inc. (JSI). She has been a welder since September 1977. Robinson is one of a very small number of female skilled craftworkers employed by JSI. Between 1977 and the present, Robinson was promoted from third-class welder to second-class welder and from second-class welder to her present position as a first-class welder.

JSI is a Florida corporation that runs several shipyards engaged in the business of ship repair, including the Commercial Yard and the Mayport Yard. As a federal contractor, JSI has affirmative action and nondiscrimination obligations. Defendant Arnold McIlwain (McIlwain) held the office of President of JSI from the time Robinson was hired by the company through the time of the trial of this case.

In addition to a welding department, JSI's other craft departments including shipfitting, sheetmetal, electrical, transportation, shipping, and receiving (including toolroom), carpenter, boilermaker, inside machine, outside machine, rigging, quality assurance, and pipe. Employees in these craft departments may be assigned to work at either the Mayport Yard, situated at the Mayport Naval Station, or the Commercial Yard, situated at a riverfront site in downtown Jacksonville and sometimes referred to as the downtown yard. Robinson's job assignments at JSI have required her to work at both the Commercial Yard and the Mayport Yard. Ship repair work is a dangerous profession; JSI acknowledges the need to "provide a working environment that is safe and healthful."

JSI is, in the words of its employees, "a boys club" and "more or less a man's world." Women craftworkers are an extreme rarity. The company's EEO-1 reports from 1980 to 1987 typically show that women form less than 5 percent of the skilled crafts.

Pictures of nude and partially nude women appear throughout the JSI work place in the form of magazines, plaques on the wall, photographs torn from magazines and affixed to the wall or attached to calendars supplied by advertising tool supply companies (vendors' advertising calendars). JSI has never distributed nor tolerated the distribution of a calendar or calendars with pictures of nude or partially nude men. Management employees from the very top down condoned these displays; often they had their own pictures.

Robinson credibly testified to the extensive, pervasive posting of pictures depicting nude women, partially nude women or sexual conduct and to the occurrence of other forms of harassing behavior perpetrated by her male co-workers and supervisors. Her testimony covered the full term of her employment, from 1977 to 1988.

Reported incidents included the following:

1. pictures in the fab shop area, in January 1985, including one of a woman wearing black tights, the top pulled down to expose her breasts to view, and one of a nude woman in an outdoor setting apparently playing with a piece of cloth between her legs.
2. a picture of a nude woman left on the tool box where Robinson returned her tools in the summer of 1986. The photograph depicted the woman's legs spread apart, knees bent up toward her chest exposing her breast and genitals. Several men were present and laughed at Robinson when she appeared upset by the picture.
3. a drawing on a heater control box, approximately one foot square, of a nude woman with fluid coming from her genital area, in 1987, at the Commercial Yard.
4. a dart board with a drawing of a woman's breast with her nipple as the bull's eye, in 1987 or 1988, at the Commercial Yard.

Robinson also testified about comments of a sexual nature she recalled hearing at JSI from co-workers. In some instances these comments were made while she also was in the presence of the pictures of nude or partially nude women. Among the remarks Robinson recalled are, "Hey pussycat, come here and give me a whiff," "The more you lick it, the harder it gets," "I'd like to get in bed with that," "I'd like to have some of that," "Black women taste like sardines," "It doesn't hurt women to have sex right after childbirth," and so on. Defendants have admitted that pictures of nude or partially nude women have been posted in the shipfitters' trailer at the Mayport Yard during Robinson's employment at JSI.

Based on the foregoing, the court finds that sexually harassing behavior occurred through the JSI working environment with both frequency and intensity over the relevant time period. Robinson did not welcome such behavior.

In April 1987, during the pendency of this lawsuit, JSI adopted a new sexual harassment policy. It was instituted unilaterally, without consulting or bargaining with the union. The official policy statement, signed by Vice-President for Operations Larry Brown, endorses the following policy:

1. It is illegal and a violation of Jacksonville Shipyards, Inc., policy for any employee, male or female, to sexually harass another employee by:
   a. making unwelcomed sexual advances or request for sexual favors or other verbal or physical conduct of a sexual nature, a condition of an employee's continued employment, or
   b. making submission to or rejection of such conduct the basis for employment decisions affecting the employee, or
   c. creating an intimidating, hostile, or offensive working environment by such conduct.
2. Any employee who believes he or she has been the subject of sexual harassment, should report the alleged act immediately to John Stewart Ext. 3716 in our Industrial Relations Department. An investigation of all complaints will be undertaken immediately. Any supervisor, agent or other employee who has been found by the Company to have sexually harassed another employee will be subject to appropriate sanctions, depending on the circumstances, from a warning in his or her file up to and including termination.

The 1987 policy had little or no impact on the sexually hostile work environment at JSI. Employees and supervisors lacked the knowledge and training in the scope of those acts that might constitute sexual harassment.

The court finds that the policies and procedures at JSI for responding to complaints of sexual harassment are inadequate. The company has done an inadequate job of communicating with employees and supervisors regarding the nature and scope of sexually harassing behavior. This failure is compounded by a pattern of unsympathetic response to complaints by employees who perceive that they are victims of harassment. This pattern includes an unwillingness to believe the accusations, an unwillingness to take prompt and stern remedial action against admitted harassers, and an express condonation of behavior that is and encourages sexually harassing conduct (such as the posting of pictures of nude and partially nude women). In some instances, the process of registering a complaint about sexual harassment became a second episode of harassment.

ORDERED AND ADJUDGED

That defendant Jacksonville Shipyards, Inc., is hereby enjoined to cease and desist from the maintenance of a work environment that is hostile to women because of their sex and to remedy the hostile work environment through the implementation, forthwith, of the Sexual Harassment Policy, which consists of the "Statement of Policy," "Statement of Prohibited Conduct," "Schedule of Penalties for Misconduct," "Procedures for Making, Investigating and Resolving Sexual Harassment and Retaliation Complaints," and "Procedures and Rules for Education and Training."

JACKSONVILLE SHIPYARDS, INC., SEXUAL HARASSMENT POLICY STATEMENT OF POLICY

Title VII of the Civil Rights Act of 1964 prohibits employment discrimination on the basis of race, color, sex, age, or national origin. Sexual harassment is included among the prohibitions.

Sexual harassment, according to the federal Equal Employment Opportunity Commission (EEOC), consists of unwelcome sexual advances, requests for sexual favors or other verbal or physical acts of a sexual or sex-based nature where (1) submission to such conduct is made either explicitly or implicitly a term or condition of an individual's employment; (2) an employment decision is based on an individual's acceptance or rejection of such conduct; or (3) such conduct interferes with an individual's work performance or creates an intimidating, hostile or offensive working environment.

CASE 13

DEWSNUP V. TIMM

502 U.S. 410, 112 S. Ct. 773, 1992 U.S. Lexis 375 (1992)
Supreme Court of the United States
Blackmun, Justice

We are confronted in this case with an issue concerning §506(d) of the Bankruptcy Code. May a debtor "strip down" a creditor's lien on real property to the value of the collateral, as judicially determined, when that value is less than the amount of the claim secured by the lien?

On June 1, 1978, respondents loaned $119,000 to petitioner Aletha Dewsnup and her husband, T. LaMar Dewsnup, since deceased. The loan was accompanied by a Deed of Trust granting a lien on two parcels of Utah farmland owned by the Dewsnups. Petitioner defaulted the following year. Under the terms of the Deed of Trust, respondents at that point could have proceeded against the real property collateral by accelerating the maturity of the loan, issuing a notice of default, and selling the land at a public foreclosure sale to satisfy the debt.

Respondents did issue a notice of default in 1981. Before the foreclosure sale took place, however, petitioner sought reorganization under Chapter 11 of the Bankruptcy Code. That bankruptcy petition was dismissed, as was a subsequent Chapter 11 petition. In June 1984, petitioner filed a petition seeking liquidation under Chapter 7 of the Code. Because of the pendency of these bankruptcy proceedings, respondents were not able to proceed to the foreclosure sale.

Petitioner-debtor takes the position that §506(a) and §506(d) are complementary and to be read together. Because, under §506(a), a claim is secured only to the extent of the judicially determined value of the real property on which the lien is fixed, a debtor can void a lien on the property pursuant to §506(d) to the extent the claim is no longer secured and thus is not "an allowed secured claim." In other words, §506(a) bifurcates classes of claims allowed under §502 into secured claims and unsecured claims; any portion of an allowed claim deemed to be unsecured under §506(a) is not an "allowed secured claim" within the lien-voiding scope of §506(d). Petition argues that there is no exception for unsecured property abandoned by the trustee.

We conclude that respondents' alternative position, espoused also by the United States, although not without its difficulty, generally is the best of the several approaches. Therefore, we hold that §506(d) does not allow petitioner to "strip down" respondents' lien, because respondents' claim is secured by a lien and has been fully allowed pursuant to §502.

The practical effect of petitioner's argument is to freeze the creditor's secured interest at the judicially determined valuation. By this approach, the creditor would lose the benefit of any increase in the value of the property by the time of the foreclosure sale. The increase would accrue to the benefit of the debtor, a result some of the parties describe as a "windfall."

We think, however, that the creditor's lien stays with the real property until the foreclosure. That is what was bargained for by the mortgagor and the mortgagee. Any increase over the judicially determined valuation during bankruptcy rightly accrues to the benefit of the creditor, not to the benefit of the debtor and not to the benefit of other unsecured creditors whose claims have been allowed and who had nothing to do with the mortgagor–mortgagee bargain.

No provision of the pre-Code statute permitted involuntary reduction of the amount of a creditor's lien for any reason other than payment on the debt.

The judgment of the court of appeals is AFFIRMED.

CASE 14

FEIST PUBLICATIONS, INC. V. RURAL TELEPHONE SERVICE CO., INC.

499 U.S. 340, 111 S.Ct. 1282, 1991 U.S. Lexis 1856 (1991)
Supreme Court of the United States
O'Connor, Justice

Rural Telephone Service Company is a certified public utility that provides telephone service to several communities in northwest Kansas. It is subject to a state regulation that requires all telephone companies operating in Kansas to issue annually an updated telephone directory. Accordingly, as a condition of its monopoly franchise, Rural publishes a typical telephone directory, consisting of white pages and yellow pages. The white pages list in alphabetical order the names of Rural's subscribers, together with their towns and telephone numbers. The yellow pages list Rural's business subscribers alphabetically by category and feature classified advertisements of various sizes. Rural distributes its directory free of charge to its subscribers, but earns revenue by selling yellow pages advertisements.

Feist Publications, Inc., is a publishing company that specializes in area-wide telephone directories. Unlike a typical directory, which covers only a particular calling area, Feist's area-wide directories cover a much larger geographical range, reducing the need to call directory assistance or consult multiple directories. The Feist directory that is the subject of this litigation covers 11 different telephone service areas in 15 counties and contains 46,878 white pages listings—compared to Rural's approximately 7,700 listings.

Of the 11 telephone companies, only Rural refused to license its listings to Feist. Rural's refusal created a problem for Feist, as omitting these listings would have left a gaping hole in its area-wide directory, rendering it less attractive to potential yellow pages advertisers. Unable to license Rural's white pages listings, Feist used them without Rural's consent.

Rural sued for copyright infringement in the District Court for the District of Kansas, taking the position that Feist, in compiling its own directory, could not use the information contained in Rural's white pages. The district court granted summary judgment to Rural, explaining that "courts have consistently held that telephone directories are copyrightable" and citing a string of lower court decisions. In an unpublished opinion, the Court of Appeals for the Tenth Circuit affirmed "for substantially the reasons given by the district court."

This case concerns the interaction of two well-established propositions. The first is that facts are not copyrightable; the other, that compilations of facts generally are. The key to resolving the tension lies in understanding why facts are not copyrightable. The *sine qua non* of copyright is originality. To qualify for copyright protection, a work must be original to the author. Original, as the term is used in copyright, means only that the work was independently created by the author (as opposed to copied from other works) and that it possesses at least some minimal degree of creativity.

Originality is a constitutional requirement. The source of Congress's power to enact copyright laws is Article 1, §8. Cl. 8, of the Constitution, which authorizes Congress to "secure for limited Times to Authors . . . the exclusive Right to their respective Writings." It is this bedrock principle of copyright that mandates the law's seemingly disparate treatment of facts and factual compilations. No one may claim originality as to facts. This is because facts do not owe their origin to an act of authorship. The distinction is one between creation and discovery: the first person to find and report a particular fact has not created the fact; he or she has merely discovered its existence.

If the selection and arrangement of facts are original, these elements of the work are eligible for copyright protection. No matter how original the format, however, the facts themselves do not become original through association.

There is no doubt that Feist took from the white pages of Rural's directory a substantial amount of factual information. At a minimum, Feist copied the names, towns, and telephone numbers of 1,309 of Rural's subscribers. Not all copying, however, is copyright infringement; two elements must be proven: (1) ownership of a valid copyright, and (2) copying of constituent elements of the work that are original. The first element is not at issue here: Feist appears to concede that Rural's directory, considered as a whole, is subject to a valid copyright because it contains some foreword text, as well as original material in its yellow pages advertisements.

The question is whether Rural has proven the second element. In other words, did Feist, by taking 1,309 names, towns, and telephone numbers from Rural's white pages, copy anything that was "original" to Rural? Certainly, the raw data does not satisfy the originality requirement. Rural may have been the first to discover and report the names, towns, and telephone numbers of its subscribers, but this data does not "owe its origin" to Rural. The question that remains is whether Rural selected, coordinated, or arranged these copyrightable facts in an original way. The selection, coordination, and arrangement of Rural's white pages do not satisfy the minimum constitutional standards for copyright protection. Rural's selection of listings could not be more obvious: it publishes the most basic information—name, town, and telephone number—about each person who applies to it for telephone service. This is "selection" of a sort, but it lacks a modicum of creativity necessary to transform mere selection into copyrightable expression. Rural extended sufficient effort to make the white pages directory useful, but insufficient creativity to make it original.

The judgment of the court of appeals is REVERSED.

CASE 15

FMC CORP. V. U.S. DEPARTMENT OF COMMERCE

786 F. Supp. 471, 1992 U.S. Dist. Lexis 2355 (E.D. Pa. 1992)
United States District Court, Eastern District of Pennsylvania
Newcomer, District Judge

This action is brought pursuant to the Comprehensive Environmental Response, Compensation and Liability Act of 1980, as amended (CERCLA), and the Declaratory Judgment Act. Plaintiff FMC Corporation (FMC) owned and operated, from 1963 to 1976, the Avtex site in Front Royal, Virginia (the Facility), a site which has been listed on the National Priorities List since 1986. FMC seeks indemnification from the defendants for some portion of its present and future costs of response in performing removal actions and other response actions at the Facility. FMC bases its claim on the United States Government (Government) activities during the period of January 1942 through 1945 relating to the operation of a rayon manufacturing facility at the Avtex site, and contends that these activities render the Government liable as an "owner," "operator," and/or "arranger" under section 107 of the CERCLA.

During World War II, after the bombing of Pearl Harbor and the Japanese conquest of Asia, the United States suffered a loss of 90 percent of its crude rubber supply. An urgent need arose for natural rubber substitute to be used in manufacturing airplane tires, jeep tires, and other war related items. The best rubber substitute available was high tenacity rayon tire cord. The Facility was one of the major producers of high tenacity rayon yarn, which was twisted and woven into high tenacity rayon tire cord. FMC presented evidence at trial showing that during the World War II period, the Government participated in managing and controlling the Facility, which was then owned by American Viscose Corporation (American Viscose), requiring the Facility to manufacture increasing quantities of high tenacity rayon yarn, which involved the treatment of hazardous materials, and necessitated the disposal of hazardous materials. FMC also presented evidence showing that the Government owned "facilities" and equipment at the plant used in the treatment and disposal of hazardous materials.

The evidence included the following:

1. During World War II, the Government took over numerous plants which, for a multitude of reasons, failed to meet production requirements, including a plant producing high tenacity rayon yarn. Beginning no later than 1943, the rayon tire cord program received constant attention from the highest officials of the War Production Board (WPB), as well as top officials of the War Department and other Government departments and agencies.
2. Once the WPB determined that there was a need for substantial expansion of the production capabilities at the Facility, Government personnel were assigned to facilitate and expedite construction. The rayon tire cord program, in general, and the implementation of the program at the Facility, in particular, required and received far more involvement, participation, and control by the Government than the vast majority of the production programs implemented during World War II.
3. The disposal or treatment of hazardous substances is inherent in the production of high tenacity rayon yarn. The Government was familiar with the Facility's process for producing high tenacity rayon yarn. The Government knew or should have known that the disposal or treatment of hazardous substances was inherent in the manufacture of high tenacity rayon yarn and that its production requirements caused a significant increase in the amount of hazardous substances generated and disposed of at the Facility.

The district court concluded that the United States, through the actions and authority of WPB and other departments, agencies, and instrumentalities of the United States Government, "operated" the Facility, from approximately January 1942 to at least November 1945, as defined by section 101(2) of the CERCLA. During the period the Government operated the Facility, wastes containing "hazardous substances," as defined by section 101(14) of CERCLA, and as identified in 40 C.F.R. Part 302, Table 302.4 (1990), were "disposed of" at the Facility.

There has been a "release or threatened release" of hazardous substances from the facilities which were owned by the United States. Such release or threatened release of hazardous substances has caused and will continue to cause FMC to incur "necessary costs of response" within the meaning of Section 107 of CERCLA, including without limitation the costs which FMC has incurred and will incur in monitoring, assessing, and evaluating the release or threatened release of hazardous substances and performing removal and/or remedial activities and taking other actions required or requested by the EPA, as well as attorneys' fees and expenses associated with this lawsuit.

Liability of an owner or operator of a facility as defined by §107(a) for the cost of removal "is strict and joint and several." The United States Government as owner is responsible for costs resulting from responses to the release of hazardous substances.

And it is SO ORDERED.

The Constitution of the United States of America

We the People of the United States, in Order to form a more perfect Union, establish Justice, insure domestic Tranquility, provide for the common defense, promote the general Welfare, and secure the Blessings of Liberty to ourselves and our Posterity, do ordain and establish this Constitution for the United States of America.

ARTICLE I

Section 1. All legislative Powers herein granted shall be vested in a Congress of the United States, which shall consist of a Senate and House of Representatives.

Section 2. The House of Representatives shall be composed of Members chosen every second Year by the People of the several states, and the Electors in each State shall have the Qualifications requisite for Electors of the most numerous Branch of the State Legislature.

No Person shall be a Representative who shall not have attained to the Age of twenty five Years, and been seven Years a Citizen of the United States, and who shall not, when elected, be an Inhabitant of that State in which he shall be chosen.

Representatives and direct Taxes shall be apportioned among the several states which may be included within this Union, according to their respective Numbers, which shall be determined by adding to the whole Number of free Persons, including those bound to Service for a Term of Years, and excluding Indians not taxed, three fifths of all other Persons. The actual Enumeration shall be made within three Years after the first Meeting of the Congress of the United States, and within every subsequent Term of ten Years, in such Manner as they shall by Law direct. The number of Representatives shall not exceed one for every thirty Thousand, but each State shall have at Least one Representative; and until such enumeration shall be made, the State of New Hampshire shall be entitled to chuse three, Massachusetts eight, Rhode Island and Providence Plantations one, Connecticut five, New York six, New Jersey four, Pennsylvania eight, Delaware one, Maryland six, Virginia ten, North Carolina five, South Carolina five, and Georgia three.

When vacancies happen in the Representation from any State, the Executive Authority thereof shall issue Writs of Election to fill such vacancies.

The House of Representatives shall chuse their Speaker and other Officers; and shall have the sole Power of Impeachment.

Section 3. The Senate of the United States shall be composed of two Senators from each State, chosen by the Legislature thereof, for six Years; and each Senator shall have one Vote.

Immediately after they shall be assembled in Consequence of the first Election, they shall be divided as equally as may be into three Classes. The Seats of the Senators of the first Class shall be vacated at the Expiration of the second Year, of the second Class at the Expiration of the fourth Year, and the third Class at the Expiration of the sixth Year, so that one third may be chosen every second Year; and if Vacancies happen by Resignation, or otherwise, during the Recess of the Legislature of any State, the Executive thereof may make temporary Appointments until the next meeting of the Legislature, which shall then fill such Vacancies.

No person shall be a Senator who shall not have attained to the Age of thirty Years, and been nine Years a Citizen of the United States, and who shall not, when elected, be an Inhabitant of that State for which he shall be chosen.

The Vice President of the United States shall be President of the Senate, but shall have no Vote, unless they be equally divided.

The Senate shall chuse their other Officers, and also a President pro tempore, in the Absence of the Vice President, or when he shall exercise the Office of President of the United States.

The Senate shall have the sole power to try all Impeachments. When sitting for that Purpose, they shall be an Oath or Affirmation. When the President of the United States is tried, the Chief Justice shall preside: And no Person shall be convicted without the Concurrence of two thirds of the Members present.

Judgment in Cases of Impeachment shall not extend further than to removal from Office, and disqualification to hold and enjoy any Office of honor, Trust or Profit under the United States: but the Party convicted shall nevertheless be liable and subject to Indictment, Trial, Judgment and Punishment, according to Law.

Section 4. The Times, Places and Manner of holding Elections for Senators and Representatives, shall be prescribed in each State by the Legislature thereof: but the Congress may at any time by Law make or alter such Regulations, except as to the Places of chusing Senators.

The Congress shall assemble at least once in every Year, and such Meeting shall be on the first Monday in December, unless they shall by Law appoint a different day.

Section 5. Each House shall be the Judge of the Elections, Returns and Qualifications of its own Members, and a Majority of each shall constitute a Quorum to do Business; but a smaller Number may adjourn from day to day, and may be authorized to compel the Attendance of absent Members, in such Manner, and under such Penalties as each House may provide.

Each House may determine the Rules of its Proceedings, punish its Members for disorderly Behaviour, and, with the Concurrence of two thirds, expel a Member.

Each House shall keep a Journal of its Proceedings, and from time to time publish the same, excepting such Parts as may in their Judgment require Secrecy; and the Yeas and Nays of the Members of either House on any question shall, at the Desire of one fifth of those Present, be entered on the Journal.

Neither House, during the Session of Congress, shall, without the Consent of the other, adjourn for more than three days, nor to any other Place than that in which the two Houses shall be sitting.

Section 6. The Senators and Representatives shall receive a Compensation for their Services, to be ascertained by Law, and paid out of the Treasury of the United States. They shall in all Cases, except Treason, Felony and Breach of the Peace, be privileged from Arrest during their Attendance at the Session of their respective Houses, and in going to and returning from the same; and for any Speech or Debate in either House, they shall not be questioned in any other Place.

No Senator or Representative shall, during the Time for which he was elected, be appointed to any civil Office under the Authority of the United States, which shall have been created, or the Emoluments whereof shall have been encreased during such time; and no Person holding any Office under the United States, shall be a Member of either House during his Continuance in Office.

Section 7. All Bills for raising Revenue shall originate in the House of Representatives; but the Senate may propose or concur with Amendments as on other Bills.

Every Bill which shall have passed the House of Representatives and the Senate, shall, before it become a Law, be presented to the President of the United States; If he approve he shall sign it, but if not he shall return it, with his Objections to that House in which it shall have originated, who shall enter the Objections at large on their Journal, and proceed to reconsider it. If after such Reconsideration two thirds of that House shall agree to pass the Bill, it shall be sent, together with the Objections, to the other House, by which it shall likewise be reconsidered, and if approved by two thirds of that House, it shall become a Law. But in all such Cases the Votes of both Houses shall be determined by Yeas and Nays, and the Names of the Persons voting for and against the Bill shall be entered on the Journal of each House respectively. If any Bill shall not be returned by the President within ten Days (Sundays excepted) after it shall have been presented to him, the Same shall be a Law, in like Manner as if he had signed it, unless the Congress by their Adjournment prevent its Return, in which Case it shall not be a Law.

Every Order, Resolution, or Vote to which the Concurrence of the Senate and House of Representatives may be necessary (except on a question of Adjournment) shall be presented to the President of the United States; and before the Same shall take Effect, shall be approved by him, or being disapproved by him, shall be repassed by two thirds of the Senate and House of Representatives, according to the Rules and Limitations prescribed in the Case of a Bill.

Section 8. The Congress shall have Power to lay and collect Taxes, Duties, Imposts and Excises, to pay the Debts and provide for the common Defence and general Welfare of the United States; but all Duties, Imposts and Excises shall be uniform throughout the United States;

To borrow Money on the credit of the United States;

To regulate Commerce with foreign Nations, and among the several States, and with the Indian Tribes;

To establish an uniform Rule of Naturalization, and uniform Laws on the subject of Bankruptcies throughout the United States;

To coin Money, regulate the Value thereof, and of foreign Coin, and fix the Standard of Weights and Measures;

To provide for the Punishment of counterfeiting the Securities and current Coin of the United States;

To establish Post Offices and post Roads;

To promote the Progress of Science and useful Arts, by securing for limited Times to Authors and Inventors the exclusive Right to their respective Writings and Discoveries;

To constitute Tribunals inferior to the supreme Court;

To define and punish Piracies and Felonies committed on the high Seas, and Offenses against the Law of Nations;

To declare War, grant Letters of Marque and Reprisal, and make Rules concerning Captures on Land and Water;

To raise and support Armies, but no Appropriation of Money to that Use shall be for a longer Term than two Years;

To provide and maintain a Navy;

To make Rules for the Government and Regulation of the land and naval Forces;

To provide for calling forth the Militia to execute the Laws of the Union, suppress Insurrections and repel Invasions;

To provide for organizing, arming, and disciplining, the Militia, and for governing such Part of them as may be employed in the Service of the United States, reserving to the States respectively, the Appointment of the Officers, and the Authority of training the Militia according to the discipline prescribed by Congress;

To exercise exclusive Legislation in all Cases whatsoever, over such District (not exceeding ten Miles square) as may, by

Cession of particular States, and the Acceptance of Congress, become the Seat of the Government of the United States, and to exercise like Authority over all Places purchased by the Consent of the Legislature of the State in which the Same shall be, for the Erection of Forts, Magazines, Arsenals, dock-Yards, and other needful Buildings;—And

To make all Laws which shall be necessary and proper for carrying into Execution the foregoing Powers, and all other Powers vested by this Constitution in the Government of the United States, or in any Department or Officer thereof.

Section 9. The Migration or Importation of such Persons as any of the States now existing shall think proper to admit, shall not be prohibited by the Congress prior to the Year one thousand eight hundred and eight, but a Tax or Duty may be imposed on such Importation, not exceeding ten dollars for each Person.

The Privilege of the Writ of Habeas Corpus shall not be suspended, unless when in Cases of Rebellion or Invasion the public Safety may require it.

No Bill of Attainder or ex post facto Law shall be passed.

No Capitation, or other direct, Tax shall be laid, unless in Proportion to the Census or Enumeration herein before directed to be taken.

No Tax or Duty shall be laid on Articles exported from any State.

No Preference shall be given by any Regulation of Commerce or Revenue to the Ports of one State over those of another; nor shall Vessels bound to, or from, one State, be obliged to enter, clear, or pay Duties in another.

No Money shall be drawn from the Treasury, but in Consequence of Appropriations made by Laws; and a regular Statement and Account of the Receipts and Expenditures of all public Money shall be published from time to time.

No Title of Nobility shall be granted by the United States: And no Person holding any Office of Profit or Trust under them, shall, without the Consent of the Congress, accept of any present, Emolument, Office, or Title, of any kind whatever, from any King, Prince, or foreign State.

Section 10. No State shall enter into any Treaty, Alliance, or Confederation; grant Letters of Marque and Reprisal; coin Money; emit Bills of Credit; make any Thing but gold and silver Coin a Tender in Payment of Debts; pass any Bill of Attainder, ex post facto Law, or Law impairing the Obligation of Contracts, or grant any Title of Nobility.

No State shall, without the Consent of the Congress, lay any Imposts or Duties on Imports or Exports, except what may be absolutely necessary for executing its inspection Laws: and the net Produce of all Duties and Imposts, laid by any State on Imports or Exports, shall be for the Use of the Treasury of the United States; and all such Laws shall be subject to the Revision and Control of the Congress.

No State shall, without the Consent of Congress, lay any Duty of Tonnage, keep Troops, or Ships of War in time of Peace, enter into any Agreement or Compact with another State, or with a foreign Power, or engage in War, unless actually invaded, or in such imminent Danger as will not admit of delay.

Article II

Section 1. The executive Power shall be vested in a President of the United States of America. He shall hold his Office during the Term of four Years, and, together with the Vice President, chosen for the same Term, be elected, as follows:

Each State shall appoint, in such Manner as the Legislature thereof may direct, a Number of Electors, equal to the whole Number of Senators and Representatives to which the State may be entitled in the Congress: but no Senator or Representative, or Person holding an Office of Trust or Profit under the United States, shall be appointed an Elector.

The Electors shall meet in their respective States, and vote by Ballot for two Persons, of whom one at least shall not be an Inhabitant of the same State with themselves. And they shall make a list of all the Persons voted for, and of the Number of Votes for each; which List they shall sign and certify, and transmit sealed to the Seat of the Government of the United States, directed to the President of the Senate. The President of the Senate shall, in the presence of the Senate and House of Representatives, open all the Certificates, and the Votes shall be counted. The Person having the greatest Number of Votes shall be the President, if such Number be a Majority of the whole Number of Electors appointed; and if there be more than one who have such Majority, and have an equal Number of Votes, then the House of Representatives shall immediately chuse by Ballot one of them for President; and if no Person have a Majority, then from the five highest on the List the said House shall in like Manner chuse the President. But in chusing the President, the Votes shall be taken by States, the Representation from each State having one Vote; A quorum for this Purpose shall consist of a Member or Members from two thirds of the States, and a Majority of all the States shall be necessary to a Choice. In every Case, after the Choice of the President, the Person having the greatest Number of Votes of the Electors shall be the Vice President. But if there should remain two or more who have equal Votes, the Senate shall chuse from them by Ballot the Vice President.

The Congress may determine the Time of Chusing the Electors, and the Day on which they shall give their Votes; which Day shall be the same throughout the United States.

No Person except a natural born Citizen, or a Citizen of the United States, at the time of the Adoption of this Constitution, shall be eligible to the Office of President; neither shall any Person be eligible to that Office who shall not have attained to the Age of thirty five Years, and been fourteen Years a Resident within the United States.

In Case of the Removal of the President from Office, or of his Death, Resignation, or Inability to discharge the Powers and Duties of the said Office, the Same shall devolve on the

Vice President, and the Congress may by Law provide for the Case of Removal, Death, Resignation or Inability, both of the President and Vice President, declaring what Officer shall then act as President, and such Officer shall act accordingly, until the Disability be removed, or a President shall be elected.

The President shall, at stated Times, receive for his Services, a Compensation, which shall neither be encreased nor diminished during the Period for which he shall have been elected, and he shall not receive within that Period any other Emolument from the United States, or any of them.

Before he enter on the Execution of his Office, he shall take the following Oath or Affirmation:—"I do solemnly swear (or affirm) that I will faithfully execute the Office of President of the United States, and will to the best of my Ability, preserve, protect and defend the Constitution of the United States."

Section 2. The President shall be Commander in Chief of the Army and Navy of the United States, and of the Militia of the several States, when called into the actual Service of the United States; he may require the Opinion, in writing, of the principal Officer in each of the executive Departments, upon any Subject relating to the Duties of their respective Offices, and he shall have Power to grant Reprieves and Pardons for Offences against the United States, except in Cases of Impeachment.

He shall have Power, by and with the Advice and Consent of the Senate, to make Treaties, provided two thirds of the Senators present concur; and he shall nominate, and by and with the Advice and Consent of the Senate, shall appoint Ambassadors, other public Ministers and Consuls, Judges of the supreme Court, and all other Officers of the United States, whose Appointments are not herein otherwise provided for, and which shall be established by Law: but the Congress may by Law vest the Appointment of such inferior Officers, as they think proper, in the President alone, in the Courts of Law, or in the Heads of Departments.

The President shall have Power to fill up all Vacancies that may happen during the Recess of the Senate, by granting Commissions which shall expire at the End of their next Session.

Section 3. He shall from time to time give to the Congress Information of the State of the Union, and recommend to their Consideration such Measures as he shall judge necessary and expedient; he may, on extraordinary Occasions, convene both Houses, or either of them, and in Case of Disagreement between them, with Respect to the Time of Adjournment, he may adjourn them to such Time as he shall think proper; he shall receive Ambassadors and other public Ministers; he shall take Care that the Laws be faithfully executed, and shall Commission all the Officers of the United States.

Section 4. The President, Vice President and all civil Officers of the United States, shall be removed from Office on Impeachment for, and Conviction of, Treason, Bribery, or other high Crimes and Misdemeanors.

ARTICLE III

Section 1. The judicial Power of the United States, shall be vested in one supreme Court, and in such inferior Courts as the Congress may from time to time ordain and establish. The Judges, both of the supreme and inferior Courts, shall hold their Offices during good Behaviour, and shall, at Times, receive for their Services, a Compensation, which shall not be diminished during their Continuance in Office.

Section 2. The judicial Power shall extend to all Cases, in Law and Equity, arising under this Constitution, the Laws of the United States, and Treaties made, or which shall be made, under their Authority;—to all Cases affecting Ambassadors, other public Ministers and Consuls;—to all Cases of admiralty and maritime Jurisdiction;—to Controversies to which the United States shall be a Party;—to controversies between two or more States;—between a State and Citizens of another State;—between Citizens of different States;—between Citizens of the same State claiming Lands under Grants of different States, and between a State, or the Citizens thereof, and foreign States, Citizens or Subjects.

In all Cases affecting Ambassadors, other public Ministers and Consuls, and those in which a State shall be Party, the supreme Court shall have original Jurisdiction. In all the other Cases before mentioned, the supreme Court shall have appellate Jurisdiction, both as to Law and Fact, with such Exceptions, and under such Regulations as the Congress shall make.

The Trial of all Crimes, except in Cases of Impeachment, shall be by Jury; and such Trial shall be held in the State where the said Crimes shall have been committed; but when not committed within any State, the Trial shall be at such Place or Places as the Congress may by Law have directed.

Section 3. Treason against the United States, shall consist only in levying War against them, or in adhering to their Enemies, giving them Aid and Comfort. No Person shall be convicted of Treason unless on the Testimony of two Witnesses to the same overt Act, or on Confession in open Court.

The Congress shall have Power to declare the Punishment of Treason, but no Attainder of Treason shall work Corruption of Blood, or Forfeiture except during the Life of the Person attainted.

ARTICLE IV

Section 1. Full Faith and Credit shall be given in each State to the public Acts, Records, and judicial Proceedings of every other State. And the Congress may by general Laws prescribe the Manner in which such Acts, Records, and Proceedings shall be proved, and the Effect thereof.

Section 2. The Citizens of each State shall be entitled to all Privileges and Immunities of Citizens in the several States.

A person charged in any State with Treason, Felony, or other Crime, who shall flee from Justice, and be found in another State, shall on Demand of the executive Authority of the State from which he fled, be delivered up, to be removed to the State having Jurisdiction of the Crime.

No Person held to Service or Labour in one State, under the Laws thereof, escaping into another, shall, in Consequence of any Law or Regulation therein, be discharged from such Service or Labour, but shall be delivered up on Claim of the Party to whom such Service or Labour may be due.

Section 3. New States may be admitted by the Congress into this Union; but no new state shall be formed or erected within the Jurisdiction of any other State; nor any State be formed by the Junction of two or more States, or Parts of States, without the Consent of the Legislatures of the States concerned as well as of the Congress.

The Congress shall have Power to dispose of and make all needful Rules and Regulations respecting the Territory or other Property belonging to the United States; and nothing in this Constitution shall be so construed as to Prejudice any Claims of the United States, or of any particular State.

Section 4. The United States shall guarantee to every State in this Union a Republican Form of Government, and shall protect each of them against Invasion; and on Application of the Legislature, or of the Executive (when the Legislature cannot be convened) against domestic Violence.

Article V

The Congress, whenever two thirds of both Houses shall deem it necessary, shall propose Amendments to this Constitution, or, on the Application of the Legislatures of two thirds of the several States, shall call a Convention for proposing Amendments, which, in either Case, shall be valid to all Intents and Purposes, as Part of this Constitution, when ratified by the Legislatures of three fourths of the several States, or by Conventions in three fourths thereof, as the one or the other Mode of Ratification may be proposed by the Congress; Provided that no Amendment which may be made prior to the Year One thousand eight hundred and eight shall in any Manner affect the first and fourth Clauses in the Ninth Section of the first Article; and that no State, without its Consent, shall be deprived of its equal Suffrage in the Senate.

Article VI

All Debts contracted and Engagements entered into, before the Adoption of this Constitution, shall be as valid against the United States under this Constitution, as under the Confederation.

This Constitution, and the Laws of the United States which shall be made in Pursuance thereof; and all Treaties made, or which shall be made, under the Authority of the United States, shall be the supreme Law of the Land; and the Judges in every State shall be bound thereby, any Thing in the Constitution or Laws of any State to the Contrary notwithstanding.

The Senators and Representatives before mentioned, and the Members of the several State Legislatures, and all executive and judicial Officers, both of the United States and of the Several States, shall be bound by Oath or Affirmation, to support this Constitution; but no religious Test shall ever be required as a Qualification to any Office or public Trust under the United States.

Article VII

The Ratification of the Conventions of nine States, shall be sufficient for the Establishment of this Constitution between the States so ratifying the Same.

Amendment I [1791]

Congress shall make no law respecting an establishment of religion, or prohibiting the free exercise thereof; or abridging the freedom of speech, or the press; or the right of the people peaceably to assemble, and to petition the Government for a redress of grievances.

Amendment II [1791]

A well regulated Militia, being necessary to the security for a free State, the right of the people to keep and bear Arms, shall not be infringed.

Amendment III [1791]

No Soldier shall, in time of peace be quartered in any house, without the consent of the Owner, nor in time of war, but in a manner to be prescribed by law.

Amendment IV [1791]

The right of the people to be secure in their persons, houses, papers, and effects, against unreasonable searches and seizures, shall not be violated, and no Warrants shall issue, but upon probable cause, supported by Oath or Affirmation, and particularly describing the place to be searched, and the persons or things to be seized.

Amendment V [1791]

No person shall be held to answer for a capital, or otherwise infamous crime, unless on a presentment or indictment of a Grand Jury, except in cases arising in the land or naval forces, or in the Militia, when in actual service in time of War or public danger; nor shall any person be subject for the same offense to be twice put in jeopardy of life or limb; nor shall be compelled in any criminal case to be a witness against himself, nor be deprived of life, liberty, or property, without due process of law; nor shall private property be taken for public use, without just compensation.

Amendment VI [1791]

In all criminal prosecutions, the accused shall enjoy the right to a speedy and public trial, by an impartial jury of the State and district wherein the crime shall have been committed, which district shall have been previously ascertained by law, and to be informed of the nature and cause of the accusation; to be confronted with the Witnesses against him; to have compulsory process for obtaining witnesses in his favor, and to have the Assistance of counsel for his defence.

Amendment VII [1791]

In suits at common law, where the value in controversy shall exceed twenty dollars, the right of trial by jury shall be preserved, and no fact tried by a jury, shall be otherwise reexamined in any Court of the United States, than according to the rules of the common law.

Amendment VIII [1791]

Excessive bail shall not be required, nor excessive fines imposed, nor cruel and unusual punishments inflicted.

Amendment IX [1791]

The enumeration in the Constitution, of certain rights, shall not be construed to deny or disparage others retained by the people.

Amendment X [1791]

The powers not delegated to the United States by the Constitution, nor prohibited by it to the States, are reserved to the States respectively, or to the people.

Amendment XI [1798]

The judicial power of the United States shall not be construed to extend to any suit in law or equity, commenced or prosecuted against one of the United States by Citizens of another State, or by Citizens or Subjects of any Foreign State.

Amendment XII [1804]

The Electors shall meet in their respective states and vote by ballot for President and Vice-President, one of whom, at least, shall not be an inhabitant of the same state with themselves; they shall name in their ballots the person voted for as President, and in distinct ballots the person voted for as Vice-President, and they shall make distinct lists of all persons voted for as President, and of all persons voted for as Vice-President, and of the number of votes for each, which lists they shall sign and certify, and transmit sealed to the seat of the government of the United States, directed to the President of the Senate;—The President of the Senate shall, in the presence of the Senate and House of Representatives, open all the certificates and the votes shall then be counted;—The person having the greatest number of votes for President, shall be the President, if such number be a majority of the whole number of Electors appointed; and if no person have such majority, then from the persons having the highest numbers not exceeding three on the list of those voted for as President, the House of Representatives shall choose immediately, by ballot, the President. But in choosing the President, the votes shall be taken by states, the representation from each state having one vote; a quorum for this purpose shall consist of a member or members from two-thirds of the states, and a majority of all the states shall be necessary to a choice. And if the House of Representatives shall not choose a President whenever the right of choice shall devolve upon them, before the fourth day of March next following, then the Vice-President shall act as President, as in the case of the death or other constitutional disability of the President. The person having the greatest number of votes as Vice-President, shall be the Vice-President, if such number be a majority of the whole number of Electors appointed, and if no person have a majority, then from the two highest numbers on the list, the Senate shall choose the Vice-President; a quorum for the purpose shall consist of two-thirds of the whole number of Senators, and a majority of the whole number shall be necessary to a choice. But no person constitutionally ineligible to the office of President shall be eligible to that of the Vice-President of the United States.

Amendment XIII [1865]

Section 1. Neither slavery nor involuntary servitude, except as a punishment for crime whereof the party shall have been duly convicted, shall exist within the United States, or any place subject to their jurisdiction.
Section 2. Congress shall have power to enforce this article by appropriate legislation.

Amendment XIV [1868]

Section 1. All persons born or naturalized in the United States, and subject to the jurisdiction thereof, are citizens of the United States and of the State wherein they reside. No State shall make or enforce any law which shall abridge the privileges or immunities of citizens of the United States; nor shall any State deprive any person of life, liberty, or property, without due process of law; nor deny to any person within its jurisdiction the equal protection of the laws.
Section 2. Representatives shall be appointed among the several States according to their respective numbers, counting the whole number of persons in each State, excluding Indians not taxed. But when the right to vote at any election for the choice of electors for President and Vice President of the United States, Representatives in Congress, the Executive and Judicial officers of a State, or the members of the Legislature thereof, is denied to any of the male inhabitants of such State, being twenty-one years of age, and citizens of the United States, or in any way abridged, except for participation in rebellion, or other crime, the basis of representation therein shall be reduced in the proportion which the number of such male citizens shall bear to the whole number of male citizens twenty-one years of age in such State.
Section 3. No person shall be a Senator or Representative in Congress, or elector of President and Vice President, or hold any office, civil or military, under the United States, or under any State, who, having previously taken an oath, as a mem-

ber of Congress, or as an officer of the United States, or as a member of any State legislature, or as an executive or judicial officer of any State, to support the Constitution of the United States, shall have engaged in insurrection or rebellion against the same, or given aid or comfort to the enemies thereof. But Congress may by a vote of two-thirds of each House, remove such disability.

Section 4. The validity of the public debt of the United States, authorized by law, including debts incurred for payment of pensions and bounties for services in suppressing insurrection or rebellion, shall not be questioned. But neither the United States nor any State shall assume or pay any debt or obligation incurred in aid of insurrection of rebellion against the United States, or any claim for the loss or emancipation of any slave; but all such debts, obligations and claims shall be held illegal and void.

Section 5. The Congress shall have power to enforce, by appropriate legislation, the provisions of this article.

Amendment XV [1870]

Section 1. The right of citizens of the United States to vote shall not be denied or abridged by the United States or by any State on account of race, color, or previous condition of servitude.

Section 2. The Congress shall have power to enforce this article by appropriate legislation.

Amendment XVI [1913]

The Congress shall have power to lay and collect taxes on incomes, from whatever source derived, without apportionment among the several States, and without regard to any census or enumeration.

Amendment XVII [1913]

The Senate of the United States shall be composed of two Senators from each State, elected by the people thereof, for six years; and each Senator shall have one vote. The electors in each State shall have the qualifications requisite for electors of the most numerous branch of the State legislatures.

When vacancies happen in the representation of any State in the Senate, the executive authority of each State shall issue writs of election to fill such vacancies; *Provided,* That the legislature of any State may empower the executive thereof to make temporary appointments until the people fill the vacancies by election as the legislature may direct.

This amendment shall not be so construed as to affect the election or term of any Senator chosen before it becomes valid as part of the Constitution.

Amendment XVIII [1919]

Section 1. After one year from the ratification of this article the manufacture, sale, or transportation of intoxicating liquors within, the importation thereof into, or the exportation thereof from the United States and all territory subject to the jurisdiction thereof for beverage purposes is hereby prohibited.

Section 2. The Congress and the several States shall have concurrent power to enforce this article by appropriate legislation.

Section 3. This article shall be inoperative unless it shall have been ratified as an amendment to the Constitution by the legislatures of the several States, as provided in the Constitution, within seven years from the date of the submission hereof to the States by the Congress.

Amendment XIX [1920]

The right of citizens of the United States to vote shall not be denied or abridged by the United States or by any State on account of sex.

Congress shall have power to enforce this article by appropriate legislation.

Amendment XX [1933]

Section 1. The terms of the President and Vice President shall end at noon on the 20th day of January, and the terms of Senators and Representatives at noon on the 3d day of January, of the years in which such terms would have ended if this article had not been ratified; and the terms of their successors shall then begin.

Section 2. The Congress shall assemble at least once in every year, and such meeting shall begin at noon on the 3rd day of January, unless they shall by law appoint a different day.

Section 3. If, at the time fixed for the beginning of the term of the President, the President elect shall have died, the Vice President elect shall become President. If a President shall not have been chosen before the time fixed for the beginning of his term, or if the President elect shall have failed to qualify, then the Vice President elect shall act as President until a President shall have qualified; and the Congress may by law provide for the case wherein neither a President elect nor a Vice President elect shall have qualified, declaring who shall then act as President, or the manner in which one who is to act shall be selected, and such person shall act accordingly until a President or Vice President shall have qualified.

Section 4. The Congress may by law provide for the case of the death of any of the persons from whom the House of Representatives may choose a President whenever the right of choice shall have devolved upon them, and for the case of the death of any of the persons from whom the Senate may choose a Vice President whenever the right of choice shall have devolved upon them.

Section 5. Sections 1 and 2 shall take effect on the 15th day of October following the ratification of this article.

Section 6. This article shall be inoperative unless it shall have been ratified as an amendment to the Constitution by the legislatures of three-fourths of the several States within seven years from the date of its submission.

Amendment XXI [1933]

Section 1. The eighteenth article of amendment to the Constitution of the United States is hereby repealed.

Section 2. The transportation or importation into any State, Territory, or possession of the United States for delivery or use therein of intoxicating liquors, in violation of the laws thereof, is hereby prohibited.
Section 3. This article shall be inoperative unless it shall have been ratified as an amendment to the Constitution by conventions in the several States, as provided in the Constitution, within seven years from the date of the submission hereof to the States by the Congress.

AMENDMENT XXII [1951]

Section 1. No person shall be elected to the office of the President more than twice, and no person who has held the office of President, or acted as President, for more than two years of a term to which some other person was elected President shall be elected to the office of the President more than once. But this Article shall not apply to any person holding the office of President when this article was proposed by the Congress, and shall not prevent any person who may be holding the office of President, or acting as President, during the term within which this Article becomes operative from holding the office of President, or acting as President during the remainder of such term.
Section 2. This article shall be inoperative unless it shall have been ratified as an amendment to the Constitution by the legislatures of three-fourths of the several States within seven years from the date of its submission to the States by the Congress.

AMENDMENT XXIII [1961]

Section 1. The District constituting the seat of government of the United States shall appoint in such manner as the Congress may direct:

A number of electors of President and Vice President equal to the whole number of Senators and Representatives in Congress to which the District would be entitled if it were a State, but in no event more than the least populous State; they shall be in addition to those appointed by the States, but they shall be considered, for the purposes of the election of President and Vice President, to be electors appointed by a State; and they shall meet in the District and perform such duties as provided by the twelfth article of amendment.
Section 2. The Congress shall have power to enforce this article by appropriate legislation.

AMENDMENT XXIV [1964]

Section 1. The right of citizens of the United States to vote in any primary or other election for President or Vice President, for electors for President or Vice President, or for Senator or Representative in Congress, shall not be denied or abridged by the United States or any State by reason of failure to pay any poll tax or other tax.
Section 2. The Congress shall have power to enforce this article by appropriate legislation.

AMENDMENT XXV [1967]

Section 1. In case of the removal of the President from office or of his death or resignation, the Vice President shall become President.
Section 2. Whenever there is a vacancy in the office of the Vice President, the President shall nominate a Vice President who shall take office upon confirmation by a majority vote of both Houses of Congress.
Section 3. Whenever the President transmits to the President pro tempore of the Senate and the Speaker of the House of Representatives his written declaration that he is unable to discharge the powers and duties of his office, and until he transmits to them a written declaration to the contrary, such powers and duties shall be discharged by the Vice President as Acting President.
Section 4. Whenever the Vice President and a majority of either the principal officers of the executive departments or of such other body as Congress may by law provide, transmit to the President pro tempore of the Senate and the Speaker of the House of Representatives their written declaration that the President is unable to discharge the powers and duties of his office, the Vice President shall immediately assume the powers and duties of the office as Acting President.

Thereafter, when the President transmits to the President pro tempore of the Senate and the Speaker of the House of Representatives his written declaration that no inability exists, he shall resume the powers and duties of his office unless the Vice President and a majority of either the principal officers of the executive department or of such other body as Congress may by law provide, transmit within four days to the President pro tempore of the Senate and the Speaker of the House of Representatives their written declaration that the President is unable to discharge the powers and duties of his office. Thereupon Congress shall decide the issue, assembling within forty-eight hours for that purpose if not in session. If the Congress, within twenty-one days after receipt of the latter written declaration, or, if Congress is not in session, within twenty-one days after Congress is required to assemble, determines by two-thirds vote of both Houses that the President shall continue to discharge the same as Acting President; otherwise, the President shall resume the powers and duties of his office.

AMENDMENT XXVI [1971]

Section 1. The right of citizens of the United States, who are 18 years of age or older, to vote, shall not be denied or abridged by the United States or any State on account of age.
Section 2. The Congress shall have the power to enforce this article by appropriate legislation.

AMENDMENT XXVII [1992]

No law, varying the compensation for the services of the Senators and Representatives, shall take effect, until an election of Representatives shall have intervened.

Analysis Using the Code of Ethics for the National Association of Legal Assistants, Inc.

The following is a summary of some of the ethical standards that should be considered when dealing with specific situations. While the canons promulgated by the National Association of Legal Assistants, Inc. are used as a framework for this analysis, all comments following each canon are not part of any document issued by that organization, and they are solely those of the author of this book.

CANON 1

A legal assistant must not perform any of the duties that attorneys only may perform nor take any actions that attorneys may not take.

In order to comply with the dictates of Canon 1, it is necessary to determine first what kinds of duties may only be performed by attorneys.

The case of *Florida Bar v. Furman*[1] demonstrates how difficult it is sometimes to draw the line between the kinds of activities that only attorneys may perform and those that may be performed by non-lawyers. In this case, Furman established a business known as Northside Secretarial Service for the alleged purpose of assisting people with the preparation of pleadings designed to meet the desires of the clients. She denied giving any of her clients legal advice and argued that she was assisting her clients in representing themselves. She further maintained that because of the relatively modest fee she was charging, indigent clients were assisted in obtaining access that they might not otherwise have to the state's domestic relations courts. It was maintained by the Florida Bar that Furman was selling "do-it-yourself divorce kits," and that she held herself out to the general public as having legal expertise. The Bar did not, however, suggest that she ever claimed to be an attorney, that her customers did not receive the services that were advertised, or that any of her customers were harmed by her assistance. Even though Furman maintained that she gave no legal advice and that her sole purpose was to assist people in helping themselves, the Bar objected to her activities as constituting the unauthorized practice of law, and it asked the court to enjoin her from all such future actions.

The Florida Supreme Court ruled in favor of the Florida Bar Association and issued an injunction against Rosemary Furman. In its ruling, the court relied upon a previous case[2] involving similar facts in which the court held that the respondent could sell legal forms and printed material purporting to explain legal practice and procedure to the public in general. It was permissible for her to type the forms for her clients as long as she only used the written information given to her and did not correct errors or omissions. She could not advise her clients as to remedies available to them, answer questions concerning which forms were necessary, help them in filling out the forms, help them in filing the forms, or assist them in preparing for their hearings.

Furman continued her business in spite of the court decision and was subsequently held in contempt of court, fined court costs, and sentenced to four months in jail. Three months of the sentence was to be suspended if she agreed to abide by the requirements of the court's injunction. After she agreed to shut down her business, the Governor of Florida suspended her entire sentence and reduced her fine.

The ethical questions surrounding the preparation of documents have been particularly difficult for paralegals, since non-lawyers in some states have been permitted to prepare business documents involving only the filling in of blanks on standard forms. Real estate brokers, for example, may in some states prepare sales contracts. The paralegal has to be familiar with the rules that govern in his or her particular state of operations.

The signing of pleadings poses difficulties inherently different from the ethical problems associated with other kinds of document preparation. Since the signing and submission of pleadings to a court of law would be tantamount to appearing before that court, such actions would be regarded as the unauthorized practice of law and would be strictly prohibited.

The second part of this canon prohibits the legal assistant from performing any duties that attorneys themselves may not engage in. Such activities would at the very least include torts[3] and crimes.

Rule 1.8 of the ABA Model Rules of Professional Conduct* indicates some of the kinds of transactions that attorneys may not engage in. They include entering into "(a) a business transaction with a client or knowingly acquiring an ownership, possessory, security or other pecuniary interest adverse to a client unless: (1) the transaction and terms on which the lawyer acquires the interest are fair and reasonable to the client and are fully disclosed and transmitted in writing in a manner that can be reasonably understood by the client; (2) the client is advised in writing of the desirability of seeking and is given a reasonable opportunity to seek the advice of independent legal counsel on the transaction; and (3) the client gives informed consent, in a writing signed by the client, to the essential terms of the transaction and the lawyer's role in the transaction, including whether the lawyer is representing the client in the transaction."[4]

***Comment**

Business Transactions Between Client and Lawyer

[1] A lawyer's legal skill and training, together with the relationship of trust and confidence between lawyer and client, create the possibility of over-reaching when the lawyer participates in a business, property or financial transaction with a client, for example, a loan or sales transaction or a lawyer investment on behalf of a client. The requirements of paragraph (a) must be met even when the transaction is not closely related to the subject matter of the representation, as when a lawyer drafting a will for a client learns that the client needs money for unrelated expenses and offers to make a loan to the client. The Rule applies to lawyers engaged in the sale of goods or services related to the practice of law, for example, the sale of title insurance or investment services to existing clients of the lawyer's legal practice. See Rule 5.7. It also applies to lawyers purchasing property from estates they represent. It does not apply to ordinary fee arrangements between client and lawyer, which are governed by Rule 1.5, although its requirements must be met when the lawyer accepts an interest in the client's business or other nonmonetary property as payment of all or part of a fee. In addition, the Rule does not apply to standard commercial transactions between the lawyer and the client for products or services that the client generally markets to others, for example, banking or brokerage services, medical services, products manufactured or distributed by the client, and utilities' services. In such transactions, the lawyer has no advantage in dealing with the client, and the restrictions in paragraph (a) are unnecessary and impracticable.

[2] Paragraph (a)(1) requires that the transaction itself be fair to the client and that its essential terms be communicated to the client, in writing, in a manner that can be reasonably understood. Paragraph (a)(2) requires that the client also be advised, in writing, of the desirability of seeking the advice of independent legal counsel. It also requires that the client be given a reasonable opportunity to obtain such advice. Paragraph (a)(3) requires that the lawyer obtain the client's informed consent, in a writing signed by the client, both to the essential terms of the transaction and to the lawyer's role. When necessary, the lawyer should discuss both the material risks of the proposed transaction, including any risk presented by the lawyer's involvement, and the existence of reasonably available alternatives and should explain why the advice of independent legal counsel is desirable. See Rule 1.0(e) (definition of informed consent).

[3] The risk to a client is greatest when the client expects the lawyer to represent the client in the transaction itself or when the lawyer's financial interest otherwise poses a significant risk that the lawyer's representation of the client will be materially limited by the lawyer's financial interest in the transaction. Here the lawyer's role requires that the lawyer must comply, not only with the requirements of paragraph (a), but also with the requirements of Rule 1.7. Under that Rule, the lawyer must disclose the risks associated with the lawyer's dual role as both legal adviser and participant in the transaction, such as the risk that the lawyer will structure the transaction or give legal advice in a way that favors the lawyer's interests at the expense of the client. Moreover, the lawyer must obtain the client's informed consent. In some cases, the lawyer's interest may be such that Rule 1.7 will preclude the lawyer from seeking the client's consent to the transaction.

[4] If the client is independently represented in the transaction, paragraph (a)(2) of this Rule is inapplicable, and the paragraph (a)(1) requirement for full disclosure is satisfied either by a written disclosure by the lawyer involved in the transaction or by the client's independent counsel. The fact that the client was independently represented in the transaction is relevant in determining whether the agreement was fair and reasonable to the client as paragraph (a)(1) further requires.

Use of Information Related to Representation

[5] Use of information relating to the representation to the disadvantage of the client violates the lawyer's duty of loyalty. Paragraph (b) applies when the information is used to benefit either the lawyer or a third person, such as another client or business associate of the lawyer. For example, if a lawyer learns that a client intends to purchase and develop several parcels of land, the lawyer may not use that information to purchase one of the parcels in competition with the client or to recommend that another client make such a purchase. The Rule does not prohibit uses that do not disadvantage the client. For example, a lawyer who learns a government agency's interpretation of trade legislation during the representation of one client may properly use that information to benefit other clients. Paragraph (b) prohibits disadvantageous use of client information unless the client gives informed consent, except as permitted or required by these Rules. See Rules 1.2(d), 1.6, 1.9(c), 3.3, 4.1(b), 8.1 and 8.3.

Gifts to Lawyers

[6] A lawyer may accept a gift from a client, if the transaction meets general standards of fairness. For example, a simple gift such as a present given at a holiday or as a token of appreciation is permitted. If a client offers the lawyer a more substantial gift, paragraph (c) does not prohibit the lawyer from accepting it, although such a gift may be voidable by the client under the doctrine of undue influence, which treats client gifts as presumptively fraudulent. In any event, due to concerns about overreaching and imposition on clients, a lawyer may not suggest that a substantial gift be made to the lawyer or for the lawyer's benefit, except where the lawyer is related to the client as set forth in paragraph (c).

[7] If effectuation of a substantial gift requires preparing a legal instrument such as a will or conveyance the client should have the detached advice that another lawyer can provide. The sole exception to this Rule is where the client is a relative of the donee.

[8] This Rule does not prohibit a lawyer from seeking to have the lawyer or a partner or associate of the lawyer named as executor of the client's estate or to another potentially lucrative fiduciary position. Nevertheless, such appointments will be subject to the general conflict of interest provision in Rule 1.7 when there is a significant risk that the lawyer's interest in obtaining the appointment will materially limit the lawyer's independent professional judgment in advising the client concerning the choice of an executor or other fiduciary. In obtaining the client's informed consent to the conflict, the lawyer should advise the client concerning the nature and extent of the lawyer's financial interest in the appointment, as well as the availability of alternative candidates for the position.

Literary Rights

[9] An agreement by which a lawyer acquires literary or media rights concerning the conduct of the representation creates a conflict between the interests of the client and the personal interests of the lawyer. Measures suitable in the representation of the client may detract from the publication value of an account of the representation. Paragraph (d) does not prohibit a lawyer representing a client in a transaction concerning literary property from agreeing that the lawyer's fee shall consist of a share in ownership in the property, if the arrangement conforms to Rule 1.5 and paragraphs (a) and (i).

Financial Assistance

[10] Lawyers may not subsidize lawsuits or administrative proceedings brought on behalf of their clients, including making or guaranteeing loans to their clients for living expenses, because to do so would encourage clients to pursue lawsuits that might not otherwise be brought and because such assistance gives lawyers too great a financial stake in the litigation. These dangers do not warrant a prohibition on a lawyer lending a client court costs and litigation expenses, including the expenses of medical examination and the costs of obtaining and presenting evidence, because these advances are virtually indistinguishable from contingent fees and help ensure access to the courts. Similarly, an exception allowing lawyers representing indigent clients to pay court costs and litigation expenses regardless of whether these funds will be repaid is warranted.

Person Paying for a Lawyer's Services

[11] Lawyers are frequently asked to represent a client under circumstances in which a third person will compensate the lawyer, in whole or in part. The third person might be a relative or friend, an indemnitor (such as a liability insurance company) or a co-client (such as a corporation sued along with one or more of its employees). Because third-party payers frequently have interests that differ from those of the client, including interests in minimizing the amount spent on the representation and in learning how the representation is progressing, lawyers are prohibited from accepting or continuing such representations unless the lawyer determines that there will be no interference with the lawyer's independent professional judgment and there is informed consent from the client. See also Rule 5.4(c) (prohibiting interference with a lawyer's professional judgment by one who recommends, employs or pays the lawyer to render legal services for another).

[12] Sometimes, it will be sufficient for the lawyer to obtain the client's informed consent regarding the fact of the payment and the identity of the third-party payer. If, however, the fee arrangement creates a conflict of interest for the lawyer, then the lawyer must comply with Rule. 1.7. The lawyer must also conform to the requirements of Rule 1.6 concerning confidentiality. Under Rule 1.7(a), a conflict of interest exists if there is significant risk that the lawyer's representation of the client will be materially limited by the lawyer's own interest in the fee arrangement or by the lawyer's responsibilities to the third-party payer (for example, when the third-party payer is a co-client). Under Rule 1.7(b), the lawyer may accept or continue the representation with the informed consent of each affected client, unless the conflict is nonconsentable under that paragraph. Under Rule 1.7(b), the informed consent must be confirmed in writing.

Aggregate Settlements

[13] Differences in willingness to make or accept an offer of settlement are among the risks of common representation of multiple clients by a single lawyer. Under Rule 1.7, this is one of the risks that should be discussed before undertaking the representation, as part of the process of obtaining the clients' informed consent. In addition, Rule 1.2(a) protects each client's right to have the final say in deciding whether to accept or reject an offer of settlement and in deciding whether to enter a guilty or nolo contendere plea in a criminal case. The rule stated in this paragraph is a corollary of both these Rules and provides that, before any settlement offer or plea bargain is made or accepted on behalf of multiple clients, the lawyer must inform each of them about all the material terms of the settlement, including what the other clients will receive or pay if the settlement or plea offer is accepted. See also Rule 1.0(e) (definition of informed consent). Lawyers representing a class of plaintiffs or defendants, or those proceeding derivatively, may not have a full client-lawyer relationship with each member of the class; nevertheless, such lawyers must comply with applicable rules regulating notification of class members and other procedural requirements designed to ensure adequate protection of the entire class.

Limiting Liability and Settling Malpractice Claims

[14] Agreements prospectively limiting a lawyer's liability for malpractice are prohibited unless the client is independently represented in making the agreement because they are likely to undermine competent and diligent representation. Also, many clients are unable to evaluate the desirability of making such an agreement before a dispute has arisen, particularly if they are then represented by the lawyer seeking the agreement. This paragraph does not, however, prohibit a lawyer from entering into an agreement with the client to arbitrate legal malpractice claims, provided such agreements are enforceable and the client is fully informed of the scope and effect of the agreement. Nor does this paragraph limit the ability of lawyers to practice in the form of a limited-liability entity, where permitted by law, provided that each lawyer remains personally liable to the client for his or her own conduct and the firm complies with any conditions required by law, such as provisions requiring client notification or maintenance of adequate liability insurance. Nor does it prohibit an agreement in accordance with Rule 1.2 that defines the scope of the representation, although a definition of scope that makes the obligations of representation illusory will amount to an attempt to limit liability.

[15] Agreements settling a claim or a potential claim for malpractice are not prohibited by this Rule. Nevertheless, in view of the danger that a lawyer will take unfair advantage of an unrepresented client or former client, the lawyer must first advise such a person in writing of the appropriateness of independent representation in connection with such a settlement. In addition, the lawyer must give the client or former client a reasonable opportunity to find and consult independent counsel.

Acquiring Proprietary Interest in Litigation

[16] Paragraph (i) states the traditional general rule that lawyers are prohibited from acquiring a proprietary interest in litigation. Like paragraph (e), the general rule has its basis in common law champerty and maintenance and is designed to avoid giving the lawyer too great an interest in the representation. In addition, when the lawyer acquires an ownership interest in the subject of the representation, it will be more difficult for a client to discharge the lawyer if the client so desires. The Rule is subject to specific exceptions developed in decisional law and continued in these Rules. The exception for certain advances of the costs of litigation is set forth in paragraph (e). In addition, paragraph (i) sets forth exceptions for liens authorized by law to secure the lawyer's fees or expenses and contracts for reasonable contingent fees. The law of each jurisdiction determines which liens are authorized by law. These may include liens granted by statute, liens originating in common law and liens acquired by contract with the client. When a lawyer acquires by contract a security interest in property other than that recovered through the lawyer's efforts in the litigation, such an acquisition is a business or financial transaction with a client and is governed by the requirements of paragraph (a). Contracts for contingent fees in civil cases are governed by Rule 1.5.

Client-Lawyer Sexual Relationships

[17] The relationship between lawyer and client is a fiduciary one in which the lawyer occupies the highest position of trust and confidence. The relationship is almost always unequal; thus, a sexual relationship between lawyer and client can involve unfair exploitation of the lawyer's fiduciary role, in violation of the lawyer's basic ethical obligation not to use the trust of the client to the client's disadvantage. In addition, such a relationship presents a significant danger that, because of the lawyer's emotional involvement, the lawyer will be unable to represent the client without impairment of the exercise of independent professional judgment. Moreover, a blurred line between the professional and personal relationships may make it difficult to predict to what extent client confidences will be protected by the attorney-client evidentiary privilege, since client confidences are protected by privilege only when they are imparted in the context of the client-lawyer relationship. Because of the significant danger of harm to client interests and because the client's own emotional involvement renders it unlikely that the client could give adequate informed consent, this Rule prohibits the lawyer from having sexual relations with a client regardless of whether the relationship is consensual and regardless of the absence of prejudice to the client.

[18] Sexual relationships that predate the client-lawyer relationship are not prohibited. Issues relating to the exploitation of the fiduciary relationship and client dependency are diminished when the sexual relationship existed prior to the commencement of the client-lawyer relationship. However, before proceeding with the representation in these circumstances, the lawyer should consider whether the lawyer's ability to represent the client will be materially limited by the relationship. See Rule 1.7(a)(2).

[19] When the client is an organization, paragraph (j) of this Rule prohibits a lawyer for the organization (whether inside counsel or outside counsel) from having a sexual relationship with a constituent of the organization who supervises, directs or regularly consults with that lawyer concerning the organization's legal matters.

Imputation of Prohibitions

[20] Under paragraph (k), a prohibition on conduct by an individual lawyer in paragraphs (a) through (i) also applies to all lawyers associated in a firm with the personally prohibited lawyer. For example, one lawyer in a firm may not enter into a business transaction with a client of another member of the firm without complying with paragraph (a), even if the first lawyer is not personally involved in the representation of the client. The prohibition set forth in paragraph (j) is personal and is not applied to associated lawyers.

Also prohibited by the rule is (1) using information relating to the representation of a client to the disadvantage of the client unless the client gives informed consent [with exceptions]; (2) soliciting from a client or preparing documents for the client that make substantial gifts from a client to the lawyer, the lawyer's relative, or a person with whom the lawyer or the client maintains a close familial relationship unless the lawyer or other recipient of the gift is related to the client; (3) making or negotiating an agreement prior to the conclusion of representation giving the lawyer literary or media rights to a portrayal or account based in substantial part on information relating to the representation; (4) providing financial assistance to a client in connection with pending or contemplated litigation other than advancing court costs and expenses where repayment may be contingent on the outcome of the matter or where the client is indigent; (5) accepting compensation from one other than the client unless the client gives informed consent, there is no interference with the lawyer's independent professional judgment or client-lawyer relationship, and the information is protected by attorney-client privilege; (6) making a settlement of claims for or against a client when there is more than one client and all others have not given their informed consents in writing with their signatures; (7) making an agreement prospectively limiting the lawyer's liability for malpractice unless the client is independently represented in making the agreement or settling a malpractice claim with an unrepresented or former client unless the person is advised in writing to obtain independent counsel; (8) acquiring a proprietary interest in the cause of action unless the attorney is acquiring a lien to obtain fees or expenses or is contracting with a client for a reasonable contingent fee in a civil case; (9) having sexual relations with a client unless a consensual sexual relationship existed between them when the client-lawyer relationship commenced; and (10) doing any of the above that would be prohibited for any other attorney associated with the firm.[5] Many of these kinds of conduct are subject to exception, so the paralegal should become familiar with the details of the rule.[6]

It is regarded as unethical for the paralegal to tell a witness not to give information to the opposing party or his or her counsel. When speaking to the witness, the paralegal should indicate whose interest the paralegal's employer represents.

Furthermore, it is generally regarded as unethical for either the attorney or the paralegal to talk to an opposing party represented by counsel without the consent of his or her attorney.

Neither the attorney nor the paralegal may tape conversations without the permission of the other party.

Canon 2

A legal assistant may perform any task which is properly delegated and supervised by an attorney, as long as the attorney is ultimately responsible to the client, maintains a direct relationship with the client, and assumes professional responsibility for the work product.

Canon 2 approves conduct that is "delegated and supervised" by the attorney under specified conditions. Questions may arise in specific situations as to what constitutes supervision by an attorney.

As a general rule, the drafting of legal documents in the absence of the attorney is not per se a violation of ethical standards. The drafting process is not considered unsupervised as long as the attorney gives the work a stamp of approval before the client sees it. However, if the paralegal turns the documents over to the client without the prior examination of the attorney, the paralegal has violated the dictates of this canon. As the canon itself states, it is the lawyer who must be responsible to the client and assume full professional responsibility for the work product. This is true even if that work product was originally the creation of the paralegal.

Similarly, it is generally permissible for a paralegal to send out to a client letters on behalf of the attorney and on the attorney's stationery as long as no legal advice is rendered or other ethical canons are violated. Such correspondence should, however, clearly indicate that the sender is not an attorney. A notation under the sender's signature indicating paralegal status is sufficient.

Questions have also arisen concerning the appropriateness of paralegals attending real estate closings or will executions. A legal assistant is, of course, prohibited from rendering legal advice in either situation, although the attendance of the paralegal at these events is not generally a problem. The extent to which the paralegal may be involved in the handling of these matters is heavily governed by state rules.

While a paralegal may not ask questions at a deposition, the requirement of supervision by an attorney does not prevent the paralegal from preparing possible deposition questions for the attorney to ask, since the attorney would not use the questions unless they were implicitly approved.

No problem is created with regard to the requirement of attorney supervision when legal assistants are hired on a freelance basis as long as any given task is performed by the legal assistant under the supervision of an attorney for that task. The exposure of freelance paralegals to civil suits for damages may be greater, however, since a law firm's liability policy generally covers paralegal employees of the firm, but excludes those working on a freelance basis.

Canon 3

A legal assistant must not

a. engage in, encourage, or contribute to any act which could constitute the unauthorized practice of law; and

b. establish attorney-client relationships, set fees, give legal opinions or advice, or represent a client before a court or agency unless so authorized by that court or agency; and

c. engage in conduct or take any action which would assist or involve the attorney in a violation of professional ethics or give the appearance of professional impropriety.

The first portion of this canon deals with the "unauthorized practice of law." This issue has posed some of the greatest difficulties for paralegals in the area of ethics, because it has never really been clearly defined in any jurisdiction. Restrictions on the unauthorized practice of law traditionally have been justified on the grounds of protecting the public from those who have not demonstrated competence to practice by fulfilling stringent educational requirements and passing the bar examination. Some critics of such restrictions have more cynically suggested that regulations against the unauthorized practice of law have been used by attorneys to protect their own businesses from competition.

In determining whether an activity constitutes the unauthorized practice of law, several factors should be considered. One is whether the activity involves the use of legal knowledge, judgment, and abilities. This is far from being a determinative test, however, since non-lawyers use their legal knowledge, judgment, and abilities in their jobs on a daily basis. Real estate brokers, bankers, insurance representatives, and those in many other occupations fall within this category. Furthermore, as noted in the discussion of Canon 4, paralegals routinely use their legal judgment in performing tasks that must ultimately be reviewed by the attorney who is to take responsibility for the final work product.

Another factor to be considered in determining whether a particular activity constitutes the unauthorized practice of law is whether the action has been traditionally handled by attorneys. Many courts have emphasized that any attempt to create an all-encompassing abstract definition of the unauthorized practice of law may not be helpful in addressing specific unauthorized practice violations.

Virtually all states have criminal law statutes prohibiting the unauthorized practice of law. Violations of unauthorized practice rules are generally handled either through criminal prosecutions or suits for injunctive relief against the wrongdoer. Failure of the legal assistant to abide by the dictates of Canon 3 can also result in trouble for the supervising attorney.

Part (b) of the NALA canon identifies four specific activities that have traditionally been regarded as constituting the unauthorized practice of law. First, paralegals may not accept cases for their employers or even suggest whether they feel their employers are likely to accept them. There are several reasons for this restriction. There is a possibility that the case might be rejected because the attorney feels that it lacks merit, and the decision to reject the case would involve the exercise of legal judgment. Also, the attorney might feel compelled to reject an apparently substantial case because of a potential conflict of interest, or the matter might be outside the firm's area of expertise. The prohibitions against accepting cases applies to a paralegal's oral statements as well as to written representations.

Second, all fee arrangements are to be determined exclusively by the attorney and the client. The reason for this is that it is the attorney, rather than the paralegal, who has the contractual relationship with the client. Furthermore, the fees may be dependent upon the complexity of the legal issues involved, and an examination of those issues requires the exercise of legal judgment.

Third, the prohibition against the giving of legal advice by a paralegal does not prevent that person from simply conveying in oral or written form the opinion of the attorney. In such situations, however, the person transmitting the information must make the paralegal status clear and must identify the opinion as that of the attorney. In some states, a distinction is made between a paralegal giving legal advice to individual "clients" as opposed to information given to the general public. An example of the latter might include information in a book written for the public by a paralegal. Those states that permit such writings stress the absence of a direct contractual relationship between the "client" and the paralegal, the lack of any communication between those parties, and the assumption that people buying a publication dispensing general legal advice are implicitly assuming the risk that the advice may not apply to their particular situation. Not all states, however, make the distinction between personal advice and public information.

Fourth, paralegals are restricted as a general rule from making appearances in virtually all courts on behalf of others in spite of the fact that a paralegal could appear on his or her own behalf in a court of law. However, the restrictions pertaining to appearances by legal assistants in administrative courts differ from those that pertain to ordinary courts of law. Administrative courts operate in administrative agencies, which are agencies created by legislatures and given the power to promulgate rules and regulations governing particularly defined subject matters. Examples of administrative agencies are the Environmental Protection Agency and the Federal Communications Commission. Procedures in federal administrative agencies are governed by the Administrative Procedure Act, 5 U.S.C. § 555. This act specifically provides that when one is forced to appear before an administrative agency, that person may be "accompanied, represented, and advised by counsel or, if permitted by the agency, by another qualified representative." This allows the agency itself to determine when to allow non-lawyer practice (whether by paralegals or other individuals). Some agencies are much more lenient in this regard than others.

Rules governing state administrative agencies vary widely, and appearances by legal assistants before administrative courts even for limited purposes may or may not be permitted.

As to part (c) of the NALA canon, it may be self-evident that a paralegal should avoid the kind of conduct prohibited by this canon, but it may be much more difficult to define the exact boundaries of this canon in specific situations.

It is unethical for paralegals to enter into partnerships, associations, or corporations with attorneys in a business involving the practice of law. Circumstances in which a paralegal agrees to split a fee with an attorney are similarly regarded as unethical, because such situations necessarily imply that the paralegal is a business partner or associate of the attorney. Nevertheless, it has been held that a paralegal may benefit from a law firm's retirement program even though the program is founded partially on the basis of profit sharing.

The question has arisen as to whether the paralegal's name together with his or her legal assistant status may appear on the letterhead of a law firm's stationery. There now seems to be a clear trend in favor of permitting it in light of the rulings of the United States Supreme Court pertaining to the right of advertising in the legal profession.

The use of business cards by the paralegal also raises similar issues pertaining to advertising. Those who object to their use contend that it is an undignified advertisement of a firm's legal services. Most states, however, allow paralegals to use business cards with the name of the law firm on them as long as the individual's non-lawyer status is clearly indicated.

Any conflicts of interest that a paralegal has with regard to a particular case can give the attorney the appearance of impropriety and, therefore, place the paralegal in direct violation of this ethical canon as well as Canon 7. The paralegal should notify the attorney at the earliest possible time of any such potential conflict. Furthermore, the paralegal should be aware of some of the basic conflict of interest rules that govern the conduct of attorneys. Attorneys may not represent a client whose interests are contrary to those of a current client unless both the client and the potential client consent. Rule 1.10(a)* indicates that "While lawyers are associated in a firm, none of them shall knowingly represent a client when any one of them practicing alone would be prohibited from doing so . . . unless the prohibition is based on a personal interest of the prohibited lawyer and does not present a significant risk of materially limiting the representation of the client by the remaining lawyers in the firm."[7]

***Comment**

Definition of "Firm"

[1] For purposes of the Rules of Professional Conduct, the term "firm" denotes lawyers in a law partnership, professional corporation, sole proprietorship or other association authorized to practice law; or lawyers employed in a legal services organization or the legal department of a corporation or other organization. See Rule 1.0(c). Whether two or more lawyers constitute a firm within this definition can depend on the specific facts. See Rule 1.0, Comments [2]–[4].

Principles of Imputed Disqualification

[2] The rule of imputed disqualification stated in paragraph (a) gives effect to the principle of loyalty to the client as it applies to lawyers who practice in a law firm. Such situations can be considered from the premise that a firm of lawyers is essentially one lawyer for purposes of the rules governing loyalty to the client, or from the

premise that each lawyer is vicariously bound by the obligation of loyalty owed by each lawyer with whom the lawyer is associated. Paragraph (a) operates only among the lawyers currently associated in a firm. When a lawyer moves from one firm to another, the situation is governed by Rules 1.9(b) and 1.10(b).

[3] The rule in paragraph (a) does not prohibit representation where neither questions of client loyalty nor protection of confidential information are presented. Where one lawyer in a firm could not effectively represent a given client because of strong political beliefs, for example, but that lawyer will do no work on the case and the personal beliefs of the lawyer will not materially limit the representation by others in the firm, the firm should not be disqualified. On the other hand, if an opposing party in a case were owned by a lawyer in the law firm, and others in the firm would be materially limited in pursuing the matter because of loyalty to that lawyer, the personal disqualification of the lawyer would be imputed to all others in the firm.

[4] The rule in paragraph (a) also does not prohibit representation by others in the law firm where the person prohibited from involvement in a matter is a nonlawyer, such as a paralegal or legal secretary. Nor does paragraph (a) prohibit representation if the lawyer is prohibited from acting because of events before the person became a lawyer, for example, work that the person did while a law student. Such persons, however, ordinarily must be screened from any personal participation in the matter to avoid communication to others in the firm of confidential information that both the nonlawyers and the firm have a legal duty to protect. See Rules 1.0(k) and 5.3.

[5] Rule 1.10(b) operates to permit a law firm, under certain circumstances, to represent a person with interests directly adverse to those of a client represented by a lawyer who formerly was associated with the firm. The Rule applies regardless of when the formerly associated lawyer represented the client. However, the law firm may not represent a person with interests adverse to those of a present client of the firm, which would violate Rule 1.7. Moreover, the firm may not represent the person where the matter is the same or substantially related to that in which the formerly associated lawyer represented the client and any other lawyer currently in the firm has material information protected by Rules 1.6 and 1.9(c).

[6] Rule 1.10(c) removes imputation with the informed consent of the affected client or former client under the conditions stated in Rule 1.7. The conditions stated in Rule 1.7 require the lawyer to determine that the representation is not prohibited by Rule 1.7(b) and that each affected client or former client has given informed consent to the representation, confirmed in writing. In some cases, the risk may be so severe that the conflict may not be cured by client consent. For a discussion of the effectiveness of client waivers of conflicts that might arise in the future, see Rule 1.7, Comment [22]. For a definition of informed consent, see Rule 1.0(e).

[7] Where a lawyer has joined a private firm after having represented the government, imputation is governed by Rule 1.11(b) and (c), not this Rule. Under Rule 1.11(d), where a lawyer represents the government after having served clients in private practice, nongovernmental employment or in another government agency, former-client conflicts are not imputed to government lawyers associated with the individually disqualified lawyer.

[8] Where a lawyer is prohibited from engaging in certain transactions under Rule 1.8, paragraph (k) of that Rule, and not this Rule, determines whether that prohibition also applies to other lawyers associated in a firm with the personally prohibited lawyer.

Because the conduct of the paralegal has the potential for reflecting either positively or negatively on the ethical reputation of the supervising attorney, it is essential that the paralegal become familiar with Rule 3.4 of the ABA Rules of Professional Conduct. That rule, dealing with fairness to the opposing party and counsel, states the following:

A lawyer shall not:

(a) unlawfully obstruct another party's access to evidence or unlawfully alter, destroy or conceal a document or other material having potential evidentiary value. A lawyer shall not counsel or assist another person to do any such act;

(b) falsify evidence, counsel or assist a witness to testify falsely, or offer an inducement to a witness that is prohibited by law;

(c) knowingly disobey an obligation under the rules of a tribunal except for an open refusal based on an assertion that no valid obligation exists;

(d) in pretrial procedure, make a frivolous discovery request or fail to make a reasonably diligent effort to comply with a legally proper discovery request by an opposing party;

(e) in trial, allude to any matter that the lawyer does not reasonably believe is relevant or that will not be supported by admissible evidence, assert personal knowledge of facts in issue except when testifying as a witness, or state a personal opinion as to the justness of a cause, the credibility of a witness, the culpability of a civil litigant or the guilt or innocence of an accused; or

(f) request a person other than a client to refrain from voluntarily giving relevant information to another party unless:

  (1) the person is a relative or an employee or other agent of a client; and

  (2) the lawyer reasonably believes that the person's interest will not be adversely affected by refraining from giving such information.[8]*

***Comment**

[1] The procedure of the adversary system contemplates that the evidence in a case is to be marshalled competitively by the contending parties. Fair competition in the adversary system is secured by prohibitions against destruction or concealment of evidence, improperly influencing witnesses, obstructive tactics in discovery procedure, and the like.

[2] Documents and other items of evidence are often essential to establish a claim or defense. Subject to evidentiary privileges, the right of an opposing party, including the government, to obtain evidence through discovery or subpoena is an important procedural right. The exercise of that right can be frustrated if relevant material is altered, concealed or destroyed. Applicable law in many jurisdictions makes it an offense to destroy material for purpose of

impairing its availability in a pending proceeding or one whose commencement can be foreseen. Falsifying evidence is also generally a criminal offense. Paragraph (a) applies to evidentiary material generally, including computerized information. Applicable law may permit a lawyer to take temporary possession of physical evidence of client crimes for the purpose of conducting a limited examination that will not alter or destroy material characteristics of the evidence. In such a case, applicable law may require the lawyer to turn the evidence over to the police or other prosecuting authority, depending on the circumstances.

[3] With regard to paragraph (b), it is not improper to pay a witness's expenses or to compensate an expert witness on terms permitted by law. The common law rule in most jurisdictions is that it is improper to pay an occurrence witness any fee for testifying and that it is improper to pay an expert witness a contingent fee.

[4] Paragraph (f) permits a lawyer to advise employees of a client to refrain from giving information to another party, for the employees may identify their interests with those of the client. See also Rule 4.2.

Sometimes potential conflict of interest problems occur when an attorney or a legal assistant leaves one law office and seeks employment at another. If the first firm is representing one party in a particular case and the second firm is representing the other, the employment of the attorney or the paralegal at the new firm could place that firm in jeopardy of disqualification from the case. For that reason, it may be necessary to establish procedures at the new firm whereby that person has no access to materials pertaining to the case. These procedures may include (among others): (1) restrictions on access to computer files by the use of special passwords and access to physical files by the use of stickers or flags; (2) notes to all office employees that materials from the case are not to get into the hands of the identified person; and (3) notations of dates when computer and hard copy files are accessed and who accesses them. Such blocks are referred to as *screens* or *Chinese walls*. Paralegals are under an ethical obligation to disclose when any conflicts of interest may require the creation of such screens.

Canon 4

A legal assistant must use discretion and professional judgment commensurate with knowledge and experience but must not render independent legal judgment in place of an attorney. The services of an attorney are essential in the public interest whenever such legal judgment is required.

While recognizing that a legal assistant must use discretion and professional judgment that is commensurate with knowledge and experience, this canon prohibits conduct by the paralegal that directly provides legal services from the paralegal to the client. For example, since the acceptance of a settlement offer in a case would involve the use of professional judgment directly on behalf of a law office client, such an acceptance by a paralegal would be regarded as unethical. Settlements are ultimately the responsibility of the attorney. However, various kinds of permissible activities require the paralegal to use legal judgment, such as the drafting of legal documents. As long as the attorney reviews and approves the documents prior to sending them out to the general public, the attorney is taking responsibility for the final product, and the dictates of this canon are not violated.

The witnessing of legal documents does not in any event involve the exercise of legal knowledge, judgment, or abilities and is therefore generally permissible.

Canon 5

A legal assistant must disclose his or her status as a legal assistant at the outset of any professional relationship with a client, attorney, a court or administrative agency or personnel thereof, or a member of the general public. A legal assistant must act prudently in determining the extent to which a client may be assisted without the presence of an attorney.

Because the contractual relationship for legal representation is between the attorney and the client, a contact by the paralegal with the attorney's clients can raise ethical questions. The requirements of Canon 5 indicate that paralegals have the duty to disclose their status at the outset of any professional relationship not only with clients of the employer, but also for contacts with other attorneys, court or administrative agencies or their personnel, or members of the general public. An obvious corollary to this is that it is grossly improper for paralegals to misrepresent their identity as paralegals. A paralegal may not, for example, fraudulently represent to a debtor that the paralegal works for a collection agency.

In addition, the duty of disclosure holds true for telephone conversations between the client and the paralegal, as well as for correspondence signed by the paralegal that is coming from the law office. It may be necessary for the paralegal to remind the client if the client ever does or says anything that suggests a misunderstanding of the paralegal's status. The reason for these rules is to avoid any possibility that members of the public will assume that legal assistants are in fact attorneys.

The attorneys, in addition to the legal assistants, have an obligation toward the public to verify that non-lawyer personnel are not being mistaken for attorneys. As Canon 2 indicates, attorneys also accept ultimate responsibility for the work product emanating from the office. If the employer fails to adequately supervise the paralegal's actions, the employer can be held responsible for the acts of the paralegal, both ethically and legally. Rule 5.3(c) of the ABA Model Rules of Professional Conduct directly addresses this issue.[9]

The second part of this canon states that the paralegal must act prudently in determining the extent to which a client may be assisted without the presence of an attorney. In order to make such a determination, the paralegal must become thoroughly familiar with the codes, rules, and case law that govern the profession. As a general rule, if the paralegal is unsure whether a particular activity is ethical, it is best to refrain from engaging in it.

Neither this canon nor any other prohibits a paralegal from talking with opposing counsel as long as the paralegal is not violating any other ethical canons, and his or her status as a paralegal is clearly indicated.

Canon 6

A legal assistant must strive to maintain integrity and a high degree of competency through education and training with respect to professional responsibility, local rules and practice, and through continuing education in substantive areas of law to better assist the legal profession in fulfilling its duty to provide legal service.

This canon imposes upon paralegals the responsibility to maintain the highest standards of integrity and competence.

There are opportunities in all states to obtain an education in many different kinds of educational institutions. Several hundred across the country have received an "approval" from the American Bar Association. While no program must obtain such an approval, it demonstrates a standard of excellence in the legal community.

In addition to the courses available through institutions of higher learning, there are always seminars and publications that can keep paralegals abreast of late-breaking developments in the law.

Canon 7

A legal assistant must protect the confidences of a client and must not violate any rule or statute now in effect or hereafter enacted controlling the doctrine of privileged communications between a client and an attorney.

Confidentiality is crucial if law office clients are to be assured that they can speak freely. The paralegal is bound just as the attorney by the same rules of confidentiality. Confidential information normally includes any information associated with the representation of the client by the law firm. Because it may sometimes be unclear exactly what information is covered, it may be best for the paralegal to refrain from a discussion of any office matters. Even a discussion of issues and problems encountered during the day's work is not appropriate if it could result in the listener knowing the identity of the client.

Rule 1.6 of the ABA Model Rules of Professional Conduct* indicates that there are a few limited situations in which the attorney may divulge confidential information. Those circumstances include (but are not limited to) when (1) "the client gives informed consent"; (2) "the disclosure is impliedly authorized in order to carry out the representation," such as when paralegals in the office are given the information so that they can work on the case; (3) "reasonably certain death or substantial bodily harm" may occur, such as when the client gives convincing information to the attorney that the client is intending to commit murder; (4) there is "a controversy between the lawyer and the client," the attorney needs "to establish a defense to a criminal charge or civil claim against the lawyer based upon conduct in which the client was involved," and the release of the information is necessary "to establish a claim or defense by the attorney"; and (5) a "law or a court order" must be followed.[10]

***Comment**

[1] This Rule governs the disclosure by a lawyer of information relating to the representation of a client during the lawyer's representation of the client. See Rule 1.18 for the lawyer's duties with respect to information provided to the lawyer by a prospective client. Rule 1.9(c)(2) for the lawyer's duty not to reveal information relating to the lawyer's prior representation of a former client and Rules 1.8(b) and 1.9(c)(1) for the lawyer's duties with respect to the use of such information to the disadvantage of clients and former clients.

[2] A fundamental principle in the client-lawyer relationship is that, in the absence of the client's informed consent, the lawyer must not reveal information relating to the representation. See Rule 1.0(e) for the definition of informed consent. This contributes to the trust that is the hallmark of the client-lawyer relationship. The client is thereby encouraged to seek legal assistance and to communicate fully and frankly with the lawyer even as to embarrassing or legally damaging subject matter. The lawyer needs this information to represent the client effectively and, if necessary, to advise the client to refrain from wrongful conduct. Almost without exception, clients come to lawyers in order to determine their rights and what is, in the complex of laws and regulations, deemed to be legal and correct. Based upon experience, lawyers know that almost all clients follow the advice given, and the law is upheld.

[3] The principle of client-lawyer confidentiality is given effect by related bodies of law: the attorney-client privilege, the work product doctrine and the rule of confidentiality established in professional ethics. The attorney-client privilege and work-product doctrine apply in judicial and other proceedings in which a lawyer may be called as a witness or otherwise required to produce evidence concerning a client. The rule of client-lawyer confidentiality applies in situations other than those where evidence is sought from the lawyer through compulsion of law. The confidentiality rule, for example, applies not only to matters communicated in confidence by the client but also to all information relating to the representation, whatever its source. A lawyer may not disclose such information except as authorized or required by the Rules of Professional Conduct or other law. See also Scope.

[4] Paragraph (a) prohibits a lawyer from revealing information relating to the representation of a client. This prohibition also applies to disclosures by a lawyer that do not in themselves reveal protected information but could reasonably lead to the discovery of such information by a third person. A lawyer's use of a hypothetical to discuss issues relating to the representation is permissible so long as there is no reasonable likelihood that the listener will be able to ascertain the identity of the client or the situation involved.

Authorized Disclosure

[5] Except to the extent that the client's instructions or special circumstances limit that authority, a lawyer is impliedly authorized to make disclosures about a client when appropriate in carrying out the representation. In some situations, for example, a lawyer may be impliedly authorized to admit a fact that cannot properly be disputed or to make a disclosure that facilitates a satisfactory conclusion to a matter. Lawyers in a firm may, in the course of the firm's practice, disclose to each other information relating to a client of the firm, unless the client has instructed that particular information be confined to specified lawyers.

Disclosure Adverse to Client

[6] Although the public interest is usually best served by a strict rule requiring lawyers to preserve the confidentiality of information relating to the representation of their clients, the confidentiality rule is subject to limited exceptions. Paragraph (b)(1) recognizes the overriding value of life and physical integrity and permits disclosure reasonably necessary to prevent reasonably certain death or substantial bodily harm. Such harm is reasonably certain to occur if it will be suffered imminently or if there is a present and substantial threat that a person will suffer such harm at a later date if the lawyer fails to take action necessary to eliminate the threat. Thus, a lawyer who knows that a client has accidentally discharged toxic waste into a town's water supply may reveal this information to the authorities if there is a present and substantial risk that a person who drinks the water will contract a life-threatening or debilitating disease and the lawyer's disclosure is necessary to eliminate the threat or reduce the number of victims.

[7] A lawyer's confidentiality obligations do not preclude a lawyer from securing confidential legal advice about the lawyer's personal responsibility to comply with these Rules. In most situations, disclosing information to secure such advice will be impliedly authorized for the lawyer to carry out the representation. Even when the disclosure is not impliedly authorized, paragraph (b)(2) permits such disclosure because of the importance of a lawyer's compliance with the Rules of Professional Conduct.

[8] Where a legal claim or disciplinary charge alleges complicity of the lawyer in a client's conduct or other misconduct of the lawyer involving representation of the client, the lawyer may respond to the extent the lawyer reasonably believes necessary to establish a defense. The same is true with respect to a claim involving the conduct or representation of a former client. Such a charge can arise in a civil, criminal, disciplinary or other proceeding and can be based on a wrong allegedly committed by the lawyer against the client or on a wrong alleged by a third person, for example, a person claiming to have been defrauded by the lawyer and client acting together. The lawyer's right to respond arises when an assertion of such complicity has been made. Paragraph (b)(3) does not require the lawyer to await the commencement of an action or proceeding that charges such complicity, so that the defense may be established by responding directly to a third party who has made such an assertion. The right to defend also applies, of course, where a proceeding has been commenced.

[9] A lawyer entitled to a fee is permitted by paragraph (b)(3) to prove the services rendered in an action to collect it. This aspect of the rule expresses the principle that the beneficiary of a fiduciary relationship may not exploit it to the detriment of the fiduciary.

[10] Other law may require that a lawyer disclose information about a client. Whether such a law supersedes Rule 1.6 is a question of law beyond the scope of these Rules. When disclosure of information relating to the representation appears to be required by other law, the lawyer must discuss the matter with the client to the extent required by Rule 1.4. If, however, the other law supersedes this Rule and requires disclosure, paragraph (b)(4) permits the lawyer to make such disclosures as are necessary to comply with the law.

[11] A lawyer may be ordered to reveal information relating to the representation of a client by a court or by another tribunal or governmental entity claiming authority pursuant to other law to compel the disclosure. Absent informed consent of the client to do otherwise, the lawyer should assert on behalf of the client all non-frivolous claims that the order is not authorized by other law or that the information sought is protected against disclosure by the attorney-client privilege or other applicable law. In the event of an adverse ruling, the lawyer must consult with the client about the possibility of appeal to the extent required by Rule 1.4. Unless review is sought, however, paragraph (b)(4) permits the lawyer to comply with the court's order.

[12] Paragraph (b) permits disclosure only to the extent the lawyer reasonably believes the disclosure is necessary to accomplish one of the purposes specified. Where practicable, the lawyer should first seek to persuade the client to take suitable action to obviate the need for disclosure. In any case, a disclosure adverse to the client's interest should be no greater than the lawyer reasonably believes necessary to accomplish the purpose. If the disclosure will be made in connection with a judicial proceeding, the disclosure should be made in a manner that limits access to the information to the tribunal or other persons having a need to know it and appropriate protective orders or other arrangements should be sought by the lawyer to the fullest extent practicable.

[13] Paragraph (b) permits but does not require the disclosure of information relating to a client's representation to accomplish the purposes specified in paragraphs (b)(1) through (b)(4). In exercising the discretion conferred by this Rule, the lawyer may consider such factors as the nature of the lawyer's relationship with the client and with those who might be injured by the client, the lawyer's own involvement in the transaction and factors that may extenuate the conduct in question. A lawyer's decision not to disclose as permitted by paragraph (b) does not violate this Rule. Disclosure may be required, however, by other Rules. Some Rules require disclosure only if such disclosure would be permitted by paragraph (b). See Rules 1.2(d), 4.1(b), 8.1 and 8.3. Rule 3.3, on the other hand, requires disclosure in some circumstances regardless of whether such disclosure is permitted by this Rule. See Rule 3.3(c).

Withdrawal

[14] If the lawyer's services will be used by the client in materially furthering a course of criminal or fraudulent conduct, the lawyer must withdraw, as stated in Rule 1.16(a)(1). After withdrawal the lawyer is required to refrain from making disclosure of the client's confidences, except as otherwise permitted by Rule 1.6. Neither this Rule nor Rule 1.8(b) nor Rule 1.16(d) prevents the lawyer from giving notice of the fact of withdrawal, and the lawyer may also withdraw or disaffirm any opinion, document, affirmation, or the like. Where the client is an organization, the lawyer may be in doubt whether contemplated conduct will actually be carried out by the organization. Where necessary to guide conduct in connection with this Rule, the lawyer may make inquiry within the organization as indicated in Rule 1.13(b).

Acting Competently to Preserve Confidentiality

[15] A lawyer must act competently to safeguard information relating to the representation of a client against inadvertent or unauthorized disclosure by the lawyer or other persons who are participating in the representation of the client or who are subject to the lawyer's supervision. See Rules 1.1, 5.1 and 5.3.

[16] When transmitting a communication that includes information relating to the representation of a client, the lawyer must take reasonable precautions to prevent the information from coming into the hands of unintended recipients. This duty, however, does not require that the lawyer use special security measures if the method of communication affords a reasonable expectation of privacy. Special circumstances, however, may warrant special precautions. Factors to be considered in determining the reasonableness of the lawyer's expectation of confidentiality include the sensitivity of the information and the extent to which the privacy of the commu-

nication is protected by law or by a confidentiality agreement. A client may require the lawyer to implement special security measures not required by this Rule or may give informed consent to the use of a means of communication that would otherwise be prohibited by this Rule.

Former Client

[17] The duty of confidentiality continues after the client-lawyer relationship has terminated. See Rule 1.9(c)(2). See Rule 1.9(c)(1) for the prohibition against using such information to the disadvantage of the former client.

Included within the protection of confidentiality is the "work product" of the law office, which includes notes and other materials prepared in anticipation of trial. Things qualifying as work product are not subject to discovery. In other words, a law office need not turn such materials over to the opposing party or counsel. Federal Rule of Civil Procedure 26(b) (3) states that one may obtain such information

> . . . only upon a showing that the party seeking discovery has substantial need of the materials in the preparation of the party's case and that the party is unable without undue hardship to obtain the substantial equivalent of the materials by other means.

This canon also addresses the "doctrine of privileged communications between a client and an attorney." The attorney-client privilege is the right of clients to refuse to allow their attorneys to divulge information that was given to the attorney in confidence as long as that information pertains to the client's rights. The privilege exists once the communication is made and is not dependent upon whether the attorney is ultimately hired or whether there was payment for services rendered. Furthermore, the privilege continues to exist even after the representation is over. As a general rule, the privilege can be waived only by the client or by the attorney directed to do so by the client. However, if either the attorney or the paralegal carelessly divulges the information that is otherwise protected, the privilege could be lost. In the event that there is such a breach of confidence, the case could be lost and the law office could be sued by the client.

It is vital that paralegals refrain from discussing confidential information or information protected by attorney-client privilege in public places such as hallways. Furthermore, the paralegal should realize that information discussed over the telephone might be overheard, and discussions over cellphones might either be overheard in the open air or intercepted by electronic means. Computer screens should not be left on where confidential information may be seen by those without authority to do so. Files and documents should not be left in open areas where members of the public may see them.

While the bar associations of a number of states do not find ethical violations in sending confidential information via e-mail (based on the conclusion that e-mail is relatively secure), it may be prudent to refrain from doing so. If it is sent, it would obviously be preferable for it to be encrypted if possible. At the very least, it is common for offices to include a warning to the client in outgoing e-mail discouraging inclusion of confidential information in e-mail responses.

Canon 8

A legal assistant must do all other things incidental, necessary, or expedient for the attainment of the ethics and responsibilities as defined by statute or rule of court.

This canon is designed as a "catchall" provision, and it is intended to stress the responsibility of the paralegal to follow rules emanating from legislatures or courts with regard to ethical issues.

There are various ethical situations that have not yet been addressed under any of the previous canons that give rise to commonly asked questions. Paralegals cannot pay witnesses for their testimony other than the ordinary witness fees that may be specifically provided by law. It is considered improper to threaten people with criminal prosecution for failure to pay an outstanding debt even though other nonlawyers may possibly be able to do so under certain circumstances. In some states, it is even impermissible to threaten debtors with the filing of a civil suit.

Canon 9

A legal assistant's conduct is guided by bar associations' codes of professional responsibility and rules of professional conduct.

Because paralegals are required to refrain from taking actions that attorneys may not take, the bar associations' codes of professional responsibility and rules of professional conduct provide helpful guidance for the paralegal. Furthermore, these rules indicate guidelines for the attorneys in dealing with and accepting responsibility for the professional conduct of employee personnel such as legal assistants.

Endnotes

1. See 376 So.2d 378 (Fla. 1979) with further proceedings at 451 So.2d 808 (Fla. 1984). While the case is older, it clearly demonstrates the difficulties that are inherent in defining the scope of acceptable paralegal activities.
2. *Florida Bar v. Brumbaugh*, 355 So.2d 1186 (Fla. 1978).
3. A *tort* is a civil wrong other than a breach of contract action. Examples of torts include fraud and libel.
4. Model Rules of Professional Conduct, copyright © 2002 by the American Bar Association. All rights reserved. Reprinted by permission of the American Bar Association. Copies of the ABA *Model Rules of Professional Conduct, 2002* are available from Service Center, American Bar Association, 321 North Clark Street, Chicago, IL 60610, 1-800-285-2221.
5. See note 4.
6. See note 4.
7. See note 4.
8. See note 4.
9. See note 4 .
10. See note 4.

APPENDIX D

Basic Citation Reference Guide

This citation information is taken from *The Bluebook, A Uniform System of Citation*, 17th edition. (Reprinted with Permission. Copyright © The Columbia Law Review Association, The Harvard Law Review Association, The University of Pennsylvania Law Review and The Yale Law Journal.)

Learning to cite correctly and consistently is essential. *The Bluebook* is a reference manual. It has more citation rules than you will ever need to learn. However, this tool is indispensable. The "rules" and conventions are all here. It takes patience to become familiar with *The Bluebook*. Take the time to look through this tool before you need to find answers quickly. The index to *The Bluebook* is excellent. Use it.

Note: many states have their own legal style or citation manual. Check with your instructor for your state guidelines.

CASE LAW

The United States Supreme Court

Most case citations follow this basic format:

Name	Volume	Reporter	Page	Year
Miranda v. Arizona,	384	U.S.	436	(1966)

Miranda v. Arizona is the name of the case. Case names are underlined or italicized. This makes them easy to see on the page.

The *Miranda* case is located in volume 384 of the United States Reports. The United States Reports is the official reporter for United States Supreme Court cases. It is "official" because it is published by the United States Government. The proper abbreviation for this reporter is: U.S.

In volume 384, the *Miranda* case is located at page 436. The case was decided in 1966. The year is placed in parentheses.

This information allows anyone looking at the citation to locate the actual decision.

All United States Supreme Court cases are located in print form in three separate reporters, published by three different publishers. The full citation for the *Miranda* case is as follows:

Miranda v. Arizona. 384 U.S. 436, 86 S. Ct. 1602, 16 L. Ed. 2d 694 (1966).

86 S. Ct. 1602 and 16 L. Ed. 2d 694 are referred to as "parallel" citations.

Remember *When you refer to or "cite" a case be sure to provide your reader with a complete citation. Use the name, volume, reporter, page number, year and, if necessary, the parallel citations.*

GO TO: *Bluebook* Table 1 (pages 183–188)

STATE CASE LAW

State cases are cited much the same as Supreme Court cases.

For example, in the state of California either of the following citations is correct for a California case.

Long Beach v. Superior Court, 64 Cal. App. 3d 65, 134 Cal. Rptr. 468 (1976).

or

Long Beach v. Superior Court (1976) 64 Cal. App. 3d 65, 134 Cal. Rptr. 468.

In California and other states, there is an unofficial publisher of state case law. In the citation above, Cal. Rptr. is the abbreviation for the California Reporter, published by West Publishing. 134 Cal. Rptr. 468 is the parallel citation.

Sometimes you will see references to "regional reporters." The regional reporter abbreviations are:

Atlantic Reporter	A.2d
North Eastern Reporter	N.E.2d
North Western Reporter	N.W.2d
Pacific Reporter	P.2d
Southern Reporter	So. 2d
South Eastern Reporter	S.E.2d
South Western Reporter	S.W.2d

The "2d" following the regional reporter abbreviation indicates that each of these reporters is in the second edition.

Remember *Most legal sources follow the general format of:*

Title
Volume
Book or Reporter (abbreviated)
Page
Year

When you are looking at an unfamiliar citation, try to identify these elements. This will enable you to understand the various citations you come across in your legal studies.

GO TO: *Bluebook* Table 1 (pages 188–244)

UNITED STATES CONSTITUTION

The fourteenth Amendment to the United States Constitution is written as follows:

U.S. Const. amend. XIV.

If you want to indicate a certain section of the Amendment you add:

§ 1

The full citation looks like this:

U.S. Const. amend. XIV, § 1.

GO TO: *Bluebook* Rule 11 (page 75)

THE UNITED STATES CODE (STATUTES)

The United States Code is cited in the following manner:

Number of Code Title	Code	Section Cited	Date
28	U.S.C.	§ 1291	(xxxx)

The proper cite is 28 U.S.C. § 1291 (xxxx).

GO TO: *Bluebook* Rule 12 (pages 76–90)

STATE CODES (STATUTES)

A statute citation must show

1. the numbers of the statutory topic,
2. the abbreviated name of the publication,

3. the specific statute or section of the statute and
4. the year of the publication.

Examples

Ariz. Rev. Stat. § ## (XXXX)	Arizona Revised Statutes
Cal. Educ. Code § ## (West XXXX)	California Education Code
Conn. Gen. Stat. § ## (XXXX)	Connecticut General Statutes
Ind. Code § ## (XXXX)	Indiana Code

GO TO: *Bluebook* Table 1 (pages 188–244)

QUOTATIONS

When you quote you must alert the reader that you are using quoted language. Usually, this means you must use quote marks. A citation must follow a quote. This citation lets the reader know where the borrowed material originated. Quotations of fifty words or more are blocked and no quotation marks are used. A blocked quote is single spaced and indented on the left and right margin. No quote marks are used with a blocked quotation.

GO TO: *Bluebook* Rule 5 (page 43–47)

SIGNALS

Signals serve a variety of purposes. Signals indicate support, suggest comparisons, indicate contradictions, or indicate background material. When there is no signal the cited authority is the source of the quoted material. A common introductory signal is *See.* When the signal *see* is placed in front of the cited authority it means that the cited authority clearly supports the proposition found in the quoted language.

GO TO: *Bluebook* Rule 1.2 (pages 22–24)
Information on the Order of Signals is found in *Bluebook* at Rule 1.3 (pages 24–25).

ELLIPSIS

When you omit a word or phrase from a quote you must alert the reader that you have done so. The ellipsis is the tool we use for this purpose. For example: "The motion to suppress, after much heated debate and loud gavel banging, was denied." could become "The motion to suppress . . . was denied." Do not use an ellipsis at the beginning of a quote. This tool is properly used in the middle of a quoted language or at the end of the quote. When used at the end of a quote, you need to use four rather than three periods. Never use more than three periods internally in a quote. Never use more than four periods at the end of a quote. The number of periods does not indicate the amount of material omitted.

GO TO: *Bluebook* Rule 5.3 (pages 45–47)

Bluebook Index (17th Edition)

When Citing	Check Bluebook Page	Rule/Table
Administrative and Executive Materials	96–97	Rule 14
A.L.R. Annotation	124	Rule 16.5.5
American Jurisprudence	113	Rule 15.7
Books	107–117	Rule 15
Brackets	44–45	Rule 5.2
Briefs	71	Rule 10.8.3
States and the District of Columbia	188–244	T.1
Capitalization	51–53	Rule 8
Case History	68–69	Rule 10.7
Case Names	56–62	Rule 10.2
CD-ROM	141–142, 144	Rules 18.3, 18.7
Commercial Electronics Databases	130–132	Rule 18.1
Constitution, The	75	Rule 11
Corpus Juris Secundum (C.J.S.)	113	Rule 15.7
Dictionaries	113	Rule 15.7
Dissenting Opinions	67–68	Rule 10.6.1
Electronic Media	128–144	Rule 18
E-Mail	141	Rule 18.2.9
Federal Cases	183–185	T.1
Federal Rules	86	Rule 12.8.3
Footnotes	34–37	Rule 3.3
Foreign Jurisdictions	245–296	T.2
Internet	132–141	Rule 18.2
Introductory Signals	22–24	Rule 1.2
Law Review Articles	117–120	Rule 16
Legislative Materials	91–96	Rule 13
LEXIS	129–132	Rule 18
Loislaw	73, 131, 144	Rule 10.9, 18, 18.7
Looseleaf Services	147–149, 343	Rule 19, T.16
Model Codes	87–88	Rule 12.8
Newspapers	120–121	Rule 16.5
Official Reporters	14–15, 62–64, 183–244	P.3, Rule 10.3, T.1
Pages	34–37	Rule 3.3
Parenthetical Explanation of Authorities	67–68, 84–85	Rules 10.6, 12.7
Pending and Unreported Cases	70	Rule 10.8.1
Periodical Abbreviations (Law Reviews)	317–341	T.14
Pinpoint Citations	34–38	Rule 3.3
Quotations	43–47	Rule 5
Restatements	87–88	Rule 12.8.5
Rules and Regulations	97–98	Rule 14.2
Short Citation Forms	40–43	Rule 4
State Cases	188–244	T.1
Statutes	76–90	Rule 12
Treatises	107–112	Rule 15
Uniform Acts	86–87	Rule 12.8.4
United States Supreme Court Cases	55–56, 63–64, 183	Rule 10, T.1
United State Jurisdictions	241–244	T.1
Versus Law	130–131	Rule 18.1.1
Westlaw	129–132	Rule 18

APPENDIX E

Glossary of Latin Terms and Phrases

a fortiori. with stronger reason; much more	ah for·she·OR·i
a posteriori. from the effect to the cause; from what comes after	ah po·steer·ee·OR·i
a prendre. to take; to seize.	ah PRAWN·dre
a priori. from the cause to the effect; from what comes before	ah pri·OR·i
ab initio. from the beginning	ab in·ish·ee·oh
actio criminalis. a criminal action	AK·shee·oh kri·mi·NAH·lis
actio damni injuria. an action for damages	AK·shee·oh DAM·ni in·JUR·ee·ah
actio ex delicto. an action arising out of fault	AK·shee·oh eks da·lik·toh
ad damnum. to the damage; money loss claimed by the plaintiff	ad DAHM·num
ad hoc. for one special purpose	ad HOK
ad infinitum. indefinitely; forever	ad in·fin·ITE·em
ad litem. for the suit	ad LY·tem
ad respondendum. to make answer	ad ree·spon·DEN·dem
additur. addition by a judge to the amount of damages awarded by a jury	AH·di·toor
amicus curiae. friend of the court	a·MEE·kes KYOOR·ee
animus furandi. intent to steal	AN·i·mus fer·AN·di
animus testandi. intent to make a will	AN·i·mus tes·TAN·di
anno Domini. (A.D.) in the year of our Lord	AN·oh DOM·eh·ni
ante. before	AN·tee
arguendo. in arguing	ar·gyoo·EN·doh
assumpsit. he promised	a·SUMP·sit
bona fide. in good faith	BONE·ah FIDE
caveat. beware	KA·vee·at
caveat emptor. let the buyer beware	KA·vee·at EMP·tor
caveat venditor. let the seller beware	KA·vee·at VEN·de·tor
certiorari. to be informed of; to be assured	ser·sho·RARE·ee
cestui que trust. beneficiary of a trust	SES·twee KAY
compos mentis. sound of mind	KOM·pes MEN·tis
consortium. fellowship of husband and wife	kon·SORE·shum
contra. against	KON·trah
coram. before; in the presence of	KOR·em
corpus delicti. body of the crime	KORE·pus de·LIK·tie
corpus juris. body of law	KORE·pus JOOR·ess
cum testamento annexo. with the will annexed	kum tes·ta·MENT·o an·EKS·o
damnum absque injuria. loss without injury in the legal sense	DAM·num AHB·skwee in·JOO·ree·ah
de facto. in fact; actually	dee FAK·toh
de jure. according to law; rightfully	dee JUR·ee
de minimus. of little importance	dee MIN·e·mes
de novo. anew, afresh, a second time	dee NOH·voh
dictum. unessential statement or remark in a court decision	DIK·tum
doli capaz. capable of criminal intent; able to distinguish between right and wrong	DO·li KAY·paks
duces tecum. bring with you	DOO·sess TEK·um
ergo. therefore; hence	EHR·go
et al. abbreviation for et alia, and others	et AHL
et seq. abbreviation for et sequentia; and the following	et SEK
et ux. abbreviation for et uxor; and wife	et UKS

Source: Brown, *Legal Terminology*, 4th Edition, © 2004. Reprinted by permission of Pearson Education, Inc. Upper Saddle River, NJ.

et vir. and husband	et VEER
ex contractu. out of a contract	eks kon·TRAK·too
ex delicto. out of a tort or wrong	eks de·LIK·toh
ex officio. by virtue of an office	eks oh·FISH·ee·oh
ex parte. apart from; one side only	eks·PAR·tay
ex post facto. after the fact	eks post FAK·toh
forum non conveniens. inconvenient court	for·em non kon·VEEN·yenz
gratis. without reward or consideration	GRAT·is
habeas corpus. you have the body	HAY·bee·ess KORE·pus
habendum. to have thus; clause in a deed that defines extent of ownership	ha·BEN·dum
ibid. abbreviation for ibidim; in the same place	IB·id
id. abbreviation for idem; the same	id
in camera. in chambers; in private	in KAM·er·ah
in curia. in court	in KYOOR·ee·ah
in flagrante delicto. in glaring fault; a crime in full light	in flay·GRAN·tee de·LIK·toh
in initio. at the beginning	in i·NISH·ee·o
in litem. during the suit	in LY·tem
in loco. in the place of	in LOH·ko
in loco parentis. in the place of a parent	in LOH·ko pa·REN·tis
in pari delicto. in equal fault	in pah·ree de·LIK·toh
in personam. against or with reference to a person	in per·SOH·nem
in re. in the matter of; concerning	in RAY
in rem. against the thing	in REM
in toto. in the whole; in total	in TOH·toh
infra. below, beneath	IN·frah
injuria absque damno. wrong without damage	in·JUR·ee·ya abs·kwee DAM·no
inter alia. among other things	IN·ter AY·lee·ah
inter vivos. between the living	IN·ter VY·vose
ipse dixit. he himself says it	IP·see DIK·sit
ipso facto. by the fact itself	IP·soh FAK·toh
juris. of right; of law	JOOR·is
jus habendi. right to have something	jes he·BEN·di
jus tertii. right of a third party	jes ter·SHEE·yi
lis pendens. pending suit	liss PEN·denz
locus sigilli. place of the seal	LOH·kus se·JIL·i
malum in se. wrong in itself	MAL·um in SEH
malum prohibita. wrong because it is prohibited	MAL·um pro·HIB·i·ta
mandamus. we command; order by a court commanding a public official to perform a duty	man·DAY·mus
mens rea. guilty mind	menz RAY·ah
modus operandi. manner of operation	MOH·dus op·er·AN·di
mortis causa. by reason of death	MORE·tis KAW·sa
n.b. abbreviation of nota bene; note well; observe	
nil. contraction of nihil; nothing	nil
nisi. unless	NIE·sie
nolle prosequi. prosection not pursued	NO·lee PROSS·e·kwi
nolo contendere. I will not contest the action	NO·lo kon·TEN·de·ree
non assumpsit. not undertaken or promised	non a·SUMP·sit
non compos mentis. not of sound mind; insane	non KOM·pes MEN·tiss
non obstante verdicto. notwithstanding the verdict	non ob·STAN·tay ver·DIK·toh
non sequitur. it does not follow	non SEK·wi·ter
nudum pactum. naked promise; bare agreement without consideration	NOO·dum PAK·tum
nul tort. no wrong has been done	nul TORT
nulla bona. no goods	null·a BONE·ah
nunc pro tunc. now for then	nunk pro tunk
obiter dictum. words of a prior decision unnecessary for the decision of the case	OH·bih·ter DIK·tum
onus probandi. burden of proof	OH·nus pro·BAN·di
pendente lite. pending suit	pen·DEN·tay lie·tay
per annum. by the year	per AN·num
per capita. by the head	per KA·pi·tah
per curiam. by the court	per KYOO·ree·am
per diem. by the day	per DEE·em
per quod. whereby	per KWOD
per se. by itself; taken alone	per SAY
per stirpes. by representation	per STER·peez
post mortem. after death	post MOR·tem
prima facie. at first sight; on the face of it	PRY·muh FAY·shee
pro bono publico. for the public good	pro BO·no POOB·lek·oh
pro forma. as a matter of form	pro FORM·ah
pro rata. proportionately	pro RAY·ta
pro se. for himself or herself	pro say
pro tanto. for as far as it goes	pro TAHN·tah
pro tempore (pro tem.). temporary; for the time being	pro TEM·po·re
quantum meruit. as much as he or she deserves	KWAN·tum MEHR·oo·it
quasi. as if; almost as it were	KWAY·zie
quasi in rem. as if against the thing	KWAY·zie in REM
quid pro quo. something for something; one thing for another	kwid proh KWOH

res. thing, object	reyz
res gestae. things that have been done	reyz JESS·tee
res ipsa loquitur. thing speaks for itself	res IP·sa LO·kwe·ter
res judicata. thing decided or judged (also res adjudicata)	res joo·di·KAY·ta
respondeat superior. let the superior answer	re·SPOND·ee·yat se·PEER·ee·or
retraxit. he or she has withdrawn	re·TRAK·sit
scienter. knowingly	si·EN·ter
scilicet. to wit; namely; that is to say	SIL·e·set
scintilla. spark	sin·TIL·ah
secundum. according to	se·KUN·dem
seriatim. separately; one by one	see·ree·AH·tem
sic. thus; in such a manner	sik
sigillum. seal	se·JIL·um
simplex obligato. single obligation	SIM·pleks ob·le·GAT·oh
sine qua non. without which, the thing cannot be	SI·nee kway NON
stare decisis. to stand by the decision	STAHR·ee de·SY·sis
sua sponte. of its own motion	SOO·ah SPON·tay
sub curia. under law	sub KURE·ee·ah
sub judice. under judicial consideration	sub JOO·de·say
sub silentio. under silence	sub se·LEN·shee·oh
subpoena. under penalty; a process to cause a witness to appear and give testimony	suh·PEEN·a
subpoena duces tecum. bring with you; a subpoena ordering a witness to produce a paper	suh·PEEN·a DOO·sess TEK·um
sui generis. one of a kind; unique	SOO·ee JEN·e·ris
sui juris. of one's own right; not under guardianship	SOO·ee JOOR·is
supersedeas. writ commanding a stay in the proceedings	soo·per·SEE·dee·es
supra. above; earlier	SOO·prah
ultra vires. beyond the powers	UL·tra VY·res
venire facias. order to the sheriff to bring people to court to serve as jurors	ven·EYE·ree FAY·she·as
versus. against	VER·ses
viz. abbreviation for videlicit; to make more specific that which has been previously stated	viz
volenti non fit injuria. volunteer suffers no wrong	voh·LEN·tie non fit in·JOOR·ee·ah

Glossary

abandoned property Property that an owner has discarded with the intent to relinquish his or her rights in it, or mislaid or lost property that the owner has given up any further attempts to locate.

abatement A principle stating that if the property the testator leaves is not sufficient to satisfy all the beneficiaries named in a will and there are both general and residuary bequests, the residuary bequest is paid last—(abated first).

acceptance A manifestation of assent by the offeree to the terms of the offer in a manner invited or required by the offer, as measured by the objective theory of contracts.

accord and satisfaction The settlement of a contract dispute.

act of monopolizing A required act for there to be a violation of Section 2 of the Sherman Act. Possession of monopoly power without such act does not violate Section 2.

act of state doctrine A doctrine that states that judges of one country cannot question the validity of an act committed by another country within that other country's borders. It is based on the principle that a country has absolute authority over what transpires within its own territory.

action for an accounting A formal judicial proceeding in which the court is authorized to (1) review the partnership and the partners' transactions and (2) award each partner his or her share of the partnership assets.

actus reus "Guilty act"—the actual performance of a criminal act.

ademption A principle stating that if a testator leaves a specific devise of property to a beneficiary but the property is no longer in the estate when the testator dies, the beneficiary receives nothing.

adjudged insane A person who has been determined to be insane by a proper court or administrative agency. A contract entered into by such a person is void.

administrative agencies Agencies that the legislative and executive branches of federal and state governments establish.

administrative law judge (ALJ) A judge presiding over administrative proceedings who decides questions of law and fact concerning the case.

Administrative Procedure Act (APA) A law establishing certain administrative procedures that federal administrative agencies must follow in conducting their affairs.

administrator or administratrix A court-appointed personal representative who administers the estate during its settlement phase when no one is named in the will or if the decedent dies intestate.

adverse action A denial or revocation of credit or a change in the credit terms offered.

adverse possession Possession in which a person who wrongfully possesses someone else's real property obtains title to that property if certain statutory requirements are met.

affirmative action A policy that provides that certain job preferences will be given to minority or other protected-class applicants when an employer makes an employment decision.

AFL-CIO The 1955 combination of the AFL and the CIO.

agency The principal–agent relationship: the fiduciary relationship "which results from the manifestation of consent by one person to another that the other shall act in his behalf and subject to his control, and consent by the other so to act."

agency by ratification An agency that occurs when (1) a person misrepresents him- or herself as another's agent when in fact he or she is not and (2) the purported principal ratifies the unauthorized act.

agency law The large body of common law that governs agency; a mixture of contract law and tort law.

agency shop An establishment in which an employee does not have to join the union but must pay a fee equal to the union dues.

agent A party who agrees to act on behalf of another.

agreement The manifestation by two or more persons of the substance of a contract.

aiding and abetting the commission of a crime Rendering support, assistance, or encouragement to the commission of a crime; harboring a criminal after he or she has committed a crime.

air pollution Pollution caused by factories, homes, vehicles, and the like that affects the air.

alien corporation A corporation that is incorporated in another country.

alternative dispute resolution (ADR) Methods other than litigation of resolving disputes.

American Inventors Protection Act A law that reorganized the U.S. Patent and Trademark Office (PTO), granting it new regulatory powers for inventions and patents and upgrading the PTO Commissioner to Assistant Secretary of Commerce with advisory powers.

Americans with Disabilities Act (ADA) of 1990 An act that imposes obligations on employers and providers of public transportation, telecommunications, and public accommodations to accommodate individuals with disabilities.

annual shareholders' meeting A meeting of the shareholders of a corporation that must be held annually by the corporation to elect directors and to vote on other matters.

answer The defendant's written response to the plaintiff's complaint, which is filed with the court and served on the plaintiff.

anticipatory breach A breach that occurs when one contracting party informs the other that he or she will not perform his or her contractual duties when due.

Anticybersquatting Consumer Protection Act Legislation aimed at preventing "cybersquatters" who register domain names based on names of famous companies and people and hold them "hostage."

antidilution statutes State laws that allow persons and companies to register trademarks and service marks.

antitrust laws Laws enacted to limit anticompetitive behavior in almost all industries, businesses, and professions operating in the United States.

apparent agency Agency that arises when a principal creates the appearance of an agency that in actuality does not exist.

appeal The act of asking an appellate court to overturn a decision after the trial court's final judgment has been entered.

appellant The appealing party in an appeal. Also known as *petitioner*.

appellate body A panel of seven justices selected from WTO member nations that hears and decides appeals from decisions by the dispute settlement body.

appellee The responding party in an appeal. Also known as *respondent*.

appropriate bargaining unit The group that a union seeks to represent.

arbitration A form of ADR in which the parties choose an impartial third party to hear and decide the dispute. A nonjudicial method of dispute resolution whereby a neutral third party decides the case.

arbitration clause A clause in contracts that requires disputes arising out of the contract to be submitted to arbitration. A clause contained in many international contracts that stipulates that any dispute between the parties concerning the performance of the contract will be submitted to an arbitrator or arbitration panel for resolution.

arraignment A hearing during which the accused is brought before a court and is (1) informed of the charges against him or her and (2) asked to enter a plea.

arrest warrant A document for a person's detainment, based on a showing of probable cause that the person committed the crime.

arson The willful or malicious burning of another's building.

article 9 of the UCC An article of the UCC that governs secured transactions in personal property.

articles of amendment A document that must be filed with the secretary of state which the amendment to the articles of incorporation is approved by the shareholders.

articles of incorporation The basic governing document of the corporation. This document must be filed with the secretary of state of the state of incorporation.

articles of limited liability partnership A public document that must be filed with the secretary of state to form a limited liability partnership.

articles of organization The formal document that must be filed with the secretary of state to form an LLC.

articles of partnership A public document that must be filed with the secretary of state to form a limited liability partnership.

assault (1) The threat of immediate harm or offensive contact or (2) any action that arouses reasonable apprehension of imminent harm. Actual physical contact is unnecessary.

assignee A party to whom a right has been transferred.

assignment The transfer of contractual rights by an obligee to another party.

assignor An obligee who transfers a right.

assumption of the risk A defense that a defendant can use against a plaintiff who knowingly and voluntarily enters into or participates in a risky activity that results in injury. A defense in which the defendant must prove that (1) the plaintiff knew and appreciated the risk and (2) the plaintiff voluntarily assumed the risk.

attempt to commit a crime A situation in which a crime is attempted but not completed.

attestation Action of a will being witnessed by two or three objective and competent people.

attorney–client privilege A rule that says a client can tell his or her lawyer anything about the case without fear that the attorney will be called as a witness against the client.

attorney-in-fact Agent who has power of attorney; does not actually have to be an attorney.

authorized shares The number of shares provided for in the articles of incorporation.

automatic stay The result of the filing of a voluntary or involuntary petition; the suspension of certain actions by creditors against the debtor or the debtor's property.

backward vertical merger A vertical merger in which the customer acquires the supplier.

bailee A holder of goods who is not a seller or a buyer (e.g., a warehouse, common carrier).

bailment A transaction in which an owner transfers his or her personal property to another to be held, stored, delivered, or for some other purpose. Title to the property does not transfer.

bailment for sole benefit of the bailee A gratuitous bailment that benefits only the bailee. The bailee owes a *duty of great care* to protect the bailed property.

bailment for the sole benefit of the bailor A gratuitous bailment that benefits only the bailor. The bailee owes only a *duty of slight care* to protect the bailed property.

bailor The owner of property in a bailment.

bait and switch A type of deceptive advertising that occurs when a seller advertises the availability of a low-cost discounted item but then pressures the buyer into purchasing more expensive merchandise.

bankruptcy estate An estate created upon the commencement of a Chapter 7 proceeding that includes all of the debtor's legal and equitable interests in real, personal, tangible, and intangible property, wherever located, that exist when the petition is filed, minus exempt property.

bargained-for exchange An exchange that parties engage in that leads to an enforceable contract.

battery Unauthorized and harmful or offensive physical contact with another person. Direct physical contact is not necessary.

bench trial Trial without a jury; also called a *waiver trial.*

beneficiary (1) A person or organization designated in the will to receive all or a portion of the testator's property at the time of the testator's death. (2) The person for whose benefit a trust is created. (3) The person who is to receive life insurance proceeds when the insured dies. (4) The creditor in a deed of trust and note transaction.

bequest (legacy) A gift of personal property by will; also known as a *legacy.*

Berne Convention An international copyright treaty to which the United States and many other nations are signatories.

bilateral contract A contract entered into by way of exchange of promises of the parties, a "promise for a promise."

Bill of Rights Constitutional Amendments I through X.

biosafety protocol An agreement sponsored by United Nations in which countries agreed that all genetically engineered foods will be clearly labeled with the phrase "May contain living modified organisms."

board of directors A panel of decision makers, the members of which are elected by the corporation's shareholders.

bona fide occupational qualification (BFOQ) Employment discrimination based on a protected class (other than race or color) that is lawful if it is *job related* and a *business necessity.* This exception is narrowly interpreted by the courts.

bond A long-term debt security that is secured by some form of collateral.

breach of the duty of care A failure to exercise care or to act as a reasonable person would act.

bribery The act of one person giving another person money, property, favors, or anything else of value for a favor in return. Often referred to as a payoff or kickback.

briefs Documents submitted by the parties' attorneys to the judge; contain legal support for their side of the case.

burden of proof The burden that the plaintiff bears to prove the allegations made in his or her complaint.

burglary The taking of personal property from another's home, office, commercial, or other type of building.

business judgment rule A rule that protects the decisions of board of directors, which acts on an informed basis, in good faith, and in the honest belief that the action taken is in the best interests of the corporation and its shareholders.

bylaws A detailed set of rules that are adopted by the board of directors after the corporation is incorporated that contains provisions for managing the business and the affairs of the corporation.

cancellation The termination of a contract by a contracting party upon the material breach of the contract by the other party.

case brief A summary of each of the following items of a case: (1) case name and citation, (2) key facts, (3) issue presented, (4) holding of the court, and (5) court's reasoning.

causation The act or process of causing. A person who commits a negligent act is not liable unless his or her act was the cause of the plaintiff's injuries. The two types of causation that must be proven are (1) causation in fact (actual cause) and (2) proximate cause (legal cause).

causation in fact, or actual cause The actual cause of negligence. A person who commits a negligent act is not liable unless causation in fact can be proven.

caveat emptor "Let the buyer beware," the traditional guideline of sales transactions.

certificate of deposit (CD) A two-party negotiable instrument that is a special form of note created when a depositor deposits money at a financial institution in exchange for the institution's promise to pay back the amount of the deposit plus an agreed-upon rate of interest upon the expiration of a set time period agreed upon by the parties.

certificate of limited partnership A document that two or more persons must execute and sign that makes the limited partnership legal and binding.

certification mark A mark certifying that goods and services are of a certain quality or originate from particular geographical areas.

chain of distribution All manufacturers, distributors, wholesalers, retailers, lessors, and subcomponent manufacturers involved in a transaction.

chain-style franchise A franchise in which the franchisor licenses the franchisee to make and sell its products or distribute services to the public from a retail outlet serving an exclusive territory.

changing conditions defense A price discrimination defense that claims that prices were lowered in response to changing conditions in the market for or the marketability of the goods.

Chapter 11 reorganization bankruptcy A bankruptcy method that allows reorganization of the debtor's financial affairs under the supervision of the bankruptcy court.

Chapter 13 consumer debt adjustment A rehabilitation form of bankruptcy that permits the courts to supervise the debtor's plan for the payment of unpaid debts by installments.

Chapter 7 liquidation bankruptcy The most familiar form of bankruptcy, in which the debtor's nonexempt property is sold for cash, the cash is distributed to the creditors, and any unpaid debts are discharged.

charitable trust A trust created for the benefit of a segment of society or society in general.

check A distinct form of draft drawn on a financial institution and payable on demand.

chief justice The U.S. Supreme Court justice responsible for administration of the Court.

choice of forum clause A clause in an international contract that designates which nation's court has jurisdiction to hear a case arising out of the contract. Also known as a *forum-selection clause.*

choice of law clause A clause in an international contract that designates which nation's laws will be applied in deciding a dispute arising out of the contract.

civil law system A major legal system derived from the Roman Empire, in which a civil code and statutes interpreting it are the sole sources of law; thus, case law and court decisions do not have the force of law.

Civil Rights Act of 1964 Law intended to eliminate job discrimination based on five protected classes: race, color, religion, sex, and national origin.

closing arguments Statements made by the attorneys to the jury at the end of the trial to try to convince the jury to render a verdict for their clients.

codicil A separate document that must be executed to amend a will; must be executed with the same formalities as a will.

codified law system Statutes organized into code books, organized by topic.

collateral Security against repayment of the note that lenders sometimes require; can be a car, a house, or other property. The property that is subject to a security interest.

collateral contract A promise in which one person agrees to answer for the debts or duties of another person.

collective bargaining The act of negotiating contract terms between an employer and the members of a union.

collective bargaining agreement The contract resulting from a collective bargaining procedure.

collective mark A mark used by cooperatives, associations, and fraternal organizations.

"coming and going" rule A rule that says a principal is generally not liable for injuries caused by its agents and employees while they are on their way to and from work.

Commerce Clause A clause of the U.S. Constitution that grants Congress the power "to regulate commerce with foreign nations, and among the several states, and with Indian tribes."

commercial impracticability Nonperformance that is excused if an extreme or unexpected development or expense makes it impractical for the promisor to perform.

commercial speech Speech used by business, such as advertising. It is subject to time, place, and manner restrictions.

common law Law developed by judges who issued their opinions when deciding a case. The principles announced in these cases became precedent for later judges deciding similar cases.

common stock A type of equity security that represents the *residual* value of the corporation.

common stock certificate A document that represents the common shareholder's investment in a corporation.

common stockholder A person who owns common stock.

comparative negligence A doctrine that applies to strict liability actions and says that a plaintiff who is contributorily negligent for his or her injuries is responsible for a proportional share of the damages. A doctrine under which damages are apportioned according to fault.

compensatory damages A remedy intended to compensate a nonbreaching party for the loss of a bargain; they place the nonbreaching party in the same position as if the contract had been fully performed by restoring the "benefits of the bargain."

competent party's duty of restitution A duty in which if a minor has transferred money, property, or other valuables to the competent party before disaffirming the contract, that party must place the minor back into status quo.

complaint The document the plaintiff files with the court and serves on the defendant to initiate a lawsuit.

complete performance A type of performance that occurs when a party to a contract renders performance exactly as required by the contract; it discharges that party's obligations under the contract.

Computer Software Copyright Act Amended the Copyright Act of 1976 to include computer programs in the list of tangible items protected by copyright law.

conciliation A form of mediation in which the parties choose an *interested* third party to act as the mediator.

concurrent jurisdiction Jurisdiction shared by two or more courts.

concurring opinion Issued by a justice who agrees with the outcome of a case but not the reason proffered by other justices, to set forth his or her reasons for deciding the case.

condition A qualification of a promise that becomes a covenant if it is met.

condition precedent A condition that requires the occurrence of an event before a party is obligated to perform a duty under a contract.

condition subsequent A condition, if it occurs, that automatically excuses the performance of an existing contractual duty to perform.

condominium A common form of ownership in a multiple-dwelling building where the purchaser has title to the individual unit and owns the common areas as a tenant in common with the other condominium owners.

confirmation The bankruptcy court's approval of a plan of reorganization.

confusion A situation that occurs if two or more persons commingle fungible goods; title is then acquired by the commingling.

conglomerate merger A merger that does not fit into any other category; a merger between firms in totally unrelated businesses.

consequential damages Foreseeable damages that arise from circumstances outside the contract. In order to be liable for these damages, the breaching party must know or have reason to know that the breach will cause special damages to the other party.

consideration Something of legal value given in exchange for a promise.

Consolidated Omnibus Budget Reconciliation Act (COBRA) A federal law that permits employees and their beneficiaries to continue their group health insurance after an employee's employment has ended.

consolidation The act of a court to combine two or more separate lawsuits into one lawsuit.

Constitution of the United States of America The supreme law of the United States.

constructive notice Usually, written notice to a third party that is put into general circulation, such as in a newspaper.

constructive trust An equitable trust imposed by law to avoid fraud, unjust enrichment, and injustice.

Consumer Leasing Act (CLA) An amendment to the TILA that extends the TILA's coverage to lease terms in consumer leases.

Consumer Product Safety Act (CPSA) A federal statute that created the Consumer Product Safety Commission and regulates potentially dangerous consumer products.

consumer protection laws Federal and state statutes and regulations that promote product safety and prohibit abusive, unfair, and deceptive business practices.

contract in restraint of trade A contract that unreasonably restrains trade.

contract contrary to public policy A contract that has a negative impact on society or interferes with the public's safety and welfare.

contributory negligence A doctrine that says a plaintiff who is partially at fault for his or her own injury cannot recover against the negligent defendant. A defense that says that a person who is injured by a defective product but has been negligent and has contributed to his or her own injuries cannot recover from the defendant.

convention A treaty that is sponsored by an international organization.

cooling-off period A period that is required so a union can give an employer at least 60 days' notice before a strike can commence.

cooperative A form of co-ownership of a multiple-dwelling building where a corporation owns the building and the residents own shares in the corporation.

co-ownership Ownership of a piece of real property by two or more persons. Also called *concurrent ownership*.

copyright The exclusive legal right to reproduce, publish, and sell a literary, musical, or artistic work.

copyright infringement An act in which a party copies a substantial and material part of the plaintiff's copyrighted work without permission. A copyright holder may recover damages and other remedies against the infringer.

Copyright Revision Act of 1976 A federal statute that (1) establishes the requirements for obtaining a copyright and (2) protects copyrighted works from infringement.

corporate citizenship A theory of responsibility that says a business has a responsibility to do good.

corporation A fictitious legal entity that (1) is created according to statutory requirements and (2) is a separate taxpaying entity for federal income tax purposes.

corporation codes State statutes that regulate the formation, operation, and dissolution of corporations.

cost justification defense A defense in a Section 2(a) action that provides that a seller's price discrimination is not unlawful if the price differential is due to "differences in the cost of manufacture, sale, or delivery" of the product.

counteroffer A response by an offeree that contains terms and conditions different from or in addition to those of the offer. A counteroffer terminates an offer.

Court of Appeals for the Federal Circuit A court of appeals in Washington, DC, that has special appellate jurisdiction to review the decisions of the Claims Court, the Patent and Trademark Office, and the Court of International Trade.

Court of Chancery A court that granted relief based on fairness. Also called equity court.

court of record A state's general-jurisdiction trial court, in which testimony and evidence are recorded and stored for future reference.

covenant An unconditional promise to perform.

covenant of good faith and fair dealing Under this implied covenant, the parties to a contract not only are held to the express terms of the contract but also are required to act in "good faith" and deal fairly in all respects in obtaining the objective of the contract.

cover A right of a licensee to engage in a commercially reasonable substitute transaction after the licensor has breached the contract.

crashworthiness doctrine A doctrine that says that automobile manufacturers are under a duty to design automobiles so they take into account the possibility of harm from a person's body striking something inside the automobile in the case of a car accident.

credit report Information about a person's credit history that can be secured from a credit bureau.

creditor The lender in a credit transaction.

creditors' committee A committee composed of the creditors holding the seven largest unsecured claims. Committees represent the interests of their class in the negotiation of a plan of organization.

crime A violation of a statute for which the government imposes a punishment.

criminal conspiracy A situation in which two or more persons enter into an agreement to commit a crime and an overt act is taken to further the crime.

criminal fraud The act of obtaining title to property through deception or trickery. Also known as false pretenses or deceit.

criminal law Federal, state, and local government laws for the purpose of defining crimes and setting forth punishments for those found guilty of violating criminal laws.

critical legal thinking The process of specifying the issue presented by a case, identifying the key facts in the case and applicable law, and then applying the law to the facts to come to a conclusion that answers the issue presented.

cross-complaint Document filed by the defendant against plaintiff to seek damages or some other remedy.

cross-examination Questioning of a witness following direct examination; precedes redirect examination and recross examination.

crossover worker A person who does not honor a strike who either (1) chooses not to strike or (2) returns to work after joining the strikers for a time.

crown jewel A valuable asset of the target corporation that the tender offeror particularly wants to acquire in the tender offer.

cruel and unusual punishment A provision of the Eighth Amendment that protects criminal defendants from torture or other abusive punishment.

custom The second source of international law, created through consistent, recurring practices between two or more nations over a period of time that have become recognized as binding.

"danger invites rescue" doctrine A doctrine that provides that a rescuer who is injured while going to someone's rescue can sue the person who caused the dangerous situation.

debenture A long-term, unsecured debt instrument that is based on the corporation's general credit standing.

debt collector An agent who collects debts for other parties.

debt securities Securities that establish a debtor–creditor relationship in which the corporation borrows money from the investor to whom the debt security is issued.

debtor The borrower in a credit transaction.

debtor-in-possession A debtor who is left in place to operate a business during a reorganization proceeding.

deed A document that describes a person's ownership interest in a piece of real property.

defamation of character False statement(s) made by one person about another. In court, the plaintiff must prove that (1) the defendant made an untrue statement of fact about the plaintiff and (2) the statement was intentionally or accidentally published to a third party.

default judgment If a defendant does not file an answer to a plaintiff's complaint, a default judgment is entered against him or her, establishing the defendant's liability.

defect Something wrong, inadequate, or improper in manufacture, design, packaging, warning, or safety measures of a product.

defect in design A defect that occurs when a product is improperly designed.

defect in manufacture A defect that occurs when the manufacturer fails to (1) properly assemble a product, (2) properly test a product, or (3) adequately check the quality of the product.

defect in packaging A defect that occurs when a product has been placed in packaging that is insufficiently tamperproof.

defendant The party against whom a lawsuit is brought.

defendant's case The process by which the defendant (1) rebuts the plaintiff's evidence, (2) proves affirmative defenses, and (3) proves allegations made in a cross-complaint.

defense attorney Attorney working on behalf of the defendant.

delegation doctrine A doctrine that says that when an administrative agency is created, it is delegated certain powers; the agency can use only those legislative, judicial, and executive powers that are delegated to it.

demand note A note payable on demand.

deponent The party who gives his or her deposition.

deposition The oral testimony given by a party or witness prior to trial. The testimony is given under oath and is transcribed.

derivative lawsuit A lawsuit a shareholder brings against an offending party on behalf of the corporation when the corporation fails to bring the lawsuit.

Digital Millennium Copyright Act (DMCA) Enacted in 1998 to protect "wrappers" and encryption technology of copyrighted works from infringement; imposes civil and criminal penalties.

direct examination The initial questioning of witnesses in a case by an attorney; often followed by cross-examination, redirect examination, and recross examination.

disaffirmance The act of a minor to rescind a contract under the infancy doctrine. Disaffirmance may be done orally, in writing, or by the minor's conduct.

discharge The termination of the legal duty of a debtor to pay debts that remain unpaid upon the completion of a bankruptcy proceeding.

discovery A legal process during which both parties engage in various activities to discover facts of the case from the other party and witnesses prior to trial.

disparagement False statements about a competitor's products, services, property, or business reputation.

disparate impact discrimination An employer's discrimination against an entire protected *class*. An example would be where a facially neutral employment practice or rule causes an adverse impact on a protected class.

disparate treatment discrimination An employer's discrimination against a specific *individual* because of his or her race, color, national origin, sex, or religion.

dispute settlement body A board comprised of one representative from each WTO member nation that reviews panel reports.

dissenting opinion Issued by a justice who does not agree with the court's decision, setting forth the reasons for his or her dissent.

dissenting shareholder appraisal rights Rights of shareholders who object to a proposed merger, share exchange, or sale or lease of all or substantially all of the property of a corporation to have their shares valued by the court and receive cash payment of this value from the corporation.

distinctive A brand name that is unique and fabricated.

distinctiveness of a mark The quality of a brand name that has acquired a secondary meaning; necessary to be trademarked.

distributorship franchise A franchise in which the franchisor manufactures a product and licenses a retail franchisee to distribute the product to the public.

district attorney–prosecutor The lawyer representing the government in a criminal lawsuit.

diversity of citizenship A case between (1) citizens of different states, (2) a citizen of a state and a citizen or subject of a foreign country, and (3) a citizen of a state and a foreign country where a foreign country is the plaintiff.

division of markets A situation in which competitors agree that each will serve only a designated portion of the market.

doctrine of sovereign immunity A doctrine that states that countries are granted immunity from suits in courts of other countries.

doctrine of strict liability in tort A tort doctrine that makes manufacturers, distributors, wholesalers, retailers, and others in the chain of distribution of a defective product liable for the damages caused by the defect, irrespective of fault.

"doing business as" (d.b.a.) Operating under a trade name.

domain name A unique name that identifies an individual's or a company's Web site.

domestic corporation A corporation in the state in which it was formed.

donee A person who receives a gift.

donor A person who gives a gift.

Double Jeopardy Clause A clause of the Fifth Amendment that protects persons from being tried twice for the same crime.

draft A three-party instrument that is an unconditional written order by one party that orders the second party to pay money to a third party.

Dram Shop Act A statute that makes taverns and bartenders liable for injuries caused to or by patrons who are served too much alcohol.

drawee of a check The financial institution on which a check is drawn.

drawee of a draft The party who must pay the money stated in the draft. Also called the *acceptor* of a draft.

drawer of a check The checking account holder and writer of a check.

drawer of a draft The party who writes the order for a draft.

dual-purpose mission An errand or another act that a principal requests of an agent while the agent is on his or her own personal business.

due diligence defense A defense to a Section 11 action that, if proven, makes the defendant not liable.

Due Process Clause A clause that provides that no person shall be deprived of "life, liberty, or property" without due process of the law.

duress Situation that occurs when one party threatens to do a wrongful act unless the other party enters into a contract.

duty not to willfully or wantonly injure The duty an owner owes a trespasser to prevent intentional injury or harm to the trespasser when the trespasser is on his or her premises.

duty of accountability A duty that an agent owes to maintain an accurate accounting of all transactions undertaken on the principal's behalf.

duty of care The obligation we all owe each other not to cause any unreasonable harm or risk of harm. A duty that corporate directors and officers have to use care and diligence when acting on behalf of the corporation.

duty of compensation A duty that a principal owes to pay an agreed-upon amount to the agent either upon the completion of the agency or at some other mutually agreeable time.

duty of cooperation A duty that a principal owes to cooperate with and assist the agent in the performance of the agent's duties and the accomplishment of the agency.

duty of indemnification A duty that a principal owes to protect the agent for losses the agent suffered during the agency because of the principal's misconduct.

duty of loyalty A duty owed by a member of a member-managed LLC or a manager of a manager-managed LLC to be honest in his or her dealings with the LLC and not to act adversely to the interests of the LLC. A duty that directors and officers have not to act adversely to the interests of the corporation and to subordinate their personal interests to those of the corporation and its shareholders.

duty of notification An agent's duty to notify the principal of information he or she learns from a third party or another source that is important to the principal.

duty of ordinary care The duty an owner owes an invitee or a licensee to prevent injury or harm when the invitee or licensee steps on the owner's premises.

duty of performance An agent's duty to a principal that includes (1) performing the lawful duties expressed in the contract and (2) meeting the standards of reasonable care, skill, and diligence implicit in all contracts.

duty of reimbursement A duty that a principal owes to repay money to the agent if the agent spent his or her own money during the agency on the principal's behalf.

duty of utmost care A duty of care that goes beyond ordinary care and that says common carriers and innkeepers have a responsibility to provide security to their passengers or guests.

easement A given or required right to make limited use of someone else's land without owning or leasing it.

e-commerce The sale of goods and services by computer over the Internet.

Economic Espionage Act A law enacted in 1996 that makes it a federal crime to steal another's trade secret.

electronic mail (e-mail) Electronic written communication between individuals using computers connected to the Internet.

embezzlement The fraudulent conversion of property by a person to whom that property was entrusted.

eminent domain Power of the government to acquire private property for public purposes. The taking of private property by the government for public use, provided just compensation is paid to the private property holder.

Employee Retirement Income Security Act (ERISA) A federal act designed to prevent fraud and other abuses associated with private pension funds.

employer lockout An act of an employer to prevent employees from entering the work premises when the employer reasonably anticipates a strike.

employer–employee relationship A relationship that results when an employer hires an employee to perform some form of service.

employment-at-will Employment without an employment contract.

employment-related injury Injury arising out of and in the course of employment, under the Workers' Compensation Act.

employment relationships (1) Business relationships, including employer–employee, (2) principal–agent, and (3) principal–independent contractor.

endorsee The person to whom a negotiable instrument is endorsed.

endorsement The signature (and other directions) written by or on behalf of the holder somewhere on the instrument.

endorser The person who endorses a negotiable instrument.

entity theory An approach holding that partnerships are separate legal entities that can have title to personal and real property, transact business in the partnership name, sue in the partnership name, and the like.

entrepreneur A person who forms and operates a new business either by him- or herself or with others.

enumerated powers Certain powers delegated to the federal government by the states.

Environmental Protection Agency (EPA) An administrative agency created by Congress in 1970 to coordinate the implementation and enforcement of federal environmental protection laws.

Equal Credit Opportunity Act (ECOA) A federal statute that prohibits discrimination in the extension of credit based on sex, marital status, race, color, national origin, religion, age, or receipt of income from public assistance programs.

equal dignity rule A rule that says that agents' contracts to sell property covered by the statute of frauds must be in writing to be enforceable.

Equal Employment Opportunity Commission (EEOC) The federal administrative agency that is responsible for enforcing most federal antidiscrimination laws.

equal opportunity in employment The right of all employees and job applicants (1) to be treated without discrimination and (2) to be able to sue employers if they are discriminated against.

Equal Pay Act of 1963 An act that protects both sexes from pay discrimination based on sex; extends to jobs that require equal skill, equal effort, equal responsibility, and similar working conditions.

Equal Protection Clause A clause that provides that a state cannot "deny to any person within its jurisdiction the equal protection of the laws."

equitable remedies Remedies that may be awarded by a judge where there has been a breach of contract and either (1) the legal remedy is not adequate or (2) the judge wants to prevent unjust enrichment.

escheat Goes to; used to describe property that goes to the state when an individual dies intestate (without a will).

Establishment Clause A clause to the First Amendment that prohibits the government from either establishing a state religion or promoting one religion over another.

estate Ownership rights in real property; the bundle of legal rights that the owner has to possess, use, and enjoy the property.

estate pour autre vie A life estate measured in the life of a third party.

ethical fundamentalism A moral theory in which a person looks to an outside source for ethical rules or commands.

ethical relativism A moral theory that holds that individuals must decide what is ethical based on their own feelings as to what is right or wrong.

ethics A set of moral principles or values that governs the conduct of an individual or a group.

European Court of Justice The judicial branch of the European Union located in Luxembourg. It has jurisdiction to enforce European Union law.

European Union (Common Market) An international region that comprises many countries of Europe. It was created to promote peace and security as well as economic, social, and cultural development.

exclusionary rule A rule that says that evidence obtained from an unreasonable search and seizure can generally be prohibited from introduction at a trial or administrative proceeding against the person searched.

exclusive agency contract A contract that a principal and an agent enter into that says the principal cannot employ any agent other than the exclusive agent.

exclusive jurisdiction Jurisdiction held by only one court.

exclusive license A license that grants the licensee exclusive rights to use information rights for a specified duration.

exculpatory clause A contractual provision that relieves one (or both) parties to the contract from tort liability for ordinary negligence.

executed contract A contract that has been fully performed on both sides; a completed contract.

executive branch The part of the government that consists of the president and vice president.

executive order An order issued by a member of the executive branch of the government.

executive powers Authority granted to administrative agencies, such as the investigation and prosecution of possible violations of statutes, administrative rules, and administrative orders.

executor or executrix A personal representative named in a will to administer an estate during its settlement phase.

executory contract A contract that has not been fully performed by either or both sides. A contract that has not been fully performed. With court approval, executory contracts may be rejected by a debtor in bankruptcy.

exempt property Property that may be retained by a debtor pursuant to federal or state law; a debtor's property that does not become part of the bankruptcy estate.

express agency An agency that occurs when a principal and an agent expressly agree to enter into an agency agreement with each other.

express contract An agreement that is expressed in written or oral words.

express trust A trust created voluntarily by the settlor.

express warranty A warranty that is created when a seller or lessor makes an affirmation that the goods he or she is selling or leasing meet certain standards of quality, description, performance, or condition.

extortion A threat to expose something about another person unless that other person gives money or property. Often referred to as *blackmail.*

extradition The act of sending a person back to a country for criminal prosecution.

failure to provide adequate instructions A defect that occurs when a manufacturer does not provide detailed directions for safe assembly and use of a product.

failure to warn A defect that occurs when a manufacturer does not place a warning on the packaging of products that could cause injury if the danger is unknown.

Fair Credit and Charge Card Disclosure Act of 1988 An amendment to the TILA that requires disclosure of credit terms on credit- and charge-card solicitations and applications.

Fair Credit Reporting Act (FCRA) An amendment to the TILA that protects customers who are subjects of a credit report by setting out guidelines for credit bureaus.

Fair Debt Collection Practices Act (FDCPA) An act enacted in 1977 that protects consumer–debtors from abusive, deceptive, and unfair practices used by debt collectors.

Fair Labor Standards Act (FLSA) A federal act enacted in 1938 to protect workers. It prohibits child labor and establishes minimum wage and overtime pay requirements.

Fair Packaging and Labeling Act A federal statute that requires the labels on consumer goods to identify the product; the manufacturer, processor, or packager of the product and its address; the net quantity of the contents of the package; and the quantity of each serving.

fair use doctrine A doctrine that permits certain limited use of a copyright by someone other than the copyright holder without the permission of the copyright holder.

false imprisonment The intentional confinement or restraint of another person without authority or justification and without that person's consent.

federal administrative agencies Administrative agencies that are part of the executive or legislative branch of government.

Federal Insurance Contributions Act (FICA) A federal act that says employees and employers must make contributions into the Social Security fund.

federalism The U.S. form of government; the federal government and the 50 state governments share powers.

Federal Patent Statute of 1952 A federal statute that establishes the requirements for obtaining a patent and protects patented inventions from infringement.

federal question A case arising under the U.S. Constitution, treaties, or federal statutes and regulations.

Federal Trade Commission (FTC) A federal government administrative agency empowered to enforce federal franchising rules, the Federal Trade Commission Act and other federal consumer protection statutes.

Federal Unemployment Tax Act (FUTA) A federal act that requires employers to pay unemployment taxes; unemployment compensation is paid to workers who are temporarily unemployed.

fee simple absolute A type of ownership of real property that grants the owner the fullest bundle of legal rights that a person can hold in real property.

fee simple defeasible A type of ownership of real property that grants the owner all the incidents of a fee simple absolute except that it may be taken away if a specified condition occurs or does not occur.

felony The most serious type of crime; inherently evil crime. Most crimes against persons and some business-related crimes are felonies.

final prospectus A final version of the prospectus that must be delivered by the issuer to the investor prior to or at the time of confirming a sale or sending a security to a purchaser.

financing statement A document filed by a secured creditor with the appropriate government office that constructively notifies the world of his or her security interest in personal property.

fixtures Goods that are affixed to real estate so as to become part thereof.

Food and Drug Administration (FDA) A federal administrative agency that administers and enforces the federal Food, Drug, and Cosmetic Act (FDCA) and other federal consumer protection laws.

Food, Drug, and Cosmetic Act (FDCA) A federal statute enacted in 1938 that provides the basis for the regulation of much of the testing, manufacture, distribution, and sale of foods, drugs, cosmetics, and medicinal products.

foreclosure A legal procedure by which a secured creditor causes the sale of the secured real estate to pay a defaulted loan.

Foreign Commerce Clause A clause of the U.S. Constitution that vests Congress with the power "to regulate commerce with foreign nations."

foreign corporation A corporation in any state or jurisdiction other than the one in which it was formed.

Foreign Sovereign Immunities Act An act that exclusively governs suits against foreign nations that are brought in federal or state courts in the United States. It codifies the principle of qualified, or restricted, immunity.

forgery The fraudulent making or altering of a written document that affects the legal liability of another person.

forum-selection clause A contract provision that designates a certain court to hear any dispute concerning non-performance of the contract.

forward vertical merger A vertical merger in which the supplier acquires the customer.

Fourteenth Amendment An amendment that was added to the U.S. Constitution in 1868. It contains the Due Process, Equal Protection, and Privileges and Immunities clauses.

franchise An arrangement that is established when one party licenses another party to use the franchisor's trade name, trademarks, commercial symbols, patents, copyrights, and other property in the distribution and selling of goods and services.

franchise agreement An agreement that a franchisor and a franchisee enter into that sets forth the terms and conditions of the franchise.

fraud by concealment Fraud that occurs when one party takes specific action to conceal a material fact from another party.

fraud in the inception Fraud that occurs if a person is deceived as to the nature of his or her act and does not know what he or she is signing.

fraud in the inducement Fraud that occurs when the party knows what he or she is signing but has been fraudulently induced to enter into the contract.

Free Exercise Clause A clause to the First Amendment that prohibits the government from interfering with the free exercise of religion in the United States.

freedom of speech The right to engage in oral, written, and symbolic speech protected by the First Amendment.

freehold estate An estate where the owner has a present possessory interest in the real property.

fresh start A debtor's discharge from burdensome debts that allows him or her to begin again.

frolic and detour A situation in which an agent does something during the course of his employment to further his own interests rather than the principal's.

FTC franchise rule A rule set out by the FTC that requires franchisors to make full presale disclosures to prospective franchisees.

future interest The right to possess property in the future; the interest that the grantor retains for him- or herself or a third party.

gambling statutes Statutes that make certain forms of gambling illegal.

general duty A duty that an employer has to provide a work environment "free from recognized hazards that are causing or are likely to cause death or serious physical harm to his employees."

general gifts Testamentary gift that does not identify the specific property from which the gift is to be made.

general partners Partners in a limited partnership who invest capital, manage the business, and are personally liable for partnership debts.

general partnership A voluntary association of two or more persons for carrying on a business as co-owners for profit. Also called a *partnership.*

general power of attorney A type of power of attorney that confers broad powers on the agent to act in any matters on the principal's behalf.

general principles of law The third source of international law, consisting of principles of law recognized by civilized nations. These are principles of law that are common to the national law of the parties to the dispute.

general-jurisdiction trial court A court that hears cases of a general nature that are not within the jurisdiction of limited-jurisdiction trial courts. Testimony and evidence at trial are recorded and stored for future reference.

generally known dangers A defense that acknowledges that certain products are inherently dangerous and are known to the general population to be so.

generic name A term for a mark that has become a common term for a product line or type of service and therefore has lost its trademark protection.

genuineness of assent The requirement that a party's assent to a contract be genuine. Genuineness of assent is an issue in the areas of mistake, misrepresentation, duress, and undue influence.

gift A voluntary transfer of title to property without payment of consideration by the donee. To be a valid gift, the following three elements must be shown: donative intent, delivery, and acceptance.

gift promise A promise that is unenforceable because it lacks consideration.

Good Samaritan law A statute that relieves medical professionals from liability for ordinary negligence when they stop and render aid to victims in emergency situations.

government contractor defense A defense that says that a contractor who was provided specifications by the government is not liable for any defect in the product that occurs as a result of those specifications.

grantee The party to whom an interest in real property is transferred.

grantor The party who transfers an ownership interest in real property.

greenmail The purchase by a target corporation of its stock from an actual or perceived tender offeror at a premium.

group boycott A situation in which two or more competitors at one level of distribution agree not to deal with others at another level of distribution.

guarantor The person who agrees to pay the debt if the primary debtor does not.

guaranty arrangement An arrangement where a third party promises to be *secondarily liable* for the payment of another's debt.

guest statute A statute that provides that if a driver of a vehicle voluntarily and without compensation gives a ride to another person, the driver is not liable to the passenger for injuries caused by the driver's ordinary negligence.

Hart-Scott-Rodino Antitrust Improvement Act An act that requires certain firms to notify the FTC and the Department of Justice in advance of a proposed merger. Unless the government challenges the proposed merger within 30 days, the merger may proceed.

hazardous waste Waste that may cause or significantly contribute to an increase in mortality or serious illness or pose a hazard to human health or the environment if improperly managed.

heirs Relatives who receive property under intestacy statutes when a person dies without a will.

holographic will Will that is entirely handwritten and signed by the testator.

horizontal merger A merger between two or more companies that compete in the same business and geographical market.

horizontal restraint of trade A restraint of trade that occurs when two or more competitors at the same level of distribution enter into a contract, combination, or conspiracy to restrain trade.

hung jury A jury that cannot come to a unanimous decision about the defendant's guilt. The government may choose to retry the case.

illegal consideration A promise to refrain from doing an illegal act. Such a promise will not support a contract.

illegal contract A contract to perform an illegal act. Cannot be enforced by either party to the contract.

illusory promise A contract into which parties enter but one or both of the parties can choose not to perform their contractual obligations. Such a contract lacks consideration.

Immigration Reform and Control Act of 1986 (IRCA) A federal statute that makes it unlawful for employers to hire illegal immigrants.

immoral contract A contract whose objective is the commission of an act that is considered immoral by society.

immunity from prosecution A situation in which the government agrees not to use any evidence given by a person granted immunity against that person.

implied agency An agency that occurs when a principal and an agent do not expressly create an agency, but it is inferred from the conduct of the parties.

implied exemptions Exemptions from antitrust laws that are implied by the federal courts.

implied trust A trust that is imposed by law or from the conduct of the parties.

implied warranty of authority A case in which an agent who enters into a contract on behalf of another party impliedly warrants that he or she has the authority to do so.

implied warranty of fitness for human consumption A warranty that applies to food or drink consumed on or off the premises of restaurants, grocery stores, fast-food outlets, and vending machines.

implied warranty of habitability A warranty that provides that the leased premises must be fit, safe, and suitable for ordinary residential use.

implied warranty of merchantability Unless properly disclosed, a warranty that is implied that sold or leased goods are fit for the ordinary purpose for which they are sold or leased, and other assurances.

implied-in-fact contract A contract in which agreement between parties has been inferred from their conduct.

impossibility of performance Nonperformance that is excused if the contract becomes impossible to perform; it must be objective impossibility, not subjective.

imputed knowledge Information that is learned by the agent that is attributed to the principal.

in personam jurisdiction Jurisdiction over the parties to a lawsuit.

in rem jurisdiction Jurisdiction to hear a case because of jurisdiction over the property of the lawsuit.

inaccessibility exception A rule that permits employees and union officials to engage in union solicitation on company property if the employees are beyond reach of reasonable union efforts to communicate with them.

inchoate crimes Incomplete crimes or crimes committed by nonparticipants, including criminal conspiracy, attempt to commit a crime, and aiding and abetting the commission of a crime.

incidental beneficiary A party who is unintentionally benefited by other people's contract.

indemnification Right of a partner to be reimbursed for expenditures incurred on behalf of a partnership.

independent contractor A person or business who is not an employee who is employed by a principal to perform a certain task on his or her behalf.

indictment The charge of having committed a crime (usually a felony), based on the judgment of a grand jury.

indirect price discrimination A form of price discrimination (e.g., favorable credit terms) that is less readily apparent than direct forms of price discrimination.

infancy doctrine A doctrine that allows minors to disaffirm (cancel) most contracts they have entered into with adults.

inferior performance Performance that occurs when a party fails to perform express or implied contractual obligations that impair or destroy the essence of the contract.

information The charge of having committed a crime (usually a misdemeanor), based on the judgment of a judge (magistrate).

injunction A court order that prohibits a person from doing a certain act.

injury Personal injury or damage that a plaintiff suffers to his or her property to recover monetary damages for the defendant's negligence.

innkeeper's statutes State statutes that provide that an innkeeper can avoid liability for loss caused to a guest's property if (1) a safe is provided in which the guest's valuable property may be kept and (2) the guest is notified of this fact.

innocent misrepresentation Misrepresentation that occurs when an agent makes an untrue statement that he or she honestly and reasonably believes to be true.

INS Form I-9 A form that must be filled out by all U.S. employers for each employee. It states that the employer has inspected the employee's legal qualifications to work.

insane, but not adjudged insane A person who is insane but has not been adjudged insane by a court or an administrative agency. A contract entered into by such person is generally *voidable*. Some states hold that such a contract is void.

Insecticide, Fungicide, and Rodenticide Act A federal statute that requires pesticides, herbicides, fungicides, and rodenticides to be registered with the EPA; the EPA may deny, suspend, or cancel registration.

inside director A member of the board of directors who is also an officer of the corporation.

insider trading Trading that occurs when an insider makes a profit by personally purchasing shares of the corporation prior to public release of favorable information or by selling shares of the corporation prior to the public disclosure of unfavorable information.

Insider Trading Sanctions Act of 1984 A federal statute that permits the SEC to obtain a civil penalty of up to three times the illegal benefits received from insider trading.

intangible property Rights that cannot be reduced to physical form, such as stock certificates, certificates of deposit, bonds, and copyrights.

intellectual property rights The right to patents, copyrights, trademarks, trade secrets, trade names, domain names, and other items of intellectual property that are very valuable business assets. Federal and state laws protect intellectual property rights from misappropriation and infringement.

intended beneficiary A third party who is not in privity of contract but who has rights under the contract and can enforce the contract against the obligor.

intentional infliction of emotional distress A tort that says that a person whose extreme and outrageous conduct intentionally or recklessly causes severe emotional distress to another person is liable for that emotional distress. Also known as the *tort of outrage*.

intentional interference with contractual relations A tort that arises when a third party induces a contracting party to breach the contract with another party.

intentional misrepresentation The intentional deception of another person out of money, property, or something else of value. A seller or lessor fraudulently misrepresenting the quality of a product and a buyer being injured thereby. A misrepresentation that occurs when one person consciously decides to induce another person to rely and act on a misrepresentation. Also called *fraud*.

intentional tort A category of torts that requires that the defendant possessed the intent to do the act that caused the plaintiff's injuries. A tort that occurs when a person has intentionally committed a wrong against (1) another person or his or her character or (2) another person's property.

intermediate appellate court An intermediate court that hears appeals from trial courts.

intermediate scrutiny test A test that is applied to classifications based on protected classes other than race (e.g., sex or age).

International Court of Justice The judicial branch of the United Nations that is located in The Hague, the Netherlands. Also called the *World Court*.

international law Law that governs affairs between nations and that regulates transactions between individuals and businesses of different countries.

Internet A collection of millions of computers that provide a network of electronic connections between computers.

internet service provider (ISP) Organization providing local or toll-free access to connect to the Internet.

interrogatories Written questions submitted by one party to another party. The questions must be answered in writing within a stipulated time.

interstate commerce Commerce that moves between states or that affects commerce between states.

inter vivos **(living)** A trust created by a grantor (settlor) during his or her lifetime.

intervention The act of others joining as parties to an existing lawsuit.

intestacy statute A state statute dictating how property is to be distributed to heirs of an individual who dies without a will.

intestate succession The application of a state's intestacy statutes to determine how property is to be distributed to heirs when an individual dies without an heir.

intoxicated person A person who is under contractual incapacity because of ingestion of alcohol or drugs to the point of incompetence.

intrastate commerce Movement of goods within states, or business that affects commerce within states.

intrastate offering exemption An exemption from registration that permits local businesses to raise from local investors capital to be used in the local economy without the need to register with the SEC.

invasion of the right to privacy A tort that constitutes the violation of a person's right to live his or her life without being subjected to unwarranted and undesired publicity.

involuntary petition A petition filed by creditors of a debtor, which alleges that the debtor is not paying his or her debts as they become due.

issued shares Shares that have been sold by the corporation.

joint and several liability Tort liability of partnership in which the partners are liable together and separately. This means that the plaintiff can sue one or more of the partners separately. If successful, the plaintiff can recover the entire amount of the judgment from any or all of the defendant-partners.

joint liability Partners are *jointly liable* for contracts and debts of the partnership. This means that a plaintiff must name the partnership and all of the partners as defendants. If successful, the plaintiff can recover the entire amount of the judgment from any or all of the partners.

joint tenancy A form of co-ownership that includes the right of survivorship.

joint will A will executed by two or more testators.

judgment The official decision of the court.

judgment notwithstanding the verdict (j.n.o.v.) In a civil case, the overturning of the jury's verdict by the judge if he or she finds bias or jury misconduct.

judicial branch The part of the government that consists of the Supreme Court and other federal courts.

judicial decision A decision about an individual lawsuit issued by federal or state courts.

judicial decisions and teachings The fourth source of international law, consisting of judicial decisions and writings of the most qualified legal scholars of the various nations involved in the dispute.

jurisdiction The authority of a court to hear a case.

jurisprudence The philosophy or science of law.

jury deliberation Process by which a jury discusses the facts and evidence they have witnessed in a trial.

jury instructions Instructions given by the judge to the jury that inform the jurors of the law to be applied in the case.

Kantian or duty ethics A moral theory that says that people owe moral duties that are based on universal rules, such as the categorical imperative "do unto others as you would have them do unto you."

land The most common form of real property; includes the land and buildings and other structures permanently attached to the land.

land pollution Pollution of the land that is generally caused by hazardous waste being disposed of in an improper manner.

land use control The collective term for the laws that regulate the possession, ownership, and use of real property.

landlord–tenant relationship A relationship created when the owner of a freehold estate (landlord) transfers a right to exclusively and temporarily possess the owner's property to another (tenant).

Lanham Trademark Act (as amended) A federal statute that (1) establishes the requirements for obtaining a federal mark and (2) protects marks from infringement.

lapse of time A stated time period after which an offer expires. If no time is stated, an offer terminates after a reasonable time.

larceny The taking of another's personal property other than from his or her person or building.

law That which must be obeyed and followed by citizens subject to sanctions or legal consequences; a body of rules of action or conduct prescribed by controlling authority and having binding legal force.

law court A court that developed and administered a uniform set of laws decreed by the kings and queens after William the Conqueror; legal procedure was emphasized over merits at that time.

lease A transfer of the right to the possession and use of real property for a set term in return for certain consideration; the rental agreement between a landlord and a tenant.

leasehold A tenant's interest in the property.

legal entity A separate legal entity—an artificial person—distinct from its members that can own property, sue and be sued, enter into and enforce contracts, and such.

legislative branch The part of the government that consists of Congress (the Senate and the House of Representatives).

libel A false statement that appears in a letter, newspaper, magazine, book, photograph, movie, video, and so on.

license A contract that transfers limited rights in intellectual property and informational rights.

licensee The party who is granted limited rights in or access to intellectual property or information rights owned by the licensor.

licensing agreement A detailed and comprehensive written agreement between the licensor and licensee that sets forth the express terms of their agreement.

licensing statute A statute that requires a person or business to obtain a license from the government prior to engaging in a specified occupation or activity.

licensor The owner of intellectual property or information rights, who transfers rights in the property or information to the licensee.

licensor's damages If a licensee breaches a contract, the licensor may sue the licensee and recover monetary damages caused by the breach.

life estate An interest in real property for a person's lifetime; upon that person's death, the interest will be transferred to another party.

limited liability Liability in which members are liable for the LLC's debts, obligations, and liabilities only to the extent of their capital contributions. A situation in which shareholders are liable for the corporation's debts and obligations only to the extent of their capital contributions. Liability that shareholders of a corporation have, only to the extent of their capital contribution. Shareholders are generally not personally liable for debts and obligations of the corporation.

limited liability company (LLC) An unincorporated business entity that combines the most favorable attributes of general partnerships, limited partnerships, and corporations.

limited liability partnership (LLP) A form of partnership in which all partners are limited partners and there are no general partners.

limited partners Partners in a limited partnership who invest capital but do not participate in management and are not personally liable for partnership debts beyond their capital contribution.

limited partnership A special form of partnership that is formed only if certain formalities are followed. A limited partnership has both general and limited partners.

limited partnership agreement A document that sets forth the rights and duties of the general and limited partners, the terms and conditions regarding the operation, termination, and dissolution of the partnership, and so on.

limited-jurisdiction trial court A court that hears matters of a specialized or limited nature.

line of commerce Products or services that consumers use as substitutes. If an increase in the price of one product or service leads consumers to purchase another product or service, the two products are substitutes for each other.

liquidated damages Damages that are specified in a contract rather than determined by a court.

litigation The process of bringing, maintaining, and defending a lawsuit.

living will A will that a person makes before catastrophe strikes and he or she becomes unable to express it because of illness or accident, stipulating that his or her life is not to be prolonged indefinitely by artificial means.

long-arm statute A statute that extends a state's jurisdiction to nonresidents who were not served a summons within the state.

lost property Property that is left somewhere by the owner because of negligence, carelessness, or inadvertence.

mail fraud The use of mail to defraud another person.

mailbox rule A rule that states that an acceptance is effective when it is dispatched, even if it is lost in transmission.

maker of a note The party who makes a promise to pay (borrower).

mala in se Term describing crimes that are inherently evil, such as murder, rape, and other crimes against persons.

mala prohibita Term describing crimes that are not inherently evil but are prohibited by society; these include non-felony crimes against property, such as robbery.

manager-managed LLC An LLC that has designated in its articles of organization that it is a manager-managed LLC.

Marine Protection, Research, and Sanctuaries Act A federal statute enacted in 1972 that extends environmental protection to the oceans.

mark The collective name for trademarks, service marks, certification marks, and collective marks that all can be trademarked.

market extension merger A merger between two companies in similar fields whose sales do not overlap.

material breach A breach that occurs when a party renders inferior performance of his or her contractual duties.

materialman's lien A contractor's and laborer's lien that makes the real property to which improvements are being made become security for the payment of the services and materials for those improvements.

maximizing profits A theory of social responsibility that says a corporation owes a duty to take actions that maximize profits for shareholders.

mediation A form of ADR in which the parties choose a *neutral third party* to act as the mediator of the dispute.

Medical Device Amendments to the FDCA Amendments enacted in 1976 that gives the FDA authority to regulate medical devices and equipment.

meeting of the creditors A meeting of the creditors in a bankruptcy case that must occur not less than 10 days nor more than 30 days after the court grants an order for relief.

meeting the competition defense A defense stipulated in Section 2(b) that says that a seller may lawfully engage in price discrimination to meet a competitor's price.

member An owner of an LLC.

member-managed LLC An LLC that has not designated that it is a manager-managed LLC in its articles of organization.

mens rea "Evil intent"—the possession of the requisite state of mind to commit a prohibited act.

Merchant Court The separate set of courts established to administer the "law of merchants."

merger A situation in which one corporation is absorbed into another corporation and ceases to exist.

minor's duty of restoration A minor's obligation to return goods or property at the time of disaffirmance. As a general rule, a minor is obligated only to return the goods or property he or she has received from the adult in the condition they are in at the time of disaffirmance.

mirror image rule A rule that states that in order for there to be an acceptance, the offeree must accept the terms as stated in the offer.

misdemeanor A less serious crime than a felony; not inherently evil but prohibited by society. Many crimes against property are misdemeanors.

mislaid property Property that is voluntarily placed somewhere and then inadvertently forgotten by the owner.

misuse A defense that relieves a seller of product liability if the user *abnormally* misused the product. Products must be designed to protect against *foreseeable* misuse.

mitigation A situation in which a nonbreaching party is under a legal duty to avoid or reduce damages caused by a breach of contract.

mobile sources Sources of air pollution such as automobiles, trucks, buses, motorcycles, and airplanes.

monetary damages Financial damages that a nonbreaching party may recover from a breaching party whether the breach was minor or material.

monopoly power The power to control prices or exclude competition, measured by the market share the defendant possesses in the relevant market.

moral minimum A theory of social responsibility that says a corporation's duty is to make a profit while avoiding harm to others.

mortgage A collateral arrangement in which a real property owner borrows money from a creditor, who uses a deed as collateral for repayment of the loan.

motion for judgment on the pleadings A motion that alleges that if all the facts presented in the pleadings are taken as true, the party making the motion would win the lawsuit when the proper law is applied to these asserted facts.

motion for summary judgment A motion that asserts that there are no factual disputes to be decided by the jury; in this case, the judge can apply the proper law to the undisputed facts and decide the case without a jury. These motions are supported by affidavits, documents, and deposition testimony.

motivation test A test to determine the liability of the principal; if the agent's motivation in committing the intentional tort is to promote the principal's business, then the principal is liable for any injury caused by the tort.

multinational corporation A single economic unit composed of companies of different nationalities connected by shareholding, managerial control, or contractual agreement.

mutual benefit bailment A bailment for the mutual benefit of the bailor and bailee. The bailee owes a *duty of reasonable care* to protect the bailed property.

mutual mistake of fact A mistake made by both parties concerning a material fact that is important to the subject matter of the contract.

mutual mistake of value A mistake that occurs if both parties know the object of the contract but are mistaken as to its value.

mutual (reciprocal) wills Wills in which two or more testators execute separate wills leaving their property to each other on the condition that the survivor leave the remaining property on his or her death as agreed by the testators; also called reciprocal wills.

national courts The courts of individual nations.

National Labor Relations Board (NLRB) A federal administrative agency that oversees union elections, prevents employers and unions from engaging in illegal and unfair labor practices, and enforces and interprets certain federal labor laws.

necessaries of life The reasonable value of food, clothing, shelter, medical care, and other items considered necessary to the maintenance of life for which a minor must pay after he or she contracts for them.

negligence A tort related to defective products in which the defendant has breached a duty of due care and caused harm to the plaintiff. Failure of a corporate director or officer to exercise the duty of care while conducting the corporation's business.

negligence per se A tort in which the violation of a statute or an ordinance constitutes the breach of the duty of care.

negligent infliction of emotional distress A tort that permits a person to recover for emotional distress caused by the defendant's negligent conduct.

Noise Control Act A federal statute enacted in 1972 that authorizes the

EPA to establish noise standards for products sold in the United States.

noise pollution Unwanted sound from planes, manufacturing plants, motor vehicles, construction equipment, stereos, and the like.

nonattainment areas Regions that do not meet air quality standards.

noncompete clause An agreement whereby a person agrees not to engage in a specified business or occupation within a designated geographical area for a specified period of time following the sale.

nonconforming uses Uses and buildings that already exist in a zoned area that are permitted to continue even though they do not fit within new zoning ordinances.

noncupative will Oral will that is made before a witness during the testator's last illness.

nonprice vertical restraints Restraints of trade that are unlawful under Section 1 of the Sherman Act if their anticompetitive effects outweigh their procompetitive effects.

note A debt security with a maturity of five years or less.

note and deed of trust An alternative to a mortgage in some states.

novation An agreement that substitutes a new party for one of the original contracting parties and relieves the exiting party of liability on the contract.

Nuclear Waste Policy Act of 1982 A federal statute that says the federal government must select and develop a permanent site for the disposal of nuclear waste.

objective theory of contracts A theory that says that the intent to contract is judged by the reasonable person standard and not by the subjective intent of the parties.

obscene speech Speech that (1) appeals to the prurient interest, (2) depicts sexual conduct in a patently offensive way, and (3) lacks serious literary, artistic, political, or scientific value.

Occupational Safety and Health Act A federal act enacted in 1970 that promotes safety in the workplace.

offensive speech Speech that is offensive to many members of society. It is subject to time, place, and manner restrictions.

offer "The manifestation of willingness to enter into a bargain, so made as to justify another person in understanding that his assent to that bargain is invited and will conclude it." [*Restatement (Second) of Contracts* § 24]

offeree The party to whom an offer to enter into a contract is made.

offeror The party who makes an offer to enter into a contract.

officers Employees of a corporation who are appointed by the board of directors to manage the day-to-day operations of the corporation.

one-year rule A rule that states that an executory contract that cannot be performed by its own terms within one year of its formation must be in writing.

opening statements Statements made by the attorneys to the jury in which they summarize the factual and legal issues of the case.

operating agreement An agreement entered into by members that governs the affairs and business of the LLC and the relations among members, managers, and the LLC.

order for relief The filing of either a voluntary petition, an unchallenged involuntary petition, or a grant of an order after a trial of a challenged involuntary petition.

ordinances Laws enacted by local government bodies such as cities and municipalities, countries, school districts, and water districts.

ordinary bailments (1) Bailments for the sole benefit of the bailor, (2) bailments for the sole benefit of the bailee, and (3) bailments for the mutual benefit of the bailor and bailee.

organizational meeting A meeting that must be held by the initial directors of the corporation after the articles of incorporation are filed.

outside director A member of the board of directors who is not an officer of the corporation.

outstanding shares Shares of stock that are in shareholder hands.

pac-man tender offer An offer in which a corporation that is the target of a tender offer makes a *reverse tender offer* for the stock of the tender offeror.

palming off Unfair competition that occurs when a company tries to pass off one of its products as that of a rival.

panel A group of three WTO judges that hears trade disputes between member nations and issues a "panel report."

par value A value assigned to common shares by the corporation that sets the lowest price at which the shares may be issued by the corporation.

partially disclosed agency An agency that occurs if the agent discloses his or her agency status but does not reveal the principal's identity and the third party does not know the principal's identity from another source.

partnership Two or more natural or artificial (corporation) persons who have joined together to share ownership and profit or loss.

partnership agreement A written agreement that the partners sign; also called *articles of partnership.*

partnership at will A partnership with no fixed duration.

partnership for a term A partnership with a fixed duration.

past consideration A prior act or performance. Past consideration (e.g., prior acts) will not support a new contract. New consideration must be given.

patent Registration of an invention that is novel, useful, and nonobvious, as conferred by the United States Patent and Trademark Office.

patent infringement Unauthorized use of another's patent. A patent holder may recover damages and other remedies against a patent infringer.

payee of a check The party to whom the check is written.

payee of a draft The party who receives the money from a draft.

payee of a note The party to whom a promise to pay is made (lender).

penal codes A collection of criminal statutes.

***per capita* distribution** A distribution of the estate that makes each grandchild and great-grandchild of the deceased inherit equally with the children of the deceased.

per se rule A rule that is applicable to those restraints of trade considered inherently anticompetitive. Once this determination is made, the court will not permit any defenses or justifications to save it.

***per stirpes* distribution** A distribution of an estate that makes grandchildren and great-grandchildren of the deceased inherit by representation of their parent.

periodic tenancy A tenancy created when a lease specifies intervals at which payments are due but does not specify how long the lease is for.

permanent trustee A legal representative of the bankruptcy debtor's estate, usually an accountant or lawyer, who is elected at the first meeting of the creditors.

personal property Property that consists of tangible property, such as automobiles, furniture, and jewelry, and intangible property, such as securities, patents, and copyrights.

petitioner The party appealing the decision of an administrative agency.

petition for certiorari A petition asking the Supreme Court to hear one's case.

physical or mental examination Examinations that may be ordered by a court to determine the extent of a defendant's alleged injuries.

picketing The action of strikers walking in front of the employer's premises, carrying signs announcing their strike.

piercing the corporate veil A doctrine that says that if a shareholder dominates a corporation and misuses it for improper purposes, a court of equity can disregard the corporate entity and hold the shareholder personally liable for the corporation's debts and obligations.

plaintiff The party who files the complaint.

plaintiff's case The process by which the plaintiff introduces evidence to prove the allegations contained in his or her complaint.

plan of reorganization A plan that sets forth a proposed new capital structure for the debtor to have when it emerges from reorganization bankruptcy. The debtor has the exclusive right to file the first plan of reorganization; any party of interest may file a plan thereafter.

plant life and vegetation Real property that is growing in or on the surface of the land.

plea bargain An agreement by an accused to admit to a lesser crime than charged; in return, the government agrees to impose a lesser sentence than might have been obtained had the case gone to trial.

pleadings The paperwork that is filed with the court to initiate and respond to a lawsuit.

point sources Sources of water pollution such as paper mills, manufacturing plants, electric utility plants, and sewage plants.

police power The power of states to regulate private and business activity within their borders.

Postal Reorganization Act An act that makes the mailing of unsolicited merchandise an unfair trade practice.

posteffective period The period of time that begins when the registration statement becomes effective and runs until the issuer either sells all of the offered securities or withdraws them from sale.

potential competition theory A theory that reasons that the real or implied threat of increased competition keeps businesses more competitive. A merger that would eliminate this perception can be enjoined under Section 7.

potential reciprocity theory A theory that says that if Company A, which supplies materials to Company B, merges with Company C (which in turn gets its supplies from Company B), the newly merged company can coerce Company B into dealing exclusively with it.

power of attorney An express agency agreement that is often used to give an agent the power to sign legal documents on behalf of the principal.

precedent A rule of law established in a court decision. Lower courts must follow the precedent established by higher courts.

preemption doctrine The concept that federal law takes precedence over state or local law.

preemptive rights Rights that give existing shareholders the option of subscribing to new shares being issued in proportion to their current ownership interest.

preexisting duty Something a person is already under an obligation to do. A promise lacks consideration in the case of preexisting duty.

preferred stock A type of equity security that is given certain preferences and rights over common stock.

preferred stockholder A person who owns preferred stock.

prefiling period A period of time that begins when the issuer first contemplates issuing the securities and ends when the registration statement is filed. The issuer may not *condition* the market during this period.

Pregnancy Discrimination Act An amendment to Title VII that forbids employment discrimination because of "pregnancy, childbirth, or related medical conditions."

pretrial hearing A hearing before the trial in order to facilitate the settlement of a case. Also called a settlement conference.

pretrial motion A motion a party can make to try to dispose of all or part of a lawsuit prior to trial.

price-fixing A situation in which competitors in the same line of business agree to set the price of the goods or services they sell; raising, depressing, fixing, pegging, or stabilizing the price of a commodity or service.

principal A party who employs another person to act on his or her behalf.

principal–agent relationship A relationship in which an employer hires an employee and gives that employee authority to act and enter into contracts on his or her behalf.

principal–independent contractor relationship A relationship that results when a person or business that is not an employee is employed by a principal to perform a certain task on his or her behalf.

private placement exemption An exemption from registration that permits issuers to raise capital from an unlimited number of accredited investors and no more than 35 nonaccredited investors without having to register the offering with the SEC.

Private Securities Litigation Reform Act of 1995 An act that provides a safe harbor from liability for companies that make forward-looking statements that are accompanied by meaningful cautionary statements of risk factors.

Privileges and Immunities Clause A clause that prohibits states from enacting laws that unduly discriminate in favor of their residents.

probability of a substantial lessening of competition A probability that a merger will substantially lessen competition or create a monopoly that prompts the court to prevent the merger under Section 7 of the Clayton Act.

probable cause The substantial likelihood that the person either committed or is about to commit a crime.

probate (settlement of the estate) The process of a deceased's property being collected, debts and taxes paid, and the remainder of the estate distributed.

procedural due process A category of due process that requires that the government give a person proper notice and hearing of the legal action before that person is deprived of his or her life, liberty, or property.

processing plant franchise A franchise in which the franchisor provides a secret formula or process to the franchisee, and the franchisee manufactures the product and distributes it to retail dealers.

production of documents A request by one party to another party to produce all documents relevant to the case prior to trial.

products liability The liability of manufacturers, sellers, and others for the injuries caused by defective products.

professional malpractice The liability of a professional who breaches his or her duty of ordinary care.

promissory estoppel An equitable doctrine that permits enforcement of oral contracts that should have been in writing. It is applied to avoid injustice.

promissory note A two-party negotiable instrument that is an unconditional written promise by one party to pay money to another party.

proof of claim A document required to be filed by an unsecured creditor that states the amount of the creditor's claim against the debtor.

prosecutor The lawyer representing the government in a criminal lawsuit.

prospectus A written disclosure document that must be submitted to the SEC along with the registration statement and given to prospective purchasers of the securities.

proximate cause, or legal cause A point along a chain of events caused by a negligent party after which this party is no longer legally responsible for the consequences of his or her actions.

proxy The written document that a shareholder signs, authorizing another person to vote his or her shares at the shareholders' meetings in the event of the shareholder's absence.

public defender Attorney provided by the government to represent a defendant who cannot afford legal representation.

public-use doctrine A doctrine that says a patent may not be granted if the public used the invention for more than one year prior to filing of the patent application.

punitive damages Damages that are awarded to punish the defendant, to deter the defendant from similar conduct in the future, and to set an example for others.

purchasing property The most common method of acquiring title to personal property.

qualified individual with a disability A person who (1) has a physical or mental impairment that substantially limits one or more of his or her major life activities, (2) has a record of such impairment, or (3) is regarded as having such impairment.

quasi in rem jurisdiction Jurisdiction allowed a plaintiff who obtains a judgment in one state to try to collect the judgment by attaching property of the defendant located in another state.

quasi-contract An equitable doctrine whereby a court may award monetary damages to a plaintiff for providing work or services to a defendant even though no actual contract existed. An equitable doctrine that permits the recovery of compensation even though no enforceable contract exists between the parties.

quorum The required number of shares that must be represented in person or by proxy to hold a shareholder's meeting.

Racketeer Influenced and Corrupt Organizations Act (RICO) A federal statute that provides for both criminal and civil penalties for engaging in a pattern of racketeering activity.

radiation pollution Emissions from radioactive wastes that can cause injury and death to humans and other life and can cause severe damage to the environment.

ratification The act of a minor after the minor has reached the age of majority by which he or she accepts a contract entered into when he or she was a minor. A principal's acceptance of an agent's unauthorized contract.

rational basis test A test that is applied to classifications not involving a suspect or protected class.

Rawls's social justice theory A moral theory that says each person is presumed to have entered into a social contract with all others in society to obey moral rules that are necessary for people to live in peace and harmony.

real property The land itself as well as buildings, trees, soil, minerals, timber, plants, and other things permanently affixed to the land.

rebuttal Presentation of a case (calling witnesses and putting forth evidence) by the plaintiff's attorney to rebut the defendant's case.

receiving stolen property (1) Knowingly receiving stolen property and (2) intending to deprive the rightful owner of that property.

record The recorded summary of a trial court proceeding, including memorandum, trial transcript, and evidence produced at trial.

record date A date that determines whether a shareholder receives payment of a declared dividend.

recording statute A statute that requires the mortgage or deed of trust to be recorded in the county recorder's office in the county in which the real property is located.

recross examination An attorney asks questions of the witness, following direct examination, cross-examination, and redirect examination.

redeemable preferred stock Stock that permits the corporation to buy back the preferred stock at some future date.

redirect examination An attorney asks questions of the witness, following direct examination and cross-examination.

reformation An equitable doctrine that permits the court to rewrite a contract to express the parties' true intentions.

registration statement A document that an issuer of securities files with the SEC that contains required information about the issuer, the securities to be issued, and other relevant information.

regular meeting A meeting held by the board of directors at the time and place established in the bylaws.

rejection Express words or conduct by the offeree that rejects an offer. Rejection terminates the offer.

relevant geographical market A relevant market that is defined as the area in which the defendant and its competitors sell a product or service.

relevant product or service market A relevant market that includes substitute products or services that are reasonably interchangeable with the defendant's products or services.

religious discrimination Discrimination against a person solely because of his or her religion or religious practices.

remainder A situation in which the right of possession returns to a third party upon the expiration of a limited or contingent estate.

remainderman The person to receive the trust corpus upon termination of a trust.

replacement worker A worker who is hired to take the place of a striking worker. A replacement worker can be hired on either a temporary or permanent basis.

reply A document filed by the original plaintiff to answer the defendant's cross-complaint.

res ipsa loquitur A tort in which the presumption of negligence arises because (1) the defendant was in exclusive control of the situation and (2) the plaintiff would not have suffered injury but for someone's negligence. The burden switches to the defendant to prove that he or she was not negligent.

resale price maintenance A *per se* violation of Section 1 of the Sherman Act that occurs when a party at one level of distribution enters into an agreement with a party at another level to adhere to a price schedule that either sets or stabilizes prices.

rescission An action to rescind (undo) a contract. Rescission is available if there has been a material breach of contract, fraud, duress, undue influence, or mistake.

residuary gift Gift of the estate left after the debts, taxes, and specific and general gifts have been paid.

resolution A decision by the board of directors that approves a transaction.

Resource Conservation and Recovery Act (RCRA) A federal statute that authorizes the EPA to regulate facilities that generate, treat, store, transport, and dispose of hazardous wastes.

respondeat superior A rule that says an employer is liable for the tortious conduct of its employees or agents while they are acting within the scope of its authority.

restitution Returning of goods or property received from the other party in order to rescind a contract; if the actual goods or property is not available, a cash equivalent must be made.

restricted securities Securities that were issued for investment purposes pursuant to the intrastate, private placement, or small offering exemptions.

resulting trust A trust created by the conduct of the parties.

reverse discrimination Discrimination against a group that is usually thought of as a majority.

reversion A right of possession that returns to the grantor after the expiration of a limited or contingent estate.

Revised Model Business Corporation Act (RMBCA) A 1984 revision of the MBCA that arranged the provisions of the original act more logically, revised the language to be more consistent, and made substantial changes in the provisions.

Revised Uniform Limited Partnership Act (RULPA) A 1976 revision of the ULPA that provides a more modern, comprehensive law for the formation, operation, and dissolution of limited partnerships.

revocation Withdrawal of an offer by the offeror that terminates an offer.

right of redemption A right that the mortgagor has to redeem real property after default and before foreclosure. It requires the mortgagor to pay the full amount of the debt incurred by the mortgagee because of the mortgagor's default.

right to cure A right of a licensor to repair a contract under certain circumstances.

River and Harbor Act A federal statute enacted in 1886 that established a permit system for the discharge of refuse, wastes, and sewage into U.S. navigable waterways.

robbery The taking of personal property from another person by use of fear or force.

Rule 10b-5 A rule adopted by the SEC to clarify the reach of Section 10(b) against deceptive and fraudulent activities in the purchase and sale of securities.

rule of reason A rule that holds that only unreasonable restraints of trade violate Section 1 of the Sherman Act. The court must examine the pro- and anticompetitive effects of the challenged restraint.

rules and regulations A legislative function adopted by administrative agencies to interpret the statutes they are authorized to enforce.

Sabbath law A law that prohibits or limits the carrying on of certain secular activities on Sundays.

Safe Drinking Water Act A federal statute enacted in 1974 and amended in 1986 that authorizes the EPA to establish national primary drinking water standards.

scienter Intentional conduct that is required for there to be a violation of Section 10(b) and Rule 10b-5.

S corporations Corporations that elect to be taxed under the Subchapter S Revision Act (as opposed to C corporations, all other corporations).

search warrant A warrant issued by a court that authorizes the police to search a designated place for specified contraband, articles, items, or documents. The search warrant must be based on probable cause.

secondary boycott picketing A type of picketing in which unions try to bring pressure against an employer by picketing his or her suppliers or customers.

secondary meaning A brand name that has evolved from an ordinary term.

Section 1 of the Sherman Act An act that prohibits *contracts, combinations*, and *conspiracies* in restraint of trade. An act that prohibits tying arrangements involving goods, services, intangible property, and real property.

Section 10(b) A provision of the Securities Exchange Act of 1934 that prohibits the use of manipulative and deceptive devices in the purchase or sale of securities in contravention of the rules and regulations prescribed by the SEC.

Section 11 A provision of the Securities Act of 1933 that imposes civil liability on persons who intentionally defraud investors by making misrepresentations or omissions of material facts in the registration statement or who are negligent for not discovering the fraud.

Section 12 A provision of the Securities Act of 1933 that imposes civil liability on any person who violates the provisions of Section 5 of the act.

Section 14(e) A provision of the Williams Act that prohibits fraudulent, deceptive, and manipulative practices in connection with a tender offer.

Section 16(a) A section of the Securities Exchange Act of 1934 that defines any person who is an executive officer, a director, or a 10 percent shareholder of an equity security of a reporting company as a *statutory insider* for Section 16 purposes.

Section 16(b) A section of the Securities Exchange Act of 1934 that requires that any profits made by a statutory insider on transactions involving *short-swing profits* belong to the corporation.

Section 2 of the Sherman Act An act that prohibits the act of monopolization and attempts or conspiracies to monopolize trade.

Section 2(a) of the Robinson-Patman Act An act that prohibits direct and indirect price discrimination by sellers of a commodity of a like grade and quality where the effect of such discrimination may be to substantially lessen competition or to tend to create a monopoly in any line of commerce.

Section 24 A provision of the Securities Act of 1933 that imposes criminal liability on any person who willfully violates the act or the rules or regulations adopted thereunder.

Section 3 of the Clayton Act An act that prohibits tying arrangements involving sales and leases of goods.

Section 32 A provision of the Securities Exchange Act of 1934 that imposes criminal liability on any person who willfully violates the 1934 act or the rules or regulations adopted thereunder.

Section 5 of the Federal Trade Commission Act A portion of the FTC Act that prohibits unfair and deceptive practices.

Section 7 of the NLRA A law that gives employees the right to join together and form a union.

Section 8(a) of the NLRA A law that makes it an *unfair labor practice* for an employer to interfere with, coerce, or restrain employees from exercising their statutory right to form and join unions.

Section 8(b) of the NLRA A law that prohibits unions from engaging in unfair labor practices that interfere with a union election.

section of the country A division of the United States that is based on the relevant geographical market; the geographical area that will feel the direct and immediate effects of a merger.

secured credit Credit that requires security (collateral) that protects payment of the loan.

secured transaction A transaction that is created when a creditor makes a loan to a debtor in exchange for the debtor's pledge of personal property as security.

Securities and Exchange Commission (SEC) A federal administrative agency that is empowered to administer federal securities laws. The SEC can adopt rules and regulations to interpret and implement federal securities laws.

Securities Act of 1933 A federal statute that primarily regulates the issuance of securities by corporations, partnerships, associations, and individuals.

Securities Exchange Act of 1934 A federal statute that primarily regulates the trading in securities.

security (1) An interest or instrument that is common stock, preferred stock, a bond, a debenture, or a warrant; (2) an interest or instrument that is expressly mentioned in securities acts; and (3) an investment contract.

Self-Employment Contributions Act A federal act that says self-employed persons must pay Social Security taxes equal to the combined employer–employee amount.

self-incrimination The giving of testimony that will likely subject a person to criminal prosecution. The Fifth Amendment states that no person shall be compelled in any criminal case to be a witness against him- or herself.

service mark A mark that distinguishes the services of the holder from those of its competitors.

service of process A summons being served on the defendant to obtain personal jurisdiction over him or her.

settlor Person who creates a trust. Also termed *trustor* or *transferor*.

sex discrimination Discrimination against a person solely because of his or her sex.

sexual harassment Lewd remarks, touching, intimidation, posting of indecent material, and other verbal or physical conduct of a sexual nature that occur on the job.

shareholders The owners of corporations, whose ownership interests are evidenced by stock certificates.

short-form merger A merger between a parent corporation and a subsidiary corporation that does not require the vote of the shareholders of either corporation or the board of directors of the subsidiary corporation.

simultaneous deaths Under the Uniform Simultaneous Death Act, a provision that each deceased person's property is distributed as if he or she survived.

slander Oral defamation of character.

small claims court A court that hears civil cases involving small dollar amounts.

small offering exemption An exemption from registration that permits the sale of securities not exceeding $1 million during a 12-month period.

social host liability rule A rule that provides that social hosts are liable for injuries caused by guests who become intoxicated at a social function. States vary as to whether they have this rule in effect.

Social Security A federal system that provides limited retirement and death benefits to covered employees and their dependents.

sole proprietorship A form of business in which the owner is actually the business; the business is not a separate legal entity.

sources of international law Those things that international tribunals rely on in settling international disputes.

special federal courts Federal courts that hear matters of specialized or limited jurisdiction.

special meeting A meeting convened by the board of directors to discuss new shares, merger proposals, hostile takeover attempts, and so forth.

special power of attorney A type of power of attorney that limits the agent to acts specifically enumerated in an agreement.

special shareholders' meetings Meetings of shareholders that may be called to consider and vote on important or emergency issues, such as a proposed merger, amending the articles of incorporation, and such.

specific duty A duty of a specific nature (e.g., requirement for a safety guard on a particular type of equipment).

specific gift Testamentary gift of a specifically named piece of property.

specific performance A judgment of a court ordering a licensor to specifically perform a license by making the contracted-for unique information available to the licensee. A remedy that orders the breaching party to perform the acts promised in the contract. Specific performance is usually awarded in cases in which the subject matter is unique, such as in contracts involving land, heirlooms, paintings, and the like.

spendthrift trust A trust that removes all control over the trust from the beneficiary.

stakeholder interest A theory of social responsibility that says a corporation must consider the effects its actions have on persons other than its stockholders.

standing to sue The plaintiff must have some stake in the outcome of the lawsuit.

stare decisis Latin: "to stand by the decision." Adherence to precedent.

state action exemptions Exemptions in which business activities that are mandated by state law are exempt from federal antitrust laws.

state administrative agencies Administrative agencies that states create to enforce and interpret state law.

state antitakeover statutes Statutes enacted by state legislatures that protect from hostile takeovers corporations incorporated in or doing business in the state.

state supreme court The highest court in a state court system; it hears appeals from intermediate state courts and certain trial courts.

stationary sources Sources of air pollution such as industrial plants, oil refineries, and public utilities.

statute Written law enacted by the legislative branch of the federal and state governments that establishes certain courses of conduct that must be adhered to by covered parties.

statute of frauds A state statute that requires certain types of contracts to be in writing.

statute of limitations A statute that establishes the period during which a plaintiff must bring a lawsuit against a defendant. A statute that requires an injured person to bring an action within a certain number of years from the time that he or she was injured by the defective product.

statute of repose A statute that limits the seller's liability to a certain number of years from the date when the product was first sold.

statutory exemptions Exemptions from antitrust laws that are expressly provided in statutes enacted by Congress.

strict liability Liability without fault.

strict, or absolute, liability A standard for imposing criminal liability without a finding of *mens rea* (intent).

strict scrutiny test A test that is applied to classifications based on race.

strike A cessation of work by union members in order to obtain economic benefits or correct an unfair labor practice.

subject matter jurisdiction Jurisdiction over the subject matter of a lawsuit.

subpoena A court order.

substantial performance Performance by a contracting party that deviates only slightly from complete performance.

substantive due process A category of due process that requires that government statutes, ordinances, regulations, or other laws be clear on their face and not overly broad in scope.

substantive rules Government regulations that have the force of law and must be adhered to by the persons and businesses covered.

subsurface rights Rights to the earth located beneath the surface of the land.

summons A court order directing the defendant to appear in court and answer the complaint.

superseding event An intervening event for which a defendant is not responsible.

supervening event An alteration or a modification of a product by a party in the chain of distribution that absolves all prior sellers from strict liability.

supervening illegality The enactment of a statute or regulation or court decision that makes the object of an offer illegal. This terminates the offer.

supramajority voting requirement A requirement that a greater than majority of shares constitutes quorum for the vote of the shareholders.

Supreme Court of the United States The Supreme Court was created by Article III of the U.S. Constitution. The Supreme Court is the highest court in the land. It is located in Washington, DC.

Supremacy Clause A clause of the U.S. Constitution that establishes that the federal Constitution, treaties, federal laws, and federal regulations are the supreme law of the land.

surety arrangement An arrangement in which a third party promises to be *primarily* liable with the borrower for the payment of the borrower's debt.

taking possession A method of acquiring ownership of unowned personal property.

tangible property Physically defined personal property, such as goods, animals, and minerals.

tangible writing Writing that can be physically seen.

target corporation The corporation that is proposed to be acquired in a tender offer situation.

tenancy at sufferance A tenancy created when a tenant retains possession of property after the expiration of another tenancy or a life estate without the owner's consent.

tenancy at will A lease that may be terminated at any time by either party.

tenancy by the entirety A form of co-ownership of real property that can be used only by married couples.

tenancy for years A tenancy created when the landlord and the tenant agree on a specific duration for the lease.

tenancy in common A form of co-ownership in which the interest of a surviving tenant in common passes to the deceased tenant's estate and not to the co-tenants.

tender offer An offer that an acquirer makes directly to a target corporation's shareholders in an effort to acquire the target corporation.

tender offeror The party that makes a tender offer.

termination by acts of the parties Termination of an agency that can occur by the following acts of the parties: (1) mutual agreement, (2) lapse of time, (3) purpose achieved, and (4) occurrence of a specified event.

termination by operation of law An agency's termination by operation of law, including: (1) death of the principal or agent, (2) insanity of the principal or agent, (3) bankruptcy of the principal, (4) impossibility of performance, (5) changed circumstances, and (6) war between the principal's and agent's countries.

testamentary capacity The Statute of Wills requirement that the testator must have been of legal age and "sound mind."

thermal pollution Pollution created by heated water or material being discharged into waterways. It upsets the ecological balance and decreases the oxygen content.

time note A note payable at a specific time.

tippee A person who receives material nonpublic information from a tipper.

tipper A person who discloses material nonpublic information to another person.

Title I of the Landrum-Griffin Act An act that is referred to as labor's "bill of rights" that gives each union member equal rights and privileges to nominate candidates for union office, vote in elections, and participate in membership meetings.

Title VII of the Civil Rights Act of 1964 (Fair Employment Practices Act) An act that is intended to eliminate job discrimination based on five protected classes: race, color, religion, sex, and national origin.

tort A wrong. There are three categories of torts: (1) intentional torts, (2) unintentional torts (negligence), and (3) strict liability.

tort of misappropriation of the right to publicity An attempt by another person to appropriate a living (and in some states dead) person's name or identity for commercial purposes.

Totten trust A trust created when a person deposits money in a bank account in his or her own name and holds it as a trustee for the benefit of another person.

toxic air pollutants Air pollutants that cause serious illness or death to humans.

toxic substances Chemicals used for agricultural, industrial, and mining uses that cause injury to humans, birds, animals, fish, and vegetation.

Toxic Substances Control Act A federal statute enacted in 1976 that requires manufacturers and processors to test new chemicals to determine their effect on human health and the environment before the EPA will allow them to be marketed.

trade dress Federal protection of the look and feel of a product, a product's packaging, or a service establishment.

trade secret A product formula, pattern, design, compilation of data, customer list, or other business secret. Ideas that make a franchise successful but that do not qualify for trademark, patent, or copyright protection.

trademark A distinctive mark, symbol, name, word, motto, or device that identifies the goods of a particular business.

trademark infringement Unauthorized use of another's mark. The holder may recover damages and other remedies from the infringer.

trademarks and service marks Distinctive marks, symbols, names, words, mottoes, or devices that identify the goods or services of a particular franchisor.

treasury shares Shares of stock repurchased by the company itself.

treaty A compact made between two or more nations. The first source of international law, consisting of an agreement or a contract between two or more nations that are formally signed by an authorized representative and ratified by the supreme power of each nation.

Treaty Clause A clause of the U.S. Constitution that states the president "shall have the power . . . to make treaties, provided two-thirds of the senators present concur."

trespass to land A tort in which a person interferes with an owner's right to exclusive possession of land.

trespass to personal property A tort that occurs whenever one person injures another person's personal property or interferes with that person's enjoyment of his or her personal property.

trial briefs Documents submitted by the parties' attorneys to the judge that contain legal support for their sides of the case.

trier of fact The jury in a jury trial; the judge where there is not a jury trial.

trust A legal arrangement established when a person (trustor) transfers title to property to another person (trustee) to be managed for the benefit of specifically named persons (beneficiaries).

trust corpus (*trust res.*) The property held in trust. Also termed *trust res.*

trustee (1) Holder of legal title of the real property in a deed of trust and note transaction. (2) Person who holds legal title to trust corpus and manages the trust for the benefit of the beneficiary(ies).

tying arrangement A restraint of trade in which a seller refuses to sell one product to a customer unless the customer agrees to purchase a second product from the seller.

UCC statute of frauds A provision for contracts that says that the sale of *goods* costing $500 or more must be in writing.

U.S. Constitution The fundamental law of the United States of America. It was ratified by the states in 1788.

U.S. courts of appeals The federal court system's intermediate appellate courts.

U.S. district courts The federal court system's trial courts of general jurisdiction.

unconscionability A doctrine under which courts may deny enforcement of unfair or oppressive contracts.

undisclosed agency An agency that occurs when the third party is unaware of either (1) the existence of an agency, or (2) the principal's identity.

undue influence One person's taking advantage of another person's mental, emotional, or physical weakness and unduly persuading that person to enter into a contract; the persuasion by the wrongdoer must overcome the free will of the innocent party.

unenforceable contract A contract in which the essential elements to create a valid contract are met but there is some legal defense to the enforcement of the contract.

unfair advantage theory A theory that holds that a merger may not give the acquiring firm an unfair advantage over its competitors in finance, marketing, or expertise.

unfair competition Competition that violates the law.

Uniform Computer Information Transactions Act (UCITA) A model act that provides uniform and comprehensive rules for contracts involving computer information transactions and software and information licenses. A model state law that creates contract law for the licensing of information technology rights.

Uniform Franchise Offering Circular (UFOC) A uniform disclosure document that requires the franchisor to make specific presale disclosures to prospective franchisees.

Uniform Limited Liability Company Act (ULLCA) A model act that provides comprehensive and uniform laws for the formation, operation, and dissolution of LLCs.

Uniform Partnership Act (UPA) A model act that codifies partnership law. Most states have adopted the UPA in whole or part.

Uniform Probate Code (UPC) A model law promulgated to establish consistent rules for the creation of wills, administration of estates, and resolution of conflicts in settling estates.

unilateral contract A contract in which the offeror's offer can be accepted only by the performance of an act by the offeree, a "promise for an act."

unilateral mistake A situation in which only one party is mistaken about a material fact regarding the subject matter of a contract.

unilateral refusal to deal A unilateral choice by one party not to deal with another party. This does not violate Section 1 of the Sherman Act because there is not concerted action.

unintentional tort or negligence A doctrine that says a person is liable for harm that is the foreseeable consequence of his or her actions.

union shop An establishment in which an employee must join the union within a certain number of days after being hired.

unprotected speech Speech that is not protected by the First Amendment and may be forbidden by the government.

unreasonable search and seizure Any search and seizure by the government that violates the Fourth Amendment.

unsecured credit Credit that does not require any security (collateral) to protect the payment of the debt.

U.S. Constitution Fundamental law of the United States of America; ratified by the states in 1788.

U.S. Supreme Court Court created by Article III of the U.S. Constitution; the highest court in the land, located in Washington, D.C.

usury law A law that sets an upper limit on the interest rate that can be charged on certain types of loans.

utilitarianism A moral theory that dictates that people must choose the action or follow the rule that provides the greatest good to society.

valid contract A contract that meets all the essential elements to establish a contract; a contract that is enforceable by at least one of the parties.

variance An exception that permits a type of building or use in an area that would not otherwise be allowed by a zoning ordinance.

venue A concept that requires lawsuits to be heard by the court with jurisdiction that is nearest the location in which the incident occurred or where the parties reside.

verdict The decision reached by the jury.

vertical merger A merger that integrates the operations of a supplier and a customer.

vertical restraint of trade A restraint of trade that occurs when two or more parties on different levels of distribution enter into a contract, combination, or conspiracy to restrain trade.

violation A crime that is neither a felony nor a misdemeanor and that is usually punishable by a fine.

void contract A contract that has no legal effect; a nullity.

voidable contract A contract in which one or both parties have the option to void their contractual obligations.

voir dire A process whereby prospective jurors are asked questions by the judge and attorneys to determine if they would be biased in their decisions.

voluntary petition A petition filed by the debtor, which states that the debtor has debts.

waiting period A period of time that begins when the registration statement is filed with the SEC and continues until the registration statement is declared effective. Only certain activities are permissible during the waiting period.

warranties of quality Seller's or lessor's assurance to the buyer or lessee that the goods meet certain standards of quality. Warranties may be expressed or implied.

warranty A buyer's or lessee's assurance that the goods meet certain standards.

water pollution Pollution of lakes, rivers, oceans, and other bodies of water.

wetlands Areas that are inundated or saturated by surface water or ground water that support vegetation typically adapted for life in such conditions.

white-collar crimes Crimes usually involving cunning and deceit rather than physical force.

will A declaration of how a person wants his or her property distributed upon death.

will or inheritance A way to acquire title to property that is a result of another's death.

Williams Act A 1968 amendment to the Securities Exchange Act of 1934 that specifically regulates all tender offers.

wire fraud Use of the telephone or telegraph to defraud another person.

witness An individual asked to testify in court, under oath.

Work product doctrine A qualified immunity from discovery for "work product of the lawyer" except on a substantial showing of "necessity or justification" of certain written statements and memoranda prepared by counsel in representation of a client, generally in preparation for trial.

workers' compensation Protection for workers providing compensation for injuries that occur on the job.

work-related test A test to determine the liability of a principal; if an agent commits an intentional tort within a work-related time or space, the principal is liable for any injury caused by the agent's intentional tort.

World Trade Organization (WTO) An international organization of more than 130 member nations created to promote and enforce trade agreements among member nations.

World Wide Web An electronic connection of millions of computers that support a standard set of rules for the exchange of information.

writ of certiorari An official notice that the Supreme Court will review one's case.

wrongful dissolution A partner's withdrawal from a partnership when he or she does not have the right to do so.

wrongful termination Termination of a franchise without just cause. The termination of an agency contract in violation of the terms of the agency contract. The nonbreaching party may recover damages from the breaching party.

zoning ordinances Local laws that are adopted by municipalities and local governments to regulate land use within their boundaries. Zoning ordinances are adopted and enforced to protect the health, safety, and general welfare of the community.

Case Index

Acuson Corp. v. Aloka Co., Ltd., 383
Alden v. Presley, 160
Allison v. ITE Imperial Corporation, 45
Amazon.com, Inc. v. Barnesandnoble.com, Inc., 364
Anheuser-Busch, Inc. v. Schmoke, 44
Anna J. v. Mark C., 221
Atwater v. City of Lago Vista, Texas, 74
Baker v. State of Vermont, 218
Billy v. USM Corporation, 299
Blyth v. Birmingham Waterworks Co., 131
Bobby Floars Toyota, Inc. v. Smith, 184
Boury v. Ford Motor Company, 54
Braun v. Soldier of Fortune Magazine, Inc., 149
Brooks v. Magnaverde Corporation, 45
Brown v. Board of Education, 6
Brumfield v. Death Row Records, Inc., 178
Burnham v. Superior Court of California, 66
Bush v. Gore, 35
Carnival Cruise Lines, Inc. v. Shute, 38
Carnival Leisure Industries, Ltd. v. Aubin, 183
Center Art Galleries–Hawaii, Inc. v. United States, 97
Chadwick v. Janecka, Warden, Delaware County Prison, Pennsylvania, 238
Chapman v. Chapman, 260
Chelsea Industries, Inc. v. Gaffney, 299
Cheong v. Antablin, 139
Church of Lukumi Babalu Aye, Inc. v. City of Hialeah, Florida, 108
Cipollone v. Liggett Group, Inc., 103
The Coca-Cola Company v. Net, 383
Conrad v. Delta Airlines, Inc., 66
Couch v. U.S., 85
Crisci v. Security Insurance Company of New Haven, Connecticut, 184
Cruzan v. Director, Missouri Department of Health, 250
Cunningham v. Hastings, 198
Dees, d/b/a David Dees Illustration v. Saban Entertainment, Inc., 157
Dewsnup v. Timm, 358
Dickerson v. United States, 86
Dothard, Director, Department of Public Safety of Alabama v. Rawlinson, 332
E. & J. Gallo Winery v. Spider Webs Ltd., 376
Exxon Oil Company v. BluePeace.org, 384
Fax.com, Inc. v. United States, 109
Federal Communications Commission v. Pacifica Foundation, 121
Federal Trade Commission v. Colgate-Palmolive Co., 394
Feist Publications, Inc. v. Rural Telephone Service Co., Inc., 382
Ferlito v. Johnson & Johnson Products, Inc., 57
Flagiello v. Pennsylvania, 12
Flood v. Fidelity & Guaranty Life Insurance Co., 163
FMC Corp. v. U.S. Department of Commerce, 410
Forsyth County Memorial Hospital Authority, Inc., 359
G.A. Modefine S.A. v. A.R. Mani WIPO, 377
Geier v. American Honda Motor Co., Inc., 102
General Electric Credit Corporation v. Stover, 271
General Motors Acceptance Corporation v. Daniels, 344
Giha v. Giha, 225
Gnazzo v. G.D. Searle & Co., 65
Gratz v. Bollinger and the Regents of the University of Michigan, 14
Greenmun v. Yuba Power Products, Inc., 140, 141
Grinder v. Bryans Road Building & Supply Co., Inc., 332
Grutter v. Bollinger and The University of Michigan Law School, 15
Guinnane v. San Francisco City Planning Commission, 205
Gupta v. Florida Bd of Regents, 331
Harris v. Forklift Systems, Inc., 25, 320, 322
Harris v. Time, Inc., 45
Haviland & Co., Incorporated v. Montgomery Ward & Co., 66
Heart of Atlanta Motel v. United States, 121
Hill v. Pinelawn Memorial Park, Inc., 212
Holiday Inns, Inc. v. Shelburne, 308
Huddleston v. Roger Dean Chevrolet, Inc., 332
In Re Air Florida System, Inc., 359
In Re Baby M, 221
In Re Estate of Potter, 260
In Re Estate of Vallerius, 259
In Re Greenbelt Cooperative, Inc., 342
In Re Tabala, 359
In Re Witwer, 348
In the Matter of Sunstate Dairy & Food Products Co., 336
In the Matter of the Estate of Jansa, 260

In the Matter of the Estate of Reed, 243
International Shoe Co. v. Washington, 37, 39
Jacobellis v. Ohio, 108
James v. Meow Media, Inc., 135
Johnson v. Kmart Enterprises, Inc., 150
Johnston v. Johnston, 237
Jones v. Jones, 260
Karns v. Emerson Electric Co., 150
Kawaauhau v. Geiger, 350
Kinney Shoe Corp. v. Polan, 283
Kyllo v. United States, 84
Largey v. Intrastate Radiotelephone, Inc., 332
Lee v. Weisman, 120
Lim v. The TV Corporation International, 171
Liz Claiborne, Inc. v. Avon Products, Inc., 184
Love v. Monarch Apartments, 212
Lundy v. Farmers Group, 173
Luque v. McLean, Trustee, 151
Mainstream Marketing Services, Inc. v. Federal Trade Commission, 389
Manning v. Grimsley, 150
Martin v. McDonald's Corporation, 290
Marvin v. Marvin, 231
MBank El Paso v. Sanchez, 314
Meinhard v. Salmon, 285
Meritor Savings Bank v. Vinson, 329
Miller v. California, 108
Miranda v. Arizona, 86
Naab v. Nolan, 212
National Association for the Advancement of Colored People, Newark Branch v. Town of Harrison, New Jersey, 319
National Lumber Company v. Advance Development Corp., 299
Nestlé Company, Inc. v. Chester's Market, Inc., 371
Neville v. Neville, 237
New York Times Co. v. Sullivan, 128
Newton v. Beastie Boys, 368
Norgart v. The Upjohn Company, 52
Nurrilab, Inc. v. Schweiker, 45
Opperman v. Anderson, 245
Palsgraf v. Long Island Railroad Co., 125, 133
Penny v. Little, 9
People v. Paulson, 97
People v. Shaw, 97
PGA Tour, Inc. v. Martin, 17, 18–23
Pizza Hut, Inc. v. Papa John's International, Inc., 32
Ray, Governor of Washington v. Atlantic Richfield Co., 121
Reddaway v. Banham, 385
Reno v. American Civil Liberties Union, 111
Reno v. Tyra, 164
Reno, Attorney General of the United States v. Condon, Attorney General of South Carolina, 105
Roach v. Stern, 130
Robinson v. Jacksonville Shipyards, Inc., 331
Robison v. Graham, 249
Roe v. Wade, 7
Rostker, Director of the Selective Service v. Goldberg, 26
Roux Laboratories, Inc. v. Clairol, Inc., 383
S&D Petroleum Company, Inc. v. Tamsett, 359
Schalk v. Texas, 96
Schweinberg v. Click, 237
Securities and Exchange Commission v. Edwards, 397
Shoshone Coca-Cola Bottling Co. v. Dolinski, 143
Sierra Club v. Morton, Secretary of the Interior, 402
Simblest v. Maynard, 66
Singer v. Microhard.com, LLC et al., 299
Sisters of Charity of the Incarnate Word v. Meaux, 191
Smith v. Workers' Compensation Appeals Board, 317
Souders v. Johnson, 212
Standefer v. United States, 6
Swierkiewicz v. Sorema N.A., 50
Tennessee Valley Authority v. Hill, Secretary of the Interior, 403
Troxel v. Granville, 236
United States v. Capital City Foods, Inc., 391
United States v. Carpenter, 411
United States v. Eichman, 122
United States v. Gel Spice Co., Inc., 411
United States v. Hoflin, 411
United States v. Hughes Aircraft Company, Inc., 79
United States v. John Doe, 97
United States v. Lopez, 104
United States v. Playboy Entertainment Group, Inc., 110
United States v. Reserve Mining Co., 411
United States v. WRW Corporation, 298
Virginia State Board of Pharmacy v. Virginia Citizens Consumer Council, Inc., 107
Vizcaino v. United States District Court for the Western District of Washington, 315
W.C. Ritchie & Co. v. Wayman, 26
Wackenhut Corporation and Delta Airlines, Inc. v. Lippert, 211
Walgreen Co. v. Sara Creek Property Co., 185
Walker v. Ayres, 201
Wallace v. Jaffree, 108
Wal-Mart Stores, Inc. v. Goodman, 127
Wal-Mart Stores, Inc. v. Samara Brothers, Inc., 88
Wickard, Secretary of Agriculture v. Filburn, 104
Willsmore v. Township of Oceola, Michigan, 190
Witt v. Miller, 200
Wrench LLC v. Taco Bell Corporation, 158
Zippo Manufacturing Company v. Zippo Dot Com, Inc., 39
Zuckerman v. Antenucci, 268

Subject Index

Abandoned property, 189–190
Abatement, 244
Absolute liability, 72
Acceptance, 156
Accommodation party, 343
Accountant-client privilege, 85
Accounting firms, as LLPs, 273
Actual cause, 132
Actual contracts, 156
Actus reus, 71
ADA, 323
ADEA, 321–323
Ademption, 244
Administrative agencies, 12, 13, 99, 113–115, 385, 387 (*see also* Administrative law)
  consumer protection and, 388–404 (*see also* Consumer protection)
  federal, 113, 387
  licensing power of, 387
  powers of, 115
  state, 114, 387
Administrative law, 114–115, 385–412
Administrative law judges (ALJ), 388
Administrative Procedure Act (APA), 115, 388
Administrator/administratix, 250
Admiralty, 36
Adoption, 221–222
Adulterated food, 388, 390
Adverse possession, real property and, 199, 200
Advertising, false and misleading, 393
Affirmative action, 14–15
Affirmative defenses, 49
Age discrimination, 321–323
Age Discrimination in Employment Act, 321–323
Agencies, administrative, *see* Administrative agencies
Agency, 302–313
  apparent, 305
  contract, 312–313
  by estoppel, *see* Apparent agency
  express, 304–305
  fully disclosed, 307
  implied, 305
  partially disclosed, 307
  by ratification, 307
  termination of contract, 312–313
  undisclosed, 309
Agency adoption, 221–222
Agent, 302–313 (*see also* Agency; Principal)
  exceeding authority, 309
  signature of, 309
  acting through, 81
Aggravated robbery, 75
Agreement, 154, 155–157
  franchise, 288
  limited partnership, 270
  operating, 272
  partnership, 266–267
  security, 341
  written, 270
Aiding and abetting, 81
Air navigation requirements, 193
Air pollution, 399
Air rights, real property and, 193
Air-space parcel, property rights and, 193
Alien corporations, 277
Alimony, 229–230
Alter-ego doctrine, 282
Alternative dispute resolution (ADR), 47, 58–60
Amazon.com, 364
Amendment, articles of, 278
American Inventors Protection Act, 364
American Revolution, 99
Americans with Disabilities Act (ADA), 323
Analytical School of jurisprudence, 6, 8
Animals, as endangered species, 402
Annulment, 223
Answer to complaint, 48, 49
Antenuptial agreements, 230
Anticybersquatting Consumer Protection Act, 376
Antideficiency statutes, 339
Anti-spam statute, 393
Antitrust, 36
Appalachian Trail, 402
Apparent agency, 305
Appeal, 58
  of administrative agency rule or decision, 116
Appellant, 13
Appellate courts, *see* Courts of appeal
Appellee, 13
Appropriate bargaining unit, unions and, 324
Arbitration:
  clauses, 58
  decision, 58
Arbitrator, 58
Army Corps of Engineers, 401
Arraignment, 72, 73–74
Arrangement:
  guaranty, 343
  surety, 343
Arrest, 72, 73
  warrant, 73
  warrantless, 73
Article 2 (Sales) of Uniform Commercial Code, 175
Article 2A (Leases) of Uniform Commercial Code, 176
Article 9 of the Uniform Commercial Code, 340
Articles of amendment, 278
Articles of Confederation, 101
Articles of:
  limited liability partnership, 271
  limited partnership, 270
  organization, 272
  partnership, 266–267
Articles of incorporation, 276, 277–278, 279
  amendment of, 278
  failure to file, 277
Artisan's lien, 343
Assault, 126
Assets, marriage termination and, 227
Assignment, of rights, 166–168
Associate justices, 31
Assumption of the risk, 138
Attachment jurisdiction, 37
Attempt to commit a crime, 81
Attestation, 240
Attorney:
  defense, 70
  district, 70
  fees, payment of, 53
  power of, 305, 306
Attorney-client privilege, 85
Attorney-in-fact, 305
Authority:
  implied warranty of, 309
  incidental, 305
  renunciation/revocation of, 313
Authority of courts, 36–37, 40
Automatic stay, suspension of creditor actions, 346
Award, 58

Bad check legislation, 77
Bailee, 188, 190, 192

Bailment, 190–192
  mutual-benefit, 192
  vs. gift, 190
Bailor, 190
Bait and switch, 393
Bald Eagle Protection Act, 402
Bankruptcy, 36, 335–336, 343–352
  Chapter 11, 351–353
  Chapter 13, 351
  Chapter 7, 345–350
  Enron and, 89
  estate, 346–349
  law, 343–352
  liquidation, 345
Bankruptcy Amendments and Federal Judgeship Act of 1984, 345
Bankruptcy Code, 345–352
Bankruptcy court, U.S., 30
Bankruptcy Reform Act of 1978, 343
Banks, hiding money in offshore, 86
Barclays Business Credit, Inc., 336
Bargaining, collective, 324
Battery, 126
Beastie Boys, 368
Bench trial, 55
Beneficiaries, 239, 248, 250–251, 253, 254 (*see also* Trusts, Wills)
  creditor as, 338
  income, 252
  third-party, 168
Bequest, 242, 248 (*see also* Gift)
BFOQ, discrimination and, 320
Bill of Rights, 101, 106
Biosafety Protocol, 392
Bioterrorism, 87
Board of directors:
  inside director, 282
  of corporations, 276–277, 282–284
  outside director, 282
  regular meetings of, 284
  special meetings of, 284
Bona fide occupational qualification (BFOQ), 320
Booking, 73
Borrower, 335
Branches of government, 100
Breach of contract:
  material, 170
  minor, 169
Breach of the duty of care, 132
Bribery, 70, 78–79
Brief, 28
  opening, 58
  responding, 58
  trial, 55
Briefing a case, 16–23
Browsers, Internet, 373
Buildings, 193
Burden of proof, 55, 69, 73
Burglary, 75
Bush, George H., 34
Bush, George W., 11
Business:
  crimes affecting, 75–80
  profits, 265–266
  subject to laws, 3
Business judgment rule, 285–288
Business organizations, 263–299
  corporations, 273–290
  general partnership, 264–268
  limited liability company (LLCs), 271–273, 274, 275, 276
  limited liability partnership (LLP), 270–271, 272, 273
  limited partnership, 268–270
  sole proprietorship, 264–265
Bylaws, corporate, 278–279, 280

Cancel a contract, 159
CAN-SPAM Act, 393
Care and diligence, 285
Case:
  briefing, 16–23
  name, 17, 18, 22
  trial, 55–56
Causation, 132–134
  in fact, 132–133
  proximate cause, 133
Caveat emptor, 388
C Corporations, 281
Centralized management, of corporations, 276
Certificate of limited partnership, 269
Certificate of recordation, 367
Certification marks, 370
Chain of distribution, 141
Chancery Court, 9–10, 30
Chapter 11 bankruptcy, 351–353
  Enron and, 89
Chapter 13 bankruptcy, 351
  vs. Chapter 7, 351
Chapter 7 bankruptcy, 345–350
  vs. Chapter 13, 351
Character, defamation of, 127–128
Charitable trusts, 253
Charter, corporate, 277
Checks and balances, 101
Check-the-Box Regulations, 272
Chicago School, 8
Chief Justice, 31
Child abuse, 220
Child, 219–222
  adopted, 221–222
  custody, 224–227
  neglect, 220
  support, 228–229
China, Constitution of, 114
Chips, computer, 367
Chrysler, 365
Cigarette companies, 101
Circuit courts, 28–31
Citation, 17, 18, 22
Citizenship, diversity of, 35
Civil law system, 10
Civil litigation, 47–58 (*see also* Litigation)
Civil Rights Act of 1964, 7, 318–321, 323
Civil tort action, 72
Claims court, U.S., 30
Clean Air Act, 399
Clean Air Act Amendments of 1990, 399
Clean Water Act, 400
Clinton, Bill, 34
Closing argument, 56
Code:
  bankruptcy, 345–352
  corporation, 277
  limited liability company, 272
Codebtor, 343
Codicil, 240
Codified law, 11, 13
Cohabitation, 231
  agreement, 231
Colgate-Palmolive, 394
Collateral, 335, 336
  possession of, 341
Collective bargaining, 324
Collective marks, 370
Color, employment discrimination and, 318
Coming and going rule, negligence and, 311
Command School of jurisprudence, 7, 8
Commerce Clause, 104, 106
  Foreign, 107
Commerce, interstate/intrastate, 104
Commercial speech, 107
Committee on Corporate Laws of the American Bar Association, 277
Common carriers, liability of, 138
Common law marriage, 219
Common stock, 281–282
  certificate, 282
Common stockholders, 282
Community property, 196, 228
Companies:
  bylaws of, 278–279, 280
  corporations, 273–290
  general partnership, 264–268
  limited liability company (LLCs), 271–273, 274, 275, 276
  limited liability partnership (LLP), 270–271, 272, 273
  limited partnership, 268–270
  organization of, 263–299
  sole proprietorship, 264–265
Comparative negligence, 140
Compensation, worker's, 315–316
Compensatory damages, 170, 172
Complaint, 48–49
Complete performance, 169
Composition, for reduction of debts, 351
Comprehensive Environmental Response, Compensation, and Liability Act (CERCLA), 401
Computer:
  crime, 81
  free speech and, 111

software, copyright of, 367
spam control and, 393
Uniform Transactions Act, 176
Computer Decency Act, 111
Computer Software Copyright Act, 367
Conciliation, 58, 59
Conciliator, 59
Concurrent jurisdiction, 35–36
Concurrent ownership:
community property, 196
condominiums, 196–197
cooperative, 197
joint tenancy, 194–195
real property and, 194–197
tenancy by the entirety, 196
tenancy in common, 195
Concurring opinion, 34
Conditions precedent, 169
Condominiums, 196–197
Confirmation, of the plan of reorganization, 352
Consequential (special) damages, 172
Consideration, 154, 157, 159
Consolidation, 49
Conspiracy, criminal, 81
Constitution of the United States, *see* U.S. Constitution
Constitution, of People's Republic of China, 114
Constitutional Convention, 101
Constitutional law, 99–122 (*see also* U.S. Constitution)
Bill of Rights, 101, 106–108
separation of powers, 100
Constitutional safeguards, 82–85
Constitutional violations, 104
Constitutions, 13 (*see also* U.S. Constitution)
Constructive notice, real property and, 197
Constructive trusts, 253
Consumer debt adjustment, *see* Chapter 13 bankruptcy
Consumer lease, 176
Consumer Product Safety Act (CPSA), 391
Consumer Product Safety Commission (CPSC), 391
Consumer protection, 388–404
Anticybersquatting Act, 376
environmental, 398–402
investors and, 395–398 (*see* Investor protection)
labeling and, 390
product safety, 391–392
regulations of drugs, 390
Contingency fees, 53
Continuation statement, 341
Contractors, independent, 303, 313–315
Contracts, 153–185
actual, 156
agency, 312–313
agreement and, 154, 155–157
assignment of rights, 166–168
capacity and, 154, 159, 161
concerning real property, 162
consideration, 154, 157, 159
contrary to public policy, 162
damages, *see* Damages
definition of, 154
evolution of modern law, 155
exclusive agency, 305
executory, 162, 352
express, 156
for the sale of goods, 164
franchises and, 288
illegal, 161–162
implied-in-fact, 156–157, 304
lawful object and, 154, 161–162
liability, 307, 309
minors and, 159
nondisclosure, 161
of adhesion, 165
option, 156
parties to, 154
performance of, 169–170
remedies, 170, 172–174 (*see also* Damages)
required signature, 165
third parties to, 307, 309
third-party beneficiaries, 168
UCC, *see* Uniform Commercial Code
unconscionable, 165
writing requirement, 162–166
Contractual capacity, 154, 159, 161
Contributory negligence, 140
Control, degree of, 313
Controlling the Assault of Non-Solicited Pornography and Marketing Act, 393
Covenants, 169
Cooling-off period, strikes and, 325
Cooperative, 197
Co-ownership, *see* Concurrent ownership
Copyright Revision Act of 1976, 366
Copyright, 36, 366–369
fair-use doctrine, 367
infringement on, 367
Corporate:
bylaws, 278–279, 280
charter, 277
criminal liability, 81
governance, rules of, 286–287
name, 278
officers, 277, 284–285
Corporations, 273–290
amending, 278
board of directors of, 276–277
centralized management of, 276
classification of, 277
codes, 277
common stock and, 281–282
hierarchy of, 275
as legal entities, 274
multinational, 287
organizational meeting of, 279–281
ownership of, 273, 282
shareholders of, 273, 276
termination of, 276
Corpus Juris Civilis, 10
Cosigner, 343
Cosmetics, regulation of, 390
Cost-benefit analysis, 49
Council on Environmental Quality, 398
Counteroffer, 156
County recorder's office, 197
Court of International Trade, U.S., 30
Courts, 17
authority of, 36–37, 40
chancery, 9–10
federal system, 29–35
jurisdiction of, 35–40
small-claims, *see* Small-claims courts
special federal, 30
state systems, 27–29
Court's reasoning, 17, 22–23
Court system:
state, 27–29
U.S., 27–45
Courts of appeal:
Federal Circuit, 31
state, 28, 29
U.S., 30–31
Courts of record, 28
Credit, 335–360
secured, 337
unsecured, 336
Credit-card crimes, 76
Creditor, 335–360
actions stayed, 346
living trusts and, 254
secured, 336, 341, 347–349
unsecured, 336, 349
Crimes:
affecting business, 75–80
aiding and abetting, 81
attempt to commit, 81
classification of, 70–71
credit card, 76
definition of, 70
essential elements of, 71–72
felony vs. misdemeanor, 70–71
inchoate, 80–81
theft, 76
violations, 71
white-collar, 77–80
Criminal:
act, 71
conspiracy, 81
fraud, 78
Criminal law, 69–87 (*see also* Crime):
classification of crimes, 70–71
constitutional protections and, 82–85
definition of a crime, 70
fraud, 78
procedure and, 72–73, 75
sentencing guidelines and, 76

Critical Legal Studies School of jurisprudence, 8
Critical legal thinking, 13–23
Cross-complaint, 48, 49
Cross-defendant, 49
Cross-examination, 55
Crossover workers, 325
Cruel and unusual punishment, 85
Culpable mental state, 71
Custodial parent, 226
Custody:
  joint, 226–227
  legal, 226
  of children, 224–227
Cyberspace, free speech in, 111

Damages, 170, 172–174
  compensatory, 170, 172
  consequential (special), 172
  liquidated, 172
  mitigation of, 172–173
  monetary, 170
  recoverable for strict liability, 142
  tort, 125
Danger invites rescue doctrine, 137
d.b.a, 264
Deathbed will, *see* Noncupative will
Debtor, 335–360 (*see also* Bankruptcy; Debts)
Debts:
  collection of, 282
  Chapter 7 bankruptcy and, 345–350
  Chapter 11 bankruptcy, 351–353
  Chapter 13 bankruptcy and, 351
  division of, 228
  liability for, 343
  of LLCs, 273
  personal guarantee of, 271
  responsibility for, 270
Deceit, 78, 310
Deceive, intent to, 167
Decisions:
  majority, 34
  plurality, 34
  tie, 34
  unanimous, 33
Declaration of Homestead, 346
Decree of divorce, 224
Deed:
  of trust, 162, 337–338
  quitclaim, 197
  warranty, 197
Defamation of character, 127–128
Default judgment, 49
Defendant, 13, 37, 70
  case of, 56
Defense of Marriage Act (DOMA), 217
Deficiency judgment, 337, 339
Degree of control, of employer over agent, 313
Delegation doctrine, 114, 386
Delegation of powers, 386–387
Deponent, 51
Depositions, 51, 53
Devise, 242
Digital Millennium Copyright Act (DMCA), 369
Direct examination, 55
Directors, board of, 276–277, 282–284
Disabilities, discrimination against people with, 323
Disaffirm a contract, 159, 161
Discharge:
  Chapter 13 bankruptcy and, 351
  of debts, 345
  of student loans, 349
  of unpaid claims, 349
  wrongful, 304
Discovery, 51, 53
Discrimination:
  against people with disabilities, 323
  age, 321–323
  color, 318
  employment, 318
  national origin, 318
  racial, 318, 319
  religious, 320
  sex, 320
  Title VII and, 318
Dissenting opinion, 21–22, 34
Dissolution, of partnerships, 267–268
Distinctiveness of a mark, 370
Distribution:
  of bankruptcy estate, 347–349
  of property, 227–228, 244–246, 254 (*see also* Wills)
  per capita, 244–246
  per stirpes, 244–246
  secured creditors and, 347–349
  unsecured creditors and, 349
District attorney, 70
District courts, U.S., 30
Diversity, of citizenship, 35, 36
Dividends, 282
Divorce, 223–224
  adoption and, 222
  community property and, 196, 228
  negotiation and settlement, 224
  no-fault, 223
  pro se, 224
DNA testing, 220–221
Doctrine of transferred intent, 126
Documents, production of, 53
Doing business as (d.b.a.), 264
Domain names, 374
Domestic:
  corporations, 277
  LLP, 271
  relations division, 29
Dominant estate, easements and, 200
Donee, 188
  beneficiary, 168
Donor, 188
Do-not-call registry, 389
Double jeopardy, 85
Dram Shop Acts, 136–137
DreamWorks SKG, 276
Drugs, regulation of, 390
Dual-purpose mission, negligence and, 311
Due Process Clause, 83, 106, 111, 112–113
Dunlop Pirelli, 287
Duty:
  not to willfully or wantonly injure, 138
  of care, 131–132, 285
  of loyalty, 285
  of ordinary care, 137–138
  of reasonable care, bailed goods and, 192
  of utmost care, 138
Dying declarations, *see* Noncupative will

Easement:
  appurtenant, 200
  in gross, 202
  land interest and, 200–202
E-commerce, 171
  federal Electronic Signature Act, 166
  UCITA and, 176
Economic Espionage Act, 362
Effective date, 396
Effects on interstate commerce test, 104
E-filings, 51
Eighth Amendment, 85
Electoral college, 100
Electronic mail, 373–374
Electronic Signature in Global and National Commerce Act (E-Sign Act), 166
Email, 373–374
Emancipation:
  children and, 219–220
  marriage and, 216
Embezzlement, 70, 77–78
Eminent domain, 204
Emotional distress:
  intentional infliction of, 129
  negligent infliction of, 134
Employees:
  at will, 304
  as crossover and replacement workers, 325
  leave for medical emergencies and, 323
  right to form a union, 324
  worker's compensation and, 315–316
Employers:
  accommodation of disabilities and, 323
  accommodation of medical emergencies and, 323
  use of crossover and replacement workers, 325
  violation of OSHA rules and, 318
  worker's compensation and, 315–316
Employment:
  discrimination, 318
  termination of contract, 312–313
Employment-at-will doctrine, 304
Employment-related injury, 316

Employment relationships, 303–304
  employer–employee relationship, 303
  principal–agent relationship, 303
  principal–independent contractor relationship, 303
Endangered species, 402
Endangered Species Act, 402
Engagement, 216
English common law, 3, 9
Enron, 89
Entity theory, 266
Entry of judgment, 55, 56
Enumerated powers, 100
Environment, hostile work, 320
Environmental Impact Statement (EIS), 398
Environmental protection, 193, 398–402
  air pollution, 399
  endangered species, 402
  hazardous waste, 401–402
  Superfund, 401
  water pollution, 399–400
Environmental Protection Agency (EPA), 386, 398–402
Equal Employment Opportunity Act of 1972, 318
Equal Protection Clause, 111–112
Equitable distribution, 227–228
Equitable remedies, 10, 170, 173–174
Equitable title, 250
Equity court, 9–10
Escheat of property, 248 (*see also* Wills)
E-Sign Act, 166
Establishment Clause, 107
Estate:
  bankruptcy, 346–349
  defined, 193
  in fee,193
  in land, 193
  probate/settlement of, 248–250
Estate *pour autre vie*, 194
Estray statues, 189
Ethics, 87–91 (*see also all* Ethical Perspective boxes)
  code of, 90
  Nike and, 16
  unconscionable contract, 165
Eviction proceedings, tenancy at sufferance and, 203
Evidence, 28
Evil intent, 71
Examinations, physical or mental, 53
Exclusive:
  agency contract, 305
  jurisdiction, 35
  remedy, 316
Executive:
  branch, 11, 100
  orders, 11–12, 13
  powers, of administrative agencies, 115
Executor/executrix, 250
Executory contract, 162, 352
Exempt property, 346
Exemptions, state bankruptcy law, 346
Express:
  agency, 304–305
  contracts, 156
  trusts, 252
Extension, for payment of debts, 351
Extortion, 76

Fact-finding, 58, 60
Fair distribution of property, 227–228
Fair Employment Practices Act, *see* Title VII
Fair Labor Standards Act (FLSA), 312
Fair Packaging and Labeling Act, 392
Fair-use doctrine, 367
False:
  and deceptive advertising, 393
  and misleading labeling, 390
  arrest, 127
  imprisonment, 126–127
  light, 128
  pretense, 78
Family and Medical Leave Act, 323
Family law, 215–238
  adoption and, 221–222
  child custody and, 224–227
  courts, 28
  engagement and, 216
  financial considerations and, 227–231
  marriage and, 216–219
  marriage termination and, 222–224
  parents and children and, 219–222
  premarriage and, 215–216
Father's registry, 220
Fault rule, of engagement, 216
Fault, liability without, 141
Federal Antiterrorism Act of 2001, 87
Federal Arbitration Act, 58
Federal Aviation Administration (FAA), 386
Federal Communications Commission (FCC), 107, 386
Federal Food, Drug, and Cosmetics Act, 386, 388, 390–391
Federal Patent Statute of 1952, 363
Federal Trade Commission (FTC), 72, 389
  living trusts and, 255
Federal Trade Commission Act, 392
Federal Water Pollution Control Act (FWPCA), 400
Federalism, 100
Fee simple estates, 193
Fees:
  contingency, 53
  payment of attorney, 53
Felony, 70–71
Feminist legal theory, 7
Fictitious business name statement, 264
Fiduciary relationship, 302
Fifth Amendment, 83
Filing, fixture, 341
Finance lease, 176
Financial considerations, of marriage termination, 227–231
Financial support, marriage and, 217–219
Financing statement, 341
Finder, mislaid/lost/abandoned property and, 188–190
Finding of fact, 58
Fine, imposition of, 70
Fireman's rule, 137
Firestone tires, 59
First Amendment, 107, 108
First-to file rule, 363
First-to-invent rule, 363
Fish and Wildlife Coordination Act, 402
Fishery Conservation and Management Act, 402
Fixture filing, 341
Fixtures, 162
  as personal property, 188
  as real property, 193
Flow-through tax benefit, 271, 272
FLSA, 312
Food:
  genetically altered, 392
  regulation of, 388, 390
Food and Drug Administration (FDA), 390
Force majeure clauses, 169
Ford Explorer rollover lawsuit, 54
Ford Motor Company, 287, 365
Foreclosure, 339
  sales, 339
Foreign Commerce Clause, 107
Foreign corporations, 277
Foreign Corrupt Practices Act of 1977 (FCPA), 80
Foreign LLP, 271
Forgery, 76
Formal will, 240
Fortas, Abe, 34
Forum-selection clause, 37, 40
Foster care, 222
Fourteenth Amendment, 82, 106
Fourth Amendment, 82–83
Fourth branch of government, 386 (*see also* Administrative law)
Franchise, 288–289
  agreement, 288
Franchisee/franchisor, 288
Frank, Jerome, 5
Fraud, 167, 310
  criminal, 78
Free Exercise Clause, 107
Free speech, in cyberspace, 111
Free transferability of shares, 276
Freedom of religion, 107
Freedom of Speech Clause, 107
Freehold estates, 193–194, 202
  estates in fee, 193
  life estates, 193–194
French civil law, 3
Fresh start, bankruptcy and, 345, 353
Frivolous lawsuits, 129
Frolic and detour, negligence and, 311
Fully disclosed agency, 307
Future interests:
  reversion and remainder, 194
  third party, 194

General gift, 242
General intent, 71
General Motors, 144
General partners, 265–266, 268–269
  liability of, 268
  vs. limited partners, 268, 270
General partnership, 264–268
General power of attorney, 305
General-jurisdiction trial courts, 27–28
Generic names, 371–372
Genetically altered foods, 392
German Civil Code, 10
Gift, 188
  causa mortis, 188
  inter vivos, 188
  promises, 159
  specific/general/residuary gift, 242
  testamentary, 242–244
  transference of real property and, 197
  vs. bailment, 190
Ginsberg, Ruth Bader, 34
Good-faith exception, 83
Good Samaritan laws, 136
Government:
  branches of, 11–12
  paternity lawsuits and, 220
  power of eminent domain and, 204
  regulation, general vs. specific, 386 (*see also* Administrative law)
Grand jury, 73
Grant, creating an easement, 200
Grantee, 197
Grantor, 197, 254
Grantor's trust, 254
Gratuitous promises, 159
Guarantor, 343
Guaranty arrangement, 343
Guardian *ad litem*, 227
Guest statutes, 137
Guilty act, 71
Gun-Free School Zone Act, 104

Hand, Learned, 3
Harassment, sexual, 320–321
Hazardous waste, 401–402
Health-care proxy, 251
Heirs, 248
Highest state court, 28–29
Historical School of jurisprudence, 6, 8
Holding, 17, 20–21, 22
Holographic will, 242
Homeland Security, Office of, 12
Honesty, found property and, 190
Hughes Aircraft, 79
Hypertext markup language (HTML), 373

Identity fraud, 72
Identity Theft and Assumption Deterrence Act, 72
IIP Act, 82
Illegality of contracts, 161–162
Immunity, 85
  from prosecution, 83
Impaneling, 55
Implied:
  agency, 305
  contract, rights to property and, 231
  trusts, 253
  warranty of authority, 309
  warranty of habitability, 203 (*see also* Landlords)
Implied-in-fact contracts, 156–157, 304
Imprisonment, false, 126–127
In rem jurisdiction, 37
Inchoate crimes, 80–81
Incidental authority, 305
Income beneficiary, 252
Income tax, LLCs and, 272
Incompetent persons, 161
Incorporation, 277–281
  articles of, 276, 277–278, 279
  doctrine, 106
Incrimination, self, 83
Independent:
  adoption, 222
  contractors, 303, 313–315
Indictment, 72, 73
Indoor air pollution, 400
Infancy doctrine, 159
Inferior performance, 170
Information (indictment), 72, 73
Information Infrastructure Protection (IIP) Act, 82
Information, sharing of, 87
Infringement:
  on copyright, 367
  on patents, 365
  on trademarks, 371
Initial public offering (IPO), 395
Injunctions, 125, 174
Injury:
  employment-related, 316
  to innocent party, 167
Innkeepers:
  liability of, 138
  loss of personal property and, 192
  statutes, 192
Innocence, presumption of, 69
Innocent misrepresentation, 310
Inside director, 282
Insiders, 396
  voidable transfers and, 347
Insider trading, 396, 398
Intangible property, 188
Intellectual property, 361–384
  copyrights, 366–369
  Economic Espionage Act, 362
  Internet and, 373–376
  licensing and, 290
  patents, 363–365
  rights, 361
  trade secrets, 362–363
  trademarks, 370–372
Intended third-party beneficiary, 168
Intent:
  to deceive, 167
  specific vs. general, 71
Intentional infliction of emotional distress, 129
Intentional misrepresentation, 310
Intentional torts, 125, 310
Inter vivos trusts, 252, 254
Interest, security, 335, 337–343
Interests, future, 194
Intermediate appellate courts, 28
Intermediate scrutiny clause, 112
Intermittent strikes, 324
Internal Revenue Code, 315
Internal Revenue Service:
  LLCs and, 272
  Microsoft and, 315
Internet:
  and the law, 5
  domain names and, 374
  e-filings, 51
  free speech and, 111
  intellectual property rights and, 373–376
  personal jurisdiction and, 39
  Service Providers, 373
  spam control and, 393
InterNIC, 374
Interrogatories, 53
Interspousal immunity, 219
Interstate commerce, 104
Interstate Commerce Commission (ICC), 386
Intervening event, 138
Intervention, 49
Intestacy statute, 248 (*see also* Wills)
Intestate, 239, 248
  succession, 248
Intoxicated persons, 161
Intrastate commerce, 104
Invasion of the right to privacy, 128–129
Invention, patents and, 363–365
Investor protection, 395–398
  insider trading and, 396, 398
  Securities and Exchange Commission (SEC), 395
Invitees, 137
Involuntary petition, 345
Irreconcilable differences, 223
IRS:
  LLCs and, 272
  Microsoft and, 315
Issue, 17, 22
Issuer, 395

Japanese legal system, 39
Joint:
  and several liability, 267
  custody, 226–227
  liability, 267
  marital debts, 228
  physical custody, 226–227
  tenancy, 194–195
  will, 247
Judgment:
  deficiency, 337, 339
  entry of, 55, 56

notwithstanding the verdict (j.n.o.v.), 56
on the pleadings, motion for, 53
Judgment-proof, 72
debtor as, 336
Judicial:
branch, 11, 100
decisions, 12, 13
powers, of administrative agencies, 115
referee, 58, 60
Jurisdiction:
attachment, 37
concurrent, 35–36
exclusive, 35
in rem, 37
obtaining personal, 39
of federal and state courts, 35–40
quasi in rem, 37
subject matter, 37
Jurisprudence, schools of, 6–8
Jury:
deliberation of, 56
instructions to, 56
right to public trial by, 85
selection, 55
sequestering of, 56
trial by, 54, 73
vote, 73
Just Compensation Clause, 113
Justice-of-the-peace courts, 28, 29
Juvenile courts, 28, 29

Key facts, summary of, 17, 18, 22
Kickback, 78
Klondike Bars, 336
Kmart, 353

Labeling:
false and misleading, 390
nutrition, 390
Labor union law, 324–325
Land, 192–205
contracts concerning, 162
laws regulating use of, 204–205
pollution, 401
rights to, 192–193
subsurface rights to, 193
surface rights to, 192
Landlords, 202–204
failure to maintain property and, 203
Landlord-tenant relationships, 202–204 (*see also* Freehold estates)
Landowners, liability of, 137–138
Land-use control, 193
real property and, 204–205
Lanham Trademark Act, 371
Lapse of time, terminating agency relationships and, 312
Larceny, grand vs. petit, 75
Last clear chance rule, 140
Law:
administrative, *see* Administrative law
and ethics, *see* Ethics
constitutional, 99–122 (*see also* Constitutional law)
courts of, 9
criminal, 69–87 (*see also* Criminal law)
defined, 4
flexibility of, 5–6
functions of, 4–5
history of American, 8–10
Internet and, 5
priority of in U.S., 12
private, 153
schools of thought, 6–8
sources of U.S., 10–13
sources of, 3
Law and Economics School of jurisprudence, 8
Lawful object, 154, 161–162
Laws:
administrative, *see* Administrative agencies
agency, employment, and equal opportunity, 301–333
bankruptcy, 335–336, 343–352
environmental protection, 193
family, 215–216
labor union, 324–325
land-use control, 193
of partnerships, 265–267
regulating land use, 204–205
regulating ownership, 204
regulating real property, 193
regulatory, *see* Administrative agencies
reproductive medicine and, 221
state bankruptcy, 346
zoning, 204–205
Lawsuit:
terminology, 13
frivolous, 129
Lease, 162, 176, 203
Leasehold, 202–203
Legacy, 242 (*see also* Gift)
Legal:
cause, 133
custody, 226
entity, corporation as, 274
person, 274
systems, comparison of Japanese and U.S., 39
thinking, critical, 13–23
title, 250
Legislative branch, 11, 100
Legislative powers, of administrative agencies, 115
Lender, 335
Lessee, 176, 202–204
Lessor, 176, 202–204
Liability, 267, 268
contracts, 307, 309
corporate criminal, 81
for debts, 343
frivolous lawsuits and, 129
limited, 270
loss of personal property and, 192
of common carriers and innkeepers, 138
of independent contractor, 314–315
of landowners, 137–138
of partners/partnership, 268
of social host, 137
product, 140–144
recovering for, 141–142
strict, 140
strict vs. absolute, 72
tort, 309–311, 314
unlimited, 270
vicarious, 311
without fault, 141
Libel, 128
Licensee/licensor, 137, 290
Licensing, 290
Lien:
artisan's, 343
material person's/mechanic's, 339, 343
preferential, 347
super-priority, 343
Life estates, 193–194
Life tenant, 194
Lifetime alimony, *see* Permanent alimony
Limited liability, 270
company, 271–273, 274, 275, 276
company codes, 272
members of LLCs and, 273
partnership, articles of, 271
partnerships, 270–271, 272, 273
Limited partnership, 268–270
Limited protection speech, 107
Limited-jurisdiction trial courts, 27–28
Lineal descendents, 244
Liquidated damages, 172
Liquidation bankruptcy, 345 (*see also* Chapter 7 bankruptcy)
Litigation, 27
civil, 47–58
defendant's case, 56
discovery, 51, 53
interrogatories, 53
jury selection, 55
plaintiff's case, 55
pleadings, 48–49, 51
settlement conference, 54
the trial, 54–56
Living trusts, 253–255
Living will, 250, 251
LLCs, 271–273, 274, 275, 276
owners as members, 273
LLPs, 270–271, 272, 273
accounting firms operating as, 273
Long-arm statute, 37
Lost property, 189

Magistrate, 73
Magna Carta, 6
Mail fraud, 78
Majority decisions, 34
Mala in se, 70
Mala prohibita, 71
Malicious prosecution, 129
Malpractice, professional, 134

Management, centralized, of corporations, 276
Marine Mammal Protection Act, 402
Marital property, 227–228
Marketable title, transference of real property and, 199
Marks, distinctiveness of, 370
Marriage, 216–219 (*see also* Marriage termination)
  common law, 219
  community property and, 196, 228
  debts, 228
  license/ceremony, 217
  obligations of, 217–219
  requirements for, 216–217
  same-sex, 217
  termination of, *see* Marriage termination
Marriage termination, 222–224 (*see also* Marriage)
  annulment, 223
  distribution of property and, 227–228, 254
  divorce, 223–224
  financial considerations of, 227–231
  prenuptial agreements and, 230
Marshall, Thurgood, 34
Mask Work Act, 367
Material breach of contract, 170
Material misrepresentation of fact, 167
Material person's lien, 339
MBCA, 277
McDonald's, 133
Mechanic's lien, 339, 343
Mediation, 58, 59, 224
Meeting, organizational, 279–281
Members, owners of LLCs as, 273
Mens rea, 71
Mental examination, 53
Mentally incompetent persons, 161
Merchant Court, 10
Merchant protection statutes, 127
Microsoft Corporation, 290
  employment law and, 315
Migratory Bird Conservation Act, 402
Migratory Bird Treaty Act, 402
Mineral rights, to land, 193
Minimum contact, 37
Minimum wage, 312
Minitrial, 58, 60
Minor breach of contract, 169
Minors, contractual capacity of, 159
Miranda rights, 86
Misappropriation, 362
Misdemeanors, 71
Mislaid property, 188–189
Misrepresentation, 167
  intentional/innocent, 310
Mitigation of damages, 172–173
Mitsubishi Group, 287
Mobile sources, 399
Model Business Corporation Act (*see* MBCA)
Model Penal Code, 71
Monetary damages, 170
Money:
  hiding in offshore banks, 86
  laundering, 77, 87
Money Laundering Control Act, 77
Moral standards, 4
Moral theory of law, 6
Mortgage, 337–339
Mortgagor/mortgagee, 337–339
Motions:
  for judgment on the pleadings, 53
  for summary judgment, 53–54
  pretrial, 53
Motivation test, 310
Multinational corporations, 287
Municipal courts, 29
Murder, 70
Murder disqualification doctrine, 248
Mutual agreement, to terminate agency relationship, 312
Mutual wills, 247–248
Mutual-benefit bailments, 192

Name, of corporation, 278
National ambient air quality standards (NAAQS), 399
National Conference of Commissioners on Uniform State Laws, 266, 272
National Environmental Policy Act (NEPA), 398
National Labor Relations Act (NLRA), 324–325
National Labor Relations Board (NLRB), 386
National origin, employment discrimination and, 318
National Priority List, 401
National Wildlife Refuge System, 402
Natural Law School, 6, 8
Necessaries of life, 159
Negligence, 56, 131–140, 285
  breach of duty of care and, 285
  comparative, 140
  compared to strict liability, 142
  contributory, 140
  defenses against, 138, 140
  elements of, 131–134
  in the selection of an independent contractor, 315
  per se, 134
  special doctrines, 134, 136–138
  tort liability, 311
Negligent infliction of emotional distress, 134
Negotiation, divorce and, 224
NET Act, 369
Nike, 16
Nineteenth Amendment, 7
NLRA, 324–325
No Electronic Theft Act, 369
No-fault divorce, 223
Nolo contendere, 73, 75
Noncitizens, detention of, 87
Nonconforming uses, of land and buildings, 204
Noncupative will, 242
Noncustodial parent, 226
Nondelegable duties, liability and, 314
Nondisclosure agreement (NDA), 161
Nonfreehold estate, 202
Norman Conquest, 9
No-strike clause, 325
Note, evidence of borrower's debt to lender, 337–338
Notice of appeal, 58
Nutrition Labeling and Education Act, 390

O'Connor, Sandra Day, 34
Objective rule, of engagement, 216
Obligations, of marriage, 217–219
Occupational Safety and Health Act, 316
Occupational Safety and Health Administration (OSHA), 316–318, 386
Occupational Safety and Health Review Commission, 318
Occurrence of a specified event, terminating agency relationships and, 313
Offensive speech, 107
Offer:
  requirements of, 155–156
  termination of, 156
Offeree, 154
Offeror, 154
Office of the Comptroller of the Currency (OCC), 386
Officers, corporate, 277, 284–285
One-click patent, 364
One-year "on sale" doctrine, 365
One-year rule, 164
Open adoption, 222
Opening brief, 58
Opening statement, 55
Operating agreement, 272
Opinions:
  of the court, 18
  dissenting, 21–22
  concurring and dissenting, 34
Option contract, 156
Order, 115
  by ALJ, 388
Ordinances, 11, 13
Ordinary prudent person, duty of care and, 285
Organizational meeting, of the corporation, 279–281
OSHA, 316–318
Outrage, tort of, 129
Outside director, 282
Overtime pay, 312
Owner, mislaid/lost/abandoned property and, 188–190
Owner-debtor, 337, 338
Ownership:
  concurrent, 194–197
  laws regulating, 204

of corporations, 273, 282
real property and, 193–202
recording statutes and, 197
transference of real property and, 197–202
wrongful possession of property and, 203

Packaging, regulation of, 392
Palimony, 231
Parents, 219–222
adoptive, 222
biological, 222
child abuse/neglect, 220
custodial/noncustodial, 226
joint custody and, 226–227
liability for children's wrongful acts, 220
rights and duties of, 219–220
Partial strikes, 324
Partially disclosed agency, 307
Parties:
to a lawsuit, 51
to a trust, 252–253
Partners:
general, 265–266, 268–269
limited, 268–269
power vs. right to dissolve partnership, 267
Partnership, 264–272
agreement, 266–267
articles of, 266–267
at will, 267
dissolution of, 267–268
for a term, 267
general, 264–268
limited, 268–270
limited liability, 270–271, 272, 273
Party, accommodation, 343
Patents, 36, 363–365
infringement on, 365
Patent Statute of 1952, 363
Paternity action, 220
Pay, overtime, 312
Payment, plan of, 351
Payoff, 778
Peace, keeping the, 4
Penal codes, 70
Penalties, 73, 172
Per capita distribution, 244–246
Per stirpes distribution, 244–246
Performance:
complete, 169
contracts and, 169–170
inferior, 170
specific, 173–174
Period of minority, 159
Periodic tenancy, 202–203
Permanent alimony, 230
Perpetual existence, of corporations, 276
Personal guarantee, of limited partnership debts, 271
Personal property, 187–192
contracts and, 162
conversion of, 131
gifts of, 188, 242
innkeepers and, 192
security interest and, 340–343
trespass to, 131
Petition, 345, 351
for certiorari, 33
for divorce, 223
voluntary/involuntary, 345
Petitioner, 13
Physical examination, 53
Picketing, 324
Piercing the corporate veil, 282
Plaintiff, 13, 37, 70, 73
case of, 55
injury to, 132
Plan:
of payment, Chapter 13 bankruptcy and, 351
of reorganization, 352
Planning, facilitating, 4
Plant life and vegetation, as type of real property, 193
Plea, 73
bargain, 72, 75
Pleadings, 48–49, 51
Plurality decisions, 34
Point sources of water pollution, 400
Poison Prevention Packaging Act, 392
Police power, 106
Possession, *see* Ownership
Possession of the collateral, 341
Pour-over will, 254
Power of attorney, 305, 306
Power of sale, 339
Precedent, 12
Preemption doctrine, 101
Preferential lien, 347
Premarital agreements, 230
Premarriage, 215–216
Prenuptial agreements, 230
President, executive orders and, 11–12
Presley, Elvis, 160
Presumed innocence, 69
Pretrial hearing, 54
Pretrial motions, 53
Principal, 302–314 (*see also* Agent)
Principal-agent relationship, 302
Privacy, invasion of right to, 128–129
Private law, 153
Privilege:
attorney-client, 85
other types of, 85
Privilege and Immunities Clause, 111, 113
Pro se divorce, 224
Probable cause, 73
Probable-cause standard, 82
Probate, 248–250, 254 (*see also* Wills)
Probate courts, 28
Procedural due process, 113
Procedural law, 386 (*see also* Administrative law)
Product liability, 140–144
Product safety, 391–392
Production of documents, 53
Professional malpractice, 134
Profits:
business, 265–266
of limited partnerships, 270
Promise to marry, actions for breach of, 216
Promisee, 168
Promises, gift/gratuitous, 159
Promisor, 168
Property:
as the bankruptcy estate, 346
cohabitation and, 231
distribution of, 227–228, 244–246, 254
escheat of, 248
exempt, 346
intangible, 188
intellectual, 290
intentional torts against, 131
living trusts and, 253–255
marital, 227–228
mislaid/lost/abandoned, 188–190
personal, *see* Personal property
real, *see* Real property
real and personal, 187–213
receiving stolen, 76
separate, 227
tangible, 188
trusts and, 250–252
wills/trusts and, 239–260
Prosecution, immunity from, 83
Prosecutor, 70
Prospectus, 396
Protected speech, 106
Protein, hidden source of, 391
Proximate cause, 133
Public defender, 70
Public domain, 363
Public policy:
contracts contrary to, 162
exception, 304
Publicity, 128
Public-use doctrine, 365
Punishment, cruel and unusual, 85
Punitive damages, 125
Purpose achieved, terminating agency relationships and, 312–313

Qualified fee, real property and, 193
Quasi in rem jurisdiction, 37
Quasi-contract, 174
Quiet title, ownership rights and, 197
Quitclaim deed, 197

Race, employment discrimination and, 318, 319
Racketeer Influenced and Corrupt Organizations (RICO) Act, 79–80
Racketeering, 80
Rape, 70
Rational basis test, 112
Reagan, Ronald, 34
Real estate, gifts of, 242

Real property, 192–205
  buildings, 193
  concurrent ownership and, 194–197
  deeds/documents concerning, 197
  fixtures, 193
  freehold estates, 193–194
  land as, 192–205
  land-use control and, 204
  laws about, 193
  ownership rights to, 193–194
  plant life and vegetation, 193
  security interest and, 337–339
  Statute of Frauds and, 162
  transferring ownership of, 197–202
Reasonable:
  accommodations, 323
  man standard, 7
  person standard, 132
  professional standard, 132
Rebuttal, 55
Receiving stolen property, 76
Reciprocal wills, 247–248
Record, 56
Recording statutes:
  certainty of ownership and, 197
  of mortgage or deed of trust, 338
Recross examination, 55
Redirect examination, 55
Reformation, 174
Registration agreement, 395
Regular meetings, 284
Regulation, 386 (*see also* Administrative law)
Regulatory statutes, 70
Rehabilitation alimony, *see* Temporary alimony
Rejoinder, 55
Relationship:
  employment, 303–304
  fiduciary, 302
  principal-agent, 302
Religion:
  annulments and, 223
  discrimination based on, 320
  freedom of, 107
Remainder, 194
Remainderman, 252
Remedies, 170, 172–174
  compensatory, 170, 172
  equitable, 173–174
  monetary, 170
Remedy, 20–21
  exclusive, 316
Remitter, 56
Renunciation of authority, 313
Reorganization bankruptcy, *see* Chapter 11 bankruptcy
Reorganization, plan of, 352
Replacement workers, 325
Reply, 48, 49
Res ipsa loquitur, 134, 136
Reservation, creating an easement, 200
Residuary gift, 242
Resource Conservation and Recovery Act (RCRA), 401
Respondeat superior, 311
Respondent, 13, 18, 115
Responding brief, 58
Restatement (Second) of Agency, rules of agency and, 302, 313
Restatement (Second) of Contracts, 155
Restatement (Second) of Torts, 140–141
Restraining order, spousal abuse and, 219
Resulting trusts, 253
Reversion, 194
Revised Model Business Corporation Act (*see* RMBCA)
Revised Uniform Gift to Minors Act, 188
Revised Uniform Limited Partnership Act (*see* RULPA)
Revocable trust, 254
Revocation of authority, 313
RICO, 79–80
Right of survivorship, joint tenancy and, 194–195
Right to die, 250
Rights, assignment of, 166–168
Rights of possession, *see* Ownership
Risk, assumption of, 138
RMBCA, 277–278, 279, 282, 284, 285
Romano-Germanic civil law system, 10
Rome, civil law and, 10
Royal Dutch/Shell Group, 287
Rule, "coming and going," 311
Rule 10b-5, 396
Rules and regulations, 100, 386, 387 (*see also* Administrative law)
RULPA, 268–270

Safety:
  product, 391–392
  standards, 316–318
Sale:
  of goods, Convention on Contracts for, 177
  power of, 339
  transference of real property and, 197
Sales, foreclosure, 339
Same-sex marriage, 217
Sanctions, 73
Sarbanes-Oxley Act of 2002, 91, 286–287
  bankruptcy fraud and, 352
Scienter, 167
S Corporations, 281
Search and seizure, 82
Search, warrantless, 82
Search warrants, 82
  nationwide, 87
Secondary meaning, 370
Secretary of the interior, 403
Section 10(b), 396
Section 24 of the Restatement (Second) of Contracts, 155
Secured:
  credit, 337
  creditor, 336, 341, 347–349
  party, 340
  transaction, 340
Securities Act of 1933, 386
Securities and Exchange Commission (SEC), 114, 386
Securities Exchange Act of 1934, 386
Securities, regulating, *see* Investor protection
Security:
  agreement, 341
  interest, 335, 337–343
  unsecured credit and, 336
Self-incrimination, 83
Semiconductor Chip Protection Act of 1884, 367
Sentencing guidelines, 76
Separate property, 227
Separation of powers, 100
September 11, 2001, 87
Sequestering, 55
Service marks, 370
Service of process, 37
Servient estate, easements and, 200
Settlement, 248–250
  agreement, 224
  conference, 54
  divorce and, 224
Settlor, 250, 252, 253, 254
Seventh Amendment, 54
Sex discrimination, 320
Sexual harassment, 320–321
Shareholders, 273, 276, 281–282
  responsible for corporation's debt, 282
Shopkeeper's privilege, 127
Sick building syndrome, 400
Signature:
  electronic, 166
  required, 165
Simultaneous death, inheritance and, 247
Sit-down strikes, 324
Sixth Amendment, 85
Slander, 128
Slavery, abolishment of, 106
Small-claims courts, 28, 29
Social host liability rule, 137
Social justice, 4
Sociological School of jurisprudence, 7, 8
Software, copyrighting, 367
Sole proprietorship, 264–265
Sonny Bono Copyright Term Extension Act of 1998 (CTEA), 366
Sources:
  of air pollution, 399
  of water pollution, 400
Spam, statute to control, 393
Spanish civil law, 3
Special:
  appearance, 37
  meetings, 284
  partnership, *see* Limited partnership
  power of attorney, 305
  risks, liability and, 314–315
Special Intelligence Court, 87

Specific:
- gift, 242
- government regulation, 386
- intent, 71
- performance, 173–174

Speech:
- commercial, 107
- free on Internet, 111
- limited protection, 107
- offensive, 107
- protected, 106–108
- unprotected, 107

Speedy Trial Act, 85
Spendthrift trusts, 253
Spousal:
- abuse, 219
- support, 229–230

Spouses:
- marriage and, 216–219
- marriage termination and, 222–224

Squatters, real property and, 200
Standards, of safety, 316–318
Standing to sue, 36
Stare decisis, 10, 12
State bankruptcy law exemptions, 346
State Farm, 173
State implementation act, 399
State supreme court, 28–29
Statement:
- continuation, 341
- financing, 341

Stationary sources, 399
Status quo, maintaining, 4
Statute of Frauds, 162–166
- business partnerships and, 266
- express agency contracts and, 305
- sales of real property and, 199

Statute of limitations, 49, 51
Statute of Wills, 240
Statutes, 11, 13
- antideficiency, 339
- recording, 338

Stolen property, receiving, 76
Straight bankruptcy, *see* Liquidation bankruptcy
Strict liability, 72, 140, 141–142
Strict scrutiny test, 112
Strikes, 324
Subchapter S Revision Act, 281
Subject-matter jurisdiction, 37
Submission agreement, 58
Subpoena, 51
Substantial performance, 169–170
Substantive:
- due process, 112
- law, 386 (*see also* Administrative law)
- rules, 115

Subsurface rights, to land, 193
Successor trustee, 254
Summary judgment, motion for, 53–54
Summons, 48–49
Sunstate Dairy & Food Products Co., 336
Superfund, 401
Super-priority liens, 343
Superseding event, 138
Support:
- child, 228–229
- spousal, 229–230

Supremacy Clause, 101, 103
Supreme court, state, 28–29
Supreme court, U.S., *see* U.S. Supreme Court
Surety, 343
Surface rights, to land, 192
Surgeon general's warning, 101
Surrogacy, 221
- contract, 221

Tangible:
- property, 188
- writings, 366

Tax:
- court, U.S., 30
- income, 272

Taxes:
- flow-through benefit, 271, 272
- living trusts and, 254

Telephone Consumer Protection Act of 1991, 389
Telephone, do not call registry and, 389
Temporary alimony, 229–230
Tenancy:
- by the entirety, 196
- in common, 195
- periodic, 202–203
- at sufferance, 203
- at will, 203
- for years, 202

Tenants, 202–204
- inability to use or enjoy property and, 203
- nonfreehold estates and, 202

Tender of performance, 169
Termination:
- of agency or employment contract, 312–313
- of corporations, 276
- of marriage, 222–224
- of trusts, 253
- wrongful, 313

Terrorism, 87
Test:
- motivation, 310
- work-related, 310–311

Testamentary:
- capacity, 240
- gifts, 242–244
- trusts, 252

Testator/testatrix, 239, 248
Testimony, 28
Theft, 76
- electronic, 369

Thermal pollution, 400–401
Thin capitalization, 282
Third parties:
- as beneficiaries, 168
- future interests and, 194
- neutral, 59
- to contracts, 307, 309

Thomas, Clarence, 34
Three-party instrument, deed of trust as, 338
Three-party secured transaction, 340
Tie decisions, 34
Title 18 of U.S. Code, 70
Title insurance, transference of real property and, 199
Title VII of Civil Rights Act of 1964, 7, 304, 318–321
- employment discrimination and, 318–319
- religious discrimination and, 320
- sexual discrimination/harassment and, 320

Title, legal/equitable, 250
Torts, 125–140
- of appropriation, 128
- franchises and, 288
- intentional, 125, 310
- intentional against persons, 125, 126–130
- intentional against property, 131
- liability, 267, 309–311, 314
- of misappropriation of the right to publicity, 128
- misrepresentation, 310
- negligence, 311
- of outrage, 129
- Restatement (Second) of, 140–141
- unintentional, 131–140 (*see also* Negligence)

Totten trusts, 253
Toxic air pollutants, 399
Trademark, 36
- infringement on, 371
- loss of, 371–372

Trademark Law Revision Act of 1988, 371
Trade name, 264
Trade secrets, 362–363
Traffic courts, 28
Transference, of real property, 197–202
Transferor, 250
Transfers, voidable, 346–347
Treaties, 11, 13
Trespass, 138
- to land, 131
- to personal property, 131

Trespasser, 138
Trial, 54–56
- bench, 55
- briefs, 55
- courts, 27–28
- judgment and, 55, 56 (*see also* Judgment)
- jury and, 56 (*see also* Jury)
- verdict of, 56
- waiver of, 55

Trier of fact, 55
Trustee, 250, 252, 254, 338
Trustor, 250, 254, 338

Trusts, 250–255
- agreement, 252
- charitable, 253
- constructive, 253
- corpus, 250, 252, 253
- express, 252
- grantor's, 254
- implied, 253
- instrument, 252
- *inter vivos*, 252, 254
- living, 253–255
- parties to, 252–253
- res, 250
- resulting, 253
- revocable, 254
- special types of, 253
- spendthrift, 253
- termination of, 253
- testamentary, 252
- totten, 253
- vs. wills, 239

Twelve Tables, 10
Two-party instrument, mortgage as, 337
Two-party secured transaction, 340

UCC, *see* Uniform Commercial Code
ULLCA, 272–273
ULPA, 269
U.N. Convention on Contracts for the International Sale of Goods (CISG), 177
Unanimous decisions, 33
Undisclosed agency, 309
Undue:
- burden, 106, 323
- hardship, 320
- influence, invalidating a will and, 248

Uniform Arbitration Act, 58–59
Uniform Commercial Code (UCC), 165, 174–176, 340–341
- Article 2 (Sales), 175
- Article 2A (Leases), 176
- Section 201, 164

Uniform Computer Information Transactions Act (UCITA), 176
Uniform Gift to Minors Act, 188
Uniform Limited Liability Company Act (*see* ULLCA)
Uniform Limited Partnership Act (*see* ULPA)
Uniform Partnership Act (*see* UPA)
Uniform Probate Code (UDC), 250
Uniform Simultaneous Death Act, 247
Uniform Trade Secrets Act, 362
Unilever, 287
Unintentional torts, 131–140 (*see also* Negligence)
Unions, 324–325
United Nations Charter, 6
Unlawful detainer actions, 203
Unlimited liability, 270
Unlimited personal liability, 264
Unprotected speech, 107
Unreasonable search and seizure, 82
Unsecured:
- credit, 336
- creditor, 336, 349

UPA, 265–267
U.S. Congress:
- authority to establish bankruptcy laws, 335–336
- job discrimination and, 318–324
- safety in the workplace and, 316–318
- same-sex marriage and, 217
- Sarbanes-Oxley Act of 2002, 286–287

U.S. Constitution, 10–11, 99, 101 (*see also* Constitutional law)
- bankruptcy laws and, 335–336, 343
- Bill of Rights, 101, 106–108
- delegation doctrine and, 386
- Due Process Clause of, 204
- Eighth Amendment, 85
- Fifth Amendment, 83, 112–113
- First Amendment, 107, 108, 111
- Fourteenth Amendment, 82, 106
- Full Faith and Credit Clause of, 217
- Just Compensation Clause of, 204
- safeguards provided by, 82–85
- Seventh Amendment, 54
- Sixth Amendment, 85

U.S. Copyright Office, 366
U.S. Patent and Trademark Office (PTO), 363
U.S. Supreme Court, 29, 31, 33–35, 104
- hostile work environment and, 320, 322
- the right to die and, 250

Variance, zoning ordinances and, 204
Vegetation, *see* Plant life and vegetation
Venue, 40
Verdict, 56
VFW/Fokker, 287
Vicarious liability, 311
Violations, 71
Violent strikes, 324
Visitation rights, 226
Voidable:
- contract, 159
- transfers, 346–347

Voir dire, 55
Voluntary petition, 345
Voting rights, in limited partnerships, 270

Wage, minimum, 312
Waiting period, 224
Waiver of trial, 55
Wal-Mart, 127
Walt Disney Company, 290
Warrantless:
- arrest, 73
- search, 82

Warranty deed, 197
Water pollution, 399–400
Wetlands, 401
White, Byron R., 34
White-collar crimes, 77–80
Wildcat strikes, 324
Will, 239–250, 254–255
- changing, 240
- dying without, 248
- formal, 240
- holographic, 242
- invalidation of, 248
- joint, 247
- mutual, 247–248
- noncupative, 242
- pour-over, 254
- reciprocal, 247–248
- requirements for making, 240–242
- revoking, 240
- sample, 241
- special issues concerning, 247–248
- special types of, 242
- vs. trust, 239

Wire fraud, 78
Wiretaps, 87
Witness, 51
Women, right to vote, 7
Worker's compensation, 315–316
Workers:
- crossover, 325
- replacement, 325

Work-related test, 310–311
World Wide Web, intellectual property rights and, 373–376 (*see also* Internet)
Writ of certiorari, 33
Writing:
- contracts and, 162–166
- formality of, 164–165

Written citation, of safety and health violations, 318
Written memorandum, 56
Wrongful:
- death action, 125
- discharge/termination, 304, 313
- dissolution of partnerships, 268

Zoning commission, 204
Zoning ordinances, land use and, 204–205

CASES DISCUSSED

Gratz v. Bollinger and the Regents of the University of Michigan, *14*

Grutter v. Bollinger and the University of Michigan Law School, *15*

1.1 W.C. Ritchie & Co. v. Wayman, *26*

1.2 Rostker, Director of the Selective Service v. Goldberg, *26*

Pizza Hut, Inc. v. Papa John's International, Inc., *32*

Carnival Cruise Lines, Inc. v. Shute, *38*

2.1 Nutrilab, Inc. v. Schweiker, *45*

2.2 Allison v. ITE Imperial Corporation, *45*

2.3 Brooks v. Magnaverde Corporation, *45*

2.4 Harris v. Time, Inc., *45*

Swierkiewicz v. Sorema N.A., *50*

Norgart v. The Upjohn Company, *52*

Ferlito v. Johnson & Johnson Products, Inc., *57*

3.1 Conrad v. Delta Airlines, Inc., *66*

3.2 Haviland & Co., Incorporated v. Montgomery Ward & Co., *66*

3.3 Simblest v. Maynard, *66*

3.4 Burnham v. Superior Court of California, *66*

Atwater v. City of Lago Vista, Texas, *74*

Kyllo v. United States, *84*

Wal-Mart Stores, Inc. v. Samara Brothers, Inc., *88*

4.1 People v. Paulson, *97*

4.2 Center Art Galleries–Hawaii, Inc. v. United States, *97*

4.3 United States v. John Doe, *97*

4.4 People v. Shaw, *97*

Geier v. American Honda Motor Co., Inc., *102*

Reno, Attorney General of the United States v. Condon, Attorney General of South Carolina, *105*

Fax.com, Inc. v. United States, *109*

United States v. Playboy Entertainment Group, Inc., *110*

5.1 Heart of Atlanta Motel v. United States, *121*

5.2 Ray, Governor of Washington v. Atlantic Richfield Co., *121*

5.3 Federal Communications Commission v. Pacifica Foundation, *121*

5.4 United States v. Eichman, *122*

Roach v. Stern, *130*

James v. Meow Media, Inc., *135*

Cheong v. Antablin, *139*

Shoshone Coca-Cola Bottling Co. v. Dolinski, *143*

6.1 Manning v. Grimsley, *150*

6.2 Johnson v. Kmart Enterprises, Inc., *150*

6.3 Karns v. Emerson Electric Co., *150*

6.4 Luque v. McLean, Trustee, *151*

Wrench LLC v. Taco Bell Corporation, *158*

Alden v. Presley, *160*

Flood v. Fidelity & Guaranty Life Insurance Co., *163*

Lim v. The .TV Corporation International, *171*

Brumfield v. Death Row Records, Inc., *178*

7.1 Bobby Floars Toyota, Inc. v. Smith, *184*

7.2 Liz Claiborne, Inc. v. Avon Products, Inc., *184*

7.3 Crisci v. Security Insurance Company of New Haven, Connecticut, *184*

7.4 Walgreen Co. v. Sara Creek Property Co., *185*

Sisters of Charity of the Incarnate Word v. Meaux, *191*

Cunningham v. Hastings, *198*

Walker v. Ayres, *201*

Guinnane v. San Francisco City Planning Commission, *205*